GLEIM®

2023 EDITION

EA REVIEW

PART 2: BUSINESSES

by

Irvin N. Gleim, Ph.D., CPA, CIA, CMA, CFM

and

James R. Hasselback, Ph.D.

Gleim EA Review for the
IRS Special Enrollment Exam
5/1/2023 - 2/29/2024

Gleim Publications, Inc.
PO Box 12848
Gainesville, Florida 32604
(800) 874-5346
(352) 375-0772
www.gleimEA.com
GleimEA@gleim.com

For updates to this 2023 edition of ***EA Review: Part 2, Businesses***

Go To: www.gleim.com/EAupdate

Or: Email update@gleim.com with **EA 2 2023-1** in the subject line. You will receive our current update as a reply.

Updates are available until the next edition is published.

ISSN: 2168-3867

ISBN: 978-1-61854-578-7 *EA 1: Individuals*
ISBN: 978-1-61854-579-4 *EA 2: Businesses*
ISBN: 978-1-61854-580-0 *EA 3: Representation, Practices & Procedures*
ISBN: 978-1-61854-586-2 *Enrolled Agent Exam Guide: A System for Success*

First Printing: January 2023

ACKNOWLEDGMENTS

The authors appreciate and thank the Internal Revenue Service and Prometric for their cooperation. Questions have been used from the 1978-2022 Special Enrollment Examinations.

The authors also appreciate the assistance of Ryan Dugger of Dugger Corcoran Illustrations, LLC, who is an illustrator living in Pensacola, Florida. He has studied fine art, graphic design, comic art, and earned his Bachelors of Fine Arts at Savannah College of Art & Design in Atlanta, Georgia. He enjoys using paint, ink, and digital mediums to bridge abstract concepts with fun, detailed imagery.

ABOUT THE AUTHORS

Irvin N. Gleim, who authored the first edition of Gleim EA Review over 20 years ago, was Professor Emeritus in the Fisher School of Accounting at the University of Florida and a member of the American Accounting Association, Academy of Legal Studies in Business, American Institute of Certified Public Accountants, Association of Government Accountants, Florida Institute of Certified Public Accountants, The Institute of Internal Auditors, and the Institute of Management Accountants. The late Dr. Gleim published articles in the *Journal of Accountancy*, *The Accounting Review*, and the *American Business Law Journal* and authored numerous accounting books, aviation books, and CPE courses.

James R. Hasselback is an Adjunct Professor at Louisiana State University. He has previously taught at Florida State University, Eastern Michigan University, the University of Florida, and Texas A&M University. A member of the American Accounting Association and the American Taxation Association, he has published over 160 papers in professional and academic journals, including *The Accounting Review*, *The Tax Adviser*, *Financial Management*, *Journal of Real Estate Taxation*, and the *American Business Law Journal*. Dr. Hasselback has presented papers at many national and regional professional meetings and has served as chairman at tax sessions of professional conferences. He regularly presents continuing education seminars for certified public accountants. In addition, he has been coauthor and technical editor of a two-volume introductory taxation series published by CCH, Inc., for the past 37 years and has served as technical editor of several publications by CCH and Harper-Collins. Dr. Hasselback has compiled over 40 editions of the *Accounting Faculty Directory*.

A PERSONAL THANKS

This edition would not have been possible without the extraordinary effort and dedication of Jedidiah Arnold, Jacob Bennett, Julie Cutlip, Fernanda Martinez, Bree Rodriguez, Veronica Rodriguez, Bobbie Stanley, Joanne Strong, Elmer Tucker, and Ryan Van Tress, who typed the entire manuscript and all revisions and drafted and laid out the diagrams, illustrations, and cover for this book.

We also appreciate the production and editorial assistance of Brianna Barnett, Rayne Chance, Ethan Good, Doug Green, Jessica Hatker, Sonora Hospital-Medina, David Sox, and Alyssa Thomas.

We are also thankful for the critical reading assistance of Ryan Guard, Mark Jones, Jess Joyson, Michael Nagarathinam, Andrew Schreiber, and Michaela Wallace.

We are also grateful for the video production expertise of Gary Brook, Philip Brubaker, and Matthew Church, who helped produce and edit our Gleim Instruct Video Series.

Finally, we appreciate the encouragement, support, and tolerance of our families throughout this project.

REVIEWERS AND CONTRIBUTORS

Garrett W. Gleim, CPA, CIA, CGMA, leads production of the Gleim CPA, CMA, CIA, and EA exam review systems. He is a member of the American Institute of Certified Public Accountants and the Florida Institute of Certified Public Accountants and holds a Bachelor of Science in Economics with a Concentration in Accounting from The Wharton School, University of Pennsylvania. Mr. Gleim is coauthor of numerous accounting and aviation books and the inventor of multiple patents with educational applications. He is also an avid pilot who holds a commercial pilot rating and is a flight instructor. In addition, as an active supporter of the local business community, Mr. Gleim serves as an advisor to several start-ups with ties to the University of Florida.

J.T. Eagan, EA, is a Clinical Assistant Professor of Accounting at Purdue University Northwest with over 15 years of professional tax experience. He is also Managing Director with NWI Tax, LLC, and a past Vice President of the Indiana Society of Enrolled Agents. Mr. Eagan is one of the EA Gleim Instruct lecturers.

Matthew Hutchens, J.D., CPA, EA, is a Lecturer of Accountancy at the University of Illinois Gies College of Business. Prior to joining the University of Illinois, he was a Staff Attorney at a Low Income Taxpayer Clinic and a Senior Staff Accountant in the National Tax Office of Crowe LLP. He received a law degree from the Indiana University Maurer School of Law and a bachelor's degree in Accounting and Finance from the Indiana University Kelley School of Business. Mr. Hutchens provided substantial editorial assistance throughout the project.

D. Scott Lawton, B.S., EA, is a graduate of Brigham Young University-Idaho and Utah Valley University. Previously, he was an auditor for the Utah State Tax Commission. Mr. Lawton provided substantial editorial assistance throughout the project.

LouAnn M. Lutter, M.S. Acc., CPA, received a Master of Science in Accounting from the University of Colorado, Boulder. Previously, she was an Accounting Manager in Corporate Accounting and Shared Business Services at Caesars Entertainment. Ms. Lutter provided substantial editorial assistance throughout the project.

Mark S. Modas, M.S.T., CPA, holds a Bachelor of Arts in Accounting from Florida Atlantic University and a Master of Science in Taxation from Nova Southeastern University. He is currently an Assistant Professor of Accounting at Santa Fe College and was formerly the head of the Internal Audit department of Perry Ellis International and the Director of Accounting and Financial Reporting for the School Board of Broward County, Florida. Additionally, he worked as the corporate tax compliance supervisor for Ryder Systems, Inc., and has worked as a tax practitioner for more than 25 years. Mr. Modas provided substantial editorial assistance throughout the project.

Nate Wadlinger, J.D., LL.M., EA, CPA, is a Lecturer of Accounting at the University of Central Florida, where he teaches tax and accounting courses in the Bachelor and Master of Accounting programs. Mr. Wadlinger received his Bachelor of Science in Accounting, Master of Accounting, and Juris Doctor from the University of Florida and his LL.M. in Taxation from Boston University. In addition, he is an EA, a CPA licensed by the State of Florida, and a member of the Florida Bar. Mr. Wadlinger is one of the EA Gleim Instruct lecturers.

TABLE OF CONTENTS

DETAILED TABLE OF CONTENTS

A MESSAGE FROM OUR AUTHORS

The purpose of this book is to help **you** prepare to pass Part 2, Businesses, of the IRS Special Enrollment Exam, which is commonly referred to as the EA (enrolled agent) exam. Our goal is to provide an affordable, effective, and easy-to-use study program. Our course

1. Explains how to maximize your score through learning strategies and exam-taking techniques perfected by Gleim EA.
2. Outlines all of the content topics described in the IRS Exam Content Outlines and tested on Part 2 of the EA exam.
3. Organizes all of the subject matter tested on Part 2 in 20 easy-to-use study units, reflecting 2022 tax law (which is what will be tested on the 2023 EA exam).
4. Presents multiple-choice questions taken or modeled from past EA examinations to prepare you for the types of questions you will find on your EA exams.
   a. In our book, the answer explanations are presented to the immediate right of each question for your convenience. Use a piece of paper to cover our detailed answer explanations as you answer the question and then review all answer choices to learn why the correct one is correct and why the other choices are incorrect.
   b. You should also practice answering these questions through our online platform, which mimics Prometric's user interface, so you are comfortable answering questions online like you will do on test day. Our adaptive course will focus and target your weak areas.
5. Provides the tax rate schedules with inflation-adjusted amounts as a detachable bookmark in the book and as an additional resource PDF in the online course for your convenience.

The outline format, spacing, and question and answer formats in this book are designed to increase readability, learning, understanding, and success on the EA exam. Our most successful candidates use the Gleim Premium EA Review System, which includes Gleim Instruct videos; our Access Until You Pass Guarantee; our innovative SmartAdapt technology; expertly authored books; the largest test bank of multiple-choice questions; audio lectures; flashcards; and the support of our team of accounting experts. To maximize the efficiency and effectiveness of your EA exam preparations, start by reviewing the *Enrolled Agent Exam Guide: A System for Success*.

Thank you for trusting us with your EA studies. We appreciate any and all feedback. Immediately after you take the exam and receive your exam score, please go to www.gleim.com/feedbackEA2 to share suggestions on how we can improve this edition. The EA exam is a **nondisclosed** exam, which means you must maintain the confidentiality of the exam by not divulging the nature or content of any EA question or answer under any circumstances. We ask only for information about our materials and any improvements that can be made regarding topics that need to be added or expanded or need more emphasis.

On behalf of our entire team, we want to thank every EA candidate who has trusted us to help them pass the EA exam and achieve career success.

Good Luck on the Exam,

Irvin N. Gleim
James R. Hasselback

GLEIM®

ACCOUNTING TITLES FROM GLEIM PUBLICATIONS

EA Review:

- Part 1: Individuals
- Part 2: Businesses
- Part 3: Representation, Practices and Procedures

CIA Review:

- Part 1: Essentials of Internal Auditing
- Part 2: Practice of Internal Auditing
- Part 3: Business Knowledge for Internal Auditing
- CIA Challenge Exam

CMA Review:

- Part 1: Financial Planning, Performance, and Analytics
- Part 2: Strategic Financial Management

CPA Review:

- Auditing & Attestation (AUD)
- Business Environment & Concepts (BEC)
- Financial Accounting & Reporting (FAR)
- Regulation (REG)

Exam Questions and Explanations (EQE) Series:

- Auditing & Systems
- Business Law & Legal Studies
- Cost/Managerial Accounting
- Federal Tax
- Financial Accounting

Gleim also publishes aviation training materials. Go to www.GleimAviation.com for a complete listing of our aviation titles.

PREPARING FOR AND TAKING THE IRS ENROLLED AGENT EXAMINATION

READ THE *ENROLLED AGENT EXAM GUIDE: A SYSTEM FOR SUCCESS*

Access the free copy of the Gleim ***Enrolled Agent Exam Guide*** by visiting www.gleim.com/PassEA and reference it throughout your studies for a deeper understanding of the EA exam. This booklet is your system for success.

OVERVIEW OF THE EA EXAMINATION

The **exam consists of three parts, with 3.5 hours for each part** (4 hours total seat time to include tutorial, survey, and optional 15-minute break). The total exam for all three parts is 10.5 hours of testing (12 hours total seat time to include tutorials, surveys, and optional 15-minute breaks). It covers **federal taxation; tax accounting; and the use of tax return forms for individuals, partnerships, corporations, trusts, estates, and gifts**. It also covers **ethical considerations and procedural requirements**.

The questions on the examination are directed toward the tasks that enrolled agents must perform to complete and file forms and tax returns and to represent taxpayers before the Internal Revenue Service. Each part of the examination consists of **100 multiple-choice questions** and covers the following tax topics:

Part 1 - Individuals
Part 2 - Businesses
Part 3 - Representation, Practices and Procedures

Based on the experience of our customers who have taken all three parts of the exam, Gleim recommends that candidates sit for Parts 1 and 2 before taking Part 3. Feedback indicates that Part 3 candidates should be knowledgeable about topics covered in Parts 1 and 2 as they relate to the topics that Part 3 tests.

IRS's NONDISCLOSURE AGREEMENT

The EA exam is nondisclosed. The following is taken from the IRS's *Candidate Information Bulletin*. It is reproduced here to remind all EA candidates about the IRS's strict policy of nondisclosure, which Gleim consistently supports and upholds.

> *This exam is confidential and proprietary. It is made available to you, the examinee, solely for the purpose of assessing your proficiency level in the skill area referenced in the title of this exam. You are expressly prohibited from disclosing, publishing, reproducing, or transmitting this exam, in whole or in part, in any form or by any means, verbal or written, electronic or mechanical, for any purpose, without the prior express written permission of the IRS.*

DATES OF THE EXAMINATION/TAX LAW COVERED

The 2023 examination test window will begin May 1, 2023, and examinations will be offered continuously through February 29, 2024.

Each testing year's EA exam (through February of the following year) covers the tax law in effect the previous December 31. For example, the May 1, 2023-February 29, 2024, testing window will test tax law in effect December 31, 2022.

Gleim consistently monitors any changes the IRS makes to the exam. Stay up to date on any EA exam changes at www.gleim.com/EAexamchanges.

GLEIM PREMIUM EA REVIEW WITH SMARTADAPT

Gleim Premium EA Review features the most comprehensive coverage of exam content and employs the most efficient learning techniques to help you study smarter and most effectively. The Gleim Premium EA Review System is powered by SmartAdapt technology, an innovative platform that identifies where you should focus (and where you should not) as you move through the following steps for optimized EA review:

Step 1:

Complete a Diagnostic Study Quiz. After you submit this quiz, you will be able to review detailed answer explanations for both the correct and incorrect answer choices. Meanwhile, your quiz results set a baseline that our SmartAdapt technology will use to create a custom learning track for each bite-sized module.

Step 2:

Solidify your knowledge by studying the suggested Knowledge Transfer Outline(s) or watching the suggested Gleim Instruct video(s). You will also be able to take notes within your online course while reviewing either of these learning tools.

Step 3:

Focus on weak areas and perfect your question-answering techniques by taking the adaptive quizzes that SmartAdapt directs you to.

Final Review:

After completing all study units, take the first full-length Mock Exam. Then, SmartAdapt will guide you through a Final Review based on your results, which will help pinpoint where you need to focus. Finally, a few days before your exam date, take the second full-length Mock Exam. SmartAdapt will tell you when you are ready to pass with confidence.

To facilitate your studies, the Gleim Premium EA Review System uses the largest bank of multiple-choice questions on the market. Our system's content and presentation precisely mimic the whole exam environment so you feel completely at ease on test day.

TIME-BUDGETING AND QUESTION-ANSWERING TECHNIQUES FOR THE EXAM

The following suggestions are to assist you in maximizing your score on Part 2 of the EA exam. Remember, knowing how to take the exam and how to answer individual questions is as important as studying/reviewing the subject matter tested on the exam.

1. **Budget your time.** We make this point with emphasis–**finish your exam before time expires**.
    a. You will have 3 hours and 30 minutes (210 minutes) to answer 100 multiple-choice questions. On your Prometric computer screen, the time remaining (starting with 03:30:00) appears in the top middle of the screen.
    b. As you work through the individual multiple-choice questions, monitor your time. If you allocate 1.5-2 minutes per question, you will require 150-200 minutes to finish all 100 questions, leaving 10-60 minutes to review your answers and "flagged" questions (see item 2.b. below). Spending 2 minutes should be reserved for only the most difficult questions. You should complete 10 questions every 15-20 minutes. If you pace yourself during the exam, you will have adequate time.
    c. The exam is broken into two halves of 50 questions each with an optional 15-minute break. The first half should take 75-100 minutes. You should finish answering and reviewing by the time you are 105 minutes through your exam. The remaining time will be spent on the second half.
    d. Gleim recommendation: Feedback from individuals who have taken Part 2 and at least one other part shows Part 2 to be more time-consuming. Plan accordingly.
2. **Answer the questions in consecutive order.**
    a. Do **not** agonize over any one question. Stay within your time budget: 1.5-2 minutes per question.
    b. Note any items you are unsure of by clicking the button with the flag icon and return to them later if time allows. Plan on going back to all flagged questions.
    c. Never leave a question unanswered. Make your best guess within your budgeted time. Your score is based on the number of correct responses. You will not be penalized for guessing incorrectly. You can always flag the question and return to it later.
3. **For each multiple-choice question,**
    a. **Try to ignore the answer choices as you determine the answer.** Do not allow the answer choices to affect your reading of the question.
        1) If four answer choices are presented, three of them are incorrect. These incorrect answers are called **distractors** for good reason. Often, distractors are written to appear correct at first glance until further analysis.
        2) In computational items, distractors are carefully calculated so that they are the result of making common mistakes. Be careful, and double-check your computations if time permits.
    b. **Read the question** carefully to determine the precise requirement.
        1) Focusing on what is required enables you to ignore extraneous information and proceed directly to determining the correct answer. This will save you valuable time.
            a) Be especially careful to note when the requirement is an **exception**; e.g., "Which of the following is **not** includible in gross income?"

c. **Determine the correct answer** before looking at the answer choices.

   1) However, some multiple-choice items are structured so that the answer cannot be determined from the stem alone. See the stem in 3.b.1)a) on the previous page.

d. **Then read the answer choices carefully.**

   1) Even if the first answer appears to be the correct choice, do not skip the remaining answer choices. Questions often ask for the "best" of the choices provided. Thus, each choice requires your consideration.
   2) Treat each answer choice as a true/false question as you analyze it.

e. **Click on the best answer.**

   1) If you are uncertain, you have a 25% chance of answering the question correctly by guessing blindly. Improve your odds with educated guessing.
   2) For many of the multiple-choice questions, two answer choices can be eliminated with minimal effort, thereby increasing your educated guess to a 50-50 proposition.

4. After you have answered the 50 questions in each exam section, return to the questions you flagged. Make sure to stay within your time budget. Then, verify that all questions have been answered.

5. **If you don't know the answer:**

   a. Again, guess but make it an educated guess. First, rule out answers you think are incorrect. Second, speculate on what the IRS is looking for and/or the rationale behind the question. Third, select the best answer or guess between equally appealing answers. Your first guess is usually the most intuitive. If you cannot make an educated guess, read the stem and each answer, and pick the most intuitive answer.
   b. Make sure you accomplish this step within the predetermined time budget.

LEARNING FROM YOUR MISTAKES

Learning from questions you answer incorrectly is very important. Each question you answer incorrectly is an **opportunity** to avoid missing actual test questions on your EA exam. Thus, you should carefully study the answer explanations provided until you understand why the original answer you chose is wrong, as well as why the correct answer indicated is correct. This learning technique is clearly the difference between passing and failing for many EA candidates.

Also, you must determine why you answered questions incorrectly and learn how to avoid the same error in the future. Reasons for missing questions include

1. Misreading the requirement (stem)
2. Not understanding what is required
3. Making a mathematical error
4. Applying the wrong rule or concept
5. Being distracted by one or more of the answers
6. Incorrectly eliminating answers from consideration
7. Not having knowledge of the topic tested
8. Employing poor intuition when guessing

HOW TO BE IN CONTROL WHILE TAKING THE EXAM

You have to be in control to be successful during exam preparation and execution. Control can also contribute greatly to your personal and other professional goals. Control is a process whereby you

1. Develop expectations, standards, budgets, and plans.
2. Undertake activity, production, study, and learning.
3. Measure the activity, production, output, and knowledge.
4. Compare actual activity with expected and budgeted activity.
5. Modify the activity to better achieve the desired outcome.
6. Revise expectations and standards in light of actual experience.
7. Continue the process or restart the process in the future.

Exercising control will ultimately develop the confidence you need to outperform most other EA candidates and PASS the EA exam!

Learn more about these strategies and other helpful tips in our free *Enrolled Agent Exam Guide: A System for Success*. You can view this booklet online at www.gleim.com/PassEA.

IF YOU HAVE QUESTIONS ABOUT GLEIM MATERIALS

Gleim has an efficient and effective way for candidates who have purchased the Premium EA Review System to submit an inquiry and receive a response regarding Gleim materials directly through their course. This system also allows you to view your Q&A session in your Gleim Personal Classroom.

Questions regarding the information in this introduction and/or the *Enrolled Agent Exam Guide* (study suggestions, studying plans, exam specifics) should be emailed to personalcounselor@gleim.com.

Questions concerning orders, prices, shipments, or payments should be sent via email to customerservice@gleim.com and will be promptly handled by our competent and courteous customer service staff.

For technical support, you may use our automated technical support service at www.gleim.com/support, email us at support@gleim.com, or call us at (800) 874-5346.

FEEDBACK

Please fill out our online feedback form www.gleim.com/feedbackEA immediately after you take the EA exam so we can adapt to changes on the exam. Our approach has been approved by the IRS.

STUDY UNIT ONE

ENTITY TYPES, METHODS, AND PERIODS

(18 pages of outline)

One of the most important decisions a business can make is its choice of entity type. Each type of business form has advantages and disadvantages from both tax and liability perspectives. Each taxpayer must figure taxable income on an annual accounting period called a tax year. The calendar year is the most common tax year. Each taxpayer must also use a consistent accounting method, which is a set of rules for determining how and when to report income and expenses. The most commonly used accounting methods are the cash method and the accrual method.

1.1 BUSINESS ENTITIES

Several different forms of businesses have been made available to taxpayers over the years. Each of these business forms has characteristics that are favorable or unfavorable to the taxpayer.

Sole Proprietorship

1. The sole proprietorship is the most common form of business entity.
    a. A sole proprietorship is not a legal entity separate and apart from its owner.
    b. Income or loss is reported by the taxpayer on Schedule C of the owner's Form 1040.
    c. The owner has unlimited liability with regard to the sole proprietorship.
        1) The owner's personal assets are exposed without limitation to any and all liabilities related to the business.
    d. Sole proprietorships are easy to establish and require no special forms.
    e. The business cannot be transferred.
        1) If the business is sold, the owner reports the sale as if each asset were sold.
    f. Spouses filing a joint return may elect out of partnership treatment by choosing to be a **qualified joint venture**.
        1) Each spouse will file a Schedule C and is treated as a sole proprietor, allowing both to receive Social Security benefits.

Corporations

2. Corporations were created to allow for the limited liability of the owners. The owners' personal assets are protected from creditors. Creditors can only look to the assets of the corporation for settlement of debts.
   a. Regular corporations are referred to as C corporations.
      1) C corporations have double taxation.
         a) First, the income is taxed to the corporation as it is earned.
         b) Second, the income is taxed when the corporation distributes the income in the form of dividends.
   b. The corporation files a return separate from its owners. The tax return is due the 15th day of the 4th month following the end of its tax year.
   c. A corporation is closely held if both of the following apply:
      1) It is not a personal service corporation.
      2) At any time during the last half of the tax year, more than 50% of the value of its outstanding stock is directly or indirectly owned by or for five or fewer individuals. "Individuals" includes certain trusts and private foundations.

S Corporations

3. The S corporation is a special type of corporation that first became available as a business form in 1958.
   a. The S corporation is not taxed, and the income is taxed to the shareholders when earned by the S corporation.
   b. The S corporation has the limited liability feature of the C corporation. However, there are several ownership restrictions placed on the S corporation.
   c. S corporations comprise over one-half of all corporations.
      1) S corporations tend to be small in size and number of owners.
      2) Over half of all S corporations have only one owner.
      3) For the most part, S corporations are required to be on a calendar tax year.
      4) The S corporation tax return is due the 15th day of the 3rd month following the end of its tax year.

Partnerships

4. There are several forms of partnerships available for taxpayers.
   a. Partnerships have the advantage that income is taxed only once.
      1) The partnership does not pay tax; the income flows through and is taxed on each owner's personal tax return.
      2) The main disadvantage of the partnership form of organization is that the owners can be held liable for the partnership's debts if there are not enough assets to cover the partnership liabilities. This form of partnership is referred to as a **general partnership**.
      3) Partnership tax returns are due by the 15th day of the 3rd month following the close of the partnership tax year.

b. **Limited partnerships** were created in the 1970s to allow for the limited liability feature of the corporation while at the same time retaining the single form of taxation.

1) The owners are divided into general partners and limited partners. Only the limited partners have the limited liability feature.

a) However, the limited partner is not allowed to participate in the operations of the business.

c. The **limited liability partnership** quickly followed the limited liability company in adoption by all states and is very similar to the limited liability company.

1) The limited liability partnership is primarily used by personal service taxpayers.

2) Several states require that the owners remain personally liable for the contracted debts of the entity.

Limited Liability Companies (LLCs)

5. An LLC is a noncorporate hybrid business structure that combines the limited liability of a corporation with the tax advantages of a general partnership.

6. An LLC is a domestic entity that is not specifically classified as a corporation, is classified as a partnership (if it has two or more members), or is disregarded as an entity separate from its owner (if it has only one owner). Thus, for federal tax purposes, the default classification for a domestic LLC with at least two members is to be treated as a partnership. However, the check-the-box regulations discussed on the next page allow an LLC to elect to be treated as a corporation.

a. LLCs are the only business entities that allow

1) Complete pass-through tax advantages and the operational flexibility of a partnership,

2) Corporation-style limited liability under state law,

3) No restrictions on the number or types of members, and

4) Management participation by all members. Members are the owners or shareholders of the LLC.

b. Most states follow Federal taxation of LLCs. Texas and Tennessee tax LLCs as corporations. Michigan imposes a 4.95% business income tax and a modified gross receipts tax on all forms of business at a tax rate of 0.8%.

c. LLCs allow the inclusion of entity-level liabilities in tax basis.

d. There is no uniform LLC agreement among states; an LLC doing business out of state may have to live with unacceptable uncertainty as to its legal status. Every state and the District of Columbia permit a single-member LLC.

Single-Member Limited Liability Companies

7. A single-member LLC is generally treated as a disregarded entity unless it elects to be taxed as a corporation.

8. For individuals, the profit or loss from a disregarded entity is simply reported on Schedule C of the member's Form 1040 along with Schedule SE. A rental real estate operation reports its income or loss on Schedule E.

a. For businesses, the profit or loss from a disregarded entity is reported on the member's return as an unincorporated branch or division of the member.

Entity Classification Election -- Check-the-box Regulations

9. An eligible entity can use Form 8832 to elect how it will be classified for federal tax purposes: as a corporation, a partnership, or an entity inseparable from its owner.
   a. An eligible entity is classified for federal tax purposes under the default rules unless it filed Form 8832 or Form 2553 to elect a classification or change its current classification.
   b. Unless an election is made on Form 8832, a domestic eligible entity is
      1) A partnership if it has two or more members
      2) Disregarded as an entity separate from its owners if it has a single owner
   c. Unless an election is made on Form 8832, a foreign eligible entity is
      1) A partnership if it has two or more members and at least one member does not have limited liability
      2) An association taxable as a corporation if all members have limited liability
      3) Disregarded as an entity separate from its owner if it has a single owner that does not have limited liability
   d. A corporation organized under a state law can only be taxed as a corporation. However, the entity may be eligible to be classified as an S corporation.

Summary of Business Entities

Business Entity	Owner's Liability	Taxation
Sole Proprietorship	Unlimited	Flow through to individual.
Corporations	Limited	At corporate level.
S Corporations	Limited	Flow through taxation on a per-day and per-share basis.
Partnership	General partners – Unlimited Limited partners – Limited	Flow through to partner.
Limited Liability Company (LLC)	Limited	Default is flow through to member. However, may elect to be treated as a different type of entity.
Single-Member LLC (disregarded entity)	Limited	Default is flow through to member. However, may elect to be treated as a different type of entity.

Trusts and Estates

10. Trusts and estates are separate entities from their owners.
    a. Trusts may be created to hold assets for the beneficiaries.
    b. The trust income is usually distributed to the beneficiaries.
    c. The beneficiary pays an income tax on the income of the trust that is required to be distributed.
    d. The trust only pays tax on income that is not required to be distributed. Thus, the income of a trust is taxed only once.

11. An estate comes into place after the taxpayer dies.
    a. The estate is required to pay tax on income that is earned on the assets of the decedent before the assets are distributed to the beneficiaries.
    b. Similar to the trust, the beneficiaries pay the tax on any income that is distributed and the estate pays tax on the remaining income.

Employer Identification Number

12. An employer identification number (EIN) is the business/entity equivalent of a taxpayer identification number (TIN).
    a. Use Form SS-4 to apply for an EIN. An EIN is a nine-digit number assigned to sole proprietors, corporations, partnerships, estates, trusts, and other entities for tax filing and reporting purposes.
    b. A sole proprietorship or self-employed farmer who establishes a qualified retirement plan or is required to file excise, employment, alcohol, tobacco, or firearms returns must have an EIN regardless of the number of employees.
    c. A partnership, corporation, real estate mortgage investment conduit, nonprofit organization, or farmers' cooperative must use an EIN for any tax-related purposes even if the entity does not have employees. Take note that sole proprietors without employees and without excise or pension plan return filings are not included in this group required to use an EIN.
    d. Generally, a sole proprietor should file only one Form SS-4 and needs only one EIN, regardless of the number of businesses operated as a sole proprietorship or trade names under which a business operates.
        1) If the proprietorship incorporates or enters into a partnership, a new EIN is required.
        2) Each corporation in an affiliated group must have its own EIN.
    e. The reporting and payment of employment taxes for employees of the LLC must be made using the name and EIN of the LLC.
    f. Do not apply for a new EIN if the existing entity only elected on Form 8832 to change the way it is taxed (or is covered by the default rules).
    g. Do not use the EIN of the prior business unless a taxpayer became the owner of a corporation by acquiring its stock.
        1) An existing corporation that is electing or revoking S corporation status should use its previously assigned EIN.
    h. In some situations, a name change may require a new EIN or a final return.

Principal Business or Professional Activity Codes

13. The codes for the principal business or professional activity, as found in the instructions for Form 1040 Schedule C, classify sole proprietorships by the type of activity they are engaged in to facilitate the administration of the Internal Revenue Code. These 6-digit codes are based on the North American Industry Classification System (NAICS).
    a. The taxpayer selects the category that best describes his or her primary business activity (e.g., real estate). Then the taxpayer selects the activity that best identifies the principal source of sales or receipts (e.g., real estate agent). Finally, the taxpayer finds the 6-digit code assigned to this activity (e.g., 531210, the code for offices of real estate agents and brokers) and enters it on Schedule C, line B.

Characteristics of Business Entities

	Formation	Capitalization	Operation	Liability	Transferability	Taxation	Termination
General Partnership	No formalities. No filings. Formed based on written or oral agreement.	Resources of general partners.	Each partner has right to equal participation in management. Can restrict management rights to one or more partners.	Partners are jointly and severally liable for any partnership obligation.	Partner may transfer financial interest without loss of rights, duties, and liabilities as partner.	Tax reporting entity only. Partners subject to tax.	Dissociation followed by dissolution and winding up.
Limited Partnership	Formalities. Must file written certificate of limited partnership with state.	Resources of general and limited partners.	General partner has full management rights. Limited partner has no management rights.	General partner has unlimited liability for partnership obligations. Limited partner liable only to extent of capital contribution.	General partner may transfer financial interest without loss of rights, duties, and liabilities as partner. Limited partner may assign interest.	Tax reporting entity only. Partners subject to tax.	Event of withdrawal of a general partner.
Limited Liability Partnership	Formalities. Must file with secretary of state and maintain professional liability insurance.	Resources of partners.	Favorable form of organization for professionals (e.g., lawyers, CPAs, etc.). All partners are general partners with limited liability.	Not personally liable for partnership obligations except to extent of LLP's assets. Partners remain personally liable for their own malpractice.	Partner may transfer financial interest without loss of rights, duties, and liabilities as partner.	Tax reporting entity only. Partners subject to tax.	Dissociation followed by dissolution and winding up.
Limited Liability Company	Formalities. Must file articles of organization with secretary of state.	Contributions of members.	Unless provided otherwise, all members have equal management rights.	Owners who participate in management have limited liability.	A member can transfer his or her distributional interest. This interest is personal property.	May elect flow-through taxation or be taxed as an entity.	Dissolution followed by liquidation.
S Corporation	Formalities. Files articles of incorporation with state. Elects S corporation status.	Members and shareholders (number of shareholders may not exceed 100).	Shareholder-elected board appoints officers to manage daily operations.	Shareholders generally are liable only to the extent of their investment.	Shareholders generally may transfer their interests to qualifying shareholders.	Flow-through taxation on a per-day and per-share basis.	If entity ceases to qualify as an S corporation, it becomes a C corporation.
C Corporation	Formalities. Files articles of incorporation with state.	May sell common and preferred stock. May issue debt.	Shareholder-elected board appoints officers to manage daily operations.	Shareholders generally are liable only to the extent of their investment.	Shareholders generally are free to transfer their interests.	Income taxed at corporate level. Shareholders pay tax on dividends received.	Perpetual existence. A shareholder's death, bankruptcy, or withdrawal does not terminate corporation.

You have completed the outline for this subunit.

Study multiple-choice questions 1 through 4 beginning on page 25.

1.2 ACCOUNTING METHODS

An accounting method is a set of rules used to determine the tax year in which an item is includible or deductible in computing taxable income. The method must clearly reflect income and remain the same from year to year.

Generally, a taxpayer can choose any permitted accounting method when filing the first tax return. The taxpayer does not need to obtain IRS approval to choose the initial accounting method. The taxpayer must, however, use the method consistently from year to year, and it must clearly reflect income.

The cash method and the accrual method are the most commonly used methods. However, other methods, such as the installment method, are allowed. Specific provisions of the Internal Revenue Code (IRC) may override and require specific treatment of certain items.

Change in Methods

1. Change in accounting methods generally requires consent of the IRS, including change in either the overall system of accounting for gross income or deductions or treatment of any material item used in the system.
   a. The taxpayer should file Form 3115 to request consent for such changes.
2. IRS consent is not required for the following changes:
   a. Adopting LIFO inventory valuation
      1) Switching to LIFO inventory requires IRS consent. Form 970, *Application to Use LIFO Inventory Method*, must be filed.
   b. Switching from declining-balance depreciation to straight-line
   c. Making an adjustment in useful life of certain assets
   d. Correcting an error in computing tax, e.g., omission
   e. Certain method situations involving small businesses (i.e., businesses with no more than $27 million in average annual gross receipts)
   f. Change in accounting for research or experimental expenditures as it pertains to Sec. 174(a)(1). This accounting change shall be treated as initiated by the taxpayer, and made with the consent of the Secretary, for any research or experimental expenditures paid or incurred in the first taxable year beginning after December 31, 2021. More information may be found in Study Unit 14, Subunit 4.
3. **Cash Method**
   a. A cash-method taxpayer accounts for income when one of the following occurs:
      1) Cash is actually received
      2) A cash equivalent is actually received
      3) Cash or its equivalent is constructively received

b. **Cash equivalent.** At the time a person receives noncash forms of income, such as property or services, the fair market value is included in gross income. This applies even if the property or service can be currently converted into cash at an amount lower than face value.

1) A cash equivalent is property that is readily convertible into cash and typically has a maturity of 3 months or less. Cash equivalents are so near to maturity that the risk of loss due to a change in value is immaterial. The following are considered cash equivalents:

a) Checks, valued at face
b) Property, e.g., land, transferable at current FMV
c) Promissory notes, valued at FMV

2) If the value of property received cannot be determined, the value of what was given in exchange for it is treated as the amount of income received.

EXAMPLE 1-1 Indeterminate Value of Property

An accountant performs various services for a start-up company in exchange for stock options. If the value of the stock options cannot be determined, the value of the services performed is included in income.

3) If both the property received and the property given are impossible to value, e.g., an unsecured promise to pay from a person with unknown creditworthiness, the transaction is treated as open, and the consideration is not viewed as income until its value can be ascertained.

c. **Constructive receipt.** Under the doctrine of constructive receipt, an item is included in gross income when a person has an unqualified right to immediate possession.

1) A person constructively receives income in the tax year during which it is credited to his or her account, set apart for him or her, or otherwise made available so that (s)he may draw upon it at any time.

a) It is more than a billing or an offer, or mere promise, to pay.

b) It includes ability to use on demand, as with escrowed funds subject to a person's order.

c) Deferring deposit of a check does not defer income. However, dishonor retroactively negates the income.

2) Income is not constructively received if the taxpayer's control of its receipt is subject to substantial restrictions or limitations, e.g., a valid deferred compensation agreement.

d. Receipt or constructive **receipt by an agent** is imputed to the principal.

e. **Economic benefit.** The courts have interpreted the definition of gross income to include any economic or financial benefit conferred on an employee as compensation. This economic benefit theory is applied by the IRS in situations in which an employee or independent contractor receives a transfer of property that confers an economic benefit that is equivalent to cash.

EXAMPLE 1-2	**Economic Benefit of Property Received Included in Gross Income**
The fair rental value of a car that a dealership provides for the personal use of its president is gross income.	

1) The economic benefit theory applies even when the taxpayer cannot choose to take the equivalent value of the income in cash.

f. Dividends are constructively received when made subject to the unqualified demand of a shareholder.

1) If a corporation declares a dividend in December and pays such that the shareholders receive it in January, the dividend is not treated as received in December.

g. When a **bond** is sold between interest payment dates, the interest accrued up to the sale date is added to the selling price of the bond. The seller includes the accrued interest in gross income.

h. **Prepaid rent** is gross income when received.

1) Security deposits are not considered income.
2) Tenant improvements, in lieu of rent, are included.
3) Lease cancellations are included.
4) Advance rental payments must be deducted as an expense by the payor during the tax periods to which the payments apply.

i. **Tips.** An employee who receives $20 or more in tips a month working for any employer must report the tips to the employer by the 10th day of the following month. The tips are gross income when reported.

j. **Deductions.** A cash-method taxpayer deducts expenditures when actually paid, except for prepaid rent.

1) A promise to pay, without more, is not payment.
2) A check represents payment when delivered or sent.
3) A third-party (e.g., bank) credit card charge transaction represents current payment with loan proceeds. A second-party (e.g., store) credit card charge transaction is not paid until the charge is paid off.
4) Bad debt. Adjusted basis in accounts receivable is deductible when the debt becomes worthless. Since a cash-method taxpayer usually has no basis in accounts receivable, (s)he may not deduct bad debts.
5) **Interest on a loan** issued at discount, or unstated (imputed) interest, is deductible pro rata over the life of the loan.
6) A person who uses the cash method to report gross income must use the cash method to report expenses.

Advance Payment of Expenses

k. In general, expenses paid in advance can be deducted only in the year to which they apply, even under the cash method of accounting.

1) However, an exception exists for farmers (but not farming syndicates). They may deduct prepaid feed when the expenditure is incurred even if it is to be consumed by the livestock in a subsequent year. Section 464(f) limits the deduction to 50% of other farm expenses.

l. The cash method cannot be used by corporations (other than S corporations), partnerships having a corporation (other than an S corporation) as a partner, or tax shelters.

1) However, an exception allows the following entities to use the cash method:

a) A farm corporation (family or otherwise) with gross receipts of $27 million or less
b) Corporations whose business is operating nurseries or sod farms and raisers and harvesters of trees (other than fruit and nut trees)
c) Qualified personal service corporations
d) A corporation or partnership with a corporate partner, other than a tax shelter, with average annual gross receipts of $27 million or less

4. **Accrual Method**

   a. An accrual-method taxpayer accounts for income in the period it is actually earned.

   b. Under the accrual method, income items generally have to be included no later than they are included for financial accounting purposes.

   c. The accrual method is required of certain persons and for certain transactions.

      1) If the accrual method is used to report expenses, it must be used to report income items.

      2) A taxpayer that maintains inventory must use the accrual method with regard to purchases and sales. Exceptions to this inventory rule include

         a) **Qualifying taxpayers** who satisfy the gross receipts test for each test year.

            i) The average annual gross receipts (consisting of the test year and the preceding 2 years) for each test year must be $27 million or less.

         b) **Qualifying small business taxpayers** who satisfy the gross receipts test for each test year.

            i) The average annual gross receipts must be $27 million or less.

            ii) The taxpayer must not be a corporation (other than an S corporation) or a partnership with a corporate partner.

            iii) The principal business activity cannot be mining, manufacturing, wholesale trade, retail trade, or information industries.

      3) Generally, C corporations, partnerships with a C corporation as a partner, charitable trusts with unrelated income, and tax shelters must use the accrual method.

         a) Tax shelters include any arrangement for which the principal purpose is avoidance of tax, any syndicates, and any enterprise in which the interests must be registered as a security.

         b) Exceptions to the general rule allow the following taxpayers to use the cash method if the entity is not a tax shelter:

            i) Qualified personal service corporations
            ii) Farming or tree-raising businesses

   d. Income is included when all the events have occurred that fix the right to receive it and the amount can be determined with reasonable accuracy.

      1) A right is not fixed if it is contingent on a future event.

EXAMPLE 1-3 **Income Not Constructively Received**
John is awarded a $10,000 bonus in 2022. If only half of the bonus is payable in 2022 with the other half paid at the end of 2023, contingent upon John completing another year of service for his employer, only $5,000 is taxable in 2022.

      2) The all-events test is satisfied when goods shipped on consignment are sold.

      3) Only in rare and unusual circumstances, in which neither the FMV received nor the FMV given can be ascertained, will the IRS respect holding a transaction open once the right to receive income is fixed. In those circumstances, income is accrued upon receipt.

         a) Proceeds from settlement of a lawsuit are determinable in amount with reasonable accuracy when received.

e. Prepaid income must generally be included in income when received.

1) Prepaid rent is includible in gross income in the year received. This rule applies to both cash-method and accrual-method taxpayers.

2) Prepaid income for services may be accrued over the period for which the services are to be performed, but only if it does not extend beyond the end of the next tax year.

a) If the taxpayer does not complete the performance within that period, the prepaid income is included in the year following receipt.

3) Merchandise sales. The right to income is fixed when it is earned, e.g., when goods are shipped.

a) Prepayments for goods must be included when reported for accounting purposes if reported earlier than when earned.

4) Taxpayers who use an accrual method of accounting, derive all their income from services, and do not charge interest or penalties for late payments may use the nonaccrual-experience method to report bad debts.

a) For example, a corporation may accrue 2% of gross sales as bad debt expense when, over the last 8 years, roughly 2% of gross sales have been uncollectible.

f. **Deductions.** Expenses are generally deductible in the period in which they accrue.

1) The accrual-method taxpayer may claim an allowable deduction when both of the following requirements are met:

a) All events have occurred that establish the fact of the liability, including that economic performance has occurred.

b) The amount can be determined with reasonable accuracy.

2) To the extent the amount of a liability is disputed, the test is not met. But any portion of a (still) contested amount that is paid is deductible.

3) Economic performance occurs as services are performed or as property is provided or used.

4) Other liabilities for which economic performance occurs as the taxpayer makes payments include liabilities for breach of contract (to the extent of incidental, consequential, and liquidated damages), violation of law, rebates and refunds, awards, prizes, jackpots, insurance, and warranty and service contracts.

Hybrid Methods

5. Any combination of permissible accounting methods may be permitted if the combination clearly reflects income and is consistently used.
   a. If inventory is used, the accrual method must be used for purchases and sales. The cash method may be used for other receipts and expenses if income is clearly reflected.
   b. A person may use different methods for separate businesses as long as the method used for each business clearly reflects the income of that particular enterprise.
   c. Any hybrid method for reporting expenses that includes the cash method is treated as the cash method and is subject to the limitations that apply to the cash method.

Related Parties

6. The Code requires matching of a deduction claimed by a payor and income reported by a payee in related-party cases of expense or interest transactions.
   a. Typically, if the payee is a cash-basis taxpayer, (s)he will include the payment in income in the taxable year received, and the payor will then deduct the payment in the same year.
   b. Related parties include a spouse; child; grandchild; parent; brother/sister (half or whole); or a related corporation, S corporation, partnership, estate, or trust.
   c. Deduction of an amount payable to a related party is allowed only when includible in gross income of the related party.

EXAMPLE 1-4 Deduction of a Payable to a Related Party

An individual cash-method taxpayer owns 55% of an accrual-method corporation. The corporation owes the individual $5,000 for rent incurred in Year 1. In Year 2, $5,000 was paid and reported as income by the individual. Because the corporation and individual are related parties, the corporation must wait to take the deduction of $5,000 until Year 2, the year it was reported as income by the related party.

Stop & Review

You have completed the outline for this subunit.

Study multiple-choice questions 5 through 13 beginning on page 27.

1.3 INVENTORY VALUATION

Identification Methods

1. There are three methods of identifying items in inventory:

Specific

a. The specific-identification method is used to identify the cost of each item of inventory by matching it with its cost of acquisition.

FIFO

b. The FIFO method assumes that the items first acquired are the first sold. Thus, the items remaining in inventory are the last items acquired.

LIFO

c. The LIFO method assumes that the latest goods to be acquired are the first to be sold. Thus, the oldest goods are considered to remain in inventory, and the cost of the oldest goods is used for valuing inventory.

Valuation Methods

2. The fundamental requirements for inventory valuation are that it conforms as nearly as possible to the best accounting practice in the trade or business and that it clearly reflects income. Approved methods include the following:

Cost Method

a. The cost method includes all direct and indirect costs associated with the inventory. The costs that must be included in inventory are found in Sec. 263A, known as the Uniform Capitalization rules (UNICAP). Section 263A states allocable costs related to property produced or to property acquired and held for resale by the taxpayer are not deductible and must be capitalized to the property. Allocable costs include direct costs as well as the property's appropriate share of indirect costs.

1) For beginning inventory, cost means the value of goods held at the end of the prior year.

2) For inventory purchased, cost means the price, minus (trade or cash) discounts, plus freight-in and other costs of acquisition. As an alternative to a reduction/deduction, cash discounts may instead be included in income.

a) If the merchant purchased inventory items and withdrew some of these items for personal use, the merchant must reduce the cost of purchases by the cost of the personal-use items.

3) For inventory produced, cost means all direct and indirect costs that are required to be capitalized under the uniform capitalization rules.

Lower-of-Cost-or-Market (LCM)

b. The LCM method values inventory at the lesser of the market value of the inventory or its cost at year end.

1) Each item in the inventory must be valued separately.
2) The LCM method cannot be used in conjunction with LIFO.

Rolling Average

c. Taxpayers using rolling-average inventory valuation for financial accounting purposes may use the same valuation method for federal income tax purposes. Use of this method is only allowed if

1) The taxpayer recomputes the rolling average cost of an inventory item on one of the following bases:
   a) Each time the taxpayer purchases or produces an additional unit or units of that item or
   b) On a regular basis but no less frequently than once per month, and
2) The taxpayer satisfies one of the following conditions:
   a) The variance percentage does not exceed 1% [(Rolling average cost – Actual cost) ÷ Rolling average cost] or
   b) The entire inventory of a taxpayer's trade or business turns at least four times per year (COGS ÷ Average inventory).

Retail Method

d. The retail inventory method may be used to value ending inventory for a department, a class of goods, or a stock-keeping unit.

1) A taxpayer maintaining more than one department or dealing in classes of goods with different percentages of gross profit must compute cost complements separately for each department or class of goods.
2) The retail selling price of ending inventory is converted to approximate cost or approximate LCM by using a cost-to-retail ratio or cost complement.
   a) A taxpayer may use the retail inventory method instead of valuing inventory at cost or LCM.
   b) The value of ending inventory is equal to the retail selling prices of goods on hand at the end of the tax year, multiplied by the cost complement.

NOTE: Once a valuation method is chosen, it cannot be changed without consent from the IRS.

FOB Shipping or Destination

3. FOB shipping point indicates that the buyer is responsible for the goods as soon as the goods are shipped.
4. FOB destination implies that the seller is responsible for the goods, and a sale is not recognized until the goods have reached the designated destination.

Consignment

5. Inventory out on consignment is included in ending inventory. The sale of consignment inventory is contingent on a future event (the person holding the inventory selling it).

Cash Method Inventory

6. Taxpayers with inventory who are allowed to use the cash method under the annual gross receipts test (i.e., less than $27 million in average annual gross receipts) treat the inventory as non-incidental materials and supplies.
   a. Non-incidental materials and supplies are those whose use or consumption are tracked and accounted for. Their cost is deducted in the year of use or consumption.

Unacceptable Inventory Valuation Methods

7. Examples of unacceptable methods of valuing inventory are found in Reg. 1.471-2(f) and include
   a. Deducting a reserve for price changes or an estimated amount for depreciation in the value of the inventory.
   b. Taking work in process, or other parts of the inventory, at a nominal price or at less than its full value.
   c. Omitting part of the stock on hand.
   d. Using a constant price or nominal value for so-called normal quantity of materials or goods in stock.
   e. Including stock in transit, shipped either to or by the taxpayer, the title to which the taxpayer does not hold.
   f. Segregating indirect production costs into fixed and variable production cost classifications and allocating only the variable costs to cost of goods produced, while treating fixed costs as period costs that are currently deductible (the direct cost method).
   g. Treating all or almost all indirect production costs (whether fixed or variable) as period costs that are currently deductible (the prime cost method).

You have completed the outline for this subunit.
Study multiple-choice questions 14 through 17 beginning on page 30.

1.4 ACCOUNTING PERIODS

The taxpayer adopts a tax year when the first income tax return is filed.

Tax Year

1. The term "tax year" is defined as follows:
   a. The annual accounting period regularly used by a taxpayer for keeping records of income, whether it be a calendar year or a fiscal year;
   b. The calendar year, if the taxpayer keeps no books, has no annual accounting period, or has an annual accounting period other than a calendar year that does not qualify as fiscal year; or
   c. The period for which the return is made, if for a period of less than 12 months.

Available Tax Years

2. The tax year may be either a calendar or fiscal year or the period for which a return is made, if the return is made for a period of less than 12 months (a short-period tax year).
   a. A calendar year is a period of 12 months ending on December 31.
   b. A fiscal year is a period of 12 months ending on the last day of any month other than December, or a 52- or 53-week tax year.
      1) A fiscal year will be recognized only if it is established as the taxpayer's annual accounting period and only if the books are kept in accord with it.
      2) A 52- or 53-week tax year. The taxpayer may elect to use a fiscal tax year that varies from 52 to 53 weeks if such period always ends on the same day of the week, either
         a) The last such day in a calendar month (e.g., January 31) or
         b) The closest such day to the last day of a calendar month (e.g., the last Friday in January).

Short Tax Year

   c. A return for a period of less than 12 months may be filed by a taxpayer that
      1) Existed during only part of what would otherwise be the taxable year or
      2) Changed the annual accounting period, e.g., from fiscal to calendar year.
         a) There are three steps to calculate the tax for a short tax year.
            i) The income must first be annualized.
            ii) The tax on the annualized income is calculated.
            iii) The short tax year portion of tax is determined.

$$\text{Annualized income} = \text{Short tax year income} \times \frac{\text{12 months}}{\text{Short tax year months}}$$

$$\text{Annualized income tax} = \text{Annualized income} \times \text{Tax rate}$$

$$\text{Short tax year tax} = \text{Annualized income tax} \times \frac{\text{Short tax year months}}{\text{12 months}}$$

d. Form 1128 is generally filed with the IRS to request the change in tax years.

1) The form must be filed by the due date (not including extensions) of the federal income tax return for the first effective year.

2) Permission to change tax years is normally granted when a substantial business purpose exists.

3) When the sole purpose of the change is to obtain a favorable tax status, the substantial business purpose test is not met.

e. Form 8716 is filed with the IRS by partnerships, S corporations, and personal service corporations (PSCs) to request a change in tax year other than a required tax year.

1) This is called a Sec. 444 election.

2) A Sec. 444 election may be made without first requesting permission to use the tax year and being denied permission.

EXAMPLE 1-5 Request for a Change of Tax Year

A partnership has a calendar year. Corporation X acquires over 50% ownership in the partnership. Corporation X has a June 30 tax year. Form 1128 is filed to change the partnership to a June 30 year end. June 30 is a required year end of the partnership. Form 8716 is filed instead of Form 1128 if the change is to a year end other than a required one.

You have completed the outline for this subunit.

Study multiple-choice questions 18 through 20 beginning on page 32.

QUESTIONS

1.1 Business Entities

1. LLCs may be an attractive small business alternative as opposed to an S corporation because LLCs offer the following advantage(s) not available in S corporations:

A. Inclusion of entity-level liabilities in tax basis.

B. Pass-through taxation.

C. Flexibility in types of owners and ownership interests.

D. Both inclusion of entity-level liabilities in tax basis and flexibility in types of owners and ownership interests.

Answer (D) is correct.

REQUIRED: The advantages available to LLCs but not S corporations.

DISCUSSION: The basis of each member in an LLC, like a partnership, is increased or decreased by the allocable share of the LLC's liabilities (IRC Sec. 752). This allows for tax loss claims in excess of capital investment and greater tax-free distributions of money and property to members. A corporation's debt may not be used by an S corporation shareholder to increase their basis, regardless of guaranteeing the debt. LLCs have no limitations on the number of owners allowed. S corporations are limited to 100 shareholders. LLCs also do not have any restrictions as to the type of owners. S corporations are restricted to estates, certain tax-exempt organizations, certain trusts, and to individuals.

Answer (A) is incorrect. Flexibility in types of owners and ownership interests are also advantages of an LLC not available to S corporations. **Answer (B) is incorrect.** Both LLCs and S corporations have the advantage of pass-through taxation. **Answer (C) is incorrect.** Inclusion of entity-level liabilities in tax basis is also an advantage of an LLC not available to S corporations.

2. Which form of business entity is NOT a legal entity separate and apart from its owner?

A. Corporation.

B. Partnership.

C. Sole proprietorship.

D. S corporation.

Answer (C) is correct.

REQUIRED: The form of business entity that is not a legal entity separate from its owner.

DISCUSSION: Several different forms of businesses have been made available to taxpayers over the years. The sole proprietorship is the most common form of business entity. It is not a legal entity separate and apart from its owner. The owner has unlimited liability with regard to the sole proprietorship.

Answer (A) is incorrect. A corporation is a separate entity from its owners. Corporations were created to allow for the limited liability of the owners. **Answer (B) is incorrect.** A partnership is separate from its owners, although income flows through and is taxed on each owner's personal tax return. **Answer (D) is incorrect.** The S corporation is a separate entity from its owners. It has the limited liability feature of the C corporation. However, there are several ownership restrictions placed on the S corporation.

3. Which of the following is an advantage of forming a limited liability company (LLC) as opposed to a partnership?

A. The entity may avoid taxation.

B. The entity may have any number of owners.

C. The owner may participate in management while limiting personal liability.

D. The entity may make disproportionate allocations and distributions to members.

Answer (C) is correct.

REQUIRED: The advantage of an LLC over a partnership.

DISCUSSION: A great advantage of the LLC is that its creditors have no claim on the personal assets of members (owners) or managers. Moreover, an LLC is assumed to be member-managed unless its articles of organization state otherwise.

Answer (A) is incorrect. Partners are taxed directly. Members of an LLC may elect to be taxed as partners. **Answer (B) is incorrect.** A partnership must have minimum of two partners. An LLC may have one or more members. **Answer (D) is incorrect.** The partners in a partnership and the members of an LLC may agree to disproportionate allocations and distributions.

4. Under which circumstance is an entity required to apply for a new employer identification number?

A. Proprietorship that incorporates.

B. Business name change.

C. Electing or revoking S corporation status.

D. 50% change of interest in partnership within 12 months.

Answer (A) is correct.

REQUIRED: The circumstance that requires a new EIN.

DISCUSSION: Generally, a sole proprietor should file only one Form SS-4 and needs only one EIN, regardless of the number of businesses operated as a sole proprietorship or trade names under which a business operates. However, if the proprietorship incorporates or enters into a partnership, a new EIN is required. Also, each corporation in an affiliated group must have its own EIN.

Answer (B) is incorrect. Existing entities do not apply for a new EIN if only changing the business name. **Answer (C) is incorrect.** An existing corporation that is electing or revoking S corporation status should use its previously assigned EIN. **Answer (D) is incorrect.** Existing partnerships do not apply for a new EIN as a result of the sale or exchange of at least 50% of the total interests in partnership capital and profits within a 12-month period.

1.2 Accounting Methods

5. John is a cash-basis taxpayer. He received the following items of income in December 2022:

1. The loan on his truck was forgiven because he performed accounting work for the dealer. He owed $2,000 at the time.
2. A retainer of $500 from a new client to guarantee that his services would be available in February when the client would need help preparing financial statements.
3. The $800 for work he completed in November of 2021.

How much of this income must John include on his 2022 tax return?

A. $500

B. $1,300

C. $2,500

D. $3,300

Answer (D) is correct.

REQUIRED: The amount of income a taxpayer must include on his or her tax return.

DISCUSSION: Gross income means all income from whatever source derived unless specifically excluded (Sec. 61). A taxpayer who is solvent generally realizes income to the extent that debts are forgiven (Sec. 108). Cash-basis taxpayers must report prepaid income when received.

Answer (A) is incorrect. The forgiven debt and the retainer are both included as gross income. **Answer (B) is incorrect.** The forgiven debt is included in gross income. **Answer (C) is incorrect.** The $800 received is included in 2022 because it is actually received in 2022.

6. You can compute your taxable income under which of the following accounting methods?

A. Hybrid method.

B. Accrual method.

C. Special method for certain items.

D. All of the answers are correct.

Answer (D) is correct.

REQUIRED: The permissible accounting method(s) used to compute taxable income.

DISCUSSION: A taxpayer is permitted to use the hybrid method, accrual method, and other special methods for certain items when computing taxable income subject to specific rules (Publication 538).

7. The Kilometer Partnership sells computers and maintains its accounting system on the accrual basis. Kilometer sold and delivered a computer on December 29, 2021, and billed the customer $3,250 on January 7, 2022. Kilometer received the $3,250 payment on February 15, 2022. The check cleared on February 22, 2022. On which date will Kilometer recognize this income?

A. January 7, 2022.

B. February 15, 2022.

C. December 29, 2021.

D. February 22, 2022.

Answer (C) is correct.

REQUIRED: The date an accrual-basis taxpayer recognizes income.

DISCUSSION: A sale is included in gross income on the date in which all the events that fix the taxpayer's right to receive income have occurred and an amount can be determined with reasonable accuracy. Kilometer Partnership recognizes the sale of the computer on December 29, 2021. This is the date of the sale and delivery of the product. Both the right to receive income and a reasonably accurate estimate of the amount to be received arise on this date (Publication 538).

Answer (A) is incorrect. The date on which a bill is sent to the customer is generally not the earliest date that a taxpayer can include a sale in gross income. **Answer (B) is incorrect.** Kilometer would recognize the sale on February 15, 2022, if it were a cash-basis taxpayer. **Answer (D) is incorrect.** The date on which a customer's check clears does not represent the time when all the events to secure the taxpayer's right to receive income occurs.

8. Generally, all of the following entities may use the cash method of accounting EXCEPT

A. A family farming corporation with gross receipts of $27 million or less.

B. An entity with no inventories and average annual gross receipts of $27 million or less.

C. A qualified personal service corporation.

D. A corporation that has long-term contracts.

Answer (D) is correct.

REQUIRED: The entity prohibited from using the cash method of accounting.

DISCUSSION: Corporations that have long-term contracts must use a special method of accounting (which is neither a pure cash nor accrual method). The following entities, however, may use the cash method of accounting: (1) any corporation or partnership (other than a tax shelter) that meets the gross receipts test ($27 million) for all tax years and (2) a qualified personal service corporation (Publication 538).

Answer (A) is incorrect. A family farming corporation with gross receipts of $27 million or less may use the cash method of accounting. **Answer (B) is incorrect.** An entity with no inventories and average annual gross receipts less than $27 million may use the cash method of accounting. **Answer (C) is incorrect.** Qualified personal service corporations may use the cash method of accounting.

9. Erin earned $1,000 in interest in 2020. Erin withdrew $700 in 2021 and $300 in 2022. How much of the original $1,000 should Erin report as interest earned in 2022?

A. $0

B. $300

C. $700

D. $1,000

Answer (A) is correct.

REQUIRED: The amount of interest to be reported in gross income.

DISCUSSION: Section 61(a) states that interest is considered income and is included on the taxpayer's tax return the year it is earned. The interest income of $1,000 earned in 2020 will have been included in Erin's 2020 tax return without regard to when the interest was withdrawn.

Answer (B) is incorrect. The full $1,000 of interest earned in 2020 was taxed, and the $300 will not be taxed again in 2022. **Answer (C) is incorrect.** The full $1,000 of interest earned in 2020 was taxed, and the $700 will not be taxed again in 2022. **Answer (D) is incorrect.** The $1,000 was taxed in 2020 when it was earned; it will not be taxed again in 2022.

10. Mark is an accrual-method taxpayer. He shipped $500 worth of merchandise to Ralph on December 30, 2022. Mark sent Ralph an invoice January 2, 2023, that was payable in 30 days. Ralph mailed his check to Mark on February 2, 2023. Mark deposited the check on February 6, 2023. Mark received and reconciled his bank statement March 3, 2023. When does Mark record the $500 in income?

A. January 2, 2023, because that is when he invoiced Ralph.

B. March 3, 2023, because that is when Mark verified that the $500 check had been accepted as a deposit.

C. December 30, 2022, the date when he shipped the merchandise to Ralph.

D. February 6, 2023, because that is when Mark deposited the check from Ralph.

Answer (C) is correct.

REQUIRED: The date that Mark should record income when using the accrual method.

DISCUSSION: An accrual-method taxpayer accounts for income in the period it is actually earned. Income is included when all the events have occurred that fix the right to receive it and the amount can be determined with reasonable accuracy. Because Mark has performed all activities necessary for the income to be earned, he must include the $500 as of December 30.

Answer (A) is incorrect. The date the invoice is sent out is irrelevant. **Answer (B) is incorrect.** The date Mark reconciles his bank statement is irrelevant. **Answer (D) is incorrect.** The date the merchandise is shipped, not the date Ralph deposited the check, is used in determining when to include the amount in gross income.

11. Generally, a substantial business inventory requires use of which method of accounting?

A. Cash.

B. Hybrid.

C. Accrual.

D. None of the answers are correct.

Answer (C) is correct.

REQUIRED: The required method of accounting when a substantial business inventory is present.

DISCUSSION: Regulation 1.446-1(c)(2) states that, when inventory is used, the accrual method of accounting must be used for purchases and sales.

Answer (A) is incorrect. Generally, the accrual, not the cash, method is required. **Answer (B) is incorrect.** Generally, the accrual, not the hybrid, method is required. **Answer (D) is incorrect.** The accrual method of accounting must be used.

12. In September 2022, Charlie, a self-employed lawyer, performed legal services for a client that has a men's clothing store. In payment for his services, Charlie received store credit of $3,500 in 2022. Charlie uses $1,500 of his store credit in 2022 and the balance in 2023. How should Charlie include the income?

	2022	2023
A.	$3,500	$0
B.	$1,500	$2,000
C.	$0	$3,500

D. None of the answers are correct.

Answer (A) is correct.

REQUIRED: The amount includible in gross income in the respective year.

DISCUSSION: The taxpayer is to include in gross income amounts received as salary or wages. If a taxpayer is an accrual method payor, items are included when the amounts receivable are reasonably estimable and all necessary events have occurred to ensure the taxpayer's right to receive income. On the other hand, a cash-method taxpayer includes items in gross income when actually or constructively received. Specifically, constructive receipt occurs when payment is made available to the taxpayer without restriction; actual possession is not necessary. Therefore, regardless of Charlie's method of accounting, all $3,500 would be included in 2022 (Publication 334).

Answer (B) is incorrect. All $3,500, not just $1,500, is included in 2022. **Answer (C) is incorrect.** All income is included in 2022, not 2023. **Answer (D) is incorrect.** One of the answers is correct.

13. Which of the following statements regarding accounting methods is false?

A. If inventories are necessary, the accrual method is used for sales and purchases.

B. A combination (hybrid) method is not an acceptable method of accounting.

C. A change from the accrual to the cash method of accounting requires consent from the IRS.

D. Under the cash method of accounting, gross income includes all items of income actually or constructively received during the year.

Answer (B) is correct.

REQUIRED: The false statement regarding accounting methods.

DISCUSSION: Under Sec. 446, one or more hybrid methods of accounting may be authorized by regulation. The regulations permit the use of a combination of methods if the combination clearly reflects income and is consistently used.

Answer (A) is incorrect. If inventory is used, the accrual method must be used for purchases and sales. The cash method may be used for other receipts and expenses if income is clearly stated. **Answer (C) is incorrect.** A change in accounting methods generally requires consent of the IRS, including change in the overall system of accounting. **Answer (D) is incorrect.** Under the cash method, all cash and constructive cash is considered income.

1.3 Inventory Valuation

14. A taxpayer is a merchant who has purchased inventory items. He withdrew some of these items for personal use. He must

A. Increase his sales by the cost of the items withdrawn.

B. Reduce the cost of purchases by the cost of the personal-use items.

C. Reduce the cost of purchases by the fair market value of the personal-use items.

D. Reduce beginning inventory by the cost of the personal-use items.

Answer (B) is correct.

REQUIRED: The cost of inventory items used for personal use.

DISCUSSION: Publication 334 states, "If you withdraw merchandise for your personal or family use, you must exclude this cost from the total amount of merchandise you bought for sale. Do this by crediting the purchases or sales account with the cost of merchandise you withdraw for personal use. You also must charge the amount to your drawing account."

15. Which of the following statements with respect to methods of valuing or identifying items in inventory is false?

A. Under the lower-of-cost-or-market method, a business compares the market value of each individual item on hand at the inventory date with its cost and uses the lower value as its inventory value.

B. If a taxpayer uses the specific-identification (cost) method or the lower-of-cost-or-market method to value inventory, (s)he may switch between the cost and the lower-of-cost-or-market methods anytime (s)he wishes, as long as the method (s)he chooses is used for a complete tax year.

C. You may adopt the LIFO method by filing either Form 970, *Application to Use LIFO Inventory Method*, or a statement that has all the information required in Form 970.

D. Deducting a reserve for price changes or an estimated amount for depreciation in the value of your inventory is not a recognized inventory practice for tax purposes.

Answer (B) is correct.

REQUIRED: The false statement regarding inventory valuation methods.

DISCUSSION: The two most common methods to value inventory are the cost method and the lower-of-cost-or-market method. Once a method is chosen, it may not be changed to another method without consent from the IRS.

Answer (A) is incorrect. Under the lower-of-cost-or-market method, the taxpayer values each item of inventory at the lesser of the item's (1) market value at the inventory date or (2) cost at year end. **Answer (C) is incorrect.** A taxpayer may adopt the LIFO method by filing either Form 970, *Application to Use LIFO Inventory Method*, or a statement that has all all the information required in Form 970. **Answer (D) is incorrect.** Taxpayers may not deduct a reserve for price changes or an estimated amount for depreciation in the value of held inventory.

16. Mr. and Mrs. Hammer own a retail hardware store. Which of the following items should they include in their December 31 current year inventory?

A. Envelopes and stationery used in the office.

B. A lawnmower that was sold to, and paid for by, a customer and has not yet been picked up.

C. In-transit cash on delivery (C.O.D.) shipment of nails to a customer.

D. Goods consigned to Mr. and Mrs. Hammer.

Answer (C) is correct.

REQUIRED: The item that is included in inventory.

DISCUSSION: Regulation 1.471-1 provides that inventory should include all finished goods, work-in-process, and raw materials and supplies that will physically become a part of merchandise intended for sale. Merchandise should be included in inventory only if title thereto is vested in the taxpayer. The title to items shipped C.O.D. does not pass to the purchaser until the items are delivered. Therefore, the Hammers still have title to the inventory.

Answer (A) is incorrect. The envelopes and stationery were not acquired for sale. **Answer (B) is incorrect.** The title has been transferred to the purchaser. **Answer (D) is incorrect.** The title remains with the consignor.

17. Which of the following items are generally included in inventory?

A. Goods for sale that someone else has consigned to you.

B. Equipment used in your business to manufacture goods.

C. Goods you have sent out on consignment for someone else to sell.

D. Goods in transit to you for which title has not yet passed to you.

Answer (C) is correct.

REQUIRED: The items included in inventory.

DISCUSSION: Ending inventory includes the cost of the raw materials, the direct and indirect labor costs that are attributable to the manufacturing of a product and are included in COGS, overhead costs, and materials and supplies used in manufacturing goods, such as hardware or chemicals. Inventory out on consignment is included in ending inventory. The sale of consignment inventory is contingent on a future event (the person holding the inventory selling it).

Answer (A) is incorrect. The inventory you hold on consignment for someone else is properly included in the other entity's inventory, not your own. **Answer (B) is incorrect.** This equipment is depreciable property and should not be included in inventory. The overhead associated with those machines should be charged to COGS and/or added to inventory. **Answer (D) is incorrect.** Those goods would properly be included in the shipping company's inventory, not your own.

1.4 Accounting Periods

18. Which form is used to change from one required tax year to another?

A. Form 1120 (Schedule H).

B. Form 1128.

C. Form 8716.

D. Form 8752.

Answer (B) is correct.

REQUIRED: The correct form for changing within required tax years.

DISCUSSION: Form 1128 is generally filed with the IRS to request the change in tax years. Permission to change tax years is normally granted when a substantial business purpose exists. However, when the sole purpose of the change is to obtain a favorable tax status, the substantial business purpose test is not met. Only partnerships, S corporations, and PSCs may change to a tax year other than a required tax year. To do so, the partnership, S corporation, or PSC files Form 8716.

Answer (A) is incorrect. Schedule H of Form 1120 is used by PSCs to figure the required minimum distribution and the maximum deductible amount for determining if a Sec. 444 election (other than required tax year) will be terminated. **Answer (C) is incorrect.** Form 8716 is filed by partnerships, S corporations, and PSCs to elect under Sec. 444 to have a tax year other than a required tax year. **Answer (D) is incorrect.** Similar to Form 1120 (Schedule H), Form 8752 is used to figure a required payment or to obtain a refund for determining if a Sec. 444 election (other than required tax year) will be terminated; however, this form is for partnerships and S corporations, not PSCs.

19. In order to adopt a fiscal tax year on its first federal income tax return, the taxpayer must

A. Maintain books and records and report income and expenses using that tax year.

B. Attach a completed Form 1128 to his or her fiscal-year-basis income tax return.

C. File a short-period return.

D. Get IRS approval.

Answer (A) is correct.

REQUIRED: The procedure that a taxpayer must follow to adopt a fiscal tax year on its first tax return.

DISCUSSION: Permission from the IRS is generally not needed to place a taxpayer's first tax year on either a calendar- or a fiscal-year basis. A taxpayer's first tax year is selected on the initial return. However, in order to adopt a fiscal year, the new taxpayer must adopt that year on the books and records before the due date for filing the return for that year (not including extensions).

Answer (B) is incorrect. A completed Form 1128 is not required to adopt a fiscal tax year on a taxpayer's first federal income tax return. **Answer (C) is incorrect.** A short-period tax year return is for a period of less than 12 months for taxpayers with special circumstances. **Answer (D) is incorrect.** IRS approval is not necessary on the initial return.

20. Which of the following dates would NOT be considered the end of a tax year?

A. The last Friday in June.

B. September 30, 2022.

C. April 15, 2022.

D. December 31, 2022.

Answer (C) is correct.

REQUIRED: The date not considered the end of a tax year.

DISCUSSION: A calendar year is a period of 12 months ending on December 31. A fiscal year is a period of 12 months ending on the last day of any month other than December, or a 52- or 53-week tax year. A fiscal year will be recognized only if it is established as the taxpayer's annual accounting period and only if the books are kept in accord with it. The taxpayer may elect to use a fiscal tax year that varies from 52 to 53 weeks if such period always ends on the same day of the week, either the last such day in a calendar month or the closest such day to the last day of a calendar month (Publication 538).

Answer (A) is incorrect. It could be an end of tax year date under a 52- or 53-week tax year. **Answer (B) is incorrect.** It could be an end of tax year date under a fiscal year or 52- or 53-week tax year. **Answer (D) is incorrect.** It is the end of a calendar-year tax year.

Go to Online Course

Access the **Gleim EA Premium Review System** featuring our SmartAdapt technology from your Gleim Personal Classroom to continue your studies.

You will experience a personalized study environment with exam-emulating multiple-choice questions.

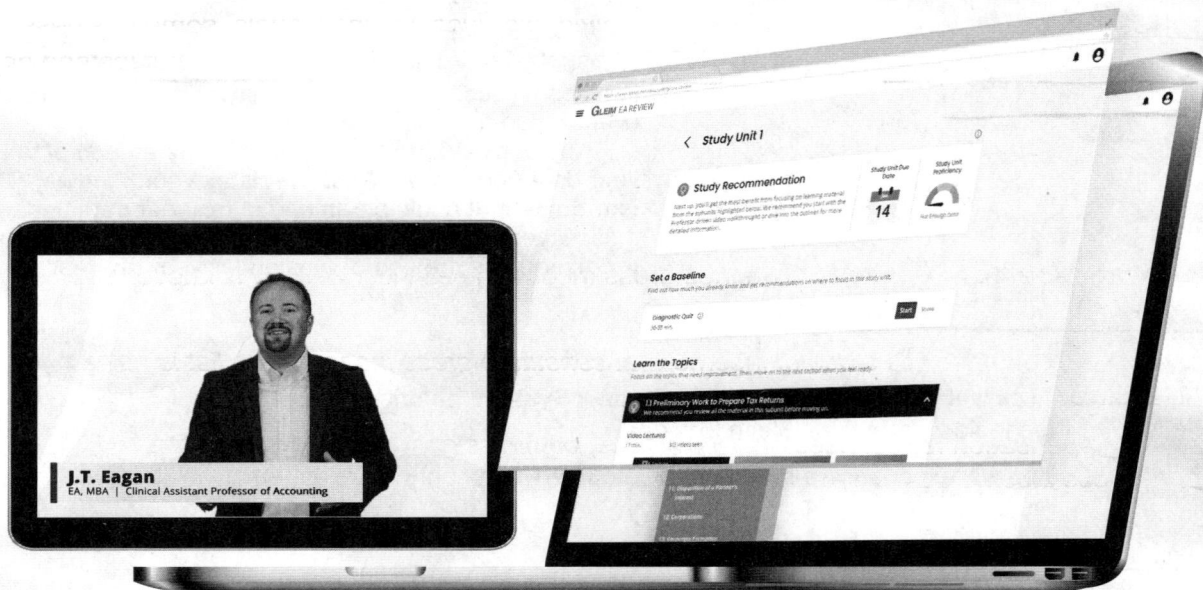

STUDY UNIT TWO

INCOME AND FARMS

(13 pages of outline)

Businesses define gross income the same as individuals. Also like individuals, some business transactions do not currently recognize or indefinitely exclude recognition of income, but instead defer recognition until a later period. This study unit also covers unique aspects of self-employment income and farm income.

2.1 GROSS INCOME

The Internal Revenue Code (IRC) defines gross income as all income from whatever source derived except as otherwise provided.

1. Section 61(a) enumerates types of income that constitute gross income. The list is not exhaustive.
   a. Compensation for services, including fees, commissions, and fringe benefits
   b. Gross income derived from business
   c. Gains derived from dealings in property
   d. Interest
   e. Rents
   f. Royalties
   g. Dividends
   h. Annuities
   i. Income from life insurance and endowment contracts
   j. Pensions
   k. Income from discharge of indebtedness
   l. Distributive share of partnership gross income
   m. Income in respect of a decedent (income earned but not received before death)
   n. Income from an interest in an estate or trust
2. Other types of income also constitute gross income unless a statute specifically provides for their exclusion.

Business Income

3. Gross income includes all income from a trade or business.
   a. Gross income from a business that sells products or commodities is

	Gross sales (receipts)
–	Cost of goods sold
+	Other gross income (e.g., rentals)
=	**Gross income from the business**

b. Cost of goods sold (COGS) is essentially treated as a return of capital. A return of capital is not income for tax purposes. Typically, COGS for a tax year is

	Beginning inventory
+	Inventory purchased during year
–	Year-end inventory
=	**COGS**

c. COGS should be determined in accordance with the method of accounting consistently used by the business.

d. State and local sales taxes imposed on a buyer, which are required to be collected and paid to state or local governments, are not income. When a sale is completed, the amount of sales tax charged to the customer becomes a liability, or money owed.

Prepaid Income

4. Generally, amounts that are received in advance for future services are required to be included in the year of receipt. However, accrual-basis taxpayers can elect to defer recognition until the time of performance, up to the year after the payment date.

Discharge of Debt

5. Gross income includes **discharge (cancellation) of indebtedness** when a debt is canceled in whole or part for consideration.

   a. If a debtor performs services to satisfy a debt, the debtor must recognize the amount of the debt as income. However, income is not recognized from a canceled debt to the extent the payment would have been a deduction.

   b. If a creditor gratuitously cancels a debt, the amount forgiven is treated as a gift.

   c. Gross income **does not include** discharges that

      1) Occur in bankruptcy.

      2) Occur when the debtor is insolvent but not in bankruptcy.

         a) The maximum amount that can be excluded is the amount by which liabilities exceed the FMV of assets.

      3) Are related to qualified farm indebtedness.

      4) Are related to a purchase-money debt reduction in which a seller reduces the debt and the debtor is not in bankruptcy and is not insolvent. The discharge is treated as a purchase price adjustment.

   d. When a taxpayer excludes discharge of indebtedness under a., b., or c. above, the taxpayer must reduce his or her tax attributes in the following order:

      1) NOLs
      2) General business credit
      3) Minimum tax credit
      4) Capital loss carryovers
      5) Basis reductions

      NOTE: However, the taxpayer may first elect to decrease the basis in depreciable property.

   e. Generally, the creditor will send the taxpayer Form 1099-C listing the amount of cancellation of debt to be reported.

6. **Examples of Other Taxable Income**

   a. Gross income includes the **recovery of tax benefit** items in a prior year.

EXAMPLE 2-1	Recovery of Tax Benefit -- Bad Debt
Taxpayer writes off bad debt in Year 1. In Year 7, the debtor pays Taxpayer the principal of the debt written off, which must be included in gross income because the deduction in Year 1 reduced the tax liability.	

      1) Amounts recovered during the tax year that did **not** provide a tax benefit in the prior year are excluded.

EXAMPLE 2-2	Recovery Not Providing a Tax Benefit
Taxpayer pays state income tax in excess of the standard deduction and itemizes deductions. Subsequent refunds in excess of the applicable standard deduction must be included in gross income. However, if Taxpayer elected the standard deduction, the refund would not be included because no tax benefit from payment of state income tax was realized.	

      2) A similar rule applies to credits.

   b. Prizes and awards

   c. Gasoline or fuel credits or refunds

   d. Gambling winnings (e.g., lottery and raffle winnings)

   e. Jury duty fees

   f. Income from the rental of personal property if the taxpayer engages in the activity for profit but is not in the business of renting property

   g. Income from an activity not engaged in for profit (e.g., hobby income)

      1) Hobby-related expenses are not deductible.

   h. Reimbursements for items deducted in an earlier tax return (e.g., state income taxes, bad debts, and medical expenses)

   i. Advances of wages and commissions

      1) Such advances are considered income when received.

   j. Supplemental wages, which are compensation paid in addition to an employee's regular wages

      1) They do not include payments for travel reimbursements paid at the federal government per diem rate.

   k. Finance reserve income

   l. Scrap sales

   m. Cooperative patronage dividends

Assignment of Income

7. Gross income includes income attributable to a taxpayer even though the income is received by other taxpayers. This doctrine imposes the tax on income on those who earn it, produce the right to receive it or enjoy the benefit of it when paid, or control property that is its source.

EXAMPLE 2-3 **Assignment of Income**
Swift, a life insurance salesperson, directs his employer to pay his commissions to his daughter. The commissions paid to Swift's daughter are gross income to Swift.

a. The doctrine applies to income earned by personal services or derived from property.

EXAMPLE 2-4 **Assignment of Interest Income Earned on Securities**
Taxpayer makes a gift of interest earned on securities to her 20-year-old daughter who attends college. The interest is gross income to Taxpayer.

b. Assignment of an income-producing asset is effective to shift the gross income to the assignee.

EXAMPLE 2-5 **Assignment of Interest Income from Transferred Securities**
Taxpayer gives the underlying securities to her 20-year-old daughter. Interest earned after the transfer is gross income to the daughter.

c. Effective assignment requires that
   1) The transfer of property be complete and bona fide,
   2) No control is retained over either the property or the income it produces, and
   3) The transfer take place before the income is actually earned.

Rental Income

8. Amounts received or accrued as rent must be included in gross income. Rental income is any payment received for the use or occupation of property.
   a. Cash-basis taxpayers report rental income in the year it is received, regardless of when it was earned. Accrual-method taxpayers generally report income when it is earned rather than when it is received. However, prepaid rent is income when received for both accrual-method and cash-basis taxpayers.
   b. Payment by a lessee of any expenses of a lessor is generally considered additional rental income to the lessor.
      1) Capital improvements made by a lessee are not income unless in lieu of paying rent or in exchange for a reduction in rent.
      2) The income is taxed when the property is sold.
   c. Consideration received by a lessor for cancellation of a lease is a substitution for rental payments and not a return of capital.

d. Property or services received as rent in lieu of cash must be included in rental income at the fair market value of the property or services.

EXAMPLE 2-6 **Service in Lieu of Rent**
Taxpayer's tenant is a painter and offers to paint Taxpayer's rental property instead of paying rent for 2 months. If Taxpayer accepts the offer, Taxpayer includes in rental income the amount the tenant would have paid for 2 months' rent.

e. Security deposits used as final payments of rent are considered advance rent and are included in income when received.

1) A security deposit is not included in income when received if the lessor plans to return it to the tenant at the end of the lease.

2) Any part of a security deposit kept during any year because the tenant does not live up to the terms of the lease is included in income for that year.

f. A lease with an option to buy is a rental agreement that gives the tenant the right to buy the rental property. Payments received under such an agreement are generally rental income.

g. An individual lessor generally reports rental real estate income and expenses on Schedule E (Form 1040), but Schedule C (Form 1040) is used if the taxpayer provided significant services to the real property lessee.

h. A corporate lessor (non-pass-through entity) generally reports rental real estate income and expenses on Form 1120.

Income from Bonds

9. For bonds issued at a premium, income is recognized to the extent of the amortized bond premium. The premium is amortized over the life of the bond.

You have completed the outline for this subunit.

Study multiple-choice questions 1 through 8 beginning on page 48.

2.2 SELF-EMPLOYMENT INCOME

A FICA tax liability is imposed on net earnings from self-employment (SE).

Included

1. Net earnings from self-employment include
   a. Net income from a trade or business,
   b. General distributive share of the ordinary income or loss of a partnership (whether active or not),
   c. Guaranteed payments for services from a partnership,
   d. Corporate directors' fees, and
   e. Payments for lost earnings.

Excluded

2. Net earnings from self-employment do not include
   a. Salaries, fees, and other income subject to Social Security or Medicare tax that a taxpayer received for performing services as an employee
   b. Rent from real estate and personal property leased with real estate unless services are provided to tenants
      1) Services generally are provided for the occupants if they are primarily for their convenience and not services normally provided with the rental of rooms for occupancy only (Publication 334).
   c. Dividends on shares of stock and interest from any bond, debenture, note, certificate, or other indebtedness issued with interest coupons or in registered form by a corporation unless they are received by a dealer in stocks or securities in the ordinary course of his or her business
   d. An S corporation shareholder's distributive share of income or loss
   e. Income received as a retired partner under a written partnership plan that provides for lifelong periodic retirement payments, assuming
      1) No other interest in the partnership
      2) Services were not performed during the year
   f. The sale, exchange, involuntary conversion (gains resulting from casualty or theft losses), or other disposition of property unless the property is stock in the business or property that is considered inventory primarily held for sale to customers in the ordinary course of business
   g. Fees received for services performed as a notary public

Self-Employment Tax

3. The FICA tax liability is imposed on net earnings from self-employment at twice the rate that applies to an employer, that is, 15.3% [2 × (6.20% Social Security tax + 1.45% Medicare tax)].

$$\text{NI from self-employment} - \left(.0765 \times \text{NI from self-employment}\right) = \text{Net earnings from self-employment}$$

a. Net income from self-employment does not include the following:
   1) Gain or loss from disposition of business property
      a) Gains from casualty losses of inventory are considered self-employment income.
   2) Capital gain or loss
   3) Nonbusiness interest
   4) Dividends
   5) Income or expenses related to personal activities
   6) Wages, salaries, or tips received as an employee

b. Rental income is normally not subject to self-employment tax unless services are provided to tenants. Services generally are provided for the occupants if they are primarily for their convenience and not services normally provided with the rental of rooms for occupancy only.

c. Payment received from lost earnings are included in net earnings from self-employment.

d. A self-employed person is allowed a deduction for the employer's portion of the FICA taxes paid to arrive at his or her AGI. For 2022, this equals
   1) 6.20% of the first $147,000 of net self-employment income plus
   2) 1.45% of net self-employment income (no cap).

e. An individual who is engaged in the business of selling real estate to customers for profit is a real estate dealer.
   1) A real estate dealer who holds property both for sale to customers in the ordinary course of business and for investment is subject to self-employment tax only on net rent from property held for sale in the ordinary course of trade or business as a real estate dealer.
   2) Rent from property held for investment or speculation is not subject to self-employment tax.

f. A partner's share of partnership income as well as any guaranteed payments from a partnership are subject to self-employment tax, whether or not the partner is an active participant. However, S corporation earnings required to be included in a shareholder's gross income are not self-employment income.

g. A limited partner's share of income from a partnership is generally not subject to self-employment tax. However, any guaranteed payments paid to the limited partner are subject to self-employment tax.

h. A decedent partner includes partnership income (or loss) through the end of the month of death on the final return of the decedent.

i. Interest earned on accounts receivable is not self-employment income.

j. An ordained, licensed, or commissioned minister must include the rental value of a home provided to him or her as part of his or her pay for duties performed as earnings from self-employment for purposes of the self-employment tax. This is true even though the rental value of such a home is not included in gross income for income tax purposes.

k. The employee's portion of the FICA taxes is not deductible.

l. The self-employment tax is computed using the total earnings from self-employment; therefore, no change in computation is necessary if the self-employed person has more than one trade or business.

m. For 2022, the maximum amount of wages subject to Social Security tax is $147,000. However, the Medicare component does not have a cap amount.

n. The employee portion includes an additional 0.9% for high-income earnings, i.e., earnings in excess of $200,000 ($250,000 MFJ, $125,000 MFS).

   1) Individuals with wages and self-employment income calculate their liabilities in three steps:

      a) Tax is calculated on any wages in excess of the applicable threshold without regard to any withholding;

      b) The applicable threshold is reduced by the total amount of Medicare wages received, but not below zero; and

      c) The tax is calculated on any self-employment income in excess of the reduced threshold.

EXAMPLE 2-7 Tax on Self-Employment Income

C, a single filer, has $130,000 in wages and $145,000 in self-employment income. C's wages are not in excess of the $200,000 threshold for single filers, so C is not liable for the surtax on these wages. Before calculating the tax on self-employment income, the $200,000 threshold for single filers is reduced by C's $130,000 in wages, resulting in a reduced self-employment threshold of $70,000. C is liable to pay the tax on $75,000 of self-employment income ($145,000 – $70,000).

o. In 2022, self-employed persons may deduct 100% of amounts paid for health insurance from gross income (AGI). The deduction does not reduce self-employment income and is taken on Schedule 1. The insurance can be for themselves, their spouses, or their dependents. There is an exception for self-employed taxpayers whose spouse's employer offers coverage.

p. Contributions to a qualified retirement plan for a self-employed individual do not constitute a business expense. Therefore, they are not deductible when computing self-employment tax.

Farm Optional Method

4. A taxpayer may use this method to figure net earnings from farm self-employment if gross farm income was $9,060 or less or net farm profits were less than $6,540.

   a. Net farm profits are the total of specified amounts from Schedule F (Form 1040), "Net farm profit or (loss)," and Schedule K-1 (Form 1065), "Net earnings (loss) from self-employment," minus the amount the taxpayer would have entered on Schedule SE, from specified social security benefits, had the taxpayer not used the optional method.

   b. There is no limit on how many years this method can be used.

   c. Under this method, the taxpayer reports in Part II, two-thirds of gross farm income, up to $6,040, as net earnings. This method can increase or decrease net earnings from farm self-employment, even if the farming business had a loss.

Figure Farm Net Earnings

IF gross income is . . .	THEN net earnings are equal to . . .
$9,060 or less	two-thirds of gross farm income.
more than $9,060	$6,040.

d. For a farm partnership, figure the taxpayer's share of gross income based on the partnership agreement. With guaranteed payments, the taxpayer's share of the partnership's gross income is the taxpayer's guaranteed payments plus the taxpayer's share of the gross income after it is reduced by all guaranteed payments made by the partnership.

1) If the taxpayer was a limited partner, only guaranteed payments for services the taxpayer actually rendered to or on behalf of the partnership would be included.

Use of the Farm Optional Method

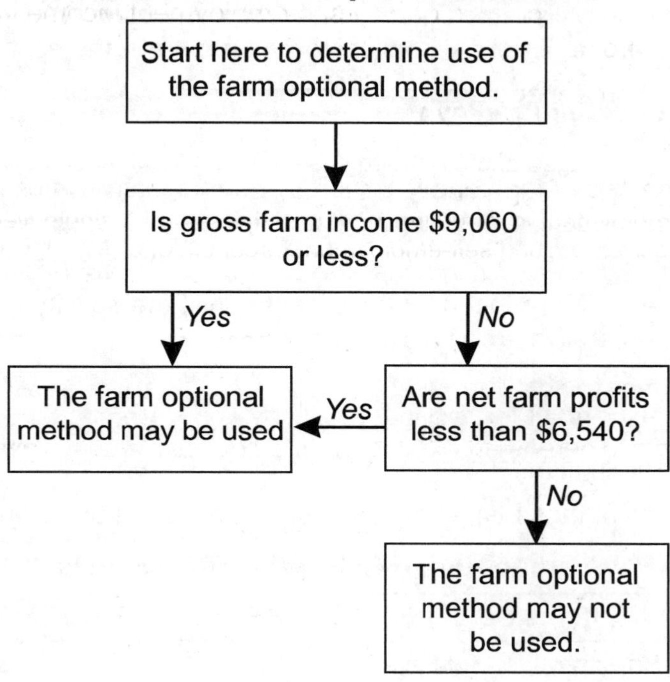

Figure 2-1

Religious Exemptions

5. A religious exemption for self-employment tax is available for a duly ordained, commissioned, or licensed minister of a church; a member of a religious order; or a Christian Science practitioner if (s)he files an exemption certificate (Form 4361).

You have completed the outline for this subunit.
Study multiple-choice questions 9 through 11 on page 51.

2.3 FARMING INCOME AND EXPENSE

Gross income from farming includes gross farm income, gross farm rental income, and gains from the sale of livestock that were raised on the farm or purchased for resale.

Gross Income from Farming

1. Gross farm income includes
   a. Income from farming -- amounts received from cultivating the soil or raising or harvesting agricultural commodities.
   b. Gains from the sale of livestock -- amounts received for livestock raised on the farm or purchased for resale. The basis of livestock is generally the cost of the animals.
   c. Income reported on Schedule F.

Gross Farm Rental Income

2. Rent received from the use of farmland is generally rental income unless it is rent received from crop shares or unless the taxpayer materially participates in the lessee's operations.
   a. Use Form 4835, *Farm Rental Income and Expenses*, to report farm rental income based on crops or livestock produced by the tenant only if the activity was a rental activity for purposes of the passive activity loss limitations.

Gains from the Sale of Livestock

3. Gains from the sale of livestock used for draft (hauling), dairy, breeding, or sporting purposes generally result in capital gains and are not reported on Schedule F.
   a. Gains on the sale of these types of livestock are reported on Form 4797.

Where to Report Sales of Farm Products

Items Sold	Schedule F	Form 4797
Farm products raised for sale	X	
Farm products bought for resale	X	
Farm assets not held primarily for sale, such as livestock held for draft, breeding, sport, or dairy purposes (bought or raised)		X

4. Agriculture program payments (i.e., farm subsidies) are reported on Schedule F and are subject to self-employment taxes.
   a. Generally, taxpayers must include in income most government payments for approved conservation practices. However, excluded are some payments received under certain cost-sharing conservation programs.

5. Taxpayers buying farm supplies through a cooperative may receive income from the cooperative in the form of patronage dividends (refunds), as reported to the taxpayer on Form 1099-PATR.
   a. Taxpayers selling their farm products through a cooperative may receive either patronage dividends or a per-unit retain certificate from the cooperative. These dividends are also reported on Schedule F.

<u>Capitalization and Depreciation</u>

6. If the taxpayer produced real or tangible personal property or acquired property for resale, certain expenses must be included in inventory costs or capitalized. These expenses include the direct costs of the property and the share of any indirect costs allocable to that property.
   a. A farmer can deduct depreciation of buildings, improvements, cars and trucks, machinery, and other farm equipment of a permanent nature.
      1) Do not deduct depreciation on a home, furniture or other personal items, land, livestock bought or raised for resale, or other property in inventory.
   b. The following are just a few examples of depreciable farm property and the corresponding recovery periods. This information does not need to be memorized for the exam.

Assets	**Recovery Period in Years**	
	GDS	**ADS**
Agricultural structures (single purpose)	10	15
Automobiles	5	5
Cattle (dairy or breeding)	5	7
Farm buildings	20	25
Farm machinery and equipment	7	10
Acquired after 2017	5	10
Fences (agricultural)	7	10
Tractor units (over-the-road)	3	4
Truck (heavy duty, unloaded weight 13,000 lbs. or more)	5	6
Truck (actual weight less than 13,000 lbs.)	5	5
Water wells	15	20

Section 1231 Gains

7. Schedule F does not include gains and losses from sales or other dispositions of farm land (Sec. 1231 property), depreciable farm equipment (Sec. 1245 property), and buildings and structures (Sec. 1250 property).

Farm Income Averaging

8. If a taxpayer is engaged in a farming or fishing business, (s)he may be able to average all or some of his or her current year's farm income by using income rates from the 3 prior years (base years) to calculate the tax on that income.
   a. An individual, a partner in a partnership, or a shareholder in an S corporation may elect farm income averaging on a timely filed return (including extensions) or later if the IRS approves.
      1) The taxpayer need not have engaged in a farming business in any base year.
   b. Corporations, partnerships, S corporations, estates, and trusts cannot use farm income averaging.
   c. To elect farm income averaging as a tax computation method, you must file a Schedule J with your income tax return for the election year.
      1) This includes late or amended returns if the period of limitations on filing a claim for credit or refund has not expired.

9. **Special Circumstances**

Weather-Related Gains on Sale of Livestock

   a. The gain from sales of livestock caused by drought, flood, or other weather-related conditions (causing the affected area to be eligible for assistance by the federal government) can be postponed for 4 years. If, because of the weather-related conditions, a farmer who uses the cash method of accounting sells more livestock (including poultry) than (s)he would have sold under normal business conditions, the farmer may choose to include the gain from the sale of the additional livestock in income next year instead of the current year.
      1) The election applies to all livestock, whether held for resale or other purposes. It applies even if the livestock was actually exchanged or sold before an area is designated as eligible for federal assistance, as long as the weather-related condition caused the exchange or sale.

Crop Insurance and Disaster Payments

   b. Crop insurance and disaster payments are generally included in income in the year they are received.
      1) An election is available to include the proceeds in income for the tax year following the tax year in which the crops were damaged.

Estimated Taxes

10. If a taxpayer qualifies as a farmer by receiving at least two-thirds of the total gross income from farming in the current year or the preceding tax year, the following special rules apply:
    a. The taxpayer shall pay all estimated taxes by January 15 and then file the 1040 return and pay any additional taxes by April 15. The required annual payment is the smaller of two-thirds of the current year's tax or 100% of the previous year's tax.
    b. In lieu of estimated payments described in 10.a., the taxpayer may file the 1040 return and pay all taxes due by March 1.
    c. The taxpayer should be sure to include any alternative minimum tax that (s)he expects to owe in the calculation for estimated tax.
    d. The following illustrates the process of determining if estimated tax payments are required by a farmer:

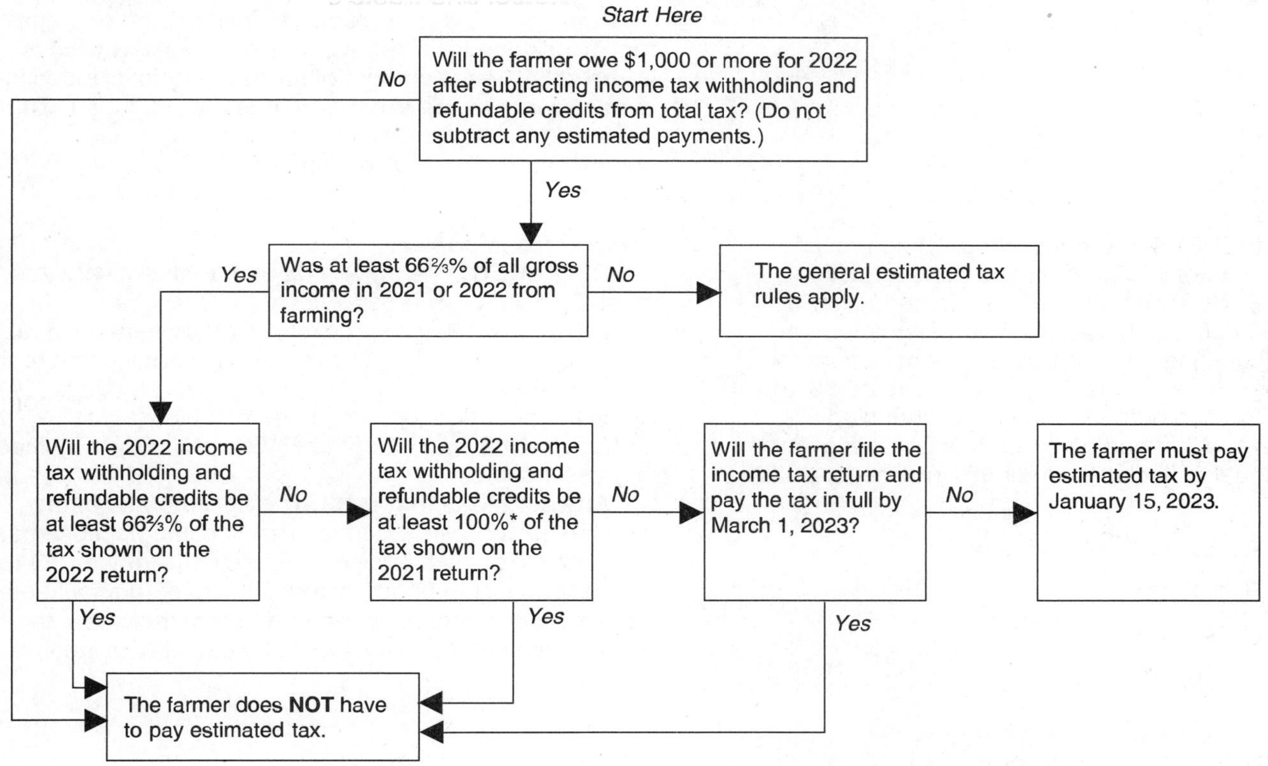

Start Here

Will the farmer owe $1,000 or more for 2022 after subtracting income tax withholding and refundable credits from total tax? (Do not subtract any estimated payments.)

No → The farmer does **NOT** have to pay estimated tax.

Yes → Was at least $66\frac{2}{3}$% of all gross income in 2021 or 2022 from farming?

No → The general estimated tax rules apply.

Yes → Will the 2022 income tax withholding and refundable credits be at least $66\frac{2}{3}$% of the tax shown on the 2022 return?

Yes → The farmer does **NOT** have to pay estimated tax.

No → Will the 2022 income tax withholding and refundable credits be at least 100%* of the tax shown on the 2021 return?

Yes → The farmer does **NOT** have to pay estimated tax.

No → Will the farmer file the income tax return and pay the tax in full by March 1, 2023?

Yes → The farmer does **NOT** have to pay estimated tax.

No → The farmer must pay estimated tax by January 15, 2023.

*110% if less than two-thirds of the farmer's gross income for 2021 and 2022 is from farming or fishing and the farmer's 2021 adjusted gross income was more than $150,000 ($75,000 if filing status for 2022 is married filing a separate return).

Figure 2-2

You have completed the outline for this subunit.
Study multiple-choice questions 12 through 20 beginning on page 52.

QUESTIONS

2.1 Gross Income

1. Mr. Zurn owns an apartment house for which he provides no services to his tenants. On December 1, 2022, he received a $2,400 payment for the first 6 months' rent in 2023. He also received a security deposit of $400. What is the amount of gross rental income Mr. Zurn should include on his 2022 income tax return?

A. $400

B. $800

C. $2,400

D. $2,800

Answer (C) is correct.

REQUIRED: The landlord's rental income.

DISCUSSION: Both cash- and accrual-basis taxpayers must include amounts in gross income upon actual or constructive receipt if the taxpayer has an unrestricted claim to such amounts under Reg. 1.61-8(b). Since Mr. Zurn has an unrestricted claim to the $2,400 of rent paid in advance, it would be included in his rental income. The security deposit of $400 would not be included in rental income since it was not intended as an advance rental payment. (Mr. Zurn does not have an unrestricted claim since it must be returned unless there are damages or rent is not paid.) Therefore, Mr. Zurn's gross rental income is $2,400.

Answer (A) is incorrect. The full amount of prepaid rent is included in current-year income. **Answer (B) is incorrect.** The full amount of prepaid rent is included in current-year income. **Answer (D) is incorrect.** Mr. Zurn does not have an unrestricted claim to the security deposit, so it is not included in income.

2. In 2021, the Birch Company had gross income of $163,000, a bad debt deduction of $5,000, and other allowable deductions of $58,500. Birch uses the accrual method of accounting and the specific charge-off method for bad debts. In 2022, Birch recovered $1,600 of the bad debt that had been deducted in 2021. What portion of the bad debt recovery should be included in Birch's income for 2022?

A. $0

B. $1,600

C. $3,400

D. $5,000

Answer (B) is correct.

REQUIRED: The amount of bad debt recovery that must be included in gross income.

DISCUSSION: The recovery of an amount previously deducted as a bad debt is included in gross income to the extent that the prior deduction reduced taxes (Sec. 111). Since the prior deduction reduced taxable income by $5,000, the full amount of the $1,600 recovery is included in gross income.

Answer (A) is incorrect. The full amount of the recovery must be included in gross income because bad debt was taken as a business deduction. **Answer (C) is incorrect.** Only the amount that is recovered should be included in income. **Answer (D) is incorrect.** Only the amount that is recovered should be included in income.

3. Sierra Corporation issued $40,000, 5-year bonds for $43,000 on March 1 of the current year. How much of the bond premium must Sierra report on its current-year income tax return?

A. $3,000

B. $600

C. $500

D. $0

Answer (C) is correct.

REQUIRED: The income reported from the issuance.

DISCUSSION: Under Reg. 1.61-12(c)(2), in the case of a bond, the amount of amortizable bond premium for the taxable year is included in income. The amount is amortized over the life of the bond. Thus, Sierra must report $600 each year [($43,000 – $40,000) ÷ 5]. In the current year, Sierra has to recognize only $500 because the bonds were issued for only 10 months [$600 × (10 months ÷ 12 months)].

Answer (A) is incorrect. The premium is amortized over the life of the bond. **Answer (B) is incorrect.** The bond was issued for only 10 months. **Answer (D) is incorrect.** The amortizable value of the premium is included in income.

4. Gross income from a hobby activity of an individual is

A. Not reported if less than $400.
B. Reported as other income on Form 1040.
C. Reported as gross income on Schedule C (Form 1040).
D. Netted against related expenses, and the excess, if any, is reported as other income on Form 1040.

Answer (B) is correct.

REQUIRED: The reporting of hobby income on Form 1040.

DISCUSSION: Income from activities from which a profit is not expected must be included on the tax return. Such activities include hobbies and farm activities operated for recreation and pleasure. Related expenses are not deductible. The income is reported on Schedule 1 of Form 1040.

Answer (A) is incorrect. There is no minimum amount that does not need to be reported. **Answer (C) is incorrect.** Income from a hobby activity is classified as other income. **Answer (D) is incorrect.** The related expenses are not netted against related income.

5. In 2021, the Hydrangea Company (a sole proprietorship) had gross income of $158,000, a bad debt deduction of $3,500, and other allowable deductions of $49,437. The business reported on the accrual method of accounting and used the specific charge-off method for bad debts. The entire bad debt deduction reduced the taxable income on the 2021 return. In 2022, the business recovered $2,000 of the $3,500 deducted in 2021. How should the recovery be treated?

A. Include $2,000 in income on the 2022 return.
B. Include $3,500 in income on the 2022 return.
C. Amend the 2021 return to add the $2,000.
D. None of the answers are correct.

Answer (A) is correct.

REQUIRED: The proper treatment of the recovery of an amount previously deducted as a bad debt.

DISCUSSION: The recovery of an amount previously deducted as a bad debt is included in gross income to the extent that the prior deduction reduced taxes (Sec. 111). Since the prior deduction reduced taxable income by $3,500, the full amount of the $2,000 recovery is included in gross income.

Answer (B) is incorrect. Only the amount of the bad debt expense recovered should be included in income in 2022. **Answer (C) is incorrect.** The amount of the recovery should be included in the return for 2022. **Answer (D) is incorrect.** A correct answer is given.

6. In Year 1, Luanne had gross income of $80,000, a bad debt deduction of $7,500, and other allowable deductions of $67,000 on her Schedule C (Form 1040). She uses the accrual method of accounting and the specific charge-off method for bad debts. During Year 2, she recovered $5,500 of the debt that she had deducted in Year 1. How must Luanne report the recovery of the bad debt?

A. She must file an amended income tax return for Year 1.
B. She must reduce her bad debt deduction for Year 2 by $5,500.
C. She must include $5,500 in nonbusiness "other income" on her Form 1040 for Year 2.
D. She must include $5,500 in "other income" on her Schedule C for Year 2.

Answer (D) is correct.

REQUIRED: The amount of bad debt recovery that must be included in gross income.

DISCUSSION: The recovery of an amount previously deducted as a bad debt is included in gross income to the extent that the prior deduction reduced taxes (Sec. 111). Since the prior deduction reduced taxable income by $7,500, the full amount of the $5,500 recovery is included in gross income. This amount is reported as "other income" on Schedule C.

Answer (A) is incorrect. Recovery of bad debt is recognized as income in the current year. **Answer (B) is incorrect.** Recovery of bad debt is recognized as income in the current year. **Answer (C) is incorrect.** The recovery of bad debt is included as "other income" on Schedule C.

7. Which of the following would generally be reported as other income on a Form 1040 Schedule C?

A. Proceeds from international sales.

B. Bad debts recovered.

C. Sales tax collected.

D. Income from bartering activities.

Answer (B) is correct.

REQUIRED: The item that would generally be reported as other income for a business.

DISCUSSION: If a deduction is claimed for a bad debt on the income tax return and later all or part of it is recovered (collected), all or part of the recovery may have to be reported in gross income. The amount included is limited to the amount actually deducted. However, the amount deducted that did not reduce the tax can be excluded. Report the recovery as "other income" on Form 1040 Schedule C.

Answer (A) is incorrect. Gross receipts from trade or business is entered on Schedule C (Form 1040), line 1, not as other income. **Answer (C) is incorrect.** Sales tax accrued in a trade or business is deductible and would not be reported as other income for a business. **Answer (D) is incorrect.** Bartered services or goods are included in gross income at the fair market value of the item(s) received in exchange for the services. Bartered exchanges are required to file Form 1099-B, and the transaction is recorded as gross receipts on Form 1040 Schedule C.

8. In Year 1, Ms. Azalea had gross income of $110,000, a bad debt deduction of $12,000, and other allowable deductions of $75,000 on her Schedule C (Form 1040). She uses the accrual method of accounting and the specific charge-off method for bad debts. During Year 2, she recovered $8,000 of the debt that she had deducted in Year 1. How must Ms. Azalea report the recovery of the bad debt?

A. She must reduce her bad debt deduction for Year 2 by $8,000.

B. She must include $8,000 in "other income" on her Schedule C for Year 2.

C. She must include $8,000 in nonbusiness "other income" on her Form 1040 for Year 2.

D. She must file an amended income tax return for Year 1.

Answer (B) is correct.

REQUIRED: The amount of bad debt recovery that must be included in gross income.

DISCUSSION: The recovery of an amount previously deducted as a bad debt is included in gross income to the extent that the prior deduction reduced taxes (Sec. 111). Since the prior deduction reduced taxable income by $12,000, the full amount of the $8,000 recovery is included in gross income. This amount is reported as "other income" on Schedule C.

Answer (A) is incorrect. Recovery of bad debt is recognized as income in the current year. **Answer (C) is incorrect.** The recovery of bad debt is included as "other income" on Schedule C. **Answer (D) is incorrect.** Recovery of bad debt is recognized as income in the current year.

2.2 Self-Employment Income

9. Mike owns a four-family apartment building and actively participates in the rental activity. Mike advertised, rented the apartments to the tenants, collected rents, and made repairs. His brother, Bryan, also owns an apartment building. Bryan spends more than half his time developing, constructing, renting, managing, and operating his apartment building as well as providing regular cleaning, linen service, and maid service for the convenience of the tenants. Which brother has self-employment income from his apartment building?

A. Mike.

B. Bryan.

C. Both brothers.

D. Neither.

Answer (B) is correct.

REQUIRED: The self-employment income obtained from the rental of an apartment building.

DISCUSSION: Rent from real estate and personal property leased with real estate is not self-employment income unless services are provided to tenants. Services generally are provided for the occupants if they are primarily for their convenience and not services normally provided with the rental of rooms for occupancy only (Publication 334). Since Bryan, but not Mike, provides these services, he is the only brother that has self-employment income from his apartment building.

Answer (A) is incorrect. Tentative net earnings from self-employment do not include rents from real estate or from personal property leased with the real estate, gain (or loss) from disposition of business property, capital gain (or loss), nonbusiness interest, or dividends. **Answer (C) is incorrect.** Mike does not have self-employment income. **Answer (D) is incorrect.** One brother does have self-employment income.

10. Which of the following individuals is NOT subject to self-employment tax?

A. Troy, a 60% owner in an S corporation, received $40,000 as his distributive share of the corporation's taxable income.

B. Lloyd, a real estate dealer providing services, had net rental income of $67,000.

C. Dave, a general partner, received a $20,000 guaranteed payment.

D. Patrick, a corporate director, received $35,000 for services performed as a director.

Answer (A) is correct.

REQUIRED: The individual not subject to the self-employment tax.

DISCUSSION: Although S corporation shareholders are treated similarly to partners for many tax purposes, they are not subject to the self-employment tax. S corporation earnings required to be included in a shareholder's gross income are not self-employment income (Rev. Rul. 59-221).

Answer (B) is incorrect. Rental income earned by a real estate dealer providing services is considered self-employment income. **Answer (C) is incorrect.** Guaranteed payments from a partnership are considered self-employment income. **Answer (D) is incorrect.** Corporate director's fees are considered self-employment income.

11. Which one of the following individuals is NOT subject to self-employment tax?

A. Mike received $10,000 for serving as a director of a corporation.

B. Laura, a paralegal, received $28,000 from her law firm's partnership as salary.

C. Gene, a real estate dealer, had net rental income of $85,000 from property held for sale.

D. Nicole, an inactive partner, received $9,000 as her distributive share of the partnership income.

Answer (B) is correct.

REQUIRED: The individual not subject to the self-employment tax.

DISCUSSION: Under Sec. 1402(a) and Reg. 1.1402(a)-1, net earnings from self-employment include the net income from a trade or business, guaranteed payments for services from a partnership, and a general partner's distributive share of income from a partnership (whether the partner is active or not). Directors' fees are self-employment income. Salary is income from employment, not self-employment.

Answer (A) is incorrect. A director's fees are self-employment income. **Answer (C) is incorrect.** Net income from a trade or business is self-employment income. **Answer (D) is incorrect.** A general partner's distributive share of income from a partnership (whether the partner is active or not) is self-employment income.

2.3 Farming Income and Expense

12. Dan, a calendar-year taxpayer, has the following amounts of gross income for 2022:

Wages	$ 10,000
Interest	2,000
Farm income	200,000

Dan has tax, including self-employment tax, of $20,000, and withholding of $1,000. To avoid any filing or estimated tax penalties, Dan must

A. File an estimated tax payment by January 15, 2023, and pay 60% of the tax due.

B. File his tax return and pay all tax due by March 1, 2023.

C. File an estimated tax payment by March 1, 2023, and pay 66 2/3% of the tax due.

D. File his tax return and pay all tax due by April 15, 2023.

Answer (B) is correct.

REQUIRED: The required filings and payments by a farmer to avoid penalties.

DISCUSSION: Dan is a qualified farmer because at least two-thirds of his gross income for 2022 was from farming (Publication 225). A qualified farmer has two filing options. The first option is to make a required payment by January 15 and file Form 1040 by April 15. The second option is to file Form 1040 and pay all tax due by March 1.

13. Farmer John, a cash-basis farmer, operates a cow-calf breeding operation. The breeder cows are not primarily held for sale. In addition to the calves raised on his farm, John also purchases calves for resale. During 2022, John had the following acquisitions and dispositions of cattle:

Purchase of 30 calves for resale	$ 3,420
Sale of 30 calves purchased for resale	6,100
Sale of 45 calves raised by John	10,400
Sale of 10 breeder cows	6,750
Original cost of breeder cows	5,500
Accumulated depreciation on breeder cows	2,860

What amount should John include in gross income on his Schedule F for 2022?

A. $13,080

B. $14,510

C. $16,500

D. $18,580

Answer (A) is correct.

REQUIRED: The total amount of income reported on Schedule F.

DISCUSSION: Income from farming reported on Schedule F includes amounts that the farmer receives from cultivating the soil or raising or harvesting any agricultural commodities, including income from the sale of livestock. Sale of livestock held for draft, dairy, breeding, or sporting purposes generally results in capital gains. John should include $13,080 [$10,400 + ($6,100 – $3,420)] in gross income on his Schedule F.

Answer (B) is incorrect. The sale of the breeder cows produces capital gains, not ordinary income. **Answer (C) is incorrect.** The original purchase price of the calves bought for resale is deducted from gross income. **Answer (D) is incorrect.** The gross income does not include the original cost of the breeder cows.

14. Bobby Rice is an unincorporated grain farmer in Louisiana with a calendar year end. Bobby does not live or farm in a disaster area. Bobby computed an estimated tax liability of $25,000 for 2022. To avoid the failure to pay estimated tax penalty, Bobby should

A. Make his first 2022 estimated tax payment by March 1, 2023.

B. Pay all his 2022 estimated taxes by February 15, 2023, and file his tax return by April 15, 2023.

C. Include any alternative minimum tax he expects to owe in his calculation of 2022 estimated taxes.

D. Pay all of his 2022 estimated taxes by the due date of his return.

Answer (C) is correct.

REQUIRED: The proper way for a farmer to avoid paying a penalty when (s)he owes an estimated tax.

DISCUSSION: If a taxpayer qualifies as a farmer by receiving at least two-thirds of the total gross income from farming in the current year or the preceding tax year, the taxpayer shall pay all estimated taxes by January 15 and then file the 1040 return and pay any additional taxes by April 15, or the required annual payment is two-thirds of the current year's tax or 100% of the previous year's tax. Alternatively, the taxpayer shall file the 1040 return and pay all taxes due by March 1. In addition, the alternative minimum tax that the taxpayer expects to owe should be included in the calculation of the estimated tax owed.

15. Which of the following statements with respect to farmers is true?

A. The sale of livestock used for breeding purposes results in capital gains.

B. A farmer is exempt from paying estimated taxes.

C. The sale of livestock raised on the farm results in capital gains.

D. Income reported on Schedule F includes gains from sale of farmland or depreciable farm equipment.

Answer (A) is correct.

REQUIRED: The true statement with respect to farmers.

DISCUSSION: Income from farming is treated in the same way as income from any other business. Gross income from farming includes gross farm income, gross farm rental income, and gains from the sale of livestock (if livestock was raised on the farm or purchased for resale). However, the sale of livestock used for draft, dairy, breeding, or sporting purposes generally results in capital gains.

Answer (B) is incorrect. Farmers are required to make estimated payments. **Answer (C) is incorrect.** The sale of livestock raised on the farm results in ordinary income. **Answer (D) is incorrect.** Gains from the sale of farmland or depreciable farm equipment are reported on Form 4797.

16. If at least two-thirds of your gross income for 2021 or 2022 was from farming, only one estimated tax payment is due. The required annual payment is the

A. Larger of two-thirds of your total tax for 2022 or 100% of the total tax shown on your full-year 2021 return.

B. Smaller of two-thirds of your total tax for 2021 or 100% of the total tax shown on your full-year 2022 return.

C. Larger of two-thirds of your total tax for 2021 or 100% of the total tax shown on your full-year 2022 return.

D. Smaller of two-thirds of your total tax for 2022 or 100% of the total tax shown on your full-year 2021 return.

Answer (D) is correct.

REQUIRED: The estimated tax payments required from farmers.

DISCUSSION: If a taxpayer qualifies as a farmer by receiving at least two-thirds of the total gross income from farming in the current year or the preceding tax year, the taxpayer shall pay all estimated taxes by January 15 and then file the 1040 return and pay any additional taxes by April 15. The required annual payment is the smaller of two-thirds of the current year's tax or 100% of the previous year's tax.

17. If you sell more livestock than you normally would in a year because of a drought, flood, or other weather-related condition, you may be able to postpone reporting the gain from selling the additional animals until the next year. You must meet all of the following conditions to make the election EXCEPT

A. You can show that, under your usual business practices, you would not have sold the animals this year except for the weather-related conditions.

B. The weather-related conditions caused an area to be designated as eligible for assistance by the federal government.

C. You use the accrual method of accounting.

D. Your principal trade or business is farming.

Answer (C) is correct.

REQUIRED: The condition not required for the election related to the postponement of the gain from a sale due to a drought, flood, or other weather-related condition.

DISCUSSION: Publication 225 states, "If you sell or exchange more livestock, including poultry, than you normally would in a year because of a drought, flood, or other weather-related condition, you may be able to postpone reporting the gain from the additional animals until the next year. You must meet all the following conditions to qualify.

- Your principal trade or business is farming.
- You use the cash method of accounting.
- You can show that, under your usual business practices, you wouldn't have sold or exchanged the additional animals this year except for the weather-related condition.
- The weather-related condition caused an area to be designated as eligible for assistance by the federal government."

Answer (A) is incorrect. This is a condition that must be met by a farmer in order to qualify for the election. **Answer (B) is incorrect.** A weather-related condition must have caused the exchange or sale in order to qualify for the election. **Answer (D) is incorrect.** The taxpayer's principal trade or business must be farming. A taxpayer qualifies as a farmer by receiving at least two-thirds of their total gross income from farming in the current year or the preceding tax year.

18. John Jacobsen is a cash-basis cattle rancher. In 2022, John sold 12 head of cattle for $9,600. The cattle were born on his ranch in 2019. During the 3 years that John used these cattle in his breeding operation, he spent $10,000 for feed and other expenses related to the cattle. How much is John's gain or loss for 2022, and where should he report the amount on his federal income tax return?

A. John should report a net gain of $9,600 on Form 4797.

B. John should report a net loss of $400 on Form 4797.

C. John should report $9,600 from the sale of the cattle on Schedule F.

D. John should report a net loss of $400 on Schedule F.

Answer (A) is correct.

REQUIRED: The correct gain or loss of a cash basis cattle ranch.

DISCUSSION: Gains from the sale of livestock used for draft, dairy, breeding, or sporting purposes generally result in capital gains and are not reported on Schedule F. These gains would be reported on Form 4797. Since cattle are considered Sec. 1231 property, the expenses incurred in raising the cattle would be deducted as a for-AGI deduction.

Answer (B) is incorrect. The expenses incurred would be deducted as a for-AGI deduction, and the entire proceeds from the sale of the cattle should be reported as a gain on Form 4797. **Answer (C) is incorrect.** Livestock used for breeding purposes are considered Sec. 1231 property, and the gain from this property should be reported on Form 4797. **Answer (D) is incorrect.** Livestock used for breeding purposes are considered Sec. 1231 property. As such, the expenses incurred would be deducted as a for-AGI deduction, and the entire proceeds from the sale of the cattle should be reported as a gain on Form 4797.

19. Who of the following may use farm income averaging, assuming farm income rules are met?

A. A natural person filing a Form 1040, a partner in a partnership, and a shareholder in an S corporation.

B. A natural person filing a Form 1040, a partnership, an S corporation, and a C corporation.

C. A natural person filing a Form 1040, a partner in a partnership, and a shareholder in a C corporation.

D. A natural person filing a Form 1040, a partner in a partnership, an estate, and a trust.

Answer (A) is correct.

REQUIRED: The taxpayer eligible to use farm income averaging.

DISCUSSION: Under Sec. 1301, a taxpayer engaged in a farming business in the year of election as an individual, a partner in a partnership, or a shareholder in an S corporation can elect to use farm income averaging. Corporations, partnerships, S corporations, estates, and trusts cannot use farm income averaging.

Answer (B) is incorrect. Partnerships, S corporations, and C corporations cannot elect farm income averaging. **Answer (C) is incorrect.** A shareholder in a C corporation cannot elect farm income averaging. **Answer (D) is incorrect.** Estates and trusts cannot elect farm income averaging.

20. Farmer Bob sold a breeding cow on March 8 for $2,500. Expenses related to the sale were $250. Farmer Bob deducted $1,000 in costs of raising the cow during the years the cow was raised. What is Farmer Bob's gain (loss) on the sale of the breeding cow, without regard to the Uniform Capitalization Rules?

A. $(350)

B. $1,150

C. $2,250

D. None of the answers are correct.

Answer (C) is correct.

REQUIRED: The gain (loss) reported without regard to the uniform capitalization rules.

DISCUSSION: Farmer Bob sold a breeding cow for $2,500. Because Farmer Bob had already received a tax benefit from the costs of raising the cow, he cannot offset those costs against the proceeds received from selling the cow. The only expenses he can deduct against the proceeds are the selling expenses. Thus, Farmer Bob's gain is $2,250 ($2,500 – $250).

Answer (A) is incorrect. The gain is calculated based on the selling price minus the selling expenses incurred. **Answer (B) is incorrect.** The gain is calculated based on the selling price minus the selling expenses incurred. **Answer (D) is incorrect.** The gain reported is $2,250.

Go to Online Course

Access the **Gleim EA Premium Review System** featuring our SmartAdapt technology from your Gleim Personal Classroom to continue your studies.

You will experience a personalized study environment with exam-emulating multiple-choice questions.

STUDY UNIT THREE

RENTAL PROPERTY AND LOSS LIMITATIONS

(9 pages of outline)

The first two subunits discuss the items included in rental property income and expenses. The last subunit discusses loss limitations associated with at-risk rules and passive activity rules.

3.1 RENTAL PROPERTY INCOME

1. Cash or the fair market value (FMV) of property or services received for the use of real estate or personal property is taxable as rental income.
   a. Rent from real estate is income from an investment, not from the operation of a business.
   b. Schedule E is not used to report income and expenses from the rental of personal property, such as equipment or vehicles. Instead, Schedule C is used if the taxpayer is in the business of renting personal property. A taxpayer is in the business of renting personal property if the primary purpose for renting the property is income or profit and the taxpayer is involved in the rental activity with continuity and regularity. If rental of personal property is not a business, any income belongs on Form 1040 (Schedule 1).
   c. A bonus received by a landlord for granting a lease is included in gross income.
   d. A lessee's refundable deposit intended to secure performance under the lease is not income to the lessor.
   e. Value received by a landlord to cancel or modify a lease is gross income.
      1) Amounts received by a lessee to cancel a lease, however, are treated as amounts realized on disposition of an asset or property (a capital gain).
   f. An amount paid by a lessee to maintain the property in lieu of rent, e.g., for property tax, is gross income to the lessor.
      1) The lessor includes the payment in gross income and may be entitled to a corresponding deduction, e.g., property tax deduction.

EXAMPLE 3-1	**Payments of Lessee in Lieu of Rent**

While a taxpayer is out of town, the furnace in the taxpayer's rental property stops working. The tenant pays for the necessary repairs and deducts the repair bill from the next rent payment. The repair bill paid by the tenant and any amount received as rent payment are included as rental income. The taxpayer may deduct the repair payment made by the tenant as a rental expense.

   g. The FMV of lessee improvements made to the property in lieu of rent is also gross income to the lessor.
      1) The FMV of the lessee improvements are also allowable as a deduction in the computation of income from the rental activity.
   h. The value of lessee improvements that are not made in lieu of rent is excluded from the lessor's gross income.

i. **Prepaid rent** is included in gross income when received (the same as for cash-method and accrual-method taxpayers).

1) Lease cancellations are included.

2) Tenant improvements, in lieu of rent, are included.

3) Security deposits are not considered income when the property owner is obligated to return them to the tenants.

4) Advance rental payments must be deducted by the payee during the tax periods to which the payments apply.

j. Rental income from a residence is included in gross income unless the residence is rented out for less than 15 days in a given year.

1) If rental income is excluded from gross income, the corresponding rental deductions are also disallowed.

k. Rental income received by an individual where no significant services are provided should be reported along with any respective rental expenses on Schedule E (Form 1040).

1) If significant services are provided, the rental income and expenses should be reported on Schedule C (Form 1040).

l. Income and expenses from business should be reported on Schedule C, *Profit or Loss From Business*.

Not-for-Profit Rental Income

2. If property is not rented to make a profit, taxpayers can deduct their rental expenses only up to the amount of their rental income. A taxpayer cannot deduct a loss or carry it forward to the next year if rental expenses are more than rental income for the year.

a. Not-for-profit rental income is reported on Form 1040 or 1040-NR. Taxpayers can include their mortgage interest (if the property is used as their main home or second home), real estate taxes, and casualty losses on the appropriate lines of Schedule A if they itemize their deductions.

b. If rental income is more than rental expenses for at least 3 years out of a period of 5 consecutive years, taxpayers are presumed to be renting property to make a profit.

Stop & Review

You have completed the outline for this subunit.

Study multiple-choice questions 1 through 7 beginning on page 66.

3.2 RENTAL PROPERTY EXPENSES

1. Expenses related to the production of rental income are generally deductible to arrive at adjusted gross income.
   a. Rental property expenditures may be deducted by depreciation. Generally, a Sec. 179 deduction includes certain depreciable tangible personal property used predominantly to furnish lodging or in connection with furnishing lodging.
2. Generally, repair and maintenance expense is considered a current-period deduction. However, certain repairs may be classified as improvements, which must be capitalized. There are safe harbor rules that allow repairs and maintenance to always be classified as current-period expenses instead of capitalized.
   a. Taxpayers who have elected to use the de minimis expense treatment must expense all repairs up to the de minimis amount (i.e., $2,500).
   b. The costs of performing certain routine maintenance activities for property may result in an improvement to the unit of property, the costs of which must be capitalized.
      1) However, a safe harbor rule allows routine repairs and maintenance to be expensed. This safe harbor rule applies to actions that maintain the asset and are reasonably expected to be performed more than once for the asset's class life under the alternative depreciation system.
3. Special rules limit deductions on the rental of a residence or a vacation home.

<u>Minimum Rental Use</u>

   a. The property must be rented for more than 14 days during the year for deductions to be allowable.
      1) When the residence is rented for less than 15 days, the rental income does not need to be reported.

<u>Minimum Personal Use</u>

   b. The vacation-home rules apply when the taxpayer uses the residence for personal purposes for the greater of (1) more than 14 days or (2) more than 10% of the number of days for which the residence is rented.
4. A residence is deemed to have been used by the taxpayer for personal purposes if the home is used by
   a. The taxpayer for personal purposes, by any other person who owns an interest in the rental property, or by the relatives of either
      1) However, if the taxpayer rented or tried to rent the property for 12 or more consecutive months, the days during which (s)he used the property as a main home do not count as personal days.
   b. Any individual under a reciprocal arrangement, whether or not rent is charged
   c. Any individual unless a fair rental is charged
5. If the taxpayer spends substantially full-time repairing or maintaining the rental property, such time does not count toward the personal-use test. This is the case regardless of use of property by other family members.

Vacation Home Rules

6. If the property passes the minimum rental-use test but fails the minimum personal-use test, the property is considered a vacation home, and rental deductions may not exceed gross income derived from rental activities.
   a. Expenses must be allocated between the personal use and the rental use based on the number of days of use of each.
   b. When deductions are limited to gross income, the order of deductions is
      1) The allocable portion of expenses deductible regardless of rental income (e.g., mortgage interest and property taxes)
      2) Deductions that do not affect basis (e.g., ordinary repairs and maintenance)
      3) Deductions that affect basis (e.g., depreciation)

EXAMPLE 3-2 Order of Deductions

A taxpayer with $4,000 of rental income, $2,000 of interest and taxes, $1,000 of repairs, and $10,000 of depreciation may only deduct $1,000 of depreciation.

Income	$ 4,000
Interest and taxes	(2,000)
Repairs	(1,000)
Depreciation	(1,000)
	$ 0

   c. Any losses disallowed may be carried forward.

7. If the property passes both the minimum rental-use test and the minimum personal-use test, then all deductions may be taken and a loss may occur, subject to the passive loss limits.

Minimum Use Tests

	Rental Use	Personal Use
Pass	> 14 days	≤ 14 days or < 10%
Fail	≤ 14 days	greater of > 14 days or > 10%

EXAMPLE 3-3 Mixed Use of Real Property

Jack owns a vacation condo on Miami Beach. He rents it out to vacationers most of the year but uses it himself a few times each year. In each of the following situations, Jack has a different ability to deduct expenses based on the amount of personal and rental use.

Situation 1: Jack uses the condo for 4 days and rents it for 200 days at fair rental value to unrelated parties. In this situation, Jack passes the rental-use and personal-use tests and is able to take all deductions applicable, subject to the passive loss rules.

Situation 2: Jack uses the condo for 24 days and rents it for 165 days at fair rental value to unrelated parties. Jack passes the rental-use test but fails the personal-use test because he personally used the rental for the greater of 14 days or 10% of the rental days. Therefore, Jack must allocate the expenses between rental use and personal use and may deduct rental expenses to the extent of rental income.

Situation 3: Jack uses the condo for 10 days and rents the condo for 10 days at fair rental value to unrelated parties. Because he fails the rental-use test, he does not need to report the rental income, but he may not deduct the related rental expenses.

8. Expense deductions for not-for-profit (NFP) rentals are limited to income from such rentals. Neither loss nor carryforward is allowed for NFP expenses in excess of NFP income.

You have completed the outline for this subunit.
Study multiple-choice questions 8 through 12 beginning on page 69.

3.3 LOSS LIMITATIONS

1. A taxpayer's deductible loss is limited to the smallest amount of the following limitations:
   a. The taxpayer's basis in the activity
   b. The at-risk rules
   c. The passive activity rules

EXAMPLE 3-4 Business Activity Loss

A taxpayer who owns both a lumber business and a boat for personal use incurred two losses during the tax year upon selling both the boat and the lumberyard to a colleague. Though the combined loss totaled $10,000, only the portion attributable to the business is potentially deductible. Losses on sales of property held for personal use are not deductible.

At-Risk Rules

2. The amount of a loss allowable as a deduction is limited to the amount a person has at risk in the activity from which the loss arose.
   a. A loss is any excess of deductions over gross income attributable to the same activity.
   b. The rules apply to individuals, partners in partnerships, members in limited liability companies, shareholders of S corporations, trusts, estates, and closely held C corporations.
      1) Personal holding companies, foreign personal holding companies, and personal service corporations are not subject to at-risk rules.
   c. The at-risk rules are applied separately to each trade or business or income-producing activity.
   d. A person's amount at risk in an activity is determined at the close of the tax year.
      1) A person's initial at-risk amount includes money contributed, the adjusted basis (AB) of property contributed, and borrowed amounts.
      2) Recourse debt requirements include the following:
         a) A person's at-risk amount includes amounts borrowed only to the extent that, for the debt, the person has either personal liability or property pledged as security (no more than the FMV when pledged minus prior or superior claims is included).
         b) The at-risk amount does not include debt if one of the following applies:
            i) Property pledged as security is used in the activity.
            ii) Insurance, guarantees, stop-loss agreements, or similar arrangements provide protection from personal liability.
            iii) A person with an interest in the activity or one related to him or her extended the credit.

3) Nonrecourse debt is generally excluded from the amount at risk.
   a) The amount at risk in the activity of holding real property includes qualified nonrecourse financing (QNRF).
   b) In qualified nonrecourse financing, the taxpayer is not personally liable, but the financing is
      i) Used in an activity of holding real estate;
      ii) Secured by the real property;
      iii) Not convertible to an ownership interest; and
      iv) Either obtained from an unrelated third party, obtained from a related party but on commercially reasonable terms, or guaranteed by a governmental entity.

EXAMPLE 3-5 Nonrecourse Debt

Kathy purchased a small apartment building for $200,000 using $25,000 of her own money and $25,000 borrowed from her father to make the down payment. She signed a note to pay the remainder of the purchase price to the seller. The debt to the seller was nonrecourse, secured only by the apartment building. Kathy is not at-risk for the loan from the seller because the seller is a person from whom the taxpayer acquired the property.

EXAMPLE 3-6 At-Risk Rules

Mooch purchased rental real estate with some money borrowed from his mother at commercially reasonable terms and the rest of the money borrowed from the seller. Both loans were nonrecourse and only secured by the property. Mooch is at risk for the loan from his mother because of the commercially reasonable terms and the nonrecourse loan is for real property. Regardless of the terms, Mooch is not at risk for the seller's loan.

4) Adjustments to an at-risk amount are made for events that vary the investors' economic risk of loss.
   a) Add contributions of money and property (its AB), recourse debt increases, QNRF increases, and income from the activity.
   b) Subtract distributions (e.g., from a partnership), liability reductions (recourse or QNRF), and tax deductions allowable (at year end).
5) Disallowed losses are carried forward.
6) If the amount at risk decreases below zero, previously allowed losses must be recaptured as income.
7) If a deduction would reduce basis in property and part or all of the deduction is disallowed by the at-risk rules, the basis is reduced anyway.

Passive Activity Loss (PAL) Limitation Rules

3. The amount of a loss attributable to a person's passive activities is allowable as a deduction or credit only against, and to the extent of, gross income or tax attributable to those passive activities (in the aggregate).
    a. The excess is deductible or creditable in a future year, subject to the same limits.

EXAMPLE 3-7 PAL Limitation

A wealthy taxpayer invested in an architecture partnership as a passive investor. Because the taxpayer does not engage in the business outside of occasional business consulting, any income or loss derived from the business is passive in nature. Therefore, any losses derived from the partnership may only offset passive activity gains.

4. The passive activity rules apply to individuals, estates, trusts, personal service corporations, and closely held corporations.
    a. Although passive activity rules do not apply to grantor trusts, partnerships, and S corporations directly, they do apply to the owners of these entities.
5. A passive activity is either rental activity or a trade or business in which the person does not materially participate.
    a. A taxpayer materially participates in an activity during a tax year if (s)he satisfies one of the following tests:
        1) Participates more than 500 hours
        2) Participation constitutes substantially all of the participation in the activity
        3) Participates for more than 100 hours and exceeds the participation of any other individual
        4) The activity is a significant participation activity in which the taxpayer participates more than 100 hours and the taxpayer's participation in all significant participation activities exceeds 500 hours
        5) Materially participated in the activity for any 5 years of the 10 years preceding the year in question
        6) Materially participated in a personal service activity for any 3 years preceding the year in question
        7) Satisfies a facts and circumstances test proving that the taxpayer participated on a "regular, continuous, and substantial" basis
            a) A taxpayer will not be considered to have materially participated in an activity under this test if (s)he participated in the activity for 100 hours or less during the year.

EXAMPLE 3-8 Business Passive Activity Loss

For 2022, Sally realized a $10,000 net loss (sales of $95,000 less expenses of $105,000) from operating a sole proprietorship, without regard to dispositions of property other than inventory. The income tax return also showed gross income of $5,000 ($2,500 of wages, $500 interest on personal savings, and a $2,000 long-term capital gain on business property). The excess of deductions over income was $18,950 ($5,000 gross income – $10,000 loss from business operations – $1,000 nonbusiness short-term capital loss on the sale of stock – $12,950 standard deduction).

Because she does not engage in the business outside of occasional business consulting, any income or loss derived from the business is passive in nature. Therefore, any losses derived from the partnership may only offset passive activity gains.

6. Rental Real Estate

   a. All rental activity is passive.

   b. Up to $25,000 of a tax year loss from rental real estate activities in excess of passive activity gross income is deductible against portfolio or active income.

EXAMPLE 3-9 PAL Limitation -- Rental Real Estate Activities

A taxpayer has wages of $30,000, $5,000 gain from a passive partnership interest, and $35,000 loss from active rental real estate activity. The taxpayer may first offset the passive gain (i.e., $5,000) with $5,000 of the passive loss. With the remaining $30,000 passive loss, $25,000 of the nonpassive gain (i.e., wages) may be offset.

      1) The $25,000 limit is reduced by 50% of the person's MAGI [i.e., AGI without regard to PALs, Social Security benefits, and qualified retirement contributions (e.g., IRAs)] over $100,000.

      2) Excess rental real estate PALs are suspended. They are treated as other PALs carried over.

EXAMPLE 3-10 PAL Limitation -- Active Participation

Lynne, a single taxpayer, has $70,000 in wages, $15,000 income from a limited partnership, and a $26,000 loss from rental real estate activities in which she actively participated and is not subject to the modified adjusted gross income phase-out rule. She can use $15,000 of her $26,000 loss to offset her $15,000 passive income from the partnership. She actively participated in her rental real estate activities, so she can use the remaining $11,000 rental real estate loss to offset $11,000 of her nonpassive income (wages).

EXAMPLE 3-11 Allowed Rental Loss

A married taxpayer filing jointly actively participated in rental activity and incurred a rental loss of $30,000 in the current year. If the taxpayer's MAGI is $120,000, what is the amount of rental loss that is deductible?

MAGI	$120,000	Loss limit	$25,000
Threshold	(100,000)	Reduction	(10,000)
Excess	$ 20,000	Allowed loss	$15,000
Reduction %	× 50%		
Reduction	$ 10,000		

   c. This exception to the general PAL limitation rule applies to a person who

      1) Actively participates in the activity,

      2) Owns 10% or more of the activity (by value) for the entire year, and

      3) Has MAGI of less than $150,000 [phaseout begins at $100,000; as discussed in b.1) above].

   d. Active participation is a less stringent requirement than material participation.

      1) It is met with participation in management decisions or arranging for others to provide services (such as repairs).

      2) There will not be active participation if at any time during the period there is ownership of less than 10% of the interest in the property (including the spouse's interest).

e. Real property trades or businesses rules include the following:

   1) The passive activity loss rules do not apply to certain taxpayers who are involved in real property trades or businesses.

   2) An individual (real estate professional) may avoid passive activity loss limitation treatment on a rental real estate activity if the following requirements are met:

      a) More than 50% of the individual's personal services performed during the year are performed in the real property trades or businesses in which the individual materially participates.

      b) The individual performs more than 750 hours of service in the real property trades or businesses in which the individual materially participates.

   3) This provision also applies to a closely held C corporation if 50% of gross receipts for the tax year are from real property trades or businesses in which the corporation materially participated.

   4) Any deduction allowed under this rule is not taken into consideration in determining the taxpayer's AGI for purposes of the phaseout of the $25,000 deduction.

   5) If 50% or less of the personal services performed are in real property trades or businesses, the individual will be subject to the PAL limitation rules.

f. A PAL continues to be treated as a PAL after the activity ceases to be passive in a subsequent tax year, except that it may also be deducted against income from that activity.

g. Disposition of a passive activity is subject to the following rules:

   1) Suspended (and current-year) losses from a passive activity become deductible in full in the year the taxpayer completely disposes of all interest in the passive activity.

   2) The loss is deductible first against net income or gain from the taxpayer's other passive activities. The remainder of the loss, if any, is then treated as nonpassive.

Excess Business Loss

7. After passing the at-risk limit and the passive activity loss rule, non-C corporate business losses are now subject to the excess business loss limit. C corporations are excluded from this limitation and allowed to offset pass-through losses received from pass-through entities against non-business income (e.g., capital gains).

   a. Excess business loss is calculated as follows:

	All deductions from trades or businesses
Gross income or gain from trades or businesses	
+ $270,000 ($540,000 MFJ) floor	
Limitation	– Limitation
	= **Excess business loss**

   b. The excess business loss is carried forward as an NOL. In carryover years, the NOL is limited to 80% of the years' TI.

You have completed the outline for this subunit.

Study multiple-choice questions 13 through 20 beginning on page 71.

QUESTIONS

3.1 Rental Property Income

1. Ms. Oak rented a small house to Mr. Acorn for $500 a month for all of the current year. The house was in serious need of rehabilitation. Mr. Acorn, an electrician, approached Ms. Oak with a proposal that he would rewire the house in lieu of payment of his January through April rent (4 months). Ms. Oak accepted Mr. Acorn's offer, and Mr. Acorn completed his work in July. In August, Ms. Oak notified Mr. Acorn that she would be out of town for 3 months starting at the beginning of September, and she asked him to "look after things." While she was away, he paid $200 to have the furnace repaired. When she returned at the end of November, he paid her $1,300 (3 months' rent for September, October, and November less the $200 he had paid for the furnace). Mr. Acorn timely paid his rent on the first of each month for May, June, July, August, and December. What amount should Ms. Oak include in her current-year gross rental income?

A. $4,000

B. $4,200

C. $6,000

D. $6,200

Answer (C) is correct.

REQUIRED: The amount of rental income to be recognized.

DISCUSSION: In general, improvements made by a lessee on the lessor's property are excluded from income under Sec. 109 unless they are in lieu of rent. In this case, Mr. Acorn rewired the house in lieu of 4 months' rent. The $2,000 ($500 × 4) of improvements must be included in income. If a lessee pays any of the expenses of his or her lessor, such payments are additional rental income to the lessor [Reg. 1.61-8(c)]. Since the expenses are in effect treated as if paid by the lessee to the lessor and then paid by the lessor to a third party, the lessor may deduct them (Publication 17). Therefore, Ms. Oak must include all 12 months of rent in income, for a total of $6,000.

Answer (A) is incorrect. The improvements were made in lieu of rent and are indirect rent. **Answer (B) is incorrect.** The improvements were made in lieu of rent and are included. **Answer (D) is incorrect.** The expenses may be deducted from income so that they are not taxed twice.

2. In the current year, Jerry signed a 5-year lease to rent space to the MacBee restaurant. That year, MacBee paid Jerry $24,000 for the first year's rent and $24,000 for the last year's rent. Jerry reports his income using the accrual method of accounting. How much of the $48,000 is included in Jerry's current-year income?

A. $24,000

B. $120,000

C. $48,000

D. $0

Answer (C) is correct.

REQUIRED: The amount includible in gross income.

DISCUSSION: Both cash- and accrual-basis taxpayers must include amounts in gross income upon actual or constructive receipt if the taxpayer has an unrestricted claim to such amounts under Reg. 1.61-8(b) (Publication 17). Since Jerry has an unrestricted claim to the $24,000 of rent paid in advance, it would be included in his rental income.

Answer (A) is incorrect. Jerry must recognize the last year's payment because he has an unrestricted claim to it. **Answer (B) is incorrect.** Jerry only has actually or constructively received $48,000. **Answer (D) is incorrect.** Income must be recognized when rent is received.

3. John and Mary had a pipe burst in the basement of your rental home. They were unable to reach you on vacation. They had the plumber come out and repair the pipe and damage. They paid the plumber $575. They deducted $575 from their rent of $5,000. How much rent should be considered income that month?

A. $5,000

B. $4,425

C. $5,575

D. $5,745

Answer (A) is correct.

REQUIRED: The correct treatment of rental income and expenses.

DISCUSSION: As a general rule, if a lessee pays any of the expenses of his or her lessor, such payments are additional rental income to the lessor [Reg. 1.61-8(c)]. Since the expenses are treated as if paid by the lessee to the lessor and then paid by the lessor to a third party, the lessor may deduct them (Publication 17).

Answer (B) is incorrect. Rental income includes the $575 of expenses paid by the tenants. **Answer (C) is incorrect.** The expenses may be deducted from income so that they are not taxed twice. **Answer (D) is incorrect.** The expenses may be deducted from income so that they are not taxed twice.

4. John and Mary moved into your rental property and paid a $10,000 security deposit. You agreed to use this security deposit as their last month's rent. Additionally, they paid a painting contractor $2,500 to paint the interior. How much of these payments should be reported as rental income for this year?

A. $0

B. $5,000

C. $10,000

D. $12,500

Answer (C) is correct.

REQUIRED: The amount of rental income given security deposits and leasehold improvements.

DISCUSSION: Section 109 states that the value of leasehold improvements that are not made in lieu of rent is excluded from the lessor's gross income. Security deposits generally are not included in income but, since it was agreed upon to use the security deposit as the last month's rent, it is considered rental income. Prepaid rent is income when received even if the lessor uses the accrual method of accounting (Publication 17).

Answer (A) is incorrect. The $10,000 security deposit will be used as the last month's rent and should be reported as rental income. **Answer (B) is incorrect.** Only the security deposit needs to be reported as rental income. **Answer (D) is incorrect.** Leasehold improvements not made in lieu of rent need not be reported as rental income.

5. You own a vacation home on Amelia Island, Florida, which you rented for 10 days during the current year. Rental expenses were $2,000 and rental income was $5,000. How much of the rental income should be reported on the tax return?

A. $5,000

B. $3,000

C. $0

D. $7,000

Answer (C) is correct.

REQUIRED: The amount of rental income to be reported.

DISCUSSION: Rent is included in gross income under Sec. 61. Section 280A(g) provides that if a dwelling unit is used as a residence and rented out for less than 15 days per year, then (1) none of the rental income is included in gross income and (2) no deduction for the rental use will be allowed (Publication 17).

6. Roger signed a 10-year lease to rent office space from Doug. In the first year, Roger paid Doug $5,000 for the first year's rent and $5,000 as rent for the last year of the lease. How much must Doug include in income in the first year of the lease?

A. $0

B. $5,000

C. $5,500

D. $10,000

Answer (D) is correct.

REQUIRED: The amount of income to recognize from rent received.

DISCUSSION: Both cash- and accrual-basis taxpayers must include amounts in gross income upon actual or constructive receipt if the taxpayer has an unrestricted claim to such amounts under Reg. 1.61-8(b) (Publication 17). Since Doug has an unrestricted claim to the $5,000 of rent paid in advance, it would be included in his rental income.

Answer (A) is incorrect. Income must be recognized when rent is received. **Answer (B) is incorrect.** Doug must recognize the last year's payment because he has an unrestricted claim to it. **Answer (C) is incorrect.** Prepaid rent is not recognized on an installment basis.

7. Paul Bristol, a cash-basis taxpayer, owns an apartment building. The following information was available for the current year:

- An analysis of the bank deposit slips showed recurring monthly rents received totaling $50,000 for the current year.
- On March 1, the tenant in apartment 2B paid Bristol $2,000 to cancel the lease expiring on December 31 of the current year.
- The lease of the tenant in apartment 3A expired on December 31 of the current year and the tenant left improvements valued at $1,000. The improvements were not in lieu of any required rent.

In computing net rental income for the current year, Bristol should report gross rents of

A. $50,000

B. $51,000

C. $52,000

D. $53,000

Answer (C) is correct.

REQUIRED: The amount of gross rents given monthly rents, leasehold improvements, and a cancellation payment.

DISCUSSION: Gross rents include the $50,000 of recurring rents plus the $2,000 lease cancellation payment. The cancellation payment is in lieu of rent so it must be included in income like rent. The $1,000 of leasehold improvements are excluded from income since they were not in lieu of rent (Sec. 109 and Publication 17).

Answer (A) is incorrect. The lease cancellation payment is also included in income. **Answer (B) is incorrect.** The improvements are not included in income but the lease cancellation payment is included. **Answer (D) is incorrect.** The improvements are excluded from income.

3.2 Rental Property Expenses

8. Which of the following is NOT considered a day of personal use of a dwelling unit for determining if it is used as a home?

A. A day on which the dwelling unit is rented to a relative at a fair rental price.

B. A day on which a related person uses the dwelling unit as her main dwelling and pays fair rental value.

C. A day on which an unrelated person uses the dwelling unit as her main dwelling and pays less than fair rental value.

D. A day on which an unrelated co-owner uses the dwelling unit for personal purposes.

Answer (B) is correct.

REQUIRED: The rental not considered a personal-use day.

DISCUSSION: If the taxpayer rents the home at a fair rental value to any person (including a relative) for use as that person's main dwelling, such use by that person is not considered personal use by the taxpayer (Publication 527).

9. Peter owned a cottage on the lake that he bought in Year 1. In Year 2, he rented the cottage for 10 days to a stranger and used the cottage for 20 days for his own personal use. The cottage was not used the rest of the year. Peter had rental income of $1,000, and he paid $600 for repairs. How should he report these activities on his Year 2 return?

A. $1,000 income, $600 expense.

B. $333 income, $200 expense.

C. $0 income, $0 expense.

D. $667 income, $400 expense.

Answer (C) is correct.

REQUIRED: The amount to be reported as income and expense from rental activity.

DISCUSSION: When a residence is rented for less than 15 days, the rental income does not need to be reported as income. However, any corresponding rental expenses cannot be deducted (Publication 527).

10. Kathy rented out her summer home for 80 days and used it personally for 20 days. She paid $1,000 for repairs and $2,000 for utilities. Rental income was $8,000. What was Kathy's net rental income?

A. $0

B. $5,000

C. $5,600

D. $8,000

Answer (C) is correct.

REQUIRED: The amount of rental income from the summer home that is both rented and used for personal purposes.

DISCUSSION: If the taxpayer uses rental property for personal purposes more than the greater of (1) more than 14 days or (2) more than 10% of the number of days the property is rented, the property is considered a vacation home. Expenses of vacation homes are limited to gross income. Expenses must be allocated between the personal use and the rental use based on the number of days of use of each (Publication 527). Kathy rented out the home for 80% (80 days used by Kathy ÷ 100 total days) of its total use. Kathy's rental income is $5,600 {$8,000 – [($2,000 + $1,000) × 80%]}.

Answer (A) is incorrect. Kathy rented out the home for more than 14 days. Therefore, she must include the income derived from the rental property. **Answer (B) is incorrect.** Twenty percent of the expenses are personal in nature and thus are not deductible. **Answer (D) is incorrect.** Kathy is allowed a deduction for the nonpersonal expenses incurred relating to the rental property.

11. Tammy owns a house at the beach, which she rented out from May 1 through October 31 of the current year. During April of the current year, she spent 10 days there on vacation. In November, she spent 9 days at Dionne's mountain home and paid Dionne fair rental value. Dionne also paid Tammy a fair rental price for using her beach house for 9 days in December of the current year. Also, during November, Tammy's grandson stayed at the beach house for 3 days without any charge. How many days would the beach house be considered to have been used for personal purposes when applying the rules to vacation homes and dwellings?

A. 0

B. 10

C. 13

D. 22

Answer (D) is correct.

REQUIRED: The number of days used for personal purposes when applying the rules to vacation homes.

DISCUSSION: The tax code restricts the deductions with respect to a dwelling unit used by the taxpayer as a residence. A taxpayer is deemed to use a dwelling unit as a residence if (s)he uses it for personal purposes for a number of days that exceeds the greater of 14 days or 10% of the number of days during the year for which the unit is rented at a fair rental. The home is deemed to be used by the taxpayer for personal purposes if, for any part of the day, the home is used by any individual under a reciprocal arrangement, whether or not rent is charged. Similarly, the home is considered to be used for personal purposes when a relative stays at the home unless it is considered a main dwelling and a fair rental is charged (Publication 527). Therefore, Tammy's beach house was used for personal purposes for 22 days (10 days for Tammy + 9 days for Dionne + 3 days for Tammy's grandson).

12. Sid and Rudy co-own a lakeside cabin that they rent to vacationers whenever possible. The cabin was not used as a main home by anyone until October 1 of the current year. During the current year, the following occurred:

1. Rudy used the cabin for a 3-week (21-day) vacation.
2. Sid's brother, Chester, rented the cabin for 2 months (61 days) at less than fair rental price.
3. Prior to October 1, Sid and Rudy spent a total of 26 days at the cabin working substantially full time repairing and maintaining the cabin.
4. Starting October 1 and continuing for the balance of the year (92 days), Sid and Rudy rented the cabin to Sid's son, Martin, who used the cabin as his main home and paid a fair rental price.

What is the number of personal-use days that Sid will use in dividing his current-year expenses between rental-use and personal-use days?

A. 61 days.

B. 82 days.

C. 174 days.

D. 200 days.

Answer (B) is correct.

REQUIRED: The number of personal-use days used for allocating rental expenses.

DISCUSSION: A vacation home is deemed to have been used by the taxpayer for personal purposes if, for any part of the day, the home is used by

1. The taxpayer, any other person who owns an interest in the home, or the relatives of either
2. Any individual who uses the home under a reciprocal agreement whether or not rent is charged
3. Any individual who uses the home unless a fair rental is charged

An exception exists when a relative rents the home at a fair rental value for use as a principal residence. Sid's personal days include the 21 days Rudy spent at the cabin and the 61 days Chester rented the cabin at less than the fair rental (Publication 527).

Answer (A) is incorrect. Any use by a co-owner is considered a personal day for all owners. **Answer (C) is incorrect.** Martin paid the fair rental price and used the cabin as his principal residence. **Answer (D) is incorrect.** Days spent working on a rental property do not constitute personal days.

3.3 Loss Limitations

13. Which of the following would be considered passive activity income?

A. Alaska Permanent Funds dividends.

B. State, local, and foreign income tax refunds.

C. Personal service income.

D. None of the answers are correct.

Answer (D) is correct.

REQUIRED: The income classified as passive activity income.

DISCUSSION: There are two kinds of passive activities: (1) trade or business activities in which the taxpayer does not materially participate and (2) rental activities, unless the taxpayer is a real estate professional (Publication 925).

Answer (A) is incorrect. Alaska Permanent Funds dividends are reported as "other income" on Form 1040. **Answer (B) is incorrect.** Tax refunds are not a kind of passive activity income. **Answer (C) is incorrect.** Personal service income is earned by performing personal services in fields such as law and architecture and is classified as active income.

14. Tom Brown, who is single, owns a rental apartment building property. This is the only rental property that Tom owns. He actively participates in this rental activity as he collects the rents and performs ordinary and necessary repairs. In the current year, Tom had a loss of $30,000 on this rental activity and had no reportable passive income. His adjusted gross income, without regard to this rental loss, is $60,000. How much of the rental loss may Tom deduct on his current year return?

A. $30,000

B. $25,000

C. $0

D. $6,000

Answer (B) is correct.

REQUIRED: The deductibility of passive activity losses when the taxpayer actively participates.

DISCUSSION: All rental activity is passive. A person who actively participates in rental real estate activity is entitled to deduct up to $25,000 of losses from the passive activity from other-than-passive income, provided that the individual's income does not exceed $100,000. Single individuals and married individuals filing jointly can qualify for the $25,000 amount. Married individuals who live together for the entire year and file separately cannot qualify. Thus, Tom may deduct $25,000 of the loss (Publication 925).

Answer (A) is incorrect. Tom is not allowed to deduct the entire amount of the loss. Tom may carry over the remaining $5,000. **Answer (C) is incorrect.** Tom can deduct $25,000 of the passive activity losses in the current tax year. **Answer (D) is incorrect.** There is no 10%-of-AGI limitation on the amount of losses that may be deducted.

15. Erica received $40,000 in wages, and her husband Paul had a net loss of $2,000 on his Schedule C. Paul materially participated in his Schedule C activity. They had interest income of $500. Paul also had a $28,000 loss from a rental real estate activity in which he actively participates. How much of the rental loss can they deduct on their current-year joint income tax return?

A. $500

B. $25,000

C. $25,500

D. $28,000

Answer (B) is correct.

REQUIRED: The deductibility of a rental loss in which the taxpayer actively participates.

DISCUSSION: Since Paul is deemed to actively participate in the rental real estate activity and Paul and Erica's adjusted gross income is less than $100,000, they are allowed to deduct $25,000 against other income (Publication 925).

Answer (A) is incorrect. Passive loss is not limited to portfolio income. **Answer (C) is incorrect.** The $500 is portfolio income, not passive income. **Answer (D) is incorrect.** The loss is limited.

16. Bill took out a $100,000 non-recourse loan and bought an apartment building. The building is not security for the loan. Bill spent $25,000 of his own money on repairs before he rented the apartment building to the public. Bill is single, works full-time, and earns $80,000 per year. Bill's loss from the rental real estate activity, in which he actively participates, is $30,000. He has no passive income. For what amount is Bill at-risk, and how much of Bill's passive loss from his rental activity is deductible?

	At-Risk	Passive Loss
A.	$100,000	$25,000
B.	$25,000	$25,000
C.	$125,000	$30,000
D.	$125,000	$25,000

Answer (B) is correct.

REQUIRED: The amount at risk and the passive loss deductible from a taxpayer's rental activity.

DISCUSSION: IRS Publication 925 states that a taxpayer is not considered at risk for his or her share of any nonrecourse loan used to finance an activity or to acquire property used in the activity unless the loan is secured by property not used in the activity. Bill took out a nonrecourse loan, and the building is not security for the loan. Therefore, Bill is at risk for the $25,000 in repairs using his own money. Since Bill is deemed to actively participate in the rental real estate activity and Bill's adjusted gross income is less than $100,000, he is allowed to deduct $25,000 against other income.

Answer (A) is incorrect. The loan is a nonrecourse loan. **Answer (C) is incorrect.** The loan is a nonrecourse loan, and Bill is limited to $25,000 of his passive loss. **Answer (D) is incorrect.** The loan is a nonrecourse loan.

Authors' note: Based on the information given, the answer is probably $25,000 at-risk and $25,000 passive loss. You are at-risk for qualified nonrecourse financing secured by real property used in the holding of real property. Since this problem stated that the building was not security for the loan (who would lend in that manner?) and no other real property was mentioned as security, we have to consider this loan to be non-risk.

17. Passive activity rules apply to

A. Closely held corporations.

B. Partnerships.

C. S corporations.

D. Grantor trusts.

Answer (A) is correct.

REQUIRED: The kinds of business entities that passive activity rules apply to.

DISCUSSION: Although passive activity rules do not apply to grantor trusts, partnerships, and S corporations directly, they do apply to the owners of these entities. The passive activity rules apply to individuals, estates, trusts, personal service corporations, and closely held corporations (Publication 925).

18. Which of the following is a true statement concerning losses from passive activities?

A. Losses from each passive activity are not deductible, regardless of income earned in other passive activities.

B. The losses may offset passive income, such as interest and dividends, but not business income or earned income.

C. The rules apply to losses but not credits.

D. Losses from one passive activity may offset income from another passive activity.

Answer (D) is correct.

REQUIRED: The true statement concerning losses from passive activities.

DISCUSSION: In general, losses from passive activities may not offset nonpassive income such as salary, interest, dividends, or active business income (Sec. 469). However, deductions from one passive activity may offset income from the same passive activity, and losses from one passive activity may generally offset income from another passive activity (Publication 925).

Answer (A) is incorrect. Losses from a passive activity are deductible to the extent of income from other passive activities. **Answer (B) is incorrect.** Losses from passive activities may not offset income such as interest and dividends, which are considered portfolio income. **Answer (C) is incorrect.** The passive loss rules apply to credits as well as losses.

19. A taxpayer who materially participates in rental real estate activities in the current year may offset some losses and credits from the activity against nonpassive income (salary, self-employment earnings, etc.) provided that the taxpayer performs more than 50% of his or her personal services for the year in real property trades or businesses in which (s)he materially participates and the number of service hours performed in those real property trades or businesses in which (s)he materially participates is more than

A. 450

B. 500

C. 750

D. 1,000

Answer (C) is correct.

REQUIRED: The minimum service hours required for rental real estate losses to offset nonpassive income.

DISCUSSION: After December 31, 1993, the losses from rental real estate activities may offset nonpassive income if the taxpayer meets two requirements: (1) More than 50% of personal services performed during the year are performed in the real property trades or businesses in which (s)he materially participates, and (2) the taxpayer performs more than 750 hours of service in the real property trades or businesses in which (s)he materially participates [Publication 925 and Sec. 469(c)(7)].

20. The at-risk rules

A. Limit a taxpayer's deductible losses from investment activities.

B. Limit the type of deductions in income-producing activities.

C. Apply to business and income-producing activities on a combined basis.

D. Apply at the entity level for partnerships and S corporations.

Answer (A) is correct.

REQUIRED: The true statement concerning the at-risk rules.

DISCUSSION: The at-risk rules are contained in Sec. 465 and limit a taxpayer's deductible losses from each business and income-producing activity to the amount for which the taxpayer is at risk with respect to that activity. Although originally designed to limit deductible losses from tax shelters, the at-risk rules apply across the board to most activities (Publication 925).

Answer (B) is incorrect. It is the losses from each activity that are limited, not the type of deductions.
Answer (C) is incorrect. The at-risk rules apply to each business and income-producing activity separately.
Answer (D) is incorrect. The at-risk rules apply at the partner or shareholder level for "pass-through" entities such as partnerships and S corporations.

Go to Online Course

Access the **Gleim EA Premium Review System** featuring our SmartAdapt technology from your Gleim Personal Classroom to continue your studies.

You will experience a personalized study environment with exam-emulating multiple-choice questions.

STUDY UNIT FOUR

BUSINESS EXPENSES

(14 pages of outline)

A deduction from gross income is allowed for all ordinary and necessary expenses paid or incurred during a tax year in carrying on a trade or business. The deduction is allowed to a sole proprietor, a partnership, or a corporation. A sole proprietor claims these deductions on Schedule C.

A trade or business is a regular and continuous activity that is entered into with the expectation of making a profit. "Regular" means the taxpayer devotes a substantial amount of business time to the activity. An activity that is not engaged in for a profit is a hobby (personal). An activity that results in a profit in any 3 of 5 consecutive tax years (2 out of 7 for the breeding and racing of horses) is presumed not to be a hobby.

An expense must be **both** ordinary and necessary to be deductible. An expense is ordinary if it normally occurs or is likely to occur in connection with businesses similar to the one operated by the person claiming the deduction. The expenditures need not occur frequently. "Necessary" implies that an expenditure must be appropriate and helpful in developing or maintaining the trade or business. Implicit in the "ordinary and necessary" requirement is a requirement that the expenditures be reasonable.

4.1 COMPENSATION

A deduction is generally allowed for salaries, wages, and other forms of payment made to officers and employees.

1. Compensation must meet all of the following tests to be deductible:

Ordinary and Necessary

   a. Payments must be ordinary and necessary expenses directly related to the trade or business.

      1) Certain wages or salaries paid by a company may be considered direct or indirect costs of producing property.

         a) If the property is inventory, the wages are added to inventory.
         b) The costs are capitalized and depreciated for any other property.

Reasonable

   b. Reasonable pay is the amount that would ordinarily be paid for the services by a like enterprise under similar circumstances at the time the services are contracted.

Paid or Incurred

   c. The expenses must have been paid or incurred during the tax year.

Paid to Employees

   d. Employees are generally individuals who perform services for a company, and the company controls when and how the work is performed.

      1) Individuals in business for themselves are generally not considered employees (Publication 15).

      2) Direct sellers and qualified real estate agents are considered nonemployees.

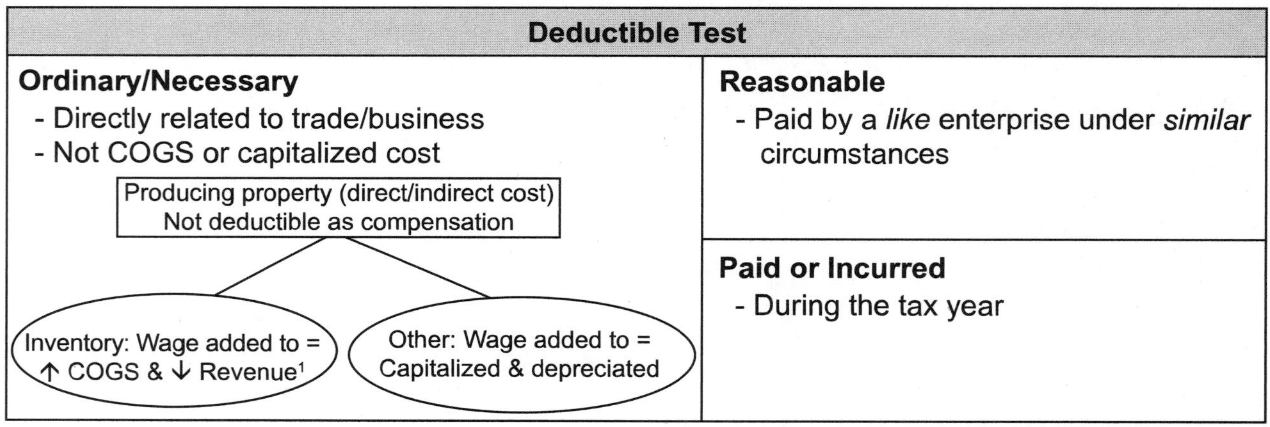

Deductible Test
Ordinary/Necessary
- Directly related to trade/business
- Not COGS or capitalized cost
Producing property (direct/indirect cost)
Not deductible as compensation
Inventory: Wage added to = ↑ COGS & ↓ Revenue[1]
Other: Wage added to = Capitalized & depreciated
Reasonable
- Paid by a *like* enterprise under *similar* circumstances
Paid or Incurred
- During the tax year

[1]Subunit 4.2 has information on cost of goods sold (COGS).

2. **Cash Payments**

   a. Bonuses paid to an employee for services actually performed may be deductible if they are reasonable for the type of services performed.

   b. Loans or advances made to employees may be deducted if it is doubtful that the employee will repay the loan.

c. Vacation pay is income to the employee whether or not the employee chooses to go on vacation.

   1) Cash- and accrual-basis taxpayers deduct vacation pay when it is paid (received by the employee).

   2) The deduction for accrual-basis taxpayers of amounts vested and paid within 2 1/2 months after the close of the tax year is not allowed.

d. Unpaid salaries may be deducted by accrual-basis taxpayers if

   1) Economic performance has occurred in the tax year,
   2) There is an unconditional agreement to pay an employee, and
   3) The payments are made within 2 1/2 months after the close of the tax year.

      a) Payments made to cash-basis related taxpayers (i.e., brothers, sisters, spouses, and lineal descendants) as wages are not deductible until the tax year in which the payment is made.

e. Sick pay is deductible but limited to amounts not compensated by insurance or other means.

3. **Noncash Payments**

a. Gifts of nominal value are deductible as nonwage business expenses. The deduction for gifts is limited to $25 per recipient per year.

b. Gifts to an employee must not be excluded from income and are taxable to the employee.

c. Transfers of property to an employee can also be considered compensation, and the fair market value of such property on the date of transfer is deductible.

   1) A gain or loss is recognized on the transfer of the difference between fair market value and the adjusted basis.

4. **Employee Benefit Programs**

a. Cafeteria plans allow employees to choose among two or more benefits consisting of cash and qualified benefits.

   1) The participant does not include any benefit amounts in gross income unless the cash is chosen.

   2) The employee must choose the benefit before the tax year begins.

   3) Any unused benefit is forfeited.

   4) If a cafeteria plan discriminates in favor of certain employees as to eligibility to participate in the plan, the favored employees are taxed on the taxable benefits they could have received under the plan.

   5) Qualified (cafeteria plan) benefits include the following benefits:

      a) Accident and health benefits (but not medical savings accounts or long-term care insurance)

      b) Adoption assistance

      c) Dependent care assistance

      d) Group-term life insurance coverage (up to $50,000 including costs that cannot be excluded from wages)

      e) Group legal services

      f) Disability benefits

6) A cafeteria plan cannot include the following benefits:

   a) Archer medical savings accounts
   b) Athletic facilities
   c) De minimis (minimal) benefits
   d) Educational assistance
   e) Employee discounts
   f) Lodging on the taxpayer's business premises
   g) Meals
   h) Moving expense reimbursements
   i) No-additional-cost services
   j) Scholarships and fellowships
   k) Transportation (commuting) benefits
   l) Tuition reduction
   m) Working condition benefits

7) Accident and health benefits apply to payments the taxpayer makes (directly or indirectly) to an employee, under an accident or health plan for employees, that are either of the following:

   a) Payments or reimbursements of medical expenses.

   b) Payments for specific injuries or illnesses (such as the loss of the use of an arm or leg).

8) Nonemployee beneficiaries (e.g., spouses) may not participate in a cafeteria plan.

b. When an employer makes payments or reimbursements for an employee's qualified educational expenses, the employer generally is allowed to deduct the expenses.

   1) Under an employer's educational assistance program, the employee may exclude up to $5,250 from his or her gross income.

   2) Graduate and undergraduate coursework qualify for the deduction.

   3) Under the CARES Act, payments made by an employer to an employee or lender between March 27, 2020, and January 1, 2026, on any qualified educational loan incurred by the employee for his or her education may be excluded by the employer from the employee's taxable wages.

c. Dependent care assistance can be deducted when

   1) The employer provides a dependent care facility for employees,

   2) The employer contracts for services with a third-party dependent care provider, or

   3) Employees are reimbursed for dependent care services. The maximum amount excludable from an employee's gross income cannot exceed $5,000 ($2,500 MFS) per year.

d. Group-term life insurance does not have to be included in an employee's income if the employer does not provide more than $50,000 of coverage.

e. An employer may deduct contributions paid or accrued to a welfare benefit fund, as long as the contributions for the year do not exceed benefits actually paid out during the year.

5. **Fringe Benefits**

   a. An employer can exclude from the employee's income certain qualified fringe benefits provided by the employer. Examples include

      1) No-additional-cost services (e.g., standby flights to flight attendants)
      2) Qualified employee discounts
      3) De minimis fringe benefits
      4) Qualified transportation fringes -- For 2022, $280 per month for commuter or transit passes and $280 per month for parking
      5) On-premises athletic facilities
      6) Qualifying adoption expenses of $14,890
      7) Occasional tickets to sporting events

   b. An employer car for personal use is included in wages.

6. **Rules of Family Employment**

<u>Child Employed by Parents</u>

   a. Payments for the services of a child under age 18 who works for his or her parents in a trade or business are not subject to Social Security and Medicare taxes if the trade or business is a sole proprietorship or a partnership in which each partner is a parent of the child.

      1) Payments for the services of a child under age 21 who works for his or her parent are not subject to federal unemployment (FUTA) tax.

         a) Although not subject to FUTA tax, the wages of a child may be subject to income tax withholding.

<u>One Spouse Employed by Another</u>

   b. The wages for the services of an individual who works for his or her spouse in a trade or business are subject to income tax withholding and Social Security and Medicare taxes, but not to FUTA tax.

<u>Covered Services of a Child or Spouse</u>

   c. The wages for the services of a child or spouse are subject to income tax withholding as well as to Social Security, Medicare, and FUTA taxes if (s)he works for

      1) A corporation, even if it is controlled by the child's parent or the individual's spouse;
      2) A partnership, even if the child's parent is a partner, unless each partner is a parent of the child;
      3) A partnership, even if the individual's spouse is a partner; or
      4) An estate, even if it is the estate of a deceased parent.

Parent Employed by Child

d. The wages for the services of a parent employed by his or her child in a trade or business are subject to income tax withholding and Social Security and Medicare taxes.

e. Social Security and Medicare taxes do not apply to wages paid to a parent for services not in a trade or business, but they do apply to domestic services if

1) The parent cares for a child who lives with a son or daughter and who is under age 18 or requires adult supervision for at least 4 continuous weeks in a calendar quarter due to a mental or physical condition and

2) The son or daughter is a widow or widower, divorced, or married to a person who, because of a physical or mental condition, cannot care for the child during such period.

f. Wages paid to a parent employed by his or her child are not subject to FUTA tax, regardless of the type of services provided.

Statutory Employees

7. An employer should indicate on the worker's Form W-2 whether the worker is classified as a statutory employee. A statutory employee is an independent contractor who is treated as an employee for employment tax purposes. The most common type of statutory employee is a driver who distributes beverages (other than milk), meat, fruit, vegetables, or bakery products.

a. Statutory employees report their wages, income, and allowable expenses on Schedule C, Form 1040.

b. Statutory employees are not liable for self-employment tax because their employers must treat them as employees for Social Security tax purposes.

8. **Documentation of Compensation Deductions**

W-2

a. Employers must file Form W-2 for wages paid to each employee from whom income, Social Security, or Medicare tax was withheld or income tax would have been withheld if the employee had claimed no more than one withholding allowance (Form W-4 for 2019 or earlier) or had not claimed exemption from withholding on Form W-4, *Employee's Withholding Certificate*.

1) Every employer engaged in a trade or business who pays remuneration for services performed by an employee, including noncash payments, must furnish a Form W-2 to each employee even if the employee is related to the employer.

2) Employers must file Copy A of Form W-2 by January 31, 2023.

a) Employers may owe a penalty for each Form W-2 that they file late.

3) Employers must furnish Copies B, C, and 2 of Form W-2 to their employees generally by January 31, 2023.

Form W-4

b. Employees provide Form W-4 to their employer to determine the amount from each paycheck to be withheld for federal income taxes. Form W-4 consists of five steps:

1) Step 1: Enter personal information (including name and filing status)

a) Tax is withheld at different rates for single and married persons.

2) Step 2: Multiple jobs or spouse works

3) Step 3: Claim dependents and other credits (e.g., Child Tax Credit and the Credit for Other Dependents)

a) Taxpayers can no longer claim personal exemptions or dependency exemptions.

4) Step 4: Other adjustments

5) Step 5: Sign the form

c. The employee's withholding amount is based solely on the standard deduction and tax rate for his or her filing status if only Step 1 and Step 5 are completed.

d. If an employee fails to give the employer a properly completed Form W-4, the employer must withhold federal income taxes from the employee's wages as if the employee selected single (or MFS) in Step 1 and made no entries to Step 2, Step 3, or Step 4.

e. A new Form W-4 need only be filed when withholding adjustments need to be made (i.e., taxes withheld are increased or decreased). The new Form W-4 should be filed within 10 days of the changing event.

f. An employee who incurred no income tax liability for his or her preceding tax year and anticipates no such liability for his or her current tax year may include statements to this effect on Form W-4. In such case, the employer may not withhold income tax from the employee's wages.

Form 1099

g. In general, by January 31 of the current year, employers/payers must provide employees/recipients with the following forms:

1) 1099-R, *Distributions From Pensions, Annuities, Retirement or Profit-Sharing Plans, IRAs, Insurance Contracts, etc.*

2) 1099-INT, *Interest Income*

3) 1099-MISC, *Miscellaneous Income*

4) 1099-NEC, *Nonemployee Compensation*

Form 8300 – $10,000

9. Each person engaged in a trade or business who, in the course of that trade or business, receives more than $10,000 in cash in one transaction or in two or more related transactions, must file Form 8300.

10. **Depositing Obligations (e.g., employment tax)**

Employment Tax Deposits

a. Employment taxes are withheld income tax, FICA contributions, and backup withholding on reportable payments. Once a tax liability arises, an employer must deposit the taxes based on their deposit schedule for the calendar year. An employer's deposit schedule is determined before the beginning of each calendar year by looking back at the total tax liability reported during a lookback period. There are two deposit schedules: monthly and semi-weekly.

Nonemployee Exemption

1) An employer does not withhold federal income tax for workers who are not common-law employees.

Monthly Deposits

b. Monthly deposits are required if the aggregate amount of employment taxes reported by the employer is $50,000 or less. Monthly deposits are due on the 15th day of the following month in which the payments were made.

Semi-Weekly Deposits

c. An employer is a semi-weekly depositor for the entire calendar year if the aggregate amount of employment taxes exceeds $50,000.

1) A monthly depositor will become a semi-weekly depositor on the first day after the employer becomes subject to the one-day rule, discussed below.
2) Semi-weekly deposits are generally due on either Wednesday or Friday, depending upon the timing of the employer's pay period.

One-Day Rule

d. If an employer has accumulated $100,000 or more of undeposited employment taxes, then the taxes must be deposited by the close of the next business day.

Form 941 Payers

e. Employers use Form 941, *Employer's Quarterly Federal Tax Return*, to

1) **Report** income taxes, Social Security tax, or Medicare tax withheld from employees' paychecks or direct deposits
2) **Pay** these taxes if total tax liability for the quarter is less than $2,500 or an underpayment for the quarter

f. The table to the right lists the due dates:

Quarter	Ending	Due Date
Jan.–Feb.–Mar.	Mar. 31	Apr. 30
Apr.–May–June	June 30	July 31
July–Aug.–Sept.	Sept. 30	Oct. 31
Oct.–Nov.–Dec.	Dec. 31	Jan. 31

Federal Unemployment Taxes

g. The calendar year is divided into four quarters for purposes of determining when deposits of federal unemployment tax are necessary.

1) The periods end on March 31, June 30, September 30, and December 31.
2) If the employer owes more than $500 in undeposited federal unemployment tax at the end of a quarter, then the tax owed must be deposited by the end of the next month.

You have completed the outline for this subunit.

Study multiple-choice questions 1 through 6 beginning on page 89.

4.2 COST OF GOODS SOLD (COGS)

Cost of goods sold is the value of inventory sold during the course of the tax year. Cost of goods sold is not a "business deduction," but it does reduce gross revenues.

1. Cost of goods sold is calculated using the following formula:

Beginning inventory		$ XXX
Plus:		
Raw materials	$XXX	
Labor	XXX	
Materials and supplies	XXX	
Overhead	XXX	
Cost of goods in inventory		XXX
Less:		
Ending inventory		(XXX)
COGS		$ XXX

   a. Beginning inventory is the ending inventory from the previous year.
   b. Raw materials include the cost of all materials or parts purchased for manufacture into a finished product. Raw materials also include the cost of freight-in.
   c. Labor includes all direct and indirect labor costs that are attributable to the manufacturing of a product and are included in COGS.
      1) Any labor costs not properly attributable to COGS may be deducted as selling or administrative expenses.
   d. Materials and supplies used in manufacturing goods, such as hardware or chemicals, are charged to COGS.
   e. Overhead expenses that are necessary for the manufacturing of a finished product are charged to COGS.
   f. The cost of inventory must be reduced by any trade discounts received.
      1) Costs to ship to the purchaser are selling expenses, not costs of inventory.
   g. Goods included in beginning inventory that are donated to charity reduce the goods available for sale in the amount of their adjusted basis.
2. Manufacturers are required to use the full absorption method of costing. Therefore, both direct and indirect production costs must be included in cost of goods sold.

You have completed the outline for this subunit.

Study multiple-choice questions 7 through 9 beginning on page 91.

4.3 INTEREST EXPENSE

Generally, the amount of interest agreed upon by the lender and the borrower can be deducted when paid or accrued.

1. **Current Deductible Interest**
   a. Interest on debt whose proceeds were used to purchase or finance a business-related property
   b. A prepayment penalty on a loan
   c. Unstated interest to the extent that the difference between interest under the contract at the applicable federal rate and the contract interest reduces the basis of the purchased property
   d. Prepaid interest in any form must be amortized over the period of the loan
   e. Investment interest to the extent of investment income
   f. Points or loan origination fees
      1) Because points are prepaid interest, they must be amortized over the life of the loan.
   g. Capitalized interest
      1) When real property is produced for use in trade or business or for sale to customers, the uniform capitalization rules require some interest expense to be capitalized.
         a) The amount of interest that is generally capitalized is an amount equal to expenditures made to produce the property.
         b) The production period must either exceed 2 years or exceed 1 year and have a cost exceeding $1 million.
   h. Interest on income tax owed is not deductible
   i. Interest on employment tax deficiency is deductible
   j. The allocation of loan proceeds and related interest is generally dependent upon how the loan proceeds are used, not the use of the property that secures the loan

<u>Refinancing</u>

2. When a debt is refinanced, the deductibility of the interest is determined by how the new loan proceeds are used.
   a. If the refinanced loan proceeds are used for personal reasons (e.g., to buy a sports boat for recreational purposes), the related interest is not deductible.
   b. If the loan proceeds are used for business purposes, the corresponding interest will be deductible as business interest expense.
3. Interest on borrowed funds used to purchase an interest in assets used in a trade or business may be deductible.
   a. The interest deduction allowed on the borrowed funds attributed to an active trade or business is limited to the proportion of the assets devoted to an active trade or business.
4. If a taxpayer borrows money from a third party to pay off a loan already outstanding and the interest is otherwise deductible, the individual may deduct the interest portion of the payment.
   a. If a cash-basis individual borrows money from the same person to whom the already outstanding loan is owed so that the borrower could pay off that first loan, then the borrower cannot deduct the interest of the first loan until payments begin on the second loan.

Limitations

5. The business interest deduction is limited to the sum of business interest income, 30% of the business's adjusted taxable income, and floor plan financing interest. Disallowed business interest may be carried forward indefinitely. For S corporations and partnerships, the limitation is generally applied at the corporate or partnership level. Any business interest deduction is taken into account in determining the non-separately stated taxable income or loss of the S corporation and partnership.
   a. The adjusted taxable income is computed without regard to
      1) Any item of income, gain, deduction, or loss that is not properly allocable to a trade or business
      2) Business interest or business interest income
      3) Net operating loss deduction
      4) Qualified business income deduction (QBID)
      5) Any deductions allowable for depreciation, amortization, or depletion
   b. Floor plan financing interest refers to interest paid or accrued on debt used to finance the acquisition of a motor vehicle held for sale or lease and secured by the inventory.
   c. The deduction limitation does not apply to small businesses with average gross receipts of $27 million or less.
   d. For S corporations and partnerships, the deduction may also be applied at the shareholder and partner level.
      1) But the adjusted taxable income of the shareholder and partner is determined without regard to the shareholder's and partner's distributive share of any items of income, gain, deduction, or loss of the S corporation or partnership.
   e. Any excess taxable income (the S corporation's and partnership's unused business interest deduction due to the limitation) is passed through to shareholders and partners.
      1) Each shareholder's and partner's deduction limit is increased by his or her distributive share of the S corporation and the partnership's excess taxable income.

EXAMPLE 4-1 Business Interest Expense

ABC Corp.'s current-year taxable income before any interest expense deduction is $300,000, including $100,000 of interest income. ABC has gross receipts exceeding $27 million. During the current year, ABC incurred interest expense of $180,000. The deductible interest expense is the sum of the interest income of $100,000 plus 30% of its adjusted taxable income of $200,000 ($300,000 – $100,000). Therefore, the deductible interest expense is $160,000 [$100,000 + ($200,000 × 30%)].

6. Interest expense incurred on borrowings used to repurchase stock is deductible in the period in which it is paid or incurred. However, other expenses related to a stock purchase on reorganization are generally not deductible.

Stop & Review

You have completed the outline for this subunit.

Study multiple-choice questions 10 through 12 beginning on page 93.

4.4 RENT EXPENSE

Rent is any amount paid for property that is not owned. Rent that is not unreasonable is deductible.

1. Prepaid rent and lease payments are deductible only for amounts that apply to the use of rented property during the tax year. The balance can be deducted only over the period to which it applies.
2. The costs of acquiring a lease (i.e., commissions, bonuses, and fees) are capitalized and amortized over the life of the lease.
3. Rent for construction equipment used to build a new building is capitalized as part of the building.

You have completed the outline for this subunit.
Study multiple-choice questions 13 through 16 beginning on page 94.

4.5 TAXES

Taxes paid or accrued in a trade or business are deductible. Taxes paid to purchase property are treated as part of the cost of the property.

Sales Tax

1. Sales tax is treated as part of the property's cost.
   a. If capitalized, the sales tax may be recoverable as depreciation.
   b. If the cost of the property is currently expensed and deductible, so is the tax.

Occupational License

2. Occupational license taxes are deductible. The Occupational License Tax and Wagering Tax are both imposed on wagering activities.

Property Tax

3. State or local personal property taxes are an itemized deduction for individuals. Tax on business property is a business expense. Real estate taxes included in monthly mortgage payments and placed in escrow cannot be deducted until the lender actually pays the taxing authority.
   a. Local improvements. Taxes assessed for local benefit that tend to increase the value of real property are added to the property's adjusted basis and are not currently deductible as tax expense.
      1) Examples are taxes assessed for streets, sidewalks, sewer lines, public parking facilities, etc.
      2) The tax must be an ad valorem tax and imposed on an annual basis.
   b. If real estate is sold, the deduction for real estate taxes must be divided between the buyer and the seller according to the number of days in the real property year.
      1) The taxes are apportioned to the seller, up to but not including the date of sale, and to the buyer beginning with the date of sale, regardless of the accrual or lien dates under local law.
   c. If a buyer agrees to pay delinquent taxes, the amount paid is added to basis and not allowed as a deduction. The seller can deduct the property taxes paid by the seller.

Income Taxes

4. State and local taxes imposed on net income of an individual are deductible.
   a. They are not a business expense of a sole proprietorship.
      1) They are a personal, itemized deduction.
   b. Federal income taxes generally are not deductible.
   c. Individual taxpayers may claim an itemized deduction for either general state and local sales taxes or state income taxes, but not both.
      1) Taxpayers can deduct either their actual sales tax amounts or a predetermined amount from an IRS table.

Employment Taxes

5. An employer may deduct the employer portion of FICA taxes. An employee may not deduct FICA taxes.
   a. Self-employed persons deduct the employer portion of FICA (self-employment) taxes to arrive at AGI based on net earnings.

Federal Excise Tax

6. Excise taxes are levied on transactions, not on income or wealth.
   a. Federal gasoline and excise taxes and import duties are not deductible as taxes.
      1) If they are paid or incurred in connection with a trade or business or with income-producing property, they may be deducted as an expense.
   b. When manufacturers' or retailers' excise taxes are reflected in the price of an article that is purchased for business or income-producing purposes, the entire price paid for such article is deductible.
      1) This applies even if the excise tax is separately stated.
      2) If the purchase price is deductible currently, the tax included in the purchase price is also deductible.
      3) If the purchase price is capitalized and amortized or depreciated, the tax included in the purchase price is also amortized or depreciated.
   c. The federal tax on automobiles may not be deducted by the ultimate purchaser.
   d. Common Excise Taxes
      1) Environmental taxes on the sale or use of ozone-depleting chemicals and imported products containing or manufactured with these chemicals
      2) Communications and air transportation taxes
      3) Fuel taxes
      4) Tax on the first retail sale of heavy trucks, trailers, and tractors
      5) Manufacturers' taxes on the sale or use of a variety of different articles
   e. The manufacturer of an item may be eligible for a credit or refund of the manufacturer's tax for certain uses, sales, exports, and price readjustments. The claim must set forth in detail the facts upon which it is based.

Real Estate Taxes

7. Any state, local, or foreign taxes on business real property are deductible when paid.
   a. If real estate is sold, the deduction for real estate taxes must be divided between the buyer and the seller according to the number of days in the real property year.
   b. Real estate taxes paid into an escrow account are deductible when the funds are withdrawn and paid to the taxing authority.

Penalties

8. Penalty taxes are generally not deductible.

You have completed the outline for this subunit.

Study multiple-choice questions 17 through 19 beginning on page 96.

QUESTIONS

4.1 Compensation

1. Which of the following tests is NOT used to determine whether an employee's pay is deductible as an expense?

A. Payments for services an employee rendered are reasonable. This test is based on the circumstances at the time you contract for the services, not on those existing when the amount of pay is questioned.

B. Payments for services an employee rendered are ordinary and necessary and are directly or indirectly connected with your trade or business.

C. Payments are made for services actually performed.

D. Depending upon the taxpayer's method of accounting, payments are made or expenses are incurred for services rendered during the year.

Answer (B) is correct.

REQUIRED: The test not used to determine whether an employee's pay is deductible.

DISCUSSION: Section 162(a)(1) allows a deduction for a reasonable allowance of salaries or other compensation for personal services actually rendered. The salary, wage, or other payment for services an employee renders must be an ordinary and necessary expense and directly connected with your trade or business. Indirectly connected services do not qualify.

Answer (A) is incorrect. Section 162(a)(1) specifically requires the amount to be reasonable and the services to be actually rendered in order to deduct compensation. **Answer (C) is incorrect.** Section 162(a)(1) specifically requires the amount to be reasonable and the services to be actually rendered in order to deduct compensation. **Answer (D) is incorrect.** Section 162 requires the expense to be paid or incurred during the year.

2. Mr. Holiday is a calendar-year, accrual-basis taxpayer. His records concerning vacation pay for his employees reflect the following:

- $20,000 paid January 30, 2022, for vacations earned in 2021. Nothing was vested by December 31, 2021.
- $100,000 vacation pay accrued and paid in 2022.
- $14,000 accrued in 2022 but vested by December 31, 2022; paid by February 28, 2023.
- $10,000 accrued but not vested by December 31, 2022.

What amount can Mr. Holiday deduct as a business expense for 2022?

A. $114,000

B. $124,000

C. $120,000

D. $154,000

Answer (C) is correct.

REQUIRED: The amount of vacation pay deductible in the current year.

DISCUSSION: Accrual-basis taxpayers deduct vacation pay when it is paid, not when it is accrued. Therefore, Mr. Holiday can deduct $120,000 in the current year.

3. Mr. Aspen, a cash basis CPA, pays Gail Smith to work during tax season as a data entry clerk. Mr. Aspen pays Gail the following:

Hourly wages	$6,275
Bonuses	500
Loan	150

How much can Mr. Aspen deduct as compensation?

A. $6,275

B. $6,775

C. $6,925

D. None of the answers are correct.

Answer (B) is correct.

REQUIRED: The amount deductible as compensation.

DISCUSSION: Section 162(a)(1) permits a deduction for a reasonable allowance for salaries or other personal services actually rendered, including bonuses. The loan is deductible only if it is doubtful the employee will repay. Otherwise, it is treated as a loan and cannot be deducted. Therefore, the wages and bonuses are deductible, but the loan is not.

Answer (A) is incorrect. The permitted deduction includes both the wages and bonuses, not just wages. **Answer (C) is incorrect.** The loan is not deductible because there is no indication for personal services actually performed. **Answer (D) is incorrect.** There is a correct answer given.

4. Allyn transferred office equipment used in his business to Wilson, an employee, as payment for services. At the time of the transfer, the equipment had a fair market value of $4,000 and an adjusted basis to Allyn of $4,750. How should Allyn report this transfer on his income tax return?

A. Wage expense $4,750; loss on sale $0.

B. Wage expense $4,000; loss on sale $750.

C. Wage expense $4,000; loss on sale $0.

D. Wage expense $0; loss on sale $4,750.

Answer (B) is correct.

REQUIRED: The proper treatment of a transfer of property as payment for services.

DISCUSSION: When property is transferred to an employee as compensation, the employer is entitled to a deduction of its fair market value on the date of the transfer. A gain or loss is realized on the date of the transfer as the difference between the fair market value and adjusted basis. Allyn will deduct $4,000 as wages and recognize a $750 loss on the sale of the equipment ($4,000 – $4,750).

Answer (A) is incorrect. A loss on sale must be recognized separately, not as a component of wage expense. **Answer (C) is incorrect.** A loss on sale must be recognized. **Answer (D) is incorrect.** The fair market value of the equipment transferred may be deducted as wages.

5. Which of the following fringe benefits is NOT excludable from an employee's wages for 2022?

A. Qualifying adoption expenses of $14,890 provided through an adoption assistance program.

B. Educational assistance expenses of $5,250 provided through an educational assistance program.

C. $60,000 of group term life insurance covering the death of an employee.

D. Dependent care assistance of $5,000 provided through a dependent care assistance program.

Answer (C) is correct.

REQUIRED: The fringe benefit not excludable from an employee's wages.

DISCUSSION: Under Sec. 79, the cost of qualified group term life insurance paid by an employer is included in the employee's gross income to the extent that such cost exceeds the cost of $50,000 of such insurance. The includible cost is determined on the basis of uniform premiums prescribed by regulations, rather than actual cost.

Answer (A) is incorrect. Qualifying adoption expenses of $14,890 are excludable. **Answer (B) is incorrect.** Under an employer's educational assistance program, the employee may exclude up to $5,250 from his or her gross income. **Answer (D) is incorrect.** In 2022, dependent care assistance of $5,000 is excludable.

6. Payments made to employees are normally currently deductible as business expenses EXCEPT

A. Vacation pay paid to an employee even when the employee chooses not to take a vacation.

B. Wages paid to employees for constructing a new building to be used in the business.

C. Reasonable salaries paid to employee-shareholders for services rendered.

D. Payments made to the beneficiary of a deceased employee that are reasonable in relation to the employee's past services.

Answer (B) is correct.

REQUIRED: The payment to an employee not currently deductible.

DISCUSSION: Normally, Sec. 162(a)(1) allows a deduction for a reasonable allowance for salaries or other compensation for personal services. However, Sec. 263A requires all direct costs and a proper share of indirect costs allocable to property produced by the taxpayer to be capitalized. Wages paid to employees for constructing a new building would be direct costs allocable to that building. Those costs are capitalized and depreciated as part of the cost of the building rather than currently deductible.

4.2 Cost of Goods Sold (COGS)

7. Lisa Arsenault operates a small basket weaving business as a sole proprietor. She incurred the following expenses in 2022:

Beginning inventory raw material	$ 5,000
Beginning inventory finished goods	10,000
Ending inventory raw material	6,250
Ending inventory finished goods	4,700
Purchases	17,500
Fabric used in finished goods	2,350
Building rent	12,000
Freight in on fabric	300
Freight out on sale of finished goods	475

What was her cost of goods sold?

A. $24,375

B. $24,675

C. $21,850

D. $24,200

Answer (D) is correct.

REQUIRED: The cost of goods sold for a manufacturing company.

DISCUSSION: Cost of goods sold is computed by starting with the beginning inventory, adding the cost of materials purchased during the year and the cost of production, and subtracting the ending inventory. Under Sec. 263A, manufacturers are required to use the full absorption method of costing, which means that both direct and indirect production costs must be included. Freight in charges are always added to the cost of the goods purchased. Freight out on sale of finished goods are selling expenses, not costs of inventory.

Beginning inventory (raw materials and finished goods)		$ 15,000
Materials and labor:		
Fabric used	$ 2,350	
Freight-in	300	
Purchases	17,500	20,150
Goods available for sale		$ 35,150
Less: Ending inventory (raw materials and finished goods)		(10,950)
Cost of goods sold		$ 24,200

Authors' note: This is a former EA exam question. The answer choices indicate that building rent is a Selling, General, and Administrative (SG&A) expense (i.e., not included in overhead and therefore not included in COGS).

Answer (A) is incorrect. Freight out are selling expenses, not cost of inventory. Freight in charges are always added to the cost of goods purchased. **Answer (B) is incorrect.** Freight out are selling expenses, not cost of inventory. **Answer (C) is incorrect.** The fabric used must be included in cost of goods.

8. The FX Partnership manufactures garden hoses for sale. In the month of January, its sales were $80,000. During that month, the partnership had the following:

Beginning inventory, January 1	$ 0
Raw materials purchased January 1	35,000
Raw materials shipping costs	1,585
Direct labor (production)	27,000
Production overhead	6,000
Ending inventory, January 31	10,000

What is the cost of goods sold for the FX Partnership for the month of January?

A. $58,000

B. $59,585

C. $69,585

D. $53,585

Answer (B) is correct.

REQUIRED: The amount reported as cost of goods sold.

DISCUSSION: Cost of goods sold is computed by starting with the beginning inventory, adding the cost of materials purchased during the year and the cost of production, and subtracting the ending inventory. Under Sec. 263A, manufacturers are required to use the full absorption method of costing, which means that both direct and indirect production costs must be included. Freight-in charges are always added to the cost of the goods purchased.

Costs to ship to the purchaser are selling expenses, not costs of inventory.

Beginning inventory		$ 0
Raw materials and labor:		
Direct labor	$27,000	
Raw materials	36,585	
Production overhead	6,000	69,585
Goods available for sale		$ 69,585
Less: Ending inventory		(10,000)
Cost of goods sold		$ 59,585

Answer (A) is incorrect. Raw material shipping costs are added to the cost of the goods purchased. **Answer (C) is incorrect.** Ending inventory must be subtracted from the goods available for sale. **Answer (D) is incorrect.** Production overhead is an indirect production cost that must be included.

9. XYZ Corporation, a clothing retailer, showed the following expenses in 2022:

Clothing purchased for resale	$72,000
Freight-in	3,550
Freight out to customers	1,750
Beginning inventory	55,650
Ending inventory	42,500

What is XYZ's cost of goods sold?

A. $88,700

B. $175,450

C. $90,450

D. $86,900

Answer (A) is correct.

REQUIRED: The calculated cost of goods sold.

DISCUSSION: Cost of goods sold is computed by starting with the beginning inventory, adding the cost of materials purchased during the year and the cost of production, and subtracting the ending inventory. Under Sec. 263A, manufacturers are required to use the full absorption method of costing, which means that both direct and indirect production costs must be included. Freight-in charges are always added to the cost of the goods purchased. Costs to ship to the purchaser are selling expenses, not costs of inventory. Therefore, the cost of goods sold is $88,700.

Beginning inventory	$ 55,650
Clothing purchased for resale	72,000
Freight-in	3,550
Goods available for sale	$131,200
Less: Ending inventory	(42,500)
Cost of goods sold	$ 88,700

Answer (B) is incorrect. The ending inventory is subtracted, not added, and the freight out to customers is not included to arrive at cost of goods sold. **Answer (C) is incorrect.** Freight out to customers is a selling expense, not an item in cost of goods sold. **Answer (D) is incorrect.** Freight out to customers is a selling expense, not an item in cost of goods sold. Freight-in charges are always added to the cost of goods purchased.

4.3 Interest Expense

10. Mr. M, a cash-basis sole proprietor, secured two business loans from two different banks. The following information pertains to the loans. Assume all costs have been paid by M.

	Loan 1	Loan 2
Date of loan	1/1/Yr 1	1/1/Yr 3
Term	10 years	10 years
Loan origination fee	$1,000	$2,000
Mortgage commission	250	500
Abstract fees	150	300
Recording fees	100	200
Interest for Year 3	5,000	7,000

On December 31, Year 3, Mr. M paid off Loan 1 and had to pay a prepayment penalty of $1,500. What deductions can Mr. M take in Year 3 with respect to these loans?

	Interest Expense	Other Costs
A.	$14,500	$500
B.	$14,000	$2,500
C.	$13,500	$3,000
D.	$12,000	$4,500

Answer (A) is correct.

REQUIRED: The amount and character of deductions for miscellaneous loan costs.

DISCUSSION: Interest is deductible under Sec. 163 as well as other payments made in lieu of interest. The prepayment penalty is in lieu of interest. The loan origination fees are also in lieu of interest since they are unreasonably large to be actual fees for processing a loan. As prepaid interest, the loan origination fees must be amortized over the period of each loan, but the balance of unpaid origination fees on Loan 1 is deductible in Year 3 when the loan was paid off.

All other expenditures are costs of obtaining a loan and are deductible over the period of each loan as Sec. 162 business expenses. The balance of the costs on Loan 1 is deductible in Year 3 when the loan was paid off.

Stated interest on both loans	$12,000
Prepayment penalty on Loan 1	1,500
Remainder of Loan 1 origination fee ($1,000 – $200 amortized in Year 1 and Year 2)	800
Loan 2 origination fees amortized in Year 3 ($2,000 ÷ 10 years)	200
Total Year 3 deductible interest	$14,500
Remainder of Loan 1 fees ($500 – $100 amortized in Year 1 and Year 2)	$ 400
Loan 2 fees ($1,000 ÷ 10 years) amortized in Year 3	100
Other deductible costs	$ 500

Answer (B) is incorrect. The origination costs should be included in interest expense. Other costs should only include the unamortized miscellaneous costs for the loan and the first-year amortization. **Answer (C) is incorrect.** The origination fees should also be included in interest expense. Other costs of $3,000 is incorrect because this is the full amount of the origination fees and other fees for Loan 2. Origination fees should be amortized with interest expense, and the other fees should be amortized with other costs with the remaining costs from Loan 1. **Answer (D) is incorrect.** The prepayment penalty and the loan origination fees are considered interest expenses. Other costs should contain the amortized portions of the other fees associated with the loans.

11. On June 30, 2022, Sally, who uses the cash method of accounting and is not subject to the business interest deduction limitations, borrowed $25,000 from a bank for use in her business. Sally was to repay the loan in one payment with $2,000 interest on December 30, 2022. On December 30, 2022, she renewed that loan plus the interest due. The new loan was for $27,000. What is the amount of interest expense that Sally can deduct for 2022?

A. $0

B. $333

C. $1,000

D. $2,000

Answer (A) is correct.

REQUIRED: The amount of interest deduction permitted for a cash-method taxpayer.

DISCUSSION: If a taxpayer borrows money from a third party to pay off a loan already outstanding and the interest is otherwise deductible, the individual may deduct the interest portion of the payment. However, if a cash-basis individual borrows money from the same person to whom the already outstanding loan is owed so that the borrower could pay off that first loan, then the borrower cannot deduct the interest of the first loan until payments begin on the second loan. Thus, Sally cannot deduct interest expense for 2022.

12. On June 30, 2022, Lily, who uses the accrual method of accounting and is not subject to the business interest deduction 30% limitation, borrowed $25,000 from a bank for use in her business. Lily was to repay the loan in one payment with interest on December 30, 2022. On December 30, 2022, she renewed that loan plus the interest due. The new loan was for $27,000. What is the amount of interest expense that Lily can deduct for 2022?

A. $0

B. $333

C. $1,000

D. $2,000

Answer (D) is correct.

REQUIRED: The amount of interest expense deductible.

DISCUSSION: If an accrual-method taxpayer borrows money from a third party to pay off a loan already outstanding and the interest is otherwise deductible, the individual may deduct the interest portion of the payment. However, if a cash-basis individual borrows money from the same person to whom the already outstanding loan is owed so that the borrower could pay off that first loan, then the borrower cannot deduct the interest until payments begin on the second loan. Since Lily is on the accrual method, she can deduct the interest expense for 2022.

4.4 Rent Expense

13. Wilma Smith leased a building for 4 years beginning in March of the current year for $1,500 per month. On March 1 of the current year, Mrs. Smith paid her landlord $33,000 in rent. How much can she deduct on her current-year tax return?

A. $33,000

B. $18,000

C. $0

D. $15,000

Answer (D) is correct.

REQUIRED: The allowable deduction for prepaid rent.

DISCUSSION: If rent is paid in advance, only the portion that applies to the current year may be deducted. The rest of the prepayment is deductible in the year in which the rent applies. Therefore, $15,000 is deductible in the current year ($1,500 × 10 months).

Answer (A) is incorrect. Only rent attributable to the current year may be deducted, not the entire amount. **Answer (B) is incorrect.** Only the rent for the remaining 10 months ($15,000) may be deducted, not an entire year's rent of $18,000 ($1,500 × 12 months). **Answer (C) is incorrect.** The amount of $15,000 is permitted as a deduction in the current year.

14. On March 1 of the current year, Sharon, a cash-basis sole proprietor, leased a dance studio from Shelby Room Renters for 3 years at $1,200 per month. During the current year, Sharon paid $28,800 on the lease. What is the amount Sharon can deduct on her income tax return for the current year?

A. $26,400
B. $12,000
C. $14,400
D. $28,800

Answer (B) is correct.
REQUIRED: The amount of rent that can be deducted in the current year.
DISCUSSION: Rental expenses are generally deductible by a cash-basis taxpayer-lessee in the tax year in which they are paid. However, the general rule does not apply to advance rental payments. Advance rental payments made by a cash-basis taxpayer-lessee are generally not deductible in the tax year in which they are made but must be allocated over the period of time for which the premises may be used as a result of such payments. Sharon will deduct $12,000 of rent expense in the current year (10 months of current year rent × $1,200 rent per month).

15. Clyde operated a food distribution business. He leased a small warehouse in 2021 for $60,000 per year for a 3-year term. The lease was to start on July 1, 2021. Clyde paid the first year's rent in advance in May 2021. Clyde then began to make monthly payments of $5,000 starting on July 1, 2022, and continuing on the first of the month for the balance of 2022. What rent expense may Clyde claim in 2022?

A. $60,000
B. $50,000
C. $30,000
D. None of the answers are correct.

Answer (A) is correct.
REQUIRED: The amount of rent that can be deducted.
DISCUSSION: Assuming that Clyde is a cash-basis taxpayer, generally, rental expenses are deductible by a cash-basis taxpayer-lessee in the tax year in which they are paid. However, the general rule does not apply to advance rental payments. Advance rental payments made by a cash-basis taxpayer-lessee are generally not deductible in the tax year in which they are made but must be allocated over the period of time for which the premises may be used as a result of such payments. Clyde will be able to deduct $60,000 of rent because he can deduct the allocated portion of the $30,000 prepaid rent and the $30,000 of current rent expenses paid.
Answer (B) is incorrect. Clyde may claim a full year's rent in the current year. **Answer (C) is incorrect.** Clyde may deduct the allocated share of prepaid rent he paid in the previous year. **Answer (D) is incorrect.** A correct answer is given.

16. In Year 1, Vicki paid $6,000 to acquire a lease, starting January 1, Year 2, for an office to use in her tax practice. The lease had 4 years remaining on it and two options to renew for 2 years each. Of the $6,000 cost, $4,000 was paid for the original lease, and $2,000 was applied to the renewal options. The term of the lease is 8 years including all renewal options. How much of the $6,000 cost can Vicki deduct for Year 2?

A. $0
B. $750
C. $1,000
D. $1,500

Answer (B) is correct.
REQUIRED: The allowable deduction in the year of acquisition for the cost of acquiring a long-term lease.
DISCUSSION: A cash-basis taxpayer normally deducts expenses in the year paid. However, the lease is an asset with a useful life that extends substantially beyond the close of the taxable year, so the cost of it must be capitalized and amortized over the life of the lease [Reg. 1.461-1(a)]. The taxpayer's allowable deduction in Year 2 is $750 ($6,000 ÷ 8-year useful life).
Answer (A) is incorrect. Vicki is allowed a deduction in the current year. **Answer (C) is incorrect.** The entire amount of rent paid is allocated over the length of the lease including renewal periods. **Answer (D) is incorrect.** The length of the lease includes the two options to renew each of the two years.

4.5 Taxes

17. Rudy, a plumber, paid the following taxes: $800 on the purchase of a new truck, $1,500 for the current year's property tax, $150 sales tax on miscellaneous office supplies, $600 sales tax on merchandise he purchased for resale. How much can he deduct as a current business expense for tax purposes?

A. $150

B. $1,650

C. $2,250

D. $3,050

Answer (B) is correct.

REQUIRED: The type of taxes deductible as a current business expense.

DISCUSSION: Section 1012 outlines general rules for certain types of commonly capitalized costs. The $800 paid in taxes on the purchase of a new truck is capitalized and added to the basis of the truck and depreciated. The $600 sales tax on merchandise purchased for resale is added to the cost basis of the merchandise and used to determine the cost of goods sold. The $1,500 for the current year's property tax (assuming the tax is related to the business) is deductible as a current business expense. The $150 in sales tax for the office supplies is deductible as a current business expense because the supplies are deemed to be consumed during the year. Therefore, the total amount Rudy may deduct during the current year as a current business expense is $1,650. However, due to the vagueness of the relationship of the property tax to the business, the IRS accepted both $150 and $1,650 as answers for this question.

Answer (A) is incorrect. The $1,500 of property tax may be deductible as a current business expense. **Answer (C) is incorrect.** The $600 of sales tax on the merchandise purchased for resale is capitalized as part of the cost of the merchandise. **Answer (D) is incorrect.** The $600 of sales tax on the merchandise purchased for resale is capitalized as part of the cost of the merchandise. Also, the $800 of tax on the purchase of the new truck is capitalized as part of the cost of the truck and will be depreciated.

18. During 2022, Ms. Smith had the following expenditures relating to commercial real estate she owns:

- County property tax, $1,975
- State property tax, $980
- Assessment for sewer construction, $1,500
- Charges for sewer and water service, $810

What is the amount Ms. Smith may deduct as real estate taxes on her commercial real estate for 2022?

A. $2,955

B. $4,455

C. $3,765

D. $5,265

Answer (A) is correct.

REQUIRED: The correct amount to be deducted as real estate taxes.

DISCUSSION: Sales and/or local property taxes are an itemized deduction for individuals and a business expense for businesses. Thus, the $1,975 and the $980 are deductions as real estate taxes. Assessments for sewer construction are local improvements. These are taxes for things not currently deductible as a tax expense that tend to increase the value of real property and are added to the property's adjusted basis. Charges for sewer and water service are not an ad valorem tax and would not be deducted as real estate tax.

Answer (B) is incorrect. Assessments for sewer construction are local improvements. These are taxes for things that tend to increase the value of real property and are added to the property's adjusted basis. These are not currently deductible as tax expense. **Answer (C) is incorrect.** Charges for sewer and water service are not an ad valorem tax and are not deductible as real estate tax. **Answer (D) is incorrect.** Assessments for sewer construction are local improvements. These are taxes for things not currently deductible as a tax expense that tend to increase the value of real property and are added to the property's adjusted basis. Charges for sewer and water service are not an ad valorem tax and would not be deducted as real estate tax.

19. Which of the following statements regarding deductible taxes is correct?

1) Local benefit taxes for business assets are deductible only if they are for maintenance, repair, or interest charges related to those benefits.
2) Real estate taxes on business property included in monthly mortgage payments placed in escrow cannot be deducted unless the lender actually paid the taxing authority.
3) Taxes on gasoline, diesel fuel, and other motor fuels that you use in your business should be deducted as part of the cost of the fuel.
4) Any tax imposed by a state or local government on personal property used in your trade or business is deductible.

A. 1, 2, and 4.

B. 2 and 4.

C. 1 and 3.

D. 1, 2, 3, and 4.

Answer (D) is correct.

REQUIRED: The correct statement about deductible taxes.

DISCUSSION: Local benefit taxes for businesses are deductible if the local benefit does not increase the value of the property. When real estate taxes are paid into an escrow account with the monthly mortgage payment, the taxes cannot be deducted until the escrow funds are withdrawn and paid to the taxing authority. Taxes on gasoline, diesel fuel, and other motor fuels are expensed. The rule is if the cost of the property is currently expensed and deductible, so is the tax. Any tax by state or local government on personal property in a trade or business is deductible.

Answer (A) is incorrect. Taxes on gasoline, diesel fuel, and other motor fuels are expensed. The rule is, if the cost of the property is currently expensed and deductible, so is the tax. **Answer (B) is incorrect.** Local benefit taxes for businesses are deductible if the local benefit does not increase the value of the property and because taxes on gasoline, diesel fuel, and other motor fuels are expensed. The rule is, if the cost of the property is currently expensed and deductible, so is the tax. **Answer (C) is incorrect.** When real estate taxes are paid into an escrow account with the monthly mortgage payment, the taxes cannot be deducted until the escrow funds are withdrawn and paid to the taxing authority. Also, any tax by state or local government on personal property in a trade or business is deductible.

Go to Online Course

Access the **Gleim EA Premium Review System** featuring our SmartAdapt technology from your Gleim Personal Classroom to continue your studies.

You will experience a personalized study environment with exam-emulating multiple-choice questions.

STUDY UNIT FIVE

OTHER DEDUCTIONS

(24 pages of outline)

This study unit continues the discussion of business expenses. A deduction from gross income is allowed for all ordinary and necessary expenses paid or incurred during a tax year in carrying on a trade or business. The deduction is allowed to a sole proprietor, a partnership, or a corporation. A sole proprietor claims these deductions on Schedule C.

5.1 BUSINESS MEALS EXPENSE

1. Prior to 2018, there was a deduction for entertainment expenses, which included recreation, e.g., entertaining guests at a nightclub, sporting event, or theater; supplying vacations, trips, etc.; and furnishing a hotel suite, automobile, food and beverages, or the like to a customer or a member of the customer's family.
   a. Now, only the food and beverage portion of the deduction remains and is referred to as the business meals deduction.

EXAMPLE 5-1 Business Meals Expense Deduction

Annie, a self-employed taxpayer, takes her client Bonnie to a baseball game where they discuss business. The cost of the tickets to the game is $100. While at the game, Annie buys Bonnie hot dogs and sodas costing $40. Because the price of the food and beverages is separately billed, Annie can deduct $40, which is 100% of the meal expense. The $100 price of the tickets is nondeductible entertainment.

2. For a business meal to be deductible, the meal must
   a. Be an ordinary and necessary expense
   b. Not be a lavish or extravagant expense, i.e., be reasonable based on facts and circumstances
   c. Be attended by the taxpayer or an employee of the taxpayer
   d. Be provided to a current or potential business customer, client, consultant, or similar business contact
   e. Be separately stated from any nondeductible entertainment expense or purchased separately from the entertainment

Deduction Limit

3. The amount deductible for meal expense is 100% of the actual expense for food or beverages provided by a restaurant between December 31, 2020, and January 1, 2023. The limits also apply to the taxpayer's own meals. However, there is a 50% limit to deductible amounts for other allowable meal expenses (i.e., meals not provided by a restaurant). Related expenses, such as taxes, tips, and parking fees, but not transportation to and from a business meal, are subject to the same limit as the meal.
   a. The IRS has denied deductions for any meal expense over $75 for which the claimant did not provide substantiating evidence, i.e., documented dates, amounts, location, purpose, and business relationship.
   b. The expenses of a spouse are not deductible (i.e., they would have to be a business associate as well).
   c. The term "restaurant" means a business that prepares and sells food or beverages to retail customers for immediate consumption, regardless of whether the food or beverages are consumed on the business's premises. However, a restaurant does not include a business that primarily sells prepackaged food or beverages not for immediate consumption, such as a grocery store; specialty food store; beer, wine, or liquor store; drug store; convenience store; newsstand; vending machine; or kiosk.
   d. A taxpayer may treat the meal portion of a per diem rate or allowance paid or incurred after December 31, 2020, and before January 1, 2023, as being attributable to food or beverages provided by a restaurant.
   e. An exclusion from employee income for employee meals furnished on the business premises of the employer applies if they are furnished to the employee for the convenience of the employer.
      1) The meals are deductible by the employer as an ordinary and necessary business expense. The deduction for these meals are now also limited to 50% of the expense.
         a) However, meal and entertainment expenses for employee recreation (e.g., a holiday party or an annual picnic) remain 100% deductible.

EXAMPLE 5-2 Business Meals Expense Deduction Limitation

ABC Accounting Firm requires its employees to work until 11 p.m. every evening the month prior to tax filing deadlines. ABC contracts a catering service to provide the employees with meals every evening on the company's premises. Such meals are for the convenience of the employer and are excluded from the employee's income. ABC would be allowed a deduction for 50% of the cost of the meals.

4. The following is a summary of the rules explained on the previous pages:

General rule	A taxpayer can deduct ordinary and necessary expenses to provide a meal to a client, customer, or employee if the expenses meet five qualifications.
Definitions	• An **ordinary** expense is one that is common and accepted in the taxpayer's field of business, trade, or profession. • A **necessary** expense is one that is helpful and appropriate, although not necessarily required, for the business.
Five qualifications	The meal must • Be an ordinary and necessary expense • Not be a lavish or extravagant expense, i.e., be reasonable based on facts and circumstances • Be attended by the taxpayer or an employee of the taxpayer • Be provided to a current or potential business customer, client, consultant, or similar business contact • Be separately stated from any nondeductible entertainment expense or purchased separately from the entertainment
Other rules	• The taxpayer cannot deduct the cost of the meal as business meal expense if claiming the meal as a travel expense. • The taxpayer generally can deduct only 50% (100% if provided by a restaurant) of business meal expenses.

Entertainment Facility

5. There still remains no deduction allowed for any expenses for entertainment facilities, such as yachts, hunting lodges, swimming pools, tennis courts, or bowling alleys. The membership or initiation fee is a capital expenditure that is not currently deductible, and any gain upon sale is a capital gain.

You have completed the outline for this subunit.

Study multiple-choice questions 1 through 3 beginning on page 123.

5.2 TRAVEL EXPENSES

While away from home overnight on business, ordinary and necessary travel expenses, including meals (subject to the 50%/100% limits), are deductible.

1. No deduction is allowed for the following:
   a. Travel that is primarily personal in nature (if more days are spent for personal purposes than for business purposes) except for
      1) Directly related business expenses while at the destination
   b. The travel expenses of a taxpayer's spouse unless there is a bona fide business purpose for the spouse's presence, the spouse is an employee, and the expenses would be otherwise deductible
   c. Commuting between home and work
      1) A taxpayer's "home" is considered to be
         a) The taxpayer's regular or principal (if there is more than one regular) place of business or
         b) If the taxpayer has no regular or principal place of business because of the nature of the work, the taxpayer's regular place of abode in a real and substantial sense.
      2) If the period of work in a new location is or becomes indefinite, travel expenses are not deductible because the individual is treated as though (s)he changed the location of his or her tax homes to his or her work location.
   d. Travel for attending investment meetings
   e. Travel as a form of education (e.g., a Spanish teacher traveling to Spain to improve her Spanish)
2. For individuals subject to Department of Transportation hours of service rules, the deductible meals percentage is 80%.

Automobile Expenses

3. Actual expenses for automobile use are deductible (e.g., services, repairs, gasoline, etc.). Alternatively, the taxpayer may deduct the standard mileage rate of $0.585 per mile for Jan.-Jun. 2022, $0.625 per mile for Jul.-Dec. 2022, plus expenses, such as parking fees and tolls, that are not actual automobile expenses.

Domestic Travel

4. For travel within the U.S., expenses other than transportation (e.g., airfare) are allocated based on personal or business purpose. Transportation expenses are
   a. 100% deductible if the primary purpose is business or
   b. 0% deductible if the primary purpose is personal (i.e., no proportional allocation for transportation costs when traveling within the U.S.).

Foreign Travel

5. Generally, traveling expenses (including meals and lodging) of a taxpayer who travels outside of the United States and away from home must be allocated between time spent on the trip for business and time spent for pleasure. However, no allocation is required for transportation, such as costs of getting to and from the destination, when one of the following three exceptions for a trip considered entirely for business applies.
   a. A trip is considered entirely for business if the traveler did not have substantial control over arranging the trip.
   b. When the trip is for not more than 1 week (7 consecutive days counting the day of return but not the day of departure) and a personal vacation was not the major consideration, the trip is considered entirely for business.
   c. When the foreign trip is longer than a week and less than 25% of the total time away from home outside the United States is spent for nonbusiness activities, the trip is considered entirely for business. For this purpose, include both the day the trip began and the day it ended.

EXAMPLE 5-3 Deductible Foreign Travel Expenses

Scott's foreign trip is for more than a week, and he spends 35% of his time as a personal vacation. However, he spends the other 65% providing business-related services.

Only 65% of the expenses related to the time providing business services, including transportation, lodging, local travel, etc., may be deducted.

Convention Expenses

6. Deductible travel expenses include those incurred when attending a convention related to the taxpayer's business.
   a. The fact that an attending individual uses vacation or leave time or that attendance at the convention is voluntary will not necessarily negate the deduction.
   b. Expenses for a convention or meeting in connection with investments, financial planning, or other income-producing property are not deductible.
   c. A taxpayer can show that his or her attendance at a convention benefits his or her trade or business by comparing the convention agenda with the official duties and responsibilities of his or her position. The fact that the convention agenda does deal with his or her specific duties lends support for the travel being ordinary and necessary in the conduct of a trade or business.

7. The following chart summarizes expenses that can be deducted when traveling away from home for business purposes:

IF there are expenses for . . .	THEN the taxpayer can deduct the cost of . . .
transportation	travel by airplane, train, bus, or car between the home and the business destination. If the taxpayer was provided with a free ticket or the taxpayer was riding free as a result of a frequent traveler or similar program, the cost is zero. Travel by ship (e.g., cruise ships) for conventions has additional rules and limits.
taxi, commuter bus, and airport limousine	fares for these and other types of transportation that take the taxpayer between • The airport or station and the hotel, and • The hotel and the work location of the customers or clients, the business meeting place, or the temporary work location.
baggage and shipping	sending baggage and sample or display material between the regular and temporary work locations.
car	operating and maintaining the car when traveling away from home on business. The taxpayer can deduct the actual expenses or the standard mileage rate, as well as business-related tolls and parking. If the taxpayer rents a car while away from home on business, (s)he can deduct only the business-use portion of the expenses.
lodging and meals	lodging and meals if the business trip is overnight or long enough to require a stop for sleep or rest to properly perform duties. Meals include amounts spent for food, beverages, taxes, and related tips and have additional rules and limits.
cleaning	dry cleaning and laundry.
telephone	business calls while on the business trip. This includes business communication by fax machine or other communication devices.
tips	tips paid for any expenses in this chart.
other	other similar ordinary and necessary expenses related to the business travel. These expenses might include transportation to or from a business meal, public stenographer's fees, computer rental fees, and operating and maintaining a house trailer.

Reimbursed Employee Expenses

8. If reimbursements equal expenses and the employee makes an accounting of expenses to the employer, the reimbursements are excluded from the employee's gross income (i.e., excluded from employee's W-2), and the employer may deduct the expenses (accountable plan).
   a. This rule also applies if reimbursements exceeding expenses are returned to the employer and the employee substantiates the expenses.
   b. If excess reimbursements are not returned or if the employee does not substantiate them, the reimbursements are included in the employee's gross income, and none of the expenses are deductible by the employee (nonaccountable plan).

Unreimbursed Employee Expenses

9. Unreimbursed employee expenses are not deductible.

Recordkeeping

10. Taxpayers generally must have documentary evidence, such as receipts, canceled checks, or bills, to support their expenses. Documentary evidence ordinarily will be considered adequate if it shows the amount, date, place, and essential character of the expense. A canceled check, together with a bill from the payee, ordinarily establishes the cost.
    a. However, a canceled check by itself does not prove a business expense without other evidence to show that it was for a business purpose. Documentary evidence is not needed for expenses, other than lodging, of less than $75.

Stop & Review

You have completed the outline for this subunit.
Study multiple-choice question 4 on page 124.

5.3 INSURANCE EXPENSES

1. Ordinary and necessary trade or business insurance expense paid or incurred during the tax year is deductible.
   a. A cash-method taxpayer may not deduct a premium before it is paid.
   b. Prepaid insurance of more than 1 year must be apportioned over the period of coverage.

<table>
<tr><th colspan="4">Ordinary & Necessary Trade/Business Insurance Expenses</th></tr>
<tr><td>Casualty insurance:
-Fire -Theft
-Accident -Other
-Storm</td><td colspan="2">Credit insurance:
-Losses from unpaid debts</td><td>Group hospitalization & medical insurance costs paid for employees</td></tr>
<tr><td>Accident & health insurance premiums paid for partners as guaranteed payments made to the partners in a partnership or the shareholders in an S corporation</td><td colspan="2">Workers' Compensation
Premiums for: / Deduct as:
Employees / Business insurance
Partners / Guaranteed payment
S corp. shareholders / Wages</td><td>Overhead insurance
-Long periods of disability from taxpayer's injury/illness (i.e., owner, not employee)</td></tr>
<tr><td>Malpractice and nonperformance insurance</td><td colspan="2">Liability insurance
-Covers injury to employee/client</td><td>Life insurance
-Covers officers & employees
-Taxpayer is not the beneficiary</td></tr>
<tr><td colspan="2">Self-employed (SE) health insurance
-100% of costs
-Covers SE/spouse/dependents
-Deduction limit = Earnings from related business</td><td colspan="2">Compensation for employees injured at work</td></tr>
<tr><td>SUTA fund contributions
-If state considers as tax</td><td colspan="2">Business auto insurance
-No deduction if mileage rate for car expenses is used</td><td>Business interruption insurance
-Profit loss due to shutdown</td></tr>
</table>

2. A taxpayer may not deduct the following:
   a. Loss of earnings except for certain overhead insurance expenses
   b. Self-insurance reserve funds
      1) Deductible when payment made
   c. Premiums on a life insurance policy covering the taxpayer, an employee, or any person with a financial interest in the taxpayer's business if the taxpayer is directly or indirectly a beneficiary
   d. Costs for a self-employed taxpayer eligible for coverage under the plan of his or her spouse's employer
3. Self-employed health insurance is not deductible on Schedule C. It would be deducted on Form 1040, Schedule 1, in the adjustments to income section.

Stop & Review

You have completed the outline for this subunit.
Study multiple-choice questions 5 through 7 beginning on page 125.

5.4 BAD DEBTS

Bad Debt Deduction

1. A bad debt deduction is allowed only for a bona fide debt arising from a debtor-creditor relationship based upon a valid and enforceable obligation to pay a fixed or determinable sum of money.
   a. Worthless debt is deductible only to the extent of adjusted basis in the debt.
   b. Money lent to a relative or friend with the understanding the relative or friend may not repay it must be considered a gift by the taxpayer, not as a loan, and it may not be deducted as a bad debt.
   c. A cash-basis taxpayer has no basis in accounts receivable and generally has no deduction for bad debts.

Business Bad Debt

2. A business bad debt is one incurred or acquired in connection with or closely related to the taxpayer's trade or business.
   a. A debt is closely related if the primary motive for incurring the debt is business related.
      1) If a taxpayer makes a loan to a client, supplier, employee, or distributor for a business reason and it becomes worthless, it becomes a business bad debt.
   b. The bad debts of corporations are always business bad debts.
   c. Partially worthless business debts may be deducted to the extent they are worthless and specifically written off.
   d. A business bad debt is treated as an ordinary loss.
   e. A bad debt written off in a previous tax year but recovered in the current tax year should be reported as other income.

Nonbusiness Bad Debt

3. A nonbusiness bad debt is a debt other than one incurred or acquired in connection with the taxpayer's trade or business.
   a. Investments are not treated as a trade or business.
   b. A shareholder loan to protect his or her investment in the corporation is not treated as a business loan.
   c. A partially worthless nonbusiness bad debt is not deductible.
   d. A wholly worthless nonbusiness debt is deducted in the year it becomes worthless, and it is then treated as a short-term capital loss.
4. Taxpayers cannot take a bad debt deduction for a loan made to a corporation if, based on the facts and circumstances, the loan is actually a contribution to capital.
   a. Worthless corporate securities are not considered bad debts. They are generally treated as a capital loss.
5. Taxpayers can take a bad debt deduction only if the amount owed was previously included in gross income. This applies to amounts owed from all sources of taxable income, including sales, services, rents, and interest.
   a. If a taxpayer uses the cash method of accounting, (s)he generally reports income when payment is received. A taxpayer cannot take a bad debt deduction for amounts owed because those amounts were never included in income.

Specific Write-Off Method

6. The specific write-off method generally must be used for tax purposes. The reserve method is used for financial accounting purposes.
   a. If the specific write-off method is used, taxpayer can deduct specific bad debts that become either partly or totally worthless during the tax year.
   b. Taxpayers can deduct specific bad debts that become partly uncollectible.
   c. The tax deduction is limited to the amount charged off on the books during the year.

Stop & Review

You have completed the outline for this subunit.
Study multiple-choice questions 8 through 12 beginning on page 126.

5.5 BUSINESS GIFTS

Expenditures for business gifts are deductible. They must be ordinary and necessary.

1. Deduction for business gift expenditure is disallowed unless the taxpayer substantiates, by adequate records, the following:
   a. Amount (cost) of the gift
   b. Date of the gift
   c. Description of the gift
   d. Business purpose for the gift
   e. Business relation of the recipient to the taxpayer
2. Deduction is limited to $25 per recipient per year for items excludable from income.
   a. If a gift is given to a member of a customer's family, the gift is generally considered an indirect gift to the customer. This rule does not apply if there is a bona fide, independent business connection with that family member and the gift is not intended for the customer's eventual use.
   b. A husband and wife are treated as one taxpayer, even if they file separate returns and have independent business relationships with the recipient.
   c. Incidental costs, such as engraving on jewelry or packaging, insuring, and mailing, are generally not included in determining the cost of a gift for purposes of the $25 limit.
   d. The $25 limit does not apply to incidental (e.g, advertising) items costing (the giver) not more than $4 each and other promotional materials including signs and displays.

Employee Achievement Awards

3. Up to $400 of the cost to the employer (not FMV) of employee achievement awards is deductible by an employer for all nonqualified plan awards. (Deduction of qualified plan awards is limited to $1,600 per year.)
   a. An employee achievement award is tangible personal property awarded to an employee as part of a meaningful presentation for safety achievement or length of service.
      1) Tangible personal property does not include cash, cash equivalents, gift cards/coupons/certificates, vacations, meals, lodging, event tickets (e.g., theater, sporting), stocks, bonds, and other securities.

Stop & Review

You have completed the outline for this subunit.
Study multiple-choice questions 13 and 14 on page 128.

5.6 OTHER BUSINESS EXPENSES

Some other items of business-related expense follow:

Depreciation

1. Deduction for obsolescence or wear and tear of property used in a trade or business has generally been tested in the context of corporations. However, depreciation can be a deductible expense of any business.

Start-Up/Organization Costs

2. Start-up/organization costs in general are capitalized and amortized proportionally over the 180-month (15-year) period beginning with the month in which the active trade or business begins.
   a. Start-up costs are amounts paid or incurred to create an active trade or business, investigate the creation or acquisition of a trade or business, or engage in any activity for profit or the production of income.
      1) If the taxpayer is not already in the business for which they have incurred start-up costs, those costs must be capitalized and amortized only if the business is entered into. No deduction is allowed if the taxpayer does not enter into the business.
      2) If the taxpayer is already in the business, a deduction is allowed for start-up costs regardless of whether the taxpayer enters the business. For example, a restaurant chain incurs qualified expenses to open a new location. These expenses may be deducted or amortized regardless of the new location opening.
   b. Organizational costs are amounts paid or incurred that are incidental to the creation of a corporation or partnership (i.e., direct costs). They are chargeable to a capital account, amortizable over the fixed life of the entity, and incurred before the first tax year ends (corporation) or when the first return is due (partnership).

c. The following table provides examples of costs that do or do not qualify as start up or organizational costs:

	Start-Up Costs	Organizational Costs
Qualifying Costs	• Surveys of potential markets, products, labor supplies, transportation facilities, etc. • Grand opening advertisements • Training costs such as salaries and wages for employees and instructors • Salaries and fees for executives and consultants or similar professional services • Acquisition of certain supplies and equipment (noncapital)	• Legal services, e.g., negotiation and preparation of the partnership agreement (partnerships) or obtaining a corporate charter (corporations) • Temporary directors (corporations) • Organizational meetings (corporations) • State incorporation fees (corporations) • Accounting fees for organization (partnerships) • Filing fees (partnerships) • Items expected to be beneficial throughout the life of the partnership
Nonqualifying Costs	• Deductible interest, taxes, or research and experimental costs	• Issuing and selling stock or securities, e.g., commissions, professional fees, printing, and stock exchange listing (corporations) • Transfer or acquisition of assets to the corporation or partnership • Admitting or removing partners after initial organization • Creation of contracts concerning operations (partnership) • Syndication fees, i.e., costs for issuing and marketing interest in a partnership, e.g., brokerage registration, legal fees, and printing costs

d. Taxpayers can deduct up to $5,000 of start-up and $5,000 of organizational expenditures in the taxable year in which the business begins. The total startup or organizational costs deducted for the first year equal the sum total of the $5,000 limit and the amortized amount allocated to the first year.

1) The $5,000 is reduced, but not below zero, by the cumulative cost of the start-up expenditures that exceed $50,000. The phaseout is computed separately for both start-up cost and organizational costs.

Vacant Land

3. Interest and taxes on vacant land are deductible.

Demolition

4. If a structure is demolished, demolition costs, undepreciated (remaining) basis, and any losses sustained are not deductible. They are allocated to the land.

Abandoned Assets

5. A loss is deductible in the year the assets are actually abandoned with no claim for reimbursement. The amount of the loss is the adjusted basis for determining a loss on the sale or other disposition of the property.

COGS

6. Cost of goods sold reduces revenue before inclusion in gross income.

Sales – COGS = Gross income

Medical Reimbursement Plans

7. The cost of such a plan for employees is deductible by the employer.

Political Contributions

8. Contributions to a political party or candidate and, generally, lobbying expenses are not deductible.

EXAMPLE 5-4 **Nondeductibility of Political Contributions**
Craft Store pays for advertising in the program for a political party's convention. Proceeds are used for the party's activities. The expense is a political contribution, which is not deductible.

   a. Lobbying activity equates to appearances before and communications with any council or similar governing body with respect to legislation of direct interest to the taxpayer.
      1) Up to $2,000 of direct cost of lobbying activity at the state or federal level is deductible.
         a) This does not include payments to professional lobbyists.
         b) If total direct costs exceed $2,000, this de minimis exception is unavailable.

Debt of Another

9. Payment of a debt of another party is generally not ordinary for a trade or business and thus is not deductible.
   a. A legal obligation or definite business requirement, e.g., if required by suppliers to stay in business, renders the payment deductible.

Intangibles

10. The cost of intangibles must generally be capitalized.
   a. Amortization is allowed if the intangible has a determinable useful life, e.g., a covenant not to compete or if a code section specifically so provides.
   b. Generally, Sec. 197 intangibles have a 15-year life.

Tax-Exempt Income

11. An expenditure related to producing tax-exempt income, e.g., interest on a loan used to purchase tax-exempt bonds, is not deductible.

Nondeductible

12. Certain trade or business expenditures that are ordinary, necessary, and reasonable are nondeductible. The following are examples of expenditures disallowed as deductions:
    a. Fines and penalties paid to the government for violation of the law
    b. Illegal bribes and kickbacks (including Medicaid and Medicare referrals) provided the law is generally enforced
    c. Two-thirds of damages for violation of federal antitrust law
    d. Expenses of dealers in illegal drugs

Moving Expenses

13. Expenses involved with an employer business move are deductible.
    a. The Tax Cuts and Jobs Act of 2017 removed the employee deduction for job-related relocation (i.e., moving expenses) except for military on active duty who move pursuant to a military order and due to a permanent change of station.
        1) When an employer reimburses an employee for moving expenses, such reimbursement is included in the gross income of the employee and is deductible by the employer.

Research Expenses

14. No deduction is allowed for research or experimental costs. The taxpayer must capitalize such expenditures and amortize them over 5 years. For research or experimental expenditures which are attributable to foreign research, the amortization period is 15 years. The change in accounting shall be applied only on a cut-off basis for any research or experimental expenditures paid or incurred in the first taxable year beginning after December 31, 2021, and shall be treated as
    a. Initiated by the taxpayer
    b. As made with the consent of the Secretary

Environmental Clean-Up Costs

15. Environmental clean-up costs are treated as land and capitalized.

Miscellaneous Business Expenses

16. Miscellaneous ordinary and necessary business expenses are deductible. Examples include costs of office supplies, advertising, professional fees, and bank fees.

Fines for Nonperformance of a Contract

17. Although fines and penalties paid to a government are generally not deductible, the payment of a penalty for late performance or nonperformance of a contract is generally deductible.
    a. This penalty usually represents damages that one contracting party was willing to incur in order to avoid performing under the contract.

Costs of Removing Barriers to the Disabled and the Elderly

18. The costs of making a trade or business facility or public transportation vehicle more accessible to those who are disabled or elderly can be deducted.
    a. The most that can be deducted for any year is $15,000.
    b. The costs incurred above the limit can be added to the basis of the property and depreciated.
    c. A tax credit for eligible access expenditures of up to 50% of $10,000 is available for small businesses (less than $1 million in gross receipts).

Charitable Contributions

19. Sole proprietorships, shareholders in S corporations, and partners in partnerships may be able to deduct charitable contributions made by their business entities.
    a. The deduction is taken on Schedule A of Form 1040.

Government-Granted License

20. A taxpayer must amortize the capitalized costs of acquiring, issuing, or renewing a license granted by a governmental unit or agency.

Deductions on Schedule C

21. A statutory employee's business expenses are deductible on Schedule C (Form 1040).

Self-Rental

22. The amount of a loss or credit attributable to a person's passive activities is allowable as a deduction or credit only against, and to the extent of, gross income or tax attributable to those passive activities.
    a. If a taxpayer rents property to a business in which (s)he materially participates (i.e., the taxpayer rents to his or her own business), net rental income is nonpassive. Stated differently, rental income from self-rented property cannot be used to trigger allowance of passive losses on Form 8582.
        1) Self-rental losses, on the other hand, are passive, deductible only to the extent of passive income.
        2) Income is still reportable on Schedule E but cannot be entered as passive income on Form 8582.

Self-Employed Education Expense Related to Business

23. Self-employed taxpayers may deduct their own education expenses on Schedule C as an other business deduction. To qualify, the education must maintain or improve the skills used in the taxpayer's trade or business, or be necessary to keep a job, status, or rate of pay under the requirements of applicable law or regulations. A taxpayer cannot deduct expenses incurred to meet minimum requirements for a trade or profession or to qualify for a new trade or profession.

Stop & Review

You have completed the outline for this subunit.

Study multiple-choice questions 15 and 16 on page 129.

5.7 BUSINESS USE OF HOME

1. Expenses incurred for the use of a person's home for business purposes are deductible only if strict requirements are met.
   a. The portion of the home must be used exclusively and regularly as
      1) The principal place of business for any trade or business of the taxpayer;
      2) A place of business that is used by patients, clients, or customers in the normal course of the taxpayer's trade or business; or
      3) A separate structure that is not attached to the dwelling unit that is used in the taxpayer's trade or business.
   b. If the taxpayer is an employee, the business use of the home is not deductible.

Exclusive-Use Test

2. Any personal use of the business portion of the home by anyone results in complete disallowance of the deductions. There are two exceptions to the exclusive-use test:
   a. Retail/wholesale
   b. Day care

Limitation

3. A taxpayer's deduction of otherwise nondeductible expenses, e.g., insurance, utilities, and depreciation (with depreciation taken last), is limited to
   a. Gross income derived from the use; minus
   b. Deductions related to the home, allowed regardless of business or personal use, e.g., mortgage interest or taxes; and
   c. Deductions allocable to the trade or business for which the home office is used that are not home office expenses, e.g., employee compensation.

Simplified Option

4. A new simplified option allows taxpayers to claim $5 per square foot of home office space, up to 300 ft^2, for a maximum deduction of $1,500.

Stop & Review

You have completed the outline for this subunit.
Study multiple-choice question 17 on page 129.

5.8 STATUTORY EMPLOYEES/NONEMPLOYEES

Worker Classification

1. It is critical that business owners correctly determine whether the individuals providing services are employees or independent contractors.
   a. Generally, employers must withhold income taxes, withhold and pay Social Security and Medicare taxes, and pay unemployment tax on wages paid to an employee.
   b. Employers do not generally have to withhold or pay any taxes on payments to independent contractors.
   c. Before an employer can determine how to treat payments made for services, the employer must first know the business relationship that exists between the employer and the person performing the services.
      1) In determining whether the person providing service is an employee or an independent contractor, all information that provides evidence of the degree of control and independence must be considered.

Common Law Rules

2. Facts that provide evidence of the degree of control and independence fall into three categories:
   a. Behavioral: Does the company control or have the right to control what the worker does and how the worker does the job?
   b. Financial: Are the business aspects of the worker's job controlled by the employer (e.g., how the worker is paid, whether expenses are reimbursed, who provides tools/supplies)?
   c. Type of Relationship: Are there written contracts or employee-type benefits (e.g., pension plan, insurance, vacation pay)? Will the relationship continue, and is the work performed a key aspect of the business?
3. Employers must weigh all these factors when determining whether a worker is an employee or independent contractor. Some factors may indicate that the worker is an employee, while other factors indicate that the worker is an independent contractor. There is no "magic" or set number of factors that "makes" the worker an employee or an independent contractor, and no one factor stands alone in making this determination. Also, factors that are relevant in one situation may not be relevant in another.
   a. The keys are to look at the entire relationship, consider the degree or extent of the right to direct and control, and, finally, to document each of the factors used in coming up with the determination.
   b. If, after reviewing the three categories of evidence, it is still unclear whether a worker is an employee or an independent contractor, Form SS-8, *Determination of Worker Status for Purposes of Federal Employment Taxes and Income Tax Withholding*, can be filed with the IRS. The form may be filed by either the employer or the worker.
      1) The IRS will review the facts and circumstances and officially determine the worker's status. It can take 6 months to get a determination, but an employer who continually hires the same types of workers to perform particular services may want to consider filing the Form SS-8.

Statutory Employees

4. If workers are independent contractors under the common law rules, such workers may still be treated as employees by statute (statutory employees) for certain employment tax purposes if they fall within any one of the following four categories and meet the three conditions described under "Social Security and Medicare Taxes" below.
   a. A driver who distributes beverages (other than milk) or meat, vegetable, fruit, or bakery products; or who picks up and delivers laundry or dry cleaning, if the driver is the payer's agent or is paid on commission.
   b. A full-time life insurance sales agent whose principal business activity is selling life insurance, annuity contracts, or both, primarily for one life insurance company.
   c. An individual who works at home on materials or goods that the payer supplies and that must be returned to the payer or to a person the payer names if the payer also furnishes specifications for the work to be done.
   d. A full-time traveling or city salesperson who works on the payer's behalf and turns in orders to the payer from wholesalers, retailers, contractors, or operators of hotels, restaurants, or other similar establishments.
      1) The goods sold must be merchandise for resale or supplies for use in the buyer's business operation.
      2) The work performed for the payer must be the salesperson's principal business activity.

Social Security and Medicare Taxes

5. Payers withhold Social Security and Medicare taxes from the wages of statutory employees if all three of the following conditions apply:
   a. The service contract states or implies that substantially all the services are to be performed personally by the statutory employees.
   b. The statutory employees do not have a substantial investment in the equipment and property used to perform the services (other than an investment in transportation facilities).
   c. The services are performed on a continuing basis for the same payer.

Statutory Nonemployees

6. There are three categories of statutory nonemployees: direct sellers, licensed real estate agents, and certain companion sitters. Direct sellers and licensed real estate agents are treated as self-employed for all federal tax purposes, including income and employment taxes, if
   a. Substantially all payments for their services as direct sellers or real estate agents are directly related to sales or other output rather than to the number of hours worked and
   b. Services are performed under a written contract providing that they will not be treated as employees for federal tax purposes.

Direct Sellers

7. Direct selling includes activities of individuals who attempt to increase direct sales activities of their direct sellers and who earn income based on the productivity of their direct sellers. Such activities include providing motivation and encouragement; imparting skills, knowledge, or experience; and recruiting. Direct sellers include persons falling within any of the following three groups:
   a. Persons engaged in selling (or soliciting the sale of) consumer products in the home or place of business other than in a permanent retail establishment
   b. Persons engaged in selling (or soliciting the sale of) consumer products to any buyer on a buy-sell basis, a deposit-commission basis, or any similar basis prescribed by regulations, for resale in the home or at a place of business other than in a permanent retail establishment
   c. Persons engaged in the trade or business of delivering or distributing newspapers or shopping news (including any services directly related to such delivery or distribution)

Licensed Real Estate Agents

8. Licensed real estate agents include individuals engaged in appraisal activities for real estate sales if they earn income based on sales or other output.

Companion Sitters

9. Companion sitters are individuals who furnish personal attendance, companionship, or household care services to children or to individuals who are elderly or disabled.
   a. A person engaged in the trade or business of putting the sitters in touch with individuals who wish to employ them (i.e., a companion sitting placement service) will not be treated as the employer of the sitters if that person does not receive or pay the salary or wages of the sitters and is compensated by the sitters or the persons who employ them on a fee basis.
   b. Companion sitters who are not employees of a companion sitting placement service are generally treated as self-employed for all federal tax purposes.

Stop & Review

You have completed the outline for this subunit.
Study multiple-choice question 18 on page 130.

5.9 QUALIFIED BUSINESS INCOME DEDUCTION (QBID)

1. Calculation

   a. **Qualified Business Income Deduction (QBID) (Section 199A)**

      1) When Congress passed the Tax Cuts and Jobs Act (TCJA), it reduced the C corporation tax rate to 21%.

      2) Congress did not want to disadvantage owners of pass-through entities (sole proprietorships, S corporations, and partnerships) by leaving them with a substantially higher tax liability (potentially 37%) than C corporations (21%). Congress reduced this burden by creating the QBID.

      3) The QBID is the last deduction before determining a taxpayer's taxable income. It is based on determining qualified business income (QBI).

      4) For the QBID, Congress divided pass-through entities into two categories: (a) specified service trades or businesses and (b) qualified trades or businesses. The reason for the two categories is that above certain thresholds of taxable income, each QBID is subject to varying limitations.

         a) The specifics of the limitations are complex and beyond the scope of the exam. Therefore, the coverage in this subunit is the general information needed to have a basic understanding of the QBID for the exam.

   b. **Specified Service Trades or Businesses**

      1) In general, a specified service trade or business (SSTB) is any trade or business in which the principal asset is the reputation or skill of one or more of its employees.

      2) Specifically, SSTBs include the following types of trades and businesses:

         a) Health (e.g., physicians, nurses, dentists, and other similar healthcare professionals)

            i) Health does not include services not directly related to a medical field, such as medical device sales, coding, billing, and payment processing.

         b) Law

         c) Accounting

         d) Actuarial science

         e) Performing arts

         f) Consulting

         g) Athletics

         h) Financial services (e.g., financial advisors, wealth planners, retirement advisors, investment bankers, and other professionals performing similar services)

            i) This includes any professional service consisting of investing, investment management, trading or dealing in securities, partnership interests, or commodities.

         i) Brokerage services

3) Also, an SSTB is any trade or business wherein a principal earns income (e.g., fees, licenses, or compensation) for any of the following activities:

   a) Endorsing products or services
   b) Use of the principal's likeness, image, name, etc.
   c) Appearance fees for an event or media performance (e.g., radio, TV, etc.)

EXAMPLE 5-5 Reputation and Skill

Bill owns Bill's Plumbing, a sole proprietorship. Bill's Plumbing's motto is "Bill is a very skilled plumber with a great reputation." According to the regulations, because Bill's Plumbing does not involve endorsements, compensation for use of one's likeness, or appearance fees, Bill's Plumbing's principal asset is not the reputation or skill of one or more of its employees or owners. Thus, Bill's Plumbing is not considered a specified service business.

4) Trades and businesses that are specifically **not** considered SSTBs include

   a) Architects
   b) Engineers
   c) Real estate agents and brokers
   d) Insurance agents and brokers

EXAMPLE 5-6 SSTB

Danny is a partner at XYZ, LLP, a public accounting firm. Danny is single with taxable income of $500,000. Because Danny's taxable income is above the upper taxable income threshold, the specified service business limitation applies. Thus, because XYZ is a specified service business (and Danny's taxable income is above the upper threshold), XYZ's business income is not QBI and thus is not eligible for the QBID. However, if Danny's taxable income had instead been $100,000, XYZ's business income would have been eligible for the QBID because the specified service business limitation would not have applied.

c. **Qualified Trades or Businesses**

1) In general, a qualified trade or business is any pass-through entity not considered an SSTB.

2) Specifically, a pass-through entity can be identified as a qualified trade or business if it has QBI.

d. The QBID on line 13 of Form 1040 is generally 20% of QBI, but it is limited due to an **overall limitation**.

   1) The overall limitation is the **lesser of**

      a) 20% × Qualified business income or
      b) 20% × (Taxable income – Net capital gains).

   2) Therefore, if a taxpayer has net capital gains, the taxpayer's net capital gains decrease his or her QBID. (For this deduction, net capital gains are long-term gains and qualified dividends, minus short-term losses.)

   3) Before a taxpayer can apply the overall limitation, (s)he has to determine the combined QBID before the taxable income limitation. Determining the combined QBID is a three-step process. After the three steps have been used to determine the combined QBID, the taxpayer must apply the overall limitation, which becomes Step 4.

e. To **calculate the combined QBID and ultimately the QBID, the following must be completed**:

   1) **Step 1** – Every pass-through entity must first determine its QBI.

      a) This information will be reported on a Schedule K-1 (or a Schedule C if the entity is a sole proprietorship).

      b) The details of this process are described in Figure 5-1 on the next page.

   2) **Step 2** – The sum of each pass-through entity's QBI must then be tested against the taxpayer's taxable income.

      a) If the taxpayer is in the phase-in range or upper threshold, the QBID for each respective pass-through entity is reduced or limited by the IRS. This reduction is the allowed amount of QBID for each respective pass-through entity.

         i) Single taxpayers reach the phase-in range once taxable income exceeds $170,050 and enter the upper threshold at $220,050.

         ii) Married filing jointly taxpayers reach the phase-in threshold when taxable income exceeds $340,100 and enter the upper threshold at $440,100.

      b) The details of this process are complex and beyond the scope of the exam.

      c) General rules that should be understood:

         i) Below the phase-in ranges, the QBID is the full 20% overall limitation.

         ii) Above the phase-in ranges, the QBID is subject to additional limitations.

         iii) For SSTBs, the QBID is completely disallowed above the upper threshold.

   3) **Step 3** – A taxpayer determines the applicable combined QBID by adding together the allowed QBID amount for each respective entity to arrive at a total (or combined) QBID.

   4) **Step 4** – The final step is for the taxpayer to apply the overall limitation to total (or combined) QBID to determine the correct amount to deduct. This amount is then reported on line 13 of Form 1040.

Step 1 – Determine What Constitutes QBI[1]

Step 1 Ensure the entity is a relevant pass-through entity (i.e., sole proprietor, S corporation, partnership, estate, or trust).

Step 2 Determine whether the entity is directly owned by the taxpayer (e.g., a K-1 is sent directly to the taxpayer as a direct owner of the pass-through entity or business income is reported on Schedule C).

Step 3 Calculate the net amount of income, gain, deduction, and loss with respect to any trade or business. This includes the sale, exchange, or distribution of unrealized receivables or inventory. Also, post-2017 adjustments from changes to accounting methods or previously disallowed losses or deductions currently allowed are treated as items attributable to the trade or business for computing QBI in the current year.

Limited to Amounts

Effectively connected with the conduct of a trade or business within the United States or Puerto Rico	AND	Included or allowed in determining taxable income for the taxable year

Step 4[2] Remove the following from the calculation of net income[3]

1) Capital gains and losses
2) Dividends
3) Nonoperating interest income
4) Interest income attributable to working capital
5) Gains or losses relating to transactions in commodities
6) Foreign currency gains[4]
7) Any less-than-reasonable salary payments to owners[5]
8) Any deduction or loss properly allocated to the items above

[1] This is the same methodology for determining income from an SSTB.

[2] Conceptually, Congress is allowing small business owners the ability to deduct income that results from the core operations of a small business because the entrepreneurial spirit of small business can drive domestic employment. Because the overarching goal is to spur growth and, ultimately, employment, Congress hopes to incentivize small business owners to grow their core business rather than speculate on side-ventures unrelated to their main business objectives. Therefore, qualified business income is the ordinary, noninvestment income of a business.

[3] There are more reductions in total, but these are the big-picture items that are most likely to affect most taxpayers.

[4] The IRS lists "excess foreign currency gains." For most taxpayers, this effectively means any foreign currency gains.

[5] If the taxpayer paid himself or herself a salary (or guaranteed payment) less than a reasonable amount to receive a higher QBI deduction, the taxpayer must reduce QBI by the amount of the less-than-reasonable salary payment.

Figure 5-1

Stop & Review

You have completed the outline for this subunit.
Study multiple-choice questions 19 and 20 on page 130.

QUESTIONS

5.1 Business Meals Expense

1. Which of the following is NOT required for a business meal to be deductible?

A. The expense must be ordinary and necessary.

B. The meal expense must be separately stated from any entertainment expense.

C. The meal must take place during the taxpayer's business hours.

D. The meal must be attended by the taxpayer or the taxpayer's employee.

Answer (C) is correct.

REQUIRED: The item not required for deducting a business meal.

DISCUSSION: To be deductible, a meal must

- Be an ordinary and necessary expense
- Not be a lavish or extravagant expense, i.e., be reasonable based on facts and circumstances
- Be attended by the taxpayer or an employee of the taxpayer
- Be provided to a current or potential business customer, client, consultant, or similar business contact
- Be separately stated from any nondeductible entertainment expense or purchased separately from the entertainment

The time of day of the meal is not relevant.

2. When an employer reimburses an employee for meals not provided by a restaurant but under an accountable plan while the employee is away from home, the employer must

A. Include 50% of the cost of meals as income to the employee.

B. Do nothing.

C. Deduct only 50% of the reimbursement on his or her tax return.

D. Add 100% of the meals as income to the employee.

Answer (C) is correct.

REQUIRED: The true statement regarding meal reimbursements.

DISCUSSION: An employer can take a deduction for travel and meals expenses if their employees are reimbursed for these expenses under an accountable plan. The amount an employer deducts for meals, however, may be subject to a 50% limit (i.e., when the meal is not provided by a restaurant). Meals purchased while away from home that are reimbursed by an employer are not gross income to the employee.

Answer (A) is incorrect. Meals purchased while away from home that are reimbursed by an employer are not gross income to the employee. **Answer (B) is incorrect.** The employer may deduct only 50%, not 100%, of the reimbursement on his or her tax return for meals not provided by a restaurant. **Answer (D) is incorrect.** Meals purchased while away from home that are reimbursed by an employer are not gross income to the employee.

3. Which of the following fringe benefits for meals is NOT subject to the 50% deduction limit?

A. Meals furnished to your employees at the work site when you operate a restaurant.

B. Meals furnished to your employees as part of the expense of a company picnic.

C. Meals furnished to your employees at your place of business when more than half of these employees are provided the meals for your convenience.

D. Meals furnished to a customer not at a restaurant during a business discussion.

Answer (B) is correct.

REQUIRED: The fringe benefits for meals not subject to the 50% deduction limit.

DISCUSSION: Generally, the amount deductible for meal expenses is 50% of the actual expense. The limit also applies to the taxpayer's own meals. Thus, meals furnished to a customer during a business discussion qualify. Beginning in 2018, the qualified meals provided for the convenience of the employer are still deductible but now limited to 50%. However, meal expenses for employee recreation, e.g., picnics, remain 100% deductible.

Answer (A) is incorrect. Section 119 provides an exclusion for meals furnished on the business premises of the employer if they are furnished to the employee for the convenience of the employer. However, since 2018, the deduction is limited to 50%. **Answer (C) is incorrect.** Section 119 provides an exclusion for meals furnished on the business premises of the employer if they are furnished to the employee for the convenience of the employer. However, since 2018, the deduction is limited to 50%. **Answer (D) is incorrect.** The business meals deduction is limited to 50%.

5.2 Travel Expenses

4. Bart, a partner in the B & A Partnership, attended the Comdex Computer Convention in Las Vegas. The partnership repairs and upgrades commercial computers for business use. At the convention, a new advanced computer hard drive was introduced that would make current machines run faster and more efficiently. Bart is responsible for purchasing hard drives for the computers used in the partnership. Bart's travel expenses, excluding meals, were $950. Part of that amount includes a rental car of $100 incurred to visit his mother and $50 for flowers and candy he bought for her. How much is deductible as a business expense?

A. $950

B. $900

C. $800

D. $850

Answer (C) is correct.

REQUIRED: The amount of travel expenses deductible as business expenses.

DISCUSSION: A taxpayer may deduct ordinary and necessary expenses incurred when traveling away from home on business. A business deduction is not allowed for personal expenses. Bart must divide the total travel expenses between the business related expenses and personal expenses. He may only deduct as a business expense the business related travel expenses. Therefore, Bart may deduct $800 ($950 – $100 – $50) of the travel expenses excluding meals as a business expense.

Answer (A) is incorrect. The $150 of personal expenses incurred during travel are not deductible as business expenses. **Answer (B) is incorrect.** The $100 Bart incurred to visit his mother is a personal travel expense and is not deductible. **Answer (D) is incorrect.** The $50 Bart spent on flowers and candy for his mother is a personal expense and is not deductible.

5.3 Insurance Expenses

5. All of the following insurance premiums are ordinarily deductible as an insurance expense EXCEPT

A. Workers' compensation on behalf of partners in a business partnership.

B. Life insurance on the life of an employee with the employee's wife as the beneficiary.

C. Group health insurance that does not contain continuation coverage to employees.

D. Malpractice insurance covering a professional's personal liability for negligence resulting in injury to business clients.

Answer (A) is correct.

REQUIRED: The insurance premium not ordinarily deductible as a business expense.

DISCUSSION: Workers' compensation insurance premiums paid on behalf of employees are deductible as a business expense. However, for this purpose, partners are not considered employees of the partnership (they are considered self-employed owners), and the insurance premiums on their behalf are deductible as guaranteed payments, not as an insurance expense.

Answer (B) is incorrect. Life insurance premiums paid on the life of an employee are deductible as long as the employer is not the beneficiary. These life insurance premiums are effectively compensation to the employee unless excluded as part of a group term life insurance plan. **Answer (C) is incorrect.** The premiums are deductible by the employer. However, an excise tax is imposed under Sec. 4980B if an employer has group health insurance not containing continuation coverage for employees. **Answer (D) is incorrect.** Malpractice insurance is deductible as an ordinary business expense.

6. During the current year, WHOOS Partnership paid insurance premiums for the following coverage:

Use and occupancy and business interruption insurance	$2,000
Overhead insurance	1,000
Accident and health insurance paid for its partners as guaranteed payments made to the partners	800
Group term life insurance on the lives of all the partners with the partnership as beneficiary	500
Life insurance on the lives of all the partners in order to get or protect a loan	700

What is the amount of WHOOS's deductible expense for the current year?

A. $5,000

B. $3,800

C. $3,700

D. $3,000

Answer (B) is correct.

REQUIRED: The amount of the partnership's deductible insurance expense.

DISCUSSION: Section 162(a) allows a deduction for all ordinary and necessary expenses paid or incurred during the taxable year in carrying on any trade or business. Insurance premiums paid for carrying on a trade or business are deductible. Under the terms of a use and occupancy insurance contract, a taxpayer may be insured for the loss of the use and occupancy of property damaged by fire. This expense is deductible. Premiums paid for overhead insurance are also deductible. Guaranteed payments are recorded as income by the partners and are deductible by the partnership. The deduction for the group term life insurance is not available because the partnership is the beneficiary. Finally, insurance premiums paid on a taxpayer's own life are personal expenses and are not deductible. Therefore, the amount of WHOOS's deductible expense for the current year is $3,800 ($2,000 business interruption insurance + $1,000 overhead insurance + $800 accident and health insurance).

Answer (A) is incorrect. All of the expenses are not deductible. **Answer (C) is incorrect.** The life insurance is not deductible. **Answer (D) is incorrect.** The accident and health insurance is deductible.

7. John owned a small advertising company, the operations of which he included on Schedule C of his current-year individual income tax return. What type of insurance may John NOT deduct on his current-year return?

A. Fire, theft, and flood insurance.

B. Employer's liability insurance.

C. Loss of earnings due to sickness or disability of John.

D. Overhead insurance, which pays John's overhead expenses in the event of his long period of disability caused by his sickness or injury.

Answer (C) is correct.

REQUIRED: The insurance that may not be deducted on the taxpayer's return.

DISCUSSION: A premium on a personal disability insurance policy is not deductible when it applies to insurance for the self-employed owner.

Answer (A) is incorrect. Fire, theft, and flood insurance is an ordinary and necessary trade or business insurance expense. **Answer (B) is incorrect.** Employer's liability insurance is an ordinary and necessary trade or business insurance expense. **Answer (D) is incorrect.** Overhead insurance is an ordinary and necessary trade or business insurance expense.

5.4 Bad Debts

8. Which is a false statement regarding business bad debts?

A. The debt does not have to be due to be worthless.

B. A bad debt can result from a loan to a supplier.

C. Cash-basis taxpayers can take a deduction for amounts never received or collected.

D. A debt can arise from the guarantee of a debt that becomes worthless.

Answer (C) is correct.

REQUIRED: The false statement regarding business bad debts.

DISCUSSION: A taxpayer may deduct a loss from a bad debt only if (s)he has a basis in the debt. For this reason, cash basis taxpayers who normally do not report income until it is required are not entitled to deductions for payments they cannot collect. Their loss is represented by the unrecovered expenses incurred in providing the goods or services.

Answer (A) is incorrect. The debt is worthless when it is determined the borrower cannot pay the debt. **Answer (B) is incorrect.** Section 166 includes debts that arise from the sale of goods or services. **Answer (D) is incorrect.** The guarantee of a debt that becomes worthless is legally enforceable as a debt.

9. Mr. Benson, who operates a small tools supply company, in order to retain the customer, guaranteed payment of a $10,000 note for Black Hardware store, one of Mr. Benson's largest clients. Black Hardware later filed for bankruptcy and defaulted on the loan. Mr. Benson made full payment to satisfy the note. Mr. Benson's payment should be considered a(n)

A. Business bad debt.

B. Nonbusiness bad debt.

C. Gift.

D. Investment.

Answer (A) is correct.

REQUIRED: The characterization of a loss on a guarantee of a customer's debt.

DISCUSSION: A business bad debt is deductible in full as an ordinary loss under Sec. 166. A loss on a guarantee of a debt is treated the same as a primary debt in determining whether it is business or nonbusiness. To be a business bad debt, it must be closely related to one's trade or business. However, guaranteeing the debt of a primary customer does not necessarily make it a business debt. If making the guarantee was required to retain the customer, the payment on the guarantee would be a business bad debt.

10. With regard to the correct treatment of business bad debts, which of the following statements is false?

A. Tom deducted a bad debt in a prior tax year and later recovered part of it. He may have to include the amount recovered in gross income for the year of recovery.

B. Bill can deduct his business bad debt as a short-term capital loss.

C. Sally received property in a partial settlement of a debt. She should reduce the debt by the fair market value of the property received. She can deduct the remaining amount as a bad debt in the year she determines it to be worthless and charges it off.

D. Jane may deduct only the difference between the amount owed to her by a bankrupt entity and the amount received from the distribution of its assets as a bad debt.

Answer (B) is correct.

REQUIRED: The false statement concerning the treatment of business bad debts.

DISCUSSION: A loss from a business debt is an ordinary loss, while a loss from a nonbusiness debt is treated as a short-term capital loss.

Answer (A) is incorrect. Recovery of a bad debt is generally included in the current year's income. **Answer (C) is incorrect.** Partially worthless business debt may be deducted to the extent they are worthless and specifically written off. **Answer (D) is incorrect.** Partially worthless business debt may be deducted to the extent they are worthless and specifically written off.

11. Mary, a seamstress, made loans of $5,000 and $1,000 to Buttons & Bows and Thread Bare, respectively. Both of these establishments are partnerships. Mary also made a loan of $2,000 to her cousin Sarah, who was starting her own business as a proprietorship. The loans to both partnerships improved Mary's business, which was the reason Mary made the loans. If all three loans become uncollectible, what amount may Mary deduct as a business bad debt?

A. $5,000

B. $6,000

C. $1,000

D. $2,000

Answer (B) is correct.

REQUIRED: The amount that can be deducted as a business bad debt.

DISCUSSION: Publication 535 states, "A business bad debt is a loss from the worthlessness of a debt that was either

- Created or acquired in your trade or business, or
- Closely related to your trade or business when it became partly or totally worthless.

A debt is closely related to your trade or business if your primary motive for incurring the debt is business related. . . . If you make a loan to a client, supplier, employee, or distributor for a business reason and it becomes worthless, you have a business bad debt." The loans to both partnerships improved Mary's business, so they are deductible. However, Mary's loan to Sarah is not deductible because it was made for personal reasons instead of business reasons.

Answer (A) is incorrect. Mary's loan to Thread Bare is deductible since it was made to improve her business. **Answer (C) is incorrect.** Mary's loan to Buttons & Bows is deductible since it was made to improve her business. **Answer (D) is incorrect.** Mary's loan to Sarah was not for business reasons, so it is not deductible.

12. Ms. R lent her sister money to buy a new personal-use automobile. The understanding was that the loan may not be repaid. The debt was subsequently forgiven since Ms. R's sister could not repay the debt. This is an example of

A. A business bad debt.

B. A nonbusiness bad debt.

C. A gift.

D. A specific charge-off.

Answer (C) is correct.

REQUIRED: The character of a forgiven debt owed by a related party.

DISCUSSION: A bad debt deduction may be taken only for a bona fide debt arising from a valid debtor-creditor relationship based upon a valid and enforceable obligation to pay a fixed or determinable sum of money [Reg. 1.166-1(c)]. Ms. R made a gift to her sister of the balance of the debt owed. Therefore, no bad debt exists, and no deduction is available.

Answer (A) is incorrect. A business bad debt arises from a debtor-creditor relationship and is based upon a valid and enforceable obligation. **Answer (B) is incorrect.** Money lent to a relative or friend with the understanding the relative or friend may not repay it must be considered a gift by the taxpayer, not a loan, and it may not be deducted as a bad debt. **Answer (D) is incorrect.** The forgiven amount constituted a gift to the sister.

5.5 Business Gifts

13. William Roberts sells products to unrelated XYZ Corporation. He gave XYZ five cheese packages to thank them for their business. Mr. Roberts paid $100 for each package for a total of $500. Five of the XYZ Corporation executives took the packages home. How much can William deduct for the gifts?

A. $125

B. $500

C. $0

D. $250

Answer (A) is correct.

REQUIRED: The amount of deductible business gifts.

DISCUSSION: Deductions for business gifts, whether made directly or indirectly, are limited to $25 per recipient per year. Since William gave five gifts to five executives, he is allowed to deduct $25 per recipient, or $125.

Answer (B) is incorrect. He is not allowed to deduct the entire cost of the gifts. **Answer (C) is incorrect.** He is allowed a deduction for the gifts. **Answer (D) is incorrect.** A 50% deduction for business gifts is not allowed.

14. Mr. Garland, a self-employed seafood wholesaler, arranged a business meeting with his five principal clients during the current year. The night the clients arrived in town, Mr. and Mrs. Garland entertained the clients and their spouses at their home. The cost of the food and beverages was $800. As each client left, they were given a cheese and fruit basket, which cost $80 each. The business meeting was held the next day at Mr. Garland's office. Assuming no other similar expenses during the current year, what amount can Mr. Garland deduct as a business expense for the current year?

A. $0

B. $125

C. $400

D. $525

Answer (D) is correct.

REQUIRED: The amount of a deduction for business expenses.

DISCUSSION: The meal expense deductible is $400 (50%) because the food or beverage was not purchased from a restaurant, and the deduction for gifts to clients is limited to $25 per person. Here, the Garlands gave each of five clients an $80 gift. The Garlands may deduct $125 of this $400 gift expense.

Answer (A) is incorrect. A portion of the meals and gifts is deductible. **Answer (B) is incorrect.** A portion of the meals is deductible. **Answer (C) is incorrect.** A gift to clients is limited to $25 per person per year.

5.6 Other Business Expenses

15. All of the following "Sec. 197 intangibles" acquired after August 10, 1993, must be amortized over 15 years EXCEPT a

A. Covenant not to compete entered in connection with the acquisition of an interest in a trade or business.

B. Patent that you created, but not in connection with the acquisition of assets constituting a trade or business or a substantial part of a trade or business.

C. Fast food franchise.

D. Governmental license including renewals.

Answer (B) is correct.

REQUIRED: The Sec. 197 intangible that is not required to be amortized over 15 years.

DISCUSSION: Under Sec. 197, the cost of acquiring any intangible assets, including non-compete covenants, is amortizable over a 15-year period, beginning in the month of acquisition. The actual useful life of the covenant is ignored. Section 197(c)(2) states that, generally, a Sec. 197 intangible created by the taxpayer is not amortizable unless it is created in connection with a transaction or series of related transactions that involves the acquisition of assets constituting a trade or business or a substantial part of a trade or business.

16. Mr. R is a self-employed over-the-road trucker who uses the cash method of accounting. Which one of the following expenses paid during the current year would be deductible on Mr. R's Schedule C?

A. Penalty for late delivery of cargo paid to Corporation V.

B. Fine for speeding in business truck paid to City A.

C. Overweight fine paid to State B.

D. Contribution to Bull Moose political party in an attempt to receive a trucking contract.

Answer (A) is correct.

REQUIRED: The deductible business expense.

DISCUSSION: Although fines and penalties paid to a government are generally not deductible, the payment of a penalty for nonperformance of a contract is generally deductible. This penalty usually represents damages that one contracting party was willing to incur in order to avoid performing under the contract. This is a business decision, and the damages are deductible under Sec. 162(a).

Answer (B) is incorrect. It is a fine or penalty paid to a government or governmental agency and is specifically not deductible under Sec. 162(f). **Answer (C) is incorrect.** It is a fine or penalty paid to a government or governmental agency and is specifically not deductible under Sec. 162(f). **Answer (D) is incorrect.** Political contributions are not deductible as business expenses.

5.7 Business Use of Home

17. Which of the following is a true statement about the exclusive-use test for business use of a home?

A. Generally, any personal use of the business portion of the home by anyone results in complete disallowance of the deductions.

B. A retailer must meet the exclusive-use test.

C. A day care must meet the exclusive-use test.

D. A wholesaler must meet the exclusive-use test.

Answer (A) is correct.

REQUIRED: The true statement about the exclusive-use test.

DISCUSSION: Any personal use of the business portion of the home by anyone results in complete disallowance of the deductions. There are two exceptions to the exclusive-use test:

1. A retailer or wholesaler
2. A day care

Answer (B) is incorrect. Retailers with no other location are exempt from the test. **Answer (C) is incorrect.** Use by a qualifying day care is exempt from the test. **Answer (D) is incorrect.** Wholesalers with no other location are exempt from the test.

5.8 Statutory Employees/Nonemployees

18. Which of the following is a statutory employee?

A. A person engaged in selling consumer products in homes, and all service payments are for sales, not hours worked.

B. A companion sitter who pays the placement service out of the payments from the sitter's client.

C. A soda beverage distribution driver who performs all the services on a continuing basis for the same payer, and does not own any of the equipment.

D. A real estate appraiser with earnings based on sales who is contracted as not being an employee.

Answer (C) is correct.

REQUIRED: The statutory employee.

DISCUSSION: If workers are independent contractors under the common-law rules, such workers may still be treated as employees by statute for certain employment tax purposes. An example of a statutory employee is a driver who distributes beverages (other than milk) if the driver is the payer's agent or is paid on commission. Other requirements include substantial performance of all services, no substantial investment in the equipment, and the continual performance of the services.

Answer (A) is incorrect. Direct sellers are statutory nonemployees. **Answer (B) is incorrect.** The placement service will not be treated as the employer of the sitter if the service does not receive or pay the salary or wages of the sitter and is compensated by the sitter. **Answer (D) is incorrect.** Nonemployee licensed real estate agents include those engaged in appraisal activities for real estate sales if earnings are based on sales or other output.

5.9 Qualified Business Income Deduction (QBID)

19. A taxpayer may NOT claim the qualified business income (QBI) deduction if (s)he has qualified business income from which of the following entities?

A. S corporations.

B. C corporations.

C. Sole proprietorships.

D. Trusts.

Answer (B) is correct.

REQUIRED: The non-pass-through entity.

DISCUSSION: The QBI deduction is available to noncorporate taxpayers who have qualified business income from qualified pass-through entities. Qualified pass-through entities include sole proprietorships, S corporations, partnerships, trusts, and estates.

20. Which of the following items are included in qualified business income (QBI)?

A. Pre-2018 previously disallowed losses or deductions that are allowed in the current year.

B. Allocable losses associated with a qualified trade or business.

C. Short-term capital losses.

D. Guaranteed payments paid for services rendered with respect to a qualified trade or business.

Answer (B) is correct.

REQUIRED: The QBI item.

DISCUSSION: QBI includes any items of income, gain, deduction, and loss to the extent that such items are effectively connected with the conduct of a trade or business within the United States and are included or allowed in determining taxable income for the taxable year.

Answer (A) is incorrect. The disallowed losses or deductions have to be from a post-2017 tax year to be included in QBI. **Answer (C) is incorrect.** QBI does not include any item of short-term capital gain, short-term capital loss, long-term capital gain, or long-term capital loss. **Answer (D) is incorrect.** QBI does not include any guaranteed payment described in Sec. 707(c) paid to a partner for services rendered with respect to the trade or business.

STUDY UNIT SIX

BASIS AND PROPERTY TRANSACTIONS

(15 pages of outline)

The concept of basis is important in federal income taxation. The assigned value of property at any particular time is the property's **basis**. Multiple factors may require a taxpayer to adjust the basis of his or her property during the time (s)he owns it. Uniform capitalization rules determine if a cost is allocated to the basis of the property or expensed in the current year.

6.1 BASIS

Overview

When a taxpayer acquires property, his or her basis in the property is initially cost, substituted, transferred, exchanged, or converted basis.

1. **Cost basis** is the sum of capitalized acquisition costs.
    a. Cost basis includes the FMV of property given up. If it is not determinable with reasonable certainty, use the FMV of property received.
    b. A rebate to the purchaser is treated as a reduction of the purchase price. It is not included in basis or in gross income.
2. **Substituted basis** is computed by reference to basis in other property.
3. **Transferred basis** is computed by reference to basis in the same property in the hands of another.
4. **Exchanged basis** is computed by reference to basis in other property previously held by the person.
5. **Converted basis** is when personal-use property is converted to business use; the basis of the property is the lower of its basis or the FMV on the date of conversion.

Unit of Property

6. Whether tangible (real or personal) property costs are deducted or capitalized is determined by examining the unit of property. The unit of property is a group of functionally interdependent components and can either be an asset, group of assets, or a defined portion of an asset. In the case of personal or real property other than a building, all the components that are functionally interdependent comprise a single unit of property. The identified units of property must be further divided into major components and substantial structural parts. Absent an available exception, costs to replace a major component or substantial structural part must be capitalized.

Capitalized Acquisition Costs

7. Initial basis in purchased property is the cost of acquiring it. Only capital costs are included, i.e., those for acquisition, title acquisition, and major improvements.
   a. Capital acquisition expenditures may be made by cash, by cash equivalent, in property, with liability, or by services.
   b. An improvement expenditure must be capitalized if it (1) results in a betterment to the unit of property, (2) adapts the unit of property to a new or different use, or (3) results in a restoration of the unit of property.
      1) An expenditure is a **betterment** if it ameliorates a condition or defect that existed before acquisition of the property or arose during the production of the property; is for a material addition to the property; or increases the property's productivity, efficiency, strength, etc.
      2) An expenditure is an **adaptation** to a new or different use if it adapts the unit of property to a use inconsistent with the taxpayer's intended ordinary use at the time the taxpayer originally placed the property into service.
      3) An expenditure is a **restoration** if it
         a) Restores a basis that has been taken into account,
         b) Returns the unit of property to working order from a nonfunctional state,
         c) Results in a rebuilding of the unit of property to a like-new condition after the end of the property's alternative depreciation system class life, or
         d) Replaces a major component or substantial structural part of the unit of property.

Common Capitalized Costs (for Sec. 1012)

Purchase Price (Stated)	Miscellaneous Costs
Liability to which property is subject NOTE: Not unstated interest	Appraisal fees Freight Installation Testing
Closing Costs	**Major Improvements**
Brokerage commissions Pre-purchase taxes Sales tax on purchase Title transfer taxes Title insurance Recording fees Attorney fees Document review, preparation	New roof New gutters Extending water line to property Demolition costs and losses New electrical wiring

EXAMPLE 6-1 Tax Basis -- Building with a Mortgage

If an individual buys a building for $20,000 cash and assumes a mortgage of $80,000 on it, his or her basis is $100,000.

4) In the case of repainting a building's exterior, the basic rules are
   a) If painting is the only thing being done, the painting costs are expensed or
   b) If painting is part of a larger project that includes capital improvements to the building's structure, the painting costs are capitalized.

c. A taxpayer must capitalize amounts paid to **facilitate** the acquisition of real or personal property. This treatment applies when the amount is paid in the process of investigating or otherwise pursuing the acquisition.
   1) Facilitative (i.e., capitalized) costs do not include amounts paid to determine whether to acquire real property or which real property to acquire. Such amounts are current deductions.
   2) Amounts paid for employee compensation and overhead are treated as amounts that do not facilitate the acquisition of real or personal property.

EXAMPLE 6-2 Facilitative Cost

Dolores is a manager of a family-owned grocery store and is assigned to determine where to open a second location. The compensation for Dolores' time is deducted, not capitalized, by the grocery store as a facilitative cost. If the work had been performed by a real estate professional and paid as commission, the amount would have to be capitalized because it was paid to facilitate the acquisition of real property.

d. Expenses not properly chargeable to a capital account. Costs of maintaining and operating property are not added to basis, e.g., interest on credit related to the property, insurance (e.g., casualty), ordinary maintenance or repairs (e.g., painting), etc.

Basis in a Rental House – How to Calculate and Treat Improvements that Happen Later

Figure 6-1

Visual Memory Aid: For candidates who are visual learners, the figure above and the description below can aid in recalling how to capitalize certain capital acquisition costs.

Basis in a rental house includes purchase price plus closing costs. Add to the basis and capitalize long-term improvements.

In Figure 6-1 above, the right side of the house shows capitalized improvements that must be depreciated over periods of up to 27 1/2 years. These include improvements to land (e.g., sidewalks, landscaping, sprinkler systems), swimming pools, new roofs, extensions of or additions to the structure, air conditioning units, central vacuum systems, security systems, and septic tanks. Improvements that are added later in the life of the rental unit must be separately capitalized and depreciated.

The left side of the house shows short-term repairs. Short-term repairs are expensed in the year in which they are made. Short-term repairs include repairing broken windows, faucets, and air conditioning units; patching leaking roofs; painting; etc.

Uniform Capitalization Rules

8. Costs of constructing real or tangible personal property to be used in trade or business and costs of producing or acquiring property for sale to customers are capitalized.
   a. Costs (both direct and most allocable indirect costs) necessary to prepare the property for its intended use must be capitalized, e.g., for permits, materials, equipment rental, compensation for services (minus any work opportunity credit), and architect fees.
      1) Costs and losses associated with demolishing a structure are allocated to the land. The costs include the adjusted basis (not FMV) of the structure and demolition costs.
   b. Construction period interest and taxes must be capitalized as part of building cost.
   c. Indirect costs not capitalized include, among other things, marketing, selling, advertising, distribution, research, experimental, Sec. 179, strike, warranty, unsuccessful bid, and deductible service costs.
   d. Uniform capitalization rules do not apply to producers and resellers if the company's average annual gross receipts for the past 3 years do not exceed $27 million.
   e. Uniform capitalization rules do not apply to the following:
      1) Property produced by the taxpayer for personal purposes
      2) Qualified creative expenses incurred by an individual as a freelance writer, photographer, or artist
      3) Property produced under a long-term contract
      4) Research and development expenses allowable as a deduction
      5) Intangible drilling and development costs
      6) Timber and certain ornamental trees (more than 6 years old)
      7) Animals, dependent on taxpayer ownership
      8) Selling, marketing, advertising and distribution costs

De Minimis Expense

9. Taxpayers can make an election to deduct a de minimis amount for each transaction relating to tangible property with an economic useful life of at least 12 months.
   a. A **de minimis amount** is a cost that is so small that it is not worth tracking. Taxpayers may expense any purchased assets with a cost of less than $2,500 provided they also use this policy for financial accounting purposes. The determination of the value of an asset includes all capitalized costs but the limit is applied on a per unit basis.
      1) The limit is raised to $5,000 for taxpayers with an applicable financial statement (e.g., a certified, audited financial statement that is accompanied by the report of an independent certified public accountant).

EXAMPLE 6-3 De Minimis Expense

Henry, a business owner, purchases 2 computers for $3,000 and pays $500 to have them installed. The cost per computer is $1,750 [($3,000 + $500) ÷ 2], which allows the computers to be expensed as a de minimis expense.

Liabilities

10. Acquisition basis is

    a. Increased for notes to the seller (minus unstated interest)
    b. Increased for liabilities to which the acquired property is subject

Property for Services

11. The FMV of property received in exchange for services is income (compensation) to the provider when it is not subject to a substantial risk of forfeiture and not restricted as to transfer. The property acquired has a tax cost basis equal to the FMV of the property.

EXAMPLE 6-4 **Tax Basis -- Property Received for Services**
Jim's neighbor needs his fence painted and offers to give Jim a rare baseball card if Jim paints his fence. The baseball card has a fair market value of $500. If Jim paints the fence, he has a $500 basis in the baseball card.

Lump Sum

12. When more than one asset is purchased for a lump sum, the basis of each is computed by apportioning the total cost based on the relative FMV of each asset.

$$\text{Allocable cost (basis)} = \frac{\text{FMV of asset}}{\text{FMV of all assets purchased}} \times \text{Lump sum purchase price}$$

Gifts

13. The donee's basis in property acquired by gift is the donor's basis, increased for any gift tax paid attributable to appreciation. The donor's basis is increased by

$$\text{Gift tax paid} \times \left[\frac{\text{FMV (at time of gift)} - \text{Donor's basis}}{\text{FMV (at time of gift)} - \text{Annual exclusion}}\right]$$

    a. If the FMV on the date of the gift is less than the donor's basis, the donee has a dual basis for the property.

        1) Loss basis. The FMV at the date of the gift is used if the property is later transferred at a loss.
        2) Gain basis. The donor's basis is used if the property is later transferred at a gain.
        3) If the property is later transferred for more than FMV at the date of the gift but for less than the donor's basis at the date of the gift, no gain (loss) is recognized.

Figure 6-2

Visual Memory Aid: For candidates who are visual learners, the figure above and the description below can aid in recalling how to calculate gains and losses of gifts with a FMV less than AB.

In the illustration above, Uncle Donor gifts his niece a vehicle. The big question: What basis should she use if she decides to sell the vehicle and how can she determine a gain or loss on her tax return?

Imagine on the day of the gift the FMV is only $10,000 (according to Internet research), but the uncle paid $40,000 (his AB) for it years ago. If the niece is only able to sell it for $9,500, she can claim a loss of $500. Note in her hand the small stack of bills. It may help to remember that if she sells it for "pennies" her **basis is the *Fair* Market Value, because it was a *Fair* Loss**.

Now, imagine the same FMV ($10,000) and AB ($40,000), but the niece was able to sell it for $41,000 and claim a gain of only $1,000. Notice the large stack of bills in her other hand. Her basis for determining a gain is the donor's adjusted basis. The memory device is ***GAIN* a *DONOR***.

Alternatively, imagine the same FMV ($10,000) and AB ($40,000), but the sale price falls between the FMV and the AB, leaving the niece with neither a gain nor a loss. Without a net gain or loss, the sale is a ***WASH***, represented in the illustration by a washing machine.

b. Depreciable basis is transferred basis adjusted for gift taxes paid. If converted from personal to business use, it is FMV on the date of conversion if less than adjusted basis.

EXAMPLE 6-5 Sale of Gift Property

Bobby received a house as a gift from his father. At the time of the gift, the house had a FMV of $80,000 and the father's adjusted basis was $100,000. If no events occurred that changed the basis and Bobby sells the house for $120,000, Bobby will have a $20,000 gain because he must use the father's adjusted basis ($100,000) at the time of the gift to figure his gain. If he sells the house for $70,000, he will have a $10,000 loss because he must use the FMV ($80,000) at the time of the gift to figure his loss.

If the sale was between $80,000 and $100,000, Bobby would not recognize a gain or a loss.

c. When property other than money is contributed by a nonshareholder (e.g., government), the transferred basis is zero.

Inherited Property

14. Basis is the FMV on the date of death or 6 months thereafter if the executor qualifies for and elects the alternate valuation date for the estate tax return.

Property Converted into Business Use

15. Basis for depreciation is the lesser of the FMV of the property at the conversion date or the adjusted basis at conversion.

Land Improvements

16. Depreciable **land improvements** generally have a recovery period of 15 years under MACRS. The 150% declining balance method applies. An issue that often arises is whether all or any portion of a **land improvement** is depreciable. In general, to be depreciable, a **land improvement** must be subject to wear and tear. Sidewalks, concrete driveways, asphalt streets and concrete curbs, playground equipment, fencing, and landscaping have been classified as **land improvements**. Sewer lines are not land improvements.

Leasehold Improvements

17. Improvements made by the lessee are not income to the lessor either at the time the improvements are made or upon termination of the lease. Thus, the basis of the improvements is zero. Gain or loss will be recognized only at the time the property is sold.

    a. However, where the lessee makes repairs that are the responsibility of the lessor or makes improvements in lieu of rent, the lessor has rental income to the extent of the market value of the improvements and the basis of the improvements is market value.

Stop & Review

You have completed the outline for this subunit.

Study multiple-choice questions 1 through 6 beginning on page 146.

6.2 ADJUSTMENTS TO BASIS

Initial basis is adjusted consistent with tax-relevant events. Adjustments include the following:

1. Certain expenditures subsequent to acquisition are property costs, and they increase basis, e.g., legal fees to defend title or title insurance premiums.
2. Basis must be increased for expenditures that prolong the life of the property by at least 1 year or materially increase its value.
   a. Assessments that increase the value of property should be capitalized.
   b. If the assessments do not add value to the property, they may be deductible.
      1) Examples include major improvements (e.g., new roof, addition to building) and zoning changes.

EXAMPLE 6-6 Adjusted Basis

In order to save money on their utility bills, Mr. and Mrs. Thrifty paid to replace their old roof with a new one with better insulation. The new roof materially increased the value of the house, so the cost of the roof should be added to the basis of the house.

      2) Generally, repairs and maintenance expenses are considered a current-period deduction. However, certain repairs may be classified as an improvement, which must be capitalized. There are multiple safe harbors that allow repairs and maintenance to always be classified as a current-period expense instead of capitalized.
         a) Taxpayers who have elected to use the de minimis expense treatment must expense all repairs up to the de minimis amount (i.e., $2,500).
         b) The costs of performing certain routine maintenance activities for property may result in an improvement to the unit of property, i.e., capitalized costs.
            i) However, a safe harbor allows routine repairs and maintenance to be expensed. This safe harbor applies to actions that maintain the asset and are reasonably expected to be performed more than once for the asset's class life under the alternative depreciation system.
3. Increase to basis may result from liability to the extent it is secured by real property and applied to extend its life.
4. Basis must be reduced by the larger of the amount of depreciation allowed or allowable (even if not claimed). Unimproved land is not depreciated.
   a. Section 179 expense is treated as a depreciation deduction.
      1) The Sec. 179 amount is $1.08 million for 2022.
      2) The limitation is reduced (but not below zero) by the amount by which the cost of Sec. 179 property placed in service during the 2022 taxable year exceeds $2,700,000.

5. A shareholder does not recognize gain on the voluntary contribution of capital to a corporation.
    a. The shareholder's stock basis is increased by the basis in the contributed property.
    b. The corporation has a transferred basis in the property.
6. The basis of stock acquired in a nontaxable distribution (e.g., stock rights) is allocated a portion of the basis of the stock upon which the distribution was made.
    a. If the new and old shares are not identical, basis is allocated in proportion to the FMV of the original stock and the distribution as of the date of distribution.
    b. If the new and old shares are identical (e.g., stock splits), the old basis is simply divided among the new total of shares.
    c. If the FMV of the stock rights is less than 15% of the FMV of the stock upon which it was issued, the rights have a zero basis (unless an election is made to allocate basis).

EXAMPLE 6-7 Basis of Rights to Purchase Stock

A taxpayer exercises (sells) rights to purchase stock at $50 per share when the rights are worth $6 per share. Since the rights are worth less than 15% of the FMV of the stock, the taxpayer is not required to allocate a portion of old basis of the stock to the stock rights.

Tax Benefit Adjustments

7. Basis adjustment is required for certain specific items that represent a tax benefit. Four examples follow:

Casualty Losses

    a. Basis is reduced by the amount of the loss, by any amounts recovered by insurance, and by any amounts for which no tax benefit was received.

Debt Discharge

    b. Specific exclusion from gross income is allowed to certain insolvent persons for debt discharged. Reduction in basis is required for certain amounts excluded.

Credits for Building Rehabilitation

    c. Sometimes, the full amount of the credit must be deducted from the basis; other times, only one-half of the credit must be deducted. In the case of low-income housing, no reduction is required.
    d. Exclusions from income of subsidies for energy conservation measures decrease the basis of property.

Partial Disposition of Property

8. The basis of the whole property must be equitably apportioned among the parts; relative FMV is generally used.

Common Examples of Decreases to Basis

Common Examples of Decreases to Basis
Exclusion from income of subsidies for energy conservation measures
Casualty or theft loss deductions and insurance reimbursements
Certain vehicle credits
Section 179 deduction
Deductions previously allowed (or allowable) for amortization, depreciation, and depletion
Depreciation
Nontaxable corporate distributions
Rebates treated as adjustments to the sales price

You have completed the outline for this subunit.
Study multiple-choice questions 7 through 12 beginning on page 149.

6.3 LIKE-KIND EXCHANGES

Section 1031 defers recognizing gain or loss to the extent that **real** property productively used in a trade or business or held for the production of income (investment) is exchanged (commonly referred to as relinquished) for property of like-kind. Realized gain (loss) is the gain (loss) from the sale or exchange. Recognized gain (loss) is the amount reported on the tax return.

Like-Kind Property

1. Only real property qualifies for like-kind treatment for transfers after 2017. Like-kind real property is alike in nature or character but not necessarily in grade or quality.
   a. Properties are of like kind if each is within a class of like nature or character, without regard to differences in use (e.g., business or investment), improvements (e.g., bare land or house), location (e.g., city or rural), or proximity.
      1) A real estate lease that runs 30 years or more is treated as real property, and the exchange of it for other real estate qualifies under Sec. 1031 as long as the parties to the exchange are not dealers in real estate.
   b. Real property located within the United States is like-kind with all other real property in the U.S. Foreign real estate is like-kind with other foreign real estate. But, U.S. real estate and foreign real estate are not like-kind. This is different from the rule for involuntary conversions by condemnation discussed in Subunit 6.4.

Boot

2. Boot is all nonqualified property transferred in an exchange transaction.
   a. Gain is recognized equal to the lesser of gain realized or boot received.
   b. Boot received includes cash, net liability relief, and other nonqualified property (its FMV).

EXAMPLE 6-8 Like-Kind Exchange with Boot

Scott owned a parcel of real estate that he was holding for investment. It had an adjusted basis of $50,000. Scott exchanged the real estate for a piece of land with a fair market value of $60,000, a boat for personal use that had a fair market value of $3,000, and $2,000 cash. Scott's basis in the land received is equal to the adjusted basis of the real estate transferred ($50,000), less the boot received of the boat ($3,000) and the cash ($2,000), plus the gain recognized on the transaction. Gain is recognized to the extent of boot received. Here, the boat and the cash are boot; therefore, a gain of $5,000 must be recognized. This recognized gain increases basis of the land to $50,000.

EXAMPLE 6-9 Like-Kind Exchange

Real property with an adjusted basis of $50,000 is exchanged for $20,000 cash and like-kind property with a FMV of $40,000. The recognized gain is $10,000 ($40,000 + $20,000 – $50,000), the lesser of the gain realized ($10,000) and the boot received ($20,000).

EXAMPLE 6-10 Like-Kind Qualified Property

Alan exchanged real property with a basis of $60,000 plus $5,000 cash for like-kind property with a FMV of $63,000. Alan's $2,000 loss [$63,000 – ($60,000 + $5,000)] is not deductible.

Liabilities

3. Liabilities are treated as money paid or received.
   a. If each party assumes a liability of the other, only the net liability given or received is treated as boot.
   b. Liabilities include mortgages on property.

Basis

4. Qualified property received in a like-kind exchange has an exchanged basis adjusted for boot and gain recognized.

	AB of property given
+	Gain recognized
+	Boot given (cash, liability incurred, other property)
–	Boot received (cash, liability relief, other property) + Exchange fees incurred
–	Loss recognized (boot given)
=	Basis in acquired property

NOTE: The IRS has ruled that exchange expenses can be deducted to compute gain or loss realized, offset against cash payments received in determining recognized gain, or included in the basis of the property received.

Realized Gain

5. Under Sec. 1031, realized gain is usually recognized only to the extent of boot received (Cash + FMV of other property + Net liability relief).

Deferred Like-Kind Exchanges

6. If a taxpayer sells property and buys similar property in two mutually dependent transactions, the taxpayer may have to treat the sale and purchase as a single nontaxable exchange.

Deadlines

7. An exchange of like-kind real properties must be completed within the earlier of
   a. 180 days after the transfer of the exchanged property or
   b. The due date (including extensions) for the transferor's tax return for the taxable year in which the exchange took place.
   c. The taxpayer has 45 days from the date of the transfer to identify the like-kind real property received in the exchange.
      1) The replacement property must be clearly described in a signed, written document. The document then must be delivered to the other person involved in the exchange.
         a) The identification of multiple replacement real properties is permitted.

Exchange Expenses

8. Any exchange expenses are subtracted from the total of the following (but not below zero):
   a. Any cash paid to the taxpayer by the other party;
   b. The FMV of other (not like-kind) property received by the taxpayer, if any; and
   c. Net liabilities assumed by the other party–the excess, if any, of liabilities (including mortgages) assumed by the other party over the total of (1) any liabilities assumed, (2) cash paid by the taxpayer to the other party, and (3) the FMV of the other (not like-kind) property given up by the taxpayer. If the exchange expenses exceed (1), (2), and (3), the excess is added to the basis of the like-kind property.

Stop & Review

You have completed the outline for this subunit.
Study multiple-choice questions 13 through 17 beginning on page 151.

6.4 INVOLUNTARY CONVERSIONS

A taxpayer defers recognition of gain if property is involuntarily converted directly into similar or related property. Also, a taxpayer may elect to defer recognition of gain if property is involuntarily converted indirectly into money (i.e., nonqualified proceeds) or property that is not similar or related in use under Sec. 1033 (i.e., nonqualified property). Nonrecognition of gain is contingent on the involuntarily converted property being reinvested in qualified replacement property within the replacement period. The source of the funds for reinvestment (i.e., insurance proceeds or loan) is immaterial. Losses on involuntary conversions are not deferred.

1. An involuntary conversion of property results from destruction, theft, seizure, requisition, condemnation, or the threat of imminent requisition or condemnation.
2. Section 1033 does not apply to any realized losses.
    a. Loss from condemnation or requisition of a personal-use asset is not deductible. But certain casualty losses are deductible.
    b. When loss is realized, basis is determined independently of Sec. 1033.

Direct Conversion

3. When property is first converted into other property that is similar or related in service or use to the converted property, the realized gain is deferred.
    a. Nonrecognition is mandatory, not elective, on direct conversion to the extent of any amount realized in the form of qualified replacement property.
    b. Basis in the proceeds (property) is exchanged, i.e., equal to the basis in the converted property.

Indirect Conversion

4. When property is first converted involuntarily into nonqualified proceeds or property and qualified property is later purchased within the replacement period, an election may be made to defer realized gain.
    a. The deferral is limited to the extent that the amount realized is invested in qualified replacement property.
    b. Basis in the qualified replacement property is decreased by the amount of any unrecognized gain.
5. The replacement period begins on the earlier of the date of disposition or the threat of condemnation and ends 2 years after the close of the first tax year in which any part of the gain is realized.
    a. Regarding real property used in business or held for investment (not inventory, dealer property, or personal-use property), if conversion is by condemnation or requisition, or threat thereof, 3 years is allowed.
    b. Construction of qualified property must be complete before the end of the replacement period for its cost to be included.

6. "Similar or related in service or use" means the following:

Owner-User

a. For an owner-user, that the property has functional similarity, i.e., meets a functional use test that requires the property to
   1) Have similar physical characteristics
   2) Be used for the same purpose

Owner-Investor

b. For an owner-investor, that the service or use of the property has a close relationship to the service or use the previous property had to the investor, such that the owner-investor's risks, management activities, services performed, etc., continue without substantial change.

Owner-General

c. For **owners (in general)**, that, if property held for investment or for productive use in a trade or business is involuntarily converted due to a **federally declared disaster**, any tangible replacement property will be deemed similar or related in service or use.

7. For real property used in business or held for investment (not inventory, dealer property, personal-use property, etc.), if conversion is by condemnation or threat thereof, like-kind property qualifies as replacement. This standard (i.e., like-kind) is less stringent than the similar or related standard. For condemnations, foreign and U.S. real property are considered like-kind property and subject to the less stringent standard. This is different from the rule for Sec. 1031 like-kind exchanges discussed in Subunit 6.3.
   a. Conversion must be direct.
8. To recap, on a Sec. 1033 involuntary conversion, realized gain is generally recognized only to the extent that any amount realized exceeds the cost of the similar or related-in-service property. Gain recognized is subject to classification as ordinary income under Sec. 1245 or Sec. 1250.

You have completed the outline for this subunit.
Study multiple-choice questions 18 through 20 beginning on page 153.

QUESTIONS

6.1 Basis

1. Mike purchased a building lot in Year 1 for $25,000 and constructed his primary residence there for an additional $175,000. In Year 4, Mike moved to a different city but kept the house he constructed in Year 1 and converted it to a rental property. On the date Mike made this change, the fair market value of the converted property was $225,000. For depreciation purposes, what is Mike's basis in this rental property?

A. $150,000

B. $175,000

C. $200,000

D. $225,000

Answer (B) is correct.

REQUIRED: The basis of property converted into business use.

DISCUSSION: Property converted into business use uses a basis of the lesser of the FMV of the property at the conversion date [$200,000 ($225,000 – $25,000 land)] or the adjusted basis at conversion [$175,000 (land is excluded for the depreciation basis)]. Because Mike's adjusted basis is less than the FMV at the date of conversion, the adjusted basis is used.

Answer (A) is incorrect. The basis of the rental property (the residence built on the land) is not reduced by the basis of the land (that is, the land is not excluded twice for depreciation). **Answer (C) is incorrect.** Because land is not depreciable, only the cost of the building is included when figuring the basis for depreciation. **Answer (D) is incorrect.** The basis used is the lower of FMV or adjusted basis on the date of conversion. In addition, land is excluded for the depreciation basis.

2. Arthur is a proprietor of Arthur's Pizza Emporium. He bought a commercial building several years ago. He made a down payment of $20,000 in cash and assumed a mortgage for $100,000. After he paid off the mortgage, Arthur later sold the building for $180,000. Straight-line depreciation taken up to the date of sale was $18,000. What is the total gain on the sale?

A. $78,000

B. $80,000

C. $60,000

D. $160,000

Answer (A) is correct.

REQUIRED: The gain on the sale of property.

DISCUSSION: The adjusted basis of property is typically the cost basis increased by certain items, such as boot given. The cost basis for the commercial building is the $20,000 down payment of cash by Arthur, increased by the assumption of the $100,000 mortgage. Therefore, Arthur's basis in the commercial building is $120,000. However, this basis is reduced by the $18,000 of depreciation taken. When Arthur sells the commercial building for $180,000, he must recognize a gain on the difference between the amount realized of $180,000 and his adjusted basis of $102,000 ($120,000 basis – $18,000 depreciation) for a total of $78,000.

Answer (B) is incorrect. The down payment of $20,000 increased Arthur's basis in the commercial building, and the $18,000 of depreciation taken reduced Arthur's basis in the commercial building. **Answer (C) is incorrect.** The $18,000 of depreciation taken reduces Arthur's adjusted basis from $120,000 to $102,000. **Answer (D) is incorrect.** The assumption of the $100,000 mortgage increases Arthur's adjusted basis in the commercial building.

3. Amounts paid or incurred to demolish a structure are

A. Deductible as a casualty loss.

B. Capitalized and amortized over a 180-month period.

C. Treated as a reduction of the basis of the structure.

D. Capitalized and added to the basis of the land where the demolished structure was located.

Answer (D) is correct.

REQUIRED: The tax treatment of demolition expenditures.

DISCUSSION: Initial basis is adjusted consistent with tax-relevant events. An adjustment is made for demolition of a structure. Costs and losses associated with demolishing a structure are allocated to the land. The costs include the adjusted basis (not FMV) of the structure and demolition costs.

Answer (A) is incorrect. The costs are capitalized to the cost of the land. **Answer (B) is incorrect.** No amortization is allowed. The cost is recovered when the land is sold and any subsequent gain is reduced by the increased basis or any loss is increased by the increased basis. **Answer (C) is incorrect.** The costs and losses associated with the demolition are added to the basis of the land.

4. John purchased a new electric automobile on July 2, 2014, for $18,000. He also claimed a $2,000 plug-in electric drive motor vehicle credit on his 2014 tax return for that vehicle. From 2014 through 2021, John used this automobile only for personal purposes. On January 1, 2022, he began using the electric automobile exclusively for business purposes. The fair market value of the automobile on that day was $17,000. What is the automobile's depreciable basis as of January 1, 2022?

A. $15,000

B. $16,000

C. $17,000

D. $18,000

Answer (B) is correct.

REQUIRED: The automobile's depreciable basis upon conversion of property from personal use to business use.

DISCUSSION: Basis for depreciation is the lesser of the FMV of the property at the conversion date or the adjusted basis at conversion. The FMV on the date of conversion was $17,000. The basis was $16,000 ($18,000 purchase price – $2,000 deduction). Thus, the basis equals $16,000.

Answer (A) is incorrect. The FMV at the date of conversion is not reduced by the amount of the deduction. **Answer (C) is incorrect.** The basis used is the lesser of the adjusted basis and the FMV on the date of conversion. **Answer (D) is incorrect.** The purchase price is irrelevant in this problem. The adjusted basis and FMV on the date of conversion are all that matter.

5. Bob purchased a building and land to use in his business for a price of $1,000,000. The land was valued at $300,000 (included in the price). He then incurred $90,000 to replace the roof of the building. The city replaced the sewage lines to his business and assessed Bob $20,000. Bob had been slow in getting insurance coverage on the real property and incurred a small fire loss of $10,000, which he plans to deduct on his business tax return. What is Bob's basis for depreciation after deducting the loss?

A. $1,100,000

B. $810,000

C. $800,000

D. $720,000

Answer (C) is correct.

REQUIRED: The depreciation basis in a purchase of a business.

DISCUSSION: To determine the basis of the building for depreciation, the value of the land ($300,000) must be subtracted from the total purchase price of $1,000,000 to get $700,000. The $90,000 spent to replace the roof and the $20,000 spent to replace the sewage lines must be capitalized because they are capital expenditures, and they increase the value of the property. The $10,000 fire loss should reduce the basis because casualty losses reduce the basis by the amount of the loss. The total depreciation basis equals $800,000 ($700,000 + $90,000 + $20,000 – $10,000).

Answer (A) is incorrect. The amount of $1,100,000 includes the value of the land. Land is not depreciated. **Answer (B) is incorrect.** The amount of $810,000 does not include the $10,000 loss due to the fire. **Answer (D) is incorrect.** The amount of $720,000 does not capitalize the $90,000 to replace the roof, and it does not deduct the $10,000 loss due to the fire.

6. Which of the following activities would subject a taxpayer to the uniform capitalization rules?

A. Taxpayer produces real or tangible property for non-business use.

B. Taxpayer acquires property not for resale.

C. Taxpayer produces real or tangible personal property for sale to customers and average annual gross receipts exceed $27 million.

D. None of the answers are correct.

Answer (C) is correct.

REQUIRED: The activity that would subject a taxpayer to the uniform capitalization rules.

DISCUSSION: Under Sec. 263A(b)(1), the uniform capitalization rules apply to real or tangible personal property produced by the taxpayer if average annual gross receipts exceed $27 million. Property produced for the taxpayer's own use is excepted, unless the use is in a trade or business or an activity conducted for profit [Sec. 263A(c)(1)]. In addition, the taxpayer is subject to the rules if property is acquired for resale (unless the property is personal property and average annual gross receipts are $27 million or less).

Answer (A) is incorrect. The property produced for non-business uses is an exception. **Answer (B) is incorrect.** The rules only apply if it is acquired for resale (unless the gross receipts test is passed). **Answer (D) is incorrect.** The uniform capitalization rules apply to real or tangible personal property produced by the taxpayer if average annual gross receipts exceed $27 million.

6.2 Adjustments to Basis

7. All of the following items decrease the basis of property EXCEPT

A. Casualty or theft loss deductions and insurance reimbursements.

B. The cost of defending and perfecting a title.

C. Section 179 deduction.

D. The exclusion from income of subsidies for energy conservation measures.

Answer (B) is correct.

REQUIRED: The item that does not decrease the basis of property.

DISCUSSION: According to Reg. 1.212-1(k), the expenses paid or incurred in defending or perfecting title of property constitute a part of the cost of property. The expenses are not deductible, and the cost is added to the basis of the property.

Answer (A) is incorrect. Casualty or theft loss deductions decrease the basis of property. **Answer (C) is incorrect.** Section 179 deductions decrease the basis of property. **Answer (D) is incorrect.** Exclusions from income of subsidies for energy conservation measures decrease the basis of property.

8. Rich, Inc., a calendar-year taxpayer employing the accrual method of accounting, acquired a business warehouse building in Year 1 for $100,000. Rich deducted $3,000 in warehouse asset depreciation expense on December 31, Year 1. In January of Year 2, Rich incurred a $2,000 legal bill, successfully defending its title to the building. Later in the year, a second-floor office was added to the warehouse at a cost of $10,000. Rich deducted $5,000 in warehouse asset depreciation expense on December 31, Year 2. What is Rich, Inc.'s adjusted basis in the warehouse asset on January 1, Year 3?

A. $100,000

B. $104,000

C. $110,000

D. $112,000

Answer (B) is correct.

REQUIRED: The adjusted basis in the warehouse asset.

DISCUSSION: Initial basis is adjusted consistent with tax-relevant events. Adjustments made for certain expenditures subsequent to acquisition are property costs, such as legal fees to defend title. Basis must be increased for expenditures that prolong the life of the property by at least 1 year or materially increase its value. Basis must be reduced by the larger of the amount of depreciation allowed or allowable. Thus, Rich, Inc.'s basis in the warehouse equals $104,000 ($100,000 purchase price – $3,000 depreciation in Year 1 + $2,000 legal fees + $10,000 expansion – $5,000 depreciation in Year 2).

Answer (A) is incorrect. The adjusted basis and original basis may not necessarily be equal. In this instance, they are not. **Answer (C) is incorrect.** Basis must also be increased for the legal fees incurred and reduced by depreciation. **Answer (D) is incorrect.** The adjusted basis has not been reduced for depreciation.

9. Which of the following items does NOT increase the basis of property?

A. Freight and installation costs.

B. Legal fees to perfect the title.

C. Zoning costs.

D. Missed depreciation deductions in tax years barred by the statute of limitations.

Answer (D) is correct.

REQUIRED: The item that does not increase basis.

DISCUSSION: The basis of property must be decreased by any item that represents a return of capital for the period during which the property has been held. The basis is adjusted for depreciation in the amount that was claimed or could have been claimed on the owner's return. This reduction of basis must be taken, whether or not the taxpayer actually claimed it and even if the statute of limitations for claiming the deduction has expired.

10. Michael wants to convert his personal residence to a rental property. He paid $300,000 for the property, and the allocation of value for tax assessment has always been 2/3 building and 1/3 land. Over the years, he incurred $50,000 in permanent improvements to the house. He claimed a (federally declared disaster) casualty loss deduction of $5,000 in 1 year. On the date of conversion, the fair market value of the property was $600,000. What is the basis for depreciation of this rental?

A. $600,000

B. $345,000

C. $245,000

D. $400,000

Answer (C) is correct.

REQUIRED: The adjusted basis in property converted from personal use to business use.

DISCUSSION: Property converted into business use has a basis for depreciation of the lesser between the FMV of the property at the conversion date and the adjusted basis. Two-thirds of the $300,000 is allocated to the building. The $50,000 in permanent improvements is capitalized, and the $5,000 claimed as a casualty loss is subtracted. Thus, the adjusted basis of the property is $245,000 ($200,000 + $50,000 – $5,000).

Answer (A) is incorrect. Property converted into business use has a basis for depreciation of the lesser between the FMV ($600,000) of the property at the conversion date and the adjusted basis ($245,000). **Answer (B) is incorrect.** The $345,000 does not subtract out the value of the land. The land is 1/3 of the $300,000, and it is subtracted because land is not depreciated. **Answer (D) is incorrect.** The personal residence's basis for depreciation is valued at 2/3 of the cost, not the FMV.

11. Which of the following does NOT reduce the basis of property?

A. Credit for qualified electric vehicles.

B. Depreciation.

C. Zoning costs.

D. Section 179 deductions.

Answer (C) is correct.

REQUIRED: The item that does not reduce the basis of property.

DISCUSSION: Publication 551 provides examples of items that increase and decrease a taxpayer's basis in property. Zoning costs do not decrease, but rather increase, the basis. Conversely, a credit for qualified electric vehicles, depreciation, and Sec. 179 deductions do decrease basis.

12. A fire in Mr. White's residence (in a federally declared disaster area) resulted in a loss of $2,600. Mr. White recovered only $1,600 from his insurance company and deducted a casualty loss of $500 ($1,000 unreimbursed loss, less $500 nondeductible on property used for personal purposes). By what amount must Mr. White reduce his basis before considering any reinvestment of the insurance proceeds in repairs on the house?

A. $1,000

B. $1,600

C. $2,100

D. $2,600

Answer (C) is correct.

REQUIRED: The adjustment to the basis of a personal residence after a casualty loss.

DISCUSSION: Mr. White received $1,600 in insurance proceeds and recognized a casualty loss of $500. These are considered recovered costs for tax purposes, and Mr. White must reduce his basis by $2,100. The remaining $500 loss for which he received no tax benefit does not reduce Mr. White's basis.

Answer (A) is incorrect. The basis must also be reduced for the insurance proceeds received. **Answer (B) is incorrect.** The basis must also be reduced for the deductible portion of the loss. **Answer (D) is incorrect.** The undeductible portion of the unreimbursed loss does not increase basis.

6.3 Like-Kind Exchanges

13. The Andee Partnership traded its farm land with an adjusted basis of $10,000 for barren land with a fair market value of $15,000. Andee also received $3,500 cash on the trade. What is the gain, if any, on this trade?

A. $0

B. $3,500

C. $5,000

D. $1,500

Answer (B) is correct.

REQUIRED: The recognized gain on the exchange of land.

DISCUSSION: A partially nontaxable exchange occurs when cash or unlike property are received in addition to like-kind real property. If boot (cash or nonqualified property) is received in addition to like-kind property, the amount of recognized gain is the lesser of the amount of boot received or the amount of gain realized. In this case, Andee Partnership received boot of $3,500 cash in addition to the like-kind real property received. The realized gain of $8,500 ($15,000 fair market value of the barren land + $3,500 cash received – $10,000 adjusted basis of the farm land) is taxed only to the extent of the cash received, or $3,500. Thus, the gain on the trade is $3,500 (Publication 544).

Answer (A) is incorrect. Andee Partnership received boot in addition to the like-kind property in the exchange and therefore recognizes a gain. **Answer (C) is incorrect.** The realized gain includes the cash received, but the recognized gain is limited to the boot received ($3,500). **Answer (D) is incorrect.** The boot received increases the realized gain. The gain is equal to the amount of boot received, but not exceeding realized gain.

14. Rebecca exchanges real estate held for investment with an adjusted basis of $400,000 and a mortgage of $100,000 for other real estate to be held for investment. The other party agrees to assume the mortgage. The fair market value of the real estate Rebecca receives is $500,000. She pays exchange expenses of $10,000. What amount of gain does Rebecca realize?

A. $100,000

B. $190,000

C. $90,000

D. $200,000

Answer (B) is correct.

REQUIRED: The realized gain on the sale of property.

DISCUSSION: This transaction is a like-kind exchange. The real estate had an adjusted basis of $400,000 and was exchanged for property that has a FMV of $500,000. She was also relieved of a $100,000 mortgage, which is the same as receiving cash, and the $10,000 in expenses reduces the realized gain. Therefore, the realized, not recognized, gain is the $100,000 in the exchange of properties plus the $100,000 in mortgage relief minus the $10,000 in expenses to give a total gain of $190,000.

Answer (A) is incorrect. The realized amount that is received is $590,000. The $100,000 mortgage that is taken over is equivalent to receiving cash. This $100,000 is added to the $500,000 FMV and then is reduced by the $10,000 exchange expense to get a total of $590,000. Subtract $400,000 from the $590,000 for a $190,000 realized gain. **Answer (C) is incorrect.** The amount of $90,000 does not take into account the $100,000 mortgage that is assumed. When someone takes over debt, it is the same as receiving cash. This $100,000 is added to the gain realized. **Answer (D) is incorrect.** The amount of $200,000 fails to take into account the $10,000 exchange expense. Expenses incurred in acquiring property are added to the basis of the property, thus reducing the amount of gain realized.

15. Nelson, Inc., owned a manufacturing building with a fair market value of $95,000 and an adjusted basis of $75,000. Nelson, Inc., entered into an agreement to exchange the manufacturing building for a warehouse with an adjusted basis of $80,000 and a fair market value of $100,000 with Roberts Corporation. In addition, Nelson, Inc., would pay Roberts Corporation $5,000 in cash. Nelson, Inc., also incurred and paid attorney and deed preparation fees of $5,000 on this exchange. What is Nelson's basis in the warehouse it received in this like-kind exchange?

A. $85,000

B. $100,000

C. $95,000

D. $110,000

Answer (A) is correct.

REQUIRED: The basis of real property acquired in a like-kind exchange.

DISCUSSION: Section 1031 defers recognizing gain or loss to the extent that real property productively used in a trade or business or held for the production of income (investment) is exchanged for property of like-kind. The basis in the property equals the adjusted basis of the property given plus any gain recognized, boot given, and legal fees incurred, and less any boot received and loss recognized. Thus, the basis in the new property equals $85,000 ($75,000 adjusted basis of property given + $5,000 boot given + $5,000 legal fees incurred).

Answer (B) is incorrect. The basis in the new property does not equal the FMV of that property. **Answer (C) is incorrect.** The basis in the new property does not equal the FMV of the transferred property. **Answer (D) is incorrect.** The basis of the new property does not equal that property's FMV plus boot given and legal fees incurred.

16. Which of the following transactions qualifies as a like-kind exchange?

A. The exchange of a copyright on a novel for a copyright on a song.

B. An exchange of the "goodwill or going concern value" of a business for the "goodwill or going concern value" of another business.

C. An exchange of land improved with an apartment house for land improved with a store building.

D. An exchange of real property used predominantly in the United States for real property used predominantly outside the United States.

Answer (C) is correct.

REQUIRED: The transaction that qualifies as a like-kind exchange.

DISCUSSION: Section 1031 defers recognizing gain or loss to the extent that real property productively used in a trade or business or held for the production of income (investment) is exchanged for property of like kind. Like-kind property is alike in nature or character but not necessarily in grade or quality. Properties are of like kind if each is within a class of like nature or character, without regard to differences in use, improvements, location, or proximity. Thus, an exchange of land improved with an apartment house for land improved with a store building qualifies as a Sec. 1031 exchange.

Answer (A) is incorrect. The underlying assets, the novel and the song, are not real property or like-kind. **Answer (B) is incorrect.** The going-concern value of one entity is never like-kind as the going-concern value of another entity. **Answer (D) is incorrect.** Section 1031 does not apply to U.S. or foreign real property.

17. The Post and Rail Partnership traded a piece of farm land with an adjusted basis of $4,000 for a farm tractor that has a fair market value of $9,000 and an adjusted basis of $8,000. What is the recognized gain or loss?

A. $5,000

B. $4,000

C. $1,000

D. None; it is a like-kind exchange.

Answer (A) is correct.

REQUIRED: The recognized gain or loss on the exchange.

DISCUSSION: The definition of fair market value (FMV) is the price at which property would change hands between a buyer and a seller, neither having to buy or sell, and both having reasonable knowledge of all necessary facts (Publication 551). Since the transaction does not qualify for a like-kind exchange, the gain should be determined by subtracting the adjusted basis of the amount given up ($4,000) from the FMV of the amount received ($9,000).

6.4 Involuntary Conversions

18. Sally's business office was condemned to make way for an expanded highway on May 1, 2022. Sally's adjusted basis in her building was $20,000 ($80,000 original cost less $60,000 in depreciation). Her proceeds from condemnation were $220,000. Sally replaced her office on November 10, 2022, at a cost of $185,000. Sally must recognize a gain of

A. $200,000

B. $0

C. $35,000

D. $60,000

Answer (C) is correct.

REQUIRED: The gain recognized on an involuntary conversion.

DISCUSSION: When property is converted involuntarily into nonqualified proceeds and qualified property is purchased within the replacement period, an election may be made to defer realized gain to the extent that the amount realized on the conversion is reinvested in qualified replacement property. The basis in qualified replacement property is decreased by any unrecognized gain. Sally's gain on the involuntary conversion is the $220,000 proceeds received less the cost of the replacement property of $185,000 for a gain of $35,000.

Answer (A) is incorrect. The gain is based upon the proceeds received and the replacement property purchased, not the basis of the old property. **Answer (B) is incorrect.** Sally must recognize a gain if the replacement property does not cost as much as the proceeds received from the involuntary conversion. **Answer (D) is incorrect.** The entire $60,000 of depreciation will not be recaptured.

19. Gwen owned a duplex and lived in one half. The other half was rental property. The cost of the property was $80,000, of which $70,000 was allocated to the building and $10,000 to the land. In the current year, the property was condemned by the city. Up to that time, she had allowed (allowable) depreciation of $23,000. The city paid $70,000. She bought another duplex for $85,000. Gwen lived in one half, and the other half is a rental. What is the basis of the replacement property?

A. $62,000

B. $67,000

C. $72,000

D. $85,000

Answer (B) is correct.

REQUIRED: The basis of the replacement property.

DISCUSSION: Gwen has two assets: one for rental and one for personal use. Each asset must be computed separately. The basis of the rental building before the sale was $17,000 ($40,000 purchase price – $23,000 depreciation taken). That portion of the building was sold for $35,000, leaving a gain of $18,000. The gain is deferred, leaving a basis of $24,500 ($42,500 – $18,000). The personal-use building has a $5,000 loss ($35,000 selling price – $40,000 basis). That loss is a nondeductible personal loss. The replacement portion has a basis of $42,500, the purchase price. The total basis is $67,000 ($24,500 rental portion + $42,500 personal-use portion).

Answer (A) is incorrect. The loss does not reduce the basis. **Answer (C) is incorrect.** The loss is not deferred. **Answer (D) is incorrect.** The deferred gain reduces the basis of the new asset.

20. A tornado destroyed a forklift Ben purchased for $16,000 and for which he had deducted $12,000 of depreciation expense. Ben received an insurance payment of $18,000, of which he spent $15,000 for a new forklift. As a result, what is the minimum amount of ordinary income Ben can report on his return?

A. $0

B. $3,000

C. $12,000

D. $14,000

Answer (B) is correct.

REQUIRED: The gross income resulting from the involuntary conversion of insured property.

DISCUSSION: Ben received insurance proceeds of $18,000 on destroyed property with an adjusted basis of $4,000 and thereby realized a gain of $14,000: $12,000 ordinary and $2,000 Sec. 1231. Since the replacement property was similar, under Sec. 1033(a)(2), Ben may elect to recognize the gain only to the extent that the amount realized ($18,000) exceeds the cost of the replacement property ($15,000), or $3,000. The ordinary income must be recognized first.

Answer (A) is incorrect. A gain must be recognized to the extent that the amount realized exceeds the cost of the replacement property. **Answer (C) is incorrect.** The gain that is recognized is limited to the amount that the amount realized exceeds the cost of the replacement property. **Answer (D) is incorrect.** Only $12,000 of the gain is ordinary income and Ben elects to report only $3,000.

Go to Online Course

Access the **Gleim EA Premium Review System** featuring our SmartAdapt technology from your Gleim Personal Classroom to continue your studies.

You will experience a personalized study environment with exam-emulating multiple-choice questions.

STUDY UNIT SEVEN

DEPRECIATION

(18 pages of outline)

Depreciation is a business deduction that allows a taxpayer to recover the cost or other basis of certain business-use property with a useful life in excess of 1 year. It is an annual allowance for the wear and tear, deterioration, or obsolescence of the property.

1) Related cost recovery methods include amortization and depletion.
2) Section 179 is a special election that allows for immediate, limited expensing of depreciable property.

7.1 DEPRECIATION METHODS

Tax accounting methods of depreciation that allow a deduction in excess of a current year's decline in economic value are accelerated cost recovery (ACR) methods.

1. Property subject to the allowance for depreciation is tangible property that is used in trade or business or is held for production of income and that has a determinable, limited useful life.
    a. The amount of a current depreciation deduction is computed by applying a rate to depreciable basis (DB).
        1) The rate is determined under a mandatory or elected depreciation method.
        2) The basis of property is decreased by the greater of the amount of depreciation allowed or allowable.
            a) Allowable depreciation is the amount that a taxpayer is entitled to deduct under any proper method.
            b) Allowed depreciation is the deduction claimed on the tax return.
2. Depreciation of property begins in the taxable year that it is placed in service.
    a. Property is considered placed in service when it is ready and available for a specific use.

Straight-Line Depreciation (S-L)

3. The annual amount allowable is the depreciable basis reduced for salvage value (SV) and divided by the useful life of the asset.

(Basis – SV) ÷ Useful life

150% Declining Balance

4. Basis (not reduced by SV) minus previously allowable deductions, which is adjusted basis (AB), is multiplied by 1 1/2 times the straight-line rate.

AB × (150% ÷ Useful life)

200% Declining Balance

5. The constant rate is twice the straight-line rate.

AB × (200% ÷ Useful life)

MACRS

6. The Modified Accelerated Cost Recovery System (MACRS) applies to property placed in service in 1987 or later.
   a. MACRS consists of two depreciation systems, the **General Depreciation System (GDS)** and the **Alternative Depreciation System (ADS)**. Generally, GDS must be used unless the taxpayer is specifically required by law to use ADS or the taxpayer elects to use ADS.
   b. The IRS has established and published percentage tables in Publication 946 to help taxpayers figure their depreciation deduction under MACRS. The percentage tables are based on the depreciation method, recovery period, placed in service date, and convention. Percentages are applied to the unadjusted basis of the property each year.
   c. The 200%-declining-balance method is used for GDS recovery periods of 3, 5, 7, and 10 years; 150% is used for 15 and 20 year property.

MACRS RECOVERY PERIODS (Personal Property)			
MACRS Recovery Period # of Years	**Midpoint of ADR for Class # of Years**	**DB Rate Applicable Percent**	**Examples**
3	≤4	200	Special tools, e.g., for rubber manufacturing
5	>4, <10	200	Computers, office machinery (e.g., copier) Cars, trucks Research and experimentation (R&E) equipment
7	≥10, <16	200	Most machinery Office furniture and equipment Property without ADR midpoint & not otherwise classified
10	≥16, <20	200	Water vessels, e.g., barge Petroleum processing equipment Food & tobacco manufacturing Agricultural structures (single-purpose)
15	≥20, <25	150	Data communication plants, e.g., for phone Sewage treatment plants Billboards, improvements to land
20	≥25	150	Utilities, e.g., municipal sewers (pre 6/13/1996) Not real property with ADR midpoint ≥ 27.5 years

Residential Rental Property

1) The straight-line rate is based on a 27 1/2-year recovery period. It is real property with at least 80% of gross rents coming from dwelling units. Partial use by the owner is included. Transient use of more than half the units excludes the property, e.g., a motel.
2) Nonresidential real estate is assigned a 39-year recovery period.

Alternative Depreciation System (ADS)

7. GDS is mandatory unless ADS is required or elected. ADS uses a straight-line rate based on longer recovery periods. Salvage value is ignored. Examples of ADS recovery periods are presented in the following table:

Recovery Period (Years)	Items
5	Cars, light trucks, certain technological equipment
12	Personal property with no class life
15	Agricultural structures (single-purpose)
30	Residential rental (40 years for acquisitions placed in service before January 1, 2018)
40	Nonresidential real estate

1) ADS is required for each of the following:
   a) Listed property
   b) Property used, leased, or financed by tax-exempt organizations
   c) Tangible property used predominantly outside the U.S.
   d) Imported property from a country that engages in discriminatory trade practices

Listed Property and Automobiles

8. Recapture income may result from modified use. Timing of capital recovery is even more specifically regulated in the case of luxury automobiles.

Passenger Automobiles

a. Specific depreciation limitations apply to passenger automobiles that cost more than a base amount.
   1) Passenger automobiles are generally four-wheeled, made for use on public roads, below the weight threshold of 6,000 pounds when loaded, not used to transport for compensation, and not otherwise exempt.
   2) Deduction, otherwise allowable, is limited to the business-use percentage of the dollar limitation amount applicable with reference to the year placed in service.
   3) The lease of a car for business use is deductible.

Listed Property

b. Depreciation of listed property is limited by reference to qualified business use (QBU). Listed property includes the following:
   1) Passenger automobiles,
   2) Other transportation vehicles (e.g., truck under 6,000 pounds when loaded),
   3) Entertainment or recreational property (e.g., video camera), and
   4) Any other property of a type specified by the Secretary by regulations.

Qualified Business Use (QBU)

c. Rules for QBU include the following:

1) Use by an employee of his or her own property is QBU only if it is in the employer's trade or business, for the convenience of the employer, and required as a condition of employment (it enables proper performance of duties).
2) If QBU exceeds 50% in the tax year in which listed property is placed in service, Sec. 179 current expensing and MACRS depreciation are allowable with respect to the QBU portion.
3) If QBU is not more than 50% during the year in which listed property is placed in service, Sec. 179 expense election is not allowable and ADS depreciation is used (S-L over the class-life).
4) When QBU exceeds 50% in the first year but not in a subsequent year, the taxpayer must recapture as gross income any excess of depreciation allowed over ADS depreciation for prior year(s).

NOTE: ADS depreciation is used for all years once QBU does not exceed 50% for any year.

Section 280F

d. Section 280F allows an additional first-year depreciation (bonus depreciation) amount of $8,000 for passenger automobiles acquired after September 17, 2017, and placed in service during calendar year 2022.

1) For passenger automobiles placed in service during 2022, and for which the additional first-year depreciation deduction under Sec. 168(k) is not claimed, the maximum amount of allowable depreciation is
   a) $11,200 for the year in which the vehicle is placed in service,
   b) $18,000 for the second year,
   c) $10,800 for the third year, and
   d) $6,460 for the fourth and later years in the recovery period.
2) The capital recovery deductions include the amount expensed under Sec. 179 and depreciation.
3) The limitations are indexed for inflation for passenger automobiles placed in service after 2022.
4) For vehicles weighing less than 6,000 pounds, each year a passenger automobile is depreciated, the deduction is limited to the lesser of
   a) The Sec. 280F limitation or
   b) The depreciation that would have been computed under Sec. 168.

Stop & Review

You have completed the outline for this subunit.
Study multiple-choice questions 1 through 5 beginning on page 173.

7.2 SECTION 179 EXPENSE

A person may elect to deduct all or part of the cost of Sec. 179 property acquired during the year, up to a maximum of $1,080,000 for 2022.

1. Section 179 property is
   a. Tangible personal property that is
      1) Recovery property (depreciable) and
      2) Section 1245 property (intangible or tangible personal property subject to depreciation or amortization)
   b. Acquired
      1) By purchase,
      2) From an unrelated party, and
      3) For use in the active conduct of a trade or business.
2. The definition of Sec. 179 property has been expanded to include
   a. Certain depreciable tangible personal property used predominantly to furnish lodging or in connection with furnishing lodging and
   b. Qualified real property to include any of the following improvements to nonresidential real property placed in service after the date such property was first placed in service:
      1) Roofs
      2) Security systems
      3) Fire protection and alarm systems
      4) Heating, ventilation, and air-conditioning property
         a) Qualified energy efficient heating and air-conditioning property means any Sec. 1250 property
            i) With respect to which depreciation (or amortization in lieu of depreciation) is allowable;
            ii) Which is installed as part of a building's heating, cooling, ventilation, or hot water system; and
            iii) Which is within the scope of Standard 90.1-2007 or any successor standard.
3. Section 179 expense is treated as depreciation. It reduces basis in the property (but not below zero) prior to computation of any other depreciation deduction allowable for the first year, but only if and to the extent that Sec. 179 deduction is elected.
   a. It is subject to depreciation recapture under Sec. 1245.
4. A deduction may be for no more than either
   a. $1,080,000 minus the excess of tangible personal property purchases for the year over $2,700,000 (no Sec. 179 deduction if total purchase cost is above $3,780,000) or
   b. Taxable income (TI) from the active conduct of any trade or business during the tax year.

5. Other Sec. 179 limitations include the following:
   a. Trusts and estates may not claim a Sec. 179 deduction.
   b. Only the business-use portion of the cost of Sec. 179 property may be expensed.
   c. No more than the statutory amount may be deducted as depreciation on cars and certain luxury items. Excess over the limit may not be expensed under Sec. 179.

EXAMPLE 7-1 Maximum Sec. 179 Deduction

In 2022, Diana's Corner Stores upgraded various equipment and computers at a total cost of $3,000,000. All assets purchased are eligible for Sec. 179 treatment. The Sec. 179 deduction is phased out dollar for dollar once the minimum threshold for purchases is exceeded. Therefore, the maximum Sec. 179 deduction Diana's Corner Stores can take is $780,000 [$1,080,000 maximum deduction – ($3,000,000 purchases – $2,700,000 phaseout)].

6. Current-year excess over TI may be carried forward and treated as Sec. 179 cost in a subsequent year.

100% Expensing (Bonus Depreciation)

7. First-year bonus depreciation is 100% for qualified property (including certain planted or grafted plants bearing fruits and nuts) acquired and placed in service after September 27, 2017, and before January 1, 2023.
   a. The property is eligible for the additional depreciation if it is the taxpayer's first use. This allows for the property to be new or used.
   b. Qualifying property must be new or used MACRS property with a 20-year or less recovery period.
   c. Qualifying property includes leasehold improvements.
   d. The property cannot be acquired from a related party.
8. Any deduction for bonus depreciation is taken before the regular depreciation is recalculated.
9. The bonus depreciation rate is phased down in subsequent years as follows:
   a. 80% -- property placed in service after December 31, 2022, and before January 1, 2024.
   b. 60% -- property placed in service after December 31, 2023, and before January 1, 2025.
   c. 40% -- property placed in service after December 31, 2024, and before January 1, 2026.
   d. 20% -- property placed in service after December 31, 2025, and before January 1, 2027.

Order of Deductions

10. Any deduction for Sec. 179 is taken before any bonus (special) depreciation. Any deduction for bonus (special) depreciation is taken before the regular depreciation is recalculated.

Recapture

11. If Sec. 179 property is disposed of prior to the end of the MACRS recovery period, gross income includes any excess of Sec. 179 deduction over MACRS deductions allowable notwithstanding Sec. 179.

NOTE: Recapture also applies when the business use of the Sec. 179 property changes to less than 50% of total use.

You have completed the outline for this subunit.

Study multiple-choice questions 6 through 9 beginning on page 174.

7.3 AMORTIZATION

Amortization accounts for recovery of capital ratably (in equal installments over the useful life of the property).

1. An amortizable asset, generally, is property that
   a. Is intangible,
   b. Is personal property (as opposed to real),
   c. Has a determinable useful life, and
   d. Is used in a trade or business or for the production of income.
2. A deduction is allowed for assets used in a trade or business or for the production of income. The deduction is ratable (straight-line) over the useful life of the asset or, in the case of Sec. 197 intangibles, 15 years.

Intangibles

3. Section 197 intangibles acquired (not created) in a trade, business, or income-producing activity are amortized over a 15-year period, beginning with the month in which the intangibles are acquired.
   a. Qualified intangibles include the following:
      1) Acquired goodwill and going-concern value
      2) Intangible assets relating to the work force, information base, patent, copyright, sound recordings, computer software, know-how, customers, suppliers, or similar items
      3) Licenses, permits, or other rights granted by governmental units
      4) Covenants not to compete
      5) Any franchise, trademark, or trade name, including professional sports franchises
   b. Qualified intangibles do not include intangibles that result from the taxpayer's own efforts, unless they are in connection with the acquisition of a trade or business.
      1) The basis of an intangible is usually the cost to buy or create it.
         a) Cost includes all costs of acquisition and expenditures necessary to make the intangible asset ready for its intended use.
         b) The basis does not include unsubstantiated expenses for creative effort, only identifiable expenses.
   c. The following are excluded from intangible amortization treatment:
      1) Interests in corporations, partnerships, trusts, and estates
      2) Interests in land
      3) Most financial instruments and contracts
      4) Leases of intangible personal property
      5) Professional sports franchises
   d. Loss realized on disposition of a qualified intangible is disallowed if the taxpayer retains other qualified intangibles acquired in the same (set of) transaction(s).
      1) The amount disallowed is added to the basis of the intangibles retained.

EXAMPLE 7-2 Amortization of Intangible Assets

EMEN Corp. purchased all the assets of a sole proprietorship, including the following intangible assets:

Goodwill	$98,000
Copyright	71,000
Interest in land	12,000
Covenant not to compete	13,000

The cost of certain intangibles acquired (not created) in connection with the conduct of a trade or business or income-producing activity is amortized over a 15-year period. Qualified intangibles include acquired goodwill, copyrights, and covenants not to compete. Therefore, EMEN should amortize $182,000 ($98,000 goodwill + $71,000 copyright + $13,000 covenant not to compete) over the 15-year period.

Start-Up Costs

4. Start-up costs of business may be amortized over 180 months, starting with the month when business begins (eligible expensing is discussed in item 6. below).
   a. Start-up costs are both
      1) Paid or incurred in connection with starting or investigating the start or acquisition of an active trade or business and
      2) Allowed as a current deduction if for expansion of an existing business (i.e., not capital and fully deductible in current year).
   b. Not included is the purchase price of property to be used in the trade or business, e.g., land, building, and equipment.
   c. If the business is not started or acquired, the costs are not deductible unless the person is already engaged in a similar line of business.

Organizational Expense

5. Organizational expense of a corporation or a partnership is generally capitalized. Amortization over at least 180 months may be elected. If not, it is recoverable only upon dissolution of the entity (eligible expensing is discussed in item 6. below).
6. Up to $5,000 each of start-up expenses and organization costs may be deducted in the first year.
   a. If the costs exceed $50,000, the $5,000 is reduced dollar-for-dollar above $50,000.
   b. A taxpayer is deemed to have made the election and is not required to attach a separate statement to the return.
7. The cost of acquiring assets is included as part of the cost of the assets.

Construction Period Interest

8. Construction period interest must be capitalized and recovered under applicable depreciation rules. Amortization is not permitted.

Lease Costs

9. Costs of acquiring a lease are amortized over the lease term. Examples are the purchase price paid to the current holder, commissions, and finders' fees.
   a. Renewal options are included in the term if less than 75% of the cost is attributable to the period prior to renewal.
   b. Improvements by the lessee are deducted under the MACRS method (according to the type of improvement).

You have completed the outline for this subunit.
Study multiple-choice questions 10 through 13 beginning on page 176.

7.4 DEPLETION

Depletion accounts for recovery of investment in natural resources property.

1. Only a person who has an economic interest in a (mineral) property is entitled to deductions for depletion.
   a. A person has an economic interest if (s)he
      1) Acquires by investment an interest in the mineral in place,
      2) Derives income from extraction of the mineral, and
      3) Looks to the extracted mineral for return of capital.
   b. Investment need not be in cash and could, for example, be in
      1) Land that ensures control over access to the mineral or
      2) Stationary equipment used to extract and produce the mineral.

Cost Depletion

2. Cost depletion is computed as follows:

$$\frac{\textbf{Adjusted basis in mineral property}}{\textbf{Estimated mineral units available at year's start}} \times \textbf{Mineral units sold during year}$$

NOTE: The total deductions are limited to unrecovered capital investment.

Percentage Depletion

3. Percentage depletion, which allows deduction in excess of capital investment, is the lower of
   a. 50% of the person's TI before depletion (100% for oil and gas property) or
   b. A percentage (specified by statute) of gross income from the property less related rents or royalties paid or incurred.
      1) For oil and gas property, the rate is 15%.
4. For mineral property, the taxpayer generally must use the method that gives the largest deduction.

You have completed the outline for this subunit.
Study multiple-choice questions 14 and 15 on page 178.

7.5 DEPRECIATION RECAPTURE

We have included Examples 7-11 through 7-14, beginning on page 171, to provide additional context. Read through the outline and be sure to pay close attention to the examples in order to see the rules in practice.

1. **Overview**
   a. Sections 1231, 1245, and 1250 recharacterize gain or loss.

   NOTE: Remember that while these Sections may change the character of gain or loss, they will not change the amount of any gain or loss.

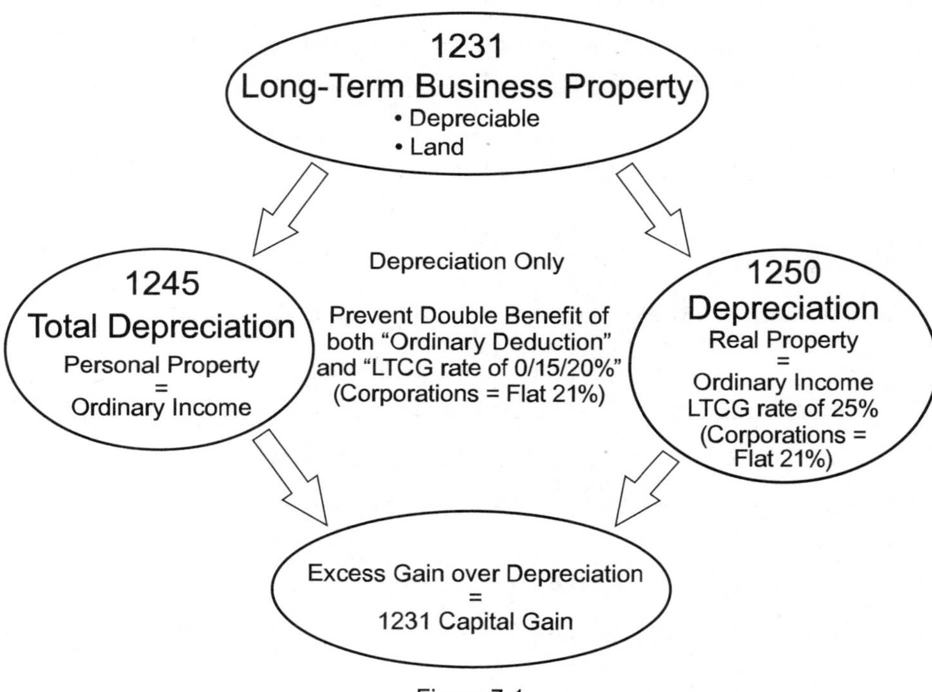

Figure 7-1

Section 1231 Property

Figure 7-2

Visual Memory Aid: For candidates who are visual learners, the figure above and the description below can aid in recalling the dual benefits of Sec. 1231 property.

Section 1231 business assets are truly "the Best of Both Worlds" because they treat losses as ordinary losses (able to offset ordinary income) and tax gains at the preferable capital gains tax rate. This memory aid uses the "31" as a "B" for "Best of Both Worlds" and an "L" for "Losses." This will remind you of the benefits of this class of assets.

2. Section 1231 property is property held for more than 1 year.
   a. It includes
      1) All real or depreciable property used in a trade or business
      2) Involuntarily converted capital assets held in connection with a trade or business or in a transaction entered into for a profit
   b. Examples of Sec. 1231 property include land, apartment buildings, parking lots, manufacturing equipment, and involuntarily converted investment artwork.
   c. Land is not depreciable. Thus, it does not fall within Sec. 1245 or Sec. 1250. Land is referred to as pure Sec. 1231 property if used for trade or business and held for more than 1 year.
   d. Examples that are not Sec. 1231 property include personal-use property and inventory.

Overview of Business Property Gains & Losses

(i.e., Beyond Depreciation Recapture)

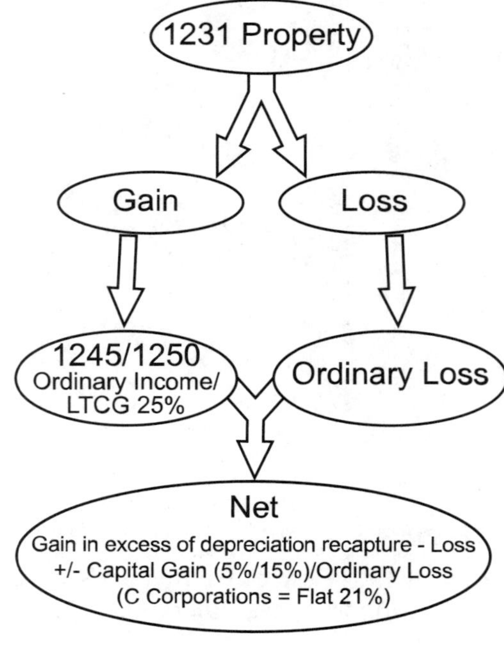

Figure 7-3

e. Section 1231 is beneficial to the taxpayer. When Sec. 1231 property gains exceed losses (a net Sec. 1231 gain), each gain or loss is treated as being from the sale of a long-term capital asset. However, if Sec. 1231 property losses exceed gains (a net Sec. 1231 loss), each gain or loss is considered ordinary. Section 1231 has a two-step test.

   1) Step 1: Determine net gain or loss from all casualties or thefts of Sec. 1231 property for the tax year. Gain or loss from involuntary conversions by other than casualty or theft is included in Step 2 but not Step 1.

      a) If the result is a net loss, each gain or loss is treated as ordinary income or loss.
      b) If the result is a net gain, each gain or loss is included in Step 2.

   2) Step 2: Determine net gain or loss from all dispositions of Sec. 1231 property for the year, including the property included in Step 1 only if Step 1 resulted in a net gain.

      a) If the result is a net loss, each gain or loss is treated as ordinary income or loss.
      b) If the result is a net gain, each gain or loss is treated as a long-term capital gain or loss.

EXAMPLE 7-3 Section 1231 Loss on Sale

A business taxpayer sold for scrap outdated equipment purchased years ago. The equipment had an adjusted basis of $5,000 and a sale price of $2,000. Business equipment held longer than a year is Sec. 1231 property, and, when sold at a loss, the loss is ordinary income, not capital gain. If this business had $10,000 taxable income from operations and no other transactions, its taxable income for the year would be $7,000 ($10,000 taxable income – $3,000 loss).

EXAMPLE 7-4 Net Section 1231 Gain/Loss, Capital/Ordinary

A taxpayer holding two lots of land used for business sells Lot 1 for a $50,000 long-term gain and Lot 2 for a $60,000 long-term loss. Because land used for business is Sec. 1231 property, the net $10,000 loss ($50,000 gain – $60,000 loss) is an ordinary loss, not a capital loss. If, however, Lot 1 was a $60,000 long-term gain and Lot 2 a $50,000 long-term loss, then the net $10,000 gain ($60,000 gain – $50,000 loss) would be a capital, not ordinary, gain.

f. Recapture. Net gain on Sec. 1231 property is treated as ordinary income (OI) to the extent of unrecaptured net Sec. 1231 losses from preceding tax years.

   1) Unrecaptured net Sec. 1231 losses are the total of net Sec. 1231 losses for the last 5 tax years, reduced by net Sec. 1231 gains characterized as ordinary income under Sec. 1231(c).

   2) Sections 1245 and 1250 recapture is computed before Sec. 1231 recapture, but Sec. 1231 recapture is computed before Steps 1 and 2 on the previous page.

NOTE: The use of the term "recapture" in reference to recapturing current-year gain as ordinary income to the extent of prior-year loss as ordinary income under Sec. 1231 is not to be confused with the recapture of depreciation as ordinary income under Secs. 1245 and 1250.

g. The installment method can apply to Sec. 1231 property. Section 1231 merely characterizes gain or loss. Any Sec. 1231 gain that is recharacterized as capital gain will first consist of 25% gain, then 0/15/20% gain.

h. Allocation is required when Sec. 1245 or Sec. 1250 property is also Sec. 1231 property and only a portion of gain recognized is Sec. 1245 or Sec. 1250 OI.

i. Sections 1245 and 1250 only involve gains. If disposition of business property results in a loss, the loss is a Sec. 1231 loss.

EXAMPLE 7-5 Section 1231 Recapture (Lookback Rule)

A taxpayer recognizes the following Sec. 1231 gains and losses:

Year	Section 1231 gain (loss)
1	$(5,000)
2	1,000
3	(3,000)
4	2,500
5	500
6	500
7	4,000

Section 1231 gains in Years 2, 4, 5, and 6 total $4,500 and are recaptured as ordinary income by the Sec. 1231 loss in Year 1. The remaining $500 loss in Year 1 is not applied to Year 7. In Year 7, $3,000 of the $4,000 gain is recaptured as ordinary income by the Sec. 1231 loss in Year 3. The remaining $1,000 ($4,000 – $3,000) gain in Year 7 is a Sec. 1231 gain. Thus, the $4,000 Sec. 1231 gain is best characterized as a net long-term capital gain of $1,000 and ordinary income of $3,000.

Section 1245 Ordinary Income

Figure 7-4

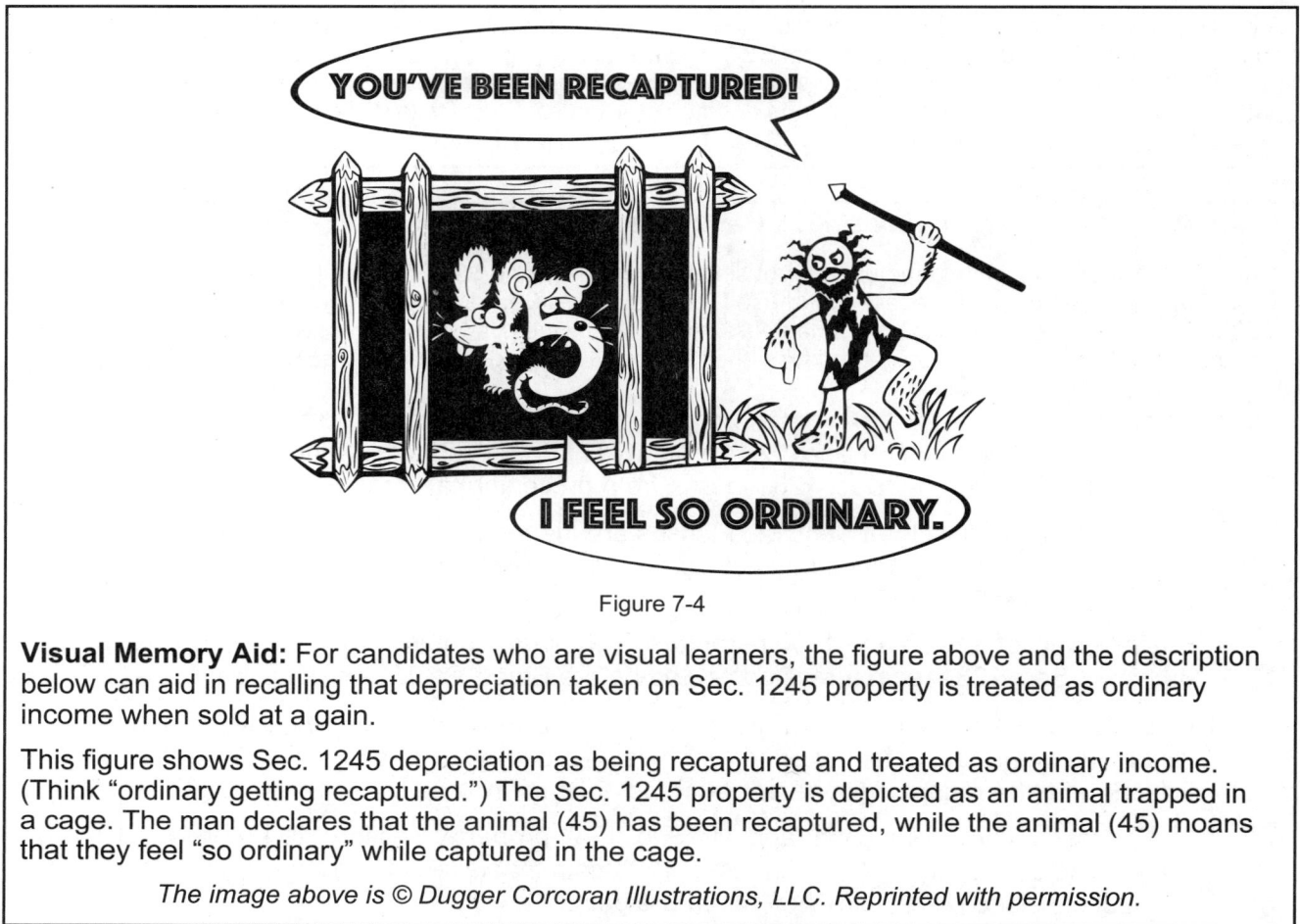

Visual Memory Aid: For candidates who are visual learners, the figure above and the description below can aid in recalling that depreciation taken on Sec. 1245 property is treated as ordinary income when sold at a gain.

This figure shows Sec. 1245 depreciation as being recaptured and treated as ordinary income. (Think "ordinary getting recaptured.") The Sec. 1245 property is depicted as an animal trapped in a cage. The man declares that the animal (45) has been recaptured, while the animal (45) moans that they feel "so ordinary" while captured in the cage.

3. Section 1245 property generally is depreciable personal property (tangible/intangible) used in a trade or business for over 12 months.
   a. Gain recognized on the disposition of Sec. 1245 property is OI to the extent of the lesser of all depreciation taken (including amounts expensed under Sec. 179) or gain realized.
      1) If gain realized is not recognized (like-kind exchanges, involuntary conversions, etc.), Sec. 1245 OI is limited to the sum of the following:
         a) Gain recognized
         b) FMV of property acquired that is not Sec. 1245 property and is not included in computing the recognized gain
      2) The recognized gain in excess of the depreciation taken may be treated as a gain from the sale or exchange of Sec. 1231 property.

EXAMPLE 7-6 Section 1245 Ordinary Income

Stewart purchased a machine for $20,000. He took $14,000 in depreciation before selling the asset for $9,000. The basis on the machine is $6,000 ($20,000 cost basis – $14,000 depreciation), so he has a $3,000 gain ($9,000 selling price – $6,000 basis). The $3,000 is ordinary income (the lesser of the gain or depreciation taken).

EXAMPLE 7-7 Section 1245 Ordinary Income and Section 1231 Gain

Assume the same information from Example 7-6 except Stewart sells the machine for $25,000. The realized gain is $19,000 ($25,000 – $6,000 basis). This gain has both Sec. 1245 gain (ordinary income) and Sec. 1231 gain (long-term capital). The $14,000 of depreciation taken on the equipment is a Sec. 1245 gain (the lesser of the gain or depreciation taken), and the remaining gain of $5,000 is a Sec. 1231 gain.

EXAMPLE 7-8 Section 1245 and 1231 Recapture

A business with a Sec. 1231 loss of $3,000 in Year 1 sells equipment in Year 2:

Sales Price	$15,000
Original Cost	10,000
Depreciation	6,000

The gain for Year 2 is $11,000 realized gain, of which $9,000 ($6,000 Sec. 1245 depreciation recapture + $3,000 Year 1 Sec. 1231 recapture of loss) is ordinary income. The remaining $2,000 ($11,000 realized – $9,000 ordinary income) is Sec. 1231 capital gain.

b. Examples of intangible amortizable personal Sec. 1245 property include

1) Leaseholds of Sec. 1245 property
2) Professional athletic contracts, e.g., baseball
3) Patents
4) Goodwill acquired in connection with the acquisition of a trade or business
5) Covenants not to compete

EXAMPLE 7-9 Intangible Section 1245 Property

The sale of a taxpayer's business includes goodwill with a tax basis of $15,000. The goodwill was acquired three years ago and amortized $1,000 per year. The goodwill was allocated $22,000 of the sale price; therefore, the $3,000 of total amortization ($1,000 × 3 years) is ordinary income to the taxpayer.

Section 1250 Ordinary Income

4. Section 1250 property is all depreciable real property, such as a building or its structural components.
   a. Examples of Sec. 1250 property include shopping malls, an apartment or office building, low-income housing, rented portions of residences, and escalators or elevators.
   b. Land is not Sec. 1250 property, but leases of land are Sec. 1250 intangible properties. Certain improvements to land may be treated as land, e.g., dams and irrigation systems.
   c. Sec. 1250 property is subject to its own recapture rules.
      1) The excess of accelerated depreciation taken over S-L depreciation is OI to the extent of gain recognized. This applies to purchases made before 1987.
         a) However, because most Sec. 1250 property (e.g., 39-year nonresidential real property and 27.5-year residential real property) has been depreciated using straight-line since 1987, it is relatively uncommon to encounter Sec. 1250 recapture.
      2) For property held less than 1 year, any depreciation taken is recaptured as OI.
      3) For corporations, the gain must be computed under both Sec. 1245 and 1250. If Sec. 1245 gain is larger than Sec. 1250 gain, 20% of the difference is characterized as ordinary income.
   d. If gain realized is not recognized (like-kind exchanges, involuntary conversions, etc.), Sec. 1250 OI is limited to the greater of the following:
      1) Recognized gain
      2) Excess of the potential Sec. 1250 OI over the FMV of Sec. 1250 property received

Section 1250 Unrecaptured Gain

5. For corporate and noncorporate taxpayers, any gain from the disposition of Sec. 1250 property that is not recaptured as ordinary income will qualify as Sec. 1231 gain.
   a. For individual taxpayers, any portion of that gain that is attributable to straight-line depreciation will be subject to a maximum capital gains rate of 25% (as opposed to 0/15/20%).

EXAMPLE 7-10 Section 1250 Unrecaptured Gain Taxed as Section 1231 Gain

Annie sold a building used in her trade or business for $110,000. Annie purchased the building several years ago for $100,000. At the time of the sale, the building has accumulated depreciation of $20,000. The building was depreciated using the straight-line method; Sec. 1250 recapture does not apply, and Annie has a Sec. 1231 gain of $30,000 ($110,000 amount realized – $80,000 adjusted basis). Of the $30,000 gain, $20,000 is attributable to straight-line depreciation and is classified as Sec. 1250 unrecaptured gain, which is subject to a maximum rate of 25%. The remaining $10,000 gain is taxed at a maximum rate of 0/15/20%.

Section 351 Exchange for Stock

6. Generally, no gain is recognized upon an exchange of property for all the stock of a newly formed corporation.
   a. Section 1245 and Sec. 1250 OI is limited to any gain recognized in a Sec. 351 transaction.

EXAMPLE 7-11 Section 1245 Recapture

On January 17, Year 1, Relief Corp. purchased and placed into service 7-year MACRS tangible property costing $100,000. On December 21, Year 4, Relief Corp. sold the property for $105,000 after taking $60,000 in MACRS depreciation deductions.

The adjusted basis of the property is $40,000 ($100,000 historical cost – $60,000 depreciation); therefore, Relief will recognize a gain of $65,000 ($105,000 selling price – $40,000 adjusted basis). Since this property qualifies for Sec. 1245 recapture, the gain is recaptured as ordinary income to the extent of the lesser of all depreciation taken or gain recognized. Thus, Relief will have $60,000 of Sec. 1245 (ordinary) gain. The remaining $5,000 of gain is Sec. 1231 (capital) gain.

EXAMPLE 7-12 Section 1245 Recapture

The facts from Example 7-11 apply, except Relief sold the property for $95,000.

Relief recognizes a gain of $55,000 ($95,000 selling price – $40,000 adjusted basis). Since this property qualifies for Sec. 1245 recapture, the gain is recaptured as ordinary income to the extent of the lesser of all depreciation taken or gain realized. Thus, Relief has $55,000 of Sec. 1245 gain.

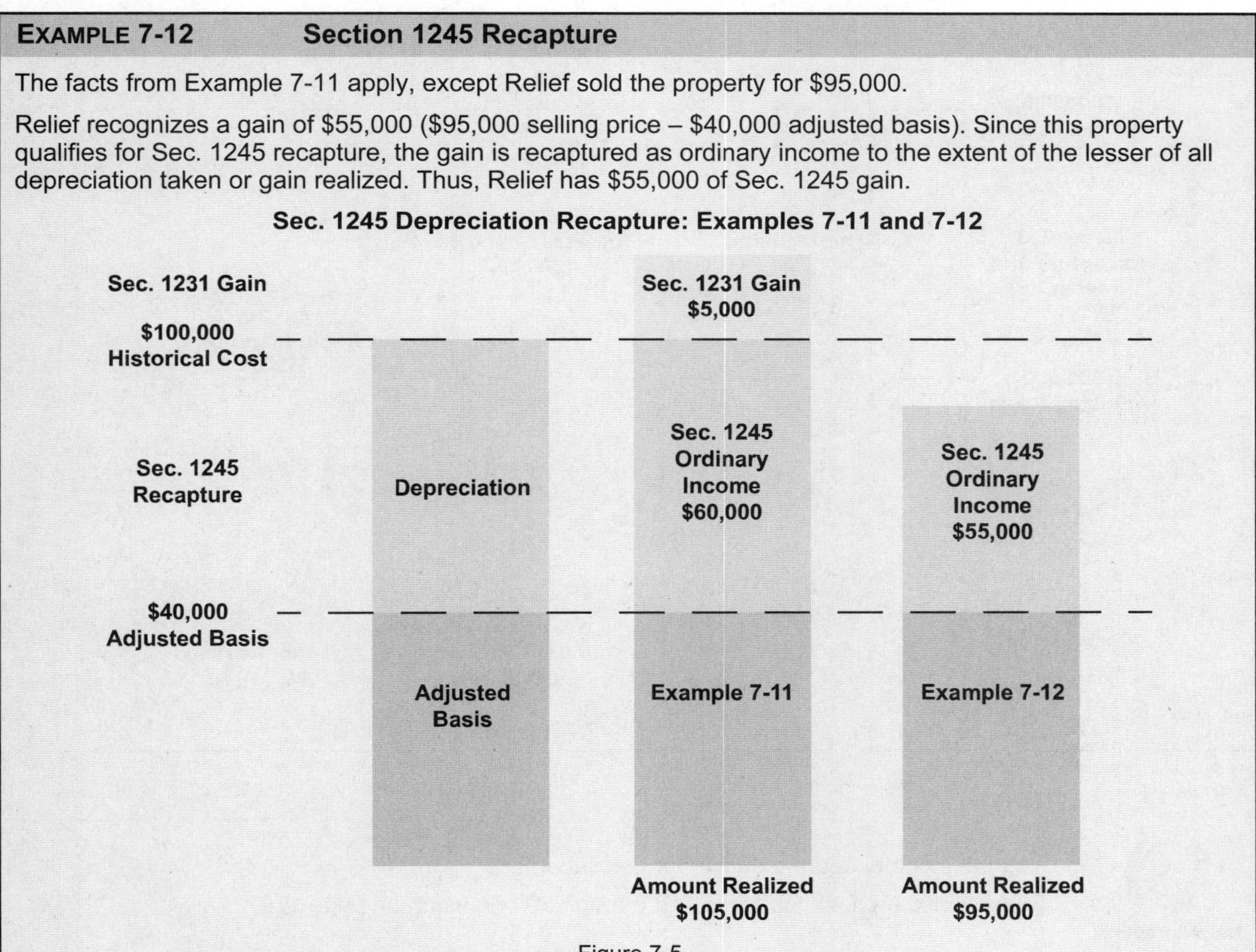

Figure 7-5

EXAMPLE 7-13 Section 1250 Unrecapture

Martha purchased and placed into service Sec. 1250 property costing $600,000. After 5 years, the property was sold for $650,000 after having taken $300,000 in straight-line depreciation deductions.

The adjusted basis of the property is $300,000 ($600,000 historical cost – $300,000 depreciation); therefore, Martha recognizes a gain of $350,000 ($650,000 selling price – $300,000 adjusted basis). Because the property was depreciated using straight-line depreciation, Sec. 1250 recapture will not apply. Thus, Martha will have $350,000 of Sec. 1231 (capital) gain, $300,000 of which is Sec. 1250 unrecaptured gain taxed at a maximum rate of 25%.

EXAMPLE 7-14 Section 1250 Unrecapture

The facts from Example 7-13 apply, except Martha sold the property for $400,000.

Martha recognizes a gain of $100,000 ($400,000 selling price – $300,000 adjusted basis). Since all of the gain is attributable to straight-line depreciation, Martha has $100,000 of Sec. 1250 unrecaptured gain.

Sec. 1250 Depreciation Recapture: Examples 7-13 and 7-14

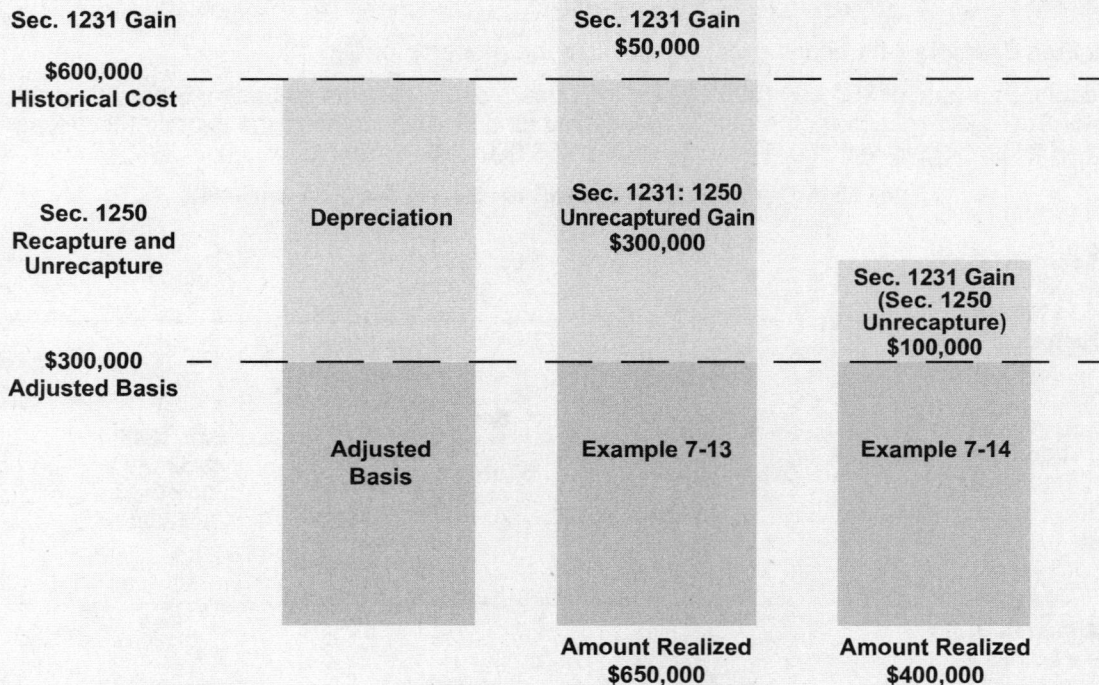

Figure 7-6

You have completed the outline for this subunit.
Study multiple-choice questions 16 through 20 beginning on page 179.

QUESTIONS

7.1 Depreciation Methods

1. In order to determine the MACRS deduction using the percentage tables, all of the following must be determined EXCEPT

A. The basis of the property.

B. The recovery period.

C. The declining balance rate.

D. The placed-in-service date.

Answer (C) is correct.

REQUIRED: The item not used in the MACRS percentage tables.

DISCUSSION: The percentage tables are based on the depreciation method, recovery period, and convention. An applicable percentage is determined each year by matching the year of the recovery period with the placed-in-service date. The percentages in the tables are applied to the unadjusted basis of the property each year to determine the MACRS deduction. Any declining balance rate is built into the tables.

2. The K&L Partnership owned the following tangible property. Which one is NOT considered listed property?

A. An automobile.

B. A video camera.

C. Recreational property used for personal use 40% of the time.

D. A truck weighing 17,000 pounds designed to carry cargo.

Answer (D) is correct.

REQUIRED: The item that is not considered listed property.

DISCUSSION: Depreciation of listed property is limited by reference to qualified business use. Listed property includes the following: passenger automobiles, other transportation vehicles (e.g., truck under 6,000 lbs.), and entertainment or recreational property (e.g., video camera).

3. Burt bought a new car for $64,000 on March 2, 2022. He will use the automobile 100% of the time in his business. The recovery period for passenger autos is 5 years. Burt elected out of additional first-year depreciation. What is Burt's depreciation for the year 2022?

A. $12,800

B. $11,200

C. $2,800

D. $18,000

Answer (B) is correct.

REQUIRED: The amount of depreciation allowed for an automobile used 100% in business.

DISCUSSION: If qualified business use exceeds 50% in the tax year in which listed property is placed in service, Sec. 179 current expensing and MACRS depreciation are allowable with respect to the qualified business use. However, in addition to the business-use requirements, limits are placed on the maximum MACRS deduction allowable for most passenger automobiles. For a vehicle placed in service in 2022, the depreciation limit in its first recovery year is $11,200 when election out of additional bonus depreciation is taken.

Answer (A) is incorrect. The amount of $12,800 is depreciation calculated under MACRS for the automobile without taking the limit of $11,200 into account.

Answer (C) is incorrect. Burt may take depreciation of $11,200 since regular MACRS exceeds the limit.

Answer (D) is incorrect. The amount of $18,000 is allowable depreciation for the second year. First year depreciation is limited to $11,200 since regular MACRS exceeds the limit.

4. Most tangible depreciable property falls within the general rule of MACRS. However, the law requires use of the ADS for certain property. ADS must be used for all of the following EXCEPT

A. Tax-exempt use property.

B. Tax-exempt bond-financed property.

C. Tangible personal property.

D. Tangible property used predominantly outside the United States during the year.

Answer (C) is correct.

REQUIRED: The property not required to use ADS.

DISCUSSION: MACRS provides two systems for depreciating property: the general depreciation system (GDS) and the alternative depreciation system (ADS). Although GDS is used for most property, ADS is required by law for any tangible property used predominantly outside the United States, any tax-exempt use property, and any tax-exempt bond-financed property. Use of ADS for tangible personal property is an election, not a requirement.

5. Which of the following is a true statement concerning depreciation of automobiles placed in service during 2022?

A. The amount of depreciation expense is limited to $11,200 in the first year, not including bonus depreciation.

B. The amount of depreciation is limited to $18,000 per year.

C. If the automobile is used 50% or less for business use, no depreciation is allowed.

D. If the use of an automobile for business decreases to 50% or less after the first year, only the current and subsequent years' depreciation will be affected.

Answer (A) is correct.

REQUIRED: The true statement concerning depreciation of automobiles placed in service in 2022.

DISCUSSION: Section 280F limits the depreciation on automobiles. The maximum amount of depreciation deductible in the first year for automobiles acquired in 2022 is $11,200 if election out of the bonus depreciation is made. This amount is reduced if business use is less than 100%.

Answer (B) is incorrect. Depreciation after the first year is limited to $18,000 in the second year, $10,800 in the third year, and $6,460 per year thereafter. **Answer (C) is incorrect.** Depreciation for an automobile used 50% or less in business is computed by the alternative depreciation system. **Answer (D) is incorrect.** If an automobile's use decreases to 50% or less in subsequent years, any depreciation in prior years in excess of the alternative depreciation system is included in gross income for the years in which the business use decreased to 50% or less.

7.2 Section 179 Expense

6. The maximum Sec. 179 expense you can elect to deduct for property you placed in service in tax year 2022 is

A. $2,700,000

B. $1,050,000

C. $1,080,000

D. $1,700,000

Answer (C) is correct.

REQUIRED: The maximum Sec. 179 expense.

DISCUSSION: A person may elect to deduct all or part of the cost of Sec. 179 property. Section 179 expense is treated as depreciation, and it reduces the basis in the property prior to any computation for depreciation for the year. The Sec. 179 expense for 2022 is $1,080,000.

Answer (A) is incorrect. The maximum amount of investment allowed is $2,700,000. **Answer (B) is incorrect.** The maximum Sec. 179 expense in 2021 was $1,050,000. **Answer (D) is incorrect.** The Sec. 179 expense for 2022 is $1,080,000.

7. On January 15, 2022, Amber purchased a car for $20,000. She used the car 75% for business during 2022. What is the maximum Sec. 179 deduction and depreciation Amber may elect to claim on her income tax return for 2022, assuming she forgoes additional first-year depreciation?

A. $8,400

B. $11,200

C. $15,000

D. $20,000

Answer (A) is correct.

REQUIRED: The Sec. 179 expense deduction in 2022.

DISCUSSION: In 2022, Sec. 179 allows a taxpayer to treat up to $1,080,000 of the cost of Sec. 179 property acquired as an expense. Only the 75% portion of the automobile used for business will qualify, however. Therefore, the Sec. 179 expense would normally be $15,000 ($20,000 × 75%).

But Sec. 280F limits the first-year capital recovery deduction for automobiles to $11,200 for 2022. The capital recovery deductions include the amount expensed under Sec. 179 and depreciation. This amount must be reduced by personal use for the automobile during the year. The redetermined amount of $8,400 is the limit times the percentage of business/investment use during the year ($11,200 × 75%).

Answer (B) is incorrect. The deduction is limited to the percentage used in business. **Answer (C) is incorrect.** The limit on first-year capital recovery deduction for automobiles is $11,200. **Answer (D) is incorrect.** The limit on first-year capital recovery deduction for automobiles is $11,200, and only the percentage used in business is allowed.

8. In 2022, Walt Sheen purchased and placed in service a packaging machine at a cost of $2,800,000. He had $6,000 taxable income from his business before considering the deduction allowed under Sec. 179. What is Walt's allowable Sec. 179 deduction for 2022?

A. $1,080,000

B. $980,000

C. $6,000

D. $0

Answer (C) is correct.

REQUIRED: The Sec. 179 expense deduction.

DISCUSSION: Section 179 allows a taxpayer to treat up to $1,080,000 of the cost of Sec. 179 property acquired in 2022 as an expense rather than as a capital expenditure. There are certain limitations that can reduce the allowable deduction. One limitation is that the amount deductible under Sec. 179 must be reduced by the amount by which the cost of Sec. 179 property placed in service during the year exceeds $2,700,000. Walt's deduction is reduced from $1,080,000 to $980,000 by this limitation. Another limitation is that the total cost that can be deducted is limited to the taxable income from the active conduct of any trade or business during the tax year. Walt had only $6,000 of taxable income. Because this amount is smaller than either the general rule or the limitation based on property placed in service, his deduction is limited to $6,000. The remaining $974,000 ($980,000 – $6,000) may be carried forward to 2023.

Answer (A) is incorrect. The entire $1,080,000 must be reduced by personal property placed in service exceeding $2,700,000 and limited to taxable income. **Answer (B) is incorrect.** The total cost that can be deducted is limited to the taxable income from the active conduct of any trade or business during the tax year. **Answer (D) is incorrect.** A Sec. 179 deduction is available for 2022.

9. In 2022, Mary Jane placed in service a machine that cost $3,300,000. If she placed no other Sec. 179 property in service during the year and forgoes additional first-year depreciation, how much is her Sec. 179 maximum dollar limit?

A. $1,050,000

B. $1,080,000

C. $0

D. $480,000

Answer (D) is correct.

REQUIRED: The allowable Sec. 179 expense deduction.

DISCUSSION: Section 179 allows a taxpayer to treat up to $1,080,000 of the cost of Sec. 179 property acquired in 2022 as an expense rather than as a capital expenditure. There are certain limitations that can reduce the allowable deduction. One limitation is that the amount deductible under Sec. 179 must be reduced by the amount by which the cost of Sec. 179 property placed in service during the year exceeds $2,700,000. Mary Jane's deduction is reduced from $1,080,000 to $480,000 [$1,080,000 – ($3,300,000 – $2,700,000)].

Answer (A) is incorrect. The amount of $1,050,000 is the 2021 limit before reduction for purchases exceeding $2,700,000. **Answer (B) is incorrect.** The entire $1,080,000 must be reduced by personal property placed in service exceeding $2,700,000 and limited to taxable income. **Answer (C) is incorrect.** A Sec. 179 deduction is available for 2022.

7.3 Amortization

10. Jeanne incurred start-up costs for her new business, which opened October 1, 2022. The costs were for advertising of $1,000, a market analysis survey of $2,500, employee training costs of $6,000, and travel costs for securing prospective distributions of $2,500. What is the maximum amount of the amortizable costs that may be deducted in 2022?

A. $12,000

B. $5,000

C. $5,117

D. $800

Answer (C) is correct.

REQUIRED: The deduction of amortizable start-up expenses.

DISCUSSION: Taxpayers may elect to deduct start-up expenditures paid or accrued up to $5,000 in the tax year the trade or business begins. A taxpayer is deemed to have made the election. The $5,000 deduction amount is reduced dollar-for-dollar when start-up costs exceed $50,000. Taxpayers must amortize the remaining balance over 180 months.

Advertising	$ 1,000
Market analysis survey	2,500
Employee training costs	6,000
Travel costs	2,500
Total start-up expenditures	$12,000

Initial deduction	$ 5,000
Current-year amortization ($7,000 × 3/180 months)	117
Total 2022 deduction	$ 5,117

Answer (A) is incorrect. After the initial $5,000 deduction, the remaining cost must be amortized over 180 months. **Answer (B) is incorrect.** Jeanne is able to include the current year's amortization as well as the $5,000. **Answer (D) is incorrect.** The amount of $800 is 1 full year's amortization of the $12,000 and does not include the $5,000 initial deduction.

11. Michael James purchased a travel agency on July 1, 2022, and immediately took over the business. The purchase contract included the following items as part of the purchase price:

- Goodwill valued at $60,000.
- Workforce in place valued at $30,000.
- Trademark valued at $60,000.
- Government permit valued at $30,000.

What is the proper amount of Michael's Internal Revenue Code Sec. 197 amortization expense for 2022, assuming Michael is a calendar-year taxpayer?

A. $90,000

B. $30,000

C. $6,000

D. $12,000

Answer (C) is correct.

REQUIRED: The amount of amortization expense of intangibles for 2022.

DISCUSSION: Section 197 states that the cost of certain intangibles acquired in connection with the conduct of a trade or business or income-producing activity is amortized over a 15-year period, beginning with the month in which the intangible is acquired. The total cost of the intangibles equals $180,000 ($60,000 goodwill + $30,000 workforce + $60,000 trademark + $30,000 government permit). This amount is amortized over 180 months. Michael James may only deduct $6,000 in 2022 [$180,000 × (6 months ÷ 180 months)].

Answer (A) is incorrect. Half of the total amount of intangibles capitalized is $90,000. These intangibles must be amortized over the 180-month period. **Answer (B) is incorrect.** The amortization period is not 6 years. **Answer (D) is incorrect.** The business was not acquired until July 1, 2022. Thus, only 6 months of amortization expense can be taken in 2022.

12. All of the following are considered Sec. 197 intangibles EXCEPT

A. Goodwill.

B. An interest under an existing lease of tangible property.

C. A trademark or trade name.

D. Information bases, including lists or other information, regarding current or future customers.

Answer (B) is correct.

REQUIRED: The item that is not a Sec. 197 intangible.

DISCUSSION: The following intangibles are Sec. 197 intangibles: goodwill, going-concern value, and covenants not to compete entered into in connection with a trade or business acquisition; workforce in place; information base; know-how; any customer- or supplier-based intangible; any license, permit, or other right granted by a governmental unit or agency; and any franchise, trademark, or trade name.

13. In 2020, Nancy leased a building for use in her business. She signed a 6-year lease with an option for an additional 3 years. In 2022, she made leasehold improvements to the building, costing a total of $8,200. Nancy must

A. Amortize the improvements over the remaining term of the initial lease period.

B. Amortize the improvements over the remaining term of the initial lease period, plus the option period.

C. Depreciate the improvements using the modified cost recovery system (MACRS).

D. Deduct the cost of the improvements as a current expense.

Answer (C) is correct.

REQUIRED: The proper method of capital recovery for leasehold improvements.

DISCUSSION: The cost of an addition or improvement made by the lessee to real property subject to MACRS is depreciated in the same manner as the property would be if the property had been placed in service at the same time as the addition or improvement without regard to the lease term.

7.4 Depletion

14. Mark, a 50% partner in the X & Y Partnership, uses the percentage method to compute his depletion allowance for the gas and oil property owned by the partnership. His allocable share of the property is $100,000. The fair market value of the property also is $100,000. His taxable income for 2022 equals $65,000. The percentage depletion rate is 15% for natural gas and oil sold. X & Y is a small producer, and the average daily production does not exceed the depletable oil and gas quantity. Mark's share of the gross sale of oil and gas deposits was $30,000. What is Mark's depletion deduction for 2022?

A. $4,500

B. $9,750

C. $9,000

D. $5,250

Answer (A) is correct.

REQUIRED: The amount of depletion deduction for a partner using the percentage method.

DISCUSSION: Percentage depletion, which allows deduction in excess of capital investment, is the lower of 50% of the person's TI before depletion (100% in the case of oil and gas property) or a percentage (specified by statute) of gross income from the property less related rents or royalties paid or incurred. Publication 535 states, "If you are an independent producer or royalty owner, you figure percentage depletion using a rate of 15% of the gross income from the property based on your average daily production of domestic crude oil or domestic natural gas up to your depletable oil or natural gas quantity." Accordingly, 15% of the gross profit is $4,500 ($30,000 × 15%). Since $4,500 is less than $65,000 (100% of taxable income limit), $4,500 is the amount of depletion Mark may take in 2022.

Answer (B) is incorrect. This amount is 15% of 65% of Mark's taxable income. **Answer (C) is incorrect.** This amount is 30% of the partnership's gross profit. **Answer (D) is incorrect.** This amount is 17.5% of the partnership's gross profit.

15. Which of the following would NOT qualify for a depletion deduction?

A. Gas well.

B. Timber lot.

C. Oil refinery.

D. Stone quarry.

Answer (C) is correct.

REQUIRED: The property not qualifying for a depletion deduction.

DISCUSSION: Depletion accounts for recovery of investment in natural resource property. A gas well, timber lot, and stone quarry are all natural resource properties and thereby qualify for the depletion deduction. The oil refinery, however, is a facility used to refine oil obtained from mineral property. It is depreciable property and does not qualify for the depletion deduction.

7.5 Depreciation Recapture

16. Maria owns a custom curtain/drapery business. She purchased three new sewing machines and, in a separate transaction, sold her three old machines for $6,000. She had bought the old machines for $5,000 and had properly claimed depreciation of $3,000. What is the amount and character of Maria's gain?

A. $0 ordinary gain and $4,000 Sec. 1231 gain.

B. $2,000 ordinary gain and $4,000 Sec. 1231 gain.

C. $3,000 ordinary gain and $1,000 Sec. 1231 gain.

D. $4,000 ordinary gain and $0 Sec. 1231 gain.

Answer (C) is correct.

REQUIRED: The amount and character of gain.

DISCUSSION: A gain on the sale or other disposition of Sec. 1245 property is taxed as ordinary income to the extent of all depreciation or amortization deductions previously claimed on the property. The amount treated as ordinary income is the lower of the excess of the amount realized or fair market value over the adjusted basis of the Sec. 1245 property or the previously allowed or allowable depreciation or amortization. The machines have an adjusted basis of $2,000 ($5,000 purchase price – $3,000 depreciation). Maria realizes a $4,000 gain on the sale ($6,000 selling price – $2,000 adjusted basis) and had previously allowable depreciation of $3,000. Therefore, Maria recognizes $3,000 of ordinary income and $1,000 of Sec. 1231 gain.

Answer (A) is incorrect. The sewing machines are subject to Sec. 1245 recapture. **Answer (B) is incorrect.** The realized gain is only $4,000. **Answer (D) is incorrect.** The previously allowable depreciation is less than the realized gain.

17. Which of the following statements is NOT true concerning residential rental property placed in service in 2022?

A. For property held less than 1 year, all depreciation is recaptured.

B. Depreciation is determined using the S-L method.

C. Depreciation is determined using an accelerated method.

D. Recovery period is 27 1/2 years.

Answer (C) is correct.

REQUIRED: The false statement concerning residential rental property.

DISCUSSION: Only residential rental property placed in service prior to 1987 used accelerated depreciation. For property placed in service after 1986, the S-L method applies.

Answer (A) is incorrect. Depreciation is recaptured when the property is held for less than a year. **Answer (B) is incorrect.** All post-1986 residential rental property uses the S-L method. **Answer (D) is incorrect.** The S-L recovery period for residential rental property is 27 1/2 years.

18. Sam files a calendar-year return. In February 2020, he purchased and placed in service for 100% use in his business a light-duty truck (5-year property) for a cost of $10,000. He used the half-year convention and figured his MACRS deductions for the truck were $2,000 in 2020 and $3,200 in 2021. He did not take the Sec. 179 deduction on it. He sold the truck in May 2022 for $7,000. The MACRS deduction in 2022, the year of sale, is $960 (1/2 of $1,920). How much of the gain will be treated as ordinary income in 2022?

A. $3,160

B. $2,200

C. $3,840

D. None of the answers are correct.

Answer (A) is correct.

REQUIRED: The amount of gain treated as ordinary income.

DISCUSSION: Sam purchased the truck for $10,000 and took $6,160 in depreciation, leaving a basis of $3,840. The gain on the sale is $3,160 ($7,000 selling price – $3,840 basis). Under Sec. 1245, if the gain is less than the depreciation taken, the entire gain is reported as ordinary income.

Answer (B) is incorrect. Sam is allowed to decrease his basis in the truck by the MACRS deduction he took in 2022 ($960). **Answer (C) is incorrect.** The amount of $3,840 represents the basis, not the amount of gain treated as ordinary income. **Answer (D) is incorrect.** Sam purchased the truck for $10,000 and took $6,160 in depreciation, leaving a basis of $3,840. The gain on the sale is $3,160 ($7,000 selling price – $3,840 basis). Under Sec. 1245, if the gain is less than the depreciation taken, the entire gain is reported as ordinary income.

19. A taxpayer acquired a rental house several years ago for $190,000. The taxpayer sold his rental house for $190,000 in May 2022. Under an accelerated method, the taxpayer's depreciation would have been $67,840. Under the S-L method, the taxpayer's depreciation is $64,960. How much Sec. 1250 gain did this taxpayer have classified as ordinary income when the house was sold?

A. $0

B. $2,880

C. $64,960

D. $67,840

Answer (A) is correct.

REQUIRED: The amount of Sec. 1250 gain that is recaptured as ordinary income.

DISCUSSION: Recapture of residential rental property as ordinary income is not required because residential rental property acquired after 1986 must be depreciated under the S-L method.

Answer (B) is incorrect. Accelerated depreciation does not apply to residential rental property acquired after 1986. **Answer (C) is incorrect.** S-L depreciation is not recaptured if the property is held for more than 1 year. **Answer (D) is incorrect.** Recapture of residential rental property as ordinary income is not required because it must be depreciated under the S-L method.

20. ABC Corp., a corporation that is not an S corporation, acquired a residential rental building on June 1, 2021, for $500,000. It sold the building March 1, 2022, for $700,000. In 2021, $13,636 of depreciation was deducted using the S-L method. What portion of ABC's gain is treated as ordinary income?

A. $0

B. $10,606

C. $13,636

D. $200,000

Answer (C) is correct.

REQUIRED: The gain recaptured as ordinary income.

DISCUSSION: The sale of the residential rental building resulted in a realized gain of $213,636 [$700,000 – ($500,000 – $13,636)]. The building is Sec. 1250 residential real property since it is excluded from Sec. 1245 property by Sec. 1245(a)(3) as in effect prior to the 1986 Tax Act. The depreciation for residential rental property is calculated using the S-L method; however, if held less than 1 year, all depreciation is recaptured as ordinary income.

Answer (A) is incorrect. The sale of the building results in Sec. 1231 gain less any depreciation recapture. **Answer (B) is incorrect.** The $10,606 for the first 2 months of depreciation in 2022 was never taken. **Answer (D) is incorrect.** The ordinary income is the depreciation previously taken, not the realized gain.

Go to Online Course

Access the **Gleim EA Premium Review System** featuring our SmartAdapt technology from your Gleim Personal Classroom to continue your studies.

You will experience a personalized study environment with exam-emulating multiple-choice questions.

STUDY UNIT EIGHT

CREDITS, LOSSES, AND ADDITIONAL TAXES

(13 pages of outline)

This is the final study unit to discuss reductions in tax liability that apply to all business entities. Business-specific credits may reduce an entity's tax due amount, while losses may reduce an entity's taxable income. Losses come from operations, casualty, and theft.

This study unit concludes with a brief explanation of additional business-related taxes for heavy vehicle use, farmers, and employer shared responsibility payments.

8.1 GENERAL BUSINESS CREDIT (SEC. 38)

Tax credits are used to achieve policy objectives, such as encouraging energy conservation. A $1 credit reduces gross tax liability by $1.

1. The General Business Credit (GBC) is a set of more than 30 credits commonly available to businesses. The GBC is taken on Form 3800.
   a. The GBC includes, among others, credits for investment, research, work opportunity, disabled access, pension plan start-up, and childcare facilities.
2. Most credits are nonrefundable, meaning that once tax liability reaches zero, no more credits can be taken to produce refunds.

Overall Limit [Sec. 38(c)]

3. For individuals, the GBC is limited to net income tax minus the greater of (a) the tentative alternative minimum tax or (b) 25% of net regular tax liability over $25,000.

EXAMPLE 8-1 General Business Credit

Taxpayer has a regular tax of $60,000 and a tentative alternative minimum tax of $57,000. The taxpayer also has $10,000 of potential general business credits. Since the regular tax exceeds the tentative minimum tax, there is no alternative minimum tax. The taxpayer is allowed a General Business Credit computed as follows:

$60,000	Regular tax
(0)	Alternative minimum tax
$60,000	Income tax
(0)	Nonrefundable credits other than General Business Credit
$60,000	Net income tax
(57,000)	Greater of tentative alternative minimum tax or 25% of net regular tax over $25,000
$ 3,000	General Business Credit

   a. Net income tax is the sum of regular income tax and alternative minimum tax liability, reduced by nonrefundable credits other than those that comprise the General Business Credit.

b. Net regular tax is the taxpayer's regular income tax liability (i.e., without alternative minimum tax) reduced by nonrefundable credits.

c. Excess over the limit may be allowable as a current deduction to the extent it is attributable to the Work Opportunity Credit, among other credits.

d. Any excess of the combined GBC over the limit (and not allowed as a current deduction) may be carried back 1 year and forward 20 years as a credit. It is carried to the earliest year to which it could be used, then to the next, and so on.

Small Employer Insurance Credit (Sec. 45R)

NOTE: Throughout this course, "PPACA" instead of "ACA" is used to identify significant topics from the Patient Protection and Affordable Care Act in order to avoid confusion with the Applicable Credit Amount for gift and estate taxes.

4. As part of PPACA, the Small Employer Health Insurance Tax Credit provides a 50% credit for the cost of premiums paid toward health insurance coverage.
   a. The small employer must contribute at least 50% of the premium cost.
   b. The credit is available to small employers with 25 or fewer employees and average annual wages of less than $57,400 (2022).
   c. A sole proprietor, a partner, a shareholder owning more than 2% of an S corporation, and any owner of more than 5% of other businesses are not employees for purposes of the credit. Family members of any business are generally excluded.
      1) Seasonal employees who work for 120 days or fewer for the business in a year are excluded.
   d. The credit is limited to 2 consecutive years.
   e. The credit reduces the deduction for health insurance premiums.

Disabled Access Credit (Sec. 44)

5. A credit for a portion of qualifying expenditures to provide access to disabled persons is available as a General Business Credit.
   a. Eligible persons are small businesses, including partnerships and S corporations, that, during the preceding tax year, did not have either more than 30 full-time employees or more than $1 million in gross receipts.
   b. Examples of qualifying access expenditures are payments to remove physical barriers, to modify equipment, and to install access ramps.
   c. Eligible access expenditures do not include expenditures related to a building that was first placed in service by the taxpayer.
   d. The credit is equal to 50% of qualifying expenditures that fall between a $250 threshold and a $10,250 cap.
   e. The credit is limited to $5,000 [($10,250 – $250) × 50%] for the tax year.
   f. The credit is not allowed for new buildings.
   g. The credit is computed on Form 8826, *Disabled Access Credit*.

Work Opportunity Tax Credit (WOTC) (Sec. 51)

6. Employers may claim a credit for wages paid to individuals from certain targeted group(s) during their first year of employment. The credit is taken on Form 5884.
   a. The employees must work at least 120 hours in a calendar year to be eligible for the credit.
      1) An employee who works at least 400 hours is eligible for the full 40% credit. An employee who works between 120 and 400 hours has a reduced credit of 25%.
   b. The maximum credit by qualifying class is shown below.

Targeted Group(s)	Applicable Wages	Maximum Credit	Calculation
Qualified summer youth employee	$3,000	$1,200	$3,000 × 40%
Long-term family assistance (first year)	$10,000	$4,000	$10,000 × 40%
Long-term family assistance (second year)	$10,000	$5,000	$10,000 × 50%
Qualified veterans	up to $24,000	$9,600	$24,000 × 40%
All other targeted groups	$6,000	$2,400	$6,000 × 40%

   c. Targeted groups include
      1) Qualified IV-A recipients of temporary assistance to needy families
      2) Qualified veterans
      3) Qualified ex-felons
      4) Designated community residents
      5) Vocational rehabilitation referrals
      6) Qualified supplemental nutrition assistance program (SNAP) benefits recipients
      7) Qualified SSI recipients
      8) Long-term family assistance recipients
      9) Qualified summer youth employees
      10) Qualified long-term unemployment recipients
   d. Qualified wages include
      1) Remuneration for employment
      2) Amount received under accident and health plans
      3) Contributions by employers to accident and health plans
      4) Educational assistance
      5) Dependent care expenses
   e. Any business deduction for the wages must be reduced by the amount of the credit.

Investment Tax Credit

7. Investment credit property is depreciable or amortizable property as listed below. To be eligible, some or all of the qualified investments must be certified by the Secretary of Treasury.

   a. The credit is claimed on Form 3468 and consists of the following five parts:

      1) (Business) Energy Credit
      2) Rehabilitation Credit
      3) Qualifying Advanced Coal Project Credit
      4) Qualifying Gasification Project Credit
      5) Qualifying Advanced Energy Project Credit

(Business) Energy Credit

   b. The credit is available to businesses that invest in energy-conserving property.

      1) The original use of the property must begin with the taxpayer.
      2) The credit is equal to the basis of the property placed in service during the year times the credit percentage.
      3) Qualified property and their corresponding energy percentages range from 10% to 30%.
      4) The property's basis for depreciation is reduced by 50% of the credit taken.

Rehabilitation Credit

   c. The credit is equal to 20% ratably over 5 years (i.e., 4% per year) for certified historic structures expenditures paid or incurred after 2017.

      1) The expenditures must exceed the larger of $5,000 or the structure's adjusted basis.
      2) The structure's basis for depreciation is reduced by the amount of the credit taken.

Qualifying Advanced Coal Project

   d. The credit is available for investment in qualified property that is used in a qualified advanced coal project. The details of a qualified project are beyond the scope of the EA exam.

      1) The original use of the property must begin with the taxpayer.
      2) The credit is equal to the basis of the property placed in service during the year times the credit percentage.
      3) Qualified property and their corresponding credit percentages are

         a) Integrated gasification combined cycle, 20%
         b) Other advanced coal-based projects, 15%
         c) Advanced coal-based generation technologies, 30%

Qualifying Gasification Project

   e. The credit is available for investments in qualified property used in a qualified gasification project. The credit is 20% of the basis, with an increase to 30% if 75% of carbon dioxide emissions are captured.

      1) Credit is disallowed for property if an Advanced Coal Credit is allowed.

Qualifying Advanced Energy Project

f. The Qualified Advanced Energy Project Credit is available for investment in qualified property used in a qualifying advanced energy project.

1) The credit is 30% of the basis.

2) Credit is disallowed for property available for the Energy Credit, the Advanced Coal Project Credit, or the Gasification Project Credit.

Research Credit

8. Eligible small businesses ($50 million or less in gross receipts) can claim a tax credit on Form 6765 for expenses relating to increasing research activities in a trade or business. This research must be undertaken for discovering information that is technological in nature, and its application must be intended for use in developing a new or improved business component of the taxpayer.

a. The following is a calculation of the credit for research:

  20% × (Qualified expenses for the year – Base period expenses)
+ 20% × (Basic research payments)
+ 20% × (Amounts paid to an energy research consortium for qualified energy research)
= Research Credit claimed

1) Qualified expenses represents all research expenses (not just in-house) for the taxpayer incurred while carrying on any trade or business.

a) Wages taken into account in determining the Work Opportunity Credit from qualified research expenses are excluded.

2) Base period expenses are calculated by multiplying the taxpayer's average gross receipts from the 4 preceding years by the taxpayer's fixed-base percentage.

a) The fixed-base percentage depends on whether the taxpayer is an existing company or a start-up company.

b) The maximum fixed-base percentage is 16%, and start-up companies must use a 3% fixed-base percentage.

b. Taxpayers may elect an alternative simplified credit equal to 14% of expenses in excess of 50% of the average expense for the preceding 3 years.

c. The credit is included as part of the General Business Credit described in Sec. 38 and may be subject to limitation and carryforward and carryback rules.

d. The cost of acquiring someone else's product or process does not qualify for the credit.

e. Research must be conducted within the U.S., including Puerto Rico, and U.S. possessions.

Pension Plan Start-Up Costs

9. A Pension Plan Start-Up Costs Credit is available for small employers (100 or fewer employees) for the first three tax years of the plan's existence.

a. The credit amount equals 50% of the start-up costs incurred to create or maintain a new employee retirement plan.

b. The credit limit is the greater of $500 or the lesser of $250 for each eligible employee who is not a highly compensated employee or $5,000.

Employer-Provided Childcare Credit

10. The Employer-Provided Childcare Credit was designed to create an incentive for small and medium-sized businesses to provide childcare for their employees.
    a. This credit applies to 25% of qualified expenses paid for employee childcare and 10% of qualified expenses paid for childcare resource and referral services.
    b. This credit is limited to $150,000 each year, and it is filed on Form 8882.
    c. Costs do not qualify for a Sec. 179 expensing election.

FICA Tip Credit

11. A nonrefundable tax credit is allowed for an employer's portion of FICA taxes paid (incurred) on employee cash tips exceeding the tips satisfying minimum wage requirements.

Paid Family and Medical Leave Credit

12. Through 2025, employers who provide paid family and medical leave to their employees may take a credit of 12.5% to 25% of those wages paid. The 12.5% applies to payments of at least 50% of the wages normally paid to the employee, and increases by 0.25% (but not above 25%), for each percentage increase above 50%. The credit is filed on Form 8994.
    a. The leave can be for any of the following relating to an employee:
        1) Birth of a child and care for that child
        2) Adoption and foster care placement of a child with the employee
        3) Care for spouse, child, or parent with a serious health condition
        4) Employee being unable to perform work functions due to health condition
        5) Urgent need due to spouse, child, or parent being on active military duty
        6) Care for a service member (spouse, child, parent, or next of kin)
    b. Any of the pay that is required by state or local law does not count towards the 50%.
    c. The employee's prior-year compensation must be $81,000 or less to qualify for the credit.
    d. The employer must provide at least 2 weeks of leave to full-time employees and a prorated amount of leave for part-time employees.
    e. The employer must have a written policy in place.

Foreign Tax Credit

13. The Foreign Tax Credit (FTC) is an alternative to deduction of the tax and equals the lesser of
    a. Foreign taxes paid/accrued during the tax year or
    b. The portion of U.S. tax liability (before credits) attributed to all foreign-earned income.

$$\text{FTC} = \text{U.S. income tax}^{1} \times \frac{\text{Foreign-earned taxable income}^{2}}{\text{Worldwide taxable income}}$$

[1] Before the FTC
[2] Not more than worldwide taxable income

        1) If the credit is limited to the amount in b. above, unused foreign tax credits will equal the difference between a. and b.
        2) Unused credits can be carried back for 1 year and then carried forward for 10 years.

Stop & Review

You have completed the outline for this subunit.
Study multiple-choice questions 1 through 9 beginning on page 194.

8.2 NET OPERATING LOSS (NOL)

1. A net operating loss occurs when business expenses exceed business income.
2. The NOL is deductible when carried to a year in which there is taxable income.
3. Applying NOLs as a deduction. The treatment of an NOL in the current year depends on the year in which the NOL originally arose (i.e., the year the loss was incurred).
   a. NOLs that arise in 2021 and later may be carried forward indefinitely, but no carryback is allowed. The carryover is limited to 80% of the taxable income for the year it is carried to. Any excess continues to carryover to future years until exhausted.
   b. NOLs for tax years 2018, 2019, and 2020 may be carried back 5 years and carried forward indefinitely. The carryback or carryforward period may offset the taxpayer's entire taxable income until 2021.
   c. When utilizing NOLs, the oldest NOL is used first.
4. Although NOLs are typically business deductions, an individual may have an NOL.
5. To calculate NOL, start with taxable income (a negative amount) and adjust as follows:
   a. Add back NOLs carried forward into the current tax year.
   b. Add back the Qualified Business Income Deduction (discussed in Study Unit 5, Subunit 9).
   c. Add back excess of nonbusiness deductions over nonbusiness income.
      1) For this purpose, nonbusiness deductions are
         a) Alimony (for divorce agreements executed before 2019),
         b) Contributions to self-employed retirement plans,
         c) Loss from the sale of investment property, and
         d) Either the standard deduction or all itemized deductions, except for casualty and theft losses, and state income tax on trade or business income.

         NOTE: Business deductions include all (even personal) casualty losses.
      2) Nonbusiness income includes
         a) Interest,
         b) Dividends,
         c) Gain on the sale of investment property, and
         d) Treasure trove.
      3) Rents and wages are business income.

EXAMPLE 8-2 NOL

For 2022, Sally realized a $30,000 net loss (sales of $200,000 less expenses of $230,000) from operating a sole proprietorship without regard to dispositions of property other than inventory. Other than this, the income tax return showed gross income of $10,000 ($4,500 of wages, $1,000 interest on personal savings, and a $4,500 long-term capital gain on business property). The excess of deductions over income was $32,950 ($10,000 gross income – $30,000 loss from business operations – $12,950 standard deduction).

To compute Sally's NOL, add back the $11,950 excess of nonbusiness deductions over nonbusiness income ($12,950 standard deduction – $1,000 interest).

Thus, Sally's NOL for the current tax year is $21,000 [$(32,950) "negative taxable income" + $11,950].

6. Capital losses. The amount of capital loss (CL) included in the NOL of a noncorporate taxpayer is limited. Before the limit is applied, the CL must be separated into business CL and nonbusiness CL. Capital losses are included in the NOL only as follows:
   a. Nonbusiness CL is deducted to the extent of nonbusiness capital gain (CG). Any excess nonbusiness CL is not deductible.
   b. If nonbusiness CG exceeds nonbusiness CL, such excess is applied against any excess of nonbusiness deductions over nonbusiness income.
   c. If nonbusiness CG exceeds excess nonbusiness deductions, the excess nonbusiness CG may offset business CL. Business CL may also be deducted to the extent of business CG.
7. Threshold for excess business loss.
   a. Excess business losses of a taxpayer other than a corporation are not allowed. An excess business loss is the excess of aggregate deduction attributable to the taxpayer's trades or businesses over the sum of the aggregate gross income or gain from all their trades or businesses plus a threshold amount. The threshold amount is adjusted annually for inflation.
   b. For partnerships and S corporations the limit on excess business losses is applied at the partner or shareholder level. Each partner's distributive share or each S corporation shareholder's pro rata share of items of income, gain, deduction, or loss of the partnership or S corporation is taken into account by the partner or shareholder in applying the excess business loss rules to the partner's or shareholder's tax year with or within which the partnership's or S corporation's tax year ends.
   c. Excess business losses above the threshold are carried forward and treated as part of the taxpayer's NOL carryforward, subject to the 80% of taxable income limitation.
   d. For 2022, in determining a taxpayer's excess business loss, the threshold amount is $270,000 ($540,000 for joint returns).
8. A hobby is an activity for which profit is not a primary motive.
   a. An activity is presumed not to be a hobby if profits result in any 3 of 5 consecutive tax years (in the case of breeding, training, showing, or racing horses, 2 of 7 consecutive years).
   b. A few factors used to determine whether an activity is carried on for profit are
      1) The manner in which the taxpayer carries on the activity;
      2) The expertise of the taxpayer or advisors;
      3) The time and effort expended by the taxpayer in carrying on the activity;
      4) The expectation that assets used in the activity may appreciate in value;
      5) The success of the taxpayer in carrying on other similar or dissimilar activities;
      6) The taxpayer's history of income or losses with respect to the activity;
      7) The amount of occasional profits, if any, that are earned;
      8) The financial status of the taxpayer; and
      9) Elements of personal pleasure or recreation.
9. **Before the TCJA**, hobby expenses to the extent of income derived from the activity were deducted as an itemized deduction on Schedule A (Form 1040), *Itemized Deductions*, subject to the 2% floor on miscellaneous deductions.

10. The TCJA suspended the deductions subject to the 2% floor on miscellaneous deductions for tax years beginning after December 31, 2017, and before January 1, 2026.
    a. For 2022, hobby expenses to the extent of income derived from the activity are not deductible.

You have completed the outline for this subunit.

Study multiple-choice questions 10 through 13 beginning on page 197.

8.3 CASUALTY AND THEFT LOSSES

The IRC allows deductions for losses caused by theft or casualties, whether business or personal. However, as of 2018, personal casualty and theft losses only apply to **federally declared disasters** and **losses to the extent of casualty gains**.

Casualty

1. Casualty loss arises from a sudden, unexpected, or unusual event caused by an external force, such as fire, storm, shipwreck, earthquake, sonic boom, etc.
    a. Losses resulting from ordinary accidents, e.g., dropping a vase, or from progressive deterioration, e.g., rust or insect damage, are not deductible.
    b. The cost of protecting property against a casualty or theft is not part of a casualty or theft loss.

Theft

2. Theft includes robbery, larceny, and the like. It also may include loss from extortion, blackmail, etc. Not generally included in the definition of theft is misplacing or losing items or having them confiscated by a foreign government.
    a. In general, the loss amount is the lesser of the decline in FMV or the AB minus insurance reimbursements. However, if business or investment property is completely lost or stolen, FMV is disregarded and AB is used to compute the loss.

EXAMPLE 8-3 Casualty Losses

Kaitlyn is a veterinarian. She had business equipment with a FMV of $15,000 and adjusted basis of $20,000 and had a business computer with a FMV of $1,000 and adjusted basis of $500. Both the equipment and computer were completely destroyed by a storm. She did not have insurance on these assets. Kaitlyn is able to deduct a loss of the combined adjusted bases since the assets are business assets equal to $20,500 ($20,000 + $500). If the same assets were personal-use assets and not business assets, and the storm was a federally declared disaster, the loss would be the lower of the adjusted basis or decline in fair market value (subject to a per-event and AGI floor). Since there was one event, look at the items' combined value. If it was not a federally declared disaster, there would be no loss deduction for personal-use assets.

    b. Reimbursement
        1) Only the amount of loss not compensated by insurance is deductible.
        2) Any excess recovered over the amount of property basis is gain.
    c. Timing
        1) A casualty loss is deductible in the tax year in which it occurs.
        2) A theft loss is deductible when it is discovered.

Loss of Inventory

3. There are two ways a taxpayer can deduct a casualty or theft loss of inventory, including items held for sale to customers.
   a. Deduct the loss through the increase in the cost of goods sold by properly reporting opening and closing inventories. When using this method, do not claim this loss again as a casualty or theft loss. Any insurance or other reimbursement received for the loss is included in gross income when received.
   b. Eliminate the affected inventory items from cost of goods sold by making a downward adjustment to opening inventory or purchases. The amount of the loss is reduced by the reimbursement received. The reimbursement is not included in gross income. If the taxpayer does not receive the reimbursement by the end of the year, the taxpayer may not claim a loss to the extent a reasonable prospect of recovery exists.

Business or Income-Producing Property

4. If a taxpayer has business or income-producing property, such as rental property, and it is stolen or completely destroyed, the decrease in FMV is not considered. The loss is calculated as shown to the right:

	Adjusted basis
–	Salvage value
–	Insurance reimbursement
=	Deductible loss

   a. When business property is partially destroyed, the deductible amount is the lesser of the decline in FMV or the property's adjusted basis (prior to the loss).

Federally Declared Disaster Election

5. A taxpayer is subject to a special rule if (s)he sustains a loss from a federally (synonymous with presidentially) declared disaster. Disaster loss treatment is available when property is rendered unsafe due to the disaster in the area and is ordered to be relocated or demolished by the state or local government.
   a. The taxpayer has the option of deducting the loss on
      1) The return for the year in which the loss actually occurred or
      2) The preceding year's return (by filing an amended return).
         a) Revocation of the election may be made before expiration of time for filing the return for the year of loss.
         b) A disaster loss deduction is computed the same as a casualty loss.
   b. The IRS grants administrative relief to taxpayers who are affected by a federally declared disaster area by suspending examination and collection actions.
      1) Examination and collection actions that can be precluded or suspended include tax return audits, mailings of notices, and other actions involving the collection of overdue taxes.
      2) The IRS may abate the interest on the underpaid income tax for the length of any extension period granted for filing income tax returns. However, abatement of interest by the IRS is not mandatory.

You have completed the outline for this subunit.

Study multiple-choice questions 14 through 17 beginning on page 199.

8.4 ADDITIONAL TAXES

Heavy Vehicle Use Tax

1. Taxpayers operating qualified vehicles are subject to an excise tax for highway use based on weight.
   a. A person is subject to the highway use tax if his or her vehicle meets all of the following tests:
      1) It is a highway motor vehicle.
      2) It is registered for highway use.
      3) It is used on public highways.
      4) It has a taxable gross weight of at least 55,000 pounds.
   b. The taxable gross weight of a vehicle (other than a bus) is the total of
      1) The actual unloaded weight of the vehicle fully equipped for service,
      2) The actual unloaded weight of any trailers or semitrailers fully equipped for service customarily used in combination with the vehicle, and
      3) The weight of the maximum load customarily carried on the vehicle and on any trailers or semitrailers customarily used in combination with the vehicle.
   c. Filing requirements. Every person with a highway motor vehicle registered in his or her name at the time of its first taxable use must file a Form 2290, *Heavy Highway Vehicle Use Tax Return*. The tax period runs from July 1 of the current year through June 30 of the next year.
      1) Form 2290 is due the last day of the month following the month that the vehicle is first used on the public highways. There is an exception if the last day of the month falls on a weekend or legal holiday.
      2) A taxpayer is eligible for credit or refund from the heavy vehicle use tax if the vehicle is destroyed, stolen, or meets the low mileage limit requirement during the tax period.
   d. If a vehicle is purchased from another registered vehicle owner who had used the vehicle during the tax period, the original owner owes the tax for the whole tax period.
      1) If the tax is not paid and the new owner uses the vehicle, the new owner is liable for the tax.
   e. If a vehicle is expected to be used on public highways for 5,000 miles or less (7,500 miles or less for agricultural vehicles) during a certain period, the liability for the heavy vehicle use tax can be suspended for that period.

Farmers' Other Taxes

2. Farmers are subject to unique tax laws for fuel tax credits and employment taxes.
   a. A farmer may claim a credit or refund of excise taxes included in the price of fuel used on a farm for farming purposes if (s)he is the owner, tenant, or operator of a farm.
      1) The credit is available for excise taxes on gasoline, special motor fuel, compressed natural gas, and aviation fuel used on a farm for farming purposes.
      2) A credit cannot be claimed for a tax on diesel fuel.
   b. Employment taxes. Farmers who have employees may have to pay employer taxes, withhold employee Social Security and Medicare taxes, and withhold income tax.
      1) A farmer-employer may have to pay Social Security and Medicare taxes if (s)he has one or more agricultural employees, including parents, children 18 years of age or older, or a spouse, and the farmer meets either of the following tests:
         a) Paid the employee $150 or more in cash wages during the year
         b) Paid wages of $2,500 or more during the year to all employees
   c. A farmer must pay federal unemployment tax if either cash wages of $20,000 or more are paid to farm workers in any calendar quarter during the current or preceding year or 10 or more farm workers are employed for at least 1 day during each of 20 different calendar weeks during the current or preceding calendar year.

Employer Shared Responsibility

3. Under PPACA, applicable large employers (ALEs) must either (a) offer minimum essential coverage to 95% of full-time employees that is (1) affordable and (2) provides minimum value to all full-time employees and their dependents or (b) make an employer shared responsibility payment (i.e., employer mandate or "pay-or-play provision"). There are two types of responsibility payments based on the above two qualifications, but an employer can only be liable for one payment, not both.
   a. ALEs are employers with an average of 50 full-time employees (including full-time-equivalent employees) during the preceding year. For purposes of the employer shared responsibility provisions, a full-time employee is, for a calendar month, an employee employed on average at least 30 hours of service per week or 120 hours of service per calendar month.
      1) All types of employers can be ALEs, including tax-exempt organizations and government entities.
      2) Generally, entities with a common owner or that are otherwise related are combined and treated as a single employer for determining ALE status.

EXAMPLE 8-4 Applicable Large Employers with Subsidiaries

Company A owns 100% of all classes of stock of Company B and Company C. Company A has no employees at any time in 2021. For every calendar month in 2021, Company B has 40 full-time employees and Company C has 60 full-time employees. Companies A, B, and C are considered a controlled group. Because Companies A, B, and C have a combined total of 100 full-time employees, they are an ALE for 2022.

NOTE: Although entities with a common owner or that are otherwise related are combined and treated as a single employer for determining ALE status, potential liability under the employer shared responsibility provisions is determined separately for each ALE member. Therefore, in Example 8-4, only Companies B and C will be required to make liability payments, because Company A does not have any employees.

b. An ALE member will owe the first type of employer shared responsibility payment if it does not offer minimum essential coverage to at least 95% of its full-time employees (and their dependents) and at least one full-time employee receives the premium tax credit for purchasing coverage through the Health Insurance Marketplace.

   1) This responsibility payment is $2,750 for each full-time employee except for the first 30 full-time employees.

c. Even if an ALE member offers minimum essential coverage to at least 95% of its full-time employees (and their dependents), it may owe the second type of employer shared responsibility payment for each full-time employee who receives the premium tax credit for purchasing coverage through the Marketplace.

   1) This responsibility payment is $4,120 for each full-time employee who received the premium tax credit.

Stop & Review

You have completed the outline for this subunit.

Study multiple-choice questions 18 through 20 beginning on page 201.

QUESTIONS

8.1 General Business Credit (Sec. 38)

1. The General Business Credit cannot lower your tax below

A. The poverty level for the year.

B. The taxpayer's tax for the prior year.

C. A number IRS announces each year.

D. 25% of net regular tax over $25,000.

Answer (D) is correct.

REQUIRED: The threshold amount for which the General Business Credit can no longer lower tax.

DISCUSSION: The General Business Credit (GBC) is limited to the greater of the tentative alternative minimum tax or net income tax minus 25% of net regular tax over $25,000. The amount that may be claimed as the GBC is limited based on tax liability. A credit cannot lower a taxpayer's liability below zero.

Answer (A) is incorrect. The GBC is limited based on tax liability. It is not limited to the poverty level for the year. **Answer (B) is incorrect.** The GBC is limited based on tax liability. The taxpayer's tax for the prior year is not used in determining the GBC limit for the current year. **Answer (C) is incorrect.** The IRS does not announce a number each year regarding the amount below which the General Business Credit cannot lower your tax. The GBC may not exceed the greater of the tentative alternative minimum tax or net income tax minus 25% of the net regular tax liability above $25,000.

2. The General Business Credit consists of the following credits EXCEPT

A. Investment Credit.

B. Pension Plan Start-Up Cost Credit.

C. Work Opportunity Credit.

D. Adoption credit.

Answer (D) is correct.

REQUIRED: The credit that is not a component of the General Business Credit.

DISCUSSION: The General Business Credit (GBC) is a set of several credits commonly available to businesses. The GBC includes credits for investment, research, work opportunity, disabled access, pension plan start-up, and childcare facilities. It does not include a credit for adoptions. The adoption credit is for individuals, not businesses.

3. A company increased its research expenses by $3,600. What is the maximum credit it qualifies for on its tax return for tax year 2022?

A. $360

B. $900

C. $2,700

D. $720

Answer (D) is correct.

REQUIRED: The maximum Research Tax Credit.

DISCUSSION: Publication 334 states, "The research credit is designed to encourage businesses to increase the amounts they spend on research and experimental activities. The credit is generally 20% of the amount by which your research expenses for the year exceed your base amount."

Answer (A) is incorrect. The maximum credit is more than 10% of research expenses. **Answer (B) is incorrect.** The maximum credit is not 25% of research expenses. **Answer (C) is incorrect.** The maximum credit is less than 75% of research expenses.

4. The Barrow and Jones partnership incurred qualified rehabilitation expenses of $50,000 on a certified historic structure. What is the Rehabilitation Investment Credit before tax limitations are applied?

A. $5,000

B. $10,000

C. $7,500

D. $6,000

Answer (B) is correct.

REQUIRED: The Rehabilitation Investment Credit before tax limitations are applied.

DISCUSSION: Instructions for Form 3468 state, "You are allowed a credit for qualified rehabilitation expenditures made for any qualified rehabilitated building." The credit is 20% of the expenditures for a certified historic structure spread over 5 years.

5. An employee who qualifies for the Work Opportunity Credit must be a member of a targeted group. All of the following are considered targeted groups EXCEPT

A. Qualified veterans.

B. Qualified relatives of the employer.

C. Qualified summer youth employees.

D. Qualified SNAP recipients.

Answer (B) is correct.

REQUIRED: The party not classified as a targeted group for purposes of the Work Opportunity Credit.

DISCUSSION: IRS Form 5884 defines a member of a targeted group to be any employee who has been certified by a state employment security agency (SESA) as a

1) Qualified IV-A recipient of temporary assistance to needy families
2) Qualified veteran
3) Qualified ex-felon
4) Designated community resident
5) Vocational rehabilitation referral
6) Qualified supplemental nutrition assistance program (SNAP) benefits recipient
7) Qualified SSI recipient
8) Long-term family assistance recipient
9) Qualified summer youth employee
10) Qualified long-term unemployment recipient

6. The F&E Partnership spent $100,000 on eligible access expenditures that qualify for the Disabled Access Credit. The partnership had gross receipts of $1 million and 30 full-time employees during the preceding tax year. What is the amount of the Disabled Access Credit for the year 2022?

A. $5,000

B. $10,000

C. $250

D. $50,000

Answer (A) is correct.

REQUIRED: The amount of the Disabled Access Credit for the year 2022.

DISCUSSION: Publication 535 states, "The disabled access credit is a nonrefundable tax credit for an eligible small business that pays or incurs expenses to provide access to persons who have disabilities." Form 8826 defines, "For purposes of the credit, an eligible small business is any business or person that (a) had gross receipts for the preceding tax year that did not exceed $1 million or had no more than 30 full-time employees during the preceding tax year . . ." The credit equals 50% of eligible expenditures in excess of $250 and less than $10,250.

Answer (B) is incorrect. The credit equals 50% of eligible expenditures in excess of $250 and less than $10,250, or $5,000. **Answer (C) is incorrect.** The credit threshold is $250. **Answer (D) is incorrect.** Although 50% of eligible access expenditures qualify for the credit, expenditures for the credit have a cap of $10,250.

7. John has three employees who are certified as members of a targeted group. Two of the employees worked for John for 2 months in 2020 and came back to work for John on January 1, 2022. The other employee began working for John on January 1, 2022. Each employee makes $1,000 per month. How much can John claim as qualified first-year wages in computing the Work Opportunity Credit?

A. $12,000

B. $6,000

C. $36,000

D. $0

Answer (B) is correct.

REQUIRED: The qualified first-year wages used in computing the Work Opportunity Credit deduction.

DISCUSSION: The Work Opportunity Credit is 40% of the first $6,000 of wages paid to each member of a target group during the first year of employment. Because only one of the employees qualifies as a first-year employee, the wages used to calculate the credit equal $6,000.

Answer (A) is incorrect. Only the first $6,000 of the wages per employee may be used in computing the credit, and only first-year wages count. **Answer (C) is incorrect.** Only one of the employees qualifies as a first-year employee, and the credit only applies to the first $6,000. **Answer (D) is incorrect.** One of the employees qualifies as a first-year employee.

8. Ryan runs a manufacturing business employing several people with young children. These employees require daycare as both parents work. He decided that, in order to make it easier for his employees to come to work each day, he would allocate some of the unused space in his manufacturing facility to a childcare facility. In 2022, he incurred $20,000 in qualified childcare facility expenditures. He had no qualified childcare resource and referral expenditures and had no pass-through credits. What is Ryan's credit for 2022?

A. $20,000

B. $2,000

C. $10,000

D. $5,000

Answer (D) is correct.

REQUIRED: The amount of the Employer-Provided Childcare Facilities Credit.

DISCUSSION: The Employer-Provided Childcare Facilities Credit was established to create an incentive for small- and medium-sized businesses to provide childcare for their employees. This credit applies to 25% of qualified expenses paid for employee childcare. Thus, Ryan can use a credit of $5,000 ($20,000 × 25%).

Answer (A) is incorrect. The credit is limited to 25% of qualified expenses. **Answer (B) is incorrect.** The 10% rule applies to qualified expenses paid for employee childcare resource and referral services. **Answer (C) is incorrect.** The correct percentage is 25%, not 50%.

9. Which one of the following statements about the Disabled Access Credit is false?

A. The credit is available in the current year only to businesses having gross receipts that were $1 million or less or no more than 30 full-time employees in the preceding tax year.

B. The credit equals 50% of eligible expenditures in excess of $250 and less than $10,250.

C. No deduction is allowed for any amount for which the Disabled Access Credit is claimed.

D. The credit is a refundable credit for individuals and corporations.

Answer (D) is correct.

REQUIRED: The incorrect statement regarding the Disabled Access Credit.

DISCUSSION: Under Sec. 44(a), a credit is available to individuals and corporations that make expenditures to provide access to disabled individuals. The Disabled Access Credit is not a refundable credit because it is part of the General Business Credit. Excess general business credits may be carried back 1 year or forward 20 years, but not refunded.

8.2 Net Operating Loss (NOL)

10. What is the amount of the net operating loss for 2022 based on the following information?

Total income:	
Interest on nonbusiness savings	$ 425
Net long-term capital gain on sale of business property	2,000
Salary	1,000
Total deductions:	
Net loss from business (sales of $86,000 less expenses of $92,000)	$ 6,000
Net nonbusiness short-term capital loss on sale of stock	1,000
Standard deduction	12,950

A. $0

B. $2,575

C. $3,000

D. $16,525

Answer (C) is correct.

REQUIRED: The taxpayer's net operating loss.

DISCUSSION: A net operating loss is defined as the excess of allowable deductions (as modified) over gross income [Sec. 172(c)]. An NOL generally includes only items that represent business income or loss. Personal casualty losses and wage or salary income are included as business items. Nonbusiness income in excess of nonbusiness deductions must be included. Interest and dividends are not business income.

Net loss from business	$(6,000)
Capital gain on business property	2,000
Salary	1,000
Net operating loss	$(3,000)

The nonbusiness capital loss cannot be offset against the business-related capital gain. The nonbusiness deductions (the standard deduction) exceed the nonbusiness income (interest), and both items are excluded from the NOL calculation.

Answer (A) is incorrect. There is a net operating loss for the year. **Answer (B) is incorrect.** The nonbusiness interest is not included in the net operating loss calculation. **Answer (D) is incorrect.** The nonbusiness interest, nonbusiness loss, and the standard deduction are not included in the net operating loss.

11. For 2022, Able Corporation had $700,000 of gross income from business operations and $750,000 of allowable business expenses. It also received $100,000 in dividends from a domestic corporation for which it can take a 65% deduction. Based on this information, compute Able's net operating loss for 2022.

A. Able Corporation did not have an NOL for 2022.

B. $(15,000)

C. $(50,000)

D. $(150,000)

Answer (B) is correct.

REQUIRED: The corporation's net operating loss when there is dividend income and an NOL carryover.

DISCUSSION: Section 172(c) defines a net operating loss as the excess of deductions over gross income, with certain modifications. One modification is that the dividends-received deduction is computed without regard to the Sec. 246(b) limitation of 65% of taxable income if taking the full 65% deduction creates or increases an NOL. Also, a deduction for a net operating loss carryover is not allowed in computing a current NOL. Consequently, Able Corporation's NOL is computed as follows:

Gross income from business operations		$700,000
Dividends received		100,000
Gross income		$800,000
Less: Business expenses		(750,000)
Dividends-received deduction ($100,000 × 65%)	(65,000)	
Net operating loss	$ (15,000)	

Answer (A) is incorrect. A $15,000 NOL exists at year end. **Answer (C) is incorrect.** The NOL is calculated as gross income less business expenses and the dividends-received deduction. **Answer (D) is incorrect.** The NOL is calculated as gross income less business expenses and the 65% dividends-received deduction.

12. Which of the following losses generally would NOT generate a net operating loss?

A. Loss from trade or business.

B. Casualty or theft loss in a federally declared disaster area.

C. Loss from rental property.

D. Loss created by sale of personal residence for less than its cost.

Answer (D) is correct.

REQUIRED: The loss that would not generate an NOL.

DISCUSSION: Any losses from the sale of a principal residence cannot be deducted (Publication 523). Therefore, an NOL will not result from the sale of the residence for less than its cost. A net operating loss must generally be caused by deductions from a trade or business, deductible casualty and theft losses, deductible moving expenses, or rental property.

Answer (A) is incorrect. A loss from trade or business can generate a net operating loss. **Answer (B) is incorrect.** Casualty or theft losses can generate a net operating loss. **Answer (C) is incorrect.** Loss from a rental property can generate a net operating loss.

13. In determining whether you are carrying on an activity for profit, all the facts and circumstances are taken into account. All of the following are factors to consider EXCEPT

A. You are carrying on two different business activities. When you combine the income and expenses together, you have a net profit.

B. Your losses are due to circumstances beyond your control.

C. You can expect to make a future profit from the appreciation of the assets used in the activity.

D. You were successful in making a profit in similar activities in the past.

Answer (A) is correct.

REQUIRED: The factor that does not determine whether you are carrying on an activity for profit.

DISCUSSION: Publication 535 states, "In determining whether you are carrying on an activity for profit, all the facts are taken into account. No one factor alone is decisive. Among the factors to consider are whether

1. You carry on the activity in a businesslike manner,
2. The time and effort you put into the activity indicate you intend to make it profitable,
3. You depend on income from the activity for your livelihood,
4. Your losses are due to circumstances beyond your control (or are normal in the start-up phase of your type of business),
5. You change your methods of operation in an attempt to improve profitability,
6. You, or your advisors, have the knowledge needed to carry on the activity as a successful business,
7. You were successful in making a profit in similar activities in the past,
8. The activity makes a profit in some years, and how much profit it makes, and
9. You can expect to make a future profit from the appreciation of the assets used in the activity."

Answer (B) is incorrect. Losses due to circumstances beyond your control are a factor to consider in determining whether you are carrying on an activity for profit. **Answer (C) is incorrect.** Expectations of a future profit from the appreciation of the assets used in the activity are a factor to consider in determining whether you are carrying on an activity for profit. **Answer (D) is incorrect.** Successfully making a profit in similar activities in the past is a factor to consider in determining whether you are carrying on an activity for profit.

8.3 Casualty and Theft Losses

14. A taxpayer suffered an $11,000 loss of inventory when his cooler malfunctioned. He had no insurance for this type of loss. He shows this loss on his tax return by

A. Taking a bad debt deduction of $22,000, the amount he would have sold the inventory for.

B. Taking an ordinary loss on Form 4797 of $11,000.

C. Taking a business loss on his Schedule C as reflected by an increase of $11,000 in cost of goods sold.

D. Taking a loss of $11,000 as a bad debt on Schedule D.

Answer (C) is correct.

REQUIRED: The correct method of presenting an inventory loss on the tax return.

DISCUSSION: Publication 547 states, "There are two ways you can deduct a casualty or theft loss of inventory, including items you hold for sale to customers.

"One way is to deduct the loss through the increase in the cost of goods sold by properly reporting your opening and closing inventories. Do not claim this loss again as a casualty or theft loss. If you take the loss through the increase in the cost of goods sold, include any insurance or other reimbursement you receive for the loss in gross income.

"The other way is to deduct the loss separately. If you deduct it separately, eliminate the inventory items from cost of goods sold by making a downward adjustment to opening inventory or purchases. Reduce the loss by the reimbursement you received. Do not include the reimbursement in gross income. If you do not receive the reimbursement by the end of the year, you may not claim a loss to the extent you have a reasonable prospect of recovery."

Answer (A) is incorrect. The deduction cannot be greater than the cost basis of the property. **Answer (B) is incorrect.** Form 4797 is used for sales and exchanges of property used in a trade or business from other than casualty or theft. **Answer (D) is incorrect.** To take the loss on Schedule D, it must be a bad debt from sales or services. Losses on inventory do not fall under this category.

15. Fred bought new office equipment 4 years ago for $1,000. In April, a fire destroyed the equipment. Fred estimates that it will cost $1,200 to replace the equipment. Fred estimates the fair market value of the equipment was $500. He had no insurance, and at the time of the fire, his adjusted basis was $437. What is Fred's business loss?

A. $1,200

B. $1,000

C. $500

D. $437

Answer (D) is correct.

REQUIRED: The casualty loss for an asset that was completely destroyed.

DISCUSSION: If business property, such as office equipment, is completely destroyed, the amount of the loss is calculated as follows:

Adjusted basis
– Salvage value
– Insurance reimbursement
= Deductible loss

Because Fred's office equipment was completely destroyed in the fire, his deductible loss is $437 ($437 adjusted basis – $0 salvage value – $0 insurance reimbursement).

Answer (A) is incorrect. The replacement value of the equipment is $1,200, which is not used to determine the casualty loss. **Answer (B) is incorrect.** The original price of the equipment is $1,000. This needs to be reduced by the amount of depreciation taken to arrive at adjusted basis. **Answer (C) is incorrect.** The change in FMV of the equipment is $500. This needs to be compared to the adjusted basis to determine the casualty loss.

16. In the current year, Ms. Brown's building was damaged by an earthquake. The building was on land Ms. Brown owned. She used 75% of the building for business purposes and lived in the other 25%. For the current year, her books and records reflect the following:

Cost of building	$400,000
Depreciation on building before earthquake	130,000
Fair market value before earthquake	800,000
Fair market value after earthquake	200,000
Insurance reimbursement	200,000

What is Ms. Brown's deductible business casualty loss for the current year?

A. $20,000

B. $40,900

C. $170,000

D. $250,000

Answer (A) is correct.

REQUIRED: The deductible business casualty loss.

DISCUSSION: When property is partially destroyed, the loss is the lesser of the adjusted basis less any reimbursement or the decrease in the FMV less any reimbursement. When the property is used only partially for business, the casualty loss is calculated separately for business and personal purposes.

	Business (75%)	Personal (25%)
Cost of building	$300,000	$100,000
Depreciation	130,000	
(1) Adjusted basis	$170,000	$100,000
(2) Decrease in FMV ($800,000 – $200,000)	$450,000	$150,000
Lesser of (1) or (2)	170,000	100,000
Less: Insurance	(150,000)	(50,000)
Loss	$ 20,000	$ 50,000

Therefore, Ms. Brown's business casualty loss is $20,000.

Answer (B) is incorrect. The business casualty loss is calculated by allocating the lesser of the adjusted basis or the decline in FMV to the proportion of time the property is used in business. **Answer (C) is incorrect.** The amount of $170,000 is the adjusted basis in the business portions of the building before the earthquake. **Answer (D) is incorrect.** The amount of $250,000 is the business portion of the decrease in FMV less the full insurance reimbursement. When the property is partially destroyed, the loss is the lesser of the adjusted basis or the decrease in the FMV. Additionally, the insurance reimbursement should be allocated between business and personal.

17. On October 2, Year 1, Pamela's store was robbed, causing her to lose $5,000 of merchandise. Her insurance company reimbursed her only $2,500 on December 7, Year 1. Pamela had a beginning inventory of $10,000, purchases of $8,000, and an ending inventory of $3,000. Which of the following is a proper method to account for this event?

A. Reduce beginning inventory by $5,000 and increase gross receipts by $2,500.

B. Reduce purchases by $5,000 and increase gross receipts by $2,500.

C. Increase gross receipts by $2,500.

D. All of the answers are correct.

Answer (C) is correct.

REQUIRED: The correct method of reporting a loss of inventory and an insurance reimbursement.

DISCUSSION: If opening and closing inventories are properly reported, a theft or casualty loss to inventory will automatically be claimed through the increase in cost of goods sold. In such an event, an insurance reimbursement must be included in ordinary income. Alternatively, the loss can be shown separately and reduced by the insurance reimbursement. But then, either opening inventory or purchases must be adjusted downward so that the loss is also not automatically claimed through cost of goods sold.

Answer (A) is incorrect. If the beginning inventory is adjusted, the loss must be deducted. **Answer (B) is incorrect.** If purchases are adjusted, the loss must be deducted. **Answer (D) is incorrect.** Gross receipts should be increased in the current year.

8.4 Additional Taxes

18. Which of the following vehicles are eligible for suspension of the heavy highway motor vehicle use tax?

A. Heavy highway motor vehicles with a gross weight of 55,000 pounds or more.

B. Commercial buses.

C. Agriculture vehicles used 7,500 or fewer miles.

D. Trucks and tractors.

Answer (C) is correct.

REQUIRED: The vehicle eligible for suspension of the heavy highway motor vehicle use tax.

DISCUSSION: Highway motor vehicles that have a taxable gross weight of 55,000 pounds or more are taxable. A highway motor vehicle includes any self-propelled vehicle designed to carry a load over public highways, whether or not also designed to perform other functions. Examples of vehicles that are designed to carry a load over public highways include buses, trucks, and truck tractors. Generally, vans, pickup trucks, panel trucks, and similar trucks are not subject to this tax because they have a taxable gross weight less than 55,000 pounds. If a vehicle is expected to be used on public highways for 5,000 miles or less (7,500 miles or less for agricultural vehicles) during a certain period, the liabilities for the heavy vehicle use tax can be suspended for that period.

19. For a tax period beginning July 1, a truck with taxable gross weight of 60,000 lbs., registered to Mason Corp., was first used on a public highway on July 10. On December 10, the truck was sold to Mr. Diaz, who registered and used it in the tax period. The total federal highway use tax for the period was $232. Which of the following statements is false in respect to who is liable for the tax?

A. Mason Corp. is liable for the full tax of $232 since it first placed the truck in service.

B. Mr. Diaz is liable for the full tax of $232 to the extent Mason has not paid the tax.

C. Mr. Diaz is the only one of the two owners during the tax period with any liability for the tax due from December through June.

D. To the extent that either Mason or Mr. Diaz pays the $232, the other party is relieved, although the truck changed ownership.

Answer (C) is correct.

REQUIRED: The false statement regarding the liability for heavy vehicle use tax.

DISCUSSION: If a heavy vehicle is purchased from another registered owner, the first owner (Mason) owes the tax for the tax period the vehicle is used. However, if the first owner owed the tax but did not pay it, the second owner (Diaz) is liable for the tax if it is used during the period that unpaid tax is due.

Answer (A) is incorrect. The first owner owes the tax for the whole tax period the vehicle is used.
Answer (B) is incorrect. Mr. Diaz is liable for the full tax of $232 to the extent Mason has not paid the tax.
Answer (D) is incorrect. To the extent that either Mason or Mr. Diaz pays the $232, the other party is relieved, although the truck changed ownership.

20. The Affordable Care Act requires an employer with at least 50 full-time or full-time-equivalent employees (FTEs) to offer them affordable essential health insurance coverage or pay a penalty. In which situation is the penalty NOT imposed?

A. An employer offers coverage to FTEs but the coverage is not affordable.

B. Any employee receives a tax credit to buy coverage and the employer does not provide affordable essential coverage.

C. An employer offers coverage to FTEs but the coverage does not provide the minimum essential care.

D. None of the answers are correct.

Answer (D) is correct.

REQUIRED: The circumstance in which the employer mandate of the PPACA does not apply.

DISCUSSION: According to the PPACA, an employer with at least 50 full-time employees or full-time-equivalent employees (FTEs) must offer them affordable essential health insurance coverage or pay a penalty. If any employee receives a tax credit to buy coverage, the annual penalty for choosing not to provide coverage is imposed. An employer offering coverage to FTEs also may be penalized if the coverage (1) is unaffordable or (2) does not meet minimum coverage or actuarial value standards.

Answer (A) is incorrect. The penalty is imposed when an employer offers coverage to FTEs but the coverage is not affordable. **Answer (B) is incorrect.** The penalty is imposed when any employee receives a tax credit to buy coverage but the employer does not provide affordable essential coverage. **Answer (C) is incorrect.** The penalty is imposed when an employer offers coverage to FTEs but the coverage does not provide the minimum essential care.

Go to Online Course

Access the **Gleim EA Premium Review System** featuring our SmartAdapt technology from your Gleim Personal Classroom to continue your studies.

You will experience a personalized study environment with exam-emulating multiple-choice questions.

STUDY UNIT NINE

CONTRIBUTIONS TO A PARTNERSHIP

(10 pages of outline)

Partnerships are collaborative ventures governed by the partnership agreement. Ownership interest in a partnership is determined by contributions to the partnership and the operations of the partnership, including assumption of liability. Despite the flow-through nature of partnerships, filing requirements do exist, with the required tax year determined by several guidelines.

9.1 PARTNERSHIP DEFINED

1. A partnership is the relationship between two or more entities who join together to carry on a trade or business. An entity, when used in this context, may refer to an individual, a corporation, a trust, an estate, or another partnership.
   a. For federal tax purposes, the term "partnership" includes a syndicate, group, pool, or joint venture that is carrying on a trade or business and is not classified as a trust, an estate, a qualified joint venture, or a corporation.
      1) Per-se corporations, such as insurance companies, cannot be classified as partnerships.
      2) Tax-exempt organizations cannot be classified as partnerships.
      3) A domestic limited liability company (LLC) with at least two members that does not file Form 8832 is classified as a partnership for federal income tax purposes.
   b. An agreement to share expenses does not constitute a partnership.
   c. Co-ownership of rental property is not a partnership unless services are provided to the tenants.
   d. A partnership is allowed to be excluded from treatment as a partnership if it is not in the active conduct of a business, for example, a partnership of individuals who pool their money for investment purposes.
      1) All partners must elect for this treatment to apply.
      2) Each member must separately include his or her share of the income and deductions.
   e. A single-member domestic LLC is treated as a disregarded entity but alternatively may elect treatment as a corporation for tax purposes.

Partnership Agreement

2. A partnership agreement includes the original agreement that determines the partner's share of income, gains, losses, deductions, and credits.
   a. The agreement must be agreed to by all partners.
   b. The agreement must have **substantial economic effect**; otherwise, the allocation will be made based on the partner's interest in the partnership.
      1) There must be a reasonable possibility that the allocation will substantially affect the dollar amount of the partner's share of ownership.
      2) The partner to whom an allocation is made actually receives the economic benefit or burden corresponding to that allocation.

Family Partnership

3. A family partnership is one consisting of a taxpayer and his or her spouse, ancestors, lineal descendants, or trusts for the primary benefit of any of them. Siblings are not treated as members of the taxpayer's family for these purposes. Income or loss from a family partnership should be reported on Form 1065 rather than on Schedule C of Form 1040.
   a. For family members to be recognized as partners in a family partnership, one of the following requirements must be met:
      1) If capital is a material income-producing factor, they acquired their capital interest in a bona fide transaction (even if by gift or purchase from another family member), actually own the partnership interest, and actually control the interest.
      2) If capital is not a material income-producing factor, they joined together in good faith to conduct a business. They agreed that contributions of each entitle them to a share in the profits, and some capital or service has been (or is) provided by each partner.
   b. **Services.** A services partnership is one in which capital is not a material income-producing factor.
      1) In a family partnership, a family member is treated as a services partner only to the extent (s)he provides services that are substantial or vital to the partnership.

c. **Capital.** A family member is treated as a partner in a partnership in which capital is a material income-producing factor.

1) However, the partnership agreement is disregarded to the extent a partner receives less than reasonable compensation for services.

EXAMPLE 9-1 Family Partnership -- Gift to Child

R gives Son a gift of $250,000. Son contributes it in exchange for a 50% interest in a newly formed partnership with R. R&R Partnership continues what was R's sole proprietorship. The reasonable value of R's services the following tax year is $75,000. Of R&R's gross income of $125,000, $75,000 must be allocated to R for his services. Son's distributive share attributable to his capital interest is no more than $25,000 [($125,000 – $75,000) × 50%].

2) The recipient of gifted interest may not receive income greater than the proportionate share of the donor.

3) This rule applies to all, not just some, family members.

d. Spouses filing a joint return may elect out of partnership treatment by choosing to be a qualified joint venture.

1) The only members of the joint venture must be the spouses, and both must materially participate and make the election.

2) Each spouse will be treated as a sole proprietor, allowing both to receive Social Security benefits.

3) All items of income, gain, loss, deduction, and credit attributable to the business must be divided between the spouses in accordance with each spouse's respective interest in the joint venture.

Constructive Ownership -- Partnership Interest

4. An individual is treated as owning the interest owned by his or her spouse, brothers and sisters, children, grandchildren, and parents.

a. An interest directly or indirectly owned by or for a corporation, partnership, estate, or trust is considered to be owned proportionately by or for its shareholders, partners, or beneficiaries.

b. Study Unit 14, Subunit 6, and item 12. in Study Unit 16, Subunit 1, have additional coverage of related party and constructive ownership.

Stop & Review

You have completed the outline for this subunit.

Study multiple-choice questions 1 through 4 beginning on page 213.

9.2 FILING REQUIREMENTS

Tax Year

1. The partnership's tax year is determined with respect to the partners' tax years.
   a. Unless an exception applies, the partnership must use a required tax year.
      1) The required tax year is the first of 2), 3), or 4) below that applies.

Majority Interest

2) Majority interest tax year is the tax year of partners owning more than 50% of partnership capital and profits if they have the same tax year as determined on the first day of the partnership's tax year.

Principal Partner

3) Principal partners' tax year is the same tax year of all principal partners, i.e., partners owning 5% or more in capital or profits, if they all have the same tax year.

Least Aggregate Deferral

4) Least aggregate deferral tax year is determined by multiplying each partner's ownership percentage by the number of months of income deferral for each possible partnership tax year and then selecting the tax year that produces the smallest total tax deferral.
   a) The deferral period begins with the possible partnership tax year-end date and extends to the partner's tax year-end date.

EXAMPLE 9-2 Least Aggregate Deferral Tax Year

A and B each have a 50% interest in a partnership that started business on July 1. A uses a calendar year, while B has a fiscal year ending September 30. Because ownership is split 50/50 and different year endings are used, the least aggregate deferral year must be used. The two calculations are as follows:

12/31 Year End	Year End	Interest in Partnership	Months of Deferral for 12/31 Year End	Interest × Deferral
A	12/31	50%	0	0
B	9/30	50%	9	4.5
			Total deferral	4.5

9/30 Year End	Year End	Interest in Partnership	Months of Deferral for 9/30 Year End	Interest × Deferral
A	12/31	50%	3	1.5
B	9/30	50%	0	0
			Total deferral	1.5

A September 30 year end is the least aggregate deferral year end for the partnership.

   b. Any time there is a change in partners or a partner changes his or her tax year, the partnership may be required to change its tax year.

2. A year other than one required may be adopted for a business purpose with IRS approval. Income deferral is not a business purpose.

Natural Business Year

a. Accounting for a natural business year, e.g., in a seasonal line of business, can be an acceptable business purpose.

1) It is any 12-month period for which at least 25% of annual gross receipts were received during the last 2 months of each of the preceding 3 years.

Fiscal Year

b. Under Sec. 444, a partnership may elect a tax year that is neither the required year nor a natural business year. The year elected may result in no more than 3 months of deferral (between the end of a tax year elected and the end of the required tax year).

1) Under Sec. 444, the partnership may make the election only if the partnership is not a member of a tiered structure and it did not previously make a Sec. 444 election other than to change to a shorter deferral period.

Existing Tax Year

c. If one or more than one qualifying tax year is also the partnership's existing tax year, the partnership must maintain its existing tax year.

Return Due Date

3. Partnership returns are due by the 15th day of the 3rd month following the close of the partnership's tax year.

a. An application for an extension of a partnership tax return is filed on Form 7004. The extension is for 6 months after the original due date of the return.

Domestic Partnership

4. Every domestic partnership must file Form 1065, unless it neither receives income nor incurs any expenses treated as deductions or credits for federal income tax purposes.

5. Schedules K-1 are filed with the return and furnished to the partners on or before the due date (including extensions) for the partnership return. A Schedule K-1 contains the partner's distributive share of partnership income and separately stated items to be reported on the partner's tax return.

Stop & Review

You have completed the outline for this subunit.

Study multiple-choice questions 5 through 9 beginning on page 214.

9.3 CONTRIBUTIONS TO A PARTNERSHIP

Contribution of Property

1. Generally, no gain or loss is recognized on the contribution of property in exchange for a partnership interest. The contribution may occur at the formation of the partnership or after it has been in existence for some time.
   a. Gain or loss is recognized when the following situations occur:
      1) The contributed property is distributed to a different partner within 7 years of the contribution date. The contributing partner's recognized gain is the lesser of the precontribution gain or the gain that would result if the property were sold at FMV.
      2) When a partner contributes property to a partnership and immediately receives a distribution, the transaction is essentially a sale. Gain realized is recognized to the extent the contributed property is deemed purchased by the other partners.

EXAMPLE 9-3 Recognized Gain -- Purchase by Other Partner

P and Q contributed land with FMVs of $250,000 and $500,000, respectively, each in exchange for a 50% interest in PQ Partnership. PQ mortgaged the land for $550,000 and distributed $250,000 of the proceeds to Q. Q recognizes any gain realized on 50% of the land she contributed. Fifty percent of the adjusted basis (AB) in the land is included in Q's basis in her partnership interest.

      3) A partner who contributed property receives a distribution of a different property (other than money) within 7 years of his or her contribution. The contributing partner recognizes gain on the lesser of
         a) FMV of the distributed property over the partner's basis in his or her partnership interest or
         b) The difference between the FMV and the AB of the contributed property on the contribution date.

EXAMPLE 9-4 Recognized Gain -- Partnership Distribution

C is a partner in CD Partnership. CD Partnership holds three assets: property #1, property #2, and property #3. C contributed property #1, with an AB of $5,000 and a FMV of $10,000, to the partnership in the current year. The other two properties were acquired by the partnership. C's basis in his partnership interest is $2,000. In Year 5, C receives property #3 (FMV $8,000) in a distribution from the partnership. C's gain is the lesser of (1) $6,000 ($8,000 FMV property distributed – $2,000 AB in partnership interest) or (2) $5,000 ($10,000 FMV property #1 at contribution date – $5,000 AB property #1 at contribution date). C recognizes $5,000 of gain on the distribution.

      4) A partner acts in an individual capacity in a transaction with the partnership.
   b. The basis of contributed property is the same in the hands of the partnership as it was in the hands of the partner. The holding period is carried over as well.

Contributions of Services

2. The value of a capital interest in a partnership that is transferred to a partner in exchange for services is taxable as ordinary income.
   a. The income recognized is added to the basis of the partnership interest.

Partnership Basis when Service is the Contributing Factor vs. Cash or Property Contribution

Figure 9-1

Visual Memory Aid: For candidates who are visual learners, the figure above and the description below can aid in recalling how partnership basis is determined for services contributed to the partnership.

The basis to a service partner for a partnership interest is the amount of income recognized. If the service partner is an existing partner, the amount recognized is added to the old basis.

In the illustration, the service basis partner is using a mop and hammer and holding a pie piece. His "piece," or share, of partnership interest is equal to the income he receives while performing his service. A cash- or property-contributing partner calculates his or her basis by the value of the cash or the adjusted basis of the property at the time of the donation. The property-contributing partner "carries" the keys of the contribution to remind you that there is a "carryover" of basis.

Liabilities

3. When a partner contributes property subject to a liability or the partnership assumes a liability of the contributing partner, the partner is treated as receiving a distribution of money from the partnership in the amount of the liability.
   a. A distribution reduces the partner's basis in the partnership interest.

EXAMPLE 9-5 **Basis in Partnership -- Contribution of Property**

John contributed an office building with an AB of $500,000 for a share in the partnership. The office building currently has a mortgage with a balance of $200,000. John's basis in the partnership is $300,000 ($500,000 AB – $200,000 mortgage).

Recognized Gain

   b. To the extent liabilities assumed by the partnership exceed the partner's aggregate AB in all property contributed, the partner recognizes gain (and basis in the partnership interest is zero).
      1) Note that a partner still bears responsibility for his or her share of the liabilities assumed by the partnership.

EXAMPLE 9-6 **Gain -- Liability Assumed by the Partnership**

In 2022, Albert acquired a 20% interest in a partnership by contributing a parcel of land and $10,000 in cash. At the time of Albert's contribution, the land had a fair market value of $50,000, had an AB to Albert of $20,000, and was subject to a mortgage of $70,000. Albert's relinquished liability creates a gain. When Albert became a 20% partner, he was relieved of 80% of the mortgage debt. Thus, 80% of his $70,000 mortgage, or $56,000, is a benefit to Albert because the other partners are assuming part of the mortgage obligation. Therefore, Albert has a recognized gain of $26,000 ($56,000 benefit – $10,000 cash – $20,000 AB of property).

	Cash contributed	$ 10,000
+	AB of property contributed	20,000
+	Any gain recognized on contributed property or services	26,000
+	Share of partnership liabilities	14,000
–	Partner's liability assumed by partnership	(70,000)
=	**Basis in partnership interest**	$ 0

You have completed the outline for this subunit.
Study multiple-choice questions 10 through 14 beginning on page 217.

9.4 PARTNERSHIP INTEREST

1. The original basis of a partner's interest acquired in exchange for contributions of property is the sum of
   a. The money contributed,
   b. The adjusted basis (AB) of property contributed, and
   c. The amount of any recognized gain by the partner under Sec. 721(b) on the contribution (partnership treated as an investment company).
2. The assumption of liabilities by the partner is treated as a contribution of money to the partnership and increases basis.
3. The amount of liabilities assumed by the partnership is treated as a distribution to the contributing partner and reduces basis.
4. A partner's basis in a cash-basis partnership includes liabilities only to the extent that the liability
   a. Creates or increases the partnership's basis in its assets
   b. Gives rise to a current deduction
   c. Gives rise to a nondeductible, noncapital expense of the partnership
5. Accrued but unpaid expenses and accounts payable are not included in the basis of a partner's interest in a cash-basis partnership.
6. A partner includes a liability only to the extent that the partner bears the economic risk of loss.

Partner's Basis

7. A partner's basis in contributed items is exchanged for basis in the partnership interest received, adjusted for gain recognized and liabilities.

EXAMPLE 9-7 Basis in Partnership Interest

Using the information from Example 9-6 on the previous page, basis is calculated as follows:

	Cash contributed	$ 10,000
+	AB of property contributed	20,000
+	Any gain recognized on contributed property or services	26,000
+	Share of partnership liabilities	14,000
–	Partner's liability assumed by partnership	(70,000)
=	**Basis in partnership interest**	$ 0

Partnership's Gain

8. The partnership realizes neither gain nor loss when it receives contributions of money or property in exchange for a partnership interest.

Partnership's Basis

9. The partnership's basis in contributed property is equal to the contributing partner's AB in the property immediately before contribution, increased by any gain recognized by the partner. It is not adjusted for liabilities.

Holding Periods

10. The holding period (HP) of the partner's interest includes the HP of contributed capital and Sec. 1231 assets. If the interest was received in exchange for ordinary income property or services, the HP starts the day following the exchange.
    a. The partnership's HP in contributed property includes the partner's HP, even if the partner recognized gain.

Partner Purchased Interest

11. The basis in a partnership interest purchased from a partner is its cost, which is the sum of the purchase price and the partner's share of partnership liabilities.
    a. The partnership may elect to adjust the basis in its assets by the difference between the transferee's basis in his or her partnership interest and his or her proportionate share of the partnership's AB in its assets. This is referred to as a Sec. 754 election.
        1) Section 743 provides that this adjustment to basis will apply only for the transferee partner.

Stop & Review

You have completed the outline for this subunit.
Study multiple-choice questions 15 through 20 beginning on page 220.

QUESTIONS

9.1 Partnership Defined

1. For federal tax purposes, the term "partnership" includes all of the following EXCEPT a

A. Syndicate.

B. Pool.

C. Joint venture.

D. Trust.

Answer (D) is correct.

REQUIRED: The item not included in the term "partnership."

DISCUSSION: Subchapter K is the part of the Code containing most of the tax rules that apply to partnerships. A partnership is defined under Sec. 761(a) as including a syndicate, group, pool, joint venture, or other unincorporated organization that carries on a business and is not a corporation, a trust, or an estate.

2. Jane gave each of her two children, Jake and Jeff, a 30% interest in her clothing store. Capital is a material income-producing factor. Jeff is 21 and has worked in the store since he was 15, has developed significant sales skills, and helps his mom with the management duties. Jake is 25, is married, has a job in another state, and does not participate in any of the store's management decisions. Who is(are) recognized as a partner(s)?

A. Jane.

B. Jane and Jake.

C. Jane, Jake, and Jeff.

D. Jane and Jeff.

Answer (C) is correct.

REQUIRED: The recognized partners in a family partnership.

DISCUSSION: Section 704 defines a family partnership as one consisting of a taxpayer and his or her spouse, ancestors, lineal descendants, or trusts for the primary benefit of any of them. A family member is treated as a partner in a partnership in which capital is a material income-producing factor, whether the interest is acquired by gift or purchase. However, the partnership agreement is disregarded to the extent a partner receives less than reasonable compensation for services.

Answer (A) is incorrect. Jeff and Jake are also considered partners because capital is a material income-producing factor and Jeff and Jake acquired their interest by gift. **Answer (B) is incorrect.** Jeff is a partner since he acquired his interest by gift. **Answer (D) is incorrect.** Jake is a partner since he acquired his interest by gift.

3. In determining the ownership rules of partnerships, which one of the following combinations would total more than 50% ownership of The Peach Company for Jake?

A.	Jake	30%
	Jake's wife	10%
	Jake's aunt	60%
B.	Jake	45%
	His uncle's trust	55%
C.	Jake	10%
	Jake's wife's corporation	90%
D.	Jake	30%
	Jake's father	10%
	Jake's nephew	60%

Answer (C) is correct.

REQUIRED: The constructive ownership percentages of a partnership.

DISCUSSION: An individual is treated as owning the stock owned by his or her spouse, siblings, children, grandchildren, and parents. If 50% or more in value of the interest in a partnership is owned, directly or indirectly, by or for any person, that person is considered to own the interest, directly or indirectly, by or for his or her partnership in the proportion that the value of the stock (s)he owns bears to the value of all the stock in the partnership. Stock owned, directly or indirectly, by or for a trust is considered to be owned by its beneficiaries in proportion to their actuarial interest in the trust. Stock owned, directly or indirectly, by or for an estate is considered to be owned proportionately by the beneficiaries. Jake is considered to own more than 50% of the partnership only in the answer choice stating that Jake has 10% direct ownership plus 90% indirect ownership from his wife's corporation.

Answer (A) is incorrect. Jake's aunt's ownership is not constructively owned by Jake. **Answer (B) is incorrect.** Jake's uncle's trust is not constructively owned by Jake. **Answer (D) is incorrect.** Jake's nephew's ownership is not constructively owned by Jake.

4. John sold his daughter 50% of his business partnership. The partnership had an $80,000 profit this year before deducting any compensation to the partner as a guaranteed payment. Capital is a material income-producing factor. John performed services worth $55,000, which is reasonable compensation. The daughter performed no services. How much income will John claim on his individual tax return?

A. $40,000

B. $55,000

C. $67,500

D. $80,000

Answer (C) is correct.

REQUIRED: The amount of income a partner who receives compensation will claim on the individual return.

DISCUSSION: In a partnership in which a partner performs services for compensation and capital is a material-producing factor, the compensation is first allocated from profits to the respective partner. Any remaining profits are then distributed to each partner in their respective share. Each partner will receive 50% of $25,000 ($80,000 profit – $55,000 services), or $12,500. Therefore, John must claim $67,500 ($55,000 + $12,500) on his return.

Answer (A) is incorrect. The compensation must first be deducted before profits are distributed. **Answer (B) is incorrect.** John's share of profits due to capital of 50%, or $12,500, must also be claimed. **Answer (D) is incorrect.** John's daughter must receive his portion of profits attributable to the capital, $12,500.

9.2 Filing Requirements

5. DCS Partnership, formed on August 8, Year 1, elected to use a fiscal year ending October 30. DCS is required to file its return by which of the following dates?

A. December 15, Year 1.

B. January 15, Year 2.

C. February 15, Year 2.

D. April 15, Year 2.

Answer (B) is correct.

REQUIRED: The required due date for a partnership tax return.

DISCUSSION: Generally, Form 1065 must be filed by the 15th day of the 3rd month following the close of the partnership's tax year. For a tax year ending October 30, the return must be filed by January 15 of the following year. The dates may be adjusted for weekends and holidays.

6. Bytes, Ltd. is a partnership formed by Warren Corporation, JCL Corporation, and Mike (an individual) to build and repair personal computers. The partners' profits interest in Bytes and their respective taxable years are stated below. Assuming there is no business purpose for any particular year and no Sec. 444 election has been made, determine the partnership's required taxable year.

Partner	Profits & Capital Interests	Taxable Year End
Warren Corporation	25%	May 31
JCL Corporation	40%	August 31
Mike	35%	December 31

A. Since no business purpose to establish a particular year exists, the partnership must adopt the calendar taxable year.

B. The partnership may adopt a taxable year ending either May 31 or August 31.

C. Under the required tax year rules, the partnership must adopt a taxable year ending August 31.

D. Under the required tax year rules, the partnership must adopt a calendar year.

Answer (B) is correct.

REQUIRED: The correct taxable year of a partnership.

DISCUSSION: A partnership's required tax year is that of the partner(s) owning more than 50% of the partnership's capital and profits. If the majority partner(s) do(es) not have the same year, the tax year of all principal (5%) partners must be adopted. If all principal partners do not have the same taxable year, the partnership must adopt the tax year of the partner that results in the least aggregate deferral of income to the partners. Least aggregate deferral tax year is determined by multiplying each partner's ownership percentage by the number of months of income deferral for each possible partnership tax year and then selecting the tax year that produces the smallest total tax deferral. Using Warren's tax year would result in aggregate deferral of 3.65 [(3 × 40%) + (7 × 35%) + (0 × 25%)]. Using Warren's tax year of May 31, JCL would have a deferral of 3 months (June, July, and August). Mike would have a deferral of 7 months (June through December). Using JCL's tax year would result in aggregate deferral of 3.65 [(4 × 35%) + (9 × 25%) + (0 × 40%)]. Using Mike's tax year would result in aggregate deferral of 4.45 [(5 × 25%) + (8 × 40%) + (0 × 35%)]. Because Warren and JCL's tax years result in the least deferral of income, the partnership can choose either one.

Answer (A) is incorrect. Partnership's required tax year is first of the partner(s) owning more than 50%, then of all principal partners, and lastly of the partner that results in the least aggregate deferral. **Answer (C) is incorrect.** JCL and Warren's tax year result in the least aggregate deferral of income, so the partnership must choose one of these two and is not obligated to either one. **Answer (D) is incorrect.** Under the required tax year rules, the partnership must pick a tax year of first of the partner(s) owning more than 50%, then of all principal partners, and lastly of the partner that results in the least aggregate referral.

7. Alpha Partnership is on a fiscal year ending March 31. Partner Alf reports income on the fiscal year ending March 31, and Partner Omega reports income on the fiscal year ending September 30. Both partners have a 50% interest in partnership profits. Assuming the partnership does not make a Sec. 444 election and does not establish a business purpose for a different period, what tax year must the partnership use to file its tax return?

A. Any month end.

B. March 31.

C. September 30.

D. December 31.

Answer (B) is correct.

REQUIRED: The tax year the partnership must use to file its tax return.

DISCUSSION: A partnership's required tax year is that of the partner(s) owning more than 50% of partnership capital and profits. If the majority partner(s) do(es) not have the same year, the tax year of all principal (5%) partners must be adopted. If all principal partners do not have the same taxable year, under Reg. 1.706-1, the partnership must adopt the tax year of the partner that results in the least aggregate deferral of income to the partners. Aggregate deferral is the sum of the products of deferral for each partner and each partner's interest in partnership profits. Using Alf's tax year results in aggregate deferral of 3.0 [(0 × 50%) + (6 × 50%)]. Using Omega's tax year would result in aggregate deferral of 3.0 [(6 × 50%) + (0 × 50%)]. Regulation 1.706-1 further provides that, if one or more than one qualifying tax year is also the partnership's existing tax year, the partnership must maintain its existing tax year.

Answer (A) is incorrect. Regulation 1.706-1 requires that the partnership adopt a tax year that results in the least aggregate deferral of income to the partners. **Answer (C) is incorrect.** If one or more than one qualifying tax years is also the partnership's existing tax year, the partnership must maintain its existing tax year. **Answer (D) is incorrect.** Regulation 1.706-1 requires that the partnership adopt a tax year that results in the least aggregate deferral of income to the partners.

8. Which of the following is one of the conditions a partnership must meet to be eligible to make a Sec. 444 election (election to use a tax year that is different from a required tax year)?

A. The partnership must not choose a tax year with a deferral period that is longer than 6 months or with the deferral period of the tax year being changed, if this period is shorter.

B. The partnership has not previously had a Sec. 444 election other than to change an election to a shorter deferral period.

C. The partnership establishes a business purpose for a different period.

D. The partnership is a member of a tiered structure.

Answer (B) is correct.

REQUIRED: The item that is a condition to make the Sec. 444 election.

DISCUSSION: A partnership may elect to use a tax year other than the tax year required. Under Sec. 444, the partnership may make the election only if the partnership is not a member of a tiered structure, it did not previously make a Sec. 444 election, and the deferral period is not longer than 3 months.

Answer (A) is incorrect. The deferral period must not be longer than 3 months. **Answer (C) is incorrect.** The partnership does not have to establish a business purpose to make a Sec. 444 election. **Answer (D) is incorrect.** The partnership must not be a member of a tiered structure.

9. New ABC Partnership is organized in the current year with three general partners. The partners include a corporation with a tax year ending on March 31 and a 60% interest in partnership capital and profits, and two individuals, each having a calendar tax year and a 20% interest in partnership capital and profits. The partnership's required tax year ends on

A. March 31.

B. September 30.

C. October 31.

D. December 31.

Answer (A) is correct.

REQUIRED: The tax year of a partnership.

DISCUSSION: Unless an exception applies, the partnership must use a required tax year. The first required tax year stipulated by the IRC is the majority interest tax year. The majority interest tax year is the tax year of partners owning more than 50% of partnership capital and profits if they have had the same tax year on the first day of the partnership tax year. Since the corporate partner owns 60% of the interest in ABC Partnership, the partnership must use a tax year ending on March 31.

9.3 Contributions to a Partnership

10. Generally, no gain or loss is recognized by the partnership or a partner when the partner contributes property to the partnership, unless

A. The partnership is being formed.

B. The contributed property is distributed to a different partner within 7 years of the contribution date.

C. The partnership is already operating.

D. Unencumbered depreciable property is contributed.

Answer (B) is correct.

REQUIRED: The correct time to record a gain or loss on contributed property to a partnership.

DISCUSSION: Generally, no gain or loss is recognized on the contribution of property in exchange for a partnership interest. However, there are exceptions to this rule. One exception is if the contributed property is distributed to a different partner within 7 years of the contribution date.

Answer (A) is incorrect. No gain or loss is recognized when property is contributed during the partnership's formation. **Answer (C) is incorrect.** No gain or loss is recognized when property is contributed to a partnership that is already running. **Answer (D) is incorrect.** It does not matter if the contributed property is unencumbered depreciable property.

11. Patti and Kae formed a partnership in which they share income and loss equally. Kae contributes land on which there is a recourse mortgage of $18,000, which the partnership assumed for legitimate business purposes. The land has an adjusted basis to Kae of $15,000 and a fair market value of $20,000 at the time of the contribution. Patti contributes $2,000 to the partnership in cash. What amount of gain should Kae recognize as a result of the contribution of property?

A. $0

B. $9,000

C. $5,000

D. $2,000

Answer (A) is correct.

REQUIRED: The amount of gain to be recognized on the contribution of property.

DISCUSSION: Generally, no gain or loss is recognized on the contribution of property in exchange for a partnership interest; however, a gain or loss could be recognized to the extent liabilities assumed by the other partner exceed the partner's aggregate adjusted basis in all property contributed. The only other partner, Patti, assumed a liability of half the mortgage, or $9,000, and the aggregate adjusted basis is $15,000 from the land plus $2,000 from the cash contributed. The liability reduces Kae's adjusted basis, but there is no gain on this transaction because the liability assumed does not exceed Kae's adjusted basis.

Answer (B) is incorrect. The liability that is assumed by the partnership is $9,000. Because Kae's AB is bigger than this amount, no gain is recognized. **Answer (C) is incorrect.** The amount of $5,000 is the difference between the FMV and the AB of the land. Kae recognizes a gain to the extent that the liabilities assumed by the partnership exceed Kae's AB in the property contributed. **Answer (D) is incorrect.** Kae's AB is larger than the amount of liability assumed; thus, there is no gain or loss recognized on this transaction.

12. Audra acquired a 50% interest in a partnership by contributing property that had an adjusted basis of $20,000 and a fair market value of $50,000. The property was subject to a liability of $44,000, which the partnership assumed for legitimate business purposes. Which of the following statements is true?

A. Audra must include a gain from the sale or exchange of a capital asset on her individual return, and her basis in her partnership interest increases.

B. Audra must include a gain on her individual return, and her basis in her partnership interest is zero.

C. Audra is not required to include a gain on her individual return, and her basis in her partnership interest is zero.

D. Audra is not required to include a gain on her individual return, but the gain increases her basis in her partnership interest.

Answer (B) is correct.

REQUIRED: The true statement regarding gain recognition on a contribution to a partnership.

DISCUSSION: When encumbered property is contributed to a partnership, a partner recognizes gain to the extent the partner is deemed to be relieved of a portion of the debt. Audra has a $42,000 basis upon contribution ($20,000 property basis plus $22,000, which is half of the $44,000 debt). She is also deemed to receive a cash distribution of $44,000 (the amount of the debt), creating a gain of $2,000 ($44,000 distribution – $42,000 basis). The distribution also reduces the basis in her partnership interest to zero.

Answer (A) is incorrect. The gain recognized does not affect the basis in the partnership interest. **Answer (C) is incorrect.** A gain is recognized when a distribution exceeds the partner's basis in the partnership interest. **Answer (D) is incorrect.** A gain is recognized when a distribution exceeds the partner's basis in the partnership interest.

13. Sharon provides services to a partnership during the year in exchange for a capital interest of 30% worth $25,000. Sharon's basis in the partnership is

A. Zero since she exchanged services for her interest.

B. $25,000, which must be reported by her as income in the year of receipt if the interest is vested.

C. The present value of $25,000, computed over the lesser of Sharon's remaining life or the average remaining life of the other partners.

D. Considered a profits interest and has a zero basis.

Answer (B) is correct.

REQUIRED: The correct basis in a partnership when the interest is exchanged for services.

DISCUSSION: The value of a capital interest in a partnership that is transferred to a partner in exchange for services is taxable as ordinary income. The income recognized is added to the basis of the partnership interest.

Answer (A) is incorrect. Services can be exchanged for a capital interest in a partnership. **Answer (C) is incorrect.** A capital interest in a partnership that is transferred to a partner in exchange for services is valued at what they are worth today, and it is not discounted over any period of time. **Answer (D) is incorrect.** A profits interest is when the partner's only interest is in the future earnings of the partnership, with no interest in the current partnership assets.

14. On April 10, Year 1, Reuben contributed land in exchange for a 25% partnership interest in Larson Partners. The fair market value of the land at that time was $60,000, and Reuben's adjusted basis was $25,000. On November 1, Year 5, Larson distributed that land to another partner. The fair market value at that time was $65,000. What is the amount of Reuben's recognized gain from the transfer of the land by Larson to another partner?

A. $5,000

B. $25,000

C. $35,000

D. $40,000

Answer (C) is correct.

REQUIRED: The amount of precontribution gain when a partnership distributes contributed property.

DISCUSSION: For property contributed to a partnership after 10/3/89 that had a deferred precontribution gain or loss, the contributing partner must recognize the precontribution gain or loss when the property is distributed to any other partner within 7 years of its contribution [Sec. 704(c)(1)(B)]. The precontribution gain or loss that is recognized equals the remaining precontribution gain or loss which would have been allocated to the contributing partner if the property had instead been sold for its fair market value on the distribution date. Reuben recognizes a $35,000 gain ($60,000 FMV at contribution date – $25,000 adjusted basis).

Answer (A) is incorrect. The gain is not calculated by subtracting the fair market value at distribution from the fair market value at the time of contribution. **Answer (B) is incorrect.** The $25,000 is the adjusted basis of the property when it is contributed. **Answer (D) is incorrect.** The difference between the fair market value of the property when distributed and the adjusted basis of the property at contribution is $40,000.

9.4 Partnership Interest

15. If the partner's distributive share of a partnership item cannot be determined under the partnership agreement, it is determined by his or her interest in the partnership. The partnership interest is determined by taking into account all of the following items EXCEPT the

A. Partner's relative contributions to the partnership.

B. Interests of all partners in economic profits and losses (if different from interests in taxable income or loss) and in cash flow and other nonliquidating distributions.

C. Amount of the partnership's nonrecourse liabilities.

D. Right of the partners to distributions of capital upon liquidation.

Answer (C) is correct.

REQUIRED: The factor that does not determine a partnership interest.

DISCUSSION: If a partner's distributive share of a partnership item cannot be determined under the partnership agreement, it is determined by his or her interest in the partnership. The partner's interest is determined by taking into account all of the following items:

- The partners' relative contributions to the partnership.
- The interests of all partners in economic profits and losses (if different from interest in taxable income or loss) and in cash flow and other nonliquidating distributions.
- The rights of the partners to distributions of capital upon liquidation.

Answer (A) is incorrect. The partner's relative contributions to the partnership are taken into account in determining a partnership interest. **Answer (B) is incorrect.** The interests of all partners in economic profits and losses (if different from interests in taxable income or loss) and in cash flow and other nonliquidating distributions are taken into account in determining a partnership interest. **Answer (D) is incorrect.** The right of the partners to distributions of capital upon liquidation is taken into account in determining a partnership interest.

16. Three individuals formed a partnership sharing in profits and losses equally. Mr. Aardvark contributed $10,000 cash. Mr. Baboon contributed $5,000 in cash and land worth $5,000 with an adjusted basis of $4,000. Mr. Camel contributed machinery with a fair market value of $16,000 subject to a mortgage of $6,000, which the partnership assumed, and with an adjusted basis of $16,000. The partnership has no other liabilities. The adjusted basis of Mr. Baboon's interest in the partnership is

A. $5,000

B. $9,000

C. $10,000

D. $11,000

Answer (D) is correct.

REQUIRED: The adjusted basis of a partner's interest received in exchange for cash and property.

DISCUSSION: The basis of a partnership interest acquired by a contribution of property and money is the adjusted basis of property contributed plus the amount of money contributed (Sec. 722). An increase in a partner's share of partnership liabilities is treated as an additional cash contribution [Sec. 752(a)], which increases the partner's basis. Mr. Baboon's adjusted basis is

Money contributed	$ 5,000
Adjusted basis of land contributed	4,000
Share of partnership's liabilities (1/3 of $6,000)	2,000
Baboon's adjusted basis	$11,000

Answer (A) is incorrect. The adjusted basis of the property and the partner's share of the partnership liabilities also increase basis. **Answer (B) is incorrect.** The partner's share of the partnership liabilities also increases basis. **Answer (C) is incorrect.** The basis does not equal the cash and the fair market value of the land.

17. Marlene acquired a 30% interest in a partnership by contributing property that had an adjusted basis to her of $25,000, a fair market value of $50,000, and a $40,000 mortgage. The partnership assumed the liability. What is Marlene's gain or loss on the contribution of her property to the partnership?

A. $0

B. $3,000 gain.

C. $12,000 gain.

D. $10,000 loss.

Answer (B) is correct.

REQUIRED: The gain or loss recognized on the contribution of encumbered property to a partnership.

DISCUSSION: To the extent liabilities assumed by the partnership exceed the partner's aggregate adjusted basis in all property contributed, the partner recognizes gain. Accordingly, Marlene recognizes a $3,000 gain [($40,000 × 70%) – $25,000]. Note that a partner still bears responsibility for his or her share of the liabilities assumed by the partnership.

Answer (A) is incorrect. The partnership recognizes no gain or loss, but Marlene does because she received boot from the partnership's assumption of her mortgage. **Answer (C) is incorrect.** The gain is not calculated on the mortgage assumed. **Answer (D) is incorrect.** The fair market value of the property exceeds the mortgage. The FMV is not used in calculating Marlene's gain or loss.

18. The holding period of property acquired by a partnership as a contribution to the contributing partner's capital account

A. Begins with the date of contribution to the partnership.

B. Includes the period during which the property was held by the contributing partner.

C. Is equal to the contributing partner's holding period prior to contribution to the partnership.

D. Depends on the character of the property transferred.

Answer (B) is correct.

REQUIRED: The holding period of contributed property.

DISCUSSION: The partnership's holding period for contributed property includes the period of time the property was held by the contributing partner [Sec. 1223(2)]. The holding period of the partner "tacks on" because the partnership receives a carryover basis in the contributed property. This is true even if the contributing partner recognizes a gain or loss.

19. Josephine acquired a 20% interest in a partnership by contributing property that had an adjusted basis to her of $8,000 and a $4,000 mortgage. The partnership assumed payment of the mortgage. What is the basis of Josephine's interest?

A. $1,600

B. $4,000

C. $4,800

D. $8,000

Answer (C) is correct.

REQUIRED: The taxpayer's basis in a partnership interest when mortgaged property is contributed.

DISCUSSION: Under Sec. 722, the basis of a partnership interest acquired by the contribution of property is the adjusted basis of the property to the contributing partner. Under Sec. 752(b), the assumption by a partnership of a partner's individual liabilities is treated as a distribution of money to the partner, which reduces the basis of the partner's interest (Sec. 733). Josephine's basis is the $8,000 adjusted basis of the equipment contributed less the relieved individual liability ($4,000 × 80% = $3,200). The basis is $4,800 ($8,000 – $3,200).

Answer (A) is incorrect. The basis is not calculated by multiplying the percent interest times the adjusted basis of the contributed property. **Answer (B) is incorrect.** The basis is the adjusted basis of the equipment less the percentage of the mortgage actually relieved. **Answer (D) is incorrect.** The basis is the basis of the equipment less any relieved individual liability.

20. Bob acquired a 50% interest in a partnership by contributing depreciable property that had an adjusted basis of $15,000 and a fair market value of $45,000. The property was subject to a liability of $32,000, which the partnership assumed for legitimate business purposes. What is the partnership's basis in the property for depreciation?

A. $0

B. $13,000

C. $15,000

D. $16,000

Answer (D) is correct.

REQUIRED: The partnership's basis in contributed property.

DISCUSSION: Under Sec. 723, the partnership's basis for contributed property is the adjusted basis (AB) of such property to the contributing partner at the time of contribution, provided it is not an investment partnership, plus any gain recognized by the partner. To the extent liabilities assumed by the partnership exceed the partner's aggregate AB in all property contributed, the partner recognizes gain (and basis in the partnership interest is zero).

Bob acquired a 50% interest in a partnership by contributing depreciable property that had an AB of $15,000 and was subject to a liability of $32,000. Bob's relinquished liability is a gain. When Bob became a 50% partner, he was relieved of 50% of the liability. Thus, 50% of his $32,000 liability, or $16,000, is a benefit to Bob because the other partners are assuming part of the liability. Therefore, Bob has a recognized gain of $1,000 ($16,000 benefit – $15,000 AB of property). The partnership's basis in the depreciable property is $16,000 ($15,000 AB of property + $1,000 recognized gain).

Answer (A) is incorrect. The partner's basis is $0, and the basis of the contributing partner carries over to the partnership. **Answer (B) is incorrect.** The FMV of the property less the assumed mortgage is not the basis of the property. **Answer (C) is incorrect.** The basis of the property must be increased by any gain recognized.

STUDY UNIT TEN

PARTNERSHIP OPERATIONS

(16 pages of outline)

A partnership is a business organization other than a corporation, a trust, or an estate, co-owned by two or more persons and operated for a profit.

The partnership, as an untaxed, flow-through entity, reports taxable income or loss and separately stated items.

1) When computing his or her personal income tax liability, an individual partner must consider his or her distributive share of the partnership's taxable income or loss and every other separately stated item for the partnership, regardless of whether any distributions were made from the partnership to the partner.

Nonseparately and separately stated partnership items are currently taxed to the partners, but distributions are generally received tax-free. You should identify the different loss limitation rules.

1) Partnership inventory and unrealized receivables are very important because they can trigger ordinary income to one partner when another partner receives a distribution (even of money).
2) Similarly, precontribution gain must be identified as it can trigger and recharacterize otherwise unrecognized capital gain.
3) Partnership liability fluctuations also have special significance because they vary the partners' bases in their partnership interests and affect treatment of distributions.
4) Be prepared to identify a payment to a partner as a guaranteed payment, as a distributive share, or in a nonpartner capacity, and the effect of the classification, e.g., a deduction to the partnership passed through ratably to all partners.

10.1 PARTNERSHIP OPERATIONS AND PARTNER'S TAXABLE INCOME

Partnership-Incurred Liabilities

1. A partner's share of partnership liabilities affects the partner's basis in his or her partnership interest and can result in increased gain being recognized by the partner. Any increase in a partner's share of liabilities increases the partner's basis. The opposite is true for a decrease in partnership liabilities.

Recourse Liabilities

a. A liability is a recourse liability if the creditor has a claim against the partnership or any partner for payment if the partnership defaults.

EXAMPLE 10-1 Recourse Liability

ABC Partnership, a general partnership, purchased a building for $100,000 with a $90,000 mortgage from XYZ Bank secured by the building. Later, the building is destroyed and becomes worthless. Because ABC is a general partnership, ABC's general partners are liable for the debts of the partnership in the event the partnership is unable to pay. If ABC defaults on the mortgage, XYZ can take legal action against the partners of ABC to pay the $90,000 debt. Thus, the loan is recourse to the partners of ABC (i.e., the partners bear the economic risk).

1) Partners generally share recourse liabilities based on their ratio for sharing losses.

a) However, regulations allocate a recourse liability to the partner(s) who would be liable for it if, at the time, all partnership debts were due, all partnership assets (including cash) had zero value, and a hypothetical liquidation occurred.

2) A limited partner cannot share in recourse debt in excess of any of his or her obligations to make additional contributions to the partnership and any additional amount(s) that (s)he would actually lose if the partnership could not pay its debt.

Nonrecourse Liabilities

b. The creditor has no claim against the partnership or any partners. At most, the creditor has a claim against a particular secured item of partnership property.

1) Generally, partners share in nonrecourse liabilities based on their ratio for sharing profits.

EXAMPLE 10-2 Nonrecourse Liabilities

ABC, LLP, purchased a building for $100,000 with a $90,000 mortgage from XYZ Bank. The loan was secured by the building itself and no partner made a personal guarantee on the loan. In the event that ABC defaults and is unable to pay the loan, XYZ's only option is to foreclose and sell the property. If the property's value has decreased and the sale proceeds are insufficient to recover the balance of the loan, XYZ has no other legal remedy. This is because ABC's partners have limited liability by being partners in an LLP and are not generally liable for the debts of the partnership. Thus, the loan is nonrecourse to the partners of ABC (i.e., the lender bears the economic risk, not the partners).

Partnership Cancellation of Debt

c. In general, if the taxpayer has cancellation of debt income because debt is canceled, forgiven, or discharged for less than the amount the taxpayer must pay, the amount of the canceled debt is taxable and the taxpayer must report the canceled debt on the tax return for the year the cancellation occurs.

Partners' Capital Accounts

2. A capital account is maintained for each partner at the partnership level.
   a. A partner's initial capital account balance is the fair market value (FMV) of the assets (net of liabilities) (s)he contributed to the partnership.
   b. It is separate from the partner's adjusted basis (AB) in his or her partnership interest.
   c. The basis in partnership interest is assessed in order to track the tax position of the investment.

EXAMPLE 10-3 Adjusted Basis of Contributed Property

Taxpayer contributes property that has an adjusted basis of $400 and a fair market value of $1,000. Taxpayer's partner contributes $1,000 cash. While each has increased their capital account by $1,000, the adjusted basis of Taxpayer's partnership interest is only $400 and the adjusted basis of Taxpayer's partner's partnership interest is $1,000.

Partner's Taxable Income

3. A partner's taxable income may be affected by his or her interest in a partnership in several ways. Examples include
   a. His or her distributive share of partnership income and separately stated items
   b. Sale of his or her partnership interest
   c. Dealings with the partnership (e.g., guaranteed payments)
4. A partner reports his or her distributive share of partnership items for the partnership's tax year that ends with or within the partner's tax year.

Partnership Taxable Income

5. Partnership taxable income is determined in the same way as for individuals except that certain deductions are not allowed for a partnership, other items are required to be separately stated, and business interest expense is limited.

Separately Stated Items

6. Each partnership item of income, gain, deduction, loss, or credit that may vary the tax liability of any partner must be separately stated. Items that must be separately stated include the following:
   a. Section 1231 gains and losses
   b. Net short- and long-term capital gain or loss from the sale or exchange of capital assets
   c. Guaranteed payments
   d. Interest and dividend income
   e. Royalties
   f. Tax-exempt income and related expenses
   g. Investment income and related expenses
   h. Rental activities, portfolio income, and related expenses
   i. Cancellation of debt
   j. Recovery items (e.g., prior taxes, bad debts)
   k. Charitable contributions
   l. Foreign income taxes paid or accrued
   m. Depletion on oil and gas wells
   n. Section 179 deductions
   o. Distributions
   p. Qualified items of income, gain, and loss for the qualified business income deduction

Ordinary Income

7. This is all taxable items of income, gain, loss, or deduction that are not separately stated.
   a. Ordinary income is different from taxable income, which is the sum of all taxable items, including the separately stated items and the partnership ordinary income or loss.
      1) Ordinary income includes such items as gross profit, administrative expenses, and employee salaries.
      2) **Exception:** Guaranteed payments are subtracted as expenses for computing ordinary business income but are separately stated as income to the recipient partner.

Deductions

8. Certain deductions, e.g., charitable contributions, are disallowed in computing partnership taxable income. These are items that must be separately stated by the partnership.
   a. Each partner may be entitled to a deduction for his or her distributive share of these items in computing his or her personal tax liability.

Contributions to Employee Retirement Accounts

9. Contributions made by a partnership for its employees under a qualified SEP, SIMPLE IRA, pension, profit sharing plan, annuity plan, or another deferred compensation plan may be deducted subject to limitations.
   a. Contributions to an employee's IRA are included in the employee's salaries and wages.

Partner's Distributive Share

10. Each partner is taxed on his or her share of partnership income whether or not it is distributed.
    a. A partner's distributive share of any partnership item is allocated by the partnership agreement as long as the allocation has substantial economic effect, which means the allocation is not for tax avoidance.
       1) For example, allocation of tax-exempt income to one partner and taxable interest (equal in amount) to another partner in a lower tax bracket has no substantial economic effect; i.e., it is motivated by tax avoidance.
    b. If the partnership agreement does not allocate a partnership item, the item must be allocated to partners according to their interests in the partnership.

Precontribution Gain or Loss

   c. To the extent of gain not recognized on contribution of property to the partnership, gain or loss subsequently recognized on the sale or exchange of an asset by the partnership must be allocated to the contributing partner.
      1) Postcontribution gain or loss is allocated among partners as distributive shares, i.e., as any other gain or loss.

EXAMPLE 10-4 Postcontribution Gain or Loss

Tony and Mary form a partnership as equal partners. Tony contributes cash of $100,000, and Mary contributes an asset with a basis of $80,000 and a FMV of $100,000. Two years later, the partnership sells the asset for $110,000. The $30,000 gain ($110,000 selling price – $80,000 basis) is allocated, $25,000 to Mary [$20,000 precontribution gain + (50% partnership interest × $10,000 postcontribution gain)] and $5,000 to Tony (50% partnership interest × $10,000 postcontribution gain).

d. A partner generally must recognize gain on the distribution of property (other than money) if the partner contributed appreciated property to the partnership during the 7-year period before the distribution.

1) The gain recognized is the lesser of the following amounts:

a) The excess of

i) The fair market value of the property received in the distribution, over

ii) The adjusted basis of the partner's interest in the partnership immediately before the distribution, reduced (but not below zero) by any money received in the distribution.

b) The "net precontribution gain" of the partner. This is the net gain the partner would recognize if all the property contributed by the partner within 7 years of the distribution and held by the partnership immediately before the distribution were distributed to another partner other than a partner who owns more than 50% of the partnership.

2) The character of the gain is determined by reference to the character of the net precontribution gain. This gain is in addition to any gain the partner must recognize if the money distributed is more than his or her basis in the partnership.

3) Subunit 10.2 has further discussion regarding property distributions.

Character

e. The character of distributive shares of partnership items is generally determined at the partnership level.

1) Any capital loss (FMV < AB) inherent at contribution is capital loss to the extent of any loss realized when the partnership disposes of the property. This applies for 5 years after contribution.

2) Partnership gain or loss on inventory and unrealized receivables is ordinary income. This treatment of the inventory (but not the receivables) disappears 5 years after contribution.

f. If the size of a partner's interest in the partnership varies (e.g., by sale, purchase, exchange, liquidation) during a partnership tax year, the distributive shares of partnership items must be apportioned on a daily basis.

Elections by Partnership or Partner

11. A few of the elections available to partnerships are made at the partnership level:
    a. Partnerships make all elections available (except for those listed in b. below), such as
        1) Methods of accounting
        2) Computing depreciation
        3) Inventory methods
        4) Installment method election
        5) Expensing intangible drilling and development costs

        These elections apply equally amongst all partners; however, no election made by a partnership has any force or effect with respect to any partner's nonpartnership interests.
    b. Partners make the following elections on the individual income tax return:
        1) Deduction or credit of foreign income taxes paid
            a) The amount is limited to the partner's distributive share from the partnership.
        2) Treatment of mining and exploration expenditures
        3) Basis reduction following discharge of indebtedness

Adjustments to Basis

12. The basis of a partner's interest in a partnership is adjusted each year for subsequent contributions of capital, partnership taxable income (loss), separately stated items, variations in the partner's share of partnership liabilities, and distributions from the partnership to the partner.

	Initial basis
+	Subsequent contributions of capital
+/–	Distributive share of partnership ordinary business income (loss)
+	Separately stated taxable and nontaxable income
–	Separately stated deductible and nondeductible expenditures
+	Increase in allocable share of partnership liabilities
–	Decrease in allocable share of partnership liabilities
–	Current-year excess business interest expense
–	Share of the adjusted basis of charitable property contributions and foreign taxes paid or accrued
–	Distributions from partnership
=	**Adjusted basis in partnership interest**

EXAMPLE 10-5 Year-End Adjusted Basis

The taxpayer's ownership and basis in the partnership are 50% and $15,000, respectively, at the beginning of the year. The partnership has ordinary income of $8,000, made charitable contributions of $3,000, and made a $5,000 distribution to the taxpayer. The taxpayer's basis at the end of the year is $12,500 [$15,000 beginning basis + ($8,000 ordinary income × 50% ownership) – ($3,000 charitable contribution × 50% ownership) – $5,000 distribution].

a. Basis is adjusted for variations in a partner's allocable share of partnership liabilities during the year, e.g., by payments on principal.
    1) Partner capital accounts are not adjusted for partnership liability variations.
b. Basis is not reduced below zero.
c. Basis is reduced without regard to losses suspended under passive activity loss rules and at-risk rules or losses creating an NOL under the excess loss rules.
d. No adjustment to basis is made for guaranteed payments received.

Loss Limits

13. A partnership ordinary loss is a negative balance of taxable income.

Basis Limit

a. A partner's distributive share of a partnership ordinary loss is allowable as a deduction to the partner only to the extent of the partner's AB in his or her interest in the partnership at the end of the year. Excess loss is deductible in a subsequent year in which AB is greater than zero.

At-Risk Rules

b. Each partner may deduct only a partnership ordinary loss to the extent (s)he is at risk with respect to the partnership.
   1) The at-risk limits also apply at the partnership level with respect to each partnership activity.
   2) The amount of a partnership loss currently deductible (up to an amount for which the partnership bears economic risk of loss with respect to each partnership activity) is allocated to partners as a deductible distributive share.
      a) Only partnership liabilities for which a partner is personally liable can be considered in a partner's at-risk limit.

c. Passive activity losses are deductible in the current tax year only to the extent of gains from passive activities (in the aggregate).
   1) Partnership ordinary loss is generally passive to a partner unless the partner materially participates in the partnership activity.

Excess Business Loss

d. When total losses from all trades or businesses exceed all gross income and gains from all sources, only $270,000 of the net loss is deductible on an individual return ($540,000 in the case of MFJ).
   1) Any nondeductible loss is treated as a net operating loss.

Gift of a Partnership Interest

14. Generally, no gain is recognized upon the gift. However, if partnership liabilities allocable to the gifted interest exceed the AB of the partnership interest, the donor must recognize gain. No loss is recognized on the gift.
   a. The donee's basis in the interest is the donor's basis after adjustment for the donor's distributive share of partnership items up to the date of the gift.
   b. For purposes of computing a loss on a subsequent sale of the interest by the donee, the FMV of the interest immediately prior to the gift is used if the FMV of the gifted partnership interest is lower than the basis at the time of the gift.

Inheritance

15. The tax year of a partnership closes with respect to a partner whose entire interest in the partnership terminates, whether by death, liquidation, or otherwise.
    a. The successor has a FMV basis in the interest.
    b. The partnership tax year does not close with respect to the other partners.

EXAMPLE 10-6 Effect of Partnership Liabilities

Ivan acquired a 20% interest in a partnership by contributing property that had an adjusted basis to him of $8,000 and a $4,000 mortgage. The partnership assumed payment of the mortgage. The basis of Ivan's interest is calculated as follows:

Adjusted basis of contributed property	$8,000
Minus: Part of mortgage assumed by other partners (80% × $4,000)	3,200
Basis of Ivan's partnership interest	$4,800

EXAMPLE 10-7 Effect of Partnership Liabilities

If, in Example 10-6, the contributed property had a $12,000 mortgage, the basis of Ivan's partnership interest would be zero. The $1,600 difference between the mortgage assumed by the other partners, $9,600 (80% × $12,000), and his basis of $8,000 would be treated as capital gain from the sale or exchange of a partnership interest. However, this gain would not increase the basis of his partnership interest.

EXAMPLE 10-8 Adjusted Basis of Partner's Interest

Enzo contributes to his partnership property that has an adjusted basis of $400 and a fair market value of $1,000. His partner contributes $1,000 cash. While each partner has increased his capital account by $1,000, which will be reflected in the partnership's books, the adjusted basis of Enzo's interest is only $400 and the adjusted basis of his partner's interest is $1,000.

EXAMPLE 10-9 Adjusted Basis of Partner's Interest

Juan and Teresa form a cash-basis general partnership with cash contributions of $20,000 each. Under the partnership agreement, they share all partnership profits and losses equally. The partnership borrows $60,000 and purchases depreciable business equipment. This debt is included in the partners' basis in the partnership because incurring it creates an additional $60,000 of basis in the partnership's depreciable property.

If neither partner has an economic risk of loss in the liability, it is a nonrecourse liability. Each partner's basis would include his or her share of the liability: $30,000.

If Teresa is required to pay the creditor if the partnership defaults, she has an economic risk of loss in the liability. Her basis in the partnership would be $80,000 ($20,000 + $60,000), while Juan's basis would be $20,000.

EXAMPLE 10-10 Sale, Exchange, or Other Transfer

Kumar became a limited partner in the ABC Partnership by contributing $10,000 in cash on the formation of the partnership. The adjusted basis of his partnership interest at the end of the current year is $20,000, which includes his $15,000 share of partnership liabilities. The partnership has no unrealized receivables or inventory items.

Kumar sells his interest in the partnership for $10,000 in cash. He had been paid his share of the partnership income for the tax year. Kumar realizes $25,000 from the sale of his partnership interest ($10,000 cash payment + $15,000 liability relief). He reports $5,000 ($25,000 realized gain – $20,000 basis) as a capital gain.

EXAMPLE 10-11 Sale, Exchange, or Other Transfer -- Partner Withdrawal

The facts are the same as in Example 10-10, except Kumar withdraws from the partnership when the adjusted basis of his interest in the partnership is zero. He is considered to have received a distribution of $15,000, his liability relief. He reports a capital gain of $15,000.

Reporting Requirements of a Partnership

16. A partnership, as a conduit, is not subject to federal income tax. But it must report information that includes partnership items of income, loss, deduction, and credit to the IRS.
    a. A partnership is required to file an initial return for the first year in which it receives income or incurs expenditures treated as deductions for federal income tax purposes.
    b. Form 1065 is used for the partnership's information return.
    c. Signature by any partner is evidence that the partner was authorized to sign the return. Only one partner is required to sign the return.
    d. Any partnership item that may vary tax liability of any partner is separately stated on Schedule K.
    e. A Schedule K-1 is prepared for each partner and contains the partner's distributive share of partnership income and separately stated items to be reported on the partner's tax return.
    f. There are penalties for not filing correct information returns and/or not furnishing correct payee statements.

Large Businesses with Gross Receipts of More Than $5 Million and Government Entities (Average annual gross receipts for the most recent 3 taxable years) IRC 6721 & IRC 6722

Time returns filed/furnished	Due 01-01-2022 thru 12-31-2022 (inflation adjusted)	Due 01-01-2023 thru 12-31-2023 (inflation adjusted)
Not more than 30 days late (by March 30 if the due date is February 28)	$50 per return/ $571,000 maximum	$50 per return/ $588,500 maximum
31 days late – August 1	$110 per return/ $1,713,000 maximum	$110 per return/ $1,766,000 maximum
After August 1 or Not At All	$280 per return/ $3,426,000 maximum	$290 per return/ $3,532,500 maximum
Intentional Disregard	$570 per return/ No limitation	$580 per return/ No limitation

Small Businesses with Gross Receipts $5 Million or Less (Average annual gross receipts for the most recent 3 taxable years) IRC 6721 & IRC 6722

Time returns filed/furnished	Due 01-01-2022 thru 12-31-2022 (inflation adjusted)	Due 01-01-2023 thru 12-31-2023 (inflation adjusted)
Not more than 30 days late (by March 30 if the due date is February 28)	$50 per return/ $199,500 maximum	$50 per return/ $206,000 maximum
31 days late – August 1	$110 per return/ $571,000 maximum	$110 per return/ $588,500 maximum
After August 1 or Not At All	$280 per return/ $1,142,000 maximum	$290 per return/ $1,177,500 maximum
Intentional Disregard	$570 per return/ No limitation	$580 per return/ No limitation

g. A partnership return is due (postmark date) on or before the 15th day of the 3rd month following the close of the partnership's tax year.

h. Inadequate filing. Penalty is imposed in the amount of the number of persons who were partners at any time during the year, multiplied by $220 (for 2022 returns filed in 2023) for each of up to 12 months (including a portion of one) that the return was late or incomplete.

Partnership Representative

17. The IRC provides for designation of a partnership representative who has sole authority to commit the partnership to tax and litigation matters.

    a. All partnerships must designate a **partnership representative** who

        1) May be a partner in the partnership,
        2) Must have a substantial presence in the U.S., and
        3) Has sole authority to act on behalf of the partnership for purposes of the new rules.

b. The partnership representative's exclusive authority also includes acting on the partnership's behalf in all matters involving examination of the partnership's tax return, conducting administrative practice before the IRS, and conducting matters of litigation regarding disputed tax adjustments.

1) A partner (other than the designated partnership representative) does not have the statutory right to notification of an audit or updates on its progress and does not have the right to participate in the audit or resulting litigation.

2) The partnership representative is designated annually on the partnership's tax return, and the effective date is the date of filing the return.

c. A partnership with 100 or fewer partners may opt out of having a partnership representative as long as all partners are "qualifying partners."

1) Qualifying partners are individuals, estates of deceased partners, and corporations (both C and S corporations).

2) If the partnership elects to opt out, the IRS will proceed with an audit of each individual partner.

d. Affirmative action of electing a partnership representative or opting out must occur on each year's tax return.

Consistent Treatment Rules

e. The partner's treatment of partnership items must be consistent with the treatment of that item by the partnership in all respects, including the amount, timing, and characterization of the item.

Reporting for Qualified Business Income Deduction (QBID)

18. In regards to a partnership, the qualified business income (QBI) deduction is determined at the partner level. To allow partners to correctly figure the deduction on the partner's Form 1040 return, the partnership must report QBI related items on the partner's Schedule K-1.

    a. Identify each trade or business that is a specified service trade or business (SSTB). The SSTBs are subject to special limitations, not applicable to the qualified trades or businesses, and generally include a trade or business where the principal asset is the reputation or skill of one or more of its employees.

    b. The QBI (e.g., income, gain, deduction, and loss) from the trade or businesses.

    c. The W-2 wage totals paid to employees by each trade or business.

19. Each partner must report his or her share of items consistently with their treatment on the partnership return.

20. When a partner dies, his or her distributive share of self-employment income is figured through the end of the month in which the death occurs.

Stop & Review

You have completed the outline for this subunit.

Study multiple-choice questions 1 through 10 beginning on page 239.

10.2 DISTRIBUTION OF PARTNERSHIP ASSETS

A distribution is a transfer of value from the partnership to a partner in reference to his or her interest in the partnership. A distribution may be in the form of money, liability relief, or other property. A draw is a distribution.

Current Distributions

1. A current (or operating) distribution reduces the partner's basis in the partnership interest.
   a. A decrease in a partner's allocable share of partnership liabilities is treated as a distribution of money.

Money Distributions

   b. The partnership recognizes no gain on money distributions.
      1) A partner recognizes gain only to the extent the distribution (FMV) exceeds the AB in the partnership interest immediately before the distribution.
         a) Gain recognized is capital gain.
         b) Basis in the interest is decreased, but not below zero.
         c) Loss is not recognized.

Property Distributions

   c. **Partnership.** Generally, no gain or loss is recognized by the partnership when it distributes property, including money.
      1) Precontribution gain or loss. If property is distributed to a noncontributing partner within 7 years of contribution, the partnership recognizes gain or loss realized to the extent of any unrealized gain or loss, respectively, that existed at the contribution date.
         a) Allocate this recognized gain (loss) to the contributing partner.
         b) The contributing partner's basis in his or her partnership interest is increased.
         c) Basis in the property is also increased.
         d) The distributee has a transferred basis.
      2) Disproportionate distributions of unrealized receivables or substantially appreciated inventory result in gain recognition.
         a) Inventory is considered substantially appreciated if its FMV exceeds 120% of the partnership's adjusted basis.
         b) Gains from such distributions are taxed as ordinary income.
   d. **Partner.** The distributee partner generally recognizes gain only to the extent that money (including liability relief) exceeds his or her AB in his or her partnership interest.
      1) However, property distributions made to a partner may cause a partner to recognize any remaining precontribution gain if the FMV of the distributed property exceeds the partner's basis in his or her partnership interest prior to the distribution. The gain recognized is the lesser of
         a) The remaining precontribution gain or
         b) The excess of the FMV of the distributed property over the adjusted basis of the partnership interest immediately before the property distribution (but after any reduction for any money distributed at the same time).

e. The partner's basis in the distributed property is the partnership's AB in the property immediately before distribution, but it is limited to the distributee's AB in his or her partnership interest minus any money received in the distribution.

1) When the above limit applies, allocate basis first to unrealized receivables and inventory, up to the partnership's AB in them, and second to other (noncash) property.

2) If the available basis is too small, the decrease (Partnership basis in assets – Basis in partnership interest) is allocated to the assets. The decrease is allocated by the following steps:

a) Assign each asset its partnership basis.

b) Calculate the decrease amount.

c) Allocate the decrease first to any assets that have declined in value.

d) Allocate any remaining decrease to the assets based on relative adjusted basis at this point in the calculation.

EXAMPLE 10-12 Allocation if Available Basis Is Inadequate

Karen has a $6,000 basis in the BK Partnership immediately before receiving a current distribution (there is no remaining precontribution gain). The distribution consists of $5,000 cash, a computer with a FMV of $1,500 and a $4,000 basis to the partnership, and a desk with a FMV of $500 and a $1,500 basis to the partnership. Karen's basis in the distributed property is determined as follows:

Beginning basis in partnership interest	$6,000
Less: Money received	(5,000)
Remaining basis to allocate	$1,000

		Computer	Desk
Step 1: Allocate partnership basis to each asset.	Partnership basis in assets	$ 4,000	$1,500
Step 2: Calculate decrease.			

Total partnership basis	$5,500
Basis to allocate	(1,000)
Decrease amount	$4,500

		Computer	Desk
Step 3: Allocate decrease to assets with a decline in FMV.	Decline in FMV	(2,500)	(1,000)
	Relative adjusted basis	$ 1,500	$ 500
Step 4: Allocate remaining decrease of $1,000 ($4,500 – $2,500 – $1,000) based on relative adjusted basis.	Remaining decrease	(750)*	(250)*
	Karen's basis in distributed property	$ 750	$ 250

* $750 = ($1,500 ÷ $2,000) × $1,000
$250 = ($500 ÷ $2,000) × $1,000

f. The partner's holding period in the distributed property includes that of the partnership.

g. The partner's basis in his or her ownership interest in the partnership is reduced by the amount of money and the AB of property received in the distribution.

Stop & Review

You have completed the outline for this subunit.

Study multiple-choice questions 11 through 15 beginning on page 243.

10.3 PARTNERS DEALING WITH THEIR OWN PARTNERSHIP

The Code recognizes that a partner can engage in property, services, and loan transactions with the partnership in a capacity other than as a partner, i.e., as an independent, outside third party. The tax result, in general, is as if the transaction took place between two unrelated persons after arm's-length negotiations.

Customary Partner Services

1. When a partner performs services for the partnership that are customarily performed by a partner, the partner's return is generally his or her share of profits of the partnership business.
   a. A partner's allocable share of partnership items is the partner's "compensation" for acting to perform the normal functions of a partner, e.g., driving the truck and keeping books of an ice cream vending partnership.
      1) It is gross income, not as compensation, but as a distributive share of partnership income.
      2) The value of the services is not deductible by the partnership.

Guaranteed Payments

2. A guaranteed payment (GP) is a payment to a partner for services rendered or capital used that is determined without regard to the income of the partnership. It is used to distinguish payments that are a function of partnership income and payments connected with partners acting in a nonpartner capacity.
   a. **Services.** The services must be a customary function of a partner. They are normal activities of a partner in conducting partnership business.
   b. **Fixed amount stated.** If the partnership agreement provides for a GP in a fixed amount, e.g., annual salary amount, the GP amount is the stated amount.
   c. **Use of capital.** The payment may be stated to be interest on the partner's capital account or to be rent on contributed property.
   d. **Stated minimum amount.** The partnership agreement may allocate a share of partnership income to the partner but guarantee payment of not less than a stated amount to the partner even if the allocable share is less.
      1) If so, the GP amount is any excess of the guaranteed minimum amount over the distributive share allocable to the partner.
   e. For purposes of determining the partner's gross income, the GP is treated as if made to a nonpartner.
      1) The partner separately states the GP from any distributive share.
      2) The payment is always ordinary income to the partner (compensation, interest, possibly rent).
      3) The GP is reported in the recipient partner's tax year that includes the end of the partnership tax year (in which the GP was made or deducted by the partnership).
      4) Receipt of the GP does not directly affect the partner's AB in his or her partnership interest.

f. For purposes of determining deductibility by the partnership, a GP is treated as if made to a nonpartner.

1) The payment is deductible if it would have been deductible if made to a nonpartner.

2) If the GP exceeds the partnership's ordinary income, the resulting ordinary loss is allocated among the partners (including the partner who receives the GP).

EXAMPLE 10-13 Guaranteed Payment to a Partner

Under a partnership agreement, Meena is to receive 30% of the partnership income, but not less than $13,000. The partnership has net income of $30,000. Meena's share, without regard to the minimum guarantee, is $9,000 (30% × $30,000). The guaranteed payment that can be deducted by the partnership is $4,000 ($13,000 – $9,000). Meena's income from the partnership is $13,000, and the remaining $17,000 of partnership income will be reported by the other partners in proportion to their shares under the partnership agreement.

If the partnership net income had been $50,000, there would have been no guaranteed payment since Meena's share, without regard to the guarantee, would have been greater than the guarantee.

g. For all other purposes, the GP is treated as if made to a partner in his or her capacity as a partner.

1) A partner is not an employee of the partnership.
2) The GP is self-employment income to the receiving partner.

EXAMPLE 10-14 Partner's Ordinary Income

Under the terms of a partnership agreement, Erica is entitled to a fixed annual payment of $10,000 without regard to the income of the partnership. Her distributive share of the partnership income is 10%. The partnership has $50,000 of ordinary income after deducting the guaranteed payment. She must include ordinary income of $15,000 [$10,000 guaranteed payment + $5,000 ($50,000 × 10%) distributive share] on her individual income tax return for her tax year in which the partnership's tax year ends.

EXAMPLE 10-15 Partner's Ordinary Income

Lamont is a calendar-year taxpayer who is a partner in a partnership. The partnership uses a fiscal year that ended January 31, 2022. Lamont received guaranteed payments from the partnership from February 1, 2021, until December 31, 2021. He must include these guaranteed payments in income for 2022 and report them on his 2022 income tax return.

Nonpartner Capacity

3. Payments to a partner without regard to income of the partnership for property or for services not customarily performed by a partner are generally treated as if the transaction took place between two unrelated persons after arm's-length negotiations.
   a. **Loans.** Interest paid to a partner on a (true) loan is all gross income to the partner and a deductible partnership item.
   b. **Services.** Payments to the partner for services rendered (of a nature not normally performed by a partner) to or for the partnership are gross income to the partner and generally an ordinary deductible expense of the partnership.
   c. **Property.** A partner acting as a nonpartner (independent third party, outsider) can sell (or exchange) property to (or with) the partnership and vice versa. Gain or loss on the transaction is recognized unless an exception applies.

EXAMPLE 10-16 **Sale to Partner Acting as a Nonpartner**
Partnership sells land to Partner. Partnership recognizes loss unless the sale is to a related party. The loss is a partnership item allocable to partners as distributive shares. Partner takes a cost basis in the property.

   d. Character and loss limit rules.
      1) **Applicability.** These loss limits apply to any transaction between the partnership and either
         a) A partner who owns more than 50% of the partnership or
         b) Another partnership if more than 50% of the capital or profits interest of each is owned by the same persons.
      2) **Character.** Any gain recognized is OI if the property is held as other than a capital asset by the acquiring partner or partnership.

EXAMPLE 10-17 **Sale of Capital Assets -- Change in Character**
Dora has held a capital asset for several years. The asset has a basis of $16,000 and a FMV of $24,000. She sells the asset to a partnership in which she is more than a 50% owner. The partnership will hold the property as a depreciable asset. Her gain of $8,000 ($24,000 – $16,000) will be ordinary income since she sold a capital asset to a more-than-50%-owned partnership that is not a capital asset to the partnership. If the partnership were to hold the asset as a capital asset, her gain would be capital gain.

      3) Related party sales.
         a) The acquiring party has a cost basis, and a subsequent taxable disposition event results in no more gain recognition than any excess of realized gain over the loss previously disallowed.
         b) Expenditures are deductible when, and not before, the amount is includible in gross income by the payee, even if the payor is an accrual-method taxpayer.

Stop & Review

You have completed the outline for this subunit.

Study multiple-choice questions 16 through 25 beginning on page 246.

QUESTIONS

10.1 Partnership Operations and Partner's Taxable Income

1. John owns a residential contracting business. Capital is a material income-producing factor. John's services to the business for Year 1 were worth $30,000. John's son, Alex, is interested in eventually working in his father's business. On January 1, Year 1, Alex receives a gift of 20% of his father's interest in the business. Alex performed no services for the business in Year 1. If the resulting partnership had a profit of $100,000 for tax year Year 1, how much of the partnership profit should be allocated to Alex?

A. $20,000

B. $35,000

C. $50,000

D. $14,000

Answer (D) is correct.

REQUIRED: The partnership profit allocated when partnership interest is received as a gift.

DISCUSSION: In a gift of a partnership interest, the donee's distributive share must be determined after due allowance has been made for the services contributed by the donor. Thus, the 20% gift is taken from the $100,000 profit minus John's services of $30,000. The calculation is [($100,000 – $30,000) × .20].

2. All of the following items must be separately stated on the partnership's Schedule K (Form 1065) and included as separate items on the partner's return EXCEPT

A. Ordinary gains and losses from Form 4797, Part II.

B. Gains and losses from sales or exchanges of capital assets.

C. Guaranteed payments to the partners.

D. Interest income.

Answer (A) is correct.

REQUIRED: The item not required to be separately stated on a partnership Schedule K.

DISCUSSION: Each partnership item of income, gain, deduction, loss, or credit that may vary the tax liability of any partner (if reported separately on the partner's personal return) must be separately stated. Items that must be separately stated include the following: (1) Sec. 1231 gains and losses; (2) net short-term and net long-term capital gain or loss from the sale or exchange of capital assets; (3) guaranteed payments; (4) interest and dividend income; (5) royalties; (6) tax-exempt income and related expenses; (7) investment income and related expenses; (8) rental activities, portfolio income, and related expenses; (9) cancellation of debt; (10) recovery items (e.g., prior taxes, bad debts); (11) charitable contributions; (12) foreign income taxes paid or accrued; (13) depletion on oil and gas wells; (14) Sec. 179 deductions; (15) distributions; and (16) qualified items of income, gain, and loss for the qualified business income deduction (QBID) (Publication 541, Form 1065 Schedule K, and the instructions to Form 1065).

3. Juan and Adelfo are equal partners in a music store. In 2022, they bought an amplifier for use in the store to demonstrate certain instruments. The amplifier cost $30,000. The partnership's taxable income before the Sec. 179 deduction is $25,000. What amount of Sec. 179 expense can Juan and Adelfo each deduct if neither has any other Sec. 179 deductions?

A. $0

B. $12,500

C. $30,000

D. $25,000

Answer (B) is correct.

REQUIRED: The Sec. 179 expense each partner can deduct if neither has any other Sec. 179 deductions.

DISCUSSION: Several types of deductions must be reported separately by the partners, including Sec. 179 deductions. With regard to elections to expense Sec. 179 property, the dollar limitations apply both to the partnership and to each individual partner. The maximum Sec. 179 deduction is $1,080,000 for 2022. The deduction for the $30,000 cost of the amplifier is further limited to the partnership's taxable income of $25,000, which is then split between the two partners.

Answer (A) is incorrect. The partners are entitled to a limited Sec. 179 deduction. **Answer (C) is incorrect.** The maximum deduction for 2022 for the partnership is $1,080,000, which is well above the $30,000 cost; however, the deduction cannot be greater than taxable income. **Answer (D) is incorrect.** The partners split the $25,000 deduction.

4. Comfy Chairs Manufacturing, Ltd. operates as a partnership and files Form 1065. Comfy manufactures inflatable lounge chairs. During the current tax year ended December 31, Comfy generated income and expenses as stated below. What is the correct amount of ordinary income (loss) from trade or business activities Comfy should report on Schedule K for the current year?

Employee wages	$15,000
Income from rental real estate	20,000
Charitable contributions	500
Cost of goods sold	10,000
Income from chair sales	75,000

A. $65,000

B. $69,500

C. $50,000

D. $30,000

Answer (C) is correct.

REQUIRED: The correct amount of ordinary income to be reported on a Schedule K.

DISCUSSION: Included in the partnership's ordinary income are such items as gross profit on sales, administrative expenses, and employee expenses. Thus, income from chair sales, employee wages, and cost of goods sold are included in ordinary income to give $50,000 ($75,000 – $15,000 – $10,000). Charitable contributions and income from rental real estate have to be separately stated. Ordinary income is different from partnership taxable income in that partnership taxable income is the sum of all taxable income items, including separately stated items and ordinary income items.

Answer (A) is incorrect. Employee wages are deductible as ordinary income of a partnership. **Answer (B) is incorrect.** Income from rental real estate and charitable contributions are not included as ordinary income (expense) of a partnership. **Answer (D) is incorrect.** Ordinary income includes gross profit on sales, administrative expenses, and employee expenses.

5. On January 1, 2020, Thomas contributed real estate he held for investment to Fog Partnership, a dealer in real estate. The real estate had an adjusted basis to Thomas of $50,000 and a fair market value at the time of the transfer of $43,000. On June 1, 2022, Fog sold the real estate for $40,000. What are the amount and the character of the partnership's loss?

A. $3,000 capital loss; $7,000 ordinary loss.

B. $7,000 capital loss; $3,000 ordinary loss.

C. $10,000 ordinary loss; $0 capital loss.

D. $10,000 capital loss; $0 ordinary loss.

Answer (B) is correct.

REQUIRED: The amount and the character of the partnership's loss on the sale of contributed property.

DISCUSSION: The partnership's basis in the property was $50,000 under Sec. 723. The loss realized and recognized on its sale was $10,000 (Sec. 1001). If property is contributed that would have generated a capital loss if sold by the partner, a loss on the disposition of the property within 5 years of its contribution is a capital loss [Sec. 724(c)]. The amount of the loss characterized as capital is the $7,000 amount of capital loss the contributing partner would have recognized if (s)he had sold the property on the contribution date ($50,000 – $43,000). The remaining loss has the character it would have to the partnership.

Answer (A) is incorrect. The amount of the loss characterized as capital is the amount of capital loss the contributing partner would have recognized if (s)he had sold the property on the contribution date. **Answer (C) is incorrect.** When property is contributed that would have generated a capital loss if sold by the partner, a loss on the disposition of the property within 5 years of its contribution is a capital loss. **Answer (D) is incorrect.** The amount of the loss characterized as capital is the amount of capital loss the contributing partner would have recognized if (s)he had sold the property on the contribution date.

6. Partnership LIFE's profits and losses are shared equally among the four partners. The adjusted basis of Partner E's interest in the partnership on December 31, Year 1, was $25,000. On January 2, Year 2, Partner E withdrew $10,000 cash. The partnership reported $200,000 as ordinary income on its Year 2 partnership return. In addition, $5,000 for qualified travel, meals, and entertainment was shown on a separate attachment to E's Schedule K-1 of Form 1065. Due to the limitation, $2,500 of the $5,000 is unallowable as a deduction. What is the amount of E's basis in the partnership on December 31, Year 2?

A. $60,000

B. $61,000

C. $65,000

D. $75,000

Answer (A) is correct.

REQUIRED: The adjusted basis of a partner's partnership interest.

DISCUSSION: The adjusted basis of a partner's interest is the original basis of such interest, increased by the partner's distributive share of the partnership's income and allocable portion of liabilities, and decreased by the partner's distributive share of partnership loss and distributions (Secs. 705, 733, and 752). Partnership basis is also reduced by both deductible and nondeductible expenses.

Beginning basis	$ 25,000
Ordinary income ($200,000 × 25%)	50,000
Cash distribution	(10,000)
Travel, meals, entertainment expense	(5,000)
Year-end basis	$ 60,000

Answer (B) is incorrect. The adjusted basis of a partner's partnership interest is increased by the ordinary income and the expenses on the Schedule K-1 and is reduced by the amount of the cash distribution. **Answer (C) is incorrect.** Partnership basis is also reduced by both deductible and nondeductible qualified travel, meals, and entertainment expenses. **Answer (D) is incorrect.** Partner E's partnership basis is reduced by the amount of the $10,000 cash distributed and both deductible and nondeductible qualified travel, meals, and entertainment expenses.

7. Partner C invested $30,000 cash for a 60% interest in ABC Partnership. C materially participates in the partnership's business, and the partnership agreement states he is liable for all of the partnership's debts. The only partnership debt at the year end was a $15,000 loan from Book Bank. Partner C and the other general partner had a separate agreement that C's liability would not exceed $10,000. The partnership reported a $70,000 ordinary loss for the year. What is the amount of C's deductible loss?

A. $40,000

B. $42,000

C. $45,000

D. $70,000

Answer (A) is correct.

REQUIRED: The partner's deductible loss when (s)he signs an agreement that states his or her liability will not exceed a certain amount.

DISCUSSION: A general partner's basis in his or her partnership interest is increased by his or her share of the partnership's recourse liabilities for which (s)he is ultimately liable [Code Sec. 752(a)]. Partner C's ultimate share of the bank debt ($10,000 per the separate agreement) plus his original basis of $30,000 gives him an adjusted basis of $40,000. Although Partner C's share of the partnership loss is 60% of $70,000, or $42,000, his deductible loss is limited to his adjusted basis of $40,000 [Code Sec. 704(d)].

Answer (B) is incorrect. Partner C's total share of the loss is $42,000, not all of which is deductible. **Answer (C) is incorrect.** The amount of $45,000 includes the total liability of $15,000 and exceeds C's share of the loss. **Answer (D) is incorrect.** The total partnership loss is not attributable to Partner C.

8. The adjusted basis of Carol's partnership interest is $50,000. She receives a distribution of $10,000 cash, land that has an adjusted basis of $30,000, and a FMV of $50,000. What is Carol's adjusted basis in the land?

A. $20,000

B. $30,000

C. $40,000

D. $50,000

Answer (B) is correct.

REQUIRED: The partner's adjusted basis for distributed property.

DISCUSSION: Publication 541 states, "Unless there is a complete liquidation of a partner's interest, the basis of property (other than money) distributed to the partner by a partnership is its adjusted basis to the partnership immediately before the distribution. However, the basis of the property to the partner cannot be more than the adjusted basis of his or her interest in the partnership reduced by any money received in the same transaction." Therefore, Carol's adjusted basis in the land is $30,000, the adjusted basis to the partnership immediately before the distribution.

Answer (A) is incorrect. The amount of $20,000 is not the adjusted basis to the partnership immediately before the distribution. **Answer (C) is incorrect.** Carol's partnership interest less the cash distribution is $40,000. **Answer (D) is incorrect.** The FMV of the distributed property is $50,000.

9. Which of the following is true concerning the qualified business income deduction from a partnership?

A. The deduction is taken by the partnership.

B. Qualified trades and businesses are subject to special limitations that specified service trades and businesses are not.

C. W-2 wage totals paid to employees are not reported.

D. The partner claims the deduction on their individual return.

Answer (D) is correct.

REQUIRED: The true statement about QBID.

DISCUSSION: The QBID is determined at the partner level, not the entity (i.e., partnership) level. However, the partnership reports the applicable amounts needed for the partner to claim the deduction on the partner's Schedule K-1.

Answer (A) is incorrect. The partnership reports the applicable amounts for the partner to take the deduction on their individual return on the partner's Schedule K-1. **Answer (B) is incorrect.** Specified service trades and businesses are subject to special limitations that qualified trades and businesses are not. **Answer (C) is incorrect.** W-2 wage totals paid to employees are among the amounts the partnership must report on the partner's Schedule K-1.

10. A partner is considered NOT at risk for which of the following amounts?

A. The money and adjusted basis of any property the partner contributed to the activity.

B. The partner's share of net income retained by the partnership.

C. An allocation of a loss, deduction, or expense attributable to a partnership nonrecourse liability.

D. Certain amounts borrowed by the partnership for use in the activity if the partner is personally liable for repayment.

Answer (C) is correct.

REQUIRED: The amount for which a partner is considered not at risk.

DISCUSSION: Section 465 states that each partner may deduct only a partnership ordinary loss to the extent (s)he is at risk with respect to the partnership. The at-risk limits also apply at the partnership level with respect to each partnership activity. The amount of a partnership loss currently deductible (up to an amount for which the partnership bears economic risk of loss with respect to each partnership activity) is allocated to partners as a deductible distributive share. Since a nonrecourse liability means that the partnership bears no economic risk of loss, there is no at-risk loss in the transaction.

Answer (A) is incorrect. A partner is at risk for the money and adjusted basis of property contributed to the activity because there is a risk of economic loss if the activity is unprofitable. **Answer (B) is incorrect.** The retention of net income by the partnership exposes the partner to the possibility of economic loss. **Answer (D) is incorrect.** Personal liability for a loan is considered an at-risk activity because the loan must be repaid.

10.2 Distribution of Partnership Assets

11. The adjusted basis of Stan's partnership interest is $15,000. He receives a distribution of cash of $6,000 and property with an adjusted basis to the partnership of $11,000. (This was not a distribution in liquidation.) What is the basis of the distributed property in Stan's hands?

A. $9,000

B. $11,000

C. $5,000

D. $17,000

Answer (A) is correct.

REQUIRED: The basis of distributive property to a partner.

DISCUSSION: Section 732(a) provides that the basis of property distributed to a partner is the property's adjusted basis to the partnership immediately before such distribution. This basis, however, cannot exceed the adjusted basis of the partner's interest in the partnership minus any money received in the same distribution [Sec. 732(a)(2)]. Stan's basis in the property distributed is

Basis of partnership interest	$15,000
Less: Cash received	(6,000)
Basis in distributed property	$ 9,000

Answer (B) is incorrect. The basis of the distributed property cannot exceed the adjusted basis of the partner's interest in the partnership. **Answer (C) is incorrect.** The basis of the distributed property will not be equal to the difference between the amount of cash received and the partnership's basis in the property. **Answer (D) is incorrect.** The amount of $17,000 includes the cash received.

12. At a time when Nedra's basis in her partnership interest was $5,000, she received a current distribution of $6,000 cash and land with an adjusted basis of $2,000 and a fair market value of $3,000. The partnership had no unrealized receivables or substantially appreciated inventory. What is the result of this distribution to Nedra?

A. $0 gain or loss, $0 basis in land, $(1,000) basis in partnership interest.

B. $3,000 capital gain, $2,000 basis in land, $0 basis in partnership interest.

C. $1,000 ordinary income, $2,000 basis in land, $0 basis in partnership interest.

D. $1,000 capital gain, $0 basis in land, $0 basis in partnership interest.

Answer (D) is correct.

REQUIRED: The tax result of a current distribution to a partner.

DISCUSSION: Gain is not recognized to a partner on a distribution except to the extent that money distributed exceeds the partner's adjusted basis in the partnership interest. Since Nedra received $6,000 when she had a $5,000 basis in the partnership interest, she will recognize a $1,000 gain, which is a capital gain under Sec. 741. The basis in the land is zero under Sec. 732(a)(2) since the basis of property received in a distribution may not exceed the partner's basis in the partnership interest minus any money received in the distribution. Nedra's basis in the partnership interest after the distribution is zero because her basis was reduced by the money distributed to her (Sec. 733).

Answer (A) is incorrect. Capital gain is recognized for the cash distributed in excess of the partnership interest basis. Nedra's basis in her partnership interest after the distribution cannot go below zero. **Answer (B) is incorrect.** Capital gain is recognized for the cash distributed in excess of the partnership interest basis, not FMV of the land. The basis of the land distributed is zero since there is no remaining partnership interest basis to allocate. **Answer (C) is incorrect.** Capital gain, not ordinary income, is recognized for the cash distributed in excess of the partnership interest basis. The basis of the land distributed is zero since there is no remaining partnership interest basis to allocate.

13. The adjusted basis of Paul's partnership interest is $10,000. He receives a distribution of $4,000 cash and property that has an adjusted basis to the partnership of $8,000. (This was not a distribution in liquidation.) What is the basis of the distributed property in Paul's hands?

A. $8,000

B. $6,000

C. $14,000

D. $2,000

Answer (B) is correct.

REQUIRED: The basis of property distributed to a partner.

DISCUSSION: Section 732(a) provides that the basis of property distributed to a partner is the property's adjusted basis to the partnership immediately before such distribution. This basis, however, cannot exceed the adjusted basis of the partner's interest in the partnership minus any money received in the same distribution [Sec. 732(a)(2)]. Paul's basis in the property distributed is

Basis of partnership interest	$10,000
Less: Cash received	(4,000)
Basis in distributed property	$ 6,000

Answer (A) is incorrect. The basis of his partnership interest cannot be reduced below zero. **Answer (C) is incorrect.** The cash received reduces Paul's partnership; it does not increase his basis. **Answer (D) is incorrect.** The basis in the property is not equal to the difference between the basis in the partnership and the partnership's basis in the property.

14. In Year 1, Bob contributed investment land with basis of $14,000 and FMV of $20,000 in exchange for a 20% capital and profits interest in the ABC Partnership. Bob recognized no gain on the contribution. In Year 3, when Bob had a basis in his partnership interest of $35,000, he received a current distribution of machinery with a basis of $34,000 and fair market value of $37,000. Bob has not recognized any of his precontribution gain prior to the distribution. On the distribution, Bob must recognize

A. No gain or loss.

B. $1,000 capital gain.

C. $2,000 capital gain.

D. $6,000 capital gain.

Answer (C) is correct.

REQUIRED: The partner's recognized gain if a current distribution is made when precontribution gain has not previously been recognized.

DISCUSSION: Property distributions made to a partner may cause a partner to recognize any remaining precontribution gain if the FMV of the distributed property exceeds the partner's basis in his or her partnership interest prior to the distribution. The gain recognized under Sec. 737 is the lesser of (1) the remaining precontribution gain or (2) the excess of the FMV of the distributed property over the adjusted basis of the partnership interest immediately before the property distribution (but after any reduction for any money distributed at the same time). The Sec. 737 gain is in addition to any gain otherwise recognized under Sec. 731.

The partnership distribution rules would require Bob to recognize no gain since the adjusted basis of the distributed property ($34,000) is less than Bob's basis in his partnership interest ($35,000). However, under Sec. 737, Bob recognizes a $2,000 capital gain, the lesser of the $6,000 remaining precontribution gain, or the excess of the property's $37,000 fair market value over Bob's $35,000 basis in the partnership interest.

Answer (A) is incorrect. A gain is recognized on the distribution. **Answer (B) is incorrect.** The gain is not calculated as the basis in the partnership interest minus the basis of the machinery received. **Answer (D) is incorrect.** Under Sec. 737, Bob should recognize the lesser of the remaining precontribution gain or the excess of the property's fair market value over the basis in the partnership interest.

15. Joan's adjusted basis in the So-Lo Partnership is $15,000. She received a non-liquidating cash distribution of $2,500 and a piece of land with an adjusted basis of $7,500 and a fair market value of $5,000. What is the gain or loss to be recognized at the time of the distribution?

A. $5,000 loss.

B. $2,500 loss.

C. $0

D. $5,000 gain.

Answer (C) is correct.

REQUIRED: The gain or loss to be recognized at the time of the distribution.

DISCUSSION: Gain is not recognized to a partner on a distribution except to the extent that money distributed exceeds the partner's adjusted basis in the partnership interest. Since the $2,500 cash distribution is less than the $15,000 basis, no gain or loss is reported. The basis is reduced by the $2,500 cash distribution and the $7,500 basis in the land.

Answer (A) is incorrect. A loss is not recognized on a distribution to a partner. **Answer (B) is incorrect.** A loss is not recognized on a distribution to a partner. **Answer (D) is incorrect.** No gain is reported when the cash distribution is less than the partner's basis.

10.3 Partners Dealing with Their Own Partnership

16. A partnership in which Jane is 50% owner had a profit of $80,000. The partnership agreement provides for a 50-50 sharing of income. Capital is a material income producing factor. During the year, Jane performed services worth $20,000. What is the total income Jane should report from the partnership?

A. $20,000

B. $40,000

C. $50,000

D. $80,000

Answer (C) is correct.

REQUIRED: The total partnership income to be reported by a 50% partner.

DISCUSSION: The partnership agreement is disregarded to the extent a partner receives less than reasonable compensation for services. The $20,000 must be subtracted from the profit of the partnership. Therefore, she receives $20,000 for services performed and $30,000 [($80,000 – $20,000) × 50%] of partnership income and reports a total of $50,000 ($20,000 + $30,000) from the partnership.

Answer (A) is incorrect. Jane also receives a proportionate share of the profits in addition to the money received for services. **Answer (B) is incorrect.** Jane does not receive a 50% share of the $80,000 profit. The $80,000 must be reduced by the amount Jane received for services, or $20,000. **Answer (D) is incorrect.** Jane does not receive the entire profit amount of $80,000. It must be reduced by $20,000 and then divided among the partners.

17. Under a partnership agreement, June is to receive 40% of the partnership income but not less than $12,000 a year. The partnership has net income of $20,000. What is the guaranteed payment that the partnership can deduct in figuring its ordinary income on Page 1 of Form 1065?

A. $0

B. $3,200

C. $4,000

D. $8,000

Answer (C) is correct.

REQUIRED: The amount of the guaranteed payment deducted on Page 1 of Form 1065.

DISCUSSION: Publication 541 states, “Guaranteed payments are those made by a partnership to a partner that are determined without regard to the partnership’s income. A partnership treats guaranteed payments . . . as if they were made to a person who is not a partner. This treatment is for purposes of determining gross income and deductible business expenses only. . . . If a partner is to receive a minimum payment from the partnership, the guaranteed payment is the amount by which the minimum payment is more than the partner’s distributive share of the partnership income before taking into account the guaranteed payment.” This is the amount that can be deducted in figuring its ordinary income on Page 1 of Form 1065. The partnership can deduct $4,000 [$12,000 guaranteed payment – ($20,000 partnership net income × 40%)].

Answer (A) is incorrect. The guaranteed payment is the amount by which the minimum payment is more than the partner’s distributive share of partnership income before taking into account the guaranteed payment. **Answer (B) is incorrect.** The guaranteed payment is not equal to 40% of the difference between partnership income and $12,000. **Answer (D) is incorrect.** The guaranteed payment is not equal to the difference between partnership income and $12,000.

18. Jasmine, a calendar-year taxpayer, is a partner in Jasmine and Prince Partnership that has a fiscal year ending March 31. Starting April 1, 2022, Jasmine receives a fixed monthly guaranteed payment of $1,000 a month without regard to the income of the partnership. How much of the guaranteed payments will Jasmine report on her 2022 tax return?

A. $0

B. $8,000

C. $9,000

D. $12,000

Answer (A) is correct.

REQUIRED: The amount of guaranteed payment included on a partner's tax return.

DISCUSSION: For purposes of determining the partner's gross income, the guaranteed payment is treated as if made to a nonpartner. The partner separately states the guaranteed payment from any distributive share. The payment is ordinary income to the partner. Guaranteed payments are included as income in the recipient's tax year, which includes the end of the partnership tax year in which they were deducted. Thus, the guaranteed payments will not be reported in the partner's income until 2023.

Answer (B) is incorrect. Jasmine received 9 months of payments, not 8. **Answer (C) is incorrect.** The guaranteed payment is reported in 2023. **Answer (D) is incorrect.** Jasmine only received payments for 9 months of her tax year.

19. Joy and Roger are partners in JR and Associates. Under the terms of the partnership agreement, Joy is to receive 25% of all partnership income or loss plus a guaranteed payment of $60,000 per year. In the current year, the partnership had $50,000 of ordinary income before any deduction for Joy's guaranteed payment. What is the amount of income or loss Joy would report on her current tax return, assuming she materially participates in partnership activities?

A. $15,000 guaranteed payment, $2,500 loss.

B. $57,500 guaranteed payment.

C. $60,000 guaranteed payment.

D. $60,000 guaranteed payment, $2,500 loss.

Answer (D) is correct.

REQUIRED: The amount of income or loss a partner who materially participates in partnership activities would report.

DISCUSSION: Even though a partnership incurs a loss for a tax year, an active partner who receives a guaranteed payment must nevertheless take into account the full amount of such payment [Sec. 707(c)]. This inclusion is required even when the partnership loss is caused by that guaranteed payment to the partner. Furthermore, the partner must also take into account his or her distributive share of the partnership loss. Accordingly, Joy must include her $60,000 guaranteed payment and 25% of the $10,000 loss ($50,000 – $60,000) on her individual return.

Answer (A) is incorrect. The entire guaranteed payment to Joy is included. **Answer (B) is incorrect.** The $60,000 guaranteed payment is completely recognized, and the partner's share of the loss is also recognized. **Answer (C) is incorrect.** The partner's share of the loss must be recognized.

20. Under a partnership agreement, Gil is to receive 40% of the partnership income, but not less than $20,000. The partnership has net income of $100,000 for Year 1 without regard to the minimum guaranteed and before any allocation. What is the amount and character of the income Gil is to receive for Year 1?

A. $40,000 distributive share.

B. $20,000 guaranteed payment; $32,000 distributive share.

C. $20,000 guaranteed payment; $20,000 distributive share.

D. $20,000 guaranteed payment; $40,000 distributive share.

Answer (A) is correct.

REQUIRED: The amount and character of income the partner is to receive for Year 1.

DISCUSSION: Since the partnership's net income is $100,000, Gil's portion of the net income is $40,000. The $40,000 is greater than the minimum guaranteed. The $40,000 will be received in its entirety regardless of the minimum guaranteed. Therefore, all of the $40,000 is considered distributive share.

Answer (B) is incorrect. Since Gil's distributive share of partnership income is more than the guaranteed payment, the guaranteed payment is not subtracted from net income before the distributive share is calculated. **Answer (C) is incorrect.** No portion of the $40,000 from net income is considered guaranteed payment. **Answer (D) is incorrect.** Gil is not guaranteed $20,000 in addition to his share of the partnership's net income.

21. Howard has a 60% interest in the profits and losses of Deck Partnership. He also owns a 65% interest in the profits and losses of Card Partnership. On February 5, 2022, Deck sold land to Card for $35,000. At the time of the sale, the land had an adjusted basis to Deck of $40,000 and a fair market value of $45,000. What is the amount of loss that Deck can recognize in 2022?

A. $0

B. $3,250

C. $5,000

D. $6,500

Answer (A) is correct.

REQUIRED: The amount of loss a partnership can recognize on the sale of property to a related partnership.

DISCUSSION: Deck realized a $5,000 loss on the sale. However, Sec. 707(b)(1) provides that losses from sales or exchanges of property between two partnerships in which the same person or persons own more than 50% of the capital or profit interest are not deductible. When the property is subsequently sold, any realized gain is recognized only to the extent that it exceeds the unrecognized loss.

22. Wolf owns a 55% interest in Red Partnership and a 75% interest in Hood Partnership. In February 2021, Red sold land to Hood for $70,000. The land had a basis to Red of $85,000. In July 2022, Hood sold the land to Ride, an unrelated individual, for $76,000. How much gain or (loss) must Hood Partnership recognize in 2022?

A. $0

B. $6,000

C. $(9,000)

D. $(15,000)

Answer (A) is correct.

REQUIRED: The amount of gain (loss) recognized on a sale to an unrelated party subsequent to the sale from a related party.

DISCUSSION: If a taxpayer purchases property from a related party who sustained a loss on the transaction but was not allowed a deduction for the loss due to the related party rules, any gain realized by the taxpayer on a subsequent sale of the property is recognized only to the extent that the gain exceeds the amount of the previously disallowed loss [Sec. 267(d)]. In this question, the $15,000 loss in the sale of the property is disallowed since the two partnerships involved are related parties. Hood Partnership recognizes no loss when it sells the property for $6,000 more than it paid for the property, and it does not recognize a gain since that $6,000 is less than the $15,000 previously disallowed loss. Therefore, the recognized gain is $0.

Answer (B) is incorrect. No portion of the gain is recognized. **Answer (C) is incorrect.** The gain on the sale to Ride does not reduce the loss to Red, and Hood does not recognize either. **Answer (D) is incorrect.** The amount that Red lost when it sold the property to Hood is $15,000. However, Sec. 707(b)(1) provides that losses from sales or exchanges of property between two partnerships in which the same person or persons own more than 50% of the capital or profit interest are not deductible.

23. In 2022, Barb and Bet Partnership sold land having a $45,000 basis to the PTA Partnership for $35,000. Pat has a 55% capital and profits interest in PTA, and his sister owns 60% of Barb and Bet. In 2023, PTA sells the land to an unrelated individual for $47,000. How much gain or loss should Barb and Bet recognize on the subsequent sale of the land?

A. 2022: $0	2023: $2,000 gain
B. 2022: $10,000 loss	2023: $0
C. 2022: $0	2023: $12,000 gain
D. 2022: $0	2023: $0

Answer (D) is correct.

REQUIRED: The gain or loss a partnership recognizes on a subsequent sale of land.

DISCUSSION: In 2022, Barb and Bet Partnership sold the land to PTA Partnership for a loss of $10,000 ($35,000 sales price – $45,000 basis). However, Barb and Bet will not recognize any of the loss because the sale is to a related party. In addition, Barb and Bet will not recognize any gain or loss on the sale of the land by PTA to the unrelated party (i.e., basically, Barb and Bet Partnership is not a party to the subsequent sale). Note that the gain on the sale that must be recognized by PTA will be recognized only to the extent that it exceeds the previously disallowed loss [i.e., $2,000 ($12,000 realized gain – $10,000 unrecognized loss)].

24. Ted owns a 60% interest in Alpha Partnership and a 55% interest in Beta Partnership. In August 2022, Alpha sold land to Beta for $85,000. The land had a basis to Alpha of $100,000. In September 2022, Beta sold the land to an unrelated individual for $125,000. How much gain or loss must Beta recognize for 2022?

A. $15,000 loss.

B. $0

C. $25,000 gain.

D. $40,000 gain.

Answer (C) is correct.

REQUIRED: The gain (loss) a partnership recognizes on a related-party transaction.

DISCUSSION: If a taxpayer purchases property from a related party who sustained a loss on the transaction but was not allowed a deduction for the loss due to the related party rules, any gain realized by the taxpayer on a subsequent sale of the property is recognized only to the extent that the gain exceeds the amount of the previously disallowed loss [Sec. 267(d)]. In this question, the $15,000 loss ($85,000 sales price – $100,000 adjusted basis) in the sale of the property is disallowed since the two partnerships involved are related parties. Beta Partnership recognizes no loss when it sells the property for $40,000 more than it paid for the property, but it does recognize a gain since that $40,000 is greater than the previously disallowed loss of $15,000. Therefore, the recognized gain is $25,000.

Answer (A) is incorrect. The amount that Alpha lost when it sold the property to Beta is $15,000. **Answer (B) is incorrect.** A portion of the gain is recognized. **Answer (D) is incorrect.** The $40,000 gain on the sale by Beta is recognized only to the extent it exceeds the previously disallowed loss.

25. The adjusted basis of Dan's interest in D & P Enterprise at the end of 2022, after allocation of his share of partnership income, was $35,000. This included his $19,000 share of partnership liabilities. The partnership had no unrealized receivables or substantially appreciated inventory items. On December 31, 2022, Dan sold his interest in D & P Enterprise to Joanne for $16,000. It was agreed that she would assume Dan's share of partnership liabilities. What is the amount of Dan's capital gain (loss)?

A. $1,000

B. $16,000

C. $0

D. $(19,000)

Answer (C) is correct.

REQUIRED: The amount of capital gain (loss) recognized when the amount realized equals the adjusted basis.

DISCUSSION: Because there were no unrealized receivables or inventory, the sale of the interest in the partnership results in capital gain or loss (Sec. 741). The relief from partnership liabilities is treated as an amount realized on the sale [Sec. 752(d)]. Because Dan's amount realized equals his adjusted basis, he will not recognize a gain or loss.

Proceeds ($16,000 cash + $19,000 liabilities assumed by purchaser)	$35,000
Minus: Adjusted basis	(35,000)
Capital gain	$ 0

Answer (A) is incorrect. No gain or loss is recognized when the amount realized equals the adjusted basis. **Answer (B) is incorrect.** A gain is calculated as amount realized minus adjusted basis. **Answer (D) is incorrect.** The relief from liabilities is treated as an amount realized.

STUDY UNIT ELEVEN

DISPOSITION OF A PARTNER'S INTEREST

(5 pages of outline)

The disposition of a partner's interest in a partnership may be accomplished by either a sale or a liquidation. Because the tax consequences differ between the two methods, it is important to understand the differences between them.

11.1 SALE OF A PARTNERSHIP INTEREST

The sale of a partnership interest generally results in a capital gain or loss. The gain or loss is the difference between the amount realized and the adjusted basis of the partnership interest.

1. The amount realized includes the relief of any liabilities that have been assumed by the buyer.

EXAMPLE 11-1 Relief from Partnership Liabilities

Tami sold her share of a partnership for $29,000. Her basis in the partnership is $24,000, including $10,000 of liabilities. The selling price is considered to be $39,000 ($29,000 cash received plus the $10,000 relief of liabilities). Thus, her gain on the sale of the partnership interest is $15,000 ($39,000 – $24,000).

2. The basis of the partnership interest must be adjusted for the current year's distributive share and other allocations.
3. The partnership may make an election for an optional adjustment to the basis of partnership assets in the year the interest is transferred.
    a. The adjustment is the difference between the transferee partner's basis for the partnership interest and the proportionate share of the basis of all partnership property.
4. The sale may be made to an outside party or another partner. A sale to the partnership is treated as a liquidating distribution.
5. Note that a sale of a partnership interest relates to a partner's outside, or adjusted, basis. Inside basis relates to the basis the partnership has in its assets and can be affected by some elections by either the partner or partnership.

Unrealized Receivables

6. If a partner receives money or property in exchange for any part of a partnership interest, the amount due to his or her share of the partnership's unrealized receivables or inventory items results in ordinary income or loss.

Termination of Partnership

7. A partnership terminates for federal tax purposes only when operations of the partnership cease. The partner's self-employment income includes the partner's distributive share of income earned by the partnership through the end of the month in which the partner's death occurs.
   a. Sale or exchange termination is treated as a distribution of assets immediately followed by the contribution of those assets to a new partnership.
   b. The tax year of a partnership closes with respect to a partner whose entire interest in the partnership terminates by death, liquidation, or other means.
      1) A deceased partner's allocable share of partnership items up to the date of death will be taxed to the decedent on his or her final return.
      2) Any items allocated after the date of death will be the responsibility of the successor in interest.
      3) A return must be filed for the short period, which is the period from the beginning of the tax year through the date of termination.
      4) The partnership's tax year does not end.
8. The conversion from a partnership to an LLC (limited liability company) is not considered a sale, exchange, or liquidation of any partnership interest.
   a. The partnership's tax year does not close, and the LLC can continue to use the partnership's taxpayer identification number.

Stop & Review

You have completed the outline for this subunit.

Study multiple-choice questions 1 through 12 beginning on page 256.

11.2 LIQUIDATING DISTRIBUTIONS

Distributions liquidating the entire interest of a partner may be due to partnership termination and/or the retirement or death of the partner. Sale to the partnership of a partner's entire interest is treated as a liquidating distribution.

1. Payments to a retired partner that are determined by partnership income are treated as a distributive share of partnership income, regardless of the period over which they are paid. The income is characterized at the partnership level.
    a. Payments to a retiring partner in liquidation of an interest that are treated as distributive shares of partnership income or as guaranteed payments are subject to self-employment tax.
2. Amounts received from the partnership in liquidation of a partnership interest are generally treated the same as other (nonliquidating) distributions.
    a. Gain is recognized to the extent money distributed exceeds the liquidating partner's adjusted basis (AB) in the partnership interest immediately before the distribution.
        1) Decrease of the partner's share of partnership liabilities is treated as a distribution of money.
        2) The gain is capital gain. However, precontribution gain or disproportionate distribution of substantially appreciated inventory (SAI) or unrealized receivables (URs) could result in ordinary income.
            a) Inventory is considered substantially appreciated if its FMV exceeds 120% of the partnership's adjusted basis.
    b. The liquidating partner is treated as a partner for tax purposes until all payments in complete liquidation have been made.
3. Distributions of inventory made in exchange for all or part of a partner's interest in other partnership property are governed by the "substantially appreciated" rule.
    a. Gain from such distributions are taxed as ordinary income if the fair market value exceeds 120% of the partnership's AB of inventory.

Loss

4. A loss is realized when money and the FMV of property distributed are less than the AB of the partnership interest.
    a. No loss is recognized if any property other than money, unrealized receivables, and inventory is distributed in liquidation of the interest.
    b. Loss recognized is limited to any excess of the AB in the partnership interest over the sum of money and the AB in the URs and inventory.
    c. Loss recognized is characterized as if from sale of a capital asset.

EXAMPLE 11-2 Loss on Partnership Interest Liquidation

Amber has a basis in a partnership of $17,000. In complete liquidation of her interest, she received $11,000 in cash and receivables with a basis of $0. Amber will report a capital loss of $6,000 ($17,000 – $11,000 – $0) from the liquidation. The basis of the receivables will be $0 to her. If she had received a capital asset instead of the receivables, she would not qualify to take a loss, and the capital asset would have a basis to her of $6,000 ($17,000 – $11,000).

5. The partner's basis in the distributed property is the partnership's AB in the property immediately before distribution, but is limited to the distributee's AB in the partnership interest immediately before distribution minus any money received in the distribution.
   a. If the total partnership basis of assets distributed exceeds the partner's basis in the partnership interest, allocate the decrease in the same manner as for current distributions (as described in item 1.e. in Study Unit 10, Subunit 2).
   b. For liquidating distributions only, if the basis in the partnership interest exceeds the total partnership basis of distributed assets, allocate the increase by the following steps:
      1) Determine the amount of basis to be allocated.

         Beginning basis
         – Money received
         – Unrealized receivables and inventory
         = **Basis to allocate**

      2) First, assign the existing basis to each property.
      3) Allocate any appreciation to each asset.
      4) Allocate any remaining basis (Basis to allocate – Appreciation of distributed assets) to the assets based on FMV prior to the distribution.

EXAMPLE 11-3 Adjusted Basis of Partnership Interest -- Liquidating Distributions

Immediately before receiving the following distribution in the complete liquidation of Scotch Associates, the adjusted basis of Hop's partnership interest in Scotch was $180,000.

	Fair Market Value	Basis Scotch
Cash	$100,000	$100,000
Real estate	96,000	70,000

Hop's basis in the real estate is $80,000 because, in the liquidating distribution, Hop's basis in his partnership interest must be reduced by the amount of money received. The remaining basis is then allocated to other property received, in this case, the real estate.

EXAMPLE 11-4 Basis of Property Distributed in Liquidation

In the complete liquidation of Taper, Inc., Mary received the following property distributions. Mary's partnership interest before the distribution was $150,000.

Equipment	$20,000 FMV	$20,000 Basis (Taper)
Building	$80,000 FMV	$50,000 Basis (Taper)

Because Mary's basis in the partnership exceeds the partnership's basis in the distributed assets,

1. The existing basis is first assigned to each asset – $20,000 for the equipment and $50,000 for the building.
2. Next, the unrealized appreciation in each property is allocated. Nothing is allocated to the equipment because there is no unrealized appreciation. The building is allocated basis of $30,000 ($80,000 – $50,000) for unrealized appreciation.
3. Accordingly, $50,000 ($150,000 – $20,000 – $50,000 – $30,000) remains to be allocated. It is allocated based on the FMVs of the properties. The equipment will be allocated $10,000 [$20,000 FMV ÷ ($20,000 FMV equipment + $80,000 FMV building) × $50,000 remaining], and the building will be allocated $40,000 [$80,000 FMV ÷ ($20,000 FMV equipment + $80,000 FMV building) × $50,000 remaining].
4. The basis in the equipment will be $30,000 ($20,000 + $10,000), and the basis in the building will be $120,000 ($50,000 + $30,000 + $40,000).

6. The distributee's holding period in the distributed property includes that of the partnership.

Disposition of Distributed Assets

7. Gain on the sale of URs distributed by the partnership is OI.
   a. Gain or loss realized on inventory distributed depends on the nature of the property in the distributee's hands.

Partnership Liquidation

Figure 11-1

Visual Memory Aid: For candidates who are visual learners, the figure above and the description below can aid in recalling the order of distributions when a partnership is liquidated.

The XYZ partnership is liquidating. The liquidation of a partnership starts with a review of the company's assets, including property and cash, and its debts. The partners then sell the company's assets, which can result in a gain or a loss. Notice the van driving off with the assets. The money received from selling the assets goes to pay the debts the company owes, even if the company sells the assets at a loss.

At the business closeout party, Partners X, Y, and Z divide the pizza, which represents the partnership's value. The animals' expressions indicate the order in which partnerships distribute liquidated assets.

Limited partners' shares are paid before general partners, but any loans must be paid first. Notice that the snake, who is a limited partner, expected to eat first but was stopped by the goat, a general partner with a loan to the partnership. The goat's loan will be paid first, the snake's share will be paid second, and whatever is left over will be divided between the remaining general partners, the goat and the lion, based on their respective ownership of partnership shares. The lion, therefore, eats last and is visibly upset.

Stop & Review

You have completed the outline for this subunit.

Study multiple-choice questions 13 through 20 beginning on page 261.

QUESTIONS

11.1 Sale of a Partnership Interest

1. Which of the following statements about the sale or exchange of a partner's interest in a partnership is true?

A. Gain or loss is the difference between the amount realized and the adjusted basis of the partner's interest in the partnership.

B. The amount realized by the selling partner does not include any partnership liabilities of which the selling partner is relieved.

C. Any amount realized due to inventory items held by the partnership results in capital gain or loss.

D. The exchange of a limited partnership interest for a limited interest in another partnership is a nontaxable exchange of like-kind property.

Answer (A) is correct.

REQUIRED: The true statement regarding the sale or exchange of a partnership interest.

DISCUSSION: The sale or exchange of an interest in a going partnership is similar to the sale of stock in a corporation. The gain or loss on the sale of the partnership interest is a capital gain or loss, subject to long- or short-term treatment depending upon the length of time the selling partner owned the interest in the partnership. The rule also applies to the sale of a partial interest in a partnership. An exception to this rule applies when the partnership owns unrealized receivables or inventory. In this case, the selling partner must allocate a portion of the sales proceeds to the unrealized receivables and to the inventory and, to that extent, will realize ordinary income.

Answer (B) is incorrect. The amount realized includes any liabilities of which the partner is relieved. **Answer (C) is incorrect.** Any amount realized due to inventory items is ordinary income. **Answer (D) is incorrect.** The exchange of limited partnership interests is not a like-kind exchange.

2. Abby sells her 50% interest in the ABC partnership to Marty for $1,000 cash. Her adjusted basis at that time is $775. The partnership has inventory and a capital asset with respective bases of $1,200 and $300 and respective fair market values of $1,500 and $450. Abby should properly recognize

A. Ordinary income of $300 and a capital loss of $75.

B. Capital gain of $225 on the sale of her partnership interest.

C. An ordinary gain of $225, since she received cash of at least that amount.

D. Ordinary income of $150 and a capital gain of $75.

Answer (D) is correct.

REQUIRED: The amount and character of the gain (loss) from the sale of a partnership interest.

DISCUSSION: The total gain Abby realizes is the amount received ($1,000) minus her adjusted basis ($775). This equals $225. Under Sec. 751, however, a partner is to recognize ordinary income on the sale or exchange of a partnership interest to the extent the consideration received is attributable to unrealized receivables and/or inventory items. The inventory increased in value by $300 ($1,500 fair market value – $1,200 basis), and Abby's share of this is $150 ($300 increase in value × 50%). Thus, $150 is ordinary income, and the remaining gain of $75 ($225 total gain – $150 ordinary income) is treated as a capital gain.

Answer (A) is incorrect. Ordinary income is recognized only to Abby's share of the unrealized inventory increase, not the whole increase. Abby's share is 50% of the $300 increase in inventory. **Answer (B) is incorrect.** Ordinary income must be recognized when there are unrealized receivables or inventory items. **Answer (C) is incorrect.** The sale of a partnership interest results in a capital gain or loss to the extent it is over the ordinary income that is recognized from unrealized receivables or inventory.

3. Scott became a limited partner in the S&N Partnership with a $10,000 contribution on the formation of the partnership. The adjusted basis of his partnership interest at the end of the current year is $20,000, which includes his $15,000 share of partnership liabilities. He had been paid his share of the partnership income for the year. There are no unrealized receivables or inventory items. Scott sells his interest in the partnership for $10,000 and is relieved of any partnership liabilities. What is the amount and character of Scott's gain (loss) when selling his partnership interest?

A. $5,000 ordinary income.

B. $5,000 capital gain.

C. $10,000 ordinary loss.

D. $25,000 capital gain.

Answer (B) is correct.

REQUIRED: The amount and character of a partner's gain (loss) when selling his or her partnership interest.

DISCUSSION: Section 741 provides the general rule that capital gain or loss is recognized on the sale of a partnership interest. A selling partner's relief of liabilities is included in the amount realized [Sec. 752(d)]. Gain or loss recognized by the selling partner is the difference between the amount realized and the adjusted basis of the partner's interest in the partnership [Reg. Sec. 1.741-1(a)]. Therefore, Scott's capital gain is $5,000 ($25,000 amount realized – $20,000 adjusted basis).

4. Joseph is a partner in JKL Partnership. The adjusted basis of his partnership interest is $38,000, which includes his $30,000 share of partnership liabilities. The partnership has no unrealized receivables or inventory items. Joseph sells his interest in the partnership for $15,000 in cash and is relieved of any partnership liabilities. He had been paid his share of the partnership income for the tax year. What is Joseph's gain or loss on the sale?

A. $7,000

B. $15,000

C. $(15,000)

D. $(23,000)

Answer (A) is correct.

REQUIRED: The gain or loss on sale of interest in partnership subject to liabilities.

DISCUSSION: Because there were no unrealized receivables or inventory, the sale of the interest in the partnership results in capital gain or loss (Sec. 741). The relief from partnership liabilities is treated as an amount realized on the sale [Sec. 752(d)]. Because Joseph's amount realized exceeds his adjusted basis, he will recognize a gain of $7,000.

Answer (B) is incorrect. The gain is not the entire cash received. **Answer (C) is incorrect.** The cash received does not reduce his liabilities of the partnership. **Answer (D) is incorrect.** The cash received is not balanced against his basis without the liabilities assumed.

5. Michael has a partnership interest with a zero basis. The partnership has inventory valued at $250,000. Michael's share of the ordinary income to be received from the sale of the inventory would be $10,000. Michael sells his partnership interest, including inventory, for $30,000. Michael will report the following gain:

A. $30,000 capital gain.

B. $20,000 ordinary gain and $10,000 capital gain.

C. $10,000 ordinary gain and $20,000 capital gain.

D. No gain or loss.

Answer (C) is correct.

REQUIRED: The gain reported from sale of interest in a partnership.

DISCUSSION: The sale of a partnership interest generally results in a capital gain or loss. The gain or loss is the difference between the amount realized and the adjusted basis of the partnership interest. Any amount of gain attributable to unrealized receivables or inventory must be reclassified as ordinary income. Michael's total gain would equal $30,000. Of this gain, $10,000 would be classified as ordinary income. The remaining $20,000 would receive capital gain treatment.

Answer (A) is incorrect. Only $10,000 of the gain would be classified as ordinary income. **Answer (B) is incorrect.** Only the portion of the gain attributable to the unrealized receivables or inventory is ordinary income. **Answer (D) is incorrect.** Michael's basis is $30,000 less than the selling price, resulting in a gain.

6. On December 31 of the current year, Rita's adjusted basis in Diamond Partnership was $40,000, which included her $30,000 share of partnership liabilities. The partnership had no unrealized receivables or inventory. Rita sold her interest for $20,000 cash and was relieved of any partnership liabilities. What is the amount and character of Rita's gain or loss?

A. $0

B. $10,000 ordinary income.

C. $10,000 capital gain.

D. $(20,000) capital loss.

Answer (C) is correct.

REQUIRED: The amount and character of a partner's gain or loss on the sale of a partnership interest.

DISCUSSION: Because there were no unrealized receivables or inventory, the sale of the interest in the partnership results in capital gain or loss (Sec. 741). The relief from partnership liabilities is treated as an amount realized on the sale [Sec. 752(d)]. Rita's gain is

Proceeds ($20,000 cash + $30,000 liabilities assumed by purchaser)	$50,000
Less: Adjusted basis	(40,000)
Capital gain	$10,000

Answer (A) is incorrect. A capital gain or loss is generally recognized on the sale of a partnership interest. **Answer (B) is incorrect.** The gain on the sale of a partnership interest is a capital gain unless the gain is attributable to inventory or unrealized receivables. **Answer (D) is incorrect.** The assumption of liabilities by the buyer is included in the amount realized.

7. Lloyd is a partner in LG Partnership. The adjusted basis of his partnership interest is $40,000, of which $35,000 represents his share of the partnership liabilities for which neither Lloyd, the other partners, nor the partnership has assumed personal liability. Lloyd's share of unrealized receivables in the partnership is $15,000. Lloyd sold his partnership interest for $60,000 cash and was relieved of any partnership liabilities. What is the amount and character of Lloyd's gain?

A. $15,000 ordinary gain; $40,000 capital gain.

B. $40,000 ordinary gain; $15,000 capital gain.

C. $20,000 capital gain.

D. $55,000 capital gain.

Answer (A) is correct.

REQUIRED: The amount and character of gain on the sale of a partnership interest including Sec. 751 items.

DISCUSSION: Section 741 provides the general rule that capital gain or loss is recognized on the sale or exchange of a partnership interest. A selling partner's relief of liabilities is included in the amount realized [Sec. 752(d)]. However, under Sec. 751(a), gain attributable to unrealized receivables or inventory is ordinary income. The answer assumes that the basis in unrealized receivables is zero.

Total gain ($95,000 amount realized – $40,000 basis)	$55,000
Sec. 751 gain (ordinary) on receivables	(15,000)
Capital gain	$40,000

Answer (B) is incorrect. The portion of gain attributable to unrealized receivables is ordinary income. **Answer (C) is incorrect.** The liabilities assumed by the buyer are included in the amount realized. **Answer (D) is incorrect.** The portion of gain attributable to unrealized receivables is ordinary income.

8. Linda sold her partnership interest for $25,000 and was relieved of any partnership liabilities. Her adjusted basis at the time of the sale is $22,500, which includes her $12,500 share of partnership liabilities. When she initially invested in the partnership, she contributed $10,000 worth of equipment. There was no profit or loss at the partnership level at the time she sold her interest. What is the amount and nature of her gain or loss from the sale of her partnership interest?

A. $7,500 ordinary loss.

B. $10,000 capital gain.

C. $12,500 ordinary gain.

D. $15,000 capital gain.

Answer (D) is correct.

REQUIRED: The gain reported from sale of a partnership interest.

DISCUSSION: The sale of a partnership interest generally results in a capital gain or loss. The gain or loss is the difference between the amount realized and the adjusted basis of the partnership interest. Her gain would be increased by the amount of liabilities in the partnership. Thus, she would report a capital gain of $15,000 ($25,000 selling price + $12,500 – $22,500 basis). The contribution of the equipment is not a factor.

Answer (A) is incorrect. A loss is not realized on the sale of the partnership interest. **Answer (B) is incorrect.** The amount of $10,000 is the difference between Linda's adjusted basis and her share of partnership liabilities. **Answer (C) is incorrect.** Gain attributable to unrealized receivables or inventory in the sale of a partnership interest is ordinary gain.

9. Cobb, Maci, Danver, and Evans each owned a one-quarter interest in the capital and profits of their calendar-year partnership. On September 18, Year 1, Cobb and Danver sold their partnership interests to Frank and immediately withdrew from all participation in the partnership. On March 15, Year 2, Cobb and Danver received full payment from Frank for the sale of their partnership interests. For tax purposes, the partnership

A. Terminated on September 18, Year 1.

B. Terminated on December 31, Year 1.

C. Terminated on March 15, Year 2.

D. Did not terminate.

Answer (D) is correct.

REQUIRED: The date a partnership terminated for tax purposes.

DISCUSSION: A partnership terminates for tax purposes only if no part of any business, financial operation, or venture of the partnership continues to be carried on by its partners in a partnership.

10. All of the following are considered in determining the basis of a partner's interest in a partnership for purposes of computing gain or loss on the sale or liquidation of that interest EXCEPT the

A. Partner's distributive share of capital losses.

B. Partnership book value of the partner's interest.

C. Partner's distributive share of nontaxable partnership income.

D. Adjusted basis of property distributed to the partner by the partnership.

Answer (B) is correct.

REQUIRED: The item not used in determining the basis of a partner's interest in a partnership.

DISCUSSION: Once an interest in a partnership is acquired, the partner's basis is adjusted to reflect various partnership activities. Basis is increased by any additional contributions, any increased share of partnership liabilities, and the distributive share of both taxable and nontaxable income. Basis is decreased by any distribution to the partner, any decrease in liabilities, and the distributive share of partnership losses. The partnership book value of a partner's interest (capital account) has no effect on basis for sale or liquidation purposes.

Answer (A) is incorrect. Basis is reduced by the partner's distributive share of capital losses. **Answer (C) is incorrect.** Basis is increased by the partner's distributive share of nontaxable partnership income. **Answer (D) is incorrect.** Basis is decreased by any distribution to the partner.

11. Which of the following statements about the liquidation of a partner's interest is false?

A. A retiring partner is treated as a partner until his or her interest in the partnership has been completely liquidated.

B. The retiring partner will recognize a gain on a liquidating distribution to the extent that any money distributed is more than the partner's adjusted basis in the partnership.

C. Payments in liquidation of a partnership interest that are not made in exchange for the interest in partnership property are reported as capital gain by the recipient.

D. Payments to a retiring partner in liquidation of an interest that are treated as distributive shares of partnership income or as guaranteed payments are subject to self-employment tax.

Answer (C) is correct.

REQUIRED: The false statement regarding liquidation of a partner's interest.

DISCUSSION: Amounts received from the partnership in liquidation of a partnership interest are generally treated as distributive shares of partnership income or guaranteed payments.

12. Candy is a partner in LX Partnership. The adjusted basis of her partnership interest is $24,000, of which $19,000 represents her share of the partnership liabilities for which neither Candy, the other partners, nor the partnership has assumed personal liability. Candy's share of unrealized receivables in the partnership is $10,000. Candy sold her partnership interest for $28,000 and was relieved of any partnership liabilities. What is the amount and character of Candy's gain?

A. $10,000 ordinary gain; $13,000 capital gain.

B. $13,000 ordinary gain; $10,000 capital gain.

C. $4,000 ordinary income.

D. $23,000 capital gain.

Answer (A) is correct.

REQUIRED: The amount and character of a gain when a partnership interest is sold.

DISCUSSION: The gain or loss on the sale of the partnership interest is a capital gain or loss, subject to long- or short-term treatment depending upon the length of time the selling partner owned the interest in the partnership. An exception to this rule applies when the partnership owns unrealized receivables or inventory. In this case, the selling partner must allocate a portion of the sale proceeds to the unrealized receivables and to the inventory and, to that extent, will realize ordinary income. Therefore, she must allocate $10,000 of her realized gain of $23,000 ($47,000 amount realized – $24,000 adjusted basis) to ordinary income. This leaves a capital gain of $13,000 ($23,000 realized gain – $10,000 unrealized receivables).

Answer (B) is incorrect. The portion of the gain attributable to unrealized receivables is ordinary income. **Answer (C) is incorrect.** The liabilities assumed by the buyer are included in the amount realized. **Answer (D) is incorrect.** The portion of the gain attributable to unrealized receivables is ordinary income.

11.2 Liquidating Distributions

13. When payments are made to a retiring partner or successor in interest of a deceased partner for an interest in the partnership property, which of the following is true?

A. Payments that are based on partnership income are not taxable as a distributive share of partnership income but for the interest in the partnership.

B. A retiring partner is treated as a partner until his or her interest in the partnership has been completely liquidated.

C. Payments made for a retiring partner's share of the partnership's unrealized receivables are treated as made in exchange for partnership property if capital is not a material income producing factor and the retiring partner was a general partner.

D. If the amount of the payment is based on partnership income, the payment is treated as a guaranteed payment.

Answer (B) is correct.

REQUIRED: The true statement about payments made to a retiring partner.

DISCUSSION: For income tax purposes, a retiring partner or successor in interest of a deceased partner is treated as a partner until his or her interest in the partnership has been completely liquidated (Publication 541).

Answer (A) is incorrect. Payments to a retired partner that are determined by partnership income are treated as a distributive share of partnership income. **Answer (C) is incorrect.** Amounts received from the partnership in liquidation of a partnership interest are generally treated the same as other (nonliquidating) distributions. **Answer (D) is incorrect.** Payments to a retiring partner in liquidation of an interest are treated as distributive shares of partnership income or as guaranteed payments.

14. Which of the following statements about the liquidation of a partner's interest is false?

A. A retiring partner is treated as a partner until his or her interest in the partnership has been completely liquidated.

B. The remaining partners' distributive shares of partnership income are reduced by payments in exchange for a retiring partner's interest in partnership property.

C. The retiring partner will recognize a gain on a liquidating distribution to the extent that any money distributed is more than the partner's adjusted basis in the partnership.

D. Payments in liquidation of an interest that are not made in exchange for the interest in partnership property are reported as ordinary income by the recipient.

Answer (B) is correct.

REQUIRED: The false statement regarding the liquidation of a partner's interest.

DISCUSSION: Payments made in liquidation of a partner's interest are considered a distribution under Sec. 736(b) to the extent the payments are made in exchange for the interest of the partner in the partnership property. The partnership is not allowed a deduction, and therefore the remaining partners' distributive shares are not affected.

Answer (A) is incorrect. The liquidating partner is treated as a partner for tax purposes until all payments in complete liquidation have been made. **Answer (C) is incorrect.** Gain is recognized to the extent money distributed exceeds the liquidating partner's adjusted basis in the partnership interest immediately before the distribution. **Answer (D) is incorrect.** Payments not made in exchange for the interest in partnership property are reported as ordinary income by the recipient.

15. John's basis in his partnership interest on October 15 of the current year was $30,000. In a distribution in liquidation of his entire interest, he received properties C and D from the partnership on that date, neither of which were inventory or unrealized receivables. On October 15 of the current year, property C had an adjusted basis of $20,000 and a fair market value of $5,000, and property D had an adjusted basis of $30,000 and a fair market value of $20,000. Based on this information, what is John's basis in property C immediately after the distribution?

A. $5,000

B. $8,000

C. $12,000

D. $20,000

Answer (B) is correct.

REQUIRED: The basis in property received in liquidation of the partnership interest.

DISCUSSION: Section 732(b) provides that the basis of property distributed by a partnership in a liquidating distribution to a partner is the adjusted basis of the partner's interest in the partnership minus any money received in the same distribution. The basis of distributed property is allocated first to inventory items and unrealized receivables up to the amount of the partnership's adjusted basis in these items, then to other property to the extent of each distributed property's adjusted basis to the partnership. The remaining basis increase or decrease is allocated depending on whether the adjusted basis of the distributed properties exceed the partner's remaining basis in the partnership interest or not.

Since the partnership's basis in the distributed properties exceed the partner's remaining basis in the partnership ($50,000 basis in properties and $30,000 basis in partnership), a decrease must be allocated among the properties in proportion to the respective amounts of unrealized depreciation inherent in each property (but only to the extent of any unrealized depreciation). John's basis in property C will be $8,000. The $20,000 basis of property C is reduced by the decline in FMV of property C ($15,000) divided by the decline in FMV of both properties ($15,000 + $10,000) times the $20,000 ($50,000 – $30,000) required reduction in basis for a reduction of $12,000 for property C. The old $20,000 basis minus the $12,000 reduction equals the new $8,000 basis.

Answer (A) is incorrect. The adjusted basis of the property is not its fair market value. **Answer (C) is incorrect.** The basis of the partnership is not allocated to property C based on the basis of the two properties, which is the former rule. **Answer (D) is incorrect.** The combined basis of the properties received cannot exceed the basis of the partnership interest.

16. DUG Partnership operates a business. Its tax year ends on December 31. A partner dies on August 20 of the current year. The deceased partner's (and his or her estate's) distributive share of partnership income for the year of death is $18,000. The partner's share of self-employment income from the partnership is

A. $18,000

B. $11,500

C. $12,000

D. $9,000

Answer (C) is correct.

REQUIRED: The partner's share of self-employment income from a partnership.

DISCUSSION: The partner's self-employment income includes the partner's distributive share of income earned by the partnership through the end of the month in which the partner's death occurs [IRC Sec. 1402(f)]. Since the partner dies in the eighth month, $12,000 ($18,000 × 8/12 months) of the distribution is considered self-employment income.

17. On January 1 of the current year, Ruth had a basis in her partnership interest of $72,500. Thereafter, in liquidation of her entire interest, she received an apartment house and an office building. The apartment house has an adjusted basis to the partnership of $10,000 and a fair market value of $50,000. The office building has an adjusted basis to the partnership of $12,500 and a fair market value of $12,500. What is Ruth's basis in each property after the distribution?

A. Apartment house, $50,000; office building, $22,500.

B. Apartment house, $58,000; office building, $14,500.

C. Apartment house, $35,000; office building, $37,500.

D. Apartment house, $60,000; office building, $12,500.

Answer (B) is correct.

REQUIRED: The partner's basis in property after a distribution in liquidation.

DISCUSSION: If a partner's interest is liquidated solely through a distribution of partnership property other than money, no gain is recognized. If the partnership distributes property other than money, the partner's basis in the partnership must be transferred to the distributed assets. When a liquidation occurs and the partner's basis in the partnership exceeds the partnership's basis in the distributed assets, the excess of the partner's basis in the partnership must also be allocated among the distributed assets. Any basis increase required is allocated first to properties with unrealized appreciation in proportion to the respective amounts of unrealized appreciation inherent in each property (but only to the extent of each property's unrealized appreciation). Any remaining increase is then allocated in proportion to the properties' fair market values.

The apartment house is first assigned its basis of $10,000, and the office building is assigned $12,500. Another $50,000 ($72,500 partnership basis – $22,500 assigned to properties) must be allocated to the two properties. The apartment house is allocated $40,000 [($40,000 increase in FMV ÷ $40,000 total increase in FMV) × $40,000]. Accordingly, $10,000 still remains to be allocated. It is allocated based on the FMVs of the properties. The apartment house will be allocated $8,000 [$50,000 FMV ÷ ($50,000 FMV of the apartment + $12,500 FMV of the building) × $10,000 remaining increase], and the building will be allocated the remaining $2,000. Thus, the basis in the apartment house will be $58,000 ($10,000 + $40,000 + $8,000), and the basis in the office building will be $14,500 ($12,500 + $2,000).

Answer (A) is incorrect. The bases in the properties will not be based solely on the FMV of the apartment house. **Answer (C) is incorrect.** The excess of the FMV over the adjusted bases of the properties is not divided equally among the assets. **Answer (D) is incorrect.** After the initial appreciation, any remaining increase is then allocated in proportion to the properties' fair market values.

18. David Beck and Walter Crocker were equal partners in the calendar-year partnership of Beck & Crocker. On July 1, Year 1, Beck died. Beck's estate became the successor in interest and continued to share in Beck & Crocker's profits until Beck's entire partnership interest was liquidated on April 30, Year 2. At what date was the partnership considered terminated for tax purposes?

A. April 30, Year 2.

B. Did not terminate.

C. July 31, Year 1.

D. July 1, Year 1.

Answer (A) is correct.

REQUIRED: The date the partnership is considered terminated for tax purposes following a partner's death.

DISCUSSION: A partnership generally does not terminate for tax purposes on the death of a partner since the deceased partner's estate or successor in interest continues to share in partnership profits and losses (Sec. 708). The Beck & Crocker partnership terminated on April 30, Year 2, because when Beck's entire partnership interest was liquidated, the business ceased to be operated as a partnership.

19. The adjusted basis of Dave's partnership interest in CDS Partnership is $60,000. In a complete liquidation of his interest, Dave received the following:

	Basis to CDS	Fair Market Value
Cash	$20,000	$20,000
Inventory items	15,000	20,000
Land	24,000	40,000
Building	8,000	10,000

What is Dave's basis in the land and in the building?

	Land	Building
A.	$18,750	$6,250
B.	$24,000	$8,000
C.	$40,000	$10,000
D.	$56,000	$14,000

Answer (A) is correct.

REQUIRED: The bases in properties received in liquidation of the partnership interest.

DISCUSSION: Section 732(b) provides that the basis of property distributed by a partnership in a liquidating distribution to a partner is the adjusted basis of the partner's interest in the partnership minus any money received in the same distribution. The basis of distributed property is allocated first to inventory items and unrealized receivables up to the amount of the partnership's adjusted basis in these items, then to other property to the extent of each distributed property's adjusted basis to the partnership. The remaining basis increase or decrease is allocated depending on whether the adjusted bases of the distributed properties exceed the partner's remaining basis in the partnership interest or not.

Since the partnership's bases in the distributed properties exceed the partner's remaining basis in the partnership, a decrease must be allocated among the properties with unrealized depreciation in proportion to their respective amounts of unrealized depreciation (to the extent of cash property's depreciation) and then in proportion to the properties' respective adjusted bases (considering the adjustments already made). In this case, a $7,000 decrease [$60,000 adjusted basis – ($20,000 cash + $15,000 inventory + $24,000 land + $8,000 building)] is allocated based on the properties' respective adjusted bases as follows:

	Building	Land
Carryover basis	$8,000	$24,000
Allocate decrease (25% to building and 75% to land)	(1,750)	(5,250)
Basis	$6,250	$18,750

Answer (B) is incorrect. The bases must be reduced by the allocation of the remaining basis in the partnership interest. **Answer (C) is incorrect.** The FMV of the property does not determine the basis. **Answer (D) is incorrect.** Basis is first allocated to cash and inventory.

20. Carl sold his interest in a partnership for $15,000 in cash when the adjusted basis of his partnership interest was zero. As part of the sales transaction, Carl was relieved of his $10,000 share of partnership liabilities. How much did Carl realize on the sale of his interest in the partnership?

A. $0

B. $10,000

C. $15,000

D. $25,000

Answer (D) is correct.

REQUIRED: The amount realized on the sale of a partnership interest when liabilities are assumed.

DISCUSSION: In a sale or exchange of a partnership interest, liabilities are treated the same as in connection with the sale or exchange of other property [Sec. 752(d)]. Therefore, liabilities assumed by the purchaser are included in the amount realized. Thus, Carl realizes $25,000 on the sale of his partnership interest ($15,000 cash received + $10,000 liabilities assumed).

Answer (A) is incorrect. The amount realized includes the FMV of all property received and the assumption of liabilities. **Answer (B) is incorrect.** The amount realized includes the amount of cash received. **Answer (C) is incorrect.** The amount realized includes the share of liabilities assumed by the purchaser.

STUDY UNIT TWELVE

CORPORATIONS

(11 pages of outline)

For tax purposes, the predominant forms of business organizations are C corporations, S corporations, partnerships, and sole proprietorships. A business must choose among the kinds of business organizations based on a number of different factors, including an organization's tax treatment.

C corporations are subject to the most rigid tax rules of all the kinds of business organizations, as their earnings are taxed twice. First, the earnings are subject to a corporate tax, and then the profits are taxed at the individual level when they are distributed to shareholders as dividends.

A corporation is a business formed by associates to conduct a business venture and divide profits among investors. A corporation files a charter, prepares bylaws, is overseen by a board of directors, and issues stock.

12.1 BUSINESSES TAXED AS CORPORATIONS

Businesses Formed before 1997

1. The following businesses formed before 1997 are taxed as corporations:
   a. A business that is legally chartered as a corporation
   b. A joint-stock company
   c. An insurance company
   d. Any other business formed before 1997 that has more than two of the following characteristics:
      1) Centralization of management
      2) Continuity of life
      3) Free transferability of interests
      4) Limited liability

Businesses Formed after 1996

2. Under a "check-the-box" system, certain business entities are automatically treated as corporations for federal tax purposes, while others may elect to be treated as corporations for federal tax purposes.
   a. If an entity has one owner and is not automatically considered a corporation, it may nevertheless elect to be treated as a corporation or, by default, it will be treated as a sole proprietorship.
   b. Similarly, if an entity has two or more owners and is not automatically considered a corporation, it can elect to be taxed as a corporation for federal tax purposes; otherwise, it will be taxed as a partnership.
   c. An eligible entity may elect its classification on Form 8832 (*Entity Classification Election*).
      1) Each member of the entity, or any member of the entity authorized to make the election, must sign the election.
      2) The taxpayers must indicate the date the election will become effective.
      3) This effective date cannot be more than 75 days before or 12 months after the date the election was filed.
      4) If an eligible entity makes an election to change its classification, the corporation cannot change its classification by election again during the 60 months succeeding the effective date of the election.
         a) EXCEPTION: The IRS may allow a corporation to change its classification (by private letter ruling) prior to the 60 months if more than 50% of the ownership interests are owned by persons other than those who made the prior election.
   d. The following businesses formed after 1996 are automatically taxed as corporations:
      1) A business formed under a federal or state law that refers to the business as a corporation, body corporate, or body politic
      2) A business formed under a state law that refers to the business as a joint-stock company or joint-stock association
      3) An insurance company
      4) Certain banks
      5) A business wholly owned by a state or local government
      6) A business specifically required to be taxed as a corporation by the Internal Revenue Code, e.g., certain publicly traded partnerships
      7) Certain foreign businesses
3. In general, any business formed before 1997 and taxed as a corporation under the old rules will continue to be taxed as a corporation.
4. A single-member limited liability company (LLC) may elect to be taxed as a corporation.
   a. If LLCs do not make this election, they are considered disregarded entities, and income is reported as part of the tax return of the owner.

5. Any nonexempt closely held corporation is classified as a personal holding company (PHC) if a significant portion of its income is passive in nature.
   a. Closely held in this case means more than 50% of the value of the corporation's shares are owned, directly or indirectly, by five or fewer shareholders.
   b. PHCs are subject to a penalty tax on undistributed PHC income.
   c. Further details about PHCs and the penalty tax are beyond the scope of the EA exam and therefore not covered in this review course.

Stop & Review

You have completed the outline for this subunit.

Study multiple-choice questions 1 through 3 on page 276.

12.2 CONTROLLED GROUPS AND PERSONAL SERVICE CORPORATIONS (PSCs)

A controlled group of corporations includes corporations with a specified degree of relationship by stock ownership.

Parent-Subsidiary

1. A parent-subsidiary type of controlled group consists of a. and b. presented below:
   a. Two corporations if one of the corporations owns stock that represents
      1) 80% or more of total voting power **or**
      2) 80% or more of total value outstanding of the stock of the other

   NOTE: Distinguish the controlled group 80% test from that of affiliated groups in which both the 80% voting and 80% value tests must be met.

   b. Any other corporation that meets the requirements above (if the two corporations discussed there and others in the group own stock in it)

EXAMPLE 12-1 Parent-Subsidiary Controlled Group

Each corporation has a single class of stock. P owns 80% of S stock. P and S own 40% each of O stock. P, S, and O own 30% each of T stock. As shown in the diagram below, per the 80% test, P, S, O, and T are a controlled group.

Diagram

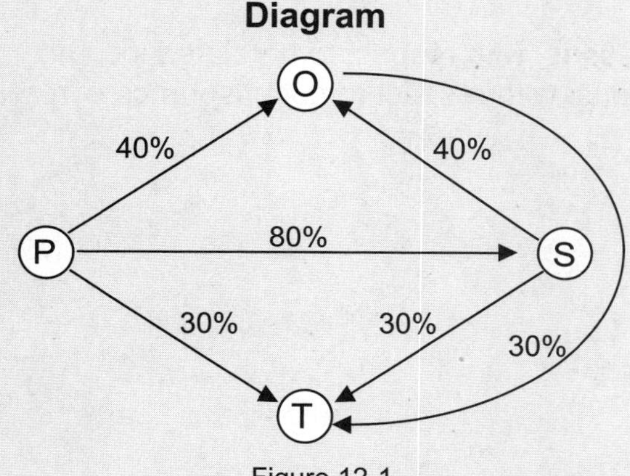

Figure 12-1

Brother-Sister

2. Any two or more corporations are considered a brother-sister controlled group if the stock of each owned by the same five or fewer persons (only individuals, trusts, or estates)
   a. Represents either
      1) 80% or more of voting power of all classes or
      2) 80% or more of value of all classes and
   b. Represents either (counting for each person only the smallest amount owned by that person in any of the corporations)
      1) More than 50% of voting power of all classes or
      2) More than 50% of value of all classes.

EXAMPLE 12-2 Brother-Sister Controlled Group

Alpha, Bravo, and Charley Corporations, each with one class of stock, have the following ownership:

	80% Test			
Shareholders	Alpha	Bravo	Charley	50% Test
Mike	45%	5%	30%	5%
Sierra	30%	65%	10%	10%
Oscar	25%	30%	60%	25%
	100%	100%	100%	40%

Alpha, Bravo, and Charley passed the 80% test but not the 50% test. Therefore, they are not a controlled brother-sister group.

3. Rights to acquire stock are treated as the stock would be.
4. Stock both actually and constructively owned is counted. Generally, a person constructively owns stock owned by a
   a. Family member [spouse (not legally separated), child, grandchild, parent, or grandparent] and
   b. Corporation, partnership, estate, or trust
      1) In which (s)he has a 5% or more interest
      2) In proportion to that interest

Excluded Corporations

5. Without regard to stock ownership, certain types of corporations are excluded from a controlled group, e.g.,
   a. Tax-exempt corporations, with respect to unrelated income
   b. Insurance corporations, with respect to non-insurance corporations

Limit on Tax Benefits

6. Each of the following is an example of a tax benefit item that must be shared by the members of a controlled group:
   a. Section 179 expensing maximum of $1,080,000.
   b. General Business Credit $25,000 offset.
   c. AET $250,000 presumed deduction base.

NOTE: A controlled group generally may choose any method to allocate the amounts among the members of the group. In default, an item is divided equally among members. If a controlled group adopts or changes an apportionment plan, each member must attach a copy of this consent to his or her tax return.

EXAMPLE 12-3 Limit on Tax Benefits -- Section 179

Alpha, Bravo, Charley, and Delta corporations are a controlled group. Each corporation purchased and placed in service $400,000 of qualified Sec. 179 equipment for a total of $1.6 million in qualified equipment for the group. Barring selection of any other allocation, each corporation's Sec. 179 deduction for the year is limited to only $270,000 ($1,080,000 ÷ 4).

Personal Service Corporations

7. A corporation is a PSC if it meets all of the following requirements:
   a. Principal activity during the "testing period" is performing personal services, including any activity performed in the fields of accounting, actuarial science, architecture, consulting, engineering, health (including veterinary services), law, and the performing arts.
      1) Generally, the testing period for any tax year is the prior tax year. If the corporation has just been formed, the testing period begins on the first day of its tax year and ends on the earlier of
         a) The last day of its tax year or
         b) The last day of the calendar year in which its tax year begins.
   b. Employee-owners substantially perform the services in item a. above.
      1) This requirement is met if more than 20% of the corporation's compensation cost for its activities of performing personal services during the testing period is for personal services performed by employee-owners.
      2) A person is an employee-owner if both of the following apply:
         a) (S)he is an employee of the corporation or performs personal services for, or on behalf of, the corporation on any day of the testing period.
         b) (S)he owns any stock in the corporation at any time during the testing period.
   c. Its employee-owners own more than 10% of the fair market value of its outstanding stock on the last day of the testing period.
8. Like corporations, PSCs are taxed at a flat rate of 21%.

Stop & Review

You have completed the outline for this subunit.
Study multiple-choice questions 4 through 8 beginning on page 277.

12.3 U.S. SOURCE INCOME

Income received by a foreign corporation is considered U.S. source income if the income is effectively connected with the conduct of a trade or business within the United States.

1. Income is considered "effectively connected" if it satisfies one of the following tests:
   a. The income was derived from assets used in, or held for use in, the conduct of a U.S. business (the "asset use" test).
   b. The U.S. trade or business was a material factor in the production of income.
2. No withholding is required from income when effectively connected.
3. Fixed, determinable, annual, or periodical (FDAP) income of a foreign corporation received from U.S. sources not effectively connected with the conduct of a U.S. trade or business is generally taxed at a flat 30% rate.
   a. Tax must be withheld from payment of income.
4. Gross income from the sale of inventory purchased for resale is sourced on the basis of where the sale occurs (i.e., where title passes).
5. An annual withholding tax return (Form 1042) for U.S. source income paid to foreign persons must be filed whether or not any income tax was withheld.

You have completed the outline for this subunit.
Study multiple-choice questions 9 and 10 on page 279.

12.4 TAX RETURN FILING

Every corporation subject to taxation must file a federal income tax return.

1. The corporate tax return is filed on Form 1120.
2. A C corporation's tax return is due by the 15th day of the 4th month after the end of the corporation's tax year. A short-period return must be filed by a new corporation or a dissolved corporation by the 15th day of the 4th month after a short period ends or the date it dissolved.
   a. If the 15th falls on a Saturday, Sunday, or holiday, the tax return is due the next succeeding day that is not a Saturday, Sunday, or legal holiday.
   b. An exception to the rule applies to C corporations with a June 30 fiscal year. These C corporations will continue to have a due date of the 15th day of the 3rd month following the close of the tax year. This will continue until tax years beginning after December 31, 2025. The extension date is April 15.
3. Calendar year C corporations and fiscal year C corporations that file Form 7004 and pay their estimated unpaid tax liability are allowed an extension of up to 6 months.
   a. However, an extension of time to file the return does not extend the time for paying the tax.
4. The penalty for late filing is 5% of the tax due for each month or part of a month the return is late, but it does not exceed 25%.
   a. However, the minimum penalty for filing a return more than 60 days late is the smaller of the tax due or $450.
5. Corporations having gross receipts for the tax year of less than $250,000 and total assets at the end of the year of less than $250,000 are not required to file a balance sheet per books (Form 1120, Sch. L), a reconciliation of income per books with income per return (Sch. M-1), or an analysis of unappropriated retained earnings per book (Sch. M-2). These forms show the difference between book and tax income.

International Information Returns

6. Generally, U.S. tax on the income of a foreign corporation is deferred until the income is distributed as a dividend or otherwise repatriated by the foreign corporation to its U.S. shareholders.
7. The IRS applies international information reporting requirements to U.S. persons with foreign activities that require extensive financial information (e.g., balance sheet, income statement, related party descriptions, etc.) for the IRS to examine.
   a. Failure to file accurate foreign forms and schedules can lead to the assessment of substantial penalties.

8. Some of the more widely used forms include the following:

   a. **Form 926**, *Return by a U.S. Transferor of Property to a Foreign Corporation*, is used to report certain transfers of tangible or intangible property to a foreign corporation, as required by Sec. 6038B.

   b. **Form 3520**, *Annual Return to Report Transactions With Foreign Trusts and Receipt of Certain Foreign Gifts*, is used to report (1) certain transactions with foreign trusts, (2) ownership of foreign trusts under the rules of Secs. 671 through 679, and (3) receipt of certain large gifts or bequests from certain foreign persons.

   c. **Form 3520-A**, *Annual Information Return of Foreign Trust With a U.S. Owner*, is the annual information return of a foreign trust with at least one U.S. owner. The form provides information about the foreign trust, its U.S. beneficiaries, and any U.S. person who is treated as an owner of any portion of the foreign trust under the grantor trust rules (Secs. 671 through 679).

   d. **Form 5471**, *Information Return of U.S. Persons With Respect to Certain Foreign Corporations*, is used by certain U.S. persons who are officers, directors, or shareholders in certain foreign corporations. The form and schedules are used to satisfy the reporting requirements of Secs. 965, 6038, and 6046.

   e. **Form 5472**, *Information Return of a 25% Foreign-Owned U.S. Corporation or a Foreign Corporation Engaged in a U.S. Trade or Business*, is used to provide information required under Secs. 6038A and 6038C when reportable transactions occur during the tax year of a reporting corporation with a foreign or domestic related party.

   f. **Form 8865**, *Return of U.S. Persons With Respect to Certain Foreign Partnerships*, is used to report the information required under Sec. 6038, Sec. 6038B, or Sec. 6046A.

   g. **Form 8858**, *Information Return of U.S. Persons With Respect to Foreign Disregarded Entities (FDEs) and Foreign Branches (FBs)*, is used by certain U.S. persons who operate an FB or own an FDE directly or, in certain circumstances, indirectly or constructively. The form and schedules are used to satisfy the reporting requirements of Secs. 6011, 6012, 6031, and 6038, as well as related regulations.

   h. **Form 8938**, *Statement of Specified Foreign Financial Assets*, is used to report certain foreign financial assets if the total value of all the specified foreign financial assets in which the interest is held is more than the appropriate reporting threshold.

   i. **Form 8991**, *Tax on Base Erosion Payments of Taxpayers With Substantial Gross Receipts*, is used to determine an applicable tax on the taxpayer's base erosion minimum tax amount for the year. The tax is based on the taxpayer's base erosion percentage, modified taxable income, and credits that reduce regular tax liability in computing the base erosion minimum tax amount. Section 59A applies to large corporations that have the ability to reduce U.S. tax liability by making deductible payments to foreign related parties.

j. **Form 8992**, *U.S. Shareholder Calculation of Global Intangible Low-Taxed Income (GILTI)*, is used to compute a U.S. shareholder's GILTI inclusion. Section 951A requires U.S. shareholders of CFCs to include in gross income their GILTI for years in which they are U.S. shareholders of CFCs.

k. **Form 8993**, *Section 250 Deduction for Foreign-Derived Intangible Income (FDII) and Global Intangible Low-Taxed Income (GILTI)*, is used to determine the allowable deduction under Sec. 250. The deduction is allowed only to domestic corporations [not including real estate investment trusts (REITs), regulated investment companies (RICs), and S corporations].

Stop & Review

You have completed the outline for this subunit.
Study multiple-choice questions 11 through 15 beginning on page 280.

12.5 ACCUMULATED EARNINGS TAX AND ALTERNATIVE MINIMUM TAX (AMT)

1. A corporation may be subject to accumulated earnings tax if it does not distribute enough profits beyond what is needed for the conduct of its business.
2. **Formula**

  Taxable Income
+ Positive Adjustments
  1. Dividends-received deduction claimed
  2. NOL deduction claimed
  3. Excess charitable contributions carried over from a preceding tax year and deducted in determining taxable income
  4. Capital loss carryover deduction
– Negative Adjustments
  1. Accrued U.S. and foreign income taxes
  2. Charitable contributions made in excess of the 10% corporate limitation
  3. Net capital losses (if capital losses for the year exceed capital gains)
  4. Net capital gain minus the amount of any income taxes attributed to it
– Dividends-paid deduction claimed
– Accumulated Earnings Credit
= Accumulated taxable income (AMTI)
× 20%
= Accumulated earnings tax (AET)

NOTE: For all other tax years, the charitable contribution deduction limitation is 10% of TI. The increased corporate limit does not automatically apply. C corporations must elect application of the increased corporate limit on a contribution-by-contribution basis. The multiple choice questions in this publication are based on the 25% limit.

3. The Accumulated Earnings Credit reduces accumulated taxable income. It also allows corporations to accumulate E&P up to $250,000 ($150,000 for certain personal service corporations) or up to the level of its earnings accumulated for the reasonable needs of the business.
   a. Reasonable needs of a business include the following:
      1) Specific, definite, and feasible plans for use of the earnings accumulation and
      2) The amount necessary to redeem a corporation's stock included in a deceased shareholder's gross estate. The proceeds are limited to the sum of estate, inheritance, legacy, or succession taxes imposed and the funeral and administrative expenses.

AMT

4. The TCJA repealed the corporate AMT for tax years beginning after December 31, 2017.

You have completed the outline for this subunit.
Study multiple-choice questions 16 and 17 on page 282.

12.6 ESTIMATED TAX PAYMENTS

A corporation is required to make estimated tax payments unless its estimated tax liability is less than $500. The payments are required on the 15th day of the 4th, 6th, 9th, and 12th months of the tax year. For a calendar-year taxpayer, required quarterly installments are due April 15, June 15, September 15, and December 15.

1. Tax includes the regular income tax, net of credits and payments.
2. Each quarterly estimated tax payment required is 25% of the lesser of
   a. 100% of the prior year's tax (provided a tax liability existed and the preceding tax year was 12 months) or
   b. 100% of the current year's tax.
3. A corporation with uneven income flows has the option of annualizing income and paying its estimated taxes accordingly.
   a. Any shortfall is made up in later quarters so that 100% of the tax due is paid on the last installment date (December 15 for calendar-year taxpayers).
   b. Corporations are required to use general annualization rules or elect to use one of two sets of optional annualization rules.

4. Paying 100% of the prior year's tax is not an option for a large corporation, i.e., one with taxable income above $1 million during any of the 3 preceding years.
   a. A large corporation must pay 100% of the current year's tax.
   b. However, a large corporation may make its first-quarter estimated tax payment based on the preceding year's tax liability and make up any difference in its second-quarter payment.
5. Generally, a corporation must make federal tax deposits (FTDs) of estimated tax payments using electronic funds transfer. Generally, electronic funds transfer is made using the Electronic Federal Tax Payment System (EFTPS).
   a. However, if the corporation does not want to use EFTPS, it can arrange for its tax professional, financial institution, payroll service, or other trusted third party to make deposits on its behalf.
   b. The corporation should keep for its records a cleared check, bank receipt, or money order as a receipt for the deposit.
6. A penalty is imposed in the amount by which any required installment exceeds estimated tax paid, multiplied by the federal short-term rate plus 3% (5% for underpayments in excess of $100,000).
   a. The penalty accrues from the installment due date until the underpayment is paid or, if earlier, the due date for filing the tax return.
   b. The penalty is not allowed as an interest deduction.
   c. If any underpayment of estimated tax is indicated by the tax return, Form 2220 should be submitted with the return.
7. No estimated tax penalty is imposed if
   a. Tax liability shown on the return for the tax year is less than $500.
   b. The IRS waives all or part of the penalty for good cause.
   c. An erroneous IRS notice to a large corporation is withdrawn by the IRS.
8. A corporation may obtain a quick refund of estimated tax paid, but adjustment is allowed only if the overpayment is both ≥ $500 and ≥ 10% of the corporation's estimate of its tax liability.
   a. The application is filed (Form 4466) after the close of the tax year but before the return due date (without extensions).

Stop & Review

You have completed the outline for this subunit.

Study multiple-choice questions 18 through 20 beginning on page 282.

QUESTIONS

12.1 Businesses Taxed as Corporations

1. Most unincorporated businesses formed after 1996 can choose whether to be taxed as a partnership or a corporation. The regulations provide for a default rule if no election is made. If an election is NOT made and the default rules apply, which of the following is true?

A. Any new domestic eligible entity having at least two or more members is classified as a partnership.

B. Any new domestic eligible entity with a single member is disregarded as an entity separate from its owner.

C. If all members of a new foreign entity have limited liability, the entity is classified as an association taxed as a corporation.

D. All of the answers are correct.

Answer (D) is correct.

REQUIRED: The true statement regarding the default rules for the taxation of business if no election is made.

DISCUSSION: Under a "check-the-box" system, certain business entities are automatically treated as corporations for federal tax purposes, while others may elect to be treated as corporations for federal tax purposes. If an entity has one owner and is not automatically considered a corporation, it may nevertheless elect to be treated as a corporation or, by default, will be treated as a sole proprietorship. Similarly, if an entity has two or more owners and is not automatically considered a corporation, it can elect to be taxed as a corporation for federal tax purposes; otherwise, it will be taxed as a partnership. Further, if all members of a new foreign entity have limited liability, the entity is classified as a corporation. One type of a corporation as defined in the Internal Revenue Code is an association.

2. All of the following businesses, formed after 1996, are automatically classified as corporations EXCEPT

A. An insurance company.

B. A partnership that possesses at least three of the following characteristics: limited liability, centralized management, free transferability of interest, and continuity of life.

C. Certain foreign businesses.

D. A business wholly owned by a state or local government.

Answer (B) is correct.

REQUIRED: The business formed after 1996 that is not automatically classified as a corporation.

DISCUSSION: After 1996, the corporate characteristics are not determinative of corporate status. Only certain entities are required to be corporations. Other entities, such as limited liability companies, can choose partnership taxation even though the entity may possess all four of the corporate characteristics of (1) continuity of life, (2) centralization of management, (3) limited liability, and (4) free transferability of interests.

Answer (A) is incorrect. Insurance companies must be taxed as corporations if they are formed after 1996. **Answer (C) is incorrect.** Certain foreign businesses must be taxed as corporations if they are formed after 1996. **Answer (D) is incorrect.** A business wholly owned by a state or local government must be taxed as a corporation if it is formed after 1996.

3. To be classified as a corporation, which of the following characteristics is a newly created entity required to possess?

A. Free transferability of interests.

B. Limited liability.

C. Centralization of management.

D. None of the answers are correct.

Answer (D) is correct.

REQUIRED: The requirement(s) to be classified as a corporation.

DISCUSSION: After 1996, the corporate characteristics are not determinative of corporate status. Other than certain entities that are required to be corporations, entities can choose to be corporations whether or not they possess any of the four corporate characteristics of (1) continuity of life, (2) centralization of management, (3) limited liability, and (4) free transferability of interests.

12.2 Controlled Groups and Personal Service Corporations (PSCs)

4. Which of the following statements about a controlled group of corporations is false?

A. John Corporation owns 80% of the voting power and value of James Corporation stock. John Corporation and James Corporation are members of a controlled group.

B. Allen Corporation owns 80% of the voting power and value of Brown Corporation stock. Brown Corporation owns 80% of the voting power and value of Cole Corporation. Allen Corporation, Brown Corporation, and Cole Corporation are members of a controlled group.

C. Members of a controlled group may be either members of an affiliated group, parent-subsidiary corporations, or brother-sister corporations.

D. None of the statements are false.

Answer (D) is correct.

REQUIRED: The false statement regarding a controlled group.

DISCUSSION: All the statements are true.

Answer (A) is incorrect. Controlled groups exist when one corporation owns 80% of voting power or 80% of total value of the other corporation. **Answer (B) is incorrect.** Allen, Brown, and Cole corporations do meet the requirements of a controlled group. **Answer (C) is incorrect.** This is a true statement. Affiliated groups, parent-subsidiary corporations, and brother-sister corporations may be members of a controlled group.

5. Which of the following requirements does NOT have to be met for a group of corporations to be considered a brother-sister controlled group?

A. Five or fewer persons (individuals, estates, or trusts) own at least 80% of the total combined voting power of all classes of voting stock, or at least 80% of the total value of all classes of stock, of each corporation in a group of two or more corporations. A person's stock ownership is considered only if that person owns stock in each of these corporations.

B. Five or fewer persons (individuals, estates, or trusts) own more than 50% of the total combined voting power of all classes of voting stock, or more than 50% of the total value of all classes of stock, of each corporation in a group of two or more corporations. A person's stock ownership is considered only to the extent it is identical with respect to each of these corporations.

C. Five or fewer persons (individuals, estates, or trusts) own 90% or more of the total voting power of all classes of stock, or more than 90% of the total value of all classes of stock.

D. None of the answers are correct.

Answer (C) is correct.

REQUIRED: The requirements that must be met for a group to be considered a brother-sister controlled group.

DISCUSSION: Under Sec. 1563(a), a brother-sister controlled group means two or more corporations of which 5 or fewer persons who are individuals, estates, or trusts own (1) at least 80% of the voting power or value of each corporation and (2) more than 50% of the voting power or value of the stock of each corporation counting only identical ownership interests (i.e., the smallest amount owned by each person in any of the corporations is all that is counted in the other corporations for the 50% test).

6. The Dana Corporation has two subsidiary corporations. In order to determine that the subsidiary corporations are in a controlled corporate group, which of the following must be true?

A. Ten or fewer persons (individuals, estates, or trusts) own at least 80% of the voting stock or value of shares of each of two or more corporations.

B. Ten or fewer persons own more than 50% of the voting power or value of shares of each corporation, considering a particular person's stock only to the extent that it is owned identically with regard to each corporation.

C. A persons' stock ownership is not taken into account for purposes of the 80% requirement unless that shareholder owns stock in all of the corporations considered to be in the group.

D. The subsidiaries must be located in the same state.

Answer (C) is correct.

REQUIRED: The ownership requirements of a controlled corporate group.

DISCUSSION: Stock, both actually and constructively owned, is counted. A person's stock ownership is not taken into account for purposes of the 80% requirement unless that shareholder owns stock in all of the corporations considered to be in the group.

Answer (A) is incorrect. The number of persons considered in the ownership of a controlled group is 5, not 10, and they must own over 50%, not 80%. **Answer (B) is incorrect.** The number of persons considered in the ownership of a controlled group is 5, not 10. **Answer (D) is incorrect.** The location of the subsidiaries in the same state does not determine whether the subsidiaries are part of a controlled corporate group.

7. Which of the following statements is false?

A. A controlled group of corporations must file a consolidated return.

B. In addition to regular income tax, a corporation may be liable for accumulated earnings tax if it accumulates profits instead of distributing them to shareholders.

C. In addition to regular income tax, a corporation may be liable for personal holding company tax if a significant portion of its income is dividends, interest, rents, and royalties.

D. Generally, a personal service corporation is one that furnishes personal services performed by employee-owners.

Answer (A) is correct.

REQUIRED: The false statement regarding a controlled group of corporations.

DISCUSSION: Under Sec. 1563(a), a controlled group of corporations may be a parent-subsidiary controlled group, a brother-sister controlled group, or a combined group. Either a parent-subsidiary controlled group or the parent-subsidiary portion of a combined group may file a consolidated tax return because there is a common parent corporation and the includible corporations are all 80%-owned. However, a brother-sister controlled group exists when two or more corporations are owned by 5 or fewer persons who own at least 80% of the voting stock or 80% of the value of the outstanding stock. There is no common parent corporation, so a consolidated tax return could not be filed. The affiliated group definition requires ownership of 80% of the voting stock and 80% of the value of the controlled corporation. The controlled group definition is an "or" test, and some controlled groups may meet one but not both of the tests and will not be able to file a consolidated return.

8. Richard Crepe, M.D., owns 100% of the outstanding stock of Crepe Corporation. All of Crepe Corporation's income and expenditures are derived from the medical services provided by Dr. Crepe. At the end of 2022, Crepe Corporation had $10,000 in reportable taxable income. How much federal income tax was Crepe Corporation required to pay for the 2022 year?

A. $1,500

B. $2,500

C. $3,400

D. $2,100

Answer (D) is correct.

REQUIRED: The taxable liability of a personal service corporation (PSC).

DISCUSSION: PSCs are taxed at a flat rate of 21%. Crepe Corporation is required to pay $2,100 (21% of $10,000).

Answer (A) is incorrect. The correct tax rate is 21%, not 15%. **Answer (B) is incorrect.** The correct tax rate is 21%, not 25%. **Answer (C) is incorrect.** The correct tax rate is 21%, not 34%.

12.3 U.S. Source Income

9. When is income received by a foreign corporation NOT considered U.S. source income?

A. The income is connected with a trade or business conducted outside the U.S.

B. The income was derived from assets used in the conduct of a U.S. business.

C. The U.S. business was a material factor in the production of income.

D. Both the income was derived from assets used in the condition of a U.S. business and the U.S. business was a material factor in the production of income.

Answer (A) is correct.

REQUIRED: The income received by a foreign corporation that is not considered U.S. source income.

DISCUSSION: Income received by a foreign corporation is considered U.S. source income if the income is effectively connected with the conduct of a trade or business within the United States.

Answer (B) is incorrect. Income derived from assets used in the conduct of a U.S. business is considered U.S. source income. **Answer (C) is incorrect.** Income is considered U.S. source income if the U.S. business was a material factor in the production of income. **Answer (D) is incorrect.** Both choices identify U.S. source income received by a foreign corporation.

10. Fixed, determinable, annual, or periodical (FDAP) income from U.S. sources is generally taxed at a rate of 30% through mandatory withholding if the income

A. Is received by a foreign corporation.

B. Is from the domestic sale of inventory purchased for resale.

C. Meets the "asset use" test.

D. Is not effectively connected with the conduct of a U.S. trade or business.

Answer (D) is correct.

REQUIRED: The FDAP income that is generally taxed at a rate of 30%.

DISCUSSION: FDAP income of a foreign corporation received from U.S. sources not effectively connected with the conduct of a U.S. trade or business is taxed at a flat 30% rate.

Answer (A) is incorrect. Income received by a foreign corporation may be considered U.S. source income if the income is effectively connected with the conduct of a U.S. trade or business. Such income is not subject to the 30% withholding rate. **Answer (B) is incorrect.** Gross income from the sale of inventory purchased for resale is sourced on the basis of where the sale occurs (i.e., where title passes). No withholding is required on sales in the U.S. **Answer (C) is incorrect.** Income meets the "asset use" test if the income was derived from assets used in, or held for use in, the conduct of a U.S. trade or business. No withholding is required.

12.4 Tax Return Filing

11. ABC Corporation, a C corporation, is dissolved on June 9, Year 1. What is the due date, without extensions, for the filing of the final corporate income tax return?

A. April 15, Year 2.

B. December 31, Year 1.

C. October 15, Year 1.

D. October 9, Year 1.

Answer (C) is correct.

REQUIRED: The filing deadline for a dissolved C corporation.

DISCUSSION: As a general rule, a C corporation's tax return is due by the 15th day of the 4th month after the end of the C corporation's tax year. However, a short-period return must be filed by a new corporation or a dissolved corporation by the 15th day of the 4th month after a short period ends. The 4th month following June is October. Thus, the return is due on October 15, Year 1.

Answer (A) is incorrect. The general rule does not apply. The short-period rule must be used in this case. **Answer (B) is incorrect.** The short-period return must be filed on the 15th day of the 4th month following the dissolution. **Answer (D) is incorrect.** The corporation has until the 15th day of the 4th month. The short-period return is not due exactly 4 months following the dissolution.

12. Generally, a short-period income tax return of a new C corporation must be filed by the 15th day of the

A. Third month after the short period ends.

B. Fourth month after the short period ends.

C. Fourth month after the end of its first full tax year.

D. Third month after the end of its first full tax year.

Answer (B) is correct.

REQUIRED: The due date for a short-period income tax return.

DISCUSSION: Section 6072(a) provides that a C corporation must file its return on or before the 15th day of the 4th month following the close of the tax year. A return may cover less than a year if a C corporation was formed during the year.

13. Jonas Corporation, a C corporation, forgot to request an extension and filed its Form 1120 late for calendar year 2022. It paid the $100 balance due when it filed the return on July 22, 2023. The delinquency penalty will be

A. $20

B. $15

C. $5

D. $100

Answer (D) is correct.

REQUIRED: The delinquency penalty on a return filed late.

DISCUSSION: The penalty for late filing is 5% for each month or part of a month. The penalty would be $20 ($100 × 5% × 4 months). However, the minimum penalty for filing a return more than 60 days late (15 days in April + 31 days in May + 30 days in June + 22 days in July > 60 days) is the smaller of the tax due ($100) or $450. Therefore, the penalty would be $100.

Answer (A) is incorrect. The return is more than 60 days late, so the penalty is not calculated related to the percentage penalty. **Answer (B) is incorrect.** The penalty is calculated as the smaller of the tax due or $450, not in reference to the 5% times number of months' penalty. **Answer (C) is incorrect.** The penalty is calculated as the smaller of the tax due or $450, not in reference to the 5% times number of months' penalty.

14. Which of the following statements concerning the extension of time to file a calendar-year-end C corporation tax return is false?

A. A C corporation will receive an automatic 6-month extension of time for filing by submitting Form 7004.

B. The Internal Revenue Service can terminate the extension to file at any time by mailing a notice of termination to the corporation.

C. Form 7004 must be filed by the due date of the corporation's income tax return.

D. An automatic extension of time for filing a corporate income tax return also extends the time for paying the tax due on the return.

Answer (D) is correct.

REQUIRED: The false statement regarding an extension of time for a C corporation tax return.

DISCUSSION: A C corporation's entire tax liability is due on the same date as the return. Under Sec. 6072(a), a calendar-year C corporation must file its income tax return on or before the 15th day of April following the close of the calendar year. Fiscal-year corporate taxpayers must file by the 15th day of the 4th month following the close of the fiscal year. Under Sec. 6081(a), in a timely filing of Form 7004, the corporation will receive an automatic 6-month extension for filing the tax return. An extension of time to file the tax return does not provide an extension of time to pay the tax liability without incurring interest and/or penalty.

Answer (A) is incorrect. An extension may be filed to extend the due date for an additional 6 months. **Answer (B) is incorrect.** The IRS is able to terminate extensions. **Answer (C) is incorrect.** Form 7004 must be filed by the regular due date of the corporation's income tax return.

15. Generally, if a C corporation has dissolved, its final income tax return must be filed by the 15th day of the

A. Third month after the end of the calendar year.

B. Fourth month after the end of its established tax year.

C. Fourth month after the date it dissolved.

D. Third month after the date it dissolved.

Answer (C) is correct.

REQUIRED: The due date for the tax return of a dissolved C corporation.

DISCUSSION: A C corporation must file a Form 1120 on or before the 15th day of the 4th month that follows the close of its tax year. In the case of a dissolved corporation, the tax year ends on the date of the dissolution, even if the corporation dissolved on a date other than the last day of the month.

Answer (A) is incorrect. The return due date is established using the dissolution date. **Answer (B) is incorrect.** The return due date is established using the dissolution date. **Answer (D) is incorrect.** The return is due 4 months after the dissolution date.

12.5 Accumulated Earnings Tax and Alternative Minimum Tax (AMT)

16. Westover Health Services, Inc., a personal service corporation, has two shareholders. Westover was incorporated 17 years ago and has made irregular and infrequent distributions to its shareholders. The balance sheet of Westover Health Services, Inc., reflects unappropriated retained earnings in the amount of $800,000 and no marketable securities. Westover has no specific, definite, and feasible plans for use of the earnings accumulation in its business. It has been determined that the amount needed to redeem a deceased shareholder's stock is $500,000 for estate taxes and administrative expenses. What is the amount of Accumulated Earnings Tax that Westover Health Services, Inc., could be subject to for tax year ended December 31, 2022?

A. $60,000

B. $30,000

C. $130,000

D. $0

Answer (A) is correct.

REQUIRED: The Accumulated Earnings Tax associated with a redemption.

DISCUSSION: The corporation is allowed an Accumulated Earnings Credit for the greater of $150,000 or the reasonable needs (if there is a definite plan for its use) of the business but not both. The $500,000 qualifies as reasonable needs. The accumulated earnings tax is $60,000 [($800,000 unappropriated retained earnings – $500,000 reasonable needs) × 20% accumulated earnings tax rate].

Answer (B) is incorrect. The corporation is allowed an Accumulated Earnings Credit for the greater of $150,000 or the reasonable needs of the business but not both. **Answer (C) is incorrect.** The corporation is allowed an Accumulated Earnings Credit for the greater of $150,000 or the reasonable needs of the business but not both. The reasonable need is greater. **Answer (D) is incorrect.** The corporation has an accumulated earnings tax.

17. If a corporation allows earnings to accumulate beyond the reasonable needs of the business, it may be subject to an accumulated earnings tax of

A. 25%

B. 15%

C. 20%

D. 10%

Answer (C) is correct.

REQUIRED: The accumulated earnings tax rate.

DISCUSSION: The accumulated earnings tax rate is 20%. IRC Section 531 imposes an accumulated earnings tax if a corporation does not distribute enough profits beyond what is needed for the conduct of its business.

Answer (A) is incorrect. The accumulated earnings tax rate is 20%. **Answer (B) is incorrect.** The tax rate of 15% is not the accumulated earnings tax rate. **Answer (D) is incorrect.** Charitable contributions made in excess of the 10% corporate limitation are negative adjustments to taxable income in calculating accumulated taxable income.

12.6 Estimated Tax Payments

18. If a corporation is required to make estimated tax payments because it expects its tax to be $500 or more for the year, the first installment payment of estimated tax is due by the 15th day of the

A. Third month of the corporation's tax year.

B. Fourth month of the corporation's tax year.

C. Fifth month of the corporation's tax year.

D. Sixth month of the corporation's tax year.

Answer (B) is correct.

REQUIRED: The due date of the first installment of estimated taxes.

DISCUSSION: A corporation that anticipates a tax bill of $500 or more must estimate its income tax liability for the current tax year and pay four quarterly estimated tax installments. Installments of fiscal-year corporations are due on the 15th day of the 4th, 6th, 9th, and 12th months of the year.

19. Sincere, Inc., a C corporation, overestimated how successful it would be in the Year 1 tax year. Final calculations show it will have an NOL for Year 1 and owe no taxes. It had overpaid its estimated taxes for the year by $700. Sincere, Inc., wants its tax refund as soon as possible. What should it do?

A. File Form 1120, *U.S. Corporation Income Tax Return*, as quickly as possible before the 15th day of the 4th month after its year ended and wait for the money.

B. File Form 7004, *Application for Automatic Extension of Time to File Certain Business Income Tax, Information, and Other Returns*, as quickly as possible and state on the form that it had overestimated its tax and wishes a quick refund as quickly as possible.

C. File Form 4466, *Corporation Application for a Quick Refund of Overpayment of Estimated Tax*, before the 15th day of the 4th month after its year end, and use it as a worksheet to show that it had overpaid its estimates by $700.

D. Write a letter to the appropriate IRS Service Center and ask for a quick refund of overpaid corporate tax estimates.

Answer (C) is correct.

REQUIRED: The proper method to obtain a quick refund of estimated tax paid.

DISCUSSION: A corporation may obtain a quick refund of estimated tax paid, but adjustment is allowed only if the overpayment is both ≥ $500 and ≥ 10% of the corporation's estimate of its tax liability. Application is filed (Form 4466) after the close of the tax year but before the return due date (without extensions).

Answer (A) is incorrect. Form 1120 is filed for corporate income taxes, not estimated taxes. **Answer (B) is incorrect.** Form 7004 is filed by a corporation to receive an automatic 6-month extension to file its corporate tax return. **Answer (D) is incorrect.** To obtain a quick refund of estimated tax, the corporation must file a Form 4466.

20. Crock Corporation has a fiscal year beginning September 1 and ending August 31. Crock's estimated tax for the fiscal year is $10,000. The first installment of Crock Corporation's estimated tax is due by

A. December 1.

B. December 15.

C. January 1.

D. January 15.

Answer (B) is correct.

REQUIRED: The due date of the first installment of estimated taxes.

DISCUSSION: A corporation that anticipates a tax bill of $500 or more must estimate its income tax liability for the current tax year and pay four quarterly estimated tax installments. Installments of fiscal-year corporations are due on the 15th day of the 4th, 6th, 9th, and 12th months of the year. Therefore, Crock's first installment is due on December 15, which is the 4th month after the year end of August 31.

Go to Online Course

Access the **Gleim EA Premium Review System** featuring our SmartAdapt technology from your Gleim Personal Classroom to continue your studies.

You will experience a personalized study environment with exam-emulating multiple-choice questions.

STUDY UNIT THIRTEEN

CORPORATE FORMATION

(5 pages of outline)

Once a decision has been reached to use the corporate form, the investors generally must transfer money, property, or services to the corporation in exchange for a debt or equity interest in the corporation. These transfers may have tax consequences to both the transferor and the corporation. Section 351 was enacted to allow taxpayers to incorporate without incurring adverse tax consequences and to prevent taxpayers from recognizing losses while maintaining ownership of the loss assets indirectly through stock ownership.

13.1 RECOGNIZED GAIN OR LOSS

Section 351 requires that no gain or loss be recognized if property is transferred to a corporation by one or more persons (i.e., individuals, trusts, estates, partnerships, associations, companies, or corporations) solely in exchange for stock (including treasury stock) in the corporation and, immediately after the exchange, such person(s) control the corporation. Examples of property include cash, tangible property, and nontangible property. This nonrecognition treatment is mandatory, not elective.

Control

1. Control is ownership of 80% or more of the voting power of stock and 80% or more of the shares of each class of nonvoting stock of the corporation.
   a. Stock exchanged for services is not counted toward the 80%-ownership test, unless property is also transferred by the service provider.
      1) The FMV of the stock is gross income to the shareholder when stock is transferred for services.
      2) The shareholder's basis in the stock exchanged for services is its FMV.
   b. **Nonqualified preferred stock** is treated as boot received and is not counted as stock toward the 80%-ownership test. Generally, nonqualified preferred stock has any of the following characteristics:
      1) The holder has the right to require the issuer or a related person to redeem or buy the stock.
      2) The issuer or a related person is required to redeem or buy the stock.
      3) The issuer or a related person has the right to redeem or buy the stock and, on the issue date, it is more likely than not that the right will be exercised.
      4) The dividend rate on the stock varies with reference to interest rates, commodity prices, or similar indices.

Solely for Stock

2. To the extent the shareholder receives the corporation's stock in exchange for property, nonrecognition is required. This is true even if the shareholder receives some boot (money or other property) in the exchange.

EXAMPLE 13-1	Transfer of Asset in a Sec. 351 Exchange

Taxpayer transfers an asset to the corporation in a Sec. 351 exchange. The asset has a basis of $10,000. Taxpayer receives $3,000 in cash and stock worth $15,000. Taxpayer has a realized gain of $8,000 and a recognized gain of $3,000.

a. Inequality of FMV of the stock and property exchanged (i.e., **disparate value**) is not relevant in itself.
   1) The shareholder may have gross income if the disparity represents an (unstated) additional transaction, e.g., payment of compensation, a constructive dividend.
b. Section 351 may apply to an exchange after formation of the corporation.
c. Section 351 can apply to contributions of property even if the corporation issues no stock in the exchange, e.g., a capital contribution by a sole shareholder who receives no stock in exchange for the contribution.
d. Section 351 may apply when the corporation exchanges treasury stock as well as newly issued stock.
e. Whenever a shareholder (or group of shareholders) makes a Sec. 351 property exchange for stock in a corporation, a statement of all facts relevant to the exchange must be attached to the individual tax returns, as well as to the corporate return, in the year of the exchange.

Boot

3. The shareholder recognizes gain realized to the extent of money and the FMV of other property (except the stock of the corporation) received in the exchange.
   a. FMV of property given up is used if FMV of property received cannot be ascertained.
   b. Character of the gain depends on the property contributed.
   c. No loss is recognized on the receipt of boot.

Liabilities

4. Section 351 applies even if the corporation assumes the shareholder's liability or takes property subject to a liability in the exchange. Liabilities generally are not treated as boot.
   a. The amount of the liabilities is treated as recognized gain from the sale or exchange of an asset only to the extent it exceeds the adjusted basis (AB) of all property contributed by the shareholder.
      1) This rule differs from like-kind exchanges, in which liabilities are treated as boot.

EXAMPLE 13-2 Liability Transfer under Sec. 351

A taxpayer transfers an asset with a basis of $60,000 and a FMV of $100,000 to a corporation for all of its stock. The asset has a liability attached of $70,000. The taxpayer must recognize $10,000 of income, the excess of the liability ($70,000) over the basis of the asset ($60,000).

   b. If tax avoidance was a purpose or if no business purpose was present for the assumption or transfer, a gain may be recognized to the extent of the liability (the full amount) plus the FMV of any property received (not including stock).
5. The corporation recognizes no gain on exchange of its stock for property (including money). No gain or loss is recognized on treasury stock.
   a. The corporation recognizes gain on exchanging other property (neither money nor its stock), even when the exchange is with a shareholder, unless an exception applies.
6. Stock is not considered issued in exchange for property if it is issued for services or unsecured debts of the transferee or for the interest accrued to the transferor on debts owed by the transferee.

EXAMPLE 13-3 Stock Issued for Services

John and Mary form a corporation. John transfers a building worth $90,000 to the corporation for stock. Mary receives 10% of the stock in the corporation for services she provided in organizing and setting up the corporation. Mary must recognize $10,000 as ordinary income when she receives the stock.

7. Even though a transaction may not qualify as a tax-free transfer under Sec. 351, shareholders may not be able to deduct a loss if they exchange property with an adjusted basis that is higher than the FMV of the property they received.
   a. If the shareholder owns more than 50% of the corporation's stock, directly or indirectly, (s)he cannot recognize any losses on an exchange of the property for the corporation's stock or other property.
8. When a transaction does not qualify as a tax-free transfer under Sec. 351, the corporation's initial basis in the property is the FMV of the stock at the time of the exchange.
   a. If the FMV of the stock at the time of the exchange cannot be determined, the basis is the FMV of the property received.

Stop & Review

You have completed the outline for this subunit.

Study multiple-choice questions 1 through 13 beginning on page 290.

13.2 BASIS OF ASSETS TRANSFERRED IN AN EXCHANGE

In a tax-free transaction under Sec. 351, the bases of assets transferred equal the bases of the assets in the hands of the prior owner, with certain adjustments.

Basis of Shareholder in Stock

1. Basis of a controlled group shareholder in the stock of the corporation is the adjusted basis in contributed property adjusted for the boot received and the gain recognized.

	Cash and AB in contributed property
–	Boot received
	Money
	FMV of property received (other than above and the corporation's stock)
–	Liability relief (corporation assumes or takes subject to)
+	Any amount treated as a dividend
+	Gain recognized (by shareholder)
=	**Basis in stock of issuing corporation**

   a. All liabilities assumed by the corporation are treated as boot when computing stock basis (but not treated as boot for gain purposes).
   b. The holding period is generally tacked; i.e., the holding period of the property exchanged for stock is added to the holding period of the stock.
   c. If capital assets and other assets (e.g., Sec. 1231 property) are contributed by a **sole proprietor** when incorporating a business, each share received in the exchange has a split holding period.

Basis of Shareholder in Boot

2. Boot generally has a basis equal to fair market value.

Basis of Shareholder in Stock Received for Services

3. The shareholder's basis in the stock exchanged for services is its fair market value.

Basis of Corporation in Property

4. The corporation's initial carryover basis in property exchanged by a control group shareholder for its stock is an adjusted carryover basis.

	AB in property to shareholder
+	Gain recognized by shareholder
=	**Basis in property to corporation**

a. This basis also applies when the shareholder receives nothing in return.

b. This basis is also the corporation's initial depreciable basis in the property.

    1) Allowable depreciation is apportioned based on the number of months the corporation owned the asset.

    2) The step-up in basis is treated as a second property whose depreciation commences on the day of the exchange.

c. When the shareholder's AB in the property exceeds the FMV (i.e., when a built-in loss exists), the basis is limited to the FMV.

d. The holding period is tacked.

Stop & Review

You have completed the outline for this subunit.

Study multiple-choice questions 14 through 20 beginning on page 296.

QUESTIONS

13.1 Recognized Gain or Loss

1. Bob and Charles, as a group, transfer a building with a basis of $100,000 to the ABC Corporation in exchange for 66.67% of each class of stock with a fair market value of $300,000. The other 33.33% of the stock was already issued to Alice. What is the gain, if any, that Bob, Charles, or the ABC Corporation must recognize?

A. Bob and Charles, $0; ABC Corporation, $0.

B. Bob and Charles, $0; ABC Corporation, $300,000.

C. Bob and Charles, $200,000; ABC Corporation, $0.

D. Bob and Charles, $0; ABC Corporation, $200,000.

Answer (C) is correct.

REQUIRED: The gain recognized by the shareholders and corporation upon contribution of property.

DISCUSSION: Bob and Charles combined do not have control over ABC Corporation; therefore, Sec. 351 treatment does not apply. Bob and Charles must recognize a gain of $200,000 ($300,000 FMV – $100,000 adjusted basis), and ABC does not recognize any gain.

Answer (A) is incorrect. Bob and Charles must recognize a gain because, combined, they do not have control of the corporation. **Answer (B) is incorrect.** Bob and Charles must recognize a gain, and ABC does not recognize a gain. **Answer (D) is incorrect.** Bob and Charles must recognize a gain, and ABC does not recognize a gain.

2. Joseph Jackson had previously incorporated his sole proprietorship by transferring property to his newly formed corporation in exchange for 100% of the stock. These assets, if sold, would produce a gain of $100,000. A week after incorporation, Joseph sells other assets for cash to the corporation that produce a loss of $20,000. Joseph is attempting to avoid Sec. 351 on the transfer of the loss assets in order to recognize the loss for tax purposes. Which statement best explains the tax consequences to him?

A. Joseph has a recognized loss of $20,000 to report.

B. Joseph has a recognized gain of $100,000 and a recognized loss of $20,000 to report.

C. Joseph has neither a recognized gain nor recognized loss to report.

D. Joseph has only a recognized gain of $100,000 to report.

Answer (C) is correct.

REQUIRED: The tax consequences of transferring property to a corporation.

DISCUSSION: Section 351(a) provides that no gain or loss is recognized if one or more persons transfer property to a corporation solely in exchange for stock in such corporation and if, immediately after the exchange, such person(s) is (are) in control of the corporation. Control is defined in Sec. 368(c) as the ownership of stock possessing at least 80% of the total combined voting power of all classes of voting stock and at least 80% of the total number of shares of all other classes of stock. Since Joseph transferred property to the corporation in exchange for a total of 100% of the stock, the initial transaction qualifies for tax-free treatment. Under Sec. 267(a)(1), losses are not allowed on sales or exchanges of property between related parties. Related parties include an individual and a corporation in which the individual owns more than 50% of the outstanding stock. Therefore, Joseph and his corporation are treated as related parties and no loss is allowed.

Answer (A) is incorrect. Losses are not allowed on sales or exchanges of property between related parties. **Answer (B) is incorrect.** Immediately after the initial exchange of property, Joseph had 100% control of the corporation. Therefore, under Sec. 351(a), the $100,000 gain is not recognized. Also, losses are not allowed on sales or exchanges of property between related parties. **Answer (D) is incorrect.** Under Sec. 351(a), Joseph does not have a recognized gain to report.

3. Bob and Sam transfer a building with a basis of $100,000 to the Redwood Corporation in exchange for 75% of each class of stock with a fair market value of $300,000. The other 25% of the stock was already issued to Betty. What is the gain, if any, that Bob, Sam, or the Redwood Corporation must recognize?

A. Bob and Sam, none; Redwood Corporation, none.

B. Bob and Sam, none; Redwood Corporation, $300,000.

C. Bob and Sam, $200,000; Redwood Corporation, none.

D. Bob and Sam, none; Redwood Corporation, $200,000.

Answer (C) is correct.

REQUIRED: The amount of recognized gain, if any, on the transfer of property to a controlled corporation.

DISCUSSION: Publication 542 states, "If you transfer property (or money and property) to a corporation solely in exchange for stock in that corporation, and immediately thereafter you are in control of the corporation, the exchange is usually not taxable." Furthermore, "To be in control of a corporation, you or your group of transferors must own, immediately after the exchange, at least 80% of the total combined voting power of all classes of stock entitled to vote and at least 80% of the outstanding shares of each class of nonvoting stock of the corporation." Thus, Bob and Sam are not in control of the corporation and this transaction does not qualify for Sec. 351 treatment. Bob and Sam must recognize the entire $200,000 realized gain ($300,000 stock received – $100,000 basis of the building). The corporation recognizes no gain on exchange of its stock for property (including money).

Answer (A) is incorrect. The transaction does not qualify for Sec. 351 treatment; thus, a gain must be recognized. **Answer (B) is incorrect.** Bob and Sam must recognize a gain from the transaction, and the corporation does not recognize any gains on the exchange of its stock for property. **Answer (D) is incorrect.** Bob and Sam must recognize a gain from the transaction, and the corporation does not recognize any gains on the exchange of its stock for property.

4. John was one of five incorporators of Builders, Inc. Each received stock valued at $100,000. The other four shareholders each contributed $100,000 for their stock. John contributed $50,000 and his services to build the corporate headquarters. He valued his services at $50,000. How much income must John recognize on this transaction?

A. $100,000 of ordinary income.

B. $50,000 of ordinary income and $50,000 of capital gain income.

C. No income recognition.

D. $50,000 of ordinary income.

Answer (D) is correct.

REQUIRED: The amount and character of income recognized from the transfer of cash and services to a corporation.

DISCUSSION: Section 351 requires that no gain or loss be recognized if property is transferred to a corporation by one or more persons solely in exchange for stock in the corporation and, immediately after the exchange, such person(s) control the corporation. Stock is not considered issued in exchange for property if it is issued for services or unsecured debts of transferee. The services John contributed to the corporation do not qualify for the Sec. 351 treatment; therefore, $50,000 must be recognized as ordinary income.

Answer (A) is incorrect. John can exclude the $50,000 contributed to the corporation under Sec. 351. **Answer (B) is incorrect.** John only recognizes the amount of the services contributed to the corporation as ordinary income. **Answer (C) is incorrect.** John must include the $50,000 of services contributed as ordinary income.

5. Robert transferred an office building that has an adjusted basis of $60,000 and a fair market value of $105,000 to the Wargo Corporation in exchange for 100% of Wargo Corporation stock and $10,000 cash. The building was subject to a mortgage of $25,000, which Wargo Corporation assumed. The fair market value of the stock was $75,000. Which of the following are the amounts of Robert's realized gain and recognized gain?

	Realized	Recognized
A.	$55,000	$30,000
B.	$50,000	$30,000
C.	$50,000	$10,000
D.	$35,000	$10,000

Answer (C) is correct.

REQUIRED: The amounts of a shareholder's realized and recognized gain on the transfer of property to a controlled corporation.

DISCUSSION: Robert realized a gain of $50,000 on the transfer of the property to the controlled corporation ($75,000 stock + $25,000 mortgage assumed + $10,000 cash – $60,000 basis in the building). Because money is received in addition to the stock, any gain realized by the shareholder is recognized up to the amount of money received. Also, Sec. 357(c) provides that, if the liabilities transferred or assumed do not exceed the basis of all the property transferred, then the liabilities are not recognized as a gain. Thus, Robert's recognized gain is $10,000, the money received from the corporation.

Answer (A) is incorrect. The $55,000 realized gain is the difference between the fair market value of the office building and its adjusted basis plus the money received. In calculating realized gain, the FMV of the building is not considered. The $30,000 recognized gain is the difference between the fair market value of the office building and the stock received. The basis of the building should be used, and recognized gain is limited to the boot received. **Answer (B) is incorrect.** The $30,000 recognized gain is the difference between the fair market value of the office building and the stock received. The basis of the building should be used, and recognized gain is limited to the boot received. **Answer (D) is incorrect.** The $35,000 realized gain is the mortgage assumed plus the money received. Additionally, the difference between the stock's FMV and the basis in the building is also realized gain.

6. Mr. Smith and Mr. Jones each transfer property with a basis of $10,000 to a corporation in exchange for stock with a fair market value of $30,000. The total stock received by them represents 75% of each class of stock of the corporation. The other 25% of each class of stock was issued earlier to Mr. Brown, an unrelated person. The taxable consequences are

A. None because it is transfer of property for stock.

B. Mr. Smith and Mr. Jones each recognize a gain of $20,000.

C. Mr. Smith and Mr. Jones each recognize a gain of $30,000.

D. 80% of the transaction is recognized as a taxable gain.

Answer (B) is correct.

REQUIRED: The tax consequences reported on the transfer of property to a corporation.

DISCUSSION: Section 351 requires that no gain or loss be recognized if property is transferred to a corporation by one or more persons solely in exchange for stock in the corporation and, immediately after the exchange, such person(s) control the corporation. Mr. Smith and Mr. Jones combined do not have control over the corporation; therefore, Sec. 351 treatment does not apply. Mr. Smith and Mr. Jones must recognize a gain of $20,000 ($30,000 FMV – $10,000 adjusted basis).

Answer (A) is incorrect. Mr. Smith and Mr. Jones must recognize a gain of $20,000 ($30,000 FMV – $10,000 adjusted basis). **Answer (C) is incorrect.** The amount of $30,000 represents the fair market value of the stock. **Answer (D) is incorrect.** The full $20,000 gain ($30,000 FMV – $10,000 adjusted basis) must be recognized.

7. Mr. Carroll transferred the title of a condo he owned in Mexico to his 100%-owned accounting corporation in exchange for stock worth $5,000. Carroll used the condo for personal purposes, and he had no bona fide business reason for the transfer. At the time of the transfer, the condo had a fair market value of $170,000, an adjusted basis of $160,000, and a mortgage of $165,000 (which was assumed by the corporation). What is the amount of Mr. Carroll's recognized gain?

A. $165,000

B. $10,000

C. $5,000

D. $0

Answer (B) is correct.

REQUIRED: The shareholder's recognized gain when (s)he transfers property to a controlled corporation for personal purposes and receives stock in return.

DISCUSSION: If there is no bona fide business purpose in making a transfer, the excess liability rule cannot be used to determine the taxable gain. Instead, the gain is taxable to the extent of all liabilities assumed by the corporation plus the FMV of any property received (other than stock). Mr. Carroll must recognize any gain to the extent of $165,000. Therefore, Mr. Carroll's recognized gain is $10,000 ($170,000 amount realized – $160,000 basis).

Answer (A) is incorrect. The amount of $165,000 equals the liabilities assumed by the transferee corporation. **Answer (C) is incorrect.** Both the gain on the liabilities assumed and the stock treated as a dividend must be recognized. **Answer (D) is incorrect.** A gain is recognized on the transfer.

8. Tech Corporation was formed by three shareholders: Able, Baker, and Charlie. Charlie agreed to provide all the legal work of organization and incorporation for $5,000 cash and $5,000 worth of stock in Tech Corporation. Which of the following statements regarding the exchange is true?

A. Charlie will recognize $5,000 in ordinary income.

B. Charlie will recognize $10,000 in ordinary income.

C. Charlie will recognize $5,000 ordinary income and $5,000 capital gain.

D. Charlie will not have to recognize any income because the transfer is nontaxable.

Answer (B) is correct.

REQUIRED: The amount of income that must be recognized.

DISCUSSION: Charlie must recognize the services performed as income, even though he was paid in stock from the corporation. The income is recognized at $10,000.

Answer (A) is incorrect. Both the $5,000 in cash and $5,000 of stock must be reported as ordinary income because they are received as payment for services rendered. **Answer (C) is incorrect.** The $5,000 of stock is recognized as ordinary income, not a capital gain. **Answer (D) is incorrect.** It is a taxable exchange because the money and property received were for services performed.

9. Ms. D transferred property having an adjusted basis to her of $20,000 and a fair market value of $27,000 to Corporation F. In exchange for the property, she received $6,000 cash and 100% of Corporation F's only class of stock. If the stock received by Ms. D had a fair market value of $21,000 at the time of the transfer, what is the amount of her recognized gain?

A. $0

B. $6,000

C. $7,000

D. $21,000

Answer (B) is correct.

REQUIRED: The shareholder's recognized gain on the transfer of property to a controlled corporation in return for stock and money.

DISCUSSION: Section 351(a) provides for nonrecognition of gain or loss if a person transfers property to a corporation solely in exchange for stock in the corporation and if, immediately after the exchange, such person is in control (owns at least 80% of the stock). Since money is received in addition to the stock, any gain realized by the recipient is recognized but not in excess of the sum of the money received ($6,000).

Answer (A) is incorrect. A gain is recognized on the transfer. **Answer (C) is incorrect.** The realized gain is not recognized in excess of the sum of the money received. **Answer (D) is incorrect.** The gain does not equal the fair market value of the stock received.

10. Fran transfers real property and a mortgage to a corporation in exchange for stock. Fran is in control of the corporation immediately after the transfer. The real property has a fair market value of $500,000, and the mortgage transferred to the corporation is $350,000. Fran has an adjusted basis in the real property of $300,000. What is the amount of income required to be recognized by Fran, if any?

A. $350,000

B. $550,000

C. $50,000

D. $0

Answer (C) is correct.

REQUIRED: The amount of recognized gain on the exchange of property for stock in a corporation.

DISCUSSION: Section 351 applies even if the corporation assumes the shareholder's liability or takes property subject to a liability in the exchange. However, the amount of the liabilities is treated as a recognized gain from the sale or exchange of an asset only to the extent it exceeds the adjusted basis of all property contributed by the shareholder. Since Fran transferred property with an adjusted basis of $300,000 and a mortgage of $350,000, Fran is required to recognize a $50,000 gain.

Answer (A) is incorrect. Fran is not required to report the entire mortgage as a gain. **Answer (B) is incorrect.** Fran is not required to report, as a recognized gain from the exchange, either the FMV of the property ($500,000) or the amount of liability in excess of the adjusted basis of the property transferred ($50,000). **Answer (D) is incorrect.** Fran is required to report a gain for the amount the liability exceeds the adjusted basis of the property transferred.

11. Jenny transferred a factory building with an adjusted basis of $70,000 and a fair market value of $110,000 to the Crystal Corporation in exchange for 100% of Crystal Corporation stock and $20,000 cash. The building was subject to a mortgage of $25,000, which Crystal Corporation assumed. The fair market value of the stock was $75,000. What is the amount of Jenny's realized gain and recognized gain?

	Realized	Recognized
A.	$25,000	$25,000
B.	$50,000	$40,000
C.	$50,000	$20,000
D.	$35,000	$20,000

Answer (C) is correct.

REQUIRED: The amount of realized and recognized gain in transfer of property to a corporation.

DISCUSSION: Jenny realized a gain of $50,000 on the transfer of property to the controlled corporation ($75,000 stock + $25,000 mortgage assumed + $20,000 cash – $70,000 basis in building). Because money is received in addition to the stock, any gain realized by the shareholder is recognized up to the amount received. Also, Sec. 357(c) provides that, if the liabilities transferred or assumed do not exceed the basis of all the property transferred, then the liabilities are not recognized as a gain. Thus, Jenny's recognized gain is $20,000, the money received from the corporation.

Answer (A) is incorrect. The amount of $25,000 is the value of the mortgage assumed. Section 357(c) provides that, if the liabilities transferred or assumed do not exceed the basis of all the property transferred, then the liabilities are not recognized as a gain. **Answer (B) is incorrect.** The amount of $40,000 is the difference between the adjusted basis of the building and the fair market value of the building and is not how gain is calculated when property is transferred for stock. **Answer (D) is incorrect.** The amount of $35,000 is the difference between the fair market value of the building and the fair market value of the stock. The basis in the building should be used, not the FMV.

12. Fern and Isabella transferred money and a business sailing ship for stock in Courier Corporation. Immediately after the exchange, Fern owned 30% of the voting power and 49% of the total shares of each of the other classes of stock; Isabella owned 55% of the voting power and 36% of the total shares of each of the other classes of stock. Fern and Isabella are not otherwise related. Assuming Fern and Isabella each realized gains on the transaction, which of the following statements would apply?

A. Only Fern will recognize gain on the exchange.

B. Only Isabella will recognize gain on the exchange.

C. Both Fern and Isabella will recognize gains on the exchange.

D. Neither Fern nor Isabella will recognize gain on the exchange.

Answer (D) is correct.

REQUIRED: The true statement regarding the realized gain of shareholders on a transfer of property to the controlled corporation in exchange for stock.

DISCUSSION: Section 351 states that no gain or loss is recognized on the transfer of property by one or more persons solely in exchange for stock if, after the exchange, such person(s) control at least 80% of the voting power and 80% of the nonvoting shares. There is no requirement that the contributions be related. Because Fern and Isabella hold a combined controlling amount in Courier, each will defer the gain from the transfer.

13. Andrew transferred an office building that had an adjusted basis of $180,000 and a fair market value of $350,000 to Barry Corporation in exchange for 80% of Barry's only class of stock. The building was subject to a mortgage of $200,000, which Barry assumed for valid business reasons. The fair market value of the stock on the date of the transfer was $150,000. What is the amount of Andrew's recognized gain?

A. $0

B. $20,000

C. $170,000

D. $350,000

Answer (B) is correct.

REQUIRED: The shareholder's recognized gain on a transfer of property to a controlled corporation.

DISCUSSION: Section 351(a) provides for nonrecognition of gain or loss if a person transfers property to a corporation solely in exchange for stock in the corporation and if, immediately after the exchange, such person is in control (owns at least 80% of the stock). However, Sec. 357(c) provides that, if the liabilities transferred or assumed ($200,000) are greater than the basis of all the property transferred ($180,000), the excess is treated as a gain from the sale or exchange of property. Thus, Andrew's recognized gain is $20,000.

Answer (A) is incorrect. A gain on the transfer is recognized. **Answer (C) is incorrect.** The amount of $170,000 is the difference between the fair market value of the stock received plus the mortgage assumed and the adjusted basis of the property transferred. It is the realized gain. **Answer (D) is incorrect.** The amount of $350,000 is the fair market value of the property transferred.

13.2 Basis of Assets Transferred in an Exchange

14. During the year, Yasmine transferred land with an adjusted basis of $40,000 and a fair market value of $95,000 to Nadir Corporation in exchange for 100% of Nadir Corporation's only class of stock. The land was subject to a liability of $45,000, which Nadir Corporation assumed. The fair market value of Nadir Corporation's stock at the time of the transfer was $50,000. What amount of gain must Yasmine recognize and what is her basis in the Nadir Corporation stock?

A. $0 recognized gain, $40,000 basis.

B. $55,000 recognized gain, $95,000 basis.

C. $5,000 recognized gain, $0 basis.

D. $5,000 recognized gain, $45,000 basis.

Answer (C) is correct.

REQUIRED: The gain recognized on the exchange and basis in stock received.

DISCUSSION: Liabilities transferred to a corporation in a Sec. 351 transaction are not boot. However, if the liabilities exceed the basis of the assets, boot is received for the excess liabilities. Gain is recognized for the excess of liabilities over basis so that there is not a negative basis in the stock [$5,000 recognized gain ($45,000 liabilities – $40,000 basis)]. The stock basis is zero. The basis of the asset to the corporation is $45,000.

Answer (A) is incorrect. A gain must be recognized to the extent of excess of the liabilities over the basis of the assets. **Answer (B) is incorrect.** The gain is simply the excess of the liabilities over the basis and the basis is zero. **Answer (D) is incorrect.** The basis is zero because the discharge of indebtedness by the corporation is part of her amount realized, not her basis in the stock.

15. Mr. Garza transferred property with an adjusted basis of $37,000 and a fair market value of $50,000 to Corporation K. In exchange, Mr. Garza received $6,000 cash and 90% of Corporation K's only class of stock. The stock received by Garza had a fair market value of $40,000. What is Corporation K's basis in the property received in this exchange?

A. $50,000

B. $43,000

C. $40,000

D. $37,000

Answer (B) is correct.

REQUIRED: The corporation's basis in property contributed by a shareholder.

DISCUSSION: Section 362(a) provides that the basis to a corporation of property acquired in a Sec. 351 transaction is the same as the basis in the hands of the transferor, increased by the gain recognized by the transferor. Here, the transfer qualifies as a Sec. 351 transaction since greater than 80% of all stock was held by the shareholder after the exchange. Mr. Garza received $6,000 cash in addition to the stock. Mr. Garza recognizes a gain on the $6,000 received. Thus, Corporation K's basis in the property is $43,000 ($37,000 Mr. Garza's adjusted basis + $6,000 gain recognized by Mr. Garza).

Answer (A) is incorrect. The basis does not equal the fair market value of the transferred property. **Answer (C) is incorrect.** The basis does not equal the fair market value for the stock received. **Answer (D) is incorrect.** The basis must be increased by the gain recognized by the shareholder.

16. The basis of stock received in exchange for property transferred to a controlled corporation is the same as the basis of the property transferred with certain adjustments. All of the following would decrease the basis of the stock EXCEPT

A. The fair market value of other property received.

B. Any amount treated as a dividend.

C. Any money received.

D. Any loss recognized on the exchange.

Answer (B) is correct.

REQUIRED: The item that does not decrease the basis of the stock received in a tax-free transfer to a controlled corporation.

DISCUSSION: Section 358(a)(1) provides that, in a Sec. 351 exchange, the basis of the stock received by the transferors (shareholders) is the basis of the property transferred decreased by the fair market value of other property received, the amount of any money received, the amount of any liability relief, and the amount of loss that was recognized by the taxpayer. The basis is increased by the amount of gain recognized by the taxpayer. Any amount treated as a dividend increases the basis.

17. Ms. White transferred property having an adjusted basis of $145,000 and a fair market value of $160,000 to Corporation T in exchange for 100% of T's only class of stock and $20,000 cash. At the time of the transfer, the stock had a fair market value of $115,000. What is the basis of the stock Ms. White received in this transaction?

A. $160,000

B. $145,000

C. $125,000

D. $115,000

Answer (C) is correct.

REQUIRED: The basis of stock received in a tax-free transfer to a controlled corporation.

DISCUSSION: Section 358(a)(1) provides that, in a Sec. 351 exchange, the basis of the stock received by the transferors (shareholders) is the basis of the property transferred decreased by the fair market value of other property received, the amount of any money received, the amount of any liability relief, and the amount of loss that was recognized by the taxpayer. The basis is increased by the amount of gain recognized by the taxpayer. When boot (the cash) is received, gain must be recognized to the extent of the lesser of the transferor's realized gain or the fair market value of boot property received. Ms. White has a realized loss of $10,000 ($115,000 stock received + $20,000 cash – $145,000 basis). A loss is never recognized in an exchange qualifying under Sec. 351, whether boot is received or not. Therefore, the basis equals the adjusted basis of the property transferred ($145,000) less the boot property received ($20,000 cash), or $125,000.

Authors' Note: When the fair market value received ($115,000) is different from fair market value of property given up ($160,000), use FMV received as the selling price.

Answer (A) is incorrect. The basis does not equal the fair market value of the property transferred. **Answer (B) is incorrect.** The basis must be reduced by the amount of cash received. **Answer (D) is incorrect.** The basis does not equal the fair market value of the stock received.

18. For bona fide business purposes, Mr. D transferred the following property to Corporation X. X assumed the $50,000 mortgage.

	Asset Basis	Mortgage	Fair Market Value
Building and land	$120,000	$50,000	$160,000
Various equipment	60,000	0	40,000

In the exchange, Mr. D received 100% of X's only class of stock. What is Corporation X's basis in the property received in the exchange?

A. $130,000

B. $150,000

C. $180,000

D. $200,000

Answer (C) is correct.

REQUIRED: The basis of assets transferred to a corporation subject to a mortgage.

DISCUSSION: Section 362(a) provides that the basis to a corporation of property acquired in a Sec. 351 transaction is the same as the basis in the hands of the transferor, increased by the gain recognized by the transferor. Here, the transfer qualifies as a Sec. 351 transaction since greater than 80% of all stock was held by the shareholder after the exchange. Section 357(c) would not cause any recognition of gain on the contribution of the mortgage since the liability ($50,000) did not exceed the adjusted basis of all property transferred ($180,000). The basis of the property received by Corporation X is therefore the adjusted basis of the property in the hands of the shareholder, which was $180,000 ($120,000 building and land + $60,000 various equipment).

19. Mr. Kahr transferred property with an adjusted basis of $17,500 and a fair market value of $21,500 to Corporation G. In exchange, Mr. Kahr received $2,000 cash and 85% of Corporation G's only class of stock. The stock received by Kahr had a fair market value of $19,500. What is Corporation G's basis in the property received in this exchange?

A. $0

B. $17,500

C. $19,500

D. $21,500

Answer (C) is correct.

REQUIRED: The corporation's basis in property contributed by a shareholder.

DISCUSSION: Section 362(a) provides that the basis to a corporation of property acquired in a Sec. 351 transaction is the same as the basis in the hands of the transferor, increased by the gain recognized by the transferor. Here, the transfer qualifies as a Sec. 351 transaction since greater than 80% of all stock was held by the shareholder after the exchange.

Mr. Kahr received $2,000 cash in addition to the stock. He recognizes a gain on the $2,000 received. Thus, Corporation G's basis in the property is $19,500 ($17,500 Mr. Kahr's adjusted basis + $2,000 gain recognized by Mr. Kahr).

Answer (A) is incorrect. The corporation has a basis in the property. **Answer (B) is incorrect.** The basis is increased by the amount of gain recognized by the transferor. **Answer (D) is incorrect.** The basis does not equal the fair market value of the property.

20. On August 15 of last year, the ABC Partnership purchased telephone equipment for $10,000. The equipment is 5-year property under the MACRS rules. Depreciation in the amount of $2,000 was claimed by ABC on the equipment last year. On April 1 of the current year, ABC Partnership was incorporated with its assets being exchanged for King Corporation stock and notes. Gain of $1,000 was recognized on the transfer of the equipment that was purchased last year. What amount of depreciation is claimed by ABC and King on the equipment in the current year?

	ABC	King
A.	$800	$2,400
B.	$800	$2,600
C.	$1,600	$1,600
D.	$888	$2,640

Answer (B) is correct.

REQUIRED: The amount of depreciation claimed by the transferor of property and the recipient of the property.

DISCUSSION: Under Sec. 1012, the basis of property is generally the cost of the property. ABC's basis in the telephone equipment is therefore initially $10,000. Section 362 provides that, when property is transferred to a corporation in a transaction to which Sec. 351 applies, the corporation's basis in the property is the same as the transferor's basis, increased in the amount of any gain recognized by the transferor on the transfer. Therefore, King's basis in the property is $8,200 [$7,200 ($10,000 – $2,000 – $800) transferor's adjusted basis + $1,000 gain recognized by ABC on the transfer].

Because the property was transferred during the second year of its life, the depreciation must be apportioned between ABC and King. The depreciation is apportioned based on the number of complete months the property was owned. The step-up in basis of $1,000 is treated as a second property whose depreciation commences on April 1 of the current year. Under IRS depreciation tables, depreciation rates of 20% and 32% are applied to 5-year property in its first and second years, respectively. ABC's depreciation deduction is $800 ($10,000 basis × 32% × 3/12). King's depreciation deduction is $2,600 [($10,000 basis × 32% × 9/12) + ($1,000 basis × 20%)].

Answer (A) is incorrect. The recognized gain that increases basis must also be depreciated by King. **Answer (C) is incorrect.** The depreciation is apportioned based on the number of months the property was held and the recognized gain that increases basis must also be depreciated by King. **Answer (D) is incorrect.** The recognized gain that increases basis is only depreciated by King.

STUDY UNIT FOURTEEN

CORPORATE INCOME, LOSSES, AND DEDUCTIONS

(22 pages of outline)

Although many of the Code's provisions apply to all forms of business organizations, some areas of the law are specially tailored for each type. Corporations have many special rules, including a different tax schedule, restrictions on losses, and rules for related party transactions. This study unit examines some of the unique corporate tax laws.

14.1 CORPORATE INCOME TAX LIABILITY AND RECONCILING BOOK TO TAXABLE INCOME

1. **Tax Rate**
    a. Section 11 imposes tax on the taxable income of corporations using a flat 21% rate. This rate applies to ordinary income, capital gains, personal service corporations, and any controlled group of corporations.

EXAMPLE 14-1 Corporate Tax Rate

Little Corporation had $175,000 of taxable income in the ordinary course of business that does not include a $30,000 capital gain. The tax on the taxable income is $36,750 ($175,000 × 21%) and the tax on the capital gain is $6,300 ($30,000 × 21%). Little Corporation's total regular federal income tax is $43,050 ($36,750 + $6,300).

2. If the corporation has less than $250,000 of assets and less than $250,000 of gross receipts, it is not required to include a balance sheet (Schedule L), a reconciliation of income per book with income per return (Schedule M-1), and an analysis of unappropriated retained earnings per book (Schedule M-2).
3. Corporations file federal returns using Form 1120.

<u>**Reconciliation**</u>

4. **Overview**
    a. Corporations file federal returns using Form 1120. Reconciliation of income (loss) per books of the corporation with income (loss) per tax is reported on Schedule M-1.
    b. Schedule M-3 is required for corporations with total assets of $10 million or more.
        1) Schedule M-3 reconciles book net income (loss) for general financial reporting with taxable income (loss) for tax accounting, indicating temporary and permanent differences by category and dollar amount.

    NOTE: Carefully review the Form 1120 Schedule M-1 in Example 14-2 on page 303 and Schedule M-3 beginning on page 305.

c. Corporate tax groups with year-end assets of less than $10 million may file the Schedule M-3 in lieu of the Schedule M-1.

d. Income tax liability (if any) is reported by

 1) **Current** income tax liability or refund receivable calculated based on temporary and permanent book-to-tax differences

 2) **Deferred** income tax liability and/or asset for the future tax consequences of temporary differences (permanent differences are not considered) recognized currently in the financial statements or tax returns

5. **Temporary and Permanent Differences**

 a. Temporary differences are timing differences and occur because tax laws require the recognition of certain items of income and expense in different tax years than are required for book purposes.

  1) Temporary differences originate in 1 tax year and reverse or terminate in 1 or more subsequent tax years.

  2) Temporary differences can be derived from

   a) Cost recovery or income recognition methods (e.g., installment sale income and accelerated depreciation);

   b) Balance sheet perspectives, such as when book basis (e.g., Reserves: Bonus compensation) exceeds or is less than its corresponding tax basis; or

   c) Any other differences that do not involve balance sheet accounts (e.g., net operating loss carryover, net capital loss carryover, and charitable contribution carryover).

 b. Permanent differences result from transactions that will not be offset by any corresponding differences in later years.

Common Temporary Differences	Common Permanent Differences

Prepayments of income
Installment sale income
Accelerated depreciation (e.g., 100%-expensing, Sec. 179, MACRS, lease-type)
Amortization
Charitable contributions
Reserves:
  Credit losses/Bad debt
  Bonus compensation
Capitalized inventory costs (i.e., Sec. 263A)
Net operating loss carryover
Net capital loss carryover
	Tax-exempt interest income (and associated expenses)
	Life insurance proceeds (and associated expenses)
	Tax credits
	Nondeductible penalties and fines
	Nondeductible meals (50%) and entertainment
	Dividends-received deduction
	Lobbying and political expenditures
	Club dues

6. **Calculation**

   a. **Current income tax.** To reconcile income (loss) per books with income (loss) per tax, the following adjustments are made to net income (loss) per books (similar to Schedule M-1):

	Net income (loss) per books
+	Federal income tax
+	Excess of capital losses over capital gains
+	Income subject to tax not recorded on books
+	Expenses recorded on books not deducted on the tax return (e.g., Book depreciation > Tax depreciation, penalties, and fines)
–	Income recorded on books not subject to tax (e.g., municipal bond interest income, life insurance proceeds associated with key personnel)
–	Deductions on this return not charged against book income (e.g., Tax depreciation > Book depreciation)
=	**Taxable income before NOL and DRD**

   NOTE: Remember that M-1 adjustments occur before the dividends-received deduction (DRD) and net operating losses (NOLs). Thus, statements such as "book income and taxable income differ by the M-1 adjustments" are incorrect.

   b. **Deferred income tax expense or benefit.** Deferred tax expense or benefit is the net change during the year in an entity's deferred tax amounts.

      1) **Deferred tax liabilities (DTLs)** record the deferred tax consequences of taxable temporary differences (e.g., future income taxes payable).

      2) **Deferred tax assets (DTAs)** record the deferred tax consequences of deductible temporary differences and carryforwards (e.g., future income taxes refundable).

   c. **Taxable temporary differences** result in future taxable amounts and DTLs.

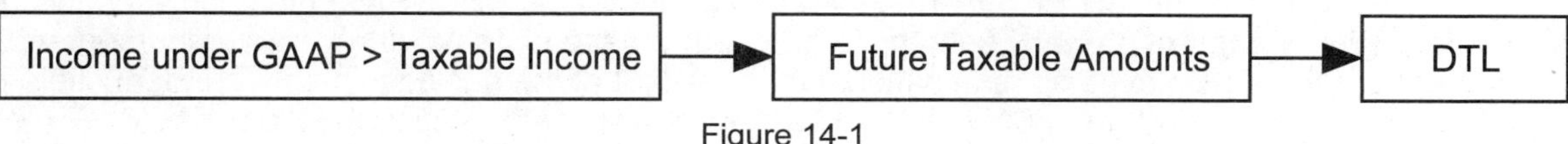

Figure 14-1

   d. **Deductible temporary differences** result in future deductible amounts and DTAs.

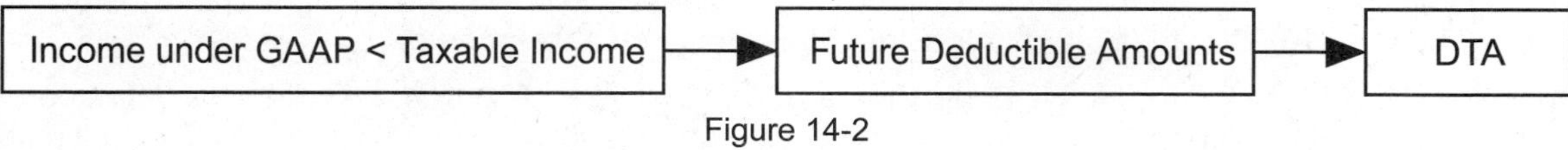

Figure 14-2

   e. Analyzing financial records such as income statements or balance sheets to assist with identifying transactions having M-1 or M-3 impacts can be accomplished by (1) proofing beginning and ending balances and (2) performing year-to-year comparisons of income statement line items, balance sheet line items, and M-1 or M-3 adjustments. Examples include the following:

      1) Advanced rents (commonly referred to as prepaid rental income), which are timing differences that, for tax purposes, are included in taxable income in the year of receipt but are reported in the period earned for book purposes

      2) Reserves for future expenses, which are not currently deductible for tax

3) Expenses incurred to earn tax-exempt income, which are not allowed as a deduction in the computation of taxable income
4) Provisions for estimated expenses, which are established for book purposes as contingencies but are not allowed for tax purposes until they become fixed and determinable
5) Officers' life insurance proceeds (Because the premiums are not deductible, income from the policy is exempt from tax.)

EXAMPLE 14-2 Schedule M-1 -- Reconciliation of Income (Loss)

The following information comes from MEEN Corporation's financial statements:

1. MEEN's net income per books **(before tax expenses)** is $51,007,500.
2. MEEN received $40,000 of interest income, of which $24,000 relates to municipal bonds and is tax exempt. Thus, a $24,000 adjustment is required to decrease taxable income.
3. MEEN received $200,000 in prepaid rent in the current year. The $200,000 prepaid rent collected in the current year is subject to tax and must be added to net income per books in order to arrive at taxable income.
4. MEEN's books showed a $40,000 short-term capital gain distribution from a mutual fund corporation and a $63,000 loss on the sale of Retro stock that was purchased 3 years ago. The stock was an investment in an unrelated corporation. There were no other gains or losses and no loss carryovers from prior years. Therefore, a $23,000 adjustment is required to increase taxable income (i.e., capital losses are limited to capital gains).
5. MEEN uses the allowance method for determining credit loss expense ($170,000) for book, and the specific write-off method is used for tax. The specific write-off method calculates $110,000 credit loss expense; thus, a $60,000 bad debt adjustment is required to increase taxable income.
6. Book depreciation on all fixed assets is $10,000,000. Tax depreciation is $20,000,000 for the fixed assets. Because tax depreciation is $10,000,000 greater than book, the adjustment is recorded on line 8a. If book depreciation were greater than tax, the amount would be recorded on line 5a.
7. MEEN's business meals (not provided by a restaurant) of $200,500 meet the conditions for deductibility and are properly substantiated under an accountable plan. The reimbursement is not treated as employee compensation. Only one-half of the business meals are deductible for tax purposes. Therefore, a $100,250 adjustment is required to increase taxable income.
8. MEEN expensed $19,000 for the term life insurance premiums on the corporation's officers. MEEN was the policy owner and the beneficiary. Key-person life insurance premiums paid by an employer are not deductible for tax purposes if the employer is a beneficiary under the policy. Thus, a $19,000 adjustment is required to increase taxable income.
9. MEEN has a $12,040,000 NOL carryforward from last year. The NOL is deductible when carried to a year in which there is taxable income. The amount applied in any carryover year is limited to 80% of that year's taxable income. Therefore, a $12,040,000 adjustment is required to decrease taxable income (100% of NOL carryover is utilized because it is less than 80% of taxable income).
10. MEEN owns 18% of EPM Industries, from which it received $48,000 in dividend income. A special corporate deduction for dividends received from domestic taxable corporations is allowed. Since MEEN owns less than 20% of EPM, a 50% deduction of $48,000 of dividend income is allowed, with a limitation of 50% of taxable income. Thus, a $24,000 adjustment is required to decrease taxable income.

The completed book-to-tax worksheet and M-1 on the next page show the reconciliation from book net income to taxable income. The explanations showing how each amount was determined are illustrated by number.

-- Continued on next page --

EXAMPLE 14-2 -- Continued

Income Statement for Current Year	Book Income	(T)emporary or (P)ermanent Differences	Book-to-Tax Differences (DR)	CR	Taxable Income
Sales revenue	$500,000,000				$500,000,000
Cost of goods sold	(410,000,000)				(410,000,000)
Gross profit	$ 90,000,000				$ 90,000,000
Other income:					
Interest income	$ 40,000	P	[2]$ (24,000)		$ 16,000
Dividend income	48,000				48,000
Rent income	0	T		[3]$200,000	200,000
Capital gains (losses)	(23,000)	T		[4] 23,000	0
Gross income	$ 90,065,000				$ 90,264,000
Expenses:					
Salaries and wages	$ (21,000,000)				$ (21,000,000)
Insurance	(900,000)				(900,000)
Licenses and permits	(250,000)				(250,000)
Credit loss expense	(170,000)	T		[5] 60,000	(110,000)
Communications	(1,400,000)				(1,400,000)
Information systems expenses	(1,600,000)				(1,600,000)
Depreciation	(10,000,000)	T	[6](10,000,000)		(20,000,000)
Advertising	(2,500,000)				(2,500,000)
Security expenses	(850,000)				(850,000)
Meals	(200,500)	P		[7] 100,250	(100,250)
Life insurance premiums	(89,000)	P		[8] 19,000	(70,000)
Other expenses	(98,000)				(98,000)
Total expenses before NOL and DRD	$ (39,057,500)				$ (48,878,250)
Income before NOL and DRD	$ 51,007,500				*$ 41,385,750
NOL carry forward from prior year	0	T	[9](12,040,000)		**(12,040,000)
Dividends-received deduction	0	P	[10] (24,000)		***(24,000)
Book/taxable income	[1]$ 51,007,500		$(22,064,000)	$402,250	$ 29,321,750
Tax rate					× 21%
			Current income tax payable		****$ **6,157,568**

*Sch. M-1 line 10; Form 1120 p.1, line 28
**Form 1120 p.1, line 29a
***Form 1120 p.1, line 29b
****Form 1120 p.1, line 30

NOTE: Items [9] (NOL carryforward) and [10] (DRD) do not appear on Schedule M-1.

Schedule M-1 **Reconciliation of Income (Loss) per Books With Income per Return**
Note: The corporation may be required to file Schedule M-3. See instructions.

1	Net income (loss) per books	[1] 51,007,500	7	Income recorded on books this year not included on this return (itemize): Tax-exempt interest $ [2] 24,000	24,000
2	Federal income tax per books				
3	Excess of capital losses over capital gains	[4] 23,000			
4	Income subject to tax not recorded on books this year (itemize): Rent Income	[3] 200,000	8	Deductions on this return not charged against book income this year (itemize): a Depreciation $[6]10,000,000; b Charitable contributions $	10,000,000
5	Expenses recorded on books this year not deducted on this return (itemize): a Depreciation $; b Charitable contributions $; c Travel and entertainment $; [5] Bad debt [7] Meals [8] Life Insurance	*179,250	9	Add lines 7 and 8	
6	Add lines 1 through 5	51,409,750	10	Income (page 1, line 28)—line 6 less line 9	41,385,750

*$60,000 (bad debt) + $100,250 (meals) + $19,000 (life insurance) = $179,250

EXAMPLE 14-3 Deferred Tax Liability Calculation for Accumulated Depreciation Basis

Book: Change in accumulated depreciation basis	
Beginning of the year	$100,000,000
End of the year	110,000,000
Net change	**$ 10,000,000**
Tax: Change in accumulated depreciation basis	
Beginning of the year	$200,000,000
End of the year	220,000,000
Net change	**$ 20,000,000**
Beginning of the year book-tax fixed assets basis difference	
Tax basis	$200,000,000
Book basis	100,000,000
Basis difference	$100,000,000
Tax rate	× 21%
Beginning of the year deferred tax liability	**$ 21,000,000**
End of the year book-tax fixed assets basis difference	
Tax basis	$220,000,000
Book basis	110,000,000
Basis difference	$110,000,000
Tax rate	× 21%
End of the year deferred tax liability	**$ 23,100,000**
Beginning of the year deferred tax liability	$21,000,000
End of the year deferred tax liability	$23,100,000
Difference: Current year deferred tax expense	**$2,100,000**

SCHEDULE M-3 (Form 1120) (Rev. December 2019) Department of the Treasury Internal Revenue Service

Net Income (Loss) Reconciliation for Corporations With Total Assets of $10 Million or More

► Attach to Form 1120 or 1120-C.
► Go to *www.irs.gov/Form1120* for instructions and the latest information.

OMB No. 1545-0123

Name of corporation (common parent, if consolidated return) | **Employer identification number**

Check applicable box(es): (1) ☐ Non-consolidated return (2) ☐ Consolidated return (Form 1120 only)
(3) ☐ Mixed 1120/L/PC group (4) ☐ Dormant subsidiaries schedule attached

Part I Financial Information and Net Income (Loss) Reconciliation (see instructions)

1a Did the corporation file SEC Form 10-K for its income statement period ending with or within this tax year?
☐ **Yes.** Skip lines 1b and 1c and complete lines 2a through 11 with respect to that SEC Form 10-K.
☐ **No.** Go to line 1b. See instructions if multiple non-tax-basis income statements are prepared.

b Did the corporation prepare a certified audited non-tax-basis income statement for that period?
☐ **Yes.** Skip line 1c and complete lines 2a through 11 with respect to that income statement.
☐ **No.** Go to line 1c.

c Did the corporation prepare a non-tax-basis income statement for that period?
☐ **Yes.** Complete lines 2a through 11 with respect to that income statement.
☐ **No.** Skip lines 2a through 3c and enter the corporation's net income (loss) per its books and records on line 4a.

2a Enter the income statement period: Beginning MM/DD/YYYY Ending MM/DD/YYYY

b Has the corporation's income statement been restated for the income statement period on line 2a?
☐ **Yes.** (If "Yes," attach an explanation and the amount of each item restated.)
☐ **No.**

c Has the corporation's income statement been restated for any of the five income statement periods immediately preceding the period on line 2a?
☐ **Yes.** (If "Yes," attach an explanation and the amount of each item restated.)
☐ **No.**

3a Is any of the corporation's voting common stock publicly traded?
☐ **Yes.**
☐ **No.** If "No," go to line 4a.

b Enter the symbol of the corporation's primary U.S. publicly traded voting common stock . . . ☐☐☐☐☐

c Enter the nine-digit CUSIP number of the corporation's primary publicly traded voting common stock . . . ☐☐☐☐☐☐☐☐☐

4a	Worldwide consolidated net income (loss) from income statement source identified in Part I, line 1	4a	
b	Indicate accounting standard used for line 4a (see instructions): (1) ☐ GAAP (2) ☐ IFRS (3) ☐ Statutory (4) ☐ Tax-basis (5) ☐ Other (specify) ______		
5a	Net income from nonincludible foreign entities (attach statement)	5a	( )
b	Net loss from nonincludible foreign entities (attach statement and enter as a positive amount)	5b	
6a	Net income from nonincludible U.S. entities (attach statement)	6a	( )
b	Net loss from nonincludible U.S. entities (attach statement and enter as a positive amount)	6b	
7a	Net income (loss) of other includible foreign disregarded entities (attach statement)	7a	
b	Net income (loss) of other includible U.S. disregarded entities (attach statement)	7b	
c	Net income (loss) of other includible entities (attach statement)	7c	
8	Adjustment to eliminations of transactions between includible entities and nonincludible entities (attach statement)	8	
9	Adjustment to reconcile income statement period to tax year (attach statement)	9	
10a	Intercompany dividend adjustments to reconcile to line 11 (attach statement)	10a	
b	Other statutory accounting adjustments to reconcile to line 11 (attach statement)	10b	
c	Other adjustments to reconcile to amount on line 11 (attach statement)	10c	
11	**Net income (loss) per income statement of includible corporations.** Combine lines 4 through 10	11	

Note: Part I, line 11, must equal Part II, line 30, column (a), or Schedule M-1, line 1 (see instructions).

12 Enter the total amount (not just the corporation's share) of the assets and liabilities of all entities included or removed on the following lines.

		Total Assets	Total Liabilities
a	Included on Part I, line 4 ►		
b	Removed on Part I, line 5 ►		
c	Removed on Part I, line 6 ►		
d	Included on Part I, line 7 ►		

Schedule M-3 (Form 1120) (Rev. 12-2019) Page 2

Name of corporation (common parent, if consolidated return)	Employer identification number

Check applicable box(es): (1) ☐ Consolidated group (2) ☐ Parent corp (3) ☐ Consolidated eliminations (4) ☐ Subsidiary corp (5) ☐ Mixed 1120/L/PC group

Check if a sub-consolidated: (6) ☐ 1120 group (7) ☐ 1120 eliminations

Name of subsidiary (if consolidated return)	Employer identification number

Part II **Reconciliation of Net Income (Loss) per Income Statement of Includible Corporations With Taxable Income per Return** (see instructions)

Income (Loss) Items (Attach statements for lines 1 through 12)	(a) Income (Loss) per Income Statement	(b) Temporary Difference	(c) Permanent Difference	(d) Income (Loss) per Tax Return
1 Income (loss) from equity method foreign corporations				
2 Gross foreign dividends not previously taxed				
3 Subpart F, QEF, and similar income inclusions				
4 Gross-up for foreign taxes deemed paid				
5 Gross foreign distributions previously taxed				
6 Income (loss) from equity method U.S. corporations				
7 U.S. dividends not eliminated in tax consolidation				
8 Minority interest for includible corporations				
9 Income (loss) from U.S. partnerships				
10 Income (loss) from foreign partnerships				
11 Income (loss) from other pass-through entities				
12 Items relating to reportable transactions				
13 Interest income (see instructions)				
14 Total accrual to cash adjustment				
15 Hedging transactions				
16 Mark-to-market income (loss)				
17 Cost of goods sold (see instructions)	( )			( )
18 Sale versus lease (for sellers and/or lessors)				
19 Section 481(a) adjustments				
20 Unearned/deferred revenue				
21 Income recognition from long-term contracts				
22 Original issue discount and other imputed interest				
23a Income statement gain/loss on sale, exchange, abandonment, worthlessness, or other disposition of assets other than inventory and pass-through entities				
b Gross capital gains from Schedule D, excluding amounts from pass-through entities				
c Gross capital losses from Schedule D, excluding amounts from pass-through entities, abandonment losses, and worthless stock losses				
d Net gain/loss reported on Form 4797, line 17, excluding amounts from pass-through entities, abandonment losses, and worthless stock losses				
e Abandonment losses				
f Worthless stock losses (attach statement)				
g Other gain/loss on disposition of assets other than inventory				
24 Capital loss limitation and carryforward used				
25 Other income (loss) items with differences (attach statement)				
26 **Total income (loss) items.** Combine lines 1 through 25				
27 **Total expense/deduction items** (from Part III, line 39)				
28 Other items with no differences				
29a Mixed groups, see instructions. All others, combine lines 26 through 28				
b PC insurance subgroup reconciliation totals				
c Life insurance subgroup reconciliation totals				
30 **Reconciliation totals.** Combine lines 29a through 29c				

Note: Line 30, column (a), must equal Part I, line 11, and column (d) must equal Form 1120, page 1, line 28.

Schedule M-3 (Form 1120) (Rev. 12-2019)

Schedule M-3 (Form 1120) (Rev. 12-2019) Page **3**

Name of corporation (common parent, if consolidated return) | **Employer identification number**

Check applicable box(es): **(1)** ☐ Consolidated group **(2)** ☐ Parent corp **(3)** ☐ Consolidated eliminations **(4)** ☐ Subsidiary corp **(5)** ☐ Mixed 1120/L/PC group

Check if a sub-consolidated: **(6)** ☐ 1120 group **(7)** ☐ 1120 eliminations

Name of subsidiary (if consolidated return) | **Employer identification number**

Part III **Reconciliation of Net Income (Loss) per Income Statement of Includible Corporations With Taxable Income per Return—Expense/Deduction Items** (see instructions)

	Expense/Deduction Items	(a) Expense per Income Statement	(b) Temporary Difference	(c) Permanent Difference	(d) Deduction per Tax Return
1	U.S. current income tax expense				
2	U.S. deferred income tax expense				
3	State and local current income tax expense				
4	State and local deferred income tax expense				
5	Foreign current income tax expense (other than foreign withholding taxes)				
6	Foreign deferred income tax expense				
7	Foreign withholding taxes				
8	Interest expense (see instructions)				
9	Stock option expense				
10	Other equity-based compensation				
11	Meals and entertainment				
12	Fines and penalties				
13	Judgments, damages, awards, and similar costs				
14	Parachute payments				
15	Compensation with section 162(m) limitation				
16	Pension and profit-sharing				
17	Other post-retirement benefits				
18	Deferred compensation				
19	Charitable contribution of cash and tangible property				
20	Charitable contribution of intangible property				
21	Charitable contribution limitation/carryforward				
22	Domestic production activities deduction (see instructions)				
23	Current year acquisition or reorganization investment banking fees				
24	Current year acquisition or reorganization legal and accounting fees				
25	Current year acquisition/reorganization other costs				
26	Amortization/impairment of goodwill				
27	Amortization of acquisition, reorganization, and start-up costs				
28	Other amortization or impairment write-offs				
29	Reserved				
30	Depletion				
31	Depreciation				
32	Bad debt expense				
33	Corporate owned life insurance premiums				
34	Purchase versus lease (for purchasers and/or lessees)				
35	Research and development costs				
36	Section 118 exclusion (attach statement)				
37	Section 162(r)—FDIC premiums paid by certain large financial institutions (see instructions)				
38	Other expense/deduction items with differences (attach statement)				
39	**Total expense/deduction items.** Combine lines 1 through 38. Enter here and on Part II, line 27, reporting positive amounts as negative and negative amounts as positive				

Schedule M-3 (Form 1120) (Rev. 12-2019)

7. Changes in the unappropriated retained earnings account from the beginning of the year to the end are reported on Schedule M-2.
   a. This schedule gives the IRS information regarding dividends paid during the year and any special transactions that caused a change in retained earnings for the year.
8. Changes in the unappropriated retained earnings account for the year are calculated as follows (similar to Schedule M-2):

	Beginning balance in unappropriated retained earnings account
+	Net income per books
+	Other increases (including a refund of federal income taxes paid in a prior year that is taken directly to the retained earnings account instead of used to reduce federal income tax expenses)
–	Dividends paid (cash or property)
–	Other decreases (including appropriation of retained earnings made during the tax year)
=	**Ending balance in unappropriated retained earnings account**

Stop & Review

You have completed the outline for this subunit.
Study multiple-choice questions 1 through 3 beginning on page 321.

14.2 DIVIDENDS-RECEIVED DEDUCTION

A special corporate dividends-received deduction (DRD) from domestic taxable corporations is allowed. However, all dividends constitute gross income.

1. Amounts deductible vary with the percentage of the stock of the distributing corporation (by voting and value) owned by the recipient.

% Ownership	% of Dividends Deductible	Limit: % of TI of Recipient
< 20%	50%	50%
≥ 20%, < 80%	65%	65%
≥ 80% & affiliated	100%	N/A

   a. A small business investment company operating under the Small Business Investment Act of 1958 may deduct 100% of dividends received.
   b. Members of an affiliated group of corporations may deduct 100% of the dividends received from a member of the same affiliated group.
2. To be eligible for the DRD, a corporation must hold the stock at least 46 days during the 91-day period that begins 45 days before the dividends are paid (i.e., the ex-dividend date).
3. A corporation cannot take a DRD if it holds a short position in substantially similar or related property.
4. Regulated investment company dividends can qualify for the DRD.
   a. However, capital gain dividends do not qualify for the deduction.
   b. The DRD may be reduced when the investment company receives substantial amounts of income from sources other than dividends from domestic corporations eligible for the DRD.

<u>Limit</u>

5. The 50% and 65% DRD is limited by the recipient corporation's adjusted taxable income (TI). The TI limit does not apply to dividends eligible for a 100% DRD.
   a. To compute the limit, use TI before the following most common adjustments:
      1) Dividends-received deduction
      2) Net operating loss (NOL) deduction
      3) Capital loss carryback
   b. If dividends are received from both 20%-owned and non-20%-owned corporations, the limit is first computed with respect to 20%-and-more-owned corporate dividends.

c. The taxable income (TI) limit does not apply if a current NOL exists or an NOL results from the DRD.

EXAMPLE 14-4 DRD

Alpha Corporation owns 10% of Beta Corporation. Alpha Corporation has $200,000 of ordinary income plus $100,000 in dividend income from Beta Corporation. Alpha Corporation has a $50,000 ($100,000 dividend × 50%) dividends-received deduction. This is less than 50% of TI before the DRD (i.e., $300,000 × 50% = $150,000); therefore, the TI limit does not apply.

EXAMPLE 14-5 DRD -- NOL

A corporation has taxable income of $1,000, including $10,000 in dividends received from a less-than-20%-owned domestic taxable corporation, before the DRD. The DRD before applying the TI limit is $5,000 ($10,000 × 50%). Because the DRD produces an NOL, it is not limited to 50% of taxable income before the deduction of $500 ($1,000 × 50%). The corporation may deduct the entire $5,000, which results in a $4,000 NOL.

Foreign Corporations

6. The DRD is allowable for dividends received from foreign corporations if the distributing corporation
   a. Is at least 10%-owned by the recipient domestic corporation,
   b. Is subject to U.S. federal income tax,
   c. Has income effectively connected with a trade or business in the U.S., and
   d. Is not a foreign personal holding company.
7. The DRD is allowable only on the portion of the dividends attributable to the effectively connected income.
8. Credit for foreign taxes deemed paid by the corporation on the dividend producing earnings and profits may be allowable.
9. An S corporation may not claim the DRD.

Disqualified Dividends

10. A deduction is not allowed, or it is further restricted, for dividends received from entities that include but are not limited to the following:
   a. Mutual savings banks (they are like interest)
   b. Real estate investment trusts
   c. Domestic international sales corporations (generally)
   d. Public utilities on preferred stock
   e. A corporation exempt (under IRC Secs. 501 or 521) from tax during the distribution year

Stop & Review

You have completed the outline for this subunit.

Study multiple-choice questions 4 through 6 beginning on page 322.

14.3 CHARITABLE CONTRIBUTIONS

A corporation's charitable contribution is deductible only if it is made to a qualified organization.

1. Deductible amounts must be paid during the tax year.
   a. An accrual-method corporation may elect to deduct amounts paid no later than the due date for filing the corporation's tax return (not including extensions) for the applicable tax year.

Ordinary Income Property

2. A corporation may deduct the adjusted basis (AB) of inventory and other ordinary income property contributed.

Capital Gain Property

3. In general, the deduction for the contribution of long-term capital gain property is the property's FMV.
   a. The deduction is FMV minus the amount of ordinary income if the asset had been sold.
4. To qualify for a FMV deduction, the tangible personal property must be used in a manner related to the organization's exempt purpose.
   a. It must not be disposed of for value.
   b. The deducting corporation must receive a statement indicating that the property use will comply with these conditions.

Limit

5. Deductions in tax year 2022 are limited to 10% of taxable income (TI) before any
   a. Charitable contributions
   b. Dividends-received deduction
   c. Capital loss carryback
   d. Deduction allowed under IRC Sec. 249 for bond premium
6. Excess over the TI limit may be carried over and is deductible during the succeeding 5 tax years.
   a. No carryback is allowed.
   b. Current-year contributions are deducted first.
   c. FIFO treatment applies to carryforwards.
   d. The charitable contribution carryover cannot be deducted to the extent it increases a net operating loss carryover to a succeeding tax year.

You have completed the outline for this subunit.

Study multiple-choice questions 7 through 9 beginning on page 324.

14.4 OTHER CORPORATE DEDUCTIONS

Gifts

1. Gifts are distinct from charitable contributions, which are made to qualified organizations. A deduction for business gifts is allowable only to the extent of $25 per donee per year. The following are not treated as gifts:
   a. Promotional materials, such as signs and display racks used on the recipient's business premises
   b. One of a number of identical items costing less than $4 and having a permanent imprint of the donor's name

Compensation

2. Compensation, e.g., salary, wages, or bonuses, is a deductible business expense unless the services are capital in nature.
   a. Accrued compensation is not deductible unless paid within 2 1/2 months after year end.
      1) If paid after 2 1/2 months, it is deferred compensation and deductible when paid.
   b. Unreasonable compensation to a shareholder is generally treated as a dividend to the extent of earnings and profits (discussed in Study Unit 15).
   c. A publicly held corporation may not deduct compensation in excess of $1 million paid in any tax year to a covered employee.
      1) A "covered employee" includes any employee who
         a) Serves as principal executive officer or principal financial officer (or acts in such capacity) at any time during the taxable year or
         b) Is among the three highest compensated officers for the taxable year (other than the principal executive officer and principal financial officer) and whose income must therefore be reported under the Exchange Act.
            i) There is no requirement that an individual must be an executive officer as of the last day of the taxable year to be a covered employee.
            ii) No amount of a "parachute payment" made to an officer, shareholder, or highly compensated person is deductible.
      2) The forms of remuneration below are not included in computing the $1 million limit:
         a) Income from pension plans, annuity plans, and specified employer trusts
         b) Benefits that are tax-free under the Code
         c) Compensation paid before being publicly held
      3) The disallowance of the deduction for the compensation payment does not change the employee's reporting of the compensation for income tax purposes.
         a) The $1 million and any excess is generally compensation gross income.
         b) The salary, bonus, or other payment is not required to be treated as a dividend. However, dividend reporting for part of the compensation may be required if part or all of the compensation is not reasonable in amount.

EXAMPLE 14-6	**Deductibility of Corporate Compensation**
David Davidson is the Chief Executive Officer (CEO) for publicly held Davidson & Sons, Inc. David is paid a $3 million cash salary, $500,000 in bonuses tied to performance, and $10,000 in tax-free fringe benefits that are accessible to all employees. David includes $3.5 million in income ($3,000,000 salary + $500,000 bonuses). Davidson & Sons can deduct $1,010,000 ($1,000,000 maximum deductible salary + $10,000 fringe benefits).	

Stock

d. FMV of property received for services is gross income to the corporate employee when it is not subject to a substantial risk of forfeiture and its value can be ascertained with reasonable certainty.

   1) If the property is sold to the employee for less than its FMV, the difference between the amount paid and the value of the property is also income. The employee's basis in the stock is cash plus the amount reported as income.

      a) If an employee is paid in cash and stock, the cash is deducted from the stock FMV and the difference is the employee's basis in the stock.

      b) If the stock splits, the split shares are allocated basis.

   2) Deduction of the compensation by the corporation is allowed when the amount is included as gross income, but only if federal income tax on the compensation is withheld.

      a) The amount of the deduction is the FMV of the stock on the date of transfer.

      b) If the stock has appreciated, the corporation must also recognize a gain on the deemed sale.

EXAMPLE 14-7	**Stock Compensation**
Employee purchases stock (FMV = $1,000) in Year 1 for $500. In Year 8, when its FMV is $2,000, Employee's rights in it are no longer subject to a substantial risk of forfeiture. Employee includes $1,500 in gross income in Year 8. Employer may deduct $1,500 in Year 8. The employee's basis in the stock is $2,000.	

   3) Sale prior to vesting in a non-arm's-length transaction results in gross income computed from the current FMV of the property. Further, gross income is includible upon a subsequent arm's-length sale.

EXAMPLE 14-8	**Stock Compensation**
Employee, from Example 14-7, sold the stock to Spouse in Year 2 for $750 when its FMV was $1,500. Spouse sold the stock for $2,000 in Year 8. Employee includes and Employer deducts $1,000 in Year 2 and $500 in Year 8.	

Education

e. Employer expenditures for employee education are deductible as a business expense.

   1) The corporate employer is not required to document incidental travel costs related to education as travel expenses.

Travel and Meals

3. Travel and meals are deductible business expenses. Meals bought while traveling or served on the business premises are deductible by 50% (100% if provided by a restaurant) of the amount incurred.
    a. Generally, expenses for **entertainment** that are ordinary and necessary to the business are no longer deductible.

EXAMPLE 14-9 **Deductibility of Meals and Entertainment**
Joe is an employee of ARC. He invited several of ARC's top clients to a presentation on new product lines. ARC often uses these presentations to entice clients to place orders. After the presentation, Joe took the clients out to dinner and a show at a cost of $1,000 ($800 show + $200 meal). If not separated into entertainment and meal expenses, none of the $1,000 is deductible. If, however, the amounts are separately stated, 100% of the meal is deductible. ARC would then deduct $200 of this expense since the amount paid is ordinary, necessary, and associated with the active conduct of trade or business, and an employee of ARC was present.

4. Limitation of deduction
    a. If the employee's meal expenses are reimbursed by his or her employer and the reimbursement is not treated as compensation, the employer's deduction is limited to 50% of the expenses for meals not provided by a restaurant.
        1) Employers are not subject to the non-restaurant 50% limit to the extent they treat the reimbursement as compensation to employees.

Insuring an Employee

5. Reasonable amounts of expenditures to promote employee health, goodwill, and welfare are deductible. This includes employee life insurance.
    a. Premiums for life insurance covering an officer or employee are not deductible if the corporation is a direct or indirect beneficiary.
        1) The excess of the insurance proceeds minus the premiums and other amounts paid for the policy is included in income.
    b. A deduction is denied for interest expense incurred with respect to corporate-owned life insurance policies or to endowment or annuity contracts.
        1) An exception is provided for debt on contracts involving key employees.

R&E Expenditures

6. Beginning in 2022, qualified research and experimental expenditures have a 5-year amortization period. For research conducted outside the United States, the amortization period is 15 years.
    a. Generally, costs incidental to development of a model, process, or similar property are included.
    b. Costs of market research, sociological research, or development of art are not included.
    c. Purchase of equipment and land receives its regular treatment and may not be deducted immediately.

Fines

7. Fines and penalties paid to a governmental entity are not deductible.

Bad Debts

8. The allowance method is not permitted (except for financial institutions). A corporation must use the direct charge-off method or the nonaccrual-experience method. The nonaccrual-experience method is a procedure for not recognizing income if it is expected to be uncollectible.

Worthless Securities

9. Loss incurred when a security becomes worthless is generally treated as a capital loss subject to the capital loss limitations.
    a. Loss incurred when a security of an affiliated corporation becomes worthless may be treated as an ordinary loss.

Stock Redemptions

10. Deduction of amounts paid or incurred with respect to a stock redemption or to the redemption of the stock of any related person is not allowed.
    a. Deductions for interest paid or accrued within the tax year on indebtedness are allowed.

Interest Expense

11. Interest expense incurred in a trade or business is generally deductible from gross income.
    a. The business interest deduction is limited to the sum of business interest income, 30% of the business's adjusted taxable income, and floor plan financing interest.
        1) Disallowed business interest may be carried forward indefinitely.
        2) The deduction limitation does not apply to small businesses with average gross receipts of $27 million or less.

Casualty Losses

12. Casualty losses are deductible by a corporation and are not limited by the federal disaster rules that apply to individuals.
    a. When business property is partially destroyed, the deductible amount is the lesser of the decline in FMV or the property's adjusted basis (prior to the loss).
    b. When business property is completely destroyed, the deductible amount is the property's adjusted basis (prior to the loss).
    c. There is no $100-per-loss floor for corporations.

Expenses between Related Taxpayers

13. A deduction for accrued expenses or interest owed by a corporation to a controlling shareholder (or any employee owner of a personal service corporation) or by a controlling shareholder (or any employee owner of a personal service corporation) to a corporation cannot be taken when
    a. The two parties use different accounting methods and
    b. The payee will include the accrued expense in gross income at a date later than when the expense is taken by the payor.

EXAMPLE 14-10 Expenses between Related Taxpayers

John, a cash-basis taxpayer, owns 100% of Gatlin, Inc., an accrual-basis taxpayer. Throughout Year 1, John leased a building to Gatlin but received no cash payments until July Year 2, when Gatlin made a payment for the entire lease. Gatlin properly accrued the expense associated with the building lease. Gatlin is not permitted to take a deduction for the accrued expense until the payment is made to John because they use different accounting methods, and the payee (John) will not include the income until Year 2. Thus, Gatlin will be allowed to deduct the expense in Year 2, and John will include the lease income in his personal income in Year 2.

1) For purposes of determining control, this includes both direct and indirect interests.

Stop & Review

You have completed the outline for this subunit.
Study multiple-choice questions 10 through 13 beginning on page 325.

14.5 NET OPERATING LOSS (NOL) AND CAPITAL LOSSES

1. The following rules apply only for corporations, not individuals.
2. **Net Operating Loss**
    a. An NOL is any excess of deductions over gross income.
    b. Modified deductions for some items are used in computing an NOL.
        1) An NOL carried over from other tax years is not allowed in computing a current NOL.
        2) A dividends-received deduction (DRD) may produce or increase an NOL. The deductible amount is based on the following:

% Ownership	% of Dividends Deductible
<20%	50%
≥20%, <80%	65%
≥80% & affiliated	100%

a) A corporation is entitled to disregard the limitations on a DRD when calculating an NOL. The DRD would increase the NOL.

EXAMPLE 14-11 NOL

MEEN Corporation had the following income and expenses for the current year:

Gross income from operations	$ 98,000
Dividend income (from less-than-20%-owned domestic corporations)	100,000
Business expenses	160,000
Prior year NOL carryover	19,000

MEEN's taxable income (TI) for the current year is computed as follows:

Gross income from business operations	$ 98,000
Dividends received	100,000
Gross income	$198,000
Less: Business expenses	(160,000)
DRD ($100,000 × 50%)	(50,000)
Taxable income (NOL)	$ (12,000)

3) Deductions for foreign-derived intangible income (FDII) and qualified business income (QBI) are not allowed in computing a current NOL.

4) Charitable contributions are not allowed in computing a current NOL.

c. Applying NOLs as a deduction. The treatment of an NOL in the current year depends on the year in which the NOL originally arose (i.e., the year the loss was incurred).

1) For NOLs arising in tax years 2021 and later, the NOL is carried forward indefinitely (i.e., does not expire), but no carryback is allowed. The carryover is limited to 80% of the TI for the year to which it is carried. Any excess continues to carry over to future years until exhausted. Any carryover from tax years 2018-2020 into post-2020 tax years is subject to an 80% limit in the post-2020 tax year.

2) For NOLs arising in tax years 2018, 2019, or 2020, the NOL is carried back 5 years and then carried forward indefinitely (i.e., does not expire) until the NOL is exhausted. A taxpayer may elect to forgo the carryback period and only carry the NOL forward. The NOL for the carryback or carryforward period may offset the taxpayer's entire taxable income of years prior to 2021.

3) For NOLs arising in 2017 and earlier, the NOL is carried forward for 20 years (after a 2-year carryback). Use of the NOL is not limited by TI. Any excess carries over to future years until the NOL is exhausted or expires after 20 years.

4) When utilizing NOLs, the oldest NOL is used first.

5) TI for the carryover year is adjusted TI.

3. **Capital Gain and Loss**

   a. Unlike individuals, corporations do not receive a preferential tax rate on long-term capital gains (LTCGs). Instead, LTCGs, or net capital gains (NCGs), are taxed at the same 21% tax rate as other corporate income.

+	Short-term capital gain (STCG)		
–	Short-term capital loss (STCL)		
+	Long-term capital gain (LTCG)		
–	Long-term capital loss (LTCL)		
=	Net capital gain (NCG)	or	Net capital loss (NCL)
	↓		↓
	× 21%		Carry forward

   b. Also unlike individuals, who can deduct up to a $3,000 NCL, corporations cannot take a net capital loss deduction. Instead, capital losses can only offset capital gains. Capital losses in excess of capital gains are nondeductible in the current year.

   c. Nondeductible net capital losses can be carried back 3 years and forward 5 years.

      1) A corporation cannot carry a capital loss from or to a year that it is an S corporation.

      2) No election to forgo the carryback is available.

      3) The capital loss carryback/carryover must be used to the extent possible in the earliest applicable tax year.

      4) When utilizing a capital loss carryback/carryover, the oldest loss is used first.

      5) The NCL is treated as an STCL in a carryover tax year. It offsets only an NCG before the carryover, but it may not produce or increase a current-year NCL or an NOL.

      6) A capital loss is carried back to the extent it does not increase or produce a net operating loss in the tax year to which it is carried.

4. **Passive Activity Loss (PAL)**

   a. The passive activity loss limitation rules explained in Study Unit 10, Subunit 1, apply to individuals, estates, and trusts (other than grantor trusts). Special PAL rules apply to closely held corporations and personal service corporations.

      1) Even though the PAL rules do not apply to grantor trusts, partnerships, and S corporations directly, they do apply to the owners of these entities.

Stop & Review

You have completed the outline for this subunit.
Study multiple-choice questions 14 through 18 beginning on page 327.

14.6 RELATED PARTY TRANSACTIONS

The following rules limit tax avoidance between related parties.

1. If gain is recognized on the transfer of an asset and the recipient can depreciate the asset, gain is ordinary income.
2. Loss realized on sale or exchange of property to a related person is not deductible. The transferee takes a cost basis. Holding periods are not added.
   a. Gain realized on a subsequent sale to an unrelated party is recognized only to the extent it exceeds the previously disallowed loss.
      1) If the gain realized on the sale to an unrelated third party is less than the amount of disallowed loss, no gain is recognized.
      2) Loss realized on a subsequent sale to a third party is recognized, but the previously disallowed loss is not added to it.

EXAMPLE 14-12 Limited Tax Avoidance

Taxpayer A sells stock with a basis of $100,000 to a related person, Taxpayer B, for $80,000, creating a $20,000 disallowed loss for Taxpayer A. If Taxpayer B then sells the stock to an unrelated party for $130,000, the realized gain will be $50,000 ($130,000 sale price – $80,000 basis) and Taxpayer B will recognize a $30,000 gain ($50,000 realized gain – $20,000 disallowed loss from original transaction between A and B).

However, if the sale to an unrelated party were for $90,000, the resulting $10,000 gain ($90,000 sale price – $80,000 basis) would not be recognized. The $10,000 gain is offset by $10,000 of the $20,000 disallowed loss.

Finally, if the unrelated sale had been for $65,000 (creating an additional $15,000 loss), Taxpayer B could only recognize a $15,000 loss, not a $35,000 loss ($20,000 disallowed loss + $15,000 unrelated-sale loss).

3. For property purchased on or after January 1, 2016, a rule precludes the above recognition of the disallowed loss when later sold to an unrelated party if the original transferor is a tax-indifferent party.
   a. Tax-indifferent parties are those not subject to federal income tax or to whom an item would have no substantial impact on its income tax. Examples of tax-indifferent parties include non-U.S. persons, tax-exempt organizations, and government entities.

EXAMPLE 14-13 Limited Tax Avoidance -- Tax-Indifferent Party

If we use the details from Example 14-12 but change Taxpayer A to a tax-indifferent party, the disallowed loss will still be $20,000 when the stock sells for $80,000 to Taxpayer B; however, on the sale from Taxpayer B to an unrelated party for $130,000, the realized and recognized gain is $50,000 ($130,000 – $80,000). The $50,000 gain is not offset by the disallowed loss.

4. For purposes of these provisions, related parties generally include
   a. An individual's brothers and sisters (whether by whole or half blood), spouse, ancestors (e.g., parent, grandparents), and lineal descendants (e.g, children, grandchildren)
   b. An individual and a corporation that the individual **controls** (directly or indirectly owns more than 50% in value of the outstanding stock)
   c. Two corporations that are members of the same **controlled group** (a chain of corporations connected through stock ownership with a common parent when at least 50% of the total combined voting power, or value, of all classes of stock is owned by one corporation)
   d. A partnership and a corporation **owned by the same person** (ownership of more than 50% of value of corporate stock and more than 50% of capital interest in the partnership)
   e. An S corporation and a C corporation if owned by the same person
   f. A personal service corporation and any employee-owner

EXAMPLE 14-14 Constructive Ownership

A corporation has 100 shares outstanding. A husband, wife, child, and grandchild (the child's child) each own 25 shares. The husband, wife, and child are each considered to own 100 shares. The grandchild is considered to own only 50 shares (25 shares of the grandchild + 25 shares of the child).

5. Generally, a corporation cannot do the following:
   a. Deduct losses on the sale or exchange of properties between itself and related parties
   b. Deduct certain unpaid business expenses and interest on transactions with related parties
   c. Treat an exchange of property between related taxpayers as a like-kind exchange if, within 2 years of the exchange, either party sells the property

You have completed the outline for this subunit.

Study multiple-choice questions 19 through 21 beginning on page 329.

QUESTIONS

14.1 Corporate Income Tax Liability and Reconciling Book to Taxable Income

1. For the tax year, Sting Corporation had net income per books of $65,000, tax-exempt interest of $1,500, excess charitable contributions of $3,000, excess tax depreciation over book depreciation of $4,500, premiums paid on term life insurance on corporate officers of $10,000 (Sting is the beneficiary), and accrued federal income tax of $9,700. Based on this information, what is Sting Corporation's taxable income as it would be shown on Schedule M-1 of its corporate tax return?

A. $59,000

B. $68,700

C. $81,700

D. $87,700

Answer (C) is correct.

REQUIRED: The taxable income on Schedule M-1.

DISCUSSION: Schedule M-1 reconciles income or loss per books with income or loss per tax return.

Net income per books	$65,000
Add back:	
Federal income taxes	9,700
Excess contributions	3,000
Life insurance premiums	10,000
	$87,700
Subtract:	
Tax-exempt interest	(1,500)
Excess depreciation	(4,500)
Taxable income	$81,700

Answer (A) is incorrect. The tax liability, excess contributions, and life insurance premiums must be added. **Answer (B) is incorrect.** The excess contributions and the life insurance premiums must be added. **Answer (D) is incorrect.** The tax-exempt interest and the excess depreciation must be subtracted.

2. HY-Text, Inc., a calendar-year cash-basis corporation, had the following transactions during the year:

Net income per books (after tax estimates)	$100,000
Federal income tax paid	22,250
Excess of capital losses over capital gains	5,000
Interest from municipal bonds	11,000
Expenses related to municipal bond interest	500

What is HY-Text's taxable income?

A. $116,750

B. $139,000

C. $127,750

D. $77,750

Answer (A) is correct.

REQUIRED: The true taxable income for a cash-method corporation.

DISCUSSION: The federal income taxes paid, excess capital losses, and expenses related to the municipal bond interest must be added back because they are not deductible for purposes of federal income tax. Additionally, the municipal bond interest is subtracted because it is tax-exempt income. Therefore,

Net income per books	$100,000
Add back:	
Federal income taxes	22,250
Excess of capital losses over capital gains	5,000
Expenses related to municipal interest	500
	$127,750
Subtract:	
Interest from municipal bonds	(11,000)
	$116,750

Answer (B) is incorrect. The federal income taxes paid are added back only once to arrive at taxable income. **Answer (C) is incorrect.** The municipal bond interest is tax-exempt income and is subtracted. **Answer (D) is incorrect.** The federal income taxes paid are added back (not subtracted) to net income before books along with the excess capital losses and the expenses related to the municipal bond interest.

3. For the current tax year, Task Corporation had an unappropriated retained earnings beginning balance of $115,000 and net income per books of $155,000. During the current year, Task had a loss on a sale of securities of $10,700, paid cash dividends of $85,000, and received a refund of last year's income taxes of $24,000. What is Task Corporation's unappropriated retained earnings ending balance for the current year?

A. $185,000

B. $209,000

C. $219,700

D. $270,000

Answer (B) is correct.

REQUIRED: The corporation's unappropriated retained earnings balance.

DISCUSSION: A corporation's unappropriated retained earnings balance is computed on Schedule M-2 of Form 1120. The balance at the end of the year is the beginning balance; plus net income per books; minus distributions of cash, property, or stock. Other adjustments may be made as necessary. Task's unappropriated retained earnings balance is as follows:

Beginning balance	$115,000
Add:	
Net income per books	155,000
Income tax refund	24,000
Less:	
Cash dividends paid	(85,000)
Unappropriated retained earnings	$209,000

The loss on the sale of securities is already included in the net income per books amount. Thus, no further adjustment is needed.

Answer (A) is incorrect. The income tax refund must be added. **Answer (C) is incorrect.** The loss on the sale of securities is already included in the net income per books. **Answer (D) is incorrect.** The income tax refund must be added, and the dividends paid must be subtracted.

14.2 Dividends-Received Deduction

4. For a domestic corporation to deduct a percentage of the dividends it receives from a foreign corporation, certain tests must be met. Which of the following conditions need NOT be present?

A. The domestic corporation owns at least 10% of the foreign corporation.

B. The foreign corporation has income effectively connected with a trade or business in the U.S.

C. The corporation is not a foreign personal holding company.

D. The foreign corporation has derived income effectively connected with its U.S. business amounting to at least 50% of its gross income from all sources for a 36-month period.

Answer (D) is correct.

REQUIRED: The condition that need not be met for a domestic corporation to deduct a percentage of dividends received from a foreign corporation.

DISCUSSION: Section 245 lists requirements that must be met for the dividends of a foreign corporation to qualify for the dividends-received deduction. These requirements include that the foreign corporation (1) not be a foreign personal holding company, (2) be subject to U.S. federal income taxation, (3) be 10% or more owned by the domestic corporation, and (4) have income from effectively connected business sources within the United States. For dividends received before 1987, prior law required the foreign corporation to have derived 50% or more of its gross income from effectively connected business sources within the U.S.

5. During the current year, Zack Corporation experienced a $15,000 loss from operations. It received $100,000 in dividends from a domestic corporation of which Zack owns 15% of total stock outstanding. Zack's taxable income before the dividends-received deduction was $85,000. What is the amount of Zack's dividends-received deduction?

A. $42,500

B. $50,000

C. $65,000

D. $100,000

Answer (A) is correct.

REQUIRED: The corporate shareholder's amount of dividends-received deduction.

DISCUSSION: The dividends-received deduction for dividends received from a 15%-owned corporation cannot exceed 50% of taxable income for the year. Zack's taxable income is $85,000 ($100,000 dividends – $15,000 loss). The tentative dividends-received deduction of $50,000 would not cause an NOL; therefore, the dividends-received deduction is limited to 50% of taxable income, or $42,500 ($85,000 × 50%).

Answer (B) is incorrect. The taxable income limitation applies. **Answer (C) is incorrect.** A 65% dividends-received deduction cannot apply. **Answer (D) is incorrect.** The deduction is limited to 50% of taxable income.

6. In Year 1, Green, Inc., had gross receipts from sales of $500,000, dividends of $100,000 from a domestic corporation in which Green owned 50% of the stock, and operating expenses of $800,000. What is the Year 1 net operating loss for Green?

A. $200,000

B. $265,000

C. $300,000

D. $330,000

Answer (B) is correct.

REQUIRED: The dividends-received deduction when increasing an NOL.

DISCUSSION: If a corporation has a 20% or greater interest in a corporation, it normally can deduct 65% of taxable income. The 65% of taxable income cap is disregarded if the corporation is determining an NOL for the year. Therefore, Green's NOL for the year is calculated as follows:

Income from business	$ 500,000
Dividends	100,000
Gross income	$ 600,000
Deductions (expenses)	(800,000)
Taxable income (loss) before special deductions	$(200,000)
Minus: Deduction for dividends received (65% of $100,000)	(65,000)
Net operating loss	$(265,000)

Answer (A) is incorrect. The DRD is computed without regard to the NOL. **Answer (C) is incorrect.** A DRD for 100% of the dividends received only applies to corporate ownership levels of greater than or equal to 80%. **Answer (D) is incorrect.** The dividends-received deduction is $65,000. The NOL should equal $265,000 ($200,000 + $65,000).

14.3 Charitable Contributions

7. Norwood Corporation is an accrual-basis taxpayer. For the year ended December 31, Year 1, it had book income before tax of $150,000 after deducting a charitable contribution of $50,000. The contribution was authorized by the board of directors in December Year 1, but was not actually paid until March 1, Year 2. How should Norwood treat this charitable contribution for tax purposes to minimize its Year 1 taxable income?

A. It cannot claim a deduction in Year 1 but must apply the payment against Year 2 income.

B. Make an election claiming a deduction for Year 1 of $20,000 with no carryover.

C. Make an election claiming a deduction for Year 1 of $37,500 with no carryover.

D. Make an election carrying the deduction back 3 years.

Answer (B) is correct.

REQUIRED: The corporation's maximum charitable contribution deduction.

DISCUSSION: Section 170(a)(2) allows an accrual-basis corporation to deduct a charitable contribution if authorized during the taxable year and paid by the due date for filing the corporation's tax return (not including extensions) for the applicable tax year. Since the contribution was paid by March 15, Year 2, it is deductible in Year 1. Section 170(b)(2) provides that the charitable contribution deduction may not exceed 10% of a corporation's taxable income computed before certain special deductions and the charitable contribution deduction. Norwood's maximum Year 1 deduction is $50,000, which is within the limit as shown below.

Taxable income after contribution	$150,000
Add: Charitable contributions made	50,000
Taxable income before contribution	$200,000
Times: Limit percentage	× 10%
Year 1 contribution deduction limit	$ 20,000

Answer (A) is incorrect. A deduction may be claimed in Year 1. **Answer (C) is incorrect.** The deduction is limited to 10% of taxable income before deducting the charitable contribution. **Answer (D) is incorrect.** Carrying the deduction back would not minimize Year 1 taxable income.

8. Grey Corporation made cash contributions totaling $20,000 to qualified charitable organizations. Grey received $30,000 in dividends from a domestic corporation in which it holds 24% stock ownership. Grey was able to deduct 65% of the dividends received from the domestic corporation. Grey's taxable income for the year was $48,300 after the dividends-received deduction but before the deduction for charitable contributions. What is Grey's charitable contribution deduction for the year?

A. $4,830

B. $15,000

C. $6,780

D. $20,000

Answer (C) is correct.

REQUIRED: The corporation's charitable contribution deduction.

DISCUSSION: Under Sec. 170, charitable contributions made to qualified organizations and paid within the taxable year may be deducted from taxable income. A corporation's charitable deduction is limited to 10% of taxable income computed before the charitable contribution deduction, capital loss carryback, and the dividends-received deduction. The dividends-received deduction of $19,500 ($30,000 × 65%) must be added back to the taxable income of $48,300. Grey's charitable contribution deduction is $6,780 ($67,800 × 10%).

Answer (A) is incorrect. The dividends-received deduction is not deducted from income before the 10% limit is applied. **Answer (B) is incorrect.** The charitable contribution deduction of 10% is applied after the dividends-received deduction is added to taxable income. **Answer (D) is incorrect.** The total cash contributions are limited to 10% of income before the charitable contributions deduction, capital loss carryback, and the dividends-received deduction.

9. Which of the following statements concerning the charitable contribution deduction by a corporation is true?

A. A corporation cannot deduct contributions in the current year that exceed 10% of its taxable income.

B. A corporation can deduct contributions to charitable organizations only if they are made in cash.

C. A corporation using the accrual basis of accounting must have made the charitable donation by the close of its tax year.

D. A corporation is not permitted to carry over any charitable contributions that were not deducted in the current year.

Answer (A) is correct.

REQUIRED: The true statement concerning the charitable contribution deduction by a corporation.

DISCUSSION: A corporation's allowable charitable contribution deduction for a given tax year cannot exceed 10% of the corporation's taxable income for the year. Any excess amount can be carried forward to the following tax year.

Answer (B) is incorrect. Noncash contributions are also deductible. **Answer (C) is incorrect.** An accrual-method corporation may elect to deduct amounts paid no later than the due date for filing the corporation's tax return (not including extensions) for the applicable tax year. **Answer (D) is incorrect.** Excess charitable contributions over the taxable income limit may be carried over and are deductible during the succeeding 5 tax years.

14.4 Other Corporate Deductions

10. Carol provides services in Year 1 to Bragg Corporation. Her service contract with Bragg listed her fee at $50,000 receivable in cash and/or stock. At the time her fee was due, Bragg stock was trading for $1,000 per share. Carol elected to receive $30,000 in cash and 20 shares of Bragg stock. In Year 4, the Bragg stock split, increasing the number of Carol's shares to 40. In Year 6, Carol sells 20 shares of her Bragg stock for $1,500 per share. What is Carol's basis in the Bragg Corporation shares she still owns?

A. $10,000

B. $20,000

C. $30,000

D. $40,000

Answer (A) is correct.

REQUIRED: The adjusted basis of a shareholder's remaining shares.

DISCUSSION: The adjusted basis of stock is usually its cost. However, since Carol rendered services for $50,000 (of which $30,000 was paid in cash), Carol's basis in her original 20 shares equals $20,000, the fair market value of the stock. The stock split reduces her basis per share to $500. Since she sold 20 shares with a $500 per share basis, her remaining 20 shares have a $500 per share basis, for a total basis of $10,000.

11. Michelle Nicole is the chief executive officer of It'll Rain Someday, Inc., a publicly held company that sells umbrellas and rainwear. During the year, Ms. Nicole was paid $1.5 million in compensation, which included a $600,000 excess golden parachute payment. What is the amount that It'll Rain Someday can deduct for Ms. Nicole's compensation?

A. $1,500,000

B. $900,000

C. $400,000

D. $1,000,000

Answer (B) is correct.

REQUIRED: The amount of compensation that can be deducted.

DISCUSSION: A corporation that enters into a contract whereby it agrees to pay an employee amounts in excess of the employee's usual compensation in the event that control or ownership of the corporation changes is barred from taking a deduction for an "excess parachute payment made to a disqualified individual." A disqualified individual is an employee who performs services for any corporation and is an officer, a shareholder, or other highly compensated individual. Therefore, the entire golden parachute payment is not deductible, and It'll Rain Someday, Inc., will deduct only $900,000 ($1,500,000 compensation – $600,000 golden parachute payment).

12. On December 31, Year 1, PSC Corporation, a personal service corporation, accrued a $25,000 bonus to Mrs. Adams, an employee-owner. She owns 3% of the outstanding stock of the corporation. Mrs. Adams is a cash-basis taxpayer and received the bonus on April 15, Year 2. PSC Corp., a calendar-year taxpayer, may take a deduction on its Year 1 return of which of the following amounts?

A. $25,000

B. $21,250

C. $3,750

D. $0

Answer (D) is correct.

REQUIRED: The deduction for a PSC when the bonus is distributed the following year to a cash-basis taxpayer.

DISCUSSION: Under Sec. 162(a), a reasonable allowance for salaries or other compensation for personal services actually rendered is deductible by the corporation if paid or incurred during the tax year. PSC Corporation is denied the deduction for the accrual in Year 1 because a deduction for accrued expenses owed between related taxpayers cannot be taken when two parties use different accounting methods, and the payee (i.e., Mrs. Adams) will include the accrued expense in gross income at a date later than when the expense is taken by the payor (i.e., PSC Corp.). In addition, even if the related parties had the same method, the deduction would be postponed to Year 2 since compensation paid to employees must not only meet the economic performance requirement but must also be paid within 2 1/2 months after the end of the employer's tax year in which the services are rendered. Payments made after the end of the 2 1/2-month period are presumed to be deferred compensation, and the deduction is deferred until the year in which payment occurs [Temp. Reg. 1.404(b)-1T(A-2)(b)(1)].

13. The Charlie Corporation, a calendar-year, accrual-basis taxpayer, distributed shares of the David Corporation stock to Charlie's employees in lieu of salaries. The salary expense would have been deductible as compensation if paid in cash. On the date of the payment, Charlie's adjusted basis in David's stock was $20,000, and the stock's fair market value was $100,000. What is the tax effect to Charlie Corporation?

A. $100,000 deduction.

B. $20,000 deduction.

C. $20,000 deduction and $80,000 recognized gain.

D. $100,000 deduction and $80,000 recognized gain.

Answer (D) is correct.

REQUIRED: The tax effect of a distribution of stock held by a corporation to its employees.

DISCUSSION: Publication 535 states, "If you transfer property (including your company's stock) to an employee as payment for services, you can generally deduct it as wages. The amount you can deduct is its fair market value on the date of the transfer minus any amount the employee paid for the property. . . . You treat the deductible amount as received in exchange for the property, and you must recognize any gain or loss realized on the transfer. Your gain or loss is the difference between the fair market value of the property and its adjusted basis on the date of transfer."

Answer (A) is incorrect. The corporation must recognize the $80,000 gain. **Answer (B) is incorrect.** The deduction is equal to the FMV of the property distributed, and the corporation must recognize the $80,000 gain. **Answer (C) is incorrect.** The deduction is equal to the FMV of the property distributed.

14.5 Net Operating Loss (NOL) and Capital Losses

14. Which of the following statements concerning capital losses by corporations other than S corporations is true?

A. Assuming no capital gains to offset the corporation's capital losses, the maximum deduction is $3,000.

B. A capital loss may never be carried forward.

C. A net capital loss may be carried back 3 years and carried forward for up to 15 years.

D. Capital losses can be deducted only up to the amount of the capital gains.

Answer (D) is correct.

REQUIRED: The true statement regarding capital losses by corporations.

DISCUSSION: Section 1211 provides that a corporation may deduct capital losses only to the extent of capital gains (without regard to whether they are short- or long-term). The remaining capital losses will be carried back 3 years or carried over to the next year.

Answer (A) is incorrect. Capital losses may be deducted only to the extent of capital gains. **Answer (B) is incorrect.** A capital loss may be carried forward for up to 5 years. **Answer (C) is incorrect.** A net capital loss may be carried back 3 years and carried forward for up to 5 years.

15. For the calendar year, Cincy Corporation had operating income of $80,000, exclusive of the following capital gains and losses:

Long-term capital gain	$14,000
Short-term capital gain	6,000
Long-term capital loss	(2,000)
Short-term capital loss	(8,000)

What is Cincy's income tax liability for the year?

A. $18,850

B. $18,900

C. $9,000

D. $18,000

Answer (B) is correct.

REQUIRED: The current-year income tax liability of a calendar-year corporation.

DISCUSSION: Section 11 imposes a tax on the taxable income of every corporation. A corporation may deduct capital losses to the extent of capital gains (without regard to whether they are short-term or long-term). Cincy Corporation's taxable income includes $80,000 of operating income and a net long-term capital gain of $10,000 [($14,000 – $2,000) + ($6,000 – $8,000)], or $90,000. The current-year tax liability of Cincy Corporation is $18,900 ($90,000 × 21%).

16. The Workit Corporation has a loss for the year 2022. In computing the current net operating loss, which of the following statements is true regarding either limiting or allowing deductions?

A. The corporation can deduct any NOL carryovers from 2021.

B. A corporation can take the deduction for dividends received, without regard to the limits based on taxable income that normally apply.

C. A corporation cannot figure the deduction for dividends paid on certain preferred stock of public utilities without limits to its taxable income for the year.

D. The corporation can deduct any NOL carryovers from prior years, subject to possible special limitations.

Answer (B) is correct.

REQUIRED: The true statement regarding net operating losses.

DISCUSSION: An NOL is any excess of deductions over gross income. A dividends-received deduction may produce or increase an NOL. A corporation is entitled to disregard the limitations on a dividends received deduction when calculating an NOL.

Answer (A) is incorrect. An NOL from other tax years is not allowed in computing a current NOL. **Answer (C) is incorrect.** A corporation can figure the deduction for dividends paid on certain preferred stock of public utilities without regard to the limits based on taxable income for the year. **Answer (D) is incorrect.** An NOL from other tax years is not allowed in computing a current NOL.

17. Sea Corporation reported gross income from operations of $100,000 and operating expenses of $150,000. Sea also received dividend income of $90,000 from a domestic corporation in which Sea is a 20% shareholder. What is the amount of Sea Corporation's net operating loss?

A. $0

B. $5,000

C. $18,500

D. $40,000

Answer (C) is correct.

REQUIRED: The net operating loss when there is dividend income.

DISCUSSION: Section 172(c) defines a net operating loss as the excess of deductions over gross income, with certain modifications. One modification is that the dividends-received deduction is computed without regard to the 65% of taxable income limitation in Sec. 246(b). Thus, Sea's NOL is $18,500 as computed below.

Gross income from operations	$100,000
Dividend income	90,000
Less: Operating expenses	(150,000)
Net income before DRD	$ 40,000
Less: Dividends-received deduction ($90,000 × 65%)	(58,500)
Net operating loss	$(18,500)

Answer (A) is incorrect. Sea's deductions exceed gross income. **Answer (B) is incorrect.** The amount of $5,000 incorrectly deducts only 50% of the dividends received. **Answer (D) is incorrect.** The amount of $40,000 is Sea's gross income.

18. Taxpayer, Inc., a C corporation, had the following transactions during 2022:

Long-term gain from sale of land	$10,000
Short-term gain from sale of stock	20,000
Long-term losses from sale of securities	(40,000)

What is the amount of long-term capital loss that may be taken as a deduction by Taxpayer in 2022?

A. $0

B. $10,000

C. $30,000

D. $40,000

Answer (C) is correct.

REQUIRED: The amount of capital losses allowed as a deduction.

DISCUSSION: Section 1211 provides that a corporation may deduct capital losses only to the extent of capital gains (without regard to whether they are short- or long-term). Therefore, Taxpayer can deduct only $30,000 of its net long-term capital loss in 2022. The remaining $10,000 long-term capital loss will be carried back 3 years or carried forward to the 5 succeeding tax years.

Answer (A) is incorrect. Capital losses are deductible when there are capital gains in the same year. **Answer (B) is incorrect.** Capital losses may be deducted up to the extent of capital gains, regardless if they are short- or long-term. **Answer (D) is incorrect.** Capital losses may be deducted only to the extent of capital gains.

14.6 Related Party Transactions

19. Chandler Corporation has 500 shares of common stock outstanding. Scott owns 150 shares; Scott's mother, Mabel, owns 50 shares; his brother, Ted, owns 40 shares; and Scott's son, Fred, owns 60 shares. Borus Corporation owns 50 shares of Chandler, and Scott owns 70% of the stock in Borus. How many shares does Scott own in Chandler, applying the rules of ownership attribution, for purposes of determining whether a loss on the sale or trade of property between related parties is deductible?

A. 335 shares.

B. 295 shares.

C. 350 shares.

D. None of the answers are correct.

Answer (A) is correct.

REQUIRED: The proper application of attribution of ownership rules in determining related parties.

DISCUSSION: Section 267 contains the constructive ownership rules of ownership of stock with respect to losses on the sale or trade of property between related taxpayers. An individual is considered to own stock owned by his or her brothers and sisters (whether by whole or half blood), spouse, ancestors, and lineal descendants [Sec. 267(c)(4)]. If a shareholder owns 50% or more in value of the stock of a corporation, (s)he is considered to own the stock the corporation owns in proportion to the value of the stock that (s)he owns in the corporation. Therefore, Scott constructively owns 35 shares (50 shares × 70%) of the stock Borus owns in Chandler. Also, Scott constructively owns the shares his relatives (Mabel, Ted, and Fred) own in Chandler. As a result, Scott constructively owns 335 shares (150 + 50 + 40 + 60 + 35) in Chandler.

Answer (B) is incorrect. Under Sec. 267, an individual is considered to own stock owned by his or her brothers and sisters. **Answer (C) is incorrect.** Since Scott owns more than 50% of Borus, he is considered to own the stock the corporation owns in proportion to the value of the stock that he owns in the corporation, not all 50 shares. **Answer (D) is incorrect.** Scott constructively owns 335 shares of Chandler.

20. Which of the following are NOT related persons for purposes of disallowing an accrual deduction for interest payable to a cash-basis person until payment of the interest is made?

A. Two corporations that are members of the same controlled group.

B. The grantor and fiduciary, and the fiduciary and beneficiary of any trust.

C. A personal service corporation and any employee-owner, regardless of the amount of stock owned by the employee-owner.

D. Any two S corporations if the same person owns 25% in value of the outstanding stock of each corporation.

Answer (D) is correct.

REQUIRED: The situation that does not describe related taxpayers.

DISCUSSION: A related person relationship exists if the same person owns more than 50% in value of the outstanding stock of each S corporation.

21. Mitchell sold his Saratoga Bombers Corporation stock to his brother Sheldon for $7,000. Mitchell's cost basis in the stock was $10,000. Sheldon later sold this stock to Morey, an unrelated party, for $10,500. What is Sheldon's recognized gain?

A. $2,100

B. $3,500

C. $500

D. $3,000

Answer (C) is correct.

REQUIRED: The amount of realized gain when stock is sold after acquisition from a related party in a loss transaction.

DISCUSSION: Under Sec. 267, losses are not allowed on sales or exchanges of property between related parties. Brothers are related parties. Mitchell realized a $3,000 ($10,000 – $7,000) loss on the sale but may not deduct it. On the subsequent sale, Sheldon realized a $3,500 gain ($10,500 sales price – $7,000 basis). However, he does not have to recognize a gain on the $3,000 because the Sec. 267(d) disallowed loss is used to offset the subsequent gain on the sale of the property. Thus, the recognized gain is $500 ($10,500 sales price – $10,000 brother's basis).

Answer (A) is incorrect. The gain is only $500.
Answer (B) is incorrect. The realized gain is $3,500.
Answer (D) is incorrect. The amount of $3,000 represents Mitchell's nondeductible loss.

Go to Online Course

Access the **Gleim EA Premium Review System** featuring our SmartAdapt technology from your Gleim Personal Classroom to continue your studies.

You will experience a personalized study environment with exam-emulating multiple-choice questions.

STUDY UNIT FIFTEEN

CORPORATE DISTRIBUTIONS

(11 pages of outline)

A **distribution** is any transfer of property by a corporation to any of its shareholders with respect to the shareholder's shares in the corporation. Property is defined as

1) Money;
2) Bonds or other obligations (also of the distributing corporation);
3) Stock in other corporations (not issued by the distributor); and
4) Other property, including receivables.

The amount of a distribution is calculated as follows:

	Money
+	Obligations (FMV), e.g., a bond
+	Property (FMV), other
–	Related liabilities, recourse or not
=	Distribution amount

15.1 EARNINGS AND PROFITS

Significance

1. The amount of a distribution is treated as a dividend to the extent of the corporation's earnings and profits (E&P).
   a. Distributions are presumed to come from the corporation's E&P, unless there are no E&P.
   b. An E&P account provides an approximate measure of a corporation's ability to pay a dividend (in the generic sense) to its shareholders.
   c. A corporate shareholder may prefer dividend treatment for a distribution it receives because of the availability of a dividends-received deduction.
      1) Between 50% and 100% of the dividend amount may represent a current deduction.

d. An individual shareholder may benefit from nondividend treatment for a portion of a distribution (Form 5452, sample below).

1) Portions treated as recovery of capital are not subject to federal income taxes.

2) Portions treated as LTCG can offset capital losses and may be taxed at a lower maximum rate of 0%, 15%, or 20%, depending on the taxpayer's total taxable income.

Form **5452**

(Rev. October 2018)

Department of the Treasury
Internal Revenue Service

Corporate Report of Nondividend Distributions

► **For calendar year ending December 31,** ______

► **Attach to the corporation's income tax return.**

► **Go to *www.irs.gov/Form5452* for instructions and the latest information.**

OMB No. 1545-0123

Name

Employer identification number

A Has the corporation filed a Form 5452 for a prior calendar year? . . . . ► ☐ **Yes** ☐ **No**
If "Yes," enter the applicable year(s) ______

B Are any of the distributions part of a partial or complete liquidation? . . . . ► ☐ **Yes** ☐ **No**
If "Yes," attach explanation.

C Are any of the distributions from an S corporation's accumulated adjustments account? . . . . ► ☐ **Yes** ☐ **No**
If "Yes," enter the balance at the beginning of the tax year ______

D Earnings and Profits (See **Supporting Information** in instructions.)

• Accumulated earnings and profits (since February 28, 1913) at the beginning of the tax year . . . ► $______

• Actual earnings and profits for the current tax year . . . . ► $______

E Shareholders at Date of Last Dividend Payment

• Number of individuals . . . . ______

• Number of partnerships . . . . ______

• Number of corporations and other shareholders . . . . ______

F Corporate Distributions (see instructions)

Date Paid	Total Amount Paid (Common (C), Preferred (P), Other (O))	Amount Per Share	Amount Paid During Calendar Year From Earnings & Profits Since February 28, 1913			Percentage Taxable	Amount Paid During Calendar Year From Other Than Earnings & Profits Since February 28, 1913	Percentage Nontaxable
			From the Current Year	Accumulated	Total			
	$	$	$	$	$	%	$	%
Totals	$		$	$	$		$	

For Paperwork Reduction Act Notice, see the instructions. Cat. No. 11881T Form **5452** (Rev. 10-2018)

Computing E&P: The Formula

2. The IRC does not provide a mechanical definition of E&P. Section 312 and regulations provide rules that indicate how certain transactions or events are reported.
   a. Taxable income (TI). TI is the starting point for computing E&P.
   b. Adjustments. TI is adjusted up and down to compute the approximate dividend-paying ability of the corporation. Adjustment items may be categorized as follows:

Adjustment Category	Adjustment to Compute E&P
1) Income excluded from TI	• Add to TI
2) Expenses and losses that are nondeductible for TI	• Subtract from TI
3) Deferred income recognition items	• Add to or subtract from TI
4) Accelerated deduction items	• Add to or subtract from TI
5) Deductions not allowed for E&P	• Add to TI

Income Excluded from TI

3. TI is adjusted upward for (most) items of economic income not included as gross income when computing TI.
   a. Add economic income that is
      1) Not a contribution to capital but
      2) Increases dividend-paying capacity.
   b. Add the following:
      1) Refunds of prior years' federal income tax
      2) Recoveries of deduction items that produced no tax benefit (e.g., bad debts, casualty losses)
      3) Tax-exempt interest income
      4) The excludable portion of life insurance proceeds paid to the corporation

Nondeductible Expenses and Losses

4. TI is adjusted downward for expenditures and losses to the extent they are not allowed as a deduction from gross income (GI) in computing TI.
   a. Subtract the following from TI:
      1) Charitable contributions (excess over 10% of TI)
      2) Capital losses (current year's carried over)
      3) Disallowed losses (e.g., sale to related party)
      4) Federal income taxes
      5) Penalties and fines
      6) Political contributions
      7) Expenses relating to tax-exempt income
      8) The excludable portion of life insurance premiums (with corporation as beneficiary)
   b. **Timing.** The adjustment for corporations using the cash method of accounting is made when the item is paid.
      1) A corporation using the accrual method of accounting generally reports the adjustment when it is accrued.
   c. **Capacity.** Each corporate item, including those previously listed, must be considered for its effect on dividend-paying capacity and on TI.
      1) For example, life insurance premiums on policies in which the corporation is the beneficiary are subtracted net of the cash surrender value increase.

Deferred Recognition Items

5. Most income for which an exception defers recognition when determining TI is not included in E&P until recognized.
   a. Exceptions
      1) Add to TI any unrecognized realized income/gain on an installment sale.

> **EXAMPLE 15-1 Installment Sale**
>
> Delaware Corp. engages in an installment sale of land that it has held as a potential plant site. Delaware is to receive 60% of the sales proceeds in the following tax year. Delaware's realized gain on the sale is $1 million. Taxable income does not include realized gain not recognized, or $600,000 ($1,000,000 × 0.60). E&P include the gain that is currently recognized as well as the $600,000 deferred gain.

      2) Recalculate income reported on a long-term contract reported using the completed-contract method as if the percentage-of-completion method were used.

Accelerated Deduction Items

6. TI is adjusted to the extent deductions reduce TI in excess of economic costs due to premature recognition of anticipated economic decline.
   a. Adjust TI upward or downward for the difference between
      1) Section 179 expense deducted and the amount deducted as if the cost is expensed ratably over 5 years
      2) Realty depreciation deducted using the MACRS rules and depreciation computed over 39 years
      3) ACRS deductions and straight-line ACRS deductions with extended recovery periods
      4) MACRS deductions and the alternative depreciation system (ADS) deductions
         a) ADS applies straight-line depreciation over the property's class life using a half-year convention.
      5) Percentage depletion deductions claimed and cost depletion amounts
      6) Intangible drilling costs (IDC) deducted and the IDC amounts amortized over 60 months

Deductions Not Allowed for E&P

7. TI is adjusted upward for items that are currently deductible from GI in computing TI but do not currently reduce capacity to pay dividends. These items may have already reduced E&P in a prior tax year or may never reduce E&P.
   a. Add to TI any amounts deducted for
      1) Charitable contribution carryovers
      2) Net operating loss carryovers
      3) Capital loss carryovers
      4) Dividends-received deductions

Distributions

8. A distribution by the corporation to one or more shareholders may trigger both upward and then downward adjustments to E&P (which may affect tax treatment of distributions to the distributee and other shareholders).
   a. Although distributions can occur at any time during the tax year, current E&P are determined at the end of the tax year.
      1) Once current E&P are determined, the tax consequences of each distribution can be determined.
   b. When a corporation distributes property that has appreciated in value, the corporation must recognize a gain as if the corporation had sold its property for its FMV.
      1) However, a corporation does not recognize any loss when it makes a distribution of property even if the sale would have resulted in a loss.
      2) Gain recognized by the corporation on the distribution of appreciated property is included in TI.
      3) Before distributions of appreciated property (other than the corporation's obligations), earnings and profits must be increased by the excess of the FMV over the adjusted basis (AB) of the appreciated property.
      4) If a liability attached to a distributed asset exceeds the FMV of the asset, the selling price is equal to the amount of the liability.
      5) When noncash property is distributed, the gain included in TI may be different from the gain that is reported for E&P purposes.
      6) When depreciable property is distributed, the gain reported for TI purposes is calculated using the property's AB after reduction for MACRS depreciation.
         a) The AB used when calculating the E&P gain is reduced for the slower ADS depreciation.
         b) This difference reduces the gain (increases the loss) reported for E&P purposes.
         c) If liabilities exceed basis, FMV is treated as not less than the liabilities assumed by the shareholder.
   c. E&P are reduced by the property's basis in the case of distributed property that is not appreciated property.
   d. Only after determining shareholder tax treatment for the tax year, reduce current E&P by the amounts constituting distributions from the corporation during the year, but not below zero. The amount of the E&P reduction is
      1) Amount of money
      2) Principal amounts of the corporation's own obligations
         a) When a bond is issued with original issue discount (OID), use the issue price
      3) FMV of appreciated property
         a) Less any liability assumed or acquired by the shareholder
      4) AB of other property
         a) Less any liability assumed or acquired by the shareholder
   e. A distribution cannot produce a deficit in (i.e., reduce below zero) current E&P.

f. For corporate distributions from E&P, there are four scenarios:

1) When both current and accumulated E&P (AE&P) are positive, the corporation is required to allocate the current portion of E&P to all of the distributions and then apply AE&P in chronological order.

2) If both are negative E&P, all distributions (to the extent of basis) are a return of basis. Any distributions in excess of basis are treated as capital gains on the stock to the investor.

3) If current E&P are positive and AE&P are negative, the corporation does not net the two. Instead, all distributions to the extent of the current E&P are dividends, and the remainder are returns of basis.

4) If current E&P are negative and AE&P are positive, the corporation prorates negative E&P up to the point of each distribution, nets it with AE&P, and all distributions to the extent of the positive E&P netted amount are considered dividends, with the remainder being returns of basis.

g. For each of the four scenarios above, once E&P are exhausted, the remainder of distributions are returns of basis to the extent of shareholder basis. Once shareholder basis is exhausted, the remainder of distributions are treated as if the underlying stock had been sold, and capital gain treatment is applied.

9. When a corporation has a loss in the current year, the loss is prorated over the year to determine the AE&P at the time of a distribution.

EXAMPLE 15-2 Distributions

A corporation has AE&P of $100,000 at the beginning of the year and a loss for the current year of $80,000. The corporation makes a distribution of $90,000 on April 1. Only $80,000 is considered a dividend because there are only $80,000 of AE&P at the time of the distribution [$100,000 – ($80,000 × 1/4)]. The $80,000 loss is prorated over the year. In addition, AE&P on December 31 is now $(60,000) ($0 basis of current E&P after April distribution – $60,000 April-December negative E&P).

You have completed the outline for this subunit.
Study multiple-choice questions 1 through 8 beginning on page 342.

Form 5452 (Rev. 10-2018) Page 3

Example of a Filled-In Worksheet for Figuring Current Year Earnings and Profits

XYZ Corporation, EIN 00-0000000
123 Main Street
Anycity, Yourstate 20200

Date Incorporated: 1/1/99
Method of Accounting: Accrual

			Retained Earnings Shown in Books		Earnings and Profits Current Year		Accumulated Earnings and Profits Credit Balance	Key
			Debit	Credit	Debit	Credit		
Balance forward 12/31/ 2021				$225,000			$20,900	
Year 2022								
1 Taxable income* from Form 1120, line 28 (or comparable line of other income tax return)				214,700		$214,700		a
2 Federal income taxes per books and tax return			$60,000		$60,000			a
3 Excess of capital losses over capital gains (tax basis)			3,600		3,600			a
4 Depreciation adjustment on earnings and profits (section 312(k))						24,000		
5 Depreciation adjustment on sale of property					4,000			
6 Total itemized expenses from line 5, Schedule M-1			11,050					
a Travel and entertainment		$200			200			a
b Life insurance premium greater than cash surrender value (CSV)		9,500			9,500			a
c Nondeductible interest paid for tax-exempt bonds		850			850			a
d Contributions carryover		500			500			a
e Other (list separately)								
7 Total itemized income from line 7, Schedule M-1				14,500				
a Life insurance proceeds greater than CSV		6,000				6,000		a
b Bad debt recovery (not charged against taxable income)		3,500						b
c Tax-exempt interest on municipal bonds		5,000				5,000		a
d Other (list separately)								
8 Refund of prior year federal income taxes								
9 Reserve for contingencies			10,000					c
10 Additional adjustments:								
11 Totals					78,650	249,700		
Current Year Earnings and Profits						171,050		
Cash Distributions:								
Preferred stock: 3/15/2022, 6/15/2022, 9/15/2022, 12/15/2022		40,000			40,000			a
10,000 Shares at $1.00/Share × 4 quarters = $40,000								
Common stock:								
1. 3/31/2022 - 90,000 Shares at $1.00 = $90,000								
From current year earnings and profits	72.81 %	65,525			65,525			a
From accumulated earnings and profits	23.22 %	20,900					(20,900)	a
Total distribution from earnings and profits	96.03 %	86,425						
From other distribution	3.97 %	3,575						
Total distribution	100 %	90,000						
2. 9/30/2022 - 90,000 Shares at $1.00 = $90,000								
From current year earnings and profits	72.81%	65,525			65,525			a
From other distribution	27.19%	24,475						
Total distribution	100%	90,000						
Total cash distributions			220,000					
Totals			304,650	229,200	171,050	171,050		
Current year change			75,450				(20,900)	
Balance forward 12/31/ 2022				$149,550			$—0—	

Form 5452 (Rev. 10-2018)

Explanation of Key
a - Identical items on the same line.
b - Item offset in 2021. Bad debt reserve method used for book accounting.
c - Item partially offset.
* Taxable income before net operating loss deduction and special deductions.

15.2 SHAREHOLDER TREATMENT OF DISTRIBUTIONS

A distribution to a shareholder is equal to the FMV of the property distributed. This amount must be decreased by any liabilities that are assumed by the shareholder or to which the property is subject.

Dividend

1. The amount of a distribution is first a dividend to the extent of any current earnings and profits (E&P) and then to the extent of any accumulated E&P (AE&P).
   a. When distributions during the year exceed current E&P, pro rata portions of each distribution are deemed to be from current E&P.
      1) If the current E&P balance is positive, the positive balance is computed as of the close of the taxable year, without regard to the amount of E&P at the time of the distribution.
      2) If the current E&P balance is negative, the negative balance is prorated to the date of each distribution made during the year.
   b. Treatment of a distribution is determined by reference to AE&P only after any current E&P have been accounted for.
      1) AE&P constitute the remaining balance of E&P from prior tax years.
      2) A deficit in AE&P never results from a distribution. It results from any aggregate excess of current E&P deficits over unused positive AE&P.
         a) A deficit in AE&P does not offset current E&P.
      3) Current E&P are added to AE&P after determining treatment of distributions.
   c. When distributions exceed both current E&P and AE&P, allocate AE&P to distributions in their chronological order.

Constructive Dividend

   d. Constructive dividends are tangible benefits to shareholders other than declared dividends and are included as income to the shareholder.
      1) The corporate deduction taken for such expenses should be reversed, thereby increasing corporate E&P.
      2) The following are examples:
         a) Excessively high salaries
         b) Forgiveness of shareholder debt
         c) Personal use of corporate equipment
         d) Excessive lease or purchase payment to shareholder
         e) Transfer of property to shareholder for less than FMV
   e. A **below-market loan** is a loan on which no interest is charged or on which interest is charged at a rate below the applicable federal rate. A below-market loan generally is treated as an arm's-length transaction in which the borrower is considered as having received both of the following:
      1) A loan in exchange for a note that requires payment of interest at the applicable federal rate and
      2) An additional payment in an amount equal to the forgone interest.

If the shareholder receives a below-market term loan other than a gift or demand loan, the shareholder is treated as receiving an additional cash payment (as a dividend, etc.) on the date the loan is made. This payment is equal to the loan amount minus the present value, at the applicable federal rate, of all payments due under the loan.

f. A constructive distribution will be treated as a dividend for tax purposes if sufficient E&P are available.

g. If the corporation makes any payment that may be a dividend but is unable to confirm whether such payment is a dividend by the time the Form 1099-DIV must be filed, the entire amount of the payment must be reported as a dividend or as an amount paid with respect to a dividend.

Capital Recovery

2. A shareholder treats the amount of a distribution in excess of dividends as tax-exempt return of capital to the extent of his or her basis in the stock.
   a. Basis in the stock is reduced (but not below zero).
   b. Apportion the distribution among the shares if they have different bases.

EXAMPLE 15-3 **Capital Recovery**

Corporation distributes $90,000 when E&P are $60,000. Shareholder N receives $30,000 of the distribution, of which $20,000 is a dividend (2/3).

	# of Shares	Basis	Dividend	Capital Recovery	Gain
Block 1	1,000	$ 3,000	$10,000	$3,000	$2,000
Block 2	1,000	15,000	10,000	5,000	0

Gain on Sale

3. Any excess of the amount of a distribution over E&P and basis is treated as gain on the sale of the stock (e.g., the $2,000 in Example 15-3).
   a. Character depends on the nature of the stock in the hands of the shareholder as a capital asset or dealer property.
   b. Loss may be recognized only if the stock becomes worthless or is redeemed.

4. The shareholder's basis in property received in a nonliquidating distribution is generally its FMV at the time of the distribution.
   a. Obligations of the distributing corporations have a basis equal to their FMV.
   b. If liabilities assumed or liabilities of property taken are
      1) Less than FMV, then basis in the property is its FMV.
      2) Greater than FMV, then the basis should equal the liability if the distributee shareholder assumes personal liability.

Stop & Review

You have completed the outline for this subunit.

Study multiple-choice questions 9 through 15 beginning on page 345.

15.3 STOCK DISTRIBUTIONS

A corporation recognizes no gain or loss on distribution of its own stock.

1. A proportionate distribution of stock issued by the corporation to the shareholders is generally not gross income to the shareholders.
   a. Generally, a shareholder does not include a distribution of stock or rights to acquire stock in gross income unless it is a
      1) Distribution in lieu of money;
      2) Disproportionate distribution;
      3) Distribution on preferred stock;
      4) Distribution of convertible preferred stock; or
      5) Distribution of common and preferred stock, resulting in receipt of preferred stock by some shareholders and common stock by other shareholders.
   b. A shareholder allocates the aggregate adjusted basis (AB) in the old stock to the old and new stock in proportion to the FMV of the old and new stock.
      1) Basis is apportioned by relative FMV to different classes of stock if applicable.
   c. The holding period of the distributed stock includes that of the old stock.
   d. Earnings and profits (E&P) are not altered for a tax-free stock dividend.

Stock Rights

2. Treat a distribution of stock rights as a distribution of the stock.
   a. Basis is allocated based on the FMV of the rights.
      1) Basis in the stock rights is zero if their aggregate FMV is less than 15% of the FMV of the stock on which they were distributed, unless the shareholder elects to allocate.
   b. Basis in the stock, if the right is exercised, is any basis allocated to the right, plus the exercise price.
   c. The holding period of the stock begins on the exercise date.
   d. No deduction is allowed for basis allocated to stock rights that lapse.
      1) Basis otherwise allocated remains in the underlying stock.

3. **Taxable Stock Distribution**
   a. The amount of a distribution subject to tax is the FMV of distributed stock or stock rights. Distributions of stock are subject to tax when
      1) Any shareholder has an option to choose between a distribution of stock or a distribution of other property.
         a) The amount of the distribution is the greater of
            i) The FMV of stock or
            ii) The cash and FMV of other property.
      2) Some shareholders receive property, and other shareholders receive an increase in their proportionate interests.
         a) Such a distribution of stock is treated as if it were a distribution of property.
      3) Some common shareholders receive common stock, but others receive preferred.
      4) Distribution is on preferred stock.
         a) Limited change in conversion ratios, by itself, does not trigger taxability.
      5) Convertible preferred stock is distributed, and the effect is to change the shareholder's proportionate stock ownership.
      6) Constructive stock distributions change proportionate interests resulting from a transaction, such as a change in conversion ratio or redemption price.
   b. E&P are reduced by the FMV of stock and stock rights distributed.
   c. Basis in the underlying stock does not change. Basis in the new stock or stock rights is their FMV.
   d. The holding period for the new stock begins on the day after the distribution date.
   e. If a distribution of a stock dividend or stock right is taxable when received, the basis is the fair market value on the date of acquisition.
      1) When the dividend is taxable, there is no tacking of the holding period for the underlying stock.
         a) The holding period begins the day following the acquisition date.

Stock Split

4. A stock split is not a distribution.
   a. Basis in the old stock is also "split" and allocated to the new stock.
   b. The holding period of the new stock includes that of the old stock.

You have completed the outline for this subunit.

Study multiple-choice questions 16 through 20 beginning on page 348.

QUESTIONS

15.1 Earnings and Profits

1. The Smart Corporation distributes an office building to Collin, a shareholder of the corporation. The fair market value of the building exceeds its basis to the corporation. Which of the following statements is true with regard to this transaction?

A. Smart realizes but does not recognize gain on this distribution.

B. Smart elects not to report the gain on this distribution.

C. Smart must recognize gain on this distribution.

D. Collin must recognize the losses on this distribution on his return as a shareholder.

Answer (C) is correct.

REQUIRED: The treatment of an office building distributed to a shareholder.

DISCUSSION: If a corporation distributes property other than its own obligations to a shareholder and the property's fair market value exceeds corporation's adjusted basis, the property is treated as sold at the time of distribution. The corporation recognizes gain on the excess of the FMV over the adjusted basis of the property.

Answer (A) is incorrect. The corporation recognizes gain on the excess of the FMV over the adjusted basis of the property. **Answer (B) is incorrect.** There is no election enabling a corporation not to report the gain on the distribution. **Answer (D) is incorrect.** There are no losses for Collin to recognize.

2. Buffalo, Inc., owned and displayed a collection of watercolors in its main office. When the 75% owner retired, he was presented with his choice from the collection. He selected a painting with a fair market value of $250,000. Buffalo's basis in the painting was $150,000. How should the distribution be reported on the return of Buffalo?

A. No reporting required.

B. $150,000 distribution reduces assets on the balance sheet but no effect on tax.

C. $100,000 taxable gain.

D. $250,000 taxable gain.

Answer (C) is correct.

REQUIRED: The treatment of distribution of property subject to appreciation.

DISCUSSION: If a corporation distributes property other than its own obligations to a shareholder and the property's FMV exceeds the corporation's adjusted basis, the property is treated as sold at the time of distribution. The corporation recognizes gain on the excess of the FMV over the adjusted basis of the property.

FMV of property distributed	$250,000
Less: Adjusted basis	(150,000)
Gain recognized under Sec. 311(b)	$100,000

Answer (A) is incorrect. A gain is recognized on the distribution of appreciated property. **Answer (B) is incorrect.** The corporation recognizes a taxable gain on the excess of the FMV over the adjusted basis of the property. **Answer (D) is incorrect.** The gain is limited to the FMV of the property less its adjusted basis.

3. Yappa Corporation distributed depreciable personal property having a fair market value of $9,500 to its shareholders. The property had an adjusted basis of $2,000 to the corporation. Yappa had correctly deducted $7,000 in depreciation on the property. What is the amount of Yappa's ordinary income due to this distribution?

A. $9,500

B. $7,500

C. $7,000

D. $0

Answer (C) is correct.

REQUIRED: The corporation's ordinary income upon the distribution of depreciable property.

DISCUSSION: Section 311(b) requires that gain on the distribution of appreciated property be recognized as if the property had been sold. Therefore, Yappa will recognize $7,500 ($9,500 fair market value – $2,000 basis) of total gain. Of this gain, $7,000 will be ordinary income as a result of Sec. 1245 depreciation recapture.

Answer (A) is incorrect. Ordinary income is limited to the depreciation actually taken. **Answer (B) is incorrect.** Ordinary income is limited to the depreciation actually taken. **Answer (D) is incorrect.** Section 1245 recaptures depreciation taken as ordinary income.

4. Heritage Corporation distributed an antique automobile to Rene, its sole shareholder. On the date of distribution, the automobile had a fair market value of $30,000 and an adjusted basis to Heritage of $22,000. What is the amount of Heritage Corporation's recognized gain on the distribution?

A. $30,000

B. $12,000

C. $8,000

D. $0

Answer (C) is correct.

REQUIRED: The corporation's recognized gain on the distribution of property.

DISCUSSION: If a corporation distributes property other than its own obligations to a shareholder and the property's FMV exceeds the corporation's adjusted basis, the property is treated as sold at the time of distribution. The corporation recognizes gain on the excess of the FMV over the adjusted basis of the property.

FMV of property distributed	$30,000
Less: Adjusted basis	(22,000)
Gain recognized under Sec. 311(b)	$ 8,000

Answer (A) is incorrect. The gain is limited to the FMV of the property less its adjusted basis. **Answer (B) is incorrect.** The gain is limited to the FMV of the property less its adjusted basis. **Answer (D) is incorrect.** A gain is recognized on the distribution of appreciated property.

5. Which of the following statements regarding corporate distributions is false?

A. Under no circumstances may a distribution, whether in cash or property, generate a deficit in E&P.

B. Under no circumstances may a distribution, whether in cash or property, add to a deficit in E&P.

C. In a corporate distribution, the E&P account is reduced by the amount of money distributed.

D. In a corporate distribution, the E&P account is reduced by the lesser of the FMV or the adjusted basis of the property distributed.

Answer (D) is correct.

REQUIRED: The false statement regarding distributions.

DISCUSSION: If a corporation distributes property other than its own obligations to a shareholder and the property's FMV exceeds the corporation's adjusted basis, the property is treated as sold at the time of distribution. The corporation recognizes gain on the excess of the FMV over the adjusted basis of the property. A distribution cannot produce a deficit in (i.e., reduce below zero) E&P. If current E&P are exhausted, the balance reduces prior-year E&P. The reductions do not produce or increase a deficit accumulated E&P. Any distributions in excess of E&P reduce paid-in capital.

Answer (A) is incorrect. If current E&P are exhausted, the balance reduces prior-year E&P. Any distributions in excess of accumulated E&P reduce paid-in capital. **Answer (B) is incorrect.** If current E&P are exhausted, the balance reduces prior-year E&P. Any distributions in excess of accumulated E&P reduce paid-in capital. **Answer (C) is incorrect.** E&P may also be reduced by the following distributions: principal amounts of the corporation's own obligations, FMV of appreciated property (less any liability assumed by the shareholder), or the adjusted basis of other property (less any liability assumed by the shareholder).

6. Foghorn Corporation, an accrual-method taxpayer, had accumulated earnings and profits of $75,000 as of December 31, Year 1. For the Year 2 tax year, Foghorn's books and records reflect the following:

Taxable income per return	$175,000
Tax-exempt interest received	2,000
Federal income taxes	60,000
Business meals in excess of 50% limitation	4,000
Contributions in excess of limitation	1,000

Based on the above, what is the amount of Foghorn Corporation's accumulated earnings and profits as of December 31, Year 2?

A. $112,000

B. $187,000

C. $250,000

D. $313,000

Answer (B) is correct.

REQUIRED: The earnings and profits (E&P) balance as of December 31, Year 2.

DISCUSSION: Calculation of E&P begins with taxable income according to the tax return. Tax-exempt income is added to the taxable income, and nondeductible expenditures are subtracted, e.g., federal income taxes, charitable contributions in excess of the 10% limitation, and excess business meals.

Acc. E&P at December 31, Year 1	$ 75,000
Taxable income for Year 2	175,000
Add: Tax-exempt interest	2,000
Deduct: Excess contributions	(1,000)
Excess business meals	(4,000)
Federal income taxes	(60,000)
Acc. E&P at December 31, Year 2	$187,000

Answer (A) is incorrect. The previous accumulated E&P are added to current-year E&P. **Answer (C) is incorrect.** E&P are adjusted by tax-exempt income and nondeductible expenditures. **Answer (D) is incorrect.** E&P are reduced by nondeductible expenses and increased by tax-exempt interest.

7. The following information is available from the records of Emute, Inc. Compute current-year earnings and profits.

Taxable income, Form 1120	$50,000
Federal income taxes paid	7,500
Nondeductible portion of meals	500
Excess of capital losses over capital gains	1,000

A. $41,500

B. $48,500

C. $41,000

D. $42,000

Answer (C) is correct.

REQUIRED: The computation of the current year's E&P.

DISCUSSION: Earnings and profits (E&P) are designed to measure a corporation's true ability to pay a dividend to its shareholders. In computing E&P, certain adjustments are made to taxable income (TI). One such adjustment is subtracting from TI expenses and losses that are nondeductible. Accordingly, current E&P are calculated as follows:

Taxable income	$50,000
Less:	
Federal income taxes paid	(7,500)
Nondeductible meals	(500)
Excess capital losses	(1,000)
Current E&P	$41,000

Answer (A) is incorrect. The nondeductible portion of meal expenses is subtracted to arrive at E&P. **Answer (B) is incorrect.** The federal income taxes paid are subtracted from taxable income. **Answer (D) is incorrect.** The excess capital losses are subtracted from taxable income to arrive at current E&P.

8. On July 1, Year 1, VAL, a calendar-year C corporation, distributed an auto used 100% in its business to its sole shareholder. At the time of the distribution, the auto, which originally cost $18,000, had an adjusted basis of $6,000 and a fair market value of $5,000. No liabilities were attached to the auto. No other distributions were made during Year 1. As of January 1, Year 1, VAL's accumulated earnings and profits were $(5,000). For Year 1, VAL's earnings and profits were $8,000. By what amount will VAL reduce its earnings and profits as a result of the distribution of the auto?

A. $3,000

B. $4,000

C. $5,000

D. $6,000

Answer (D) is correct.

REQUIRED: The reduction of E&P resulting from a distribution of unappreciated property.

DISCUSSION: In the case of distributed property that is not appreciated property, E&P are reduced by the property's basis. However, the distribution cannot create negative E&P. In determining whether negative E&P are created, first look to current year's E&P. Since the distributed property's basis ($6,000) is less than current year's E&P ($8,000), no deficit in E&P is created. Thus, E&P are reduced by the full $6,000.

15.2 Shareholder Treatment of Distributions

9. Rose Corporation, a calendar-year corporation, had accumulated earnings and profits of $40,000 as of January 1, Year 1. However, for the first 6 months of Year 1, Rose had an operating loss of $36,000 and finished the year with a total net operating loss for Year 1 tax year of $55,000. Rose distributed $15,000 to its shareholders on July 1, Year 1. Which of the following is true?

A. The entire distribution of $15,000 is taxable.

B. The entire distribution is not taxable.

C. The part of the distribution that is taxable is $12,500.

D. The part of the distribution that is taxable is $14,000.

Answer (C) is correct.

REQUIRED: The amount of a distribution taxable when it exceeds current and accumulated E&P.

DISCUSSION: When a distribution is made during the course of the year, and the current E&P balance is negative, the E&P must be prorated to reflect the accumulated E&P balance on the date of the distribution. Because the distribution occurred on July 1, the accumulated E&P were $12,500 {$40,000 – [$55,000 × (6 months ÷ 12 months)]}. A corporate distribution is a dividend that must be included in the recipient's gross income under Sec. 301(c)(1) to the extent it comes from current or accumulated E&P of a corporation. To the extent the distribution exceeds current and accumulated E&P, it is treated as a return of capital to the shareholder. Once the basis of the stock has been reduced to zero, any distributions received are treated as a gain from the sale of the stock. Therefore, each shareholder will recognize $12,500 of ordinary income.

10. During the current calendar year, the Lance Corporation made a $40,000 cash distribution to its sole shareholder. Lance's current-year earnings and profits (as of the close of the year and without reduction for distributions during the year) is $25,000. Accumulated earnings and profits is $10,000. What amount of dividend should be reported on Form 1099-DIV issued to the shareholder for the current year?

A. $40,000

B. $5,000

C. $0

D. $35,000

Answer (D) is correct.

REQUIRED: The dividend amount reported for the current year.

DISCUSSION: The amount of a distribution is a dividend to the extent, first, of any current E&P, and then, of any accumulated E&P. The first $25,000 of the distribution comes from current E&P, and the next $10,000 of the distribution comes from accumulated E&P; therefore, Lance Corporation must report $35,000 of dividend on its Form 1099-DIV.

Answer (A) is incorrect. Only dividends to the extent of current and accumulated E&P are reported. **Answer (B) is incorrect.** The amount of $5,000 represents the capital gain to be reported by the shareholder. **Answer (C) is incorrect.** There is dividend income to be reported.

11. Olympic Corporation distributed real estate with a FMV of $500,000 to its sole shareholder, Joshua. Olympic's basis in the real estate is $400,000. What is the tax effect of the distribution to Olympic and what is Joshua's basis in the real estate?

A. $0 gain (loss) to Olympic; $400,000 basis to Joshua.

B. $100,000 gain to Olympic; $400,000 basis to Joshua.

C. $0 gain (loss) to Olympic; $500,000 basis to Joshua.

D. $100,000 gain to Olympic; $500,000 basis to Joshua.

Answer (D) is correct.

REQUIRED: The tax effect of a corporation's distribution of appreciated property to its sole shareholder.

DISCUSSION: Section 301(b) provides that the amount distributed to a shareholder (corporate or noncorporate) is equal to the amount of money received, plus the fair market value of other property received. Additionally, Sec. 311(b) provides that if a corporation distributes property to a shareholder and the FMV is greater than the adjusted basis, the gain shall be recognized by the distributee corporation.

Answer (A) is incorrect. The corporation must recognize the gain on the appreciation and the basis to the shareholder is the property's FMV. **Answer (B) is incorrect.** The basis to Joshua is the FMV, not the corporation's basis. **Answer (C) is incorrect.** The $100,000 gain must be recognized on the appreciated property to the corporation.

12. For 10 years, Ben has owned all 100 outstanding shares of N and M Corporation's stock. Ben's basis for the stock is $50,000. In the current year, N and M has earnings and profits of $100,000. The corporation redeemed 25 shares of Ben's stock for $75,000 in the current year. How will Ben report this?

A. $75,000 gain.

B. $75,000 dividend.

C. $50,000 gain.

D. None of the answers are correct.

Answer (B) is correct.

REQUIRED: The treatment of a distribution to a shareholder owning 100% of the corporation when the distribution is less than E&P.

DISCUSSION: Because Ben owns 100% of the stock before and after the redemption, the transaction is a dividend to the extent that N and M Corporation has earnings and profits. Because the distribution ($75,000) is less than earnings and profits ($100,000), the entire amount is taxable as a dividend.

Answer (A) is incorrect. Ben owns 100% of the stock before and after the redemption, and the transaction is a dividend to the extent that N and M has earnings and profits. **Answer (C) is incorrect.** The distribution is less than earnings and profits; the entire amount is taxable as a dividend. **Answer (D) is incorrect.** Ben owns 100% of the stock before and after the redemption, and the transaction is a dividend to the extent that N and M has earnings and profits.

13. Walnut, Inc., is a C corporation that was started 10 years ago. At the beginning of the current year, Walnut has accumulated earnings and profits of $100,000. During the current year, Walnut makes a $5,000 distribution to its 100% shareholder in the first month of each quarter. At the end of the current year, Walnut had $150,000 in gross income and $140,000 in allowable expenses from ordinary business operations. Walnut also received $5,000 in fully tax-exempt interest from state bonds. What part of the second quarter distribution is treated as a distribution of accumulated earnings and profits?

A. $1,250

B. $2,500

C. $3,750

D. $5,000

Answer (A) is correct.

REQUIRED: The amount of the distribution from accumulated earnings and profits.

DISCUSSION: Distributions are deemed to come from current E&P and then from accumulated E&P if the current E&P are insufficient. The amount of the distribution from accumulated earnings and profits is calculated as follows:

Gross income	$150,000
Add: Tax-exempt income	5,000
Total income	$155,000
Less: Annual expenses	(140,000)
Total annual current E&P	$ 15,000

Current earnings and profits ÷ 4 quarters
= $3,750 current E&P/quarter

Amount of distributions per quarter	$ 5,000
Less: Amount of distribution from current E&P	(3,750)
Amount of distribution from accumulated E&P	$ 1,250

Answer (B) is incorrect. The amount of $2,500 does not include the tax-exempt interest in current E&P. **Answer (C) is incorrect.** The amount deemed from current E&P is $3,750. **Answer (D) is incorrect.** The total distribution for the quarter is $5,000. Only the excess distribution over current E&P is from accumulated E&P.

14. Heron, Inc., made a distribution of real estate with a FMV of $100,000 to its only shareholder, Jennifer, on December 31, Year 1. Heron's basis in the property was $60,000. Current year earnings and profits of Heron (before the distribution) is $10,000, and it has accumulated $20,000 earnings and profits from prior years. Jennifer's basis in her Heron stock is $5,000. What will be the tax effect to Jennifer?

A. $30,000 dividend and $25,000 capital gain.

B. $30,000 dividend and $65,000 capital gain.

C. $100,000 dividend.

D. $70,000 dividend and $25,000 capital gain.

Answer (D) is correct.

REQUIRED: The tax effect of a property distribution.

DISCUSSION: The $100,000 distribution of an asset with a $60,000 basis will create a $40,000 gain. The $40,000 gain will be added to current earnings and profits. Thus, dividend income would be $70,000 because of the earnings and profits ($10,000 + $40,000 + $20,000). A corporate distribution is a dividend that must be included in the recipient's gross income under Sec. 301(c)(1) to the extent it comes from current or accumulated E&P of a corporation. To the extent the distribution exceeds current and accumulated E&P, it is treated as a return of capital to the shareholder. Once the basis of the stock has been reduced to zero, any distributions received are treated as a gain from the sale of the stock. Therefore, Jennifer will treat $5,000 of the $30,000 excess ($100,000 property distribution – $70,000 current and accumulated E&P) as return of capital and $25,000 of the excess as a capital gain.

Answer (A) is incorrect. The $40,000 gain will increase current earnings and profits. **Answer (B) is incorrect.** The $40,000 gain will increase current earnings and profits. **Answer (C) is incorrect.** Dividend income is limited to earnings and profits.

15. Corporation A, a calendar-year C corporation that began conducting business 18 years ago, had accumulated earnings and profits of $26,000 as of January 1 of the current year. On April 1, A distributed $40,000 in cash to Ms. X, Corporation A's sole shareholder. Corporation A had earnings and profits of $4,000 for the current year. Ms. X had an adjusted basis of $18,000 in her stock before the distribution. What are Ms. X's ordinary dividend income and the return of capital due to this distribution?

	Dividend Income	Return of Capital
A.	$40,000	$0
B.	$22,000	$18,000
C.	$30,000	$10,000
D.	$10,000	$30,000

Answer (C) is correct.

REQUIRED: The dividend income and return of capital resulting from a distribution.

DISCUSSION: A corporate distribution is a dividend that must be included in the recipient's gross income under Sec. 301(c)(1) to the extent it comes from accumulated or current E&P of a corporation. To the extent the distribution exceeds current and accumulated E&P, it is treated as a return of capital to the shareholder. Once the basis of the stock has been reduced to zero, any distributions received are treated as a gain from the sale of the stock. The distribution of $40,000 exceeds the corporation's total E&P balance of $30,000 ($26,000 accumulated + $4,000 current). Therefore, $30,000 of the distribution will be dividend income, and the remaining $10,000 will be a return of capital and will reduce the shareholder's basis.

Answer (A) is incorrect. The distribution exceeds E&P. **Answer (B) is incorrect.** A distribution depletes E&P before it is considered a return of capital. **Answer (D) is incorrect.** The distribution is dividend income to the extent that an E&P balance exists.

15.3 Stock Distributions

16. Which one of the following statements is false with regard to property distributions?

A. All stock distributions are treated as property distributions.

B. Property distributions to shareholders are measured by their FMV on the distribution date adjusted for liabilities.

C. The distributing corporation treats the property distributed as though sold to the shareholder at FMV or the amount of liabilities the shareholder assumes, whichever is greater.

D. The shareholder's basis in the property distributed is usually the FMV on the date of distribution.

Answer (A) is correct.

REQUIRED: The false statement with regard to property distributions.

DISCUSSION: According to Publication 542, in order for a stock distribution to be treated as a property distribution, one of the following five conditions must be met:

1. The shareholder has a choice to receive cash or other property instead;
2. The distribution gives cash or other property to some and an increase in percentage interests to others;
3. The distribution is comprised of convertible preferred stock and results like 2. above;
4. Some common shareholders get preferred stock, while others get common shares; or
5. The distribution is preferred stock.

Answer (B) is incorrect. The property distributions are measured by their FMV on the distribution date adjusted for liabilities. **Answer (C) is incorrect.** The distributed property is treated as though it was sold to the shareholder at its FMV or the amount of liabilities assumed, whichever greater, by the distributing corporation. **Answer (D) is incorrect.** The basis to the shareholder normally is the FMV on the date of the distribution.

17. Corporation H, a calendar-year, accrual-basis taxpayer, distributed shares of Corporation B stock to H's employees in lieu of salaries. The salary expense would have been deductible as compensation if paid in cash. On the date of the payment, H's adjusted basis in Corporation B stock was $15,000 and the stock's fair market value was $85,000. What is the tax effect to Corporation H?

A. $85,000 deduction.

B. $15,000 deduction.

C. $85,000 deduction and $70,000 recognized gain.

D. $15,000 deduction and $70,000 recognized gain.

Answer (C) is correct.

REQUIRED: The tax effect to Corporation H of satisfying a salary liability with appreciated property.

DISCUSSION: Under Sec. 83(a), the employee includes in income the fair value of property received for services. Under Sec. 83(h), the employer is allowed a deduction for the amount the employee must include in income when the employee includes it in income. However, when property other than cash is distributed in exchange for services, the employer must recognize a gain on the deemed sale. Since the employees will include the $85,000 FMV of shares in income, Corporation H may deduct the $85,000. However, H must also recognize a $70,000 gain ($85,000 FMV – $15,000 adjusted basis) on the deemed sale.

Answer (A) is incorrect. A $70,000 gain is recognized as if the shares were sold to a third party. **Answer (B) is incorrect.** The employer may deduct the FMV of property relinquished and must recognize a gain. **Answer (D) is incorrect.** H's adjusted basis in the stock is $15,000, not the FMV of the property given up.

18. A distribution of stock or rights to acquire stock in the distributing corporation is not included in the recipient's gross income unless

A. It is a disproportionate distribution.

B. It is a distribution instead of money or other property.

C. The distribution of stock or rights is greater than 15% of the value of the stock or rights with respect to which the rights were distributed.

D. It is either a disproportionate distribution, or a distribution instead of money or other property.

Answer (D) is correct.

REQUIRED: The situation in which a distribution of stock, or rights to acquire stock in the distributing corporation, is included in the recipient's gross income.

DISCUSSION: Usually, a shareholder does not include a distribution of stock or rights to acquire stock in gross income unless it is (1) a distribution in lieu of money, (2) a disproportionate distribution, (3) a distribution on preferred stock, (4) a distribution of convertible preferred stock, or (5) a distribution of common and preferred stock, resulting in receipt of preferred stock by some shareholders and common stock by other shareholders.

Answer (A) is incorrect. A distribution of stock or rights to acquire stock in the distributing corporation is also included in the recipient's income if it is a distribution instead of money or other property. **Answer (B) is incorrect.** A distribution of stock or rights to acquire stock in the distributing corporation is also included in the recipient's income if it is a disproportionate distribution. **Answer (C) is incorrect.** It is not a requirement for inclusion in the recipient's gross income.

19. A distribution of taxable stock rights or dividends generally is treated the same as

A. Any other property distribution, and the holding period begins on the day after the distribution date.

B. The distribution of an obligation of the distributing corporation.

C. A cash distribution.

D. Any other property distribution, but the holding period begins on the day of the issue of the underlying stock.

Answer (A) is correct.

REQUIRED: The proper treatment of a distribution of taxable stock rights or dividends.

DISCUSSION: If a distribution of a stock dividend or stock right is taxable when received, the basis is the fair market value on the date of distribution. When the dividend is taxable, there is no tacking of the holding period for the underlying stock. The holding period begins the day following the acquisition date.

Answer (B) is incorrect. A distribution of taxable stock rights or dividends is not treated the same as the distribution of an obligation of the distributing corporation. **Answer (C) is incorrect.** A distribution of taxable rights or dividends is not treated the same as a cash distribution. **Answer (D) is incorrect.** The holding period of the stock begins on the day following the acquisition date.

20. A distribution of stock or stock rights is generally considered a dividend unless it is which of the following?

A. Distribution of convertible preferred stock.

B. Distribution in lieu of money.

C. Distribution with respect to preferred stock.

D. Proportionate distribution.

Answer (D) is correct.

REQUIRED: The distribution of stock or stock rights that would not be considered a dividend.

DISCUSSION: A proportionate distribution of stock or stock rights would not be considered a dividend under Sec. 305(a) and would not be included in the gross income of the distributee.

Answer (A) is incorrect. A distribution of convertible preferred stock is an exception under Sec. 305(b) to the general rule, and such a distribution would receive dividend treatment. **Answer (B) is incorrect.** A distribution in lieu of money is an exception under Sec. 305(b) to the general rule, and such a distribution would receive dividend treatment. **Answer (C) is incorrect.** A distribution with respect to preferred stock is an exception under Sec. 305(b) to the general rule, and such a distribution would receive dividend treatment.

Go to Online Course

Access the **Gleim EA Premium Review System** featuring our SmartAdapt technology from your Gleim Personal Classroom to continue your studies.

You will experience a personalized study environment with exam-emulating multiple-choice questions.

STUDY UNIT SIXTEEN

CORPORATE REDEMPTIONS AND LIQUIDATIONS

(8 pages of outline)

A stock redemption occurs when a corporation acquires its stock from its shareholders in return for cash or property. Whether the redemption is treated as a sale, an exchange, or a dividend depends on numerous factors.

1) For instance, if the distribution is considered a partial liquidation under Sec. 302, noncorporate shareholders will receive sale or exchange treatment.
2) In contrast, at some point in the life of a corporation, it may be determined that the corporation should be liquidated. If so, the corporation's shareholders will surrender all of their stock in the corporation and receive their pro rata shares of any remaining assets after all creditors are paid.

16.1 REDEMPTIONS

Stock is redeemed when a corporation acquires its own stock from a shareholder in exchange for property. The stock may be canceled, retired, or held as treasury stock. A shareholder is required to treat the amount realized on redemption (not in liquidation) as either a distribution (a corporate dividend) or a sale of the stock redeemed.

1. Redemptions of stock by a corporation are treated as dividends unless certain conditions are met. If any of the following conditions are met, the exchange is treated as a sale, and the gains or losses are capital gains and losses.
    a. The redemption is not essentially equivalent to a dividend.
    b. The redemption is substantially disproportionate.
    c. The distribution is in complete redemption of all of a shareholder's stock in the corporation.
    d. The distribution is to a noncorporate shareholder in partial liquidation.
    e. The distribution is received by an estate.

<u>Corporation</u>

2. A corporation recognizes gain realized on a distribution
    a. As if the property distributed were sold at FMV to the distributee immediately prior to the distribution
    b. Even if stock is redeemed by the distribution
3. A corporation recognizes ordinary income on the distribution of depreciated property to the extent of depreciation or amount realized, whichever is less.
4. No recognition of loss realized is allowed the corporation, unless the redemption is
    a. In complete liquidation of the corporation or
    b. Of stock held by an estate (to pay death taxes).

Shareholder

5. A shareholder treats a nonqualifying redemption in the same manner as a regular distribution. The amount is a dividend to the extent of earnings and profits (E&P).
   a. Any unrecovered basis in the redeemed stock is added to the shareholder's basis in stock retained.
   b. A distribution that redeems all of a shareholder's shares is treated as a sale irrespective of earnings and profits.

EXAMPLE 16-1 Shareholder Treatment -- Nonqualifying Redemption of Stock

Since 2016, Paige has owned all 1,010 outstanding shares of E and E Corporation's stock. Paige's basis for the stock is $10,100. In 2022, E and E has earnings and profits of $110,000. The corporation redeemed 450 shares of Paige's stock for $98,000 in 2022. Because Paige owns 100% of the stock before and after the redemption, the transaction is a dividend to the extent that E and E has earnings and profits. Because the distribution ($98,000) is less than earnings and profits ($110,000), the entire amount is taxable as a dividend.

NOTE: Do not confuse this with noncorporate shareholder treatment of a partial liquidation. (Details of partial liquidation requirements are covered in Subunit 16.3.)

6. The expenses incurred in connection with any reacquisition by a corporation of its own stock or the stock of a related person (50% relationship test) are not deductible.
   a. An exception exists for any cost allocable to an indebtedness and amortized over the life of the indebtedness (e.g., financial advisory costs).

Sale Treatment

7. The shareholder treats qualifying redemptions as if the shares redeemed were sold to a third party.
   a. Gain or loss recognized is any difference between the adjusted basis (AB) of the shares and the fair market value (FMV) of property received.
   b. Character of gain or loss depends on the nature of the stock in the shareholder's hands.
   c. Basis in distributed property is its FMV.
   d. Holding period for the property starts the day after the redemption exchange.
   e. This treatment applies only to redemptions that
      1) Terminate a shareholder's interest
      2) Are substantially disproportionate between shareholders
      3) Are not essentially equivalent to a dividend
      4) Are received by an estate
      5) Are from a shareholder, other than a corporation, in partial liquidation
   f. Treatment of a redemption as a sale is determined separately for each shareholder.

Not Essentially Equivalent

8. Not essentially equivalent to a dividend means that there is a meaningful reduction in the shareholder's proportionate interest in the corporation.
   a. Reduction in voting power is generally required for a redemption.
      1) Shareholders in control of a corporation must generally lose control to qualify as not essentially equivalent to a dividend.
      2) Majority control (over 50%) reduction to deadlock (50%) has been determined sufficient.
      3) Minimal reduction by a minority shareholder may be meaningful.
   b. Attribution can be used to determine essential equivalence.

Substantially Disproportionate

9. Substantially disproportionate means that the amount received by shareholders is not in the same proportion as their stock holdings.
   a. It is tested by determining the shareholders' applicable ownership percentages (including constructive ownerships) both before and after the redemption.
   b. A redemption is substantially disproportionate with respect to a shareholder if, immediately after the redemption, the shareholder owns
      1) Less than 50% of the voting power of outstanding voting stock and
      2) Less than 80% each of interest in
         a) The voting stock owned before the redemption and
         b) The common stock owned before the redemption.

EXAMPLE 16-2 Substantially Disproportionate Redemption

Carol, an individual shareholder, owns 275 shares of Allegiance Corporation. Allegiance has 1,000 shares of common stock outstanding and redeems 200 shares of common stock from its shareholders. The least number of Carol's shares that will need to be redeemed in order for the redemption to be substantially disproportionate to Carol is determined as follows:

Carol owned 27.5% of Allegiance Corporation before the redemption (275 shares ÷ 1,000 shares). Carol must reduce her interest to below 22% for the redemption to be substantially disproportionate (80% × 27.5%). Carol needs to own less than 176 shares after the redemption [22% × (1,000 shares – 200 shares)]. Thus, more than 99 shares (275 shares – 176 shares) need to be redeemed to reduce Carol's interest below 22%. Accordingly, Carol needs to have a minimum of 100 shares redeemed for the redemption to be substantially disproportionate.

Termination

10. Termination of a shareholder's interest must be complete to qualify.
   a. All the stock owned by the shareholder in the corporation, actually and through family attribution, must be redeemed in the exchange for the property.
   b. The family attribution rules may be waived if the following three requirements are met:
      1) The shareholder may not retain any interest (e.g., an employee, officer, director, or shareholder), except as a creditor, in the corporation.
      2) The shareholder may not acquire an interest, except by bequest or inheritance, for 10 years.
      3) A written agreement must be filed with the IRS stating that the IRS will be notified if a prohibited interest is acquired.

Estate

11. An estate may treat a qualifying redemption (to pay death taxes) as a sale.
    a. Redeemed stock must be valued at more than 35% of the gross estate net of deductions allowed.
        1) Deductions allowed are administration expenses, funeral expenses, claims against the estate (including death taxes), and unpaid mortgages.

Constructive Ownership

12. The (redeemed) shareholder is treated as owning shares owned by certain related parties. The following ownership is considered to be constructively owned by the shareholder through related parties:
    a. Stock owned directly or indirectly by or for the shareholder's spouse, children, grandchildren, or parents (excludes siblings and grandparents)

EXAMPLE 16-3 Constructive Ownership

A corporation has 100 shares outstanding. A husband, wife, child, and grandchild (the child's child) each own 25 shares. The husband, wife, and child are each considered as owning 100 shares. The grandchild is considered as owning only 50 shares (25 shares of the grandchild + 25 shares of the child).

    b. Stock owned directly or indirectly by or for a partnership (or S corporation) in which the shareholder is a partner
        1) The reverse also applies (i.e., partnership owns stock owned by a partner).
    c. Stock owned directly or indirectly by an estate or trust in which the shareholder is treated as a beneficiary or an owner
    d. Stock owned directly or indirectly by or for a corporation (other than an S corporation) in which the shareholder owns directly or indirectly at least 50% of the value of the stock
    e. Stock on which the shareholder holds an option to buy

You have completed the outline for this subunit.

Study multiple-choice questions 1 through 8 beginning on page 359.

16.2 COMPLETE LIQUIDATION

Under a plan of complete liquidation, a corporation redeems all of its stock in a series of distributions. The distributions of assets to the shareholders are made from the remaining assets after all creditors have been paid first.

Corporate Liquidation

Figure 16-1

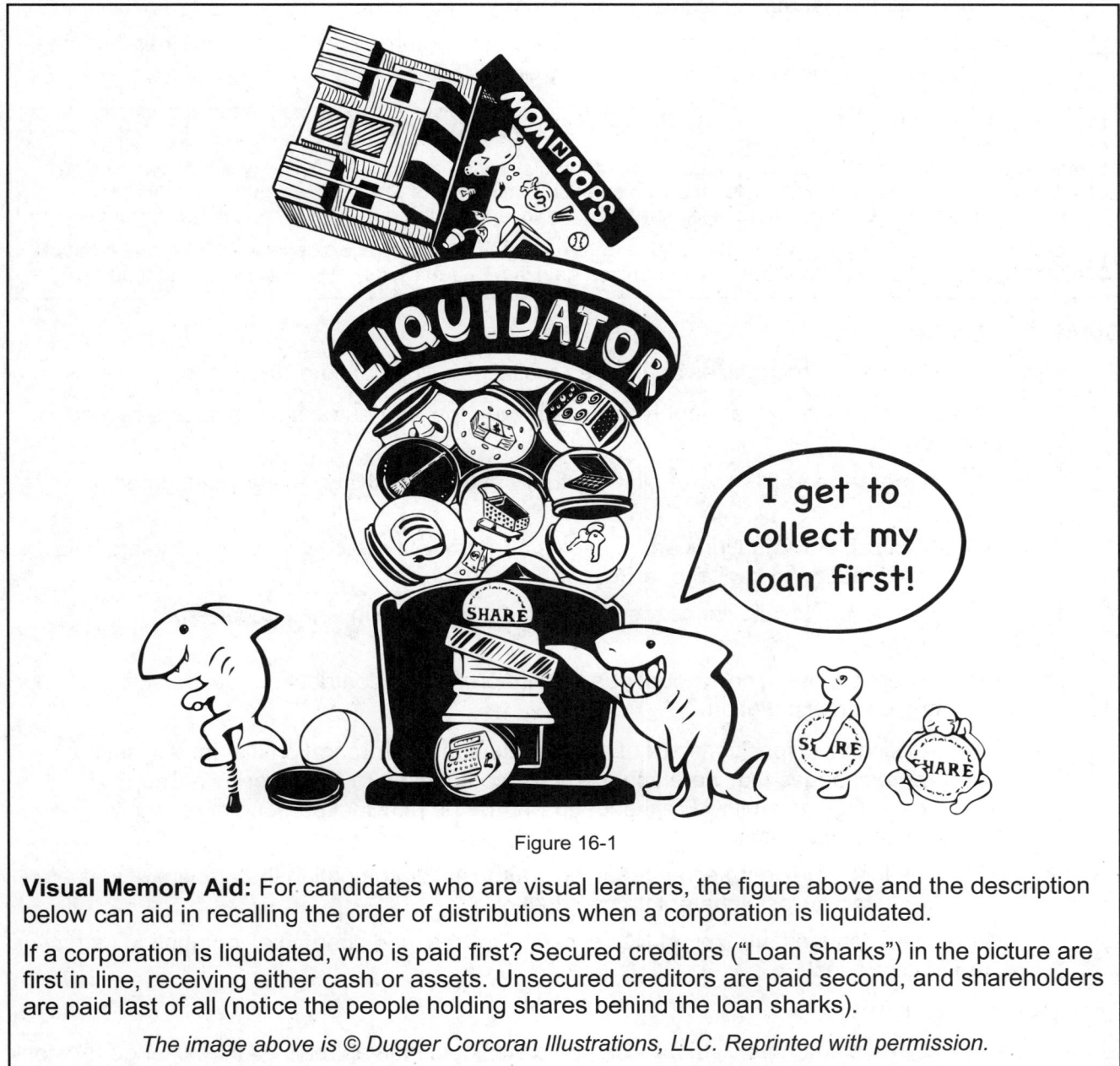

Visual Memory Aid: For candidates who are visual learners, the figure above and the description below can aid in recalling the order of distributions when a corporation is liquidated.

If a corporation is liquidated, who is paid first? Secured creditors ("Loan Sharks") in the picture are first in line, receiving either cash or assets. Unsecured creditors are paid second, and shareholders are paid last of all (notice the people holding shares behind the loan sharks).

Corporate Gains

1. A corporation recognizes any gain or loss realized on distributions in complete liquidation as if the property were sold at its FMV to the shareholder immediately before its distribution.
   a. Gain or loss is computed on an asset-by-asset basis.
   b. FMV of distributed property is treated as not less than related liabilities that the shareholder assumes or to which the property is subject.
   c. Character of amounts recognized depends on the nature of the asset in the hands of the distributing corporation, e.g., Secs. 1245 and 1250.

EXAMPLE 16-4 Complete Liquidation -- Corporate Gains

Under a plan of complete liquidation, Zaige Corporation distributed land having an adjusted basis to Zaige of $19,000 to its sole shareholder. The land was subject to a liability of $98,000, which the shareholder assumed for legitimate business purposes. The FMV of the land on the date of distribution was $71,000.

Generally, the FMV of $71,000 would be used to determine any gain; however, because the liability relief of $98,000 is greater than the FMV, Zaige's recognized gain is $79,000 ($98,000 liability relief – $19,000 AB).

Corporate Losses

2. A corporation generally recognizes any losses realized on liquidating distributions.
   a. Certain realized losses are not recognized when the distributee shareholder is related to the corporation.
      1) A more-than-50% shareholder, actually or constructively, is a typical related distributee.
      2) Applicable distributions are of assets non-pro rata or acquired within 5 years by a contribution to capital or a Sec. 351 exchange.
      3) Permanent disallowance results, even if the decline in value occurred postcontribution.
   b. Precontribution loss. The amount of a loss inherent on a contribution reduces loss recognized on distribution.
      1) Applicable dispositions are of assets a liquidating corporation distributes, sells, or exchanges that were acquired by a contribution to capital or by a Sec. 351 exchange when its AB exceeded FMV for the principal purpose of recognizing the loss on liquidation.
      2) The loss limit operates by requiring that basis for computing the amount of loss be reduced by loss inherent on contribution.
   c. Carryovers. Unused, unexpired NOLs; capital losses; and charitable contribution carryover amounts are lost.

Shareholder Treatment

3. A shareholder treats amounts distributed in complete liquidation as realized in exchange for stock.
   a. Capital recovery to the extent of basis is permitted before recognizing gain or loss.
   b. Holding period will not include that of the liquidated corporation.
   c. Amounts realized include money and the FMV of other distributed property received.
      1) Liabilities assumed or to which property is subject reduce the amount realized.
      2) Allocation of amounts realized to each block of stock is required.

EXAMPLE 16-5 Liquidating Distribution to Shareholder

Consider a single liquidating distribution to Shareholder R on February 1, 2022, of $70 cash and a car (FMV = $25) subject to a liability of $15. R's amount realized is $80 [$70 + ($25 – $15)].

Block	Shares	Acquired	Basis	Amount Realized	Gain (Loss) Realized
A	1	5/10	$10	$20	$10
B	3	10/16	$90	$60	$(30)

d. When a series of liquidating distributions is made, the shareholder must use the cost recovery method for recognition of gain or loss.

1) Each payment received is first applied against the basis of the stock.
2) When basis is exceeded, a gain must be recognized.

e. Character of recognized gain or loss depends on the nature of each block of the stock in the hands of the shareholder.

EXAMPLE 16-6 Character of Recognized Gain or Loss

If R, in Example 16-5, held the stock for investment, R would recognize LTCG on Block A and STCL on Block B.

f. Basis in distributed property is its FMV but only after gain or loss on its receipt has been recognized.

Reporting

4. A corporation must file an information return (Form 966, *Corporate Dissolution or Liquidation*) reporting adoption of a plan or resolution for its dissolution, or partial or complete liquidation, within 30 days of adoption.

a. The IRS requires a corporation to file Form 1099-DIV for each calendar year it makes partial distribution(s) of $600 or more under a plan of complete liquidation.

b. Expenses incurred in connection with the liquidation are deductible by the dissolved corporation.

c. A corporation may file Form 4810 with the IRS requesting a prompt assessment of tax liability. If granted, this request limits the time for assessment to 18 months from the date the request was filed.

1) The period for assessing the tax will not be shortened if the taxpayer

a) Filed a false return,
b) Willfully attempted to evade tax,
c) Did not file a return, or
d) Omitted from gross income greater than 25% of the amount of gross income stated in the return.

Stop & Review

You have completed the outline for this subunit.

Study multiple-choice questions 9 through 16 beginning on page 363.

16.3 PARTIAL LIQUIDATION

A noncorporate shareholder treats a distribution as a sale to the extent it is (in redemption) in partial liquidation of the corporation.

1. The corporation making the distribution recognizes gain but not loss.
2. A corporation receiving a distribution in redemption for partial liquidation of another corporation treats the distribution as a dividend to the extent of E&P of the distributing corporation.
   a. The distributee corporation is eligible for the dividends-received deduction.
3. Partial liquidation refers to contraction of the corporation's business. Focus is not on the shareholders but on genuine reduction in size of the corporation's business.
   a. Partial liquidation must be pursuant to a plan, and the distribution must not be essentially equivalent to a dividend. The partial liquidation must be complete within either
      1) The tax year of plan adoption or
      2) The succeeding tax year.
   b. Pro rata distributions do not preclude partial liquidation sale treatment. Furthermore, shareholders are not required to surrender stock to the corporation.
   c. Safe harbor. Noncorporate shareholders apply partial liquidation sale treatment to distributions received if the following conditions are satisfied:
      1) The corporation ceases conduct of a trade or business that it actively conducted for at least 5 years ending with the date of the distribution.
         a) The distribution must be attributable to the discontinued operations.
      2) Immediately after the distribution, the corporation continues to conduct at least one active trade or business it has conducted for 5 years.

Stop & Review

You have completed the outline for this subunit.

Study multiple-choice questions 17 through 20 beginning on page 366.

QUESTIONS

16.1 Redemptions

1. Two unrelated individuals, Ward and June, own all the stock of Wally Corporation, which has earnings and profits of $300,000. Because of his inactivity in the business for the last several years, Ward has decided to retire from the business completely and move to Oregon. Accordingly, Wally will redeem all the stock owned by Ward and, in return, Ward will receive a distribution of $450,000. Ward's adjusted basis in the stock is $250,000. What will be the tax effect to Ward?

A. $150,000 capital gain.

B. $300,000 dividend.

C. $450,000 dividend.

D. $200,000 capital gain.

Answer (D) is correct.

REQUIRED: The tax effect of a redemption to a shareholder.

DISCUSSION: Under Sec. 302(b)(3), if a corporation redeems all of its stock owned by a shareholder, the redemption is treated as a distribution in partial payment or full payment in exchange for the stock. Since Wally Corporation redeemed all of Ward's stock, the $450,000 distribution is treated as payment for the stock, and any gain is treated as capital gain. The amount of the gain is computed under Sec. 1001 and is the amount by which the distribution exceeds the shareholder's basis in the stock. In this case, the gain is $200,000 ($450,000 distribution – $250,000 basis). Because the stock is a capital asset, the recognized gain is a capital gain. Because the distribution is treated as an exchange for the stock and not as a dividend, the amount of the corporation's earnings and profits is irrelevant. Earnings and profits affect distributions only when those distributions have the character of dividends.

Answer (A) is incorrect. The gain is reduced by the shareholder's basis in the stock, not the earnings and profits. **Answer (B) is incorrect.** A complete redemption is treated as an exchange and therefore recognizes a gain, not a dividend. Also, the $300,000 is the amount of the earnings and profits, which is irrelevant when determining the gain in an exchange. **Answer (C) is incorrect.** The gain is reduced by the shareholder's basis in the stock, and the distribution is in redemption of a shareholder's entire interest.

2. With respect to the redemption of stock, which of the following tests does NOT establish that the redemption can be treated as an exchange of stock rather than as a dividend?

A. The redemption is substantially disproportionate with respect to the shareholder.

B. The redemption is not substantially equivalent to a dividend.

C. The redemption terminates the shareholder's entire interest in the corporation.

D. The redemption is of stock held by a corporate shareholder and is made in partial liquidation of the redeeming corporation.

Answer (D) is correct.

REQUIRED: The test that does not establish that the redemption can be treated as an exchange of stock rather than a dividend.

DISCUSSION: A redemption qualifies for sale or exchange treatment if the redemption is (1) substantially disproportionate, (2) a complete termination of the shareholder's interest, (3) not essentially equivalent to a dividend, (4) a partial liquidation of the distributing corporation in redemption of part or all of a noncorporate shareholder's stock, or (5) the distribution is received by an estate. A redemption of stock held by a noncorporate shareholder in a partial liquidation will receive sale or exchange treatment but not a redemption of stock held by a corporate shareholder.

3. Gus Corporation, a C corporation, is owned equally by Al, Bill, and Charlie. Their stock basis on December 31 is as follows: Al $20,000, Bill $40,000, and Charlie $40,000. Gus Corporation has earnings and profits of $90,000 at the end of the calendar year and will continue as a viable entity. Al wants to exit the corporation and pursue other interests. He surrenders all his shares and receives $15,000. What are the tax consequences to Al of this complete redemption?

A. $5,000 capital loss.

B. $5,000 capital gain.

C. $15,000 ordinary dividend.

D. None of the answers are correct.

Answer (A) is correct.

REQUIRED: The tax consequences of a complete redemption of shareholder's stock.

DISCUSSION: Under Sec. 302(b)(3), if a corporation redeems all of its stock owned by a shareholder, the redemption is treated as a distribution in part or full payment in exchange for the stock. Since Gus Corporation redeemed all of Al's stock, the $15,000 distribution is treated as payment for the stock, and any loss is treated as capital loss. The amount of the loss is computed under Sec. 1001 and is the amount by which the distribution is less than the shareholder's basis in the stock. Because the distribution is treated as an exchange for the stock and not as a dividend, the amount of the corporation's earnings and profits is irrelevant. Earnings and profits affect distributions only when those distributions have the character of dividends. In this case, the loss is $5,000 ($15,000 distribution – $20,000 basis). Additionally, since the stock is a capital asset, the recognized loss is a capital loss.

Answer (B) is incorrect. The redemption generates a $5,000 loss, not gain. **Answer (C) is incorrect.** The complete redemption is treated as a payment for the stock, not a dividend. **Answer (D) is incorrect.** Al will experience a $5,000 capital loss because of his complete redemption.

4. Belle Corporation owns as an investment 10% of the stock of Ton Corporation, with an adjusted basis of $4,000 and a fair market value of $44,000. Belle uses the Ton stock to redeem approximately 1%, or $10,000 par value, of its own outstanding stock from unrelated, noncorporate shareholders. As a result of this transaction, Belle must report a gain of

A. $0

B. $2,000

C. $40,000

D. $44,000

Answer (C) is correct.

REQUIRED: The gain a corporation must report on the redemption of stock with property.

DISCUSSION: A corporation that distributes property in redemption of its stock generally recognizes gain, but not loss, if it pays all or part of the redemption price by transferring property whose fair market value exceeds its basis to the corporation. Thus, Belle Corporation must recognize the $40,000 gain inherent in the difference between the value of the Ton stock ($44,000) and its basis ($4,000).

Answer (A) is incorrect. The corporation must recognize a gain. **Answer (B) is incorrect.** The corporation's gain does not equal $2,000. **Answer (D) is incorrect.** The corporation's gain does not equal the fair market value of the property.

5. Danny owns 35% of Batch Corporation's only class of stock outstanding. His daughter Ann and son-in-law Tony each own 20%. Ann is legally separated from Tony. Danny's father owns 25% of Batch's outstanding stock. What is Ann's percentage of stock ownership under the attribution rules for stock redemption?

A. 55%

B. 75%

C. 80%

D. 100%

Answer (A) is correct.

REQUIRED: The shareholder's percentage of stock ownership under the attribution rules for stock redemption.

DISCUSSION: A shareholder is treated as owning shares owned by certain related parties. Stock owned directly or indirectly by or for a spouse, child, grandchild, or parent is considered to be constructively owned. However, a spouse who is legally separated is not considered a related party. Danny's father constructively owns Ann's shares, but Ann does not constructively own Danny's father's shares. Therefore, Ann is considered to own 55% of Batch's stock (20% personally owned + 35% of father's stock).

Answer (B) is incorrect. A spouse that is legally separated is not a related party for calculating a grandchild's ownership. This is not the same as a grandchild being related for calculating the grandparent's ownership. **Answer (C) is incorrect.** A grandfather is not a related party. **Answer (D) is incorrect.** A legally separated spouse and a grandfather are not related parties.

6. Turbo Corporation distributed land to shareholder Lea in partial liquidation of her interest. At the time of the distribution, the land had an adjusted basis of $80,000 and a fair market value of $125,000. Lea exchanged 90 of 100 shares of Turbo stock for the land. At the time of the partial liquidation, Lea's adjusted basis in the 90 shares was $60,000. Other unrelated shareholders of Turbo own a combined 150 shares outstanding. Just prior to the distribution, Turbo had earnings and profits of $150,000. What are the amounts and the character of income that Turbo Corporation and Lea must recognize on the partial liquidation?

	Turbo	Lea
A.	$0	$65,000 capital gain
B.	$0	$65,000 dividend
C.	$45,000 capital gain	$65,000 capital gain
D.	$45,000 capital gain	$125,000 dividend

Answer (C) is correct.

REQUIRED: The amount and the character of income that a shareholder and a corporation recognize on a partial liquidation.

DISCUSSION: A redemption distribution is substantially disproportionate with respect to a shareholder (and qualifies for capital gains treatment) if, after the redemption, (s)he owns less than 50% of the total combined voting power of all classes of voting stock and his or her percentage of voting stock and ownership percentage of common stock after the redemption are less than 80% of each such stock owned immediately before the redemption. Lea meets these criteria and has $65,000 of capital gain ($125,000 land value – $60,000 stock basis). Turbo has capital gain of $45,000 because a corporation that makes an in-kind distribution of property that has a fair market value ($125,000) that exceeds its basis ($80,000) recognizes gain as if it had sold the property to the shareholder at its fair market value.

Answer (A) is incorrect. The corporation must recognize a gain on the partial liquidation. **Answer (B) is incorrect.** The redemption is substantially disproportionate with respect to the shareholder. **Answer (D) is incorrect.** The redemption is substantially disproportionate with respect to the shareholder and is reduced by basis in the stock.

7. Art, Betty, and Cora are equal partners in ABC Partnership. ABC Partnership and Betty are the only two shareholders in Angel, Inc., with direct ownership of 60% and 40%, respectively. Based upon the constructive-ownership rules for stock redemptions, what are ABC's and Betty's percentages of constructive ownership of Angel?

	ABC	Betty
A.	60%	60%
B.	100%	40%
C.	100%	60%
D.	100%	100%

Answer (C) is correct.

REQUIRED: The percentage of stock a taxpayer is considered to own under the constructive-ownership rules.

DISCUSSION: Stock owned by a partnership is considered to be owned proportionately by the partners. Accordingly, Art, Betty, and Cora each own 33.33% of the ABC Partnership. ABC owns 60% of the stock of Angel, Inc.; therefore, all of the partners of ABC Partnership constructively own 20% (60% × 33%) of Angel. Betty directly owns 40% of the stock of Angel and constructively owns 20%. Betty owns 60% in total (20% + 40%). Stock owned, directly or indirectly, by a partner shall be considered as owned by the partnership. Therefore, all of the stock Betty owns in Angel must be considered as being owned by the partnership, resulting in the partnership owning 100% of Angel's stock.

8. A stock redemption is the acquisition by a corporation of its stock from a shareholder. A shareholder who owns all of the stock of a corporation sells back one half of his stock for cash. Assume that the current E&P is greater than the redemption amount. Which of the following statements is true with regard to this stock redemption?

A. This sale back to the corporation of one half will cause no percentage change in the shareholder's ownership.

B. After the redemption the shareholder will own all of the stock in the corporation.

C. The stock redemption resembles a dividend distribution and will be taxed accordingly.

D. All of the answers are correct.

Answer (D) is correct.

REQUIRED: The true statement regarding stock redemptions.

DISCUSSION: Stock is redeemed when a corporation acquires its own stock from a shareholder in exchange for property. The redemption occurs whether or not the stock is canceled, retired, or held as treasury stock. A shareholder is required to treat amounts realized on a redemption (not in liquidation) either as a distribution (a corporate dividend) or as a sale of the stock redeemed. Because the shareholder owns 100% of the stock before and after the redemption, the transaction is a dividend to the extent that the corporation has earnings and profits.

16.2 Complete Liquidation

9. A fiduciary representing a dissolving corporation may request a prompt assessment of tax under Internal Revenue Code Section 6501(d). This will limit the time the Internal Revenue Service has to assess additional tax or to begin court action to collect the tax from the date the fiduciary files the request to

A. 6 months.

B. 12 months.

C. 18 months.

D. 24 months.

Answer (C) is correct.

REQUIRED: The time limit for a prompt assessment of tax for a dissolving corporation.

DISCUSSION: Section 6501(d) allows a corporation to file Form 4810 with the IRS requesting a prompt assessment of tax liability. If granted, this request limits the time for assessment to 18 months from the date the request was filed.

10. Which of the following will NOT shorten the period for assessing the tax when a fiduciary representing a dissolving corporation requests a prompt assessment of tax under Internal Revenue Code Section 6501(d) by filing a Form 4810?

A. Where the taxpayer did not report substantial amounts of gross income.

B. Where the taxpayer was filing a final return.

C. Where the taxpayer filed a false return.

D. Both where the taxpayer did not report substantial amounts of gross income and where the taxpayer filed a false return.

Answer (D) is correct.

REQUIRED: The event(s) that will not shorten the period for assessing tax for a dissolving corporation.

DISCUSSION: Under Sec. 6501, the period for assessing the tax will not be shortened if the taxpayer filed a false return, willfully attempted to evade tax, did not file a return, or omitted from gross income greater than 25% of the amount of gross income stated in the return.

Answer (A) is incorrect. A case where the taxpayer did not report substantial amounts of gross income is one of two exceptions to prompt assessment under Sec. 6501. **Answer (B) is incorrect.** A case where the taxpayer was filing a final return is not an exception under Sec. 6501. **Answer (C) is incorrect.** A case where the taxpayer filed a false return is one of two exceptions to prompt assessment under Sec. 6501.

11. In Year 1, pursuant to a complete liquidation, Richards Corporation distributes the following to a shareholder: inventory, basis $10,000, FMV $20,000; and land held as an investment, basis $5,000, FMV $40,000. The land is subject to a $30,000 liability. What are the amounts and character of income to be recognized by Richards Corporation?

A. $10,000 ordinary income; $35,000 capital gain.

B. $10,000 ordinary income; $65,000 capital gain.

C. $0 ordinary income; $0 capital gain.

D. $10,000 ordinary income; $5,000 capital gain.

Answer (A) is correct.

REQUIRED: The amounts and character of income to be recognized by Richards Corporation.

DISCUSSION: Section 311(b) requires that gain on the distribution of appreciated property be recognized as if the property had been sold. Therefore, Richards Corporation recognizes $10,000 as ordinary income for the inventory ($20,000 FMV – $10,000 basis) and $35,000 as capital gain for the land ($40,000 FMV – $5,000 basis). The $30,000 liability is irrelevant when considering the corporate gain. If the liability exceeds the FMV of the property, however, the liability amount would be considered the new “selling price” and shareholder basis in the property.

Answer (B) is incorrect. The amount of $65,000 incorrectly includes the $30,000 liability. **Answer (C) is incorrect.** Richards Corporation must recognize a gain on appreciated property. **Answer (D) is incorrect.** The amount of $35,000 must be reported as a capital gain.

12. Individual Y owns 55% of Beta Corporation. Five years ago, Y contributed property with an adjusted basis of $20,000 and a fair market value of $8,000 to Beta in a transaction qualifying under Sec. 351. In the current year, Beta adopted a plan of complete liquidation and distributed this same property to Y. At this time, the property had an adjusted basis of $18,000 and a fair market value of $5,000. How much loss will Beta recognize on the distribution?

A. $0

B. $1,000

C. $12,000

D. $13,000

Answer (A) is correct.

REQUIRED: The loss recognized in a liquidation on the distribution of recently contributed property to a related shareholder.

DISCUSSION: Normally gain or loss is recognized on a liquidating distribution of assets [Sec. 336(a)]. However, under Sec. 336(d)(1), a loss is not recognized in a liquidation on the distribution of property to a related person (which includes a greater-than-50% shareholder) unless the property is distributed to all shareholders on a pro rata basis and the property was not acquired in a Sec. 351 transaction or contribution to capital during the 5 preceding years (also known as disqualified property). Since the distribution was of property acquired in a Sec. 351 transaction within the 5 preceding years, no loss is recognized on the distribution of the disqualified property to the related person. The fact that the distribution was not pro rata does not affect the ability to recognize the loss.

13. Six years ago, Adam purchased 100 shares of Call Corporation stock for $50 per share. During the current year, Call completely liquidated. After paying its liabilities, Call distributed to its shareholders $10,000 in cash and appreciated property sold for $90,000. Adam's portion received a liquidating distribution from Call of $10,000. Adam must report what amount of capital gains income from this distribution?

A. $4,500

B. $5,000

C. $22,500

D. $25,000

Answer (B) is correct.

REQUIRED: The shareholder treatment of proceeds received from a complete liquidation.

DISCUSSION: A shareholder treats amounts distributed in complete liquidation as realized in exchange for stock. Capital recovery to the extent of basis is permitted before recognizing gain or loss. Amounts realized include money and the FMV of other distributed property received. Adam should recognize $5,000 of gain ($10,000 value of distribution received – $5,000 basis in stock).

Answer (A) is incorrect. A gain of $5,000 is reported. The value of the distribution received less the basis in the stock is the amount of gain reported. **Answer (C) is incorrect.** A gain of $5,000 is reported. The value of the distribution received less the basis in the stock is the formula used to calculate the gain income from the distribution. **Answer (D) is incorrect.** A gain of $5,000 is reported. The value of the distribution received less the basis in the stock is the formula used to calculate the gain income from the distribution.

14. Vernon receives a truck from Berry Trucking Company as a distribution in complete liquidation. Vernon's basis in the stock of Berry Trucking Company is $2,000. The fair market value of the truck on the date of the distribution is $30,000. There is a $15,000 loan on the truck, which Vernon assumed. What is the basis of the truck to Vernon?

A. $28,000

B. $13,000

C. $15,000

D. $30,000

Answer (D) is correct.

REQUIRED: The basis of property subject to a liability received by a shareholder in a complete liquidation of a corporation.

DISCUSSION: If a shareholder assumes a liability of the liquidating corporation, or receives property that is subject to a liability, then the liability reduces the amount realized by the shareholder, thus reducing the shareholder's gain or increasing the shareholder's loss. Nevertheless, the shareholder's basis for the property is the property's fair market value, in this case $30,000.

Answer (A) is incorrect. The basis does not equal the fair market value less basis of stock. **Answer (B) is incorrect.** The basis does not equal the fair market value less the loan and the basis of the stock. **Answer (C) is incorrect.** The basis does not equal the fair market value less the loan.

15. In Year 1, Daniel inherited 100% of Candy Corporation's outstanding stock from his mother. The stock had a fair market value of $250,000 at the date of death and was reflected on Candy's balance sheet as follows:

Cash	$250,000
Capital stock	150,000
Accumulated earnings & profits	100,000

Daniel immediately withdrew $50,000 out of Candy Corporation as a dividend distribution. Later in Year 1, pursuant to a plan of liquidation, Daniel withdrew the remaining $200,000 out of Candy. For Year 1, how much will Daniel be required to report as ordinary dividend income and capital gain or loss?

	Ordinary Dividend	Capital Gain or Loss
A.	$0	$0
B.	$50,000	$(50,000)
C.	$100,000	$(100,000)
D.	$50,000	$(250,000)

Answer (B) is correct.

REQUIRED: The reporting of a complete liquidation.

DISCUSSION: Because Daniel received the stock through inheritance, he takes a stepped-up basis of $250,000 (FMV at the date of the transferor's death). The $50,000 dividend is ordinary dividend income and does not affect Daniel's basis. Thus, when he liquidated the corporation and received the remaining $200,000, he had a capital loss of $50,000 ($200,000 distribution – $250,000 basis).

Answer (A) is incorrect. Daniel must report the distributions made by the corporation. **Answer (C) is incorrect.** The stock basis is stepped up because Daniel received the stock through inheritance. **Answer (D) is incorrect.** The loss does not equal the basis in the stock.

16. Ann owned two blocks of Lou Corporation stock, which had the following characteristics:

Block	Shares	Acquired	Basis
1	200	6/01/Yr 1	$20,000
2	50	7/01/Yr 2	12,500

Ann's two blocks of stock combined represented 10% of Lou Corporation's outstanding stock. Pursuant to Lou's complete liquidation, Ann received a $50,000 cash distribution on December 1, Year 2, in exchange for her 250 shares. Lou's earnings and profits balance immediately before any liquidating distributions was $50,000. What are the amount and the character of Ann's gain or loss?

A. $50,000 dividend income.

B. $17,500 long-term capital gain.

C. $20,000 long-term capital gain and $2,500 short-term capital loss.

D. No gain or loss.

Answer (C) is correct.

REQUIRED: The amount and the character of gain or loss to be reported as a result of a complete liquidation.

DISCUSSION: Section 331 provides capital gain or loss treatment for distributions received by a shareholder in complete liquidation of a corporation. The gain or loss will be long-term or short-term, depending on the length of time the stock has been held (Sec. 1222).

The shareholder's gain or loss is the difference between the amount realized and the basis in the stock. The amount realized by Ann is $200 per share ($50,000 distribution ÷ 250 shares owned). The sale of Block 1 produces a gain of $20,000 [200 shares × ($200 selling price – $100 per share basis)]. The gain is long-term because the stock was held for more than 1 year. The sale of Block 2 produces a loss of $2,500 [50 shares × ($250 per share basis – $200 per share selling price)]. The loss is short-term because the stock was held less than 1 year.

Answer (A) is incorrect. The figure of $50,000 is the amount of the distribution, not the amount of the gain (loss). **Answer (B) is incorrect.** The gain and loss should be allocated to the different blocks of stock. The amounts should not be aggregated ($50,000 distribution – $32,500 total basis). **Answer (D) is incorrect.** A gain and a loss are recognized because the transaction is treated as a sale.

16.3 Partial Liquidation

17. Oak Corporation had earnings and profits of $500,000 before distributions. Due to economic conditions, Oak, in partial liquidation, distributed land having an adjusted basis to Oak of $135,000 and a fair market value of $150,000 to Mr. Brown for 95% of his interest in Oak Corporation. Mr. Brown's adjusted basis in the stock at the time of the distribution was $180,000. What is the amount of Oak Corporation's recognized gain or loss?

A. $(45,000)

B. $(30,000)

C. $0

D. $15,000

Answer (D) is correct.

REQUIRED: The amount of gain or loss recognized by the corporation when it distributes property in a partial liquidation.

DISCUSSION: If a corporation makes a distribution of property to a noncorporate shareholder in partial liquidation, the distribution is treated as being in exchange for stock. Since the corporation makes a distribution of property whose fair market value ($150,000) exceeds its basis ($135,000), the corporation will recognize a gain of $15,000 as if it had sold the property to the shareholder at its fair market value.

18. Ivana Dolla received property with a fair market value of $60,000 and an adjusted basis of $33,000 from Candid Corporation in partial liquidation. Candid's earnings and profits for the year prior to the distribution were $250,000. Ms. Dolla's basis in the stock she exchanged was $44,000. What is the amount of Ms. Dolla's recognized gain?

A. $11,000

B. $16,000

C. $27,000

D. $60,000

Answer (B) is correct.

REQUIRED: The amount of gain recognized by a noncorporate shareholder in a partial liquidation.

DISCUSSION: Under Sec. 302(b)(4), a redemption of an interest held by a noncorporate shareholder made in partial liquidation of the corporation is treated as a distribution in exchange for the stock. The shareholder will treat any gain on the redemption as a capital gain. The amount of the gain is computed under Sec. 1001. Under Sec. 301(b)(1), the amount of the distribution is the fair market value of the property. Ms. Dolla will recognize a gain of $16,000 on the distribution ($60,000 fair market value of the distributed property – $44,000 basis in the stock).

Answer (A) is incorrect. The gain is not the difference between the adjusted basis of the stock and the adjusted basis of the property. **Answer (C) is incorrect.** The gain is not the difference between the fair market value of the property and the adjusted basis of the property. **Answer (D) is incorrect.** The gain does not equal the fair market value of the property.

19. Which of the following statements is true in order for a distribution of corporate assets to be treated as being in exchange for stock in a partial liquidation of a corporation?

A. A distribution must be essentially equivalent to a dividend.

B. A distribution must occur in the taxable year the plan is adopted.

C. A distribution of corporate assets to a corporate shareholder is treated as being in exchange for stock.

D. A distribution of corporate assets is treated as an exchange for stock in a partial liquidation of a corporation, whether or not the stock is actually surrendered.

Answer (D) is correct.

REQUIRED: The true statement regarding an exchange for stock in a partial liquidation of a corporation.

DISCUSSION: A distribution of corporate assets is treated as an exchange for stock in a partial liquidation of a corporation, regardless of whether the stock is actually surrendered.

Answer (A) is incorrect. A distribution must not be essentially equivalent to a dividend. **Answer (B) is incorrect.** The distribution can occur in a year after the plan is adopted. **Answer (C) is incorrect.** The partial liquidation treatment applies only to noncorporate shareholders.

20. Which of the following is NOT a requirement for a distribution to be treated as a partial liquidation of a corporation?

A. The distribution is not essentially equivalent to a dividend, which is determined at the shareholder level rather than at the corporate level.

B. The distribution is attributable to the distributing corporation's ceasing to conduct a qualifying trade or business that was actively conducted throughout the 5-year period ending on the date of the redemption.

C. The distribution is pursuant to a plan and occurs within the taxable year in which the plan is adopted or within the succeeding taxable year.

D. All of the answers would be treated as a distribution in partial liquidation of a corporation.

Answer (A) is correct.

REQUIRED: The statement that is not a requirement for a distribution to be treated as a partial liquidation of a corporation.

DISCUSSION: The determination of whether a distribution is not essentially equivalent to a dividend is made at the corporate level. The distribution must be the result of a bona fide contraction of the corporation's business. A distribution satisfies the "not essentially equivalent to a dividend" standard if it meets the safe harbor rule under Sec. 302(e)(2).

Answer (B) is incorrect. A distribution must be attributable to the distributing corporation's ceasing to conduct a qualifying trade or business that was actively conducted throughout the 5-year period ending on the date of the redemption for it to be treated as a partial liquidation of a corporation. **Answer (C) is incorrect.** A distribution must be pursuant to a plan and occur within the taxable year in which the plan is adopted or within the succeeding taxable year for it to be treated as a partial liquidation of a corporation. **Answer (D) is incorrect.** One of the statements is not a requirement for a distribution to be treated as a partial liquidation of a corporation.

STUDY UNIT SEVENTEEN

S CORPORATIONS

(14 pages of outline)

An S corporation is generally not subject to a federal tax on its income. The corporation's items of income, loss, deduction, and credit are passed through to its shareholders on a per-day and per-share basis. Each shareholder is taxed on his or her share of the S corporation's income as it is earned. Distributions of cash or property generally are not income to its shareholders.

17.1 ELIGIBILITY AND ELECTION

A corporation is treated as an S corporation only for those days for which each specific eligibility requirement is met and the required election is effective.

Eligibility

1. Eligibility depends on the nature of the corporation, its shareholders, and its stock.
   a. An S corporation must have only one class of stock.
      1) One class of stock means that the outstanding shares of the corporation must be identical as to the rights of the holders in the profits and in the assets of the corporation on liquidation or distribution.
         a) Variation in voting rights of that one class of stock is permitted.
      2) Debt may be treated as a disqualifying second class of stock.
   b. The number of shareholders may not exceed 100. Related taxpayers and their estates are considered a single shareholder for this purpose.
      1) A husband and wife are considered a single shareholder for this purpose.
      2) Family members in a six-generation range are also considered one shareholder.
      3) A nonresident alien (NRA) may not own any shares.
      4) Each shareholder must be an individual (including an individual owner of a single-member LLC), an estate (including estates of individuals in bankruptcy), or a qualified trust.
         a) Certain small business trusts and tax-exempt organizations (e.g., qualified retirement plans) can be shareholders.
         b) Partnerships and corporations may not be shareholders.

         NOTE: Single-member LLCs are not partnerships or corporations. However, they may elect corporation status.

         c) Charitable Remainder Unitrusts and Charitable Remainder Annuity Trusts are not eligible shareholders.

c. The corporation must be domestic and eligible.

   1) Ineligible corporations include insurance companies and financial institutions, such as banks that use the reserve method of accounting for bad debts.

d. S corporations can own C corporations or Qualified Subchapter S Subsidiaries (QSSS).

   1) A QSSS is an electing domestic corporation that qualifies as an S corporation and is 100% owned by an S corporation parent.

      a) The IRS refers to a QSSS as a QSub.

   2) A C corporation cannot own shares in an S corporation.

Election

2. An eligible corporation must make the election for S corporation status.

   a. All shareholders at the time the election is made must file a consent.

      1) A shareholder's consent is binding and may not be withdrawn after a valid election is made by the corporation unless the shareholders vote to terminate the election.

      2) Each person who is a shareholder at the time of the election must consent by signing Form 2553, *Election by a Small Business Corporation*.

      3) In addition, each person who was a shareholder at any time during the part of the tax year before the election is made must also consent.

      4) If any former shareholders do not consent, the election is considered made for the following year.

   b. Election made within the first 2 months and 15 days of the beginning of the corporation's tax year is effective from the first day of that tax year.

   c. Election made after the first 2 months and 15 days of the corporation's tax year will become effective on the first day of the following tax year.

   d. The IRS can treat a late-filed election as having been timely filed if a determination is made that reasonable cause existed for a corporation's failure to file the election in a timely manner.

   e. The IRS can waive the effect of an invalid election resulting from a corporation's failing to qualify as an S corporation and/or failing to obtain the necessary shareholder consents.

Termination

3. Upon the occurrence of a terminating event, an S corporation becomes a C corporation.
   a. An S corporation election is terminated by any of the following:
      1) An effective revocation. Shareholders collectively holding more than 50% of the outstanding shares of stock on the day of the revocation (voting and nonvoting) must consent.
         a) In order for the revocation to be effective as of the first day of the current tax year, the election must be made within the first 2 months and 15 days unless a prospective date is selected.
      2) Any eligibility requirement not being satisfied on any day.
      3) Passive investment income (PII) termination.
   b. The termination is effective as of the date the disqualifying event, other than a PII termination, occurs.
   c. **PII termination** occurs when, for 3 consecutive tax years, the corporation has both Subchapter C E&P on the last day and PII that is greater than 25% of gross receipts.
      1) An S corporation does not have E&P unless it was formerly a C corporation or acquired E&P in a tax-free reorganization, e.g., a merger.
      2) Gross receipts are gross receipts of the S corporation for the tax year reduced by capital losses (other than on stock and securities) to the extent of capital gains.
      3) PII is generally the total amount received or accrued from investments, as opposed to operations, with some adjustments.
         a) PII consists of gross receipts from dividends, interest, royalties, rents, and annuities, reduced by
            i) Interest on accounts receivable (notes) for inventory sold in the ordinary course of trade or business
            ii) Rents from a lease under which significant services are rendered to the lessee (those not customarily rendered)
         b) Interest includes tax-exempt interest
         c) Receipts from sales and exchanges of stock and securities are not considered PII. Therefore, losses to the extent of gains from such sales and exchanges do not reduce PII.
      4) A PII termination is effective as of the first day of the first tax year beginning after the third consecutive taxable year referred to in item 3.c. above.

Reinstatement

4. If an election is terminated, a new election cannot be made for 5 tax years without the consent of the IRS.
5. The IRS may waive termination.
   a. The terminating event must have been inadvertent and corrected within a reasonable time.

Accounting Method

6. An S corporation is not required to use the accrual method.
   a. Accounting method election is generally made by the S corporation.
   b. Shareholders, however, personally elect
      1) Credit or a deduction for foreign income taxes
      2) Percentage or cost depletion for oil and gas properties
      3) Treatment of mining exploration expenditures

Tax Year

7. An S corporation generally must adopt a calendar tax year.
   a. With IRS consent, it may adopt a fiscal year (if it establishes a valid business purpose for doing so) that
      1) Does not result in deferral of income to shareholders but
      2) Coincides with a natural business year.
         a) A natural business year may end with or after the end of the peak period of a cyclical business.
         b) A natural business year also exists if greater than 25% of gross receipts occur in the last 2 months of the proposed year over a 3-year period.

EXAMPLE 17-1 Fiscal Year Natural Business Year

Acme, Inc., an S corporation, provides tax preparation services. Normally its required tax year would be a calendar year. However, because greater than 25% of Acme's gross receipts have occurred in March and April over the past 3 years, Acme has a business purpose for a fiscal year ending on April 30.

   b. An S corporation that deposits the equivalent amount of the deferred tax may elect a fiscal year under Sec. 444.
      1) A new S corporation is limited to no more than 3 months' deferral of income to its shareholders.
      2) An existing S corporation may continue to use the fiscal year previously adopted.

EXAMPLE 17-2 Fiscal Year Sec. 444 Election

Ace, Inc., a newly formed S corporation, has a required tax year ending on December 31 (i.e., a calendar year). However, Ace can make a Sec. 444 election to change its tax year so that it provides no more than 3 months of deferral. This means that Ace can elect a September 30 year end (3 months of deferral), an October 31 year end (2 months of deferral), or a November 30 year end (1 month of deferral). In order to make the election, Ace will have to make a noninterest-bearing deposit with the IRS (the deposit eliminates the time value of money savings provided by deferral).

c. To change its tax year, other than by a Sec. 444 election, an S corporation should file Form 1128.

d. A Sec. 444 election may be made on Form 2553 when the corporation elects S corporation status or, if subsequent to the election, by filing Form 8716.

e. A Sec. 444 election may be terminated by filing a short-year return and writing "Sec. 444 election terminated" across the top.

f. When S status is terminated and creates a short year, nonseparately computed income is allocated on a pro rata basis unless certain exceptions apply or an election is made.

Administration

8. The tax treatment of S corporation items of income, loss, deduction, and credit is determined at the corporate level.
   a. The S corporation files a Form 1120-S tax return.
   b. Each shareholder must report his or her pro rata share of items on his or her personal tax return.
      1) The shareholder's reporting must be consistent with the Form 1120-S tax return.
         a) An exception applies if the shareholder notifies the IRS of the inconsistency.
   c. Administrative and judicial proceedings to determine proper treatment of items are unified at the level of the S corporation.
      1) Shareholders are notified and given the opportunity to participate.

EXAMPLE 17-3 Time of Reporting S Corporation Items

Compliance Corporation is a calendar-year S corporation. Compliance has two shareholders: Shelly, with a year end of June 30 of the current year, and Julie, with a year end of December 31 of the current year. Because Julie is a calendar-year taxpayer, she will report any current-year income from Compliance on her current-year return. Shelly, on the other hand, will report any current-year income from Compliance on her return for the following year.

Stop & Review

You have completed the outline for this subunit.
Study multiple-choice questions 1 through 5 beginning on page 383.

17.2 OPERATIONS

Governance and Exempt Taxes

Provisions that govern taxation of C corporations also govern taxation of S corporations, unless a specific exception applies. S corporations are expressly exempt from the following taxes:

- Corporate income tax
- Accumulated earnings tax (AET)
- Personal holding company (PHC) tax

Pro Rata Share and Separately Stated Items

1. The items of income, deduction (including losses), and credit of an S corporation are reported by the corporation.
   a. A shareholder is required to take the pro rata share of items passed through into account in computing the shareholder's personal taxable income for his or her tax year within which the tax year of the S corporation (in which the S corporation accounted for and reported the items) ended.

EXAMPLE 17-4 Shareholder Inclusion of S Corporation Items

Super, Inc., an S corporation, properly reported non-separately stated net income from operations of $100,000 for its tax year ending November 30, 2022. Steve, a calendar-year taxpayer who owns 5% of the shares of Super, Inc., must include $5,000 of ordinary income in his tax return for 2022, which is due on or before April 15, 2023.

2. S corporation items of income, deduction, and credit, which could alter the tax liability of shareholders if taken into account by them on their personal returns, are required to be stated (and are passed through) separately. Separately stated items include
   a. Section 1231 gains and losses
   b. Net short-term capital gains and losses
   c. Net long-term capital gains and losses
   d. Dividends
   e. Charitable contributions
   f. Taxes paid to a foreign country or to a U.S. possession
   g. Tax-exempt interest and related expense
   h. Investment income and related expense
   i. Amounts previously deducted (e.g., bad debts)
   j. Real estate activities
   k. Section 179 deduction
   l. Credits
   m. Deductions disallowed in computing S corporation income (i.e., deductions whose separate treatment could affect a shareholder's tax liability)

EXAMPLE 17-5 Separately Stated Items

ABC Corp., an S corporation, has a Sec. 1231 gain. But, because the ultimate treatment of Sec. 1231 gains depends on whether a taxpayer has a net Sec. 1231 gain or loss, the treatment of ABC's Sec. 1231 gain could vary at the shareholder level and must be separately stated. For example, for a shareholder with Sec. 1231 losses, a Sec. 1231 gain from ABC will reduce the Sec. 1231 loss amount that can offset ordinary income. Conversely, the share of ABC's Sec. 1231 gain for a shareholder with a net Sec. 1231 gain will be taxed at preferential long-term capital gains rates.

3. Items not required to be separately stated (e.g., organizational costs) are combined at the corporate level, and the net amount of ordinary income or loss is passed through to shareholders.
4. A shareholder's Sec. 179 deduction is subject to limits. For 2022, the maximum Sec. 179 deduction is $1.08 million.
   a. If the cost of Sec. 179 property placed in service during the year exceeds $2.7 million, the maximum deduction limit must be reduced by the amount of cost that exceeds $2.7 million.
   b. The maximum deduction limit is applied to each taxpayer, not each separate business.
5. If an S corporation makes a contribution of property to a charity, each shareholder reduces his or her basis in the stock of the S corporation by his or her pro rata share of the AB of the contributed property.

EXAMPLE 17-6 Charitable Contributions -- S Corporations

The S corporation contributed a capital asset held long term to a charity. The basis of the asset was $12,000, and the fair market value was $20,000. The sole shareholder has a $20,000 charitable contribution and reduces basis in the stock by $12,000.

6. The shareholder characterizes each item (e.g., long-term capital gain) as the corporation would.

Debt Discharge

7. Ordinarily, a taxpayer realizes income when indebtedness is forgiven or otherwise canceled. However, if the discharge of debt occurs in a bankruptcy case, when the taxpayer is insolvent, or when the discharge of indebtedness is with respect to qualified real property business indebtedness, the income realized upon the discharge is excluded from income (excluded from ordinary income, not capital gains), and the amount excluded is applied to reduce the tax attributes of the taxpayer, including any net operating loss (NOL) of the taxpayer.
   a. Income from the discharge of indebtedness of an S corporation that is excluded from the S corporation's income is not taken into account as an item of income by any shareholder. As a result, it does not increase the basis of any shareholder's stock in the corporation.

Carryovers

8. Carryovers (e.g., NOL) between S and C corporations are not permitted. This rule applies to corporations that change their status from C to S or from S to C.

Reporting for Qualified Business Income Deduction (QBID)

9. In regards to an S corporation, the QBID is determined at the shareholder level. To allow shareholders to correctly figure the deduction on the shareholder's Form 1040 return, the S corporation must report on the shareholder's Schedule K-1.

Stock Basis

10. Generally, if a shareholder purchases stock, the shareholder's original basis in the stock is its cost.
    a. If a shareholder receives stock in exchange for property, the basis is the same as the property's basis.
    b. If a shareholder lends money to the S corporation, the basis is usually the amount of the loan, and a separately tracked type of basis called debt basis is created.
    c. If a shareholder guarantees a third-party loan to an S corporation, the loan does not increase the shareholder's basis.
        1) If, however, the shareholder makes payments on the loan, the payments increase the shareholder's basis.
        2) The shareholder receives basis if the shareholder is the primary signer on the note and the S corporation is the guarantor.
    d. The FMV of the stock exchanged for services is gross income to the shareholder.
        1) The shareholder's basis in the stock exchanged for services is its FMV.
11. Almost every transaction of an S corporation affects shareholder basis. The adjusted basis of the shareholder's stock is calculated at year end with increases for the shareholder's pro rata share of the following:
    a. All income items of the S corporation, including tax-exempt income, that are separately stated
    b. Any non-separately stated income of the S corporation
    c. The amount of the deduction for depletion (other than oil and gas) that is more than the basis of the property being depleted

EXAMPLE 17-7 Adjusted Basis of Shareholder's Stock -- Increases

The taxpayer's basis in the S corporation is $12,000 at the beginning of the year. The corporation has ordinary income of $6,000, tax-exempt interest of $2,000, and a long-term capital gain of $1,500. The taxpayer's basis will be increased by $9,500 ($6,000 + $2,000 + $1,500) to $21,500 at the end of the year.

12. The adjusted basis of the shareholder's stock must also be decreased by the shareholder's pro rata share of the following:
    a. Distributions by the S corporation that were not included in income (this is done before determining the allowable loss deduction)
    b. All separately stated loss and deduction items
    c. Any non-separately stated loss of the S corporation
    d. Any expenses of the S corporation that are not deductible in figuring its taxable income or are not properly capitalized
    e. The shareholder's deduction for depletion of oil and gas property held by the S corporation to the extent it is not more than the shareholder's share of the adjusted basis of the property

EXAMPLE 17-8 Adjusted Basis of Shareholder's Stock -- Decreases

The taxpayer's basis at the beginning of the year is $22,000. The taxpayer withdraws $16,000 during the year, and the corporation has an ordinary loss of $9,000. Basis in the corporation is first reduced by the $16,000 distribution to $6,000. Only $6,000 of the loss is deductible by the shareholder, limited to basis. The remaining $3,000 loss ($9,000 – $6,000) is carried forward.

13. The basis is not reduced below zero. After basis in the shareholder's S corporation stock has been reduced to zero, the shareholder's basis in debt of the S corporation to that shareholder is reduced (but not below zero) by his or her share of items of loss and deduction.
    a. In a subsequent tax year, items passed through must restore the basis in the debt before basis in the stock.
    b. **Limit.** A shareholder's share of loss and deduction items in excess of basis in the debt is not deductible.
        1) The excess is suspended and carried over indefinitely. It may be deducted in a subsequent tax year in which basis is restored to debt or to stock.

EXAMPLE 17-9 Adjusted Basis of Shareholder's Stock and Debt

Using the data from Example 17-8, if the taxpayer's $22,000 basis in the corporation is made up of $19,500 stock basis and $2,500 debt basis, the stock basis is reduced to $3,500 by the $16,000 distribution and then to zero by the $9,000 loss pass-through. Next, the loan basis is reduced to zero by the remaining loss pass-through, with $3,000 of loss carried forward ($9,000 – $3,500 – $2,500).

At-Risk Rules

14. At-risk rules are applied at the shareholder level.
    a. Any excess of each shareholder's pro rata share of passed-through losses for the tax year over his or her amount at risk at the close of his or her tax year is not deductible in the current tax year.
        1) It is suspended and carried forward indefinitely until the shareholder's amount at risk with regard to the particular activity has increased.
    b. Each shareholder's at-risk amount equals, basically, the sum of the following:
        1) Money and the adjusted basis of property contributed to the corporation (to the extent unencumbered)
        2) Amounts borrowed and lent to the corporation to the extent the shareholder has personal liability for repayment or (s)he has pledged as security for repayment property not used in the activity (of the corporation)
            a) However, it does not include other debts of the corporation to third parties, even if the repayment is guaranteed by the shareholder.
    c. The shareholder's amount at risk is increased or decreased by the shareholder's pro rata share of passed-through income and deduction (tax-exempt related also) and by distributions to the shareholder.
    d. The shareholder's basis in his or her stock and debt of the corporation is reduced (subject to prior application of the basis loss limitation) even if current deductibility of the loss is prohibited by the at-risk rules.

Passive Activity Loss Rules

15. If the S corporation engages in rental activity or if a shareholder does not materially participate (even if the S corporation materially participates) in the trade or business conducted by the corporation, current deductibility of any losses passed through is limited at the shareholder level to passive activity income.
    a. A shareholder's amount at risk must be reduced by the full amount allowable as a current deduction after application of the at-risk rules, even if part of it must be suspended (i.e., disallowed as a current deduction) by the passive loss rules.

Balance Sheet and Reconciliation of Income per Book

16. If the S corporation's total receipts and its total assets at the end of the year are less than $250,000, the corporation is not required to complete the balance sheet and the reconciliation of income per book with income per return.

Return Due Date

17. An S corporation's tax return is due by the 15th day of the 3rd month after the end of the corporation's tax year. An application for an extension of an S corporation tax return is filed on Form 7004. The extension is for 6 months after the original due date of the return.

Failure to File Penalty

18. The penalty base amount (regardless of any tax amount owed) is imposed in the amount of the number of persons who were shareholders during any part of the year, multiplied by $220 (for 2022 tax returns filed in 2023) for each of up to 12 months (including a portion of one) that the return was late or incomplete.

EXAMPLE 17-10 Failure to File Penalty

An S corporation has 5 shareholders and the tax return is filed 1 1/4 months late. The penalty is calculated by multiplying $220 by the 5 shareholders multiplied by 2 (1 1/4 months rounded to 2). The total penalty is $2,200.

    a. **If tax is due**, the penalty is the amount stated above plus 5% of the unpaid tax for each month or part of a month the return is late, up to a maximum of 25% of the unpaid tax. The minimum penalty for a return that is more than 60 days late is the smaller of the tax due or $450.

EXAMPLE 17-11 Failure to File Penalty -- Tax Due

Expand Example 17-10 to include a $10,000 tax liability. The penalty is calculated by multiplying the $10,000 by 10% (5% times 2 months) plus $2,200, which equates to a $3,200 failure to file penalty.

Stop & Review

You have completed the outline for this subunit.
Study multiple-choice questions 6 through 14 beginning on page 385.

17.3 DISTRIBUTIONS

These include nonliquidating and liquidating distributions of money or other property but not of the S corporation's own stock or obligations. The amount of a particular distribution is the sum of any money plus the FMV of property distributed.

AAA and OAA

1. S corporations maintain two types of records for each shareholder: accumulated adjustments account (AAA) and other adjustments account (OAA).
   a. These records, together with a shareholder's basis in his or her stock and any Subchapter C E&P (i.e., accumulated earnings and profits) in the corporation, are used to determine the shareholder's tax treatment of distributions.
   b. Distributions from an S corporation are funded in the following source order:
      1) AAA
      2) AE&P
      3) OAA
      4) Stock basis
   c. Note that AAA and OAA records and information are needed by S corporations only for purposes of helping shareholders determine taxability of distributions when the S corporation has Subchapter C E&P.
   d. The AAA represents the current cumulative balance of all the separately stated items and non-separately stated items (ordinary) of the S corporation.
      1) AAA adjustments parallel those made to basis for separately and non-separately stated items.
         a) It is calculated without regard to any net negative adjustments (excess of losses and deductions over income and gains).
         b) AAA is not affected by any transactions related to when it was a C corporation (i.e., federal income tax).
      2) Expenditures that are not deductible by the S corporation decrease basis in stock and the AAA.
         a) Charitable contributions pass through to the shareholder and reduce stock basis. The reduction of basis is equal to AB of contributed property rather than FMV.
      3) Adjustment is not made to the AAA for tax-exempt income (which increases basis) or nondeductible expenses related thereto (which reduce basis).
         a) These adjustments are made to OAA.
      4) The AAA balance can be reduced below zero. (Basis may not.)
         a) Distributions do not reduce AAA below zero.
   e. The OAA represents a cumulative balance of tax-exempt interest earned and life insurance proceeds, reduced by expenses incurred in earning it.
   f. Subchapter C E&P. An S corporation does not have E&P unless it was formerly a C corporation or acquired E&P in a tax-free reorganization, e.g., a merger.
      1) Subchapter C E&P are not adjusted for any S corporation items of income (or loss, deduction, or credit) passed through to shareholders.

2. **Distributions of Property**

   a. An S corporation recognizes gain realized on the distribution of appreciated property (FMV > basis).

      1) The amount and character of the gain and its treatment are determined as if the distributed property were sold to the shareholder at its FMV.

         a) Ordinary income results if the property is depreciable in the hands of a more-than-50% shareholder.

      2) The gain is passed through pro rata to each shareholder, and the shareholder's basis in his or her stock and the AAA is increased by his or her shares as if the S corporation had sold the property.

         a) The distributee shareholder must determine the proper treatment of the distribution.

EXAMPLE 17-12 **Gain on Property Distribution**
The S corporation sells an investment asset with a basis of $15,000 for $23,000. The corporation reports an $8,000 gain, which flows through to the shareholders.

   b. When loss property (basis > FMV) is distributed, no loss may be recognized by the S corporation.

      1) The loss is passed through to the shareholders and is nondeductible.

         a) Each shareholder must reduce the basis in his or her stock in the S corporation and take a FMV basis in the property distributed.

         b) The distributee shareholder must determine the proper treatment of the distribution.

      2) Sale to a non-related party instead of distribution results in pass-through of loss.

EXAMPLE 17-13 **Loss on Property Distribution**
The S corporation has a capital asset with a basis of $7,000 and a FMV of $5,000, which it distributes to the sole shareholder. The corporation has a nondeductible loss of $2,000. The shareholder reduces basis by $7,000 and has a $5,000 basis in the asset. If the corporation sold the asset and distributed the proceeds, the shareholder would have a $2,000 deductible loss.

   c. An S corporation is not required to recognize gain on the liquidating distributions of certain installment obligations.

      1) The shareholder treats each payment as a passed-through item from the S corporation.

Shareholder Treatment

3. Shareholder treatment of distributions from the S corporation is determined at the end of the S corporation's tax year. The AAA, OAA, basis in shareholders' stock, and basis in corporate-shareholder debt must be adjusted for the S corporation's items of income, deduction, etc., for the entire tax year before determining the proper treatment by the shareholders for the distributions.

   a. S corporations with no E&P (i.e., accumulated earnings and profits). Shareholder treatment of distributions is straightforward when the S corporation has no Subchapter C E&P.

      1) That portion of distributions that does not exceed the basis in the shareholder's stock in the S corporation is treated as tax-free return of capital.

      2) Excess over basis is treated as gain on sale of the stock.

         a) The character depends on the nature of the stock in the hands of the shareholder and his or her holding period.

   b. If there are Subchapter C E&P, the distribution is first treated as return of capital (tax-free) to the extent of the shareholder's AAA balance (up to any basis in the shareholder's stock).

      1) Excess distribution beyond the AAA is dividend income to the extent of Subchapter C E&P in the corporation.

      2) Excess distribution beyond Subchapter C E&P is return of capital to the extent of OAA.

      3) Excess distribution beyond OAA is return of capital to the extent of any remaining basis in the stock.

      4) Any excess distribution over remaining basis distributed is treated as gain from the sale of the stock.

S Corporation without Subchapter C E&P

Shareholder Distribution	Tax Result
To extent of basis in stock	Not subject to tax; reduces basis in stock
In excess of basis of stock	Taxed as capital gain

S Corporation with Subchapter C E&P

Shareholder Distribution	Tax Result
To extent of AAA	Not subject to tax; reduces AAA and basis in stock
To extent of C corporation E&P	Taxed as a dividend; reduces E&P, but not basis in stock
To extent of OAA	Not subject to tax; reduces OAA and basis in stock
To extent of basis in stock	Not subject to tax; reduces basis in stock
In excess of basis	Taxed as capital gain

NOTE: In the above determination of shareholder treatment of distributions, any amount to be treated as tax-free return of capital reduces the shareholder's basis in his or her stock.

EXAMPLE 17-14 Shareholder Treatment of Distributions

A single-owner S corporation has an AAA of $12,000 and E&P of $8,000. The shareholder's basis is $25,000. The first $12,000 of any distribution reduces AAA to $0 ($12,000 AAA – $12,000 of distribution) and shareholder basis by $12,000 to $13,000 ($25,000 basis – $12,000 of distribution) and is nontaxable. The next $8,000 of distributions is classified as dividend income and reduces E&P to $0 ($8,000 E&P – $8,000 of distribution). The next $13,000 (i.e., the balance of basis calculated previously) of distributions is a tax-free reduction of basis and is classified as return of capital. Any distributions above $33,000 ($25,000 basis + $8,000 E&P) will be taxed as capital gain income.

c. An election may be made to treat distributions as coming first from Subchapter C E&P.

   1) This results in ordinary dividend income to the distributee shareholder to the extent of the E&P.

      a) Any excess distribution is treated as a return of capital or gain on the sale of stock.

d. Cash distributions within a relatively short transition period subsequent to termination of an S-election are treated as return of capital to the extent of the AAA.

   1) Basis in shareholder stock is reduced.

e. Form 1099-DIV is used to report any distribution that is in excess of the accumulated adjustments account and that is treated as a dividend to the extent of accumulated earnings and profits.

Stop & Review

You have completed the outline for this subunit.
Study multiple-choice questions 15 through 21 beginning on page 388.

QUESTIONS

17.1 Eligibility and Election

1. Which of the following characteristics can disqualify a corporation from S corporation status?

A. Corporation Z has variation in voting rights in its one class of stock.

B. Corporation M has 101 shareholders, including a husband and wife.

C. Corporation B has voting and nonvoting stock.

D. Corporation T has as its shareholders an individual, an estate, and a partnership.

Answer (D) is correct.

REQUIRED: The action that will prevent a current-year S corporation election.

DISCUSSION: An S corporation may not have more than 100 shareholders; shareholders who are not individuals, estates, or certain kinds of trusts and exempt organizations; a nonresident alien as a shareholder; or more than one class of stock [Sec. 1361(b)]. Having a partnership as a shareholder will prevent a corporation from making an S corporation election.

Answer (A) is incorrect. Variation in voting rights of one class of stock is permitted and will not disqualify a corporation from S corporation status. **Answer (B) is incorrect.** Related taxpayers are considered one taxpayer for purposes of qualifying under the 100 shareholder limit. **Answer (C) is incorrect.** These characteristics will not disqualify a corporation from S corporation status.

2. Which of the following is NOT eligible to be a shareholder of an S corporation?

A. A domestic partnership.

B. Individuals who are not nonresident aliens.

C. Estates.

D. Exempt organizations described in Sec. 401(a) or 501(c)(3).

Answer (A) is correct.

REQUIRED: The participants that are not eligible in an S corporation.

DISCUSSION: The number of shareholders may not exceed 100. A husband and wife, and their estates, are considered a single shareholder for this purpose. A nonresident alien (NRA) may not own any shares. Each shareholder must be either an individual, an estate (including estates of individuals in bankruptcy), or a qualified trust. Certain small business trusts and tax-exempt organizations can be shareholders. Partnerships and corporations may not be shareholders. Additionally, Charitable Remainder Unitrusts and Charitable Remainder Annuity Trusts are not eligible to be shareholders.

Answer (B) is incorrect. These individuals are eligible to qualify as a shareholder of an S corporation. **Answer (C) is incorrect.** Estates are eligible to qualify as a shareholder of an S corporation. **Answer (D) is incorrect.** Exempt organizations described in Sec. 401(a) or 501(c)(3) are eligible to qualify as a shareholder of an S corporation.

3. All of the following events would cause an S corporation to cease qualifying as an S corporation EXCEPT

A. Having more than 100 shareholders.

B. The transfer of its stock to a corporation.

C. The transfer of its stock to a resident alien.

D. The election is revoked with the consent of shareholders who, at the time the revocation is made, had 55% of the stock.

Answer (C) is correct.

REQUIRED: The event that would not cause an S corporation disqualification.

DISCUSSION: A resident alien is an individual who qualifies to be a shareholder of an S corporation. Therefore, the transfer of stock to a resident alien does not disqualify a corporation from S corporation status.

Answer (A) is incorrect. An S corporation may not have more than 100 shareholders. **Answer (B) is incorrect.** Partnerships and corporations may not be shareholders. **Answer (D) is incorrect.** This event would cause an S corporation to cease qualifying as an S corporation.

4. All of the following events will cause the termination of an S corporation's S election EXCEPT

A. Transaction that results in over 100 shareholders.

B. Donation of stock to a tax-exempt organization under 501(c)(4).

C. Sale of stock to a resident alien.

D. Failing the passive income test for 3 consecutive years.

Answer (C) is correct.

REQUIRED: The event that will not cause the termination of an S corporation's S election.

DISCUSSION: Upon the occurrence of a terminating event, an S corporation becomes a C corporation. The IRS may waive termination that is a result of the corporation's ceasing to be a small business corporation or failing the passive income test for 3 consecutive years when it has Subchapter C earnings and profits (E&P) if the terminating event is found to be inadvertent and is corrected within a reasonable time after it is discovered. An S corporation election is terminated by any of the following: (1) an effective revocation, which requires the consent of a majority of the shareholders (voting and nonvoting); (2) any eligibility requirement not being satisfied on any day; or (3) passive investment income (PII) termination. One eligibility requirement is that shareholders be individuals who are citizens or resident aliens of the United States. Therefore, sale of stock to a resident alien does not terminate the election.

Answer (A) is incorrect. An S corporation cannot have over 100 shareholders. **Answer (B) is incorrect.** Only charitable organizations under Sec. 501(c)(3), not civic leagues under Sec. 501(c)(4), are eligible shareholders. **Answer (D) is incorrect.** The election is terminated if the corporation has passive investment income exceeding 25% of its gross receipts for 3 consecutive years.

5. Which of the following statements regarding the termination of an S corporation election is true?

A. The election may be revoked with the consent of shareholders who, at the time the revocation is made, hold more than 50% of the number of issued and outstanding shares.

B. The election may be revoked by the board of directors of the corporation only if they are not shareholders.

C. The election terminates automatically if the corporation derives more than 25% of its gross receipts from passive investment income during the year.

D. The election may be revoked by the Internal Revenue Service if there is a history of 10 years of operating losses.

Answer (A) is correct.

REQUIRED: The true statement regarding the termination of an S corporation election.

DISCUSSION: Upon the occurrence of a terminating event, an S corporation becomes a C corporation. An S corporation election is terminated if shareholders collectively holding more than 50% of the outstanding shares of stock on the day of the revocation (voting and nonvoting) consent, any eligibility requirement not being satisfied on any day, and/or a passive income investment income (PII) termination.

Answer (B) is incorrect. Shareholders holding more than 50% of both the voting and nonvoting shares of the corporation may consent to the termination in an effective revocation. The board of directors may not terminate the election. **Answer (C) is incorrect.** The passive investment income (PII) termination occurs when, for 3 consecutive tax years, the corporation has both Subchapter C E&P on the last day and PII that is greater than 25% of gross receipts. **Answer (D) is incorrect.** No such rule exists. The IRS will not terminate an S corporation election if the corporation has 10 years of operating losses.

17.2 Operations

6. Foster's RV Sales, Inc., is an S corporation with the following activity during 2022:

Gross sales of RVs and campers	$500,000
Operating expenses	300,000
Interest income	1,000
Charitable contributions	3,000
Sec. 179 expense	10,000

How much ordinary income from trade or business activities will be reported on Schedule K, *Shareholder's Pro Rata Items*?

A. $188,000

B. $190,000

C. $198,000

D. $200,000

Answer (D) is correct.

REQUIRED: The income reported on Schedule K for an S corporation.

DISCUSSION: Items of income, gain, expense, loss, and credit must be separately stated if those items are specially treated for tax purposes at the shareholder level. These items include interest income, charitable contributions, and the Sec. 179 expense. Therefore, Foster will report $200,000 ($500,000 – $300,000) as ordinary income on Schedule K.

Answer (A) is incorrect. Interest income, charitable contributions, and Sec. 179 expense are separately stated items. **Answer (B) is incorrect.** The Sec. 179 expense is not included in ordinary income. **Answer (C) is incorrect.** The interest income and charitable contributions are not included in ordinary income.

7. What is the non-separately stated income amount of a calendar-year S corporation operating on an accrual basis with the following items?

Gross receipts	$300,000
Interest income	25,000
Royalty income	10,000
Salary paid to shareholder	20,000

A. $300,000

B. $55,000

C. $320,000

D. $280,000

Answer (D) is correct.

REQUIRED: The non-separately stated income amount for an S corporation.

DISCUSSION: Items of income, gain, expense, loss, and credit must be separately stated if those items are specially treated for tax purposes at the shareholder level. These items include interest income and royalty income. Therefore, $280,000 ($300,000 – $20,000) is ordinary income and not separately stated.

Answer (A) is incorrect. Compensation paid to a shareholder is not separately stated. **Answer (B) is incorrect.** Interest income and royalty income are not included, but gross receipts are included. Also, the salary paid to the shareholder is an expense. **Answer (C) is incorrect.** The salary paid to the shareholder is not income; it is an expense.

8. Which of the following would NOT reduce a shareholder's basis in S corporation stock?

A. A shareholder's pro-rata share of an expense not deductible in computing the corporation's taxable income and not chargeable to the capital account.

B. A shareholder's share of all loss and deduction items of the S corporation that are separately stated and passed through to the shareholder.

C. A shareholder's pro-rata share of any non-separately stated loss of the S corporation.

D. The excess of the corporation's deductions for depletion over the basis of the property subject to depletion.

Answer (D) is correct.

REQUIRED: The item that would not reduce a shareholder's basis in an S corporation's stock.

DISCUSSION: Per Sec. 1367(a)(2)(E), the shareholder's basis in S corporation stock is reduced by the amount of the shareholder's deduction for depletion only to the extent it is not in excess of the shareholder's proportionate share of the adjusted basis of the property.

Answer (A) is incorrect. The pro rata share of a nondeductible expense and one not chargeable to a capital account would reduce the basis. **Answer (B) is incorrect.** The separately stated items of loss and deduction do decrease the basis. **Answer (C) is incorrect.** The pro rata share of non-separately stated losses reduces the shareholder's basis in the stock.

9. Magnolia Corporation, a calendar-year S corporation, was formed on January 1, Year 1. Kathy owns 25% of Magnolia's outstanding stock, which she purchased for $20,000. In Year 1, Kathy guaranteed a corporate loan for $40,000. In Year 2, Kathy made payments on the loan totaling $10,000. Magnolia had losses of $90,000 and $60,000 in Year 1 and Year 2, respectively. What is the amount of the unallowed loss that Kathy can carry over to Year 3?

A. $0

B. $7,500

C. $10,000

D. $17,500

Answer (B) is correct.

REQUIRED: The amount of loss deductible by an S corporation shareholder carried over to future years.

DISCUSSION: A shareholder of an S corporation may include a pro rata share of loss in income, limited to the shareholder's basis in the stock. Generally, the shareholder's original basis is its cost. If a shareholder guarantees a loan to an S corporation, the loan does not increase the shareholder's basis. If, however, the shareholder makes payments on the loan, the payments increase the shareholder's basis. Kathy's basis in the stock was $20,000, the cost. Kathy may deduct only $20,000 of her $22,500 loss in Year 1 ($90,000 × 25%). After deducting the loss, her basis is $0. In Year 2, Kathy makes loan payments of $10,000. This makes her basis $10,000 for Year 1. Kathy may deduct the remaining loss of $2,500 from Year 1 in Year 2 ($22,500 – $20,000). Therefore, Kathy may deduct up to $7,500 ($10,000 – $2,500) of her $15,000 loss from Year 2 ($60,000 × 25%). She may, however, carry the remaining $7,500 loss over to Year 3.

Answer (A) is incorrect. Kathy may not deduct all of the losses in Year 1 and Year 2. The loss deduction is limited to the basis in the stock. **Answer (C) is incorrect.** The loss deduction is limited to the basis in the stock. **Answer (D) is incorrect.** The payment of an S corporation's loan obligations increases basis.

10. Which of the following are considered separately stated items for Form 1120-S shareholders?

A. Charitable contributions.

B. Low-income housing credit.

C. Section 179 expense deduction.

D. All of the answers are correct.

Answer (D) is correct.

REQUIRED: The items considered separately stated items for Form 1120-S.

DISCUSSION: An S corporation passes a pro rata share of its total income (loss) through to the individual shareholders except for items that require separate treatment by the shareholder. Charitable contributions made by the corporation, Sec. 179 deduction, and low-income housing credit are all items that must be separately stated.

11. Which of the following would NOT increase the basis of a shareholder's stock in an S corporation?

A. All separately stated income items of the S corporation, including tax-exempt income.

B. Any non-separately stated income of the S corporation.

C. Capital gains tax paid by the shareholder.

D. The amount of deductions for depletion that is more than the basis of the property being depleted.

Answer (C) is correct.

REQUIRED: The item that would not increase the basis of a shareholder's stock in an S corporation.

DISCUSSION: If the shareholder paid capital gains in disposing of the stock, this tax does not increase the basis of the shareholder's remaining stock.

12. Rap, Inc., was organized in January 2022 and immediately made an S election. Rap's stock is entirely owned by Howard, who contributed $40,000 to start the business. Rap reported the following results for the 2022 year:

Ordinary income	$36,000
Short-term capital loss	4,000
Charitable contributions	1,000
Tax-exempt income	1,000
Sec. 179 deduction	10,000

On April 12, 2022, Howard received a $30,000 cash distribution from the corporation. What is the adjusted basis of his stock on January 1, 2023?

A. $41,000

B. $32,000

C. $31,000

D. $10,000

Answer (B) is correct.

REQUIRED: The basis of an S corporation shareholder's stock after a distribution.

DISCUSSION: The adjusted basis of the shareholder's stock is figured at year end with increases for the shareholder's pro rata share of all income items, including tax-exempt income, that are separately stated and any nonseparately stated income. Also, all separately and nonseparately stated losses and deduction items decrease the basis of the shareholder's stock on a pro rata basis. Howard's stock basis on January 1, 2023, is $32,000.

Original basis	$ 40,000
Ordinary income	36,000
Tax-exempt income	1,000
Short-term capital loss	(4,000)
Charitable contributions	(1,000)
Sec. 179 deduction	(10,000)
Cash distribution	(30,000)
Adjusted basis	$ 32,000

Answer (A) is incorrect. The Sec. 179 deduction and charitable contributions reduce the basis. **Answer (C) is incorrect.** The charitable contributions reduce the basis. **Answer (D) is incorrect.** Other factors besides the cash distribution are considered.

13. John is the sole shareholder of Maple Corporation, a qualified S corporation. At January 1, Year 1, John has a basis in Maple Corporation of $2,000. The corporation's Year 1 tax return shows the following:

Ordinary income	$10,000
Interest income	$ 1,000
Nondeductible expenses	$ 2,000
Real estate rental loss	$ 5,000
Section 179 deduction	$ 1,500
Distributions to John	$ 3,000

What is John's basis in Maple Corporation at the end of Year 1?

A. $0

B. $3,500

C. $4,500

D. $1,500

Answer (D) is correct.

REQUIRED: The resulting shareholder's basis in an S corporation.

DISCUSSION: The shareholder of an S corporation's stock must increase his or her basis for all items of income to the S corporation that are both separately and nonseparately stated. The basis in John's stock would equal the following:

Beginning basis	$ 2,000
Ordinary income	10,000
Interest income	1,000
Nondeductible expenses	(2,000)
Real estate rental loss	(5,000)
Sec. 179 deduction	(1,500)
Distributions to John	(3,000)
Ending basis	$ 1,500

14. On January 1, Year 1, Mr. Karl purchased 50% of Olive, Inc., an S corporation, for $75,000. At the end of Year 1, Olive, Inc., incurred an ordinary loss of $160,000. How much of the loss can Mr. Karl deduct on his personal income tax return for Year 1?

A. $160,000

B. $80,000

C. $75,000

D. $37,500

Answer (C) is correct.

REQUIRED: The amount of loss a shareholder can deduct on his or her personal income tax return.

DISCUSSION: The amount of losses and deductions an S corporation shareholder can claim is limited to the adjusted basis of the shareholder's stock. Thus, for Year 1, Karl can deduct only $75,000 of the $80,000 loss ($160,000 ordinary loss × 50%) allocated to him.

Answer (A) is incorrect. The shareholder may not deduct the entire ordinary loss. **Answer (B) is incorrect.** The loss may not reduce Mr. Karl's basis below zero. **Answer (D) is incorrect.** Half of the shareholder's basis is not the limit on deductibility.

17.3 Distributions

15. If an S corporation has no accumulated earnings and profits from prior operations as a C corporation, any amount distributed to a shareholder

A. Must be returned to the S corporation.

B. Increases the shareholder's basis in the stock.

C. Decreases the shareholder's basis in the stock.

D. Has no effect on the shareholder's basis in the stock.

Answer (C) is correct.

REQUIRED: The distribution treatment of an S corporation, previously a C corporation, when no accumulated earnings and profits exist.

DISCUSSION: Section 1368(d) provides that if there are no accumulated earnings and profits, the S corporation treats distributions as a reduction in the shareholder's basis and therefore a nontaxable return of capital. If the entire basis is exhausted, any additional distribution is treated as a gain on the sale or exchange of property [Reg. 1.1368–1(c)].

Answer (A) is incorrect. The distribution does not have to be returned to the corporation. **Answer (B) is incorrect.** It decreases, not increases, the shareholder's basis. **Answer (D) is incorrect.** There is an effect on the basis: a decrease.

16. Twister, an S corporation, has no earnings and profits. In Year 1, Twister distributed property with a fair market value of $65,000 and an adjusted basis of $52,000 to Carlos, its sole shareholder. After recognizing his share of any corporate gain or loss, his adjusted basis in Twister's stock at year end was $50,000. How should the distribution be handled by Carlos?

A. $50,000 as return of capital and $15,000 as nontaxable distributions.

B. $50,000 as return of capital and $15,000 as taxable capital gain.

C. $50,000 as return of capital and $2,000 as taxable capital gain.

D. $50,000 as nontaxable distributions.

Answer (B) is correct.

REQUIRED: The treatment of an S corporation distribution when the S corporation has no accumulated earnings and profits (E&P).

DISCUSSION: If the S corporation has no accumulated E&P, any distribution a shareholder receives is a return of capital to the extent of the shareholder's basis. Any excess will be a gain from the sale of property. Therefore, Carlos will treat the distribution as a $50,000 return of capital and the remaining $15,000 as a taxable capital gain.

Answer (A) is incorrect. The remaining $15,000 is treated as a taxable capital gain. **Answer (C) is incorrect.** If property other than cash is distributed, the amount of the distribution is the FMV of the property. **Answer (D) is incorrect.** The distribution is nontaxable only to the extent of the shareholder's basis.

17. If an S corporation, which has accumulated earnings and profits (AE&P), is allowed to treat shareholder distributions as being made from the AE&P account, how will those distributions be taxed, if at all?

A. They will be taxed as dividend income.

B. They will be taxed as ordinary earned income.

C. They will be taxed as capital gain income.

D. They will not be taxed, as it would be deemed a return of shareholder capital.

Answer (A) is correct.

REQUIRED: The tax treatment of AE&P distributions.

DISCUSSION: Any part of a distribution from either current or accumulated earnings and profits is reported to the shareholder as dividend income.

18. Jenny Corporation (an S corporation) is owned entirely by Craig. At the beginning of Year 1, Craig's adjusted basis in his Jenny Corporation stock was $20,000. Jenny reported ordinary income of $5,000 and a capital loss of $10,000. Craig received a cash distribution of $35,000 in November Year 1. What is Craig's gain from the distribution?

A. $0

B. $10,000

C. $20,000

D. $35,000

Answer (B) is correct.

REQUIRED: The sole shareholder's gain from the distribution from an S corporation.

DISCUSSION: The basis is increased by the ordinary income to $25,000. The $35,000 distribution is taken next, and there is a $10,000 gain since it exceeds the basis. The capital loss is nondeductible because there is no basis, and it is carried over.

Answer (A) is incorrect. If the distribution is greater than the basis, the excess is taxable as a sale or an exchange of property (a taxable capital gain). **Answer (C) is incorrect.** The distribution is taken before the deduction for the capital loss. **Answer (D) is incorrect.** Only the difference between the distribution and the basis, not the entire distribution, is taxable.

19. At the end of 2014, Green, Inc., was a C corporation with $50,000 in earnings and profits. Green elected to be treated as an S corporation beginning with the 2015 year. At the end of 2022, Green has a balance of $10,000 in its other adjustments account, a balance of $20,000 in its accumulated adjustment account, and a balance of $50,000 in earnings and profits. Green made cash distributions of $25,000 to each of its 50% shareholders. Green makes no elections relating to the source of distributions. What is the remaining Green, Inc., earnings and profits balance after the shareholder distributions?

A. $50,000

B. $40,000

C. $30,000

D. $20,000

Answer (D) is correct.

REQUIRED: The effect on earnings and profits after a distribution.

DISCUSSION: The accumulated adjustments account represents the cumulative income and loss recognized for S corporations after 1982. Regulation Sec. 1.1368-2 provides that distributions from an S corporation reduce stock basis to the extent the AAA is positive and sufficient basis exists in the stock. The distribution is tax-free to the extent of AAA. If the distribution exceeds the AAA, then the additional distribution is taxable and is treated as coming from accumulated E&P. Since Green, Inc., had $20,000 in its accumulated adjustment account and $50,000 in its earnings and profits, the first $20,000 is treated as coming from the AAA. The remaining $30,000 distribution is subtracted from E&P. The remaining balance in E&P is $20,000 ($50,000 E&P – $30,000 distribution).

Answer (A) is incorrect. E&P was reduced by $30,000. **Answer (B) is incorrect.** Distributions cannot be treated as coming from the other adjustments account (OAA). **Answer (C) is incorrect.** Distributions cannot come from the OAA.

20. Thunder, an S corporation, has no earnings and profits (E&P). Thunder distributed $100,000 to Ben, its only shareholder. His adjusted basis in Thunder's stock is $40,000. The amount that exceeds his adjusted basis in the stock is treated as

A. Previously taxed income.

B. A nontaxable distribution.

C. A taxable dividend.

D. A taxable capital gain.

Answer (D) is correct.

REQUIRED: The treatment of a distribution to a shareholder that exceeds the shareholder's adjusted basis.

DISCUSSION: S corporation distributions to a shareholder are generally a nontaxable return of the shareholder's basis if the S corporation does not have any accumulated E&P. However, if the distributions are more than the shareholder's basis, the excess is taxable as a sale or an exchange of property (a taxable capital gain).

Answer (A) is incorrect. The amount does not constitute previously taxed income. **Answer (B) is incorrect.** The amount exceeds the shareholder's adjusted basis. **Answer (C) is incorrect.** The corporation had no accumulated E&P.

21. Quantum Leap, an S corporation, has $10,000 in accumulated earnings and profits. In Year 1, Quantum Leap distributed property with a fair market value of $75,000 and an adjusted basis of $62,000 to Edward, its sole shareholder. After recognizing his share of any corporate gain or loss, his adjusted basis in Quantum Leap's stock at the end of the year was $60,000. How should Edward handle the distribution?

A. $60,000 as return of capital and $15,000 is nontaxable distributions.

B. $10,000 as dividend income, $60,000 as return of capital, and $5,000 as taxable capital gain.

C. $60,000 as return of capital and $2,000 as taxable capital gain.

D. $70,000 is a nontaxable distribution.

Answer (B) is correct.

REQUIRED: The character of a distribution to an S corporation shareholder.

DISCUSSION: The problem does not give the amount of the accumulated adjustment account (AAA), which is distributed first as a tax-free return of basis. However, the amount of AAA cannot exceed $60,000 since the basis of the stock is $60,000. Therefore, the accumulated earnings and profits would be fully distributed as dividend income of $10,000. Next, the remaining basis ($60,000 minus the AAA balance) is distributed tax-free. The remaining $5,000 is a taxable capital gain ($75,000 distribution minus the $60,000 basis in the stock and the $10,000 dividend).

Answer (A) is incorrect. The $15,000 is taxable. **Answer (C) is incorrect.** The shareholder treats the distribution as a dividend only up to the accumulated E&P amount. The shareholder treats the remaining distribution as a return of capital up to the amount of basis. Any amount left over is treated as a taxable capital gain. **Answer (D) is incorrect.** The shareholder treats the distribution as a dividend only up to the accumulated E&P amount. The shareholder also treats the remaining distribution as a return of capital up to the amount of basis. Any amount left over is treated as a taxable capital gain.

Go to Online Course

Access the **Gleim EA Premium Review System** featuring our SmartAdapt technology from your Gleim Personal Classroom to continue your studies.

You will experience a personalized study environment with exam-emulating multiple-choice questions.

STUDY UNIT EIGHTEEN

DECEDENT, ESTATE, AND TRUST INCOME TAX RETURNS

(17 pages of outline)

This study unit addresses different kinds of income taxes. Estates and trusts (also called fiduciaries) are legal entities defined by the assets they hold. These assets produce income. The entities are subject to tax on that income. This is referred to as fiduciary income taxation. The formula for computing this fiduciary tax is the individual income tax formula, modified for the distribution deduction and other special rules. Furthermore, the beneficiaries of these fiduciary entities, rather than the fiduciary, are personally subject to income tax on certain fiduciary income.

18.1 DECEDENT'S FINAL INCOME TAX RETURN

The final individual income tax return is due at the same time the decedent's return would have been due had death not occurred.

Inclusions in Income

1. The decedent's income includible on the final return is generally determined as if the person were still alive except that the taxable period ends on the date of death.
   a. Cash-method taxpayers include only the income that was actually received or constructively received before the date of death, that is, income that was made available for use by the decedent without restriction.
   b. Accrual-method taxpayers include any amounts earned and accrued before death.
   c. For partnership income, the death of a partner does not generally close the partnership's tax year.
      1) For partnership tax years ending on or before a partner's death, the distributive share should be included on the final return.
      2) For partnership tax years ending after the date of death, the partner's distributive share before death is included on the final tax return.
      3) These rules apply for cash- and accrual-method taxpayers in all situations except for self-employment tax purposes.
   d. The person who is required to file the final income tax return of the decedent can elect to include all interest earned on bonds transferred as a result of death if the cash-method decedent had chosen not to report the interest each year.

2. **Deductions and Credits**
   a. A full standard deduction may be taken unless deductions are itemized.
   b. If deductions are itemized, **medical expenses** paid before death by the decedent are deductible.
      1) This includes amounts paid for the decedent, the decedent's spouse, and the decedent's dependents.
      2) If medical expenses are paid out of the estate during the 1-year period beginning with the day after death, an election may be made to also deduct them on the return for the year incurred.
      3) Any medical expenses claimed on the decedent's final income tax return may not be claimed on the estate tax return.
   c. A decedent's deduction for **NOLs** from business must be taken on the final return.
      1) Any deduction for capital losses must be taken on the final return.
         a) The capital loss deduction is limited to $3,000 in any year.
      2) There are no carryforwards of unused losses and deductions, and the limitations on losses and deductions still apply in this situation.
   d. Any **credits, taxes, and payments** that the decedent would have applied had (s)he not died during the year are applied in full in the final return.

<u>**Self-Employment Tax**</u>

3. Self-employment income for a decedent includes income actually or constructively received or accrued, depending on the decedent's accounting method.
   a. For self-employment tax purposes only, the decedent's self-employment income includes the decedent's distributive share of a partnership's income or loss through the end of the month in which death occurred.
4. The return should only be signed by the personal representative and/or an individual who prepares the return for pay.
   a. If an individual prepares the return free of charge, (s)he should not sign the return.

You have completed the outline for this subunit.
Study multiple-choice questions 1 through 3 beginning on page 408.

18.2 INCOME IN RESPECT OF A DECEDENT (IRD)

IRD is all amounts to which a decedent was entitled as gross income but that were not properly includible in computing taxable income on the final return. The person had a right to receive it prior to death, e.g., salary was earned, or a sale contract was entered into.

1. Not includible on the final income tax return of a cash-method (CM) taxpayer are amounts not received. Not includible on the final income tax return of an accrual-method (AM) taxpayer are amounts not properly accrued.

Items of Income in Respect of a Decedent

IRD	Not IRD
Salary earned prior to, but not received before, death of a CM taxpayer	**Salary** earned and accrued by AM taxpayer
Collection after death of A/R of CM taxpayer	**Collection** of A/R by AM taxpayer
Gain on sale of property by CM taxpayer received not before death	**Gain** on sale of property received before death
Rent accrued but not received before death by CM taxpayer	**Rent** received before death
Interest on installment debt accrued before death by CM taxpayer	**Interest** on installment debt accrued after death by AM taxpayer
Installment income recognized after death on contract entered into before death	**Installment** contract income recognized before death

2. IRD is reported by the person receiving the income as if the recipient were the decedent.
   a. The cash method applies to income once designated IRD.
   b. IRD received by a trust or estate is **fiduciary income**.
3. A right to receive IRD has a transferred basis. The basis is not stepped-up to FMV on the date of death, as is generally the case for property acquired from a decedent.

EXAMPLE 18-1 Right to Receive IRD -- Transferred Basis

Mrs. Hart earned 2 weeks' salary of $2,000 that had not been paid when she died. As a cash-method taxpayer, her basis in the right to receive the $2,000 was $0. When her estate received the income, it had $2,000 of ordinary income because its basis in the right to receive it was also $0. Note that the $2,000 is not reported on Mrs. Hart's final return.

4. IRD has the same character and tax status it would have had in the hands of the decedent.

5. IRD is taxable as income to the recipient and is includible in the gross estate. Double tax is mitigated by deductions.
   a. Deductions in respect of a decedent.
      1) Expenses accrued before death, but not deductible on the final return because the decedent used the cash method, are deductible when paid if otherwise deductible.
         a) They are deductible on the return of the taxpayer reporting the IRD (Form 1041).
         b) They are also deductible on the estate tax return (Form 706).
   b. Deduction for estate tax. Estate taxes attributable to IRD included in the gross estate are deductible on the recipient's income tax return and the fiduciary income tax return (Form 1041).
      1) Administrative expenses and debts of a decedent are deductible on the estate tax return [Form 706, *United States Estate (and Generation-Skipping Transfer) Tax Return*]. Some of them may also be deductible on the estate's income tax return (Form 1041, *U.S. Income Tax Return for Estates and Trusts*).
         a) Double deductions are disallowed.
         b) The right to deduct the expenses on Form 706 must be waived in order to claim them on Form 1041.
      2) Deduction (on Form 1041) is allowed for any excess of the federal estate tax over the amount of the federal estate tax if the IRD had been excluded from the gross estate.
   c. The tax returns that would report IRD include, but are not limited to, the following:
      1) The decedent's estate, Form 1041, if the decedent's estate receives right to the income.
      2) The beneficiary's Form 1040, if the right to income arising out of the decedent's death is passed directly to the beneficiary and is never acquired by the decedent's estate.
      3) The Form 1040 of any person to whom the decedent's estate properly distributes the income.

      NOTE: The decedent's final Form 1040 would not include IRD.

EXAMPLE 18-2 IRD -- Return Presentation

Frank Johnson owned and operated an apple orchard. He used the cash method of accounting. He sold and delivered 1,000 bushels of apples to a canning factory for $2,000, but did not receive payment before his death. The proceeds from the sale are income in respect of a decedent. When the estate was settled, payment had not been made and the estate transferred the right to the payment to his widow. When Frank's widow collects the $2,000, she must include that amount in her return. The amount is not reported on the final return of the decedent or on the return of the estate.

EXAMPLE 18-3 IRD -- Recognized Income

Assume the same facts as in Example 18-2, except that Frank used the accrual method of accounting. The amount accrued from the sale of the apples would be included on his final return. Neither the estate nor the widow would realize income in respect of a decedent when the money is later paid.

EXAMPLE 18-4 IRD -- Recognized Gain

On February 1, George High, a cash-method taxpayer, sold his tractor for $3,000, payable March 1 of the same year. His adjusted basis in the tractor was $2,000. George died on February 15, before receiving payment. The gain to be reported as income in respect of a decedent is the $1,000 difference between the decedent's basis in the property and the sale proceeds. In other words, the income in respect of a decedent is the gain the decedent would have realized had he lived.

EXAMPLE 18-5 IRD -- Recognized Income Assignment

Cathy O'Neil was entitled to a large salary payment at the date of her death. The amount was to be paid in five annual installments. The estate, after collecting two installments, distributed the right to the remaining installments to the beneficiary. The payments are income in respect of a decedent. None of the payments were includible on Cathy's final return. The estate must include in its income the two installments it received, and the beneficiary must include in income each of the three installments as the installments are received.

EXAMPLE 18-6 IRD -- Recognized Income Assignment

Paige inherited the right to receive renewal commissions on life insurance sold by her father before his death. Paige inherited the right from her mother, who acquired it by bequest from Paige's father. Paige's mother died before she received all the commissions she had the right to receive, so Paige received the rest. The commissions are income in respect of a decedent. None of these commissions were includible on Paige's father's final return. The commissions received by Paige's mother were included in her income. The commissions Paige received are not includible in Paige's mother's income, even on her final return. Paige must include them in her income.

Stop & Review

You have completed the outline for this subunit.
Study multiple-choice questions 4 and 5 on page 409.

18.3 INCOME TAXATION OF ESTATES AND TRUSTS

Tax is imposed on taxable income of a trust or estate at the following rates for 2022:

Fiduciary Taxable Income Brackets	Applicable Rate
$ 0 – $ 2,750	10%
> 2,750 – 9,850	24% (+ $275)
> 9,850 – 13,450	35% (+ $1,979)
> 13,450	37% (+ $3,239)

Fundamentals

1. Following are some basic definitions and a discussion of filing requirements:
   a. A **simple trust** is formed under an instrument having the following characteristics:
      1) Requires current distribution of all its income
      2) Requires no distribution of the res (i.e., principal)
      3) Provides for no charitable contributions by the trust
   b. A **complex trust** is any trust other than a simple trust. A complex trust can
      1) Accumulate income,
      2) Provide for charitable contributions, and
      3) Distribute amounts other than income.
   c. A **grantor trust** is any trust to the extent the grantor is the effective beneficiary. Income attributable to a trust principal that is treated as owned by the grantor is taxed to the grantor. The trust is disregarded.
      1) A trust is considered a grantor trust when the grantor retains a greater than 5% reversionary interest.
      2) Under Sec. 677(a), a grantor is treated as the owner of a trust, the income of which may be distributed or accumulated for the grantor's spouse (without the approval or consent of an adverse party).
      3) The grantor is also taxed on income from a trust in which the income may be applied for the benefit of the grantor.
         a) Use of income for the support of a dependent is considered the application of income for the benefit of the grantor.
         b) Under Sec. 677(b), however, the income of a trust that may be applied for the support of a dependent is not taxable to the grantor if it is not actually used.
      4) The grantor or other owners with substantial interests have not given up complete dominion and control over the trust property. The trust is not considered a separate legal entity for tax purposes.
      5) All revocable trusts are grantor trusts.

d. The rules for classifying trusts are applied on a year-to-year basis.

e. An estate with gross income greater than or equal to $600 is required to file a tax return. A trust is required to file a return if it has either any taxable income or more than $600 of gross income.

   1) The trustee, executor, or administrator must file the return no later than the 15th day of the 4th month after the close of the entity's tax year.

   2) Form 1041, *U.S. Income Tax Return for Estates and Trusts*, must be used.

   3) If a domestic estate has a beneficiary who is a nonresident alien, the representative must file a return regardless of income.

   4) Estate gross income includes the gain from the sale of property (not gross proceeds).

2. An estate may adopt any tax year ending within 12 months after death.

   a. Most trusts must adopt a calendar tax year.

   b. Tax-exempt and wholly charitable trusts may qualify to use a fiscal tax year.

   c. A beneficiary includes his or her share of trust income in his or her return for his or her tax year in which the trust's tax year ends.

      1) When distributions are made is irrelevant.

3. Any permissible accounting method may be adopted.

4. The alternative minimum tax applies to trusts and estates. It is determined in the same manner as for individuals.

Principal vs. Income

5. Tax is imposed on taxable income (TI) of trusts and estates, not on items treated as fiduciary principal.

   a. State law defines principal and income of a trust or estate for federal income tax purposes.

      1) Many states have adopted the Revised Uniform Principal and Income Act, some with modifications.

         a) The act and state laws provide that the trust instrument controls designations of fiduciary principal and interest components.

         b) The act and state laws also provide default designations.

   b. Generally, principal is property held eventually to be delivered to the remainderman (the person who inherits or is entitled to inherit the property).

      1) Income is return on, or for use of, the principal. It is held for or distributed to the income beneficiary.

         a) Principal is also referred to as the corpus or res.

      2) Change in form of principal is not taxable income.

Allocation of Fiduciary Receipts and Disbursements

Principal	Income
Receipts	
Consideration for property (e.g., gain on sale)	Business income
Replacement property	Insurance proceeds for lost profits
Nontaxable stock dividends	Interest
Stock splits	Rents
Stock rights	Dividends (taxable)
Liquidating dividends	Extraordinary dividends
Depletion allowance (natural resource property) - Royalties (90%)	Taxable stock dividends
	Depletion allowance (natural resource property) - Royalties (10%)
Disbursements	
Principal payments on debt	Business (ord. & nec.) expenses (e.g., interest expense)
Capital expenditures Major repairs Modifications	Production of income expenses (e.g., maintenance or repair, insurance, rent collection fee)
Fiduciary fees (e.g., management of principal)	Tax on fiduciary income
Tax on principal items (e.g., capital gains)	Depreciation
	Fiduciary fees (e.g., probate court fees and costs)

Income Tax Formula

6. TI of a trust or an estate is computed similarly to that of an individual.
   a. Gross income is computed as for individuals.
      1) It includes dividends, interest, rents, royalties, gain from the sale of property, and income from business, partnerships, trusts, and other sources.
   b. Life insurance proceeds are generally includible in the value of the gross estate but are not considered income of the estate.
   c. Income in respect of a decedent is also taxed as income if it is received by the estate.
   d. Capital gains are taxed to the estate; then the gain must be added to the principal of the estate.
   e. Losses from a passive activity owned by the estate or trust cannot be used to offset portfolio income (interest, dividends, royalties, annuities, etc.) of the estate or trust in determining taxable income.
   f. AGI does apply to fiduciaries for purposes of computing deduction limits.
      1) The standard deduction is not allowed.

g. Deductions. Deductions generally follow those allowable to an individual. Trustee, or administrator, fees and tax return preparation fees are deductible in full if not deducted on the estate tax return.

   1) Depreciation. In default of a trust instrument designation, the act charges depreciation to income.

      a) Absent provisions in the estate instrument apportioning the deduction, the allowable amount must be allocated between the estate and each beneficiary in proportion to the amount of fiduciary income taxable to each party.

      b) Trusts. The trust may deduct depreciation only to the extent a reserve is required or permitted under the trust instrument or local law, and income is set aside for the reserve and actually remains in the trust.

         i) Any part of the deduction in excess of the trust income set aside for the reserve is then allocated between the parties according to the trust instrument.

         ii) If the instrument is silent, allocation of the excess between the trust and each beneficiary is in proportion to the amount of fiduciary income taxable to each.

   2) Fiduciary NOLs are computed without regard to charitable contributions or distribution deductions. Carryover by the fiduciary is permitted.

      a) Pass-through for deduction on personal returns of beneficiaries is allowed only in the year the trust or estate terminates.

      b) Pass-through NOLs and capital loss carryovers are used to calculate the beneficiary's AGI and taxable income.

      c) Estates can claim a deduction for an NOL. The NOL is calculated in the same manner as an individual taxpayer's deduction, except that an estate cannot deduct any distributions to beneficiaries or charitable contributions in arriving at the NOL or NOL carryover.

      d) An unused NOL in the final year of the estate may carry over to the beneficiaries succeeding to the property of the estate.

   3) A fiduciary may deduct a capital loss to the extent of capital gains plus $3,000. Carryover is permitted.

   4) Charitable contributions are deductible only if the governing instrument (e.g., trust) authorizes them. Deductions are not subject to limits based on AGI.

   5) Expenses attributable to tax-exempt income are not deductible.

   6) Personal exemption. A deduction is allowable but not for the year the trust or estate terminates. The amount is $600 for an estate, $300 for a simple trust, and $100 for a complex trust.

h. Credits. Gross regular tax of a fiduciary is offset by most of the same credits available to individuals.

   1) Certain "personal" credits are unavailable.

      a) A fiduciary, for example, has no dependents.

Distribution Deduction

7. The deduction for distributions allocates TI of a trust or estate (gross of distributions) between the fiduciary and its beneficiaries.
   a. Simple trust. The deduction is the lesser of the amount of the distributions (required) minus net tax-exempt income or distributable net income (DNI) minus tax-exempt interest.

Calculating Income Distribution Deduction of Trusts

= Reduce or Eliminate Tax on 1041

Figure 18-1

Visual Memory Aid: For candidates who are visual learners, the figure above and the description below can aid in recalling how the trust distribution deduction is calculated.

Trusts can have mighty high tax rates. That is why it is advantageous to calculate the income distribution deduction, so the income is taxed at the individual rate, which is lower.

The trust fund baby illustrated above is receiving income via the vacuum cleaner with the word "deduct" on it. If the baby receives the money, the baby will pay tax on that income. The distribution deduction will be the **lesser** of the items on the scale: The distributable net income (DNI) versus the required distribution (RD).

1) Generally, DNI is current net accounting income of the fiduciary reduced by any amounts allocated to principal.

Calculating Net Income of Simple Trusts

Figure 18-2

Visual Memory Aid: For candidates who are visual learners, the figure above and the description below can aid in recalling how net income is calculated for simple trusts.

Distributable net income (DNI) = Taxable income – Capital gains + Tax-exempt income

The fisherman illustrated above is hauling in "net" income. Taxable income and tax-exempt income are "stuck" in the net and are included in net income. However, a fish escapes with a capital gain "cap" and dives into the body of water. Remember to subtract capital gains when calculating DNI for simple trusts. The body of water should remind you of "corpus" (i.e., body or principal) of the trust instrument. If capital gains are allocable to the corpus, they are excluded from DNI calculation.

b. Estates and complex trusts. The deduction is the lesser of DNI (minus tax-exempt interest) or distributions.

1) The amount distributed is the lesser of the FMV of the property or the basis of the property in the hands of the beneficiary.

2) The trustee(s) of a complex trust may elect to treat distributions made during the first 65 days of the (trust's) tax year as if they were made on the last day of the preceding tax year.

3) Specific bequests distributed or credited to a beneficiary in no more than three installments are not included as amounts distributed.

4) The fiduciary recognizes no gain on distribution of property unless an estate executor so elects.

5) A fiduciary's basis in distributed property is transferred, along with adjustments for any gain recognized, to the beneficiary. Every $1 of value distributed is treated as if (first) from any current DNI.

a) The instrument might allocate the $1 to current income, accumulated income, or principal.

b) Principal (after DNI) is distributed tax-free.

Distributable Net Income (DNI)

8. DNI is the maximum deductible at the fiduciary level for distributions and the maximum taxable at the beneficiary level. It is taxable income of the fiduciary (trust or estate), adjusted by the following items:

	TI of fiduciary (before the distribution deduction)
+	Personal exemption deduction ($600 estate, $300 simple trust, $100 complex trust)
+	Capital gain allocated to beneficiaries
+	Tax-exempt interest minus any related expenses
+	Charitable deduction adjustment, Form 1041 Schedule A
+	Capital losses allocated to principal
–	Capital gains allocated to principal
–	Taxable stock dividends allocated to principal
–	Extraordinary dividends allocated to principal
=	**DNI**

a. Expenses directly related are allocated first (e.g., interest expense allocated to taxable and exempt interest income). The remaining balance is used to allocate indirect expenses to all income.

b. No adjustment to fiduciary TI is made for the following:

1) Dividends, other than as previously noted
2) NOL deductions
3) Depreciation, if a reserve is established and all income is not distributable
4) Certain expenditures charged to principal, such as trustee fees

a) They reduce income taxable to the beneficiary.

9. **Beneficiary's Taxable Income**

Simple Trust

a. A beneficiary of a simple trust is taxed on the lower of the two amounts listed below.

1) Trust income required to be distributed (even if not distributed)
2) The beneficiary's proportionate share of the trust's DNI

Estates and Complex Trusts

b. A beneficiary of an estate or a complex trust is taxed on amounts of fiduciary income required to be distributed plus additional amounts distributed to the beneficiary.

1) The taxable amount is limited to the beneficiary's share of DNI.

Character

c. The character of the income in the hands of the beneficiary is the same as in the hands of the trust or estate.

EXAMPLE 18-7 Tax-Exempt Income from a Simple Trust
A simple trust distributes all its $10,000 income to its sole beneficiary. Its DNI is also $10,000. Included in the trust income was $1,000 of tax-exempt income. The beneficiary treats $1,000 of the income from the trust as tax-exempt interest and excludes it from his or her personal gross income.

Schedule K-1

d. Schedule K-1 (Form 1041) is used to report the beneficiary's share of income, deductions, and credits from a trust or an estate. The income is reported on the beneficiary's tax return for the year in which the trust or estate year ends.

1) Schedule K-1 also contains detailed content that is required for the taxpayer to calculate the qualified business income deduction.

10. Trusts and estates are required to remit payments of estimated tax. The required amount and due dates of installments are determined in the same manner as for individuals.

a. An estate is not required to pay estimated tax for its first 2 tax years.

b. A trustee may elect to treat any portion of an estimated tax payment by the estate as made by the beneficiary.

1) The amount would also be treated as paid or credited to the beneficiary on the last day of the tax year.

c. An estate of a domestic decedent or a domestic trust that had no tax liability for the full 12-month preceding tax year is not required to make estimated tax payments in the current year.

11. Most estate and trust income tax returns are due on April 15. An extension of up to 5 1/2 months may be granted.

Penalties

Late Filing	Failure to Provide K-1 to Beneficiaries or Recipients of Property Distribution
• 5% (of tax), per month up to 25% • 15%, per month up to 75% if fraudulent • More than 60 days late, minimum equals lesser of $450 or tax due	• $290 (per failure) up to $3,532,500 ($1,177,500 for small businesses with gross receipts ≤ $5 million) per year • Greater of $580 or 10% of reportable items, without any limit if failure is intentional

12. In general, the U.S. owner of a foreign trust is taxed on the income of that trust.
    a. A U.S. person is treated as the owner of a foreign trust under the grantor trust rules, which include someone who transfers assets to a foreign trust that has a U.S. beneficiary of any portion of the trust.
        1) Each U.S. owner should receive a *Foreign Grantor Trust Owner Statement* (Form 3520-A), which includes information about the foreign trust income (s)he must report.
    b. In general, the U.S. beneficiary of a foreign trust will report his or her share of foreign trust income to the extent it is not reported by the transferors to the trust under the grantor trust rules.
        1) The U.S. beneficiary should receive a *Foreign Grantor Trust Beneficiary Statement* (Form 3520-A) or a *Foreign Non Grantor Trust Beneficiary Statement*, which includes information about the taxability of distributions the beneficiary has received and foreign trust income the beneficiary must report.
    c. Gain on certain transfers of appreciated assets to a foreign trust must be recognized.

Net Investment Income Tax (NIIT)

13. Under PPACA, estates and trusts are subject to the NIIT, at a rate of 3.8%, if they have undistributed net investment income and also have adjusted gross income over the dollar amount at which the highest tax bracket for an estate or trust begins ($13,450 for 2022).
    a. Net investment income includes interest, dividends, capital gains, rental and royalty income, and nonqualified annuities.

EXAMPLE 18-8 NIIT -- Return of Principal

As beneficiary, a taxpayer chooses to receive $100,000 of life insurance proceeds in 10 annual installments of $11,000. Each year, the taxpayer can exclude from his or her income $10,000 ($100,000 ÷ 10) as a return of principal. The balance of the installment, $1,000, is taxable as interest income.

EXAMPLE 18-9 NIIT -- Interest Income

The face amount of a policy is $200,000, and as beneficiary a taxpayer chooses to receive annual installments of $12,000. The insurer's settlement option guarantees the taxpayer this amount for 20 years based on a guaranteed rate of interest. It also provides that extra interest may be credited to the principal balance according to the insurer's earnings. The excludable part of each guaranteed installment is $10,000 ($200,000 ÷ 20 years). The balance of each guaranteed installment, $2,000, is interest income to the taxpayer. The full amount of any additional payment for interest is income to the taxpayer.

EXAMPLE 18-10 NIIT -- Reportable Gross Income

Under the terms of the will of Gerald Peters, $5,000 is to be paid to his widow each year and $2,500 is to be paid to his daughter each year out of the estate's income during the period of administration. There are no charitable contributions. For the year, the estate's DNI is only $6,000. The DNI is less than the currently distributable income, so the widow must include in her gross income only $4,000 [($5,000 ÷ $7,500) × $6,000], and the daughter must include in her gross income only $2,000 [($2,500 ÷ $7,500) × $6,000].

EXAMPLE 18-11 NIIT -- Reportable Gross Income

Henry Frank's will provides that $500 be paid to the local Community Chest out of income each year. It also provides that $2,000 a year is currently distributable out of income to his brother, Fred, and an annuity of $3,000 is to be paid to his sister, Sharon, out of income or corpus. Capital gains are allocable to corpus, but all expenses are to be charged against income. Last year, the estate had income of $6,000 and expenses of $3,000. The personal representative paid $500 to the Community Chest and made the distributions to Fred and Sharon as required by the will. The estate's DNI (figured before the charitable contribution) is $3,000. The currently distributable income totals $2,500 ($2,000 to Fred and $500 to Sharon). The income available for Sharon's annuity is only $500 because the will requires that the charitable contribution be paid out of current income. The $2,500 treated as distributed currently is less than the $3,000 DNI (before the contribution), so Fred must include $2,000 in his gross income and Sharon must include $500 in her gross income.

EXAMPLE 18-12 NIIT -- Reportable Gross Income

Assume the same facts from Example 18-11, except the estate has an additional $1,000 of administration expenses, commissions, etc., chargeable to corpus. The estate's DNI (figured before the charitable contribution) is now $2,000 ($3,000 – $1,000 additional expense). The amount treated as currently distributable income is still $2,500 ($2,000 to Fred and $500 to Sharon). The $2,500 treated as distributed currently is more than the $2,000 DNI, so Fred has to include only $1,600 [($2,000 ÷ $2,500) × $2,000] in his gross income and Sharon has to include only $400 [($500 ÷ $2,500) × $2,000] in her gross income. Fred and Sharon are beneficiaries of amounts that must be distributed currently, so they don't benefit from the reduction of distributable net income by the charitable contribution deduction.

14. If no charitable contribution is made during the tax year, distributions should be treated as consisting of the same proportion of each class of items entering into the computation of DNI as the total of each class bears to the total DNI.

EXAMPLE 18-13 NIIT -- Gross Income Allocation

Steve's estate has DNI of $3,000, consisting of $1,800 in rents and $1,200 in taxable interest. There is no provision in the will or local law for the allocation of income. The personal representative distributes $1,500 each to Jim and Ted, beneficiaries under Steve's will. Each will be treated as having received $900 in rents ($1,800 × 50%) and $600 of taxable interest ($1,200 × 50%).

EXAMPLE 18-14 NIIT -- Gross Income Allocation

Assume that the will from Example 18-13 provides for the payment of the taxable interest to Jim and the rental income to Ted and that the personal representative distributed the income under those provisions. Jim is treated as having received $1,200 in taxable interest and Ted is treated as having received $1,800 of rental income.

15. If a charitable contribution is made by an estate and the terms of the will or local law provide for the contribution to be paid from specified sources, that provision governs. If no provision or requirement exists, the charitable contribution deduction must be allocated among the classes of income entering into the computation of the income of the estate before allocation of other deductions among the items of distributable net income.

EXAMPLE 18-15 NIIT -- Reportable Gross Income

The will of Harry Thomas requires a current distribution from income of $3,000 to his wife, Betty, each year during the administration of the estate. The will also provides that the personal representative may distribute the balance of the current earnings either to Harry's son, Tim, or to one or more designated charities. Last year, the estate's income consisted of $4,000 of taxable interest and $1,000 of tax-exempt interest. There were no deductible expenses. The personal representative distributed the $3,000 to Betty, made a contribution of $2,500 to the local heart association, and paid $1,500 to Tim. The DNI for determining the character of the distribution to Betty is $3,000. The charitable contribution deduction to be taken into account for this computation is $2,000 ($5,000 estate income – $3,000 currently distributable income). The $2,000 charitable contribution deduction must be allocated as follows: $1,600 [($4,000 ÷ $5,000) × $2,000] to taxable interest and $400 [($1,000 ÷ $5,000) × $2,000] to tax-exempt interest. Betty is considered to have received $2,400 ($4,000 – $1,600) of taxable interest and $600 ($1,000 – $400) of tax-exempt interest. She must include the $2,400 in her gross income. She must report the $600 of tax-exempt interest, but it is not taxable. The entire charitable contribution must be taken into account to determine the amount to be included in Tim's gross income. The currently distributable income is greater than the estate's income after taking into account the charitable contribution deduction, so none of the amount paid to Tim must be included in his gross income for the year.

EXAMPLE 18-16 NIIT -- Income Distribution Deduction

An estate has DNI of $2,000, consisting of $1,000 of dividends and $1,000 of tax-exempt interest. Distributions to the beneficiary total $1,500 {$750 of dividends [$1,500 distribution × ($1,000 dividends ÷ $2,000 DNI)] and $750 of tax-exempt interest [$1,500 distribution × ($1,000 tax-exempt interest ÷ $2,000 DNI)]}. The income distribution deduction is limited to $750, because no deduction is allowed for the tax-exempt interest distributed.

Stop & Review

You have completed the outline for this subunit.

Study multiple-choice questions 6 through 19 beginning on page 410.

18.4 FRAUDULENT TRUSTS

1. All trusts must comply with the tax laws as set forth by the Congress in the Internal Revenue Code (IRC), Secs. 641-685.
   a. Trusts established to hide the true ownership of assets and income or to disguise the substance of financial transactions are considered fraudulent trusts.
   b. Abusive techniques used to reduce income taxes include
      1) Depreciating personal assets (such as a home);
      2) Deducting personal expenses;
      3) Splitting income over multiple entities, often filed in multiple locations;
      4) Underreporting income;
      5) Avoiding filing returns;
      6) Wiring income overseas and failing to report it; and
      7) Attempting to protect transactions through bank secrecy laws in tax haven countries.
   c. Violations of the IRC may result in civil penalties and/or criminal prosecution.
      1) **Civil sanctions** can include a fraud penalty up to 75% of the underpayment of tax attributable to the fraud in addition to the taxes owed.
      2) **Criminal convictions** may result in fines up to $250,000 for individuals ($500,000 for corporations) and/or up to 5 years in prison for each offense.

You have completed the outline for this subunit.
Study multiple-choice question 20 on page 415.

QUESTIONS

18.1 Decedent's Final Income Tax Return

1. Alice, a cash-basis taxpayer, died August 31 of the current year. During the current year, the following amounts were paid to her estate:

- $1,000 dividend from the ABC Corp., which was declared on August 25 and received in the mail on September 2.
- $5,000 distributive share of XYZ Partnership income received on October 3 of the current year. This distribution was for the partnership's tax year ended September 30 of the current year.

What income must be included on Alice's final individual income tax return for the dividend and partnership payments?

A. The $1,000 dividend and a pro rata portion of the $5,000 partnership income.

B. The $1,000 dividend but no portion of the partnership income.

C. A pro rata portion of the partnership income but not the $1,000 dividend.

D. No income from either payment.

Answer (C) is correct.

REQUIRED: The amount of income included on the final income tax return.

DISCUSSION: If the decedent accounted for income under the cash method, only the items actually or constructively received before the date of death are included on the final return. Constructive receipt would have occurred if the income had become available for use by the decedent without restriction. Because the dividends were not available for use before the date of death, they were not constructively received. For a partnership whose tax year ends after the partner's date of death, the decedent's distributive share of income is income in respect of the decedent and will be reported on the final tax return to the extent of the pro rata portion prior to death.

Answer (A) is incorrect. The dividend income is not included in income. **Answer (B) is incorrect.** The dividend is not included in income and a pro rata portion of the $5,000 is included in income. **Answer (D) is incorrect.** A portion of the partnership income should be included.

2. Mr. Benson, a cash-method, calendar-year taxpayer, leased his farm for pasture land each August for 1 year at $2,000 per year, payable when the lease was signed. He died on June 30 of the current year. Your review of his records, as a personal representative, reflected that, as of the date of his death, he had received interest of $8,000. You also found a dividend check in the amount of $650, which was undeposited and had been received on June 15 of the current year. What is the amount of income to be included on Mr. Benson's final income tax return?

A. $8,000

B. $8,650

C. $10,000

D. $10,650

Answer (B) is correct.

REQUIRED: The amount of income included on the final income tax return.

DISCUSSION: If the decedent accounted for income under the cash method, only the items actually or constructively received before the date of death are included on the final return. Constructive receipt occurred if the income became available for use by the decedent without restriction. The interest received ($8,000) and the dividends constructively received ($650) are included in income. The rent is not included because it was not constructively received.

Answer (A) is incorrect. The dividend check was available for use by the decedent. **Answer (C) is incorrect.** The rent was not constructively received, but the dividend check was because it was available for use by the decedent. **Answer (D) is incorrect.** The rent was not constructively received.

3. John, a self-employed carpenter, died on January 8 of the current year. Which of the following, if allowable, could be deducted on John's final Form 1040?

A. Unused net operating loss carryover from last year.

B. Standard deduction.

C. Medical expenses paid by the estate within 1 year of death.

D. All of the answers are correct.

Answer (D) is correct.

REQUIRED: The allowable deductions on a decedent's final return.

DISCUSSION: A full standard deduction may be taken for a decedent's final return unless the deductions are itemized. If medical expenses are paid out of the estate during the 1-year period beginning with the day after death, an election may be made to also deduct them on the final return. A deduction for NOLs must be taken on the final return.

18.2 Income in Respect of a Decedent (IRD)

4. Which one of the following statements concerning the consequences of income being classified as "income in respect of a decedent" is true?

A. It receives no step-up in basis upon the decedent's death.

B. It is all treated as ordinary income to recipient.

C. It is all taxable to the decedent's estate.

D. It must be included in the decedent's final return.

Answer (A) is correct.

REQUIRED: The true statement of the consequences of income in respect of a decedent.

DISCUSSION: Section 1014(a) provides that the basis of property acquired from a decedent is generally the fair market value of the property on the date of the decedent's death. Section 1014(c) provides that property that constitutes a right to receive income in respect of a decedent does not receive a step-up in basis. Therefore, it has a carryover basis.

Answer (B) is incorrect. Income in respect of a decedent is treated as having the same character it would have had in the hands of the decedent [Sec. 691(a)(3)]. **Answer (C) is incorrect.** Income in respect of a decedent is included when received (as if on a cash basis) by the person who receives it [Sec. 691(a)(1)]. **Answer (D) is incorrect.** Income in respect of a decedent is income that is earned by the taxpayer but not received prior to his or her death nor accrued prior to his or her death if on the accrual method, so it is not included in the decedent's final return.

5. Fred, a calendar-year, cash-basis taxpayer who died in June of the current year, was entitled to receive a $10,000 accounting fee that had not been collected before the date of death. The executor of Fred's estate collected the full $10,000 in July of the current year. This $10,000 should appear in

A. Only the decedent's final individual income tax return.

B. Only the estate's fiduciary income tax return.

C. Only the decedent's estate tax return.

D. Both the fiduciary income tax return and the estate tax return.

Answer (D) is correct.

REQUIRED: The true treatment of income earned before death but not received until after death.

DISCUSSION: Income that a decedent had a right to receive prior to death but that was not includible on his or her final income tax return is income in respect of a decedent. The $10,000 is properly includible in the estate's (fiduciary) income tax return because Fred was a cash-basis taxpayer and would not properly include income not yet received at the time of death in his final return. Since the money was owed to Fred (he has a right to receive it), it is an asset of the estate and must be included on the estate tax return also.

Answer (A) is incorrect. Fred was a cash-basis taxpayer and would not properly include income not received at the time of death. **Answer (B) is incorrect.** The $10,000 is an asset of the estate and must also be included on the estate tax return. **Answer (C) is incorrect.** The $10,000 is income to the estate and must also be included on its income tax return.

18.3 Income Taxation of Estates and Trusts

6. Which of the following statements is true regarding estate income tax returns filed on Form 1041?

A. Form 1041 has its own tax rate schedule.

B. Estates are never liable for the alternative minimum tax.

C. All estates are subject to the same estimated tax rules that apply to Form 1040.

D. None of the answers are correct.

Answer (A) is correct.

REQUIRED: The true statement regarding estate income tax returns filed on Form 1041.

DISCUSSION: Form 1041 is subject to a tax rate schedule that reaches the 37% tax bracket in 2022 for taxable incomes exceeding $13,450.

Answer (B) is incorrect. Estates may be subject to the alternative minimum tax. **Answer (C) is incorrect.** Estates may be subject to estimated payments after 2 years. **Answer (D) is incorrect.** One of the answers is correct.

7. Which of the following statements is NOT true regarding the income taxation of trusts?

A. A trust (except for a grantor-type trust) is a separate legal entity for federal tax purposes.

B. A trust may be created only during the life of the grantor.

C. A trust figures its gross income in much the same manner as an individual.

D. A trust is allowed an income distribution deduction for distributions to beneficiaries.

Answer (B) is correct.

REQUIRED: The false statement about income taxation of trusts.

DISCUSSION: A trust is created when a grantor conveys title to property to a trustee. A trust may be created before or after the death of a grantor. A trust created by the terms of a will is called a testamentary trust. A testamentary trust does not come into existence until the estate's personal representative completes the administration of the estate or transfers assets to the trust prior to the close of the estate. An inter vivos trust is created while the grantor is still alive.

8. Which of the following statements regarding the various types of trusts is NOT true?

A. A trust may qualify as a simple trust if all income must be distributed currently.

B. A trust may qualify as a simple trust if the trust does not distribute amounts allocated to the corpus of the trust.

C. A grantor trust is a separate taxable entity in which the grantor has not relinquished complete dominion and control over the trust.

D. A complex trust is any trust that does not qualify as a simple or grantor trust.

Answer (C) is correct.

REQUIRED: The false statement regarding the various types of trusts.

DISCUSSION: A grantor-type trust is a legal trust under applicable state law that is not recognized as a separate taxable entity for income tax purposes because the grantor or other substantial owners have not relinquished complete dominion and control over the trust.

9. Christopher wants to create a revocable grantor trust that will own all of his stocks and rental properties. Which statement regarding income of the trust is true?

A. Christopher will be taxed only income that is distributed to him.

B. Christopher will be taxed on all income of the trust, regardless of distributions.

C. State law will determine how much of the trust income is taxable to Christopher.

D. If the rental income is passive, it will not be taxable to him.

Answer (B) is correct.

REQUIRED: The true statement regarding grantor trusts.

DISCUSSION: In general, a grantor trust is ignored for tax purposes, and all of the income, deductions, etc., are treated as belonging directly to the grantor. This also applies to any portion of a trust that is treated as a grantor trust.

Answer (A) is incorrect. Christopher will be taxed on the income earned by the trust whether distributed to him or not. **Answer (C) is incorrect.** Federal law states that all income earned by the trust, whether distributed to him or not, is taxable the year earned. State law defines the criteria to be classified as a grantor trust. **Answer (D) is incorrect.** The passive rental income may be taxed to Christopher.

10. James Smith, a cash-basis taxpayer, received $35,000 in wages before his death on July 7 of the current year. In addition, his stock portfolio paid $12,000 in dividends, $11,500 of which was paid to him before his death. By what date is Form 1041 required to be filed?

A. Form 1041 is not required to be filed.

B. Nine months after date of death.

C. By the 15th day of the 4th month after the end of the tax year selected by the estate's personal representative.

D. By the 15th day of the 3rd month after the end of the tax year selected by the estate.

Answer (A) is correct.

REQUIRED: The due date for Form 1041.

DISCUSSION: Under Sec. 6012(a)(3), every estate that has gross income of $600 or more must file an income tax return. Under Reg. 1.6012-3, the return to be filed by a fiduciary for an estate or a trust is Form 1041. Section 6072 requires the return to be filed on or before the 15th day of the 4th month after the end of the tax year. Because Mr. Smith's income after death is less than $600, the estate does not have to file a return.

11. Which of the following receipts should be allocated exclusively to income by a trustee?

A. A stock dividend.

B. A very large year-end cash dividend.

C. A stock split.

D. A liquidating dividend whether in complete or partial liquidation.

Answer (B) is correct.

REQUIRED: The receipts that should be allocated exclusively to income.

DISCUSSION: Cash dividends are exclusively allocable to income. Cash dividends are not a change in the form of the principal; rather, they represent earnings from the principal (corpus). For simple trusts (i.e., trusts that must distribute all of their income currently), extraordinary dividends (whether paid in cash or property) or taxable stock dividends can be excluded from income if they are not distributed or credited to a beneficiary because the fiduciary in good faith determines that the governing instrument and local law allocate such amounts to corpus [Sec. 643(a)(4)].

Answer (A) is incorrect. Stock dividends are allocated exclusively to principal. **Answer (C) is incorrect.** Stock splits are allocated exclusively to principal. **Answer (D) is incorrect.** Liquidating dividends are allocated exclusively to principal.

12. Trust B has distributable net income of $60,000, which includes $5,000 of tax-exempt income. The trustee distributed $75,000 to the trust's sole beneficiary. What amount will be shown as the distribution deduction on the trust's Form 1041?

A. $55,000

B. $60,000

C. $70,000

D. $75,000

Answer (A) is correct.

REQUIRED: The distribution deduction for a trust.

DISCUSSION: The distribution deduction for a trust is equal to the lesser of distributable net income (DNI) of the trust reduced by any tax-exempt income or the distributed amount reduced by any tax-exempt income. The DNI is less than the distribution. The $60,000 of DNI for Trust B is reduced by the $5,000 of tax-exempt income for a total of $55,000. This amount is then shown as the distribution deduction on the trust's Form 1041.

Answer (B) is incorrect. The DNI is reduced by the $5,000 of tax-exempt income. **Answer (C) is incorrect.** The DNI is reduced by the $5,000 of tax-exempt income, not the actual amount distributed. **Answer (D) is incorrect.** The actual amount distributed is not used on the Form 1041.

13. Which of the following statements is false?

A. The beneficiary of an estate or trust may be taxed on money required to be distributed whether actually distributed or not.

B. Money distributed to a beneficiary from an estate is taxed twice–on the estate return and on the beneficiary's return.

C. Tax-exempt interest distributed to a beneficiary is not taxable to the beneficiary.

D. Losses of estates and trusts are generally not deductible by the beneficiaries.

Answer (B) is correct.

REQUIRED: The false statement about estate taxes.

DISCUSSION: Money distributed to a beneficiary from an estate is not taxed twice. DNI is allocated to either the estate or beneficiary and is only taxed to whichever of the two it is allocated.

Answer (A) is incorrect. According to Sec. 662, the beneficiary may be taxed on money required to be distributed, whether actually distributed or not. **Answer (C) is incorrect.** The character of income in the hands of the beneficiary is the same as in the hands of the trust or estate. **Answer (D) is incorrect.** This is generally a true statement. However, an estate's unused net operating loss carryover or capital loss carryover existing upon termination of the estate can be used by a beneficiary succeeding to property of the estate. A beneficiary entitled to an unused loss carryover or an excess deduction is the beneficiary who, upon the estate's termination, bears the burden of any loss for which a carryover is allowed or of any deductions more than gross income.

14. If you are the beneficiary of an estate that must distribute all its income currently (and none is tax-exempt), you must report your share of

A. The distributable net income plus all other amounts actually paid to you.

B. The distributable net income that you have actually received.

C. The distributable net income whether or not you have actually received it.

D. None of the answers are correct.

Answer (C) is correct.

REQUIRED: The amount of income to be reported by a beneficiary of an estate.

DISCUSSION: Under Sec. 662, a beneficiary of an estate (or complex trust) must include in gross income the amounts required to be distributed currently and any additional amounts actually distributed, but both amounts are limited to distributable net income (DNI). Therefore, if all income is taxable and required to be distributed currently, the beneficiary must include all DNI in income even if not actually received.

Answer (A) is incorrect. DNI is the limit on a beneficiary's taxable income from an estate (or complex trust). **Answer (B) is incorrect.** DNI is included when required to be distributed even if not actually received. **Answer (D) is incorrect.** DNI must be included in income when required to be distributed even if it is not actually received.

15. Ms. Brown died on June 30 last year. During the current year, her estate received the following:

Interest income	$2,500
Dividend income	5,000
Long-term capital gain	2,500

Pursuant to her will, 50% of all income was to be distributed to a specific qualifying charitable organization. The executor complied with the provision in a timely manner. Assuming all income was accumulated, what is the estate's taxable income for the current year?

A. $10,000

B. $2,500

C. $5,000

D. $4,400

Answer (D) is correct.

REQUIRED: The taxable income of an estate.

DISCUSSION: The total income of the estate is $10,000. A deduction for the charitable contribution reduces the income to $5,000. A $600 exemption deduction is then permitted, making the taxable income $4,400.

Answer (A) is incorrect. A deduction for the charitable contribution and an exemption deduction is permitted. **Answer (B) is incorrect.** The long-term capital gain and interest income are includible. **Answer (C) is incorrect.** An exemption deduction of $600 is permitted.

16. Stan is the personal representative of his brother, Bruce, who died June 30, 2022. Stan has obtained an identification number for Bruce's estate and has notified the IRS on Form 56 that he has been appointed executor. He has filed his brother's final return for 2022 and has the following information regarding Bruce's remaining estate. What will be the taxable income of the estate?

Unpaid salary not received by Bruce before he died	$ 6,000
Dividend check on XYZ stock received August 15, 2022	600
Form 1099 interest earned on savings after death	2,000
Sales price of coin collection sold to unrelated person	10,000
Value of the coins at the date of death	9,000
Attorney's fees for administration of the estate	1,000

A. $8,600

B. $17,600

C. $8,000

D. None of the answers are correct.

Answer (C) is correct.

REQUIRED: The taxable income of the estate.

DISCUSSION: Administration expenses (and debts of a decedent) are deductible on the estate tax return under Sec. 2053, and some may also qualify as deductions for income tax purposes on the estate's income tax return. Section 642(g), however, disallows a double deduction and requires a waiver of the right to deduct them on Form 706 in order to claim them on Form 1041. Therefore, the attorney's fees for administration of the estate can be deducted on the estate return since it is not stated that a waiver was filed. The income earned by the decedent but taxable to the estate is calculated as follows:

Unpaid salary	$ 6,000
Dividend income	600
Interest income	2,000
Gain on sale of coins	1,000
Less: Administrative expense	(1,000)
Exemption deduction	(600)
Estate's taxable income	$ 8,000

Answer (A) is incorrect. An exemption deduction of $600 is allowed for estates. **Answer (B) is incorrect.** The sales price of the coins must be reduced by their basis, and an exemption deduction of $600 is allowed. **Answer (D) is incorrect.** The taxable income of the estate is $8,000.

17. Mrs. A died on June 30 of the current year. According to the terms of her will, $20,000 was paid to each of her three children prior to the end of the year. Additionally, the estate was to pay from earnings $20,000 to each child in the current year. In the current year, the estate had net earnings of $30,000. Assuming no charitable contributions were made, how much income will each child report?

A. $30,000 ordinary income.

B. $40,000 ordinary income.

C. $10,000 ordinary income.

D. $0

Answer (C) is correct.

REQUIRED: The amount each beneficiary should include in gross income from an estate.

DISCUSSION: Under Sec. 662, beneficiaries of an estate (and a complex trust) are required to include in gross income the amounts of fiduciary income that are required to be distributed and all other amounts that are distributed, limited to DNI. The amounts included in the beneficiaries' gross income retain the same character as in the hands of the estate or trust and are treated as consisting of the same proportion of each classified item entering into the computation of DNI. Since DNI is $30,000, each of the three children must include $10,000 in gross income.

Answer (A) is incorrect. DNI is distributed among the three children when calculating the amount of income to include. **Answer (B) is incorrect.** The amount includible in income is limited to the estate's DNI. Inheritances specified in the will are not included. **Answer (D) is incorrect.** DNI is $30,000 and must be distributed among three children.

18. In which circumstance must an estate of a decedent make estimated tax payments?

A. An estate is never required to make estimated tax payments.

B. The estate has a first tax year that covers 12 months.

C. The estate has income in excess of $400.

D. The estate has a tax year ending 2 or more years after the date of the decedent's death.

Answer (D) is correct.

REQUIRED: The true statement concerning estimated tax payments for an estate.

DISCUSSION: Section 6654(l) requires an estate to make estimated payments of income tax in all tax years except during its first 2 taxable years of existence. No estimated payments are required during its first 2 taxable years.

Answer (A) is incorrect. Estates are required to make payments of estimated tax after the first 2 years of existence. **Answer (B) is incorrect.** Estimated tax payments are required only after the estate's first 2 years of existence without regard to the length of the first tax year. **Answer (C) is incorrect.** An estate need not make estimated tax payments for its first 2 years of existence without regard to the amount of its gross income.

19. On December 15, Year 1, Kyle received a $10,000 distribution from his father's estate. On March 30, Year 2, Kyle was issued Schedule K-1 for the estate's first fiscal year (February 1, Year 1, through January 31, Year 2). The Schedule K-1 from the estate showed taxable interest income of $200 and had no other entries. Based on the information above, which of the following statements are true?

A. Kyle must report income of $10,000 on his Year 2 return.

B. Kyle must report $200 interest income on his Year 2 return.

C. Kyle may claim a deduction on Schedule A for a pro rata share of the estate tax that was paid by the estate.

D. Kyle must report $200 interest income on his Year 2 return and he may also claim a deduction on Schedule A for a pro rata share of the estate tax that was paid by the estate.

Answer (B) is correct.

REQUIRED: The true statement concerning the amount of estate income to be reported on the beneficiary's return.

DISCUSSION: Publication 559 states, "income in respect of a decedent is . . . taxed when received by the recipient (estate or beneficiary). However, an income tax deduction is allowed to the recipient for the estate tax paid on the income." The information in the question does not indicate whether there was any IRD. From the information, it must be assumed that the $10,000 was a nontaxable distribution of estate assets. It also should be assumed that the $200 represented income earned by the estate that flowed through to Kyle and was not IRD. Thus, Kyle would report only the $200 as income.

Answer (A) is incorrect. The $10,000 distribution was a nontaxable distribution of estate assets. **Answer (C) is incorrect.** No estate tax would have been paid since there was no income in respect of a decedent. Therefore, no deduction may be claimed. **Answer (D) is incorrect.** No estate tax would have been paid since there was no income in respect of a decedent. Therefore, no deduction may be claimed.

18.4 Fraudulent Trusts

20. Which of the following is NOT an abusive technique used to reduce income taxes?

A. Depreciation of personal assets.

B. Reporting income wired overseas.

C. Deduction of personal expenses.

D. Splitting income over multiple entities.

Answer (B) is correct.

REQUIRED: The transaction that is not considered abusive.

DISCUSSION: Some abusive techniques used to reduce income tax include

1. Depreciation of personal assets (such as a home)
2. Deduction of personal expenses
3. Splitting income over multiple entities, often filed in multiple locations
4. Underreporting income
5. Avoiding filing returns
6. Wiring income overseas and failing to report it
7. Attempting to protect transactions through bank secrecy laws in tax haven countries

Go to Online Course

Access the **Gleim EA Premium Review System** featuring our SmartAdapt technology from your Gleim Personal Classroom to continue your studies.

You will experience a personalized study environment with exam-emulating multiple-choice questions.

STUDY UNIT NINETEEN

RETIREMENT PLANS FOR SMALL BUSINESSES

(17 pages of outline)

This study unit discusses retirement plans that the owner of a small business, including a self-employed person, can set up and maintain for employees. The IRS tests three types of plans: simplified employee pension (SEP) plans, SIMPLE plans, and qualified plans. A SEP is a simple plan that allows contributions to retirement plans without involvement with the more complex qualified plan. However, some advantages available to qualified plans, such as special tax treatment that may apply to qualified plan lump-sum distributions, do not apply to SEP.

19.1 SIMPLIFIED EMPLOYEE PENSION (SEP)

1. A simplified employee pension (SEP) is a written agreement (a plan) that allows an employer to make contributions toward his or her retirement (if a self-employed individual) and his or her employees' retirement without becoming involved in more complex retirement plans.
   a. Under a SEP, an employer contributes directly to traditional individual retirement accounts (SEP-IRAs) for each qualifying employee and/or self-employed individual.
      1) The employer can set up a SEP plan for a year as late as the due date (including extensions) for the business income tax return for the year.
      2) The employer must make contributions to the SEP plan by the due date of the employer's return, including extensions.
         a) Contributions are reported on Form 5498.
      3) A SEP-IRA is owned and controlled by the employee.
   b. The employer can have another retirement plan.

Self-Employed Individual

2. A self-employed individual is an employee for SEP purposes. (S)he is also the employer.
   a. Even if the self-employed individual is the only qualifying employee, (s)he can have a SEP-IRA.
   b. Self-employment services must represent a material income-producing factor. In addition, any salaries and wages that are received in addition to self-employment income should be included in compensation. In the occasion of a net loss from self-employment, it should not be subtracted from any salaries and wages received when determining compensation.
   c. The deduction is taken on Form 1040, Schedule 1.

Qualifying Employee

3. A qualifying (eligible) employee is one who meets all of the following conditions:
   a. (S)he is at least 21 years old.
   b. (S)he has worked for the employer during at least 3 of the 5 years immediately preceding the tax year.
   c. (S)he has received from the employer at least $650 in compensation during the tax year.

Excludable Employees

4. The following groups of employees can be excluded from coverage under a SEP:
   a. Employees who are covered by a collective bargaining agreement and whose retirement benefits were bargained for in good faith
   b. Nonresident alien employees who have no U.S. source earned income from their employer
5. A leased employee may have to be included in the SEP of the organization receiving the services if certain conditions are met.
6. A SEP does not require contributions every year, but it must not discriminate in favor of highly compensated employees.

Highly Compensated Employee

   a. A highly compensated employee is any employee who meets either of the following two conditions:
      1) The employee owns (or owned last year) more than 5% of
         a) The capital or profits interest in the employer,
         b) The outstanding stock, or
         c) The total voting power of all stock of the employer corporation.
      2) The employee's compensation from the employer for the preceding year is more than $135,000 if the preceding year is 2021, and (if the employer elects to apply this clause for last year) the employee was in the top 20% when ranked on the basis of last year's compensation.

Contributions

7. An employer is permitted to make contributions to each participating employee's SEP each year. The employer may deduct the amount of the contributions from the business's gross income.
   a. The contributions are limited to the lesser of
      1) 25% of the employee's compensation or
      2) $61,000.
   b. These limits apply to contributions the employer makes for employees to all defined contribution plans, which includes SEPs. Compensation up to $305,000 in 2022 may be considered.
   c. A 10% excise tax is generally imposed on the employer on contributions in excess of the deductible amount.

8. Unlike contributions to IRAs, contributions to SEP-IRAs are excluded from an employee's income rather than deducted from it. Any excess employer contributions must be included in income without any offsetting deduction.
9. An employee's deduction for contributions to a qualified plan, including a SEP, is generally allowed for the tax year in which contributions are paid.
   a. Contributions paid on or before the due date of returns, including extensions, for a particular tax year are deemed paid on the last day of that tax year.

Self-Employed

10. Special rules apply for self-employed individuals who contribute to their own SEPs.
    a. Compensation for the self-employed is equal to net earnings from self-employment.
       1) For SEP purposes, the individual's net earnings must take into account the deduction for contributions to a SEP.
          a) Because the deduction amount and net earnings are dependent on each other, the worksheets below must be used.
          b) The maximum rate becomes 20% after the computation.
       2) First, a new rate must be determined to take into account the contribution deduction.

Self-Employed Person's Rate Worksheet	
(1) Plan contribution rate as a decimal (for example, 10 1/2% would be 0.105)	________
(2) Rate in line 1 plus one (for example, 0.105 plus one would be 1.105)	________
(3) Self-employed rate as a decimal rounded to at least 3 decimal places (divide line 1 by line 2) (for example, 0.105 ÷ 1.105 = 0.095)	________

       3) Then the maximum deduction may be computed.

Self-Employed Person's Deduction Worksheet	
Step 1: Enter the rate from the "Self-Employed Person's Rate Worksheet."	________
Step 2: Enter net profit from Schedule C.	$ ________
Step 3: Enter the deduction for self-employment tax.	$ ________
Step 4: Subtract Step 3 from Step 2 and enter the result.	$ ________
Step 5: Multiply Step 4 by Step 1 and enter the result.	$ ________
Step 6: Multiply $305,000 by the plan contribution rate. Enter the result but not more than $61,000.	$ ________
Step 7: Enter the smaller of Step 5 or Step 6. This is the **maximum deductible contribution**.	$ ________

11. Income passed through to shareholders of S corporations is not considered to be earnings from self-employment (i.e., it is not subject to self-employment taxes).

Credits

12. When an employer starts up a SEP, SIMPLE, or qualified retirement plan, the firm may be eligible for a credit, which is equal to 50% of all ordinary and necessary costs of starting up the plan for the first 3 years of the plan. (The maximum credit limit ranges from $500 to $5,000. The details of calculating this limit are beyond the scope of the exam.)
    a. Eligible small businesses are those that have 100 or fewer employees who receive at least $5,000 in compensation from the employer in the year preceding the start-up of the retirement plan.

You have completed the outline for this subunit.
Study multiple-choice questions 1 through 5 beginning on page 434.

19.2 SAVINGS INCENTIVE MATCH PLANS FOR EMPLOYEES (SIMPLE)

1. Employers with 100 or fewer employees who received at least $5,000 in compensation from the employer in the preceding year may adopt a SIMPLE individual retirement account plan (SIMPLE IRA) if they do not maintain another qualified plan.

EXAMPLE 19-1	SIMPLE Plan Eligibility
A corporation has 70 eligible employees, and its subsidiary has 50 eligible employees. The corporation is not eligible for a SIMPLE plan.	

2. Self-employed individuals may participate in a SIMPLE plan.
3. If a SIMPLE plan has been adopted, it must be available to every employee who (a) received at least $5,000 in compensation from the employer during any 2 preceding years and (b) is reasonably expected to receive at least $5,000 in compensation during the current year. Individuals who are self-employed may also participate in a SIMPLE plan.
    a. Generally, compensation means the sum of wages, tips, and other compensation subject to federal income tax withholding as well as elective salary deferral contributions the participant made to the SIMPLE IRA plan.
    b. An employer may establish a SIMPLE plan even if none of its employees wish to participate.
4. The plan allows employees to make elective contributions of up to $14,000 for 2022 ($17,000 if 50 or older) and requires employers to make matching contributions.
    a. Employee contributions are salary reductions.
5. A SIMPLE plan is not subject to nondiscrimination rules or other complex requirements applicable to qualified plans.
    a. An employer can choose to cover all employees without restriction, or (s)he can limit the employees covered to those who received at least $5,000 in compensation during any 2 preceding years and who are reasonably expected to receive at least $5,000 in the current year.

6. SIMPLE plans may be structured as an IRA or as a 401(k) qualified cash or deferred compensation.
7. Contributions to a SIMPLE IRA account are limited to employee elective contributions and require employer matching contributions or nonelective contributions.
8. There are two formulas for employer matching:

Matching

a. Matching contribution formula

1) Employers are generally required to match employee contributions on a dollar-for-dollar basis up to 3% of an employee's compensation for the year (not limited by the annual compensation limit).

EXAMPLE 19-2 SIMPLE Plan Contribution
Mary Jones has compensation of \$95,000 for the year. Mary contributes \$8,000 to her SIMPLE IRA. Mary's employer makes a matching contribution of 3% of compensation. The employer's matching contribution is \$2,850 (\$95,000 × 3%).

2) However, an employer also may elect to match contributions for all eligible employees for a given year at a rate not less than 1% of each employee's compensation upon notification to the employees.

3) The lower percentage cannot drop below 3% of employee compensation in more than 2 years in a 5-year period ending with that year.

Alternative

b. Alternative formula

1) An employer may elect to make a nonelective contribution of 2% of compensation for each eligible employee who has earned at least \$5,000 in compensation from the employer during the year.

a) Only the first \$305,000 of compensation is considered.

Employer Contributions

9. Employer contributions are expressed as a percentage of compensation, not as a flat dollar amount.

a. Employers must continue to make contributions even in lean years of at least 1% of employee compensation.

b. Employers must contribute an employee's elective deferral to the employee's SIMPLE account no later than 30 days after the last day of the month for which the contributions are made.

c. An employer must make matching contributions by the due date of the tax return, including extensions.

d. Contributions by the employer must be 100% vested.

Deduction

10. Employers may deduct contributions for the year in which they are made.
    a. Matching contributions are deductible for the year only if made by the due date of the tax return, including extensions.

Distributions

11. Distributions from a SIMPLE IRA plan are generally taxed like distributions from an IRA and are generally includible in income for the year received.

Penalties

12. Withdrawals
    a. Withdrawals before age 59 1/2 are subject to a 10% tax.
    b. Withdrawals within the first 2 years are subject to a 25% tax.
13. An employee's elective contributions will be treated as wages for purposes of employment tax.
    a. The employer's matching or nonelective contributions are not wages.

Rollover

14. A participant may roll over distributions tax-free from one SIMPLE account to another SIMPLE account. In addition, a participant may roll over distributions from a SIMPLE account to an IRA or a qualified plan without penalty if the individual has participated in the SIMPLE plan for at least 2 years.
15. Tax-free rollovers to tax sheltered annuities are not allowed.

You have completed the outline for this subunit.

Study multiple-choice questions 6 through 10 beginning on page 436.

19.3 QUALIFIED PLANS

1. A qualified employer plan set up by a self-employed person is sometimes called a Keogh or HR10 plan.
   a. The plans described here can be set up and maintained by employers that are corporations, sole proprietors, or partnerships.
   b. A common-law employee or a partner cannot set up one of these plans. A common-law employee is a person who performs services for an employer who has the right to control and direct the results of the work and the way in which it is done. For example, the employer
      1) Provides the employee's tools, materials, and workplace and
      2) Can fire the employee.
   c. Qualified plans must be set up by year end.
2. For qualified plan purposes, a self-employed person is both an employer and an employee.
3. To set up a qualified plan, an employer must either
   a. Adopt an IRS-approved prototype or master plan offered by a sponsoring organization and communicate it to the employees or
   b. Prepare and adopt a written plan that satisfies the qualification requirements of the Internal Revenue Code and communicate it to the employees.
      1) Although advance IRS approval is not required, approval may be applied for by paying a fee and requesting a determination letter.

<u>Minimum Participation Requirements</u>

4. An employee must be allowed to participate in the plan if (s)he
   a. Has reached age 21 and
   b. Has at least 1 year of service (2 years if the plan is not a 401(k) plan and provides that, after not more than 2 years of service, the employee has a nonforfeitable right to all of his or her accrued benefits).
5. A plan cannot exclude an employee because (s)he has reached a specified age.

6. **Two Basic Kinds of Qualified Plans**

Defined Contribution Plan

a. A defined contribution plan provides an individual account for each participant in the plan. It provides benefits to a participant largely based on the amount contributed to that participant's account. Benefits are also affected by any income, expenses, gains and losses, and any forfeitures of other accounts that may be allocated to an account. There are two types of defined contribution plans:

1) **Profit-sharing plan.** A profit-sharing plan is a plan for sharing employer profits with the firm's employees.

a) An employer does not have to make contributions out of net profits to have a profit-sharing plan.

2) **Money purchase pension plan.** Contributions to a money purchase pension plan are fixed and are not based on the employer's profits.

a) This applies even if the compensation of a self-employed individual as a participant is based on earned income derived from business profits.

Defined Benefit Plan

b. A defined benefit plan is any plan that is not a defined contribution plan. Contributions to a defined benefit plan are based on a computation of the contributions needed to fulfill the requirements established by an employer.

c. To be a qualified plan, a defined benefit plan must benefit at least the lesser of 50 employees or the greater of 40% of all employees or two employees.

Contributions

7. Generally, contributions made to a qualified plan, including those made for a self-employed individual's own benefit, are deductible and subject to limits.

a. Self-employed individuals may make contributions on their own behalf only if they have net earnings from self-employment.

1) Common-law employees are not self-employed and cannot set up retirement plans for income from their work, even if that income is self-employment income for Social Security tax purposes.

a) Common-law employees who are ministers, members of religious orders, full-time insurance salespeople, and U.S. citizens employed in the U.S. by foreign governments cannot set up retirement plans for their earnings from those employments, even though their earnings are treated as self-employment income.

2) A person who is a common-law employee also can be considered self-employed in other circumstances. For example,

a) An attorney can be a corporate common-law employee during regular working hours and also practice law in the evening as a self-employed person.

b) A minister employed by a congregation for a salary is a common-law employee even though the salary is treated as self-employment income for Social Security tax purposes. However, fees reported on Form 1040, Schedule C, *Profit or Loss From Business*, for performing marriages, baptisms, and other personal services are self-employment earnings for qualified plan purposes.

b. Limits

1) **Defined contribution plan.** For 2022, a defined contribution plan's annual contributions and other additions (excluding earnings) to the account of a participant cannot exceed the lesser of

a) 100% of the employee's compensation or
b) $61,000.

NOTE: For purposes of these limits, contributions to more than one such plan must be added. Since a SEP is considered a defined contribution plan for purposes of these limits, employer contributions to a SEP must be added to other contributions to defined contribution plans.

2) **Defined benefit plan.** For 2022, the annual benefit for a participant under a defined benefit plan cannot be more than the lesser of

a) 100% of the participant's average compensation for his or her highest 3 consecutive calendar years or

b) $245,000.

NOTE: Compensation is the pay a participant receives from an employer for personal services for a year. It includes wages and salaries, fees, commissions, tips, fringe benefits, and bonuses. It does not include reimbursement or other expense allowances.

3) Each year, the annual limit on deductions to a qualified plan starts again. If contributions made in a prior year were less than the deductible limit, the unused limitation may not be carried forward to another year.

Excess Contributions

8. If the total of an employee's elective deferrals (salary reduction) under a qualified 401(k) plan exceeds the limit for the year, the employee can elect to withdraw the excess or leave the excess in the plan.

a. If the employee takes out the excess deferral by April 15 of the year following the contribution year, it will be reported in the employee's gross income for the year of contribution.

b. If the employee takes out any income earned on the excess deferral, it will be taxable in the tax year in which it is taken out. The distribution is not subject to the additional 10% tax on premature distributions.

c. If the employee takes out the excess deferral by April 15 of the year following the contribution year, the amount will be considered contributed for purposes of satisfying (or not satisfying) the nondiscrimination requirements of the plan.

d. If the employee does not take out the excess deferral by April 15 of the year following the contribution year, the excess, though taxable in the contribution year, will not be included in the employee's cost basis in figuring the taxable amount of any eventual benefits or distributions under the plan.

Employer Deduction

9. The deduction is limited based on the type of plan.
   a. **Profit-sharing plan.** The deduction for contributions to a profit-sharing plan cannot be more than 25% of the compensation from the business paid to all common-law employees participating in the plan.
   b. **Money purchase pension plan.** The deduction for contributions to a money purchase pension plan is generally limited to 25% of the compensation paid to participating common-law employees.
   c. **Defined benefit plan.** Because the deduction for contributions to a defined benefit plan is based on actuarial assumptions, an actuary must compute the deduction.
   d. If an employer contributes more than can be deducted in the current year, the excess may be carried over and deducted in later years, in addition to contributions for those years.
10. **Elective Deferrals [401(k) Plans]**
   a. A qualified plan can include a cash or deferred arrangement under which eligible employees can elect to have part of their before-tax pay contributed to the plan rather than receive the pay in cash.
      1) This contribution, called an elective deferral, remains tax-free until it is distributed.
   b. An employer may, under a qualified 401(k) plan, also make contributions (other than matching contributions) for participating employees without giving them a choice to take cash instead.
   c. For 2022, the basic limit on elective deferrals is $20,500 ($27,000 if 50 or older).
   d. If an excess deferral exists and is not withdrawn by April 15 of the following year, the amount will be included in income and not included in cost basis when determining a future gain.
      1) If it is withdrawn by April 15, it will be included in gross income but no penalty will apply.

11. **Rollovers**
    a. The recipient of an eligible rollover distribution from a qualified plan can defer the tax on it by rolling it over into an IRA or another eligible retirement plan.
    b. Rollovers may be subject to withholding tax. If a recipient receives an eligible rollover distribution that is expected to total more than $200, the payor must withhold 20% of each distribution for federal income tax.
        1) Tax will not be withheld if the taxpayer has the plan administrator pay the eligible rollover distribution directly to another qualified plan or an IRA in a direct rollover.
    c. An eligible rollover distribution is any distribution that is not
        1) A required minimum distribution
        2) An annual (or more frequent) distribution under a long-term (10 years or more) annuity contract or as part of a similar long-term series of substantially equal periodic distributions
        3) The portion of a distribution that represents the return of an employee's nondeductible contributions to the plan
        4) A corrective distribution, such as a return of excess contributions or deferrals under a 401(k) plan
        5) A hardship distribution
        6) Loans treated as distributions
        7) Dividends on employer securities
        8) The cost of any life insurance coverage provided under a qualified retirement plan

Stop & Review

You have completed the outline for this subunit.
Study multiple-choice questions 11 through 15 beginning on page 438.

19.4 RETIREMENT DISTRIBUTIONS AND LOANS

1. Distributions from Qualified Plans

Annuity Distributions

a. Annuity distributions are taxed using an exclusion ratio.
    1) Joint and survivorship annuity stops being paid when both spouses are deceased.
    2) Single life annuity stops being paid when the employee dies.
    3) A nonannuity distribution made on or after an annuity starting date is generally included in full in gross income.

2. Excess Accumulations and Required Minimum Distributions (RMDs)

a. If distributions are less than the required minimum distribution (RMD) for the year, a 50% excise tax will be imposed on the amount not distributed.

b. Generally, a taxpayer must begin receiving distributions by April 1 of the calendar year following the later of the employee attaining age 72 or retiring from the employer offering the plan.
    1) For a traditional IRA, the beginning distribution date is April 1 of the calendar year following the taxpayer attaining age 72.
    2) For each year following the initial distribution, the required distribution date is December 31.

3. Borrowing from the Plan

a. The terms of a qualified plan may permit the plan to lend money to participants without adverse income or excise tax results if certain requirements are met.

b. Loans are basically treated as distributions.
    1) A loan will not be treated as a distribution to the extent loans to the employee do not exceed the lesser of
        a) $50,000 or
        b) The greater of one-half of the present value of the employee's vested accrued benefit under such plans or $10,000.
    2) The $50,000 maximum sum is reduced by the participant's highest outstanding balance during the preceding 12-month period.

EXAMPLE 19-3 Multiple Loans Distribution Limitation

Participant A has a vested account balance of $100,000 and took a plan loan of $40,000 on January 1, Year 1, to be paid in 20 quarterly installments of $2,491. On January 1, Year 2, when the outstanding balance is $33,322, Participant A wants to take another plan loan. The difference between the highest outstanding loan balance for the preceding year ($40,000) and the outstanding balance on the day of the loan ($33,322) is $6,678. Since the new loan plus the outstanding loan cannot be more than $43,322 ($50,000 – $6,678), the maximum amount that the new loan can be is $10,000 ($43,322 – $33,322).

c. Plan loans generally have to be repaid within 5 years, unless the funds are to acquire a principal residence for the participant.

d. Plan loans must be amortized in level payments, made not less frequently than quarterly over the term of the loan.

e. A pledge of the participant's interest under the plan or an agreement to pledge such interest as security for a loan by a third party, as well as a direct or indirect loan from the plan itself, is treated as a loan.

f. Any outstanding loan balance when a plan terminates (e.g., due to death or severance from employment of the plan participant) must be contributed (i.e., rolled over) to a qualified plan (i.e., an IRA) before the tax return due date (instead of the usual 60-day rollover period) in order to avoid taxation as a distribution.

4. **Tax on Premature Distributions**

a. If a distribution is made to the taxpayer under the plan before (s)he reaches age 59 1/2, the taxpayer may have to pay a 10% additional tax on the premature distribution. This tax applies to the amount received that the taxpayer must include in income.

Exceptions

b. The 10% tax will not apply if distributions before age 59 1/2

1) Are made to a beneficiary (or to the estate of the taxpayer) on or after the death of the taxpayer
2) Result from the taxpayer having a qualifying disability
3) Are part of a series of substantially equal periodic payments beginning after separation from service and made at least annually for the life or life expectancy of the taxpayer or the joint lives or life expectancies of the taxpayer and his or her designated beneficiary
4) Are made to the taxpayer after (s)he separated from service if the separation occurred during or after the calendar year in which the taxpayer reached age 55 (not applicable to SEP or traditional IRAs)
5) Are made to the taxpayer for medical care up to the amount allowable as a medical expense deduction (determined without regard to whether the taxpayer itemizes deductions)
6) Are made to an alternate payee under a qualified domestic relations order (QDRO)
7) Are made because of an IRS levy on the plan
8) Are made as a qualified U.S. reservist distribution (those called to active duty)
9) Are from federal retirement funds of a phased program
10) Are qualified hurricane or wildfire distributions
11) Are qualified higher education expenses, including those related to graduate-level courses (IRAs only)
    a) However, the amount of qualified higher education expenses is reduced by the amount of any qualified scholarship, educational assistance allowance, or payment (other than by gift, bequest, device, or inheritance) for an individual's educational enrollment, which is excludable from gross income.
12) Are used to pay medical insurance premiums of an unemployed individual (IRAs only)
13) Are used to pay up to $10,000 used in a qualified first-time home purchase (IRAs only)
14) Are timely made to reduce excess contributions or excess deferrals (IRAs only)
15) Are used to pay up to $5,000 for each qualified birth or adoption
16) Are from a government plan to a qualified public safety employee who is at least age 50

Withholding on Distributions

c. If a participant receives a distribution that is not eligible for rollover treatment, such as a long-term periodic distribution or a required distribution, the 20% withholding requirement does not apply.

   1) Although other withholding rules may apply, a taxpayer may still choose not to have tax withheld from these distributions.

5. **Prohibited Transactions**

   a. Certain transactions between a plan and a disqualified person are prohibited and are subject to a 15% excise tax on the amount involved.

      1) If the transaction is not corrected within the taxable period, an **additional** tax of 100% of the amount involved is imposed.

         a) Both taxes are payable by any disqualified person who participated in the transaction.

   b. Prohibited transactions generally include

      1) A transfer of plan income or assets to, or use of them by or for the benefit of, a disqualified person
      2) Dealing with plan income or assets by a fiduciary in his or her own interest
      3) The receiving of consideration by a fiduciary for his or her own account from a party that is dealing with the plan in a transaction that involves plan income or assets
      4) Any of the following acts between the plan and a disqualified person:

         a) Selling, exchanging, or leasing property
         b) Lending money or extending credit
         c) Furnishing goods, services, or facilities

Disqualified Persons

c. The following are disqualified persons:

1) A fiduciary of the plan
2) A person providing services to the plan
3) An employer, if any employees are covered by the plan
4) An employee organization, if any members are covered by the plan
5) Any direct or indirect owner of 50% or more of any of the following:
    a) The combined voting power of all classes of stock entitled to vote, or the total value of shares of all classes of stock of a corporation that is an employer or employee organization described in 3) or 4).
    b) The capital interest or profits interest of a partnership that is an employer or employee organization described in 3) or 4).
    c) The beneficial interest of a trust or unincorporated enterprise that is an employer or employee organization described in 3) or 4).
6) A member of the family of any individual described in 1), 2), 3), or 5).
    a) A member of a family is the spouse, ancestor, lineal descendant, or any spouse of a lineal descendant.
7) A corporation, partnership, trust, or estate of which (or in which) any direct or indirect owner described in 1) through 5) holds 50% or more of any of the following:
    a) The combined voting power of all classes of stock entitled to vote or the total value of shares of all classes of stock of a corporation.
    b) The capital interest or profits interest of a partnership.
    c) The beneficial interest of a trust or estate.
8) An officer, director (or an individual having powers or responsibilities similar to those of officers or directors), a 10% or more shareholder, or highly compensated employee (earning 10% or more of the yearly wages of an employer) of a person described in 3), 4), 5), or 7).
9) A 10% or more (in capital or profits) partner or joint venturer of a person described in 3), 4), 5), or 7).

Exemption

d. Prohibited transactions do not take place if a disqualified person receives benefits to which (s)he is entitled as a plan participant and beneficiary. However, the same terms apply as for other qualified persons.

EXAMPLE 19-4	**Age Requirement for Distributions**
The owner of a business with an established plan must meet the age requirement of 59 1/2 before receiving a distribution.	

Qualified Plan Qualification Rules

6. To qualify for the tax benefits available, a qualified plan must meet certain requirements of the tax law, which include but are not limited to the following:
   a. Plan assets must not be diverted.
   b. Minimum coverage requirements must be met. To be a qualified plan, a defined benefit plan must benefit at least the lesser of
      1) 50 employees or
      2) The greater of
         a) 40% of all employees or
         b) 2 employees.

   NOTE: If there is only one employee, the plan must benefit that employee.

   c. Contributions or benefits must not discriminate in favor of highly compensated employees.
   d. Contribution and benefit limits must not be exceeded.
   e. Minimum vesting standards must be met. A benefit becomes vested when it becomes nonforfeitable.
   f. Benefit payments must begin when required, except in the case of early retirement payments.
   g. Benefits must not be assigned or alienated.
   h. Benefits must not be reduced for Social Security increases.
   i. Elective deferrals must be limited.

Reporting Requirements

7. Generally, an annual return/report form is required to be filed by the last day of the 7th month after the plan year ends.
   a. **Form 5500-SF,** ***Short Form Annual Return/Report of Small Employee Benefit Plan***, is a simplified annual reporting form that can be used if the plan meets all of the following conditions:
      1) The plan is a small plan (generally fewer than 100 participants at the beginning of the plan year).
      2) The plan meets the conditions for being exempt from the requirement that the plan's books and records be audited by an independent qualified public accountant.
      3) The plan has 100% of its assets invested in certain secure investments with a readily determinable fair value.
      4) The plan holds no employer securities.
      5) The plan is not a multi-employer plan.

b. **Form 5500-EZ, *Annual Return of One-Participant (Owners and Their Spouses) Retirement Plan***, is used for a one-participant plan if either of the following is true:

1) The plan covers only the participant (or the participant and the participant's spouse), and the participant (or the participant and the participant's spouse) owns the entire business (whether incorporated or unincorporated).
2) The plan covers only one or more partners [or partner(s) and spouse(s)] in a business partnership.

NOTE: Beginning January 1, 2021, every one-participant plan that is required to file an annual return for 2022 must file Form 5500-EZ. If the one-participant plan(s) had total assets of $250,000 or less at the end of the plan year, Form 5500-EZ for that plan year is not required. All plans **must file** a Form 5500-EZ for the **final plan year** to show that all plan assets have been distributed.

c. **Form 5500, *Annual Return/Report of Employee Benefit Plan***, is used when the requirements for filing Form 5500-EZ or Form 5500-SF are not met and a return or report is required.

d. **Form 1099-R, *Distributions From Pensions, Annuities, Retirement or Profit-Sharing Plans, IRAs, Insurance Contracts, etc.***, is generally the form on which distributions from pensions, annuities, profit-sharing and retirement plans (including Sec. 457 state and local government plans), IRAs, insurance contracts, etc., are reported to recipients.

e. **Period statements** of the participants' account benefits are to be provided by the plan providers.

1) The following organizations generally can provide IRS-approved master or prototype plans:
   a) Banks (including some savings and loan associations and federally insured credit unions)
   b) Trade or professional organizations
   c) Insurance companies

Electronic Filing

8. All Forms 5500, 5500-SF, and 5500-EZ are required to be filed electronically with the Department of Labor through EFAST2.

Stop & Review

You have completed the outline for this subunit.

Study multiple-choice questions 16 through 20 beginning on page 439.

QUESTIONS

19.1 Simplified Employee Pension (SEP)

1. Joaquin is a small business owner who maintains a SEP for his employees:

- Jan, a 42-year-old part-timer who has worked for Joaquin in this business since 2012. She works 15 hours per week. She earned $13,650 in 2022.
- Malik, a 72-year-old seasonal worker who works from September through December. He has worked for Joaquin in this business since 2014 and earned $6,150 in 2022.
- Monica is 21 years old and works 10 hours per week all year. She has worked for Joaquin since June 2020 and earned $4,950 in 2022.

Joaquin's business had net taxable income in 2021 of $62,300. All employees and Joaquin are U.S. citizens, and none of them are union members. Which of the individuals listed below can be excluded from coverage under the SEP in 2022?

A. Jan.

B. Malik.

C. Monica.

D. Joaquin.

Answer (C) is correct.

REQUIRED: The excludable individual from coverage under the SEP.

DISCUSSION: In order for an employee to be eligible for coverage under a SEP, the employee must be 21 years old, have worked for the employer in at least 3 of the last 5 years, and have earned at least $650 in compensation. Therefore, Monica is excludable because she has not been working for Joaquin for the necessary amount of time.

2. Which of the following is required for an individual to qualify for a simplified employee pension (SEP)?

A. The individual must not be covered by another retirement plan.

B. Self-employment net loss is subtracted from any salaries and wages when figuring total compensation.

C. The individual must not be age 72 by the end of the tax year.

D. None of the answers are correct.

Answer (D) is correct.

REQUIRED: The requirement for an individual to qualify for a self-employed retirement plan.

DISCUSSION: A self-employed individual is an employee for SEP purposes. (S)he is also the employer. Even if the self-employed individual is the only qualifying employee, (s)he can have a SEP-IRA. A qualifying employee is one who meets all of the following conditions: (1) (S)he is at least 21 years old, (2) (s)he has worked for the employer during at least 3 of the 5 years immediately preceding the tax year, and (3) (s)he has received from the employer at least $650 in compensation in the tax year.

Answer (A) is incorrect. This is not a requirement to qualify for a SEP. **Answer (B) is incorrect.** This is not a requirement to qualify for a SEP. **Answer (C) is incorrect.** There is no age limitation.

3. Mike is self-employed. He is a calendar-year taxpayer. If he wants to set up a SEP plan for his business for the year 2022, he must do so by (including extensions)

A. December 31, 2022.

B. January 31, 2023.

C. April 15, 2023.

D. October 15, 2023.

Answer (D) is correct.

REQUIRED: The latest date that a SEP plan can be set up for a given year.

DISCUSSION: A deduction for contributions to a qualified plan, including a SEP, is generally allowed for the tax year in which contributions are paid. Contributions paid on or before the due date of returns, including extensions, for a particular tax year are deemed paid on the last day of that tax year. Therefore, Mike would be allowed until October 15, 2023 (the normal due date of April 15, 2023, plus a 6-month extension).

Answer (A) is incorrect. Mike is allowed beyond the 2022 tax year. He is entitled to the normal due date plus an extension. **Answer (B) is incorrect.** January 31, 2023, is before the normal due date of April 15, 2023. **Answer (C) is incorrect.** April 15, 2023, does not include the 6-month extension allowed by the IRS to set up a SEP.

4. John, a self-employed taxpayer, has a SEP plan for his business. He has three eligible employees, Sara (age 35), Joseph (age 37), and Jean (age 45), who have worked for him for the past 10 years. For the year 2022, Sara earned $15,000, Joseph earned $25,000, and Jean earned $30,000. John wants to elect the 25% contribution rate so he can put as much as possible in for himself. If he elects 25%, how much must he contribute to the plan for his employees?

A. $0

B. $14,500

C. $17,500

D. $61,000

Answer (C) is correct.

REQUIRED: The amount of money that must be contributed to a SEP plan.

DISCUSSION: A SEP does not require contributions every year, but it must not discriminate in favor of highly compensated employees. If John wants to contribute 25% to his own SEP, he must also contribute the lesser of 25% of the participating employee's compensation (limited to $305,000 of compensation) or $61,000. Therefore, 25% of $70,000 total employee compensation ($15,000 from Sara + $25,000 from Joseph + $30,000 from Jean) is $17,500, which is less than the $61,000 upper limit.

Answer (A) is incorrect. John is required to contribute to the plan if he elects the 25% contribution rate. **Answer (B) is incorrect.** John must contribute 25% of the total of his three employees' salaries and not 25% of the upper limit of how much John would be able to contribute if his employees were eligible. **Answer (D) is incorrect.** The amount of $61,000 is the upper limit of how much John would be able to contribute if his employees were eligible.

5. Crispian is employed by P, Inc. P, Inc., has a simplified employee pension (SEP) plan for its employees in which Crispian participates. Crispian's compensation for 2022, before P's contribution to his SEP-IRA, was $320,000. What is the maximum contribution that P, Inc. can contribute to Crispian's SEP-IRA?

A. $80,000

B. $61,000

C. $32,000

D. $72,500

Answer (B) is correct.

REQUIRED: The maximum deductible contribution that can be made to a SEP.

DISCUSSION: Under Sec. 404(h), the amount of deductible contributions for a simplified employee pension shall not exceed 25% of the employee's compensation (limited to $305,000) during the taxable year. P's maximum deductible contribution is $61,000 (limited to the lesser of $305,000 × 25%, or $61,000).

19.2 Savings Incentive Match Plans for Employees (SIMPLE)

6. The SIMPLE plan must be available to every employee who

A. Received at least $5,000 in compensation from the employer during any 2 preceding years and is reasonably expected to receive at least $5,000 in compensation during the current year.

B. Received at least $5,000 in compensation from the employer during each of the 2 preceding years and is reasonably expected to receive at least $5,000 in compensation during the current year.

C. Received at least $5,000 in compensation from the employer during any 2 preceding years.

D. Is reasonably expected to receive at least $5,000 in compensation during the current year.

Answer (A) is correct.

REQUIRED: The employee who is eligible to participate in a SIMPLE plan.

DISCUSSION: The SIMPLE plan must be available to every employee who (1) received at least $5,000 in compensation from the employer during any 2 preceding years and (2) is reasonably expected to receive at least $5,000 in compensation during the current year. Individuals who are self-employed may also participate in a SIMPLE plan. However, certain nonresident aliens and employees who are covered by a collective bargaining agreement may be unable to participate (Publication 4334).

Answer (B) is incorrect. The employee is required to have received at least $5,000 in compensation during any 2 preceding years, not in each of the preceding 2 years. **Answer (C) is incorrect.** The employee is also required to reasonably expect to receive at least $5,000 in compensation during the current year. **Answer (D) is incorrect.** The employee is also required to have received at least $5,000 in compensation during any 2 preceding years.

7. Participants of SIMPLE plans who take early withdrawals are generally subject to

A. A 10% withdrawal penalty.

B. A 25% withdrawal penalty.

C. A 25% withdrawal penalty on the first $10,000 and a 10% withdrawal penalty on the remainder.

D. A 25% withdrawal penalty on withdrawals made during the 2-year period beginning on the date the participant began participating in the plan and a 10% withdrawal penalty on all other early distributions.

Answer (D) is correct.

REQUIRED: The applicable early withdrawal penalty for SIMPLE plans.

DISCUSSION: Participants are considered to have taken early withdrawals if the distributions are made before age 59 1/2. These distributions are generally subject to a 10% early withdrawal penalty. However, employees who withdraw contributions during the 2-year period beginning on the date the participant began participating in the SIMPLE plan will be assessed a 25% early withdrawal penalty tax.

8. Lenore, who is 43 years old, opened a SIMPLE IRA on January 19, 2021. On September 22, 2022, she withdrew the entire $10,000 value of the account. The distribution does not meet any early withdrawal exceptions to the additional tax on early distributions. How much additional tax (penalty) is the distribution subject to?

A. $600

B. $1,000

C. $1,500

D. $2,500

Answer (D) is correct.

REQUIRED: The additional tax (penalty) assessed on early distributions from a SIMPLE IRA.

DISCUSSION: If an early distribution occurs from a SIMPLE IRA within 2 years of commencing to participate in the program, the penalty assessed increases from 10% to 25%. Therefore, Lenore would be penalized $2,500 ($10,000 × .25) (Publication 560).

Answer (A) is incorrect. The penalty is 25%, not 6%. **Answer (B) is incorrect.** The penalty assessed is 25%, not 10%. **Answer (C) is incorrect.** The penalty is 25%, not 15%.

9. The SIMPLE 401(k) plan is a qualified retirement plan. It is not subject to nondiscrimination and top-heavy rules if it meets all of the following conditions EXCEPT

A. Under the plan, the employee may choose salary reduction contributions to a trust up to $14,000 for 2022.

B. Participants age 50 and over can make a catch-up contribution up to $3,000.

C. Employers must make matching contributions of 3% of compensation for the year or nonelective contributions of 2% of compensation on behalf of each eligible employee who has at least $5,000 of compensation from his employer for the year.

D. The employee's rights to any contributions are forfeitable.

Answer (D) is correct.

REQUIRED: The condition not required to exclude the SIMPLE 401(k) plan from nondiscrimination and top-heavy rules.

DISCUSSION: The SIMPLE 401(k) plan is available to employers with 100 or fewer employees who received at least $5,000 in compensation from the employer in the preceding year. Employers are not permitted to maintain another qualified plan. Employers are generally required to match employee contributions on a dollar-for-dollar basis up to 3% of an employee's compensation for the year. An employer may elect to make a nonelective contribution of 2% of compensation for each eligible employee who has earned at least $5,000 in compensation from the employer during the year. The employees vest immediately in employer SIMPLE contributions; therefore, the funds are not forfeitable.

Answer (A) is incorrect. An employee is permitted to make salary reduction contributions to a trust up to $14,000 for 2022. **Answer (B) is incorrect.** Participants age 50 and up are allowed to make a catch-up contribution of $3,000 a year. **Answer (C) is incorrect.** The contribution percentages are properly stated.

10. All of the following are true statements about contributions to SIMPLE IRA plans EXCEPT

A. Employer contributions have to be expressed as a percentage of the employee's compensation and cannot exceed $14,000 in 2022 for employees under age 50.

B. Unless an election is made otherwise, the employer must match the elective contribution of an employee in an amount not exceeding 3% of the employee's compensation.

C. An employee's SIMPLE IRA contribution cannot exceed 3% of the employee's compensation.

D. An employer may elect to limit its matching contribution for all eligible employees to a smaller percentage of compensation, but not less than 1%.

Answer (C) is correct.

REQUIRED: The contribution requirements to a SIMPLE IRA plan.

DISCUSSION: A SIMPLE IRA must allow each eligible employee to elect to have the employer make payments either directly to the employee in cash or as a contribution, expressed as a percentage of compensation, to the SIMPLE account. Elective contributions are limited to $14,000 for employees under age 50 for 2022, but there is no limit based on a percentage of compensation. The employer must match the elective contribution of an employee in an amount not exceeding 3% of the employee's compensation. However, an employer may elect to limit its match to a smaller percentage of compensation not to fall below 1%.

Answer (A) is incorrect. Employer contributions must be expressed as a percentage of compensation and cannot exceed $14,000 if the employee is under age 50. **Answer (B) is incorrect.** The employer must match the employee's elective contribution that does not exceed 3% of compensation unless an election is made otherwise. **Answer (D) is incorrect.** An employer may elect to match a smaller elective contribution, but not less than 1% of compensation.

19.3 Qualified Plans

11. Your qualified 401(k) plan can include what type of contribution arrangement?

A. Cash.

B. Elective deferral.

C. Both cash and elective deferral arrangements.

D. None of the answers are correct.

Answer (C) is correct.

REQUIRED: The permissible qualified 401(k) contribution arrangements.

DISCUSSION: Qualified 401(k) plans can include contribution arrangements that are either cash or elective deferral arrangements (Publication 560).

12. Which of the following statements is false with respect to qualified plans?

A. If a plan is a defined benefit plan subject to the minimum funding requirements, the employer must make quarterly installment payments of the required contributions.

B. If a defined contribution plan is a profit-sharing plan, the employer can make contributions for common-law employees out of net profits only.

C. An employer can have more than one qualified plan.

D. A separate account is set up for each participant under a defined contribution plan.

Answer (B) is correct.

REQUIRED: The false statement regarding qualified plans.

DISCUSSION: A profit-sharing plan is a plan for sharing employer profits with the firm's employees. However, an employer does not have to make contributions out of net profits to have a profit-sharing plan.

Answer (A) is incorrect. The employer must make quarterly installment payments of required contributions if the plan is defined benefit subject to minimum funding requirements. **Answer (C) is incorrect.** Employers can have multiple qualified plans. **Answer (D) is incorrect.** Separate accounts are set up for each participant of a defined contribution plan.

13. Chip, a waiter, is a common-law employee of Tiger Company. Tiger Company, a sole proprietorship, has a defined contribution qualified plan in which Chip is eligible to participate. The following items represent Chip's income from Tiger in 2022:

Wages	$25,000
Bonus	5,000
Commissions	1,000
Reimbursement for travel expenses	5,000

How much can Tiger Company contribute to Chip's retirement account for 2022?

A. $25,000

B. $31,000

C. $7,750

D. $36,000

Answer (B) is correct.

REQUIRED: The maximum amount that can be contributed to a defined contribution qualified plan.

DISCUSSION: A defined contribution plan's annual contributions to the account of a participant cannot exceed the lesser of $61,000 or 100% of the compensation actually paid to the participant. Compensation includes wages and salary, fees, tips, commissions, and bonuses, but it does not include reimbursements or expense allowances. Therefore, Tiger Company may contribute a maximum of $31,000 [100% of ($25,000 wages + $5,000 bonus + $1,000 commissions)].

Answer (A) is incorrect. Bonuses and commissions are included in compensation. **Answer (C) is incorrect.** Tiger's maximum contribution is equal to 100% (not 25%) of the employee's compensation. **Answer (D) is incorrect.** Reimbursements for travel expenses are not included as compensation.

14. Which of the following statements with respect to a Sec. 401(k) plan is false?

A. Any qualified plan can include a 401(k) plan.

B. Eligible employees can elect to have their employer contribute part of their before-tax pay to the 401(k) plan rather than receive the pay in cash.

C. The amount contributed to a 401(k) plan within applicable limits, and any earnings on it, remain tax-free until it is distributed by the plan.

D. A 401(k) plan may not require, as a condition of participation, that an employee complete a period of service beyond the later of age 21 or the completion of 1 year of service.

Answer (A) is correct.

REQUIRED: The false statement regarding a Sec. 401(k) plan.

DISCUSSION: A qualified plan can include a cash or deferred arrangement [401(k) plan] under which eligible employees can elect to have an employer contribute part of their before-tax pay to the plan rather than receive the pay in cash. However, a qualified plan can include a 401(k) plan only if it is

1) A profit-sharing plan or
2) A money purchase pension plan in existence on June 27, 1974.

Answer (B) is incorrect. Eligible employees can elect to have their employer contribute part of their before-tax pay to the 401(k) plan rather than receive the pay in cash. **Answer (C) is incorrect.** The amount contributed to a 401(k) plan within applicable limits, and any earnings on it, remains tax-free until it is distributed by the plan. **Answer (D) is incorrect.** A 401(k) plan may not require, as a condition of participation, that an employee complete a period of service beyond the later of age 21 or the completion of 1 year of service.

15. The 2022 basic limit on elective deferrals in 401(k) plans (excluding SIMPLE plans) for participants under age 50 is

A. $14,000

B. $17,000

C. $20,500

D. $27,000

Answer (C) is correct.

REQUIRED: The 2022 basic limit on elective deferrals in 401(k) plans for participants under age 50.

DISCUSSION: A 401(k) plan can include a cash or deferred arrangement under which eligible employees can elect to have part of their before-tax pay contributed to the plan rather than receive the pay in cash. This contribution, called an elective deferral, remains tax-free until it is distributed. For 2022, the basic limit on elective deferrals is $20,500 ($27,000 if 50 or older).

19.4 Retirement Distributions and Loans

16. Charles retired 3 years ago at age 72 from working at his family's laminating business. His required minimum distribution for 2022 is $2,000. Charles elects to only withdraw $1,500 from his IRA account. How much excise tax may Charles have to pay for that year?

A. $50

B. $100

C. $200

D. $250

Answer (D) is correct.

REQUIRED: The amount of excise tax Charles may have to pay for excess accumulation.

DISCUSSION: Failure to meet the required minimum distributions can result in a 50% penalty (excise tax) for the year on the amount not distributed as required. The amount not distributed as required is $500 ($2,000 – $1,500). Therefore, the excise tax Charles has to pay for the year is $250 ($500 × 50%).

17. Max, a fiduciary, pledged his client's traditional IRA of $300,000 as security for a loan. If Max is found liable for engaging in a prohibited transaction, what is the minimum penalty he is most likely to pay if the transaction is not corrected?

A. $45,000

B. $30,000

C. $300,000

D. $345,000

Answer (D) is correct.

REQUIRED: The minimum penalty for engaging in a prohibited transaction.

DISCUSSION: Certain transactions between a plan and a disqualified person are prohibited and are subject to a 15% excise tax on the amount involved ($300,000 × 15% = $45,000). If the transaction is not corrected within the taxable period, an additional tax of 100% of the amount involved is imposed. Both taxes are payable by any disqualified person who participated in the transaction. The receiving of consideration by a fiduciary for his or her own account from a party that is dealing with the plan in a transaction that involves plan income or assets is prohibited. The combined total is $345,000 ($45,000 from excise tax + $300,000 amount involved).

Answer (A) is incorrect. Max must also pay an additional 100% penalty for failure to correct the transaction. **Answer (B) is incorrect.** The amount of $30,000 is only a 10% excise tax, and the correct excise tax is 15% plus an additional penalty for failure to correct the violation. **Answer (C) is incorrect.** The amount of $300,000 only includes the 100% additional penalty.

18. Which of the following distributions would be subject to the 10% additional tax that is imposed upon premature distributions from a qualified plan prior to an employee reaching age 59 1/2?

A. A distribution made to an employee after separation from service, if the separation occurred during or after the calendar year in which the employee reached age 55.

B. A distribution made to an employee for medical care to the extent that the distribution does not exceed the amount allowable as a medical expense deduction (determined without regard to whether the employee itemizes deductions).

C. A timely made distribution to reduce excess employee or matching employer contributions (excess aggregate contributions).

D. A distribution made to permit the employee to purchase a vacation home.

Answer (D) is correct.

REQUIRED: The distribution subject to the 10% additional tax.

DISCUSSION: Section 72(t)(2) lists many exceptions to the 10% tax on early distributions from qualified retirement plans. One of these exceptions is an early distribution up to $10,000 used in a qualified first-time home purchase. A qualified first-time home buyer distribution is a payment received to the extent the payment is used before the close of the 120th day after the day on which the distribution is received to pay qualified acquisition costs with respect to a principal residence of a first-time home buyer. However, the purchase of a second personal residence does not meet the exception from the additional tax.

19. Which of the following statements with respect to self-employed retirement plan prohibited transactions is false?

A. The tax on a prohibited transaction is 15% of the amount involved.

B. Disqualified persons include a fiduciary of the plan.

C. Exchanging property between a disqualified person and a plan is a prohibited transaction.

D. If the prohibited transaction is not corrected within the taxable period, an additional tax of 80% of the amount involved is imposed.

Answer (D) is correct.

REQUIRED: The false statement regarding prohibited transactions.

DISCUSSION: The tax on a prohibited transaction is 15% of the amount involved for each year in the taxable period. If the transaction is not corrected within the taxable period, an additional tax of 100% of the amount involved is imposed. Both taxes are payable by any disqualified person who participated in the transaction.

Answer (A) is incorrect. The tax on prohibited transactions is 15% of the amount involved. **Answer (B) is incorrect.** A fiduciary of the plan is a disqualified person. **Answer (C) is incorrect.** Exchanging property between a disqualified person and a plan is a prohibited transaction.

20. With regard to a qualified plan, which of the following statements is true?

A. Only a sole proprietor or a partner can establish a qualified plan.

B. An employee must be allowed to participate in the plan if the employee is at least age 21, but not over age 59 1/2, and has at least 1 year of service (2 years if the plan provides that, after not more than 2 years of service, the employee has a nonforfeitable right to all of his or her accrued benefits).

C. For qualified plan purposes, a self-employed individual is both an employer and an employee. As an employer, the individual can usually deduct, subject to limits, contributions made to a qualified plan, excluding those made for his or her own retirement.

D. You can choose not to have tax withheld on long-term periodic distributions and required distributions.

Answer (D) is correct.

REQUIRED: The true statement regarding qualified plans.

DISCUSSION: If a participant receives a distribution that is not eligible for rollover treatment, such as a long-term periodic distribution or a required distribution, the 20% withholding requirement does not apply. Although other withholding rules may apply, a taxpayer may still choose not to have tax withheld from these distributions.

Answer (A) is incorrect. A partnership, not a partner, can establish a qualified plan. Additionally, employers that are corporations can set up and maintain plans. **Answer (B) is incorrect.** A plan cannot exclude an employee because (s)he has reached a certain age. **Answer (C) is incorrect.** A self-employed individual may deduct contributions to his or her own account.

Go to Online Course

Access the **Gleim EA Premium Review System** featuring our SmartAdapt technology from your Gleim Personal Classroom to continue your studies.

You will experience a personalized study environment with exam-emulating multiple-choice questions.

STUDY UNIT TWENTY
EXEMPT ORGANIZATIONS

(7 pages of outline)

Certain organizations may qualify for exemption from federal income tax under Sec. 501(a). They are referred to as nonprofit organizations. Most organizations seeking recognition of exemption from federal income tax must use application forms specifically prescribed by the IRS.

20.1 EXEMPT ORGANIZATIONS

Exempt Status

1. Exempt status generally depends on the nature and purpose of an organization.
   a. An organization is tax-exempt only if specifically designated as such by the IRC.
   b. It may be organized as a corporation (including a limited liability company), trust, foundation, fund, society, etc., but cannot be a sole proprietorship, an individual, or a partnership.
      1) An organization operated for the primary purpose of carrying on a trade or business for profit is generally not tax-exempt.
   c. Examples of organization types that may be exempt are
      1) Religious or apostolic organizations
         a) The Salvation Army is an example of a religious organization.
      2) Political organizations
      3) Chambers of commerce
      4) Real estate boards
      5) Labor organizations
      6) American Red Cross
      7) State-chartered credit unions
      8) Civic welfare organizations
         a) Organizations that combat community deterioration and juvenile delinquency, such as a Boys & Girls Club, qualify.
      9) Certain domestic and foreign corporations
      10) Child and animal protection organizations
      11) Public safety testing organizations
      12) Athletic clubs
         a) Organizations that foster national or international amateur sports competition provided they do not provide athletic facilities or equipment
      13) Fraternal beneficiary associations
         a) Associations that operate under a lodge system and provide payment of life, sick, accident, or other benefits to members and their dependents

14) Social organizations
   a) No part of net earnings may benefit a private shareholder.
   b) Exempt status is lost if 35% or more of its receipts are from sources other than membership fees, dues, and assessments.
      i) Up to 15% of gross receipts can be from public use of a social club's facilities.

15) Schools

Prohibited Transactions

d. Certain employee trusts lose exempt status if they engage in prohibited transactions.
   1) Examples include lending without adequate security or reasonable interest or paying unreasonable compensation for personal services.

e. An exempt organization that loses its tax-exempt status cannot receive tax-deductible contributions and will not be identified in the IRS Exempt Organizations Business Master File Extract as eligible to receive tax-deductible contributions, or be included in Exempt Organizations Select Check.

Religious, Charitable, Scientific, Educational, Literary

f. Organizations formed and operated exclusively for religious, charitable, scientific, educational, literary, or similar purposes are a broad class of exempt organizations.
   1) No part of net earnings may inure to the benefit of any private shareholder or individual.
   2) No substantial part of its activities may attempt to influence legislation or a political candidacy (e.g., political action committees).
      a) In general, if a substantial part of the activities of an organization consists of attempting to influence legislation, the organization will lose its exempt status.
         i) However, most organizations can elect to replace the substantial part of activities test with a lobbying expenditure limit.
      b) If an election for a tax year is in effect for an organization and that organization exceeds the lobbying expenditure limits, an excise tax of 25% will be imposed on the excess amount.
      c) Exempt status may be lost if the organization directly participates in a political campaign.

Private Foundations

g. Each domestic or foreign exempt organization is a private foundation unless, generally, it receives more than a third of its support (annually) from its members and the general public. In this case, the private foundation status terminates, and the organization becomes a public charity.
   1) Exempt status of a private foundation is subject to statutory restrictions, notification requirements, and excise taxes.
   2) A charitable, religious, or scientific organization is presumed to be a private foundation unless it either
      a) Is a church or has annual gross receipts under $5,000 or
      b) Notifies the IRS that it is not a private foundation (on Form 1023) within 27 months from the end of the month in which it was organized.

Feeder Organization

h. A feeder organization must independently qualify for exempt status. It is not enough that all of its profits are paid to exempt organizations.

Homeowners' Association

i. A homeowners' association is treated as a tax-exempt organization.

1) A homeowners' association is one organized for acquisition, construction, management, maintenance, etc., of residential real estate or condominiums. A cooperative housing corporation is excluded.

2) A condominium management association, to be treated as a tax-exempt housing association, must file a separate election for each tax year by the return due date of the applicable year.

Tax-Exempt Organization Internal Revenue Code Chart

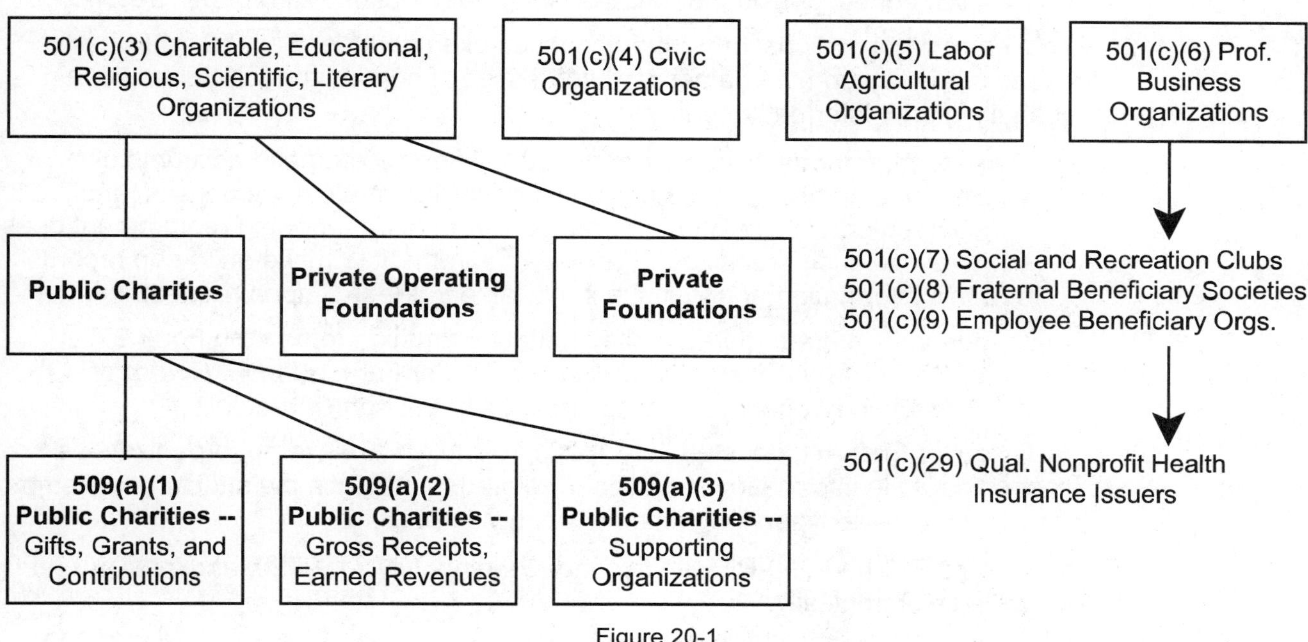

Figure 20-1

Requirements for Exemption

2. An organization other than an employee's qualified pension or profit-sharing trust must apply in writing to its IRS district director for a ruling or a determination that it is tax-exempt.

a. To establish its exemption, an organization must file a **written application** with the key director for the district in which the principal place of business or principal office of the organization is located.

1) Religious, charitable, scientific, educational, etc., organizations (public charities) use Form 1023. Form 1024 is used by most others.

2) If filed within the 15-month period (27 months per Form 1023), retroactive treatment is available.

Annual Information Return

b. Exempt organizations are generally required to file annual information returns on or before the 15th day of the 5th month following the close of the taxable year.

1) Exempt status may be denied or revoked for failure to file.
2) The organization reports all gross income, receipts, and disbursements.
    a) The amount of contributions received is reported.
    b) All substantial contributions are identified.
3) Those exempted from the filing requirement include
    a) A church or church-affiliated organization;
    b) An exclusively religious activity or any religious order;
    c) An organization (other than a private foundation) having annual gross receipts that are not more than $50,000; and
    d) A stock bonus, pension, or profit-sharing trust that qualified under Sec. 401.
4) Tax exempt organizations, other than charities exempt under Sec. 501(c)(3), are able to stop reporting the names and addresses of contributors on Schedule B when filing their information returns.
    a) Tax-exempt organizations are required to keep records and accounts of gross income and receipts (including donor information), expenses, and disbursements. Relief from the annual information reporting requirement does not relieve such organizations of the requirement to make and keep records of this information and to make it available to the IRS upon request.
5) Private foundations are required to file annual information returns on Form 990, *Return of Organization Exempt from Income Tax*, or Form 990-PF, *Return of Private Foundation*, regardless of the amounts of their gross receipts.
6) The Taxpayer First Act, enacted July 1, 2019, requires tax-exempt organizations to electronically file information returns and related forms. The law affects tax-exempt organizations in tax years beginning after July 1, 2019.
    a) Forms 990 and 990-PF with tax years ending July 31, 2020, and later **must** be filed electronically.
    b) Form 990 and 990-PF filings for tax years ending on or before June 30, 2020, may still be on paper.

7) Organizations with $50,000 or less in gross receipts that do not have to file an annual notice will be required to file a Form 990-N, *Electronic Notice (e-Postcard) for Tax-Exempt Organizations Not Required to File Form 990 or 990-EZ.*

   a) The form is due by the 15th day of the 5th month following the close of the tax year and can be filed electronically and free of charge.
   b) Form 990-N requires the organization to provide the name and mailing address of the organization, any other names used, a web address (if one exists), the name and address of the principal officer, and a statement confirming the organization's annual gross receipts are $50,000 or less.
   c) Failure to file the annual report for 3 years in a row will subject the organization to loss of its exempt status, requiring the organization to reapply for recognition.

8) A central or parent organization may file Form 990 for two or more local organizations that are not private foundations. However, this return is in addition to the central or parent organization's separate annual return if it must file one.

   a) Form 990-EZ is a shortened version of Form 990. It is designed for use by small exempt organizations and nonexempt charitable trusts. An organization may file Form 990-EZ instead of Form 990 if it meets both of the following requirements:

      i) Gross receipts during the year were less than $200,000
      ii) Total assets at the end of the year were less than $500,000

9) Exempt organizations must make the Form 990-T, *Exempt Organization Business Income Tax Return*, open for public inspection for a period of 3 years from the date the Form 990-T is required to be filed or is actually filed, whichever is later.

10) Annual information returns, employment tax returns, and a report of cash received are all returns that might be required of a tax-exempt organization.

Filing Extension

11) Form 8868, *Application for Automatic Extension of Time to File an Exempt Organization Return*, is used to request an automatic 6-month extension to file Forms 990, 990-EZ, 990-PF, or 990-T.

Failure to File Penalties

12) Generally, an exempt organization that fails to file a required return must pay a penalty of $20 a day for each day the failure continues. The same penalty will apply if the organization does not give all the information required on the return or does not give the correct information. The maximum penalty for any one return is the smaller of $11,000 or 5% of the organization's gross receipts for the year. For an organization that has gross receipts of over $1,129,000 for the year, the penalty is $110 a day (for 2022 tax returns filed in 2023), up to a maximum of $56,000.

    a) No penalty will be imposed if reasonable cause for failure to file timely can be shown.

Unrelated Business Taxable Income Tax

3. Tax-exempt organizations are generally subject to tax on income from unrelated business taxable income (UBTI).
   a. An unrelated business is a trade or business activity regularly carried on for the production of income (even if a loss results) that is not substantially related to performance of the exempt purpose or function, i.e., that does not contribute more than insubstantial benefits to the exempt purposes.
      1) Certain qualified sponsorship payments received by an exempt organization are not subject to UBTI tax.
         a) A qualified sponsorship payment is one from which the payor does not expect any substantial return or benefit, other than the use or acknowledgment of the payor's name or logo. The payor may not receive a substantial return.
      2) Income is not subject to tax as UBTI if substantially all the work is performed for the organization by unpaid volunteers.
      3) Bingo games that are not an activity ordinarily carried out on a commercial basis or do not violate state or local law are not considered an unrelated trade or business.
      4) Exempt organizations subject to tax on UBTI are required to comply with the Code provisions regarding installment payments of estimated income tax by corporations.
      5) Exempt organizations with 2 or more unrelated businesses must compute UBTI separately for each business.
      6) A UBTI tax return (Form 990-T) is required of an exempt organization with at least $1,000 of gross income used in computing the UBTI tax for the tax year.
      7) UBTI of a tax-exempt corporation over $1,000 is subject to tax at the corporate regular income tax rate.
   b. Quarterly estimated tax payments are due if the organization expects to owe $500 or more in tax including unrelated business income. Form 990-W is used to figure the organization's estimated tax payments.

Charitable Deduction

4. Solicitations for contributions or other payments by tax-exempt organizations must include a statement if payments to that organization are not deductible as charitable contributions for federal income tax purposes. Donations to the following organizations are tax deductible:
   a. Corporations organized under an Act of Congress
   b. 501(c)(3) organizations except those testing for public safety
   c. Cemetery companies
   d. Cooperative hospital service organizations
   e. Cooperative service organizations of operating educational organizations
   f. Childcare organizations
5. If an organization receives charitable deduction property and within 3 years sells, exchanges, or otherwise disposes of the property, the organization must file Form 8282, *Donee Information Return*.
   a. However, an organization is not required to file Form 8282 if
      1) The property is valued at $500 or less or
      2) The property is consumed or distributed for charitable purposes.
   b. Form 8282 must be filed with the IRS within 125 days after the disposition. Additionally, a copy of Form 8282 must be given to the donor. If the organization fails to file the required information return, penalties may apply.
6. A charitable organization must give a donor a disclosure statement for a quid pro quo contribution over $75. This is a payment a donor makes to a charity partly as a contribution and partly for goods or services. Failure to make the required disclosure may result in a penalty to the organization.
7. The required written disclosure statement must
   a. Inform the donor that the amount of the contribution that is deductible for federal income tax purposes is limited to the excess of any money (and the value of any property other than money) contributed by the donor over the fair market value of goods or services provided by the charity and
   b. Provide the donor with a good faith estimate of the fair market value of the goods or services that the donor received.

Stop & Review

You have completed the outline for this subunit.

Study multiple-choice questions 1 through 15 beginning on page 450.

QUESTIONS

20.1 Exempt Organizations

1. Which of the following is NOT an exempt organization?

A. American Society for the Prevention of Cruelty to Animals.

B. Red Cross.

C. State-chartered credit unions.

D. Privately owned nursing home.

Answer (D) is correct.

REQUIRED: The organization that does not qualify as exempt.

DISCUSSION: Exempt status generally depends on the nature and purpose of an organization. Among the types of organizations that may qualify as exempt are corporations, trusts, foundations, funds, community funds, etc. A more complete list can be found in Sec. 501(c) along with the permitted stated purposes and requirements.

Answer (A) is incorrect. The American Society for the Prevention of Cruelty to Animals is an exempt organization according to Sec. 501(c). **Answer (B) is incorrect.** The Red Cross is an exempt organization according to Sec. 501(c). **Answer (C) is incorrect.** State-chartered credit unions are exempt organizations [Sec. 501(c)(14)(A)].

2. Which of the following organizations may request exempt status under the Internal Revenue Code as exempt organizations?

A. Religious organization.

B. School.

C. Animal welfare organization.

D. All of the answers are correct.

Answer (D) is correct.

REQUIRED: The organization that could request tax-exempt status under Sec. 501(c)(3) as a charitable organization.

DISCUSSION: Exempt status generally depends on the nature and purpose of an organization. An organization is tax-exempt only if it is a class specifically described by the IRC as one on which exemption is conferred. An organization operated for the primary purpose of carrying on a trade or business for profit is generally not tax-exempt. Religious organizations, schools, and animal welfare organizations are all considered exempt because their activities do not involve making a profit.

3. Of the organizations listed below, which organization could NOT receive approval for tax-exempt status under Internal Revenue Code Sec. 501(c)(3)?

A. A local chapter of the Salvation Army.

B. A partnership for scientific research.

C. A college alumni association.

D. A local boys club.

Answer (B) is correct.

REQUIRED: The organization that qualifies as a tax-exempt organization.

DISCUSSION: Organizations formed and operated exclusively for religious, charitable, scientific, educational, literary, or similar purposes are a broad class of exempt organizations. In order to maintain exempt status, no part of the net earnings may accrue to the benefit of any private shareholder or individual. Since a partnership for scientific research could allow part of its net earnings to accrue to the benefit of any private shareholder or individual, a partnership for scientific research could not receive approval for tax-exempt status.

Answer (A) is incorrect. The Salvation Army operates exclusively for charitable purposes, with no part of net earnings accrued for the benefit of a private shareholder or individual. **Answer (C) is incorrect.** A college alumni association does not accrue any part of its net earnings for the benefit of an individual. **Answer (D) is incorrect.** A boys club operates exclusively for charitable purposes, with no part of net earnings accrued for the benefit of a private shareholder or individual.

4. Which of the following is NOT an organization exempt from federal income taxes under Subchapter F of the Internal Revenue Code (Sec. 501 et seq.)?

A. Civic leagues or organizations operated exclusively for the promotion of social welfare.

B. Fraternal benefit societies.

C. Labor, agricultural, or horticultural organizations.

D. Blue Cross and Blue Shield organizations.

Answer (D) is correct.

REQUIRED: The organization that is not tax-exempt.

DISCUSSION: Tax-exempt status is available to various classes of nonprofit organizations under Sec. 501(a). Section 501(c)(2) through (25) lists several organizations that may qualify for tax-exempt status, including civic leagues; fraternal benefit societies; and labor, agricultural, or horticultural organizations. Blue Cross and Blue Shield organizations are not qualifying organizations.

5. Which of the following organizations, exempt from federal income tax under Sec. 501(a), must file an annual information return on Form 990 or Form 990-PF?

A. An organization, other than a private foundation, having gross receipts in each year that normally are not more than $50,000.

B. A school below college level, affiliated with a church or operated by a religious order, that is not an integrated auxiliary of a church.

C. A private foundation exempt under Sec. 501(c)(3) of the Internal Revenue Code.

D. A stock bonus, pension, or profit-sharing trust that qualifies under Sec. 401 of the Internal Revenue Code.

Answer (C) is correct.

REQUIRED: The organization that is required to file an annual information return.

DISCUSSION: Most exempt organizations are required to file various returns and reports at some time during or following the close of their accounting periods. Private foundations are required to file annual information returns on Form 990 or Form 990-PF regardless of the amounts of their gross receipts.

6. Which return might a tax-exempt organization be required to file?

A. Employment tax returns.

B. Annual information return, Form 990.

C. Report of cash received.

D. All of the answers are correct.

Answer (D) is correct.

REQUIRED: The return that a tax-exempt organization might be required to file.

DISCUSSION: Publication 557 states that annual information returns, employment tax returns, and a report of cash received are all returns that might be required of a tax-exempt organization.

7. Which of the following statements is true with respect to tax-exempt organizations?

A. A foundation may qualify for exemption from federal income tax if it is organized for the prevention of cruelty to animals.

B. A partnership may qualify as an organization exempt from federal income tax if it is organized and operated exclusively for one or more of the purposes found in Sec. 501(c)(3).

C. An individual can qualify as an organization exempt from federal income tax.

D. In order to qualify as an exempt organization, the organization must be a corporation.

Answer (A) is correct.

REQUIRED: The true statement with respect to tax-exempt organizations.

DISCUSSION: Exempt status generally depends on the nature and purpose of an organization. Among the types of organizations that may qualify as exempt are corporations, trusts, foundations, funds, community funds, etc. Neither a sole proprietorship, an individual, nor a partnership can qualify as a tax exempt organization. A more complete list can be found in Sec. 501(c) along with the permitted stated purposes and requirements.

Answer (B) is incorrect. A partnership is, by definition, a for-profit association. Also, a partnership is not listed as a type of organization that may qualify for exempt status in Sec. 501(c) or (d). **Answer (C) is incorrect.** An individual is not an organization described in Sec. 501(c) or (d) that may qualify for exempt status. **Answer (D) is incorrect.** Other types of organizations listed in Sec. 501(c) or (d) may also qualify.

8. With respect to tax-exempt organizations, which of the following statements is false?

A. A foundation may qualify for exemption from federal income tax if it is organized for the prevention of cruelty to children.

B. An individual may qualify as an organization exempt from federal income tax.

C. A corporation organized for the prevention of cruelty to animals may qualify for exemption from federal income tax.

D. A trust organized and operated for the purpose of testing for public safety may qualify for exemption from federal income tax.

Answer (B) is correct.

REQUIRED: The false statement regarding tax-exempt organizations.

DISCUSSION: To qualify for tax-exempt status, an organization must be a corporation, community chest fund, or foundation. An individual or a partnership cannot qualify.

9. With respect to the filing requirements of an exempt organization (including private foundations), which of the following statements is true?

A. A central or parent organization may file Form 990, *Return of Organization Exempt from Income Tax*, for two or more local organizations that are not private foundations. However, this return is in addition to the central or parent organization's separate annual return if it must file one.

B. Every organization exempt from income tax must file an annual information return.

C. Forms 990, 990-EZ, and 990-PF are required to be filed by the 15th day of the third month after the end of the organization's accounting period.

D. An exempt organization must have at least $5,000 gross income from an unrelated business before it is required to file Form 990-T, *Exempt Organization Business Income Tax Return*.

Answer (A) is correct.

REQUIRED: The true statement regarding the filing requirements of an exempt organization.

DISCUSSION: A parent or central exempt organization files a separate return for itself. If it chooses, the organization may also file a group information return for two or more local organizations as long as none of the local organizations are private foundations.

Answer (B) is incorrect. Several organizations are exempt from filing an annual information return. **Answer (C) is incorrect.** The return is required to be filed by the 15th day of the 5th month after the end of the organization's accounting period. **Answer (D) is incorrect.** Some organizations, including private foundations, must file a return regardless of the amount of gross income.

10. A tax-exempt organization with a calendar tax year was required to file Form 990, *Return of Organization Exempt from Income Tax*, for Year 1. Disregarding any extensions, when is the return due (do not consider Saturdays, Sundays, or holidays)?

A. March 15, Year 2.

B. April 15, Year 2.

C. May 15, Year 2.

D. June 15, Year 2.

Answer (C) is correct.

REQUIRED: The date the tax-exempt organization's tax return is due.

DISCUSSION: Under Sec. 6072(e), the income tax return of an organization exempt from tax under Sec. 501(a) must be filed on or before the 15th day of the 5th month following the close of the taxable year.

11. Individuals may claim a charitable deduction for a contribution to which of the following?

A. Civic leagues or organizations operated exclusively for the promotion of social welfare.

B. Organizations operated exclusively for scientific or educational purposes.

C. Cemetery companies operated exclusively for the benefit of their members.

D. Civic leagues or organizations operated exclusively for the promotion of social welfare and organizations operated exclusively for scientific or educational purposes.

Answer (D) is correct.

REQUIRED: The organization(s) to which individuals may make a deductible charitable contribution.

DISCUSSION: Solicitations for contributions or other payments by tax-exempt organizations must include a statement if payments to that organization are not deductible as charitable contributions for federal income tax purposes. Donations to the following organizations are tax deductible:

1. Corporations organized under an Act of Congress,
2. All 501(c)(3) organizations except those testing for public safety,
3. Cemetery companies,
4. Cooperative hospital service organizations,
5. Cooperative service organizations of operating educational organizations, or
6. Childcare organizations.

Although contributions to cemetery companies are generally tax deductible, a cemetery company that operates exclusively for the benefit of its members is not a tax-exempt organization.

Answer (A) is incorrect. Organizations operated for scientific or educational purposes also qualify for deductible contributions. **Answer (B) is incorrect.** Civic leagues operated for the promotion of social welfare also qualify for deductible contributions. **Answer (C) is incorrect.** If it operates exclusively for the benefit of its members, a cemetery company is not a tax-exempt organization.

12. Which of the following organizations, which are exempt from federal income tax, must generally file an annual information report?

A. An organization, other than a private foundation, with annual gross receipts that normally are not more than $50,000.

B. A private foundation.

C. A church.

D. A religious order.

Answer (B) is correct.

REQUIRED: The organization that must file an annual information return.

DISCUSSION: Most organizations exempt from tax under Sec. 501(a) must file annual information returns on Form 990, *Return of Organization Exempt from Income Tax*. Those excepted from the requirement are

1. A church or church-affiliated organization
2. An exclusively religious activity or religious order
3. An organization (other than a private foundation) having annual gross receipts that are not more than $50,000
4. A stock bonus, pension, or profit-sharing trust that qualified under Sec. 401

Answer (A) is incorrect. Such an organization is specifically exempt from filing annual information returns. **Answer (C) is incorrect.** A church is specifically exempt from filing annual information returns. **Answer (D) is incorrect.** A religious order is specifically exempt from filing annual information returns.

13. Which of the following organizations is NOT required to file an annual information return, such as Form 990, *Return of Organization Exempt from Income Tax*?

A. All are required to file with no exceptions.

B. Any exempt organization with annual gross receipts exceeding $50,000.

C. A convention or an association of churches with annual gross receipts exceeding $50,000.

D. Any chamber of commerce with annual gross receipts exceeding $50,000.

Answer (C) is correct.

REQUIRED: The organization that is not required to file an annual information return.

DISCUSSION: Most organizations exempt from tax under Sec. 501(a) must file annual information returns on Form 990, *Return of Organization Exempt from Income Tax*. Those exempt from the requirement are

1. A church or church-affiliated organization
2. An exclusively religious activity or religious order
3. An organization (other than a private foundation) having annual gross receipts that are not more than $50,000
4. A stock bonus, pension, or profit-sharing trust that qualified under Sec. 401

Answer (A) is incorrect. Most organizations exempt from tax under Sec. 501(a) must file annual information returns on Form 990, *Return of Organization Exempt from Income Tax*. **Answer (B) is incorrect.** An organization having annual gross receipts of not more than $50,000 is not required to file Form 990. **Answer (D) is incorrect.** An organization having annual gross receipts of not more than $50,000 is not required to file Form 990.

14. An incorporated exempt organization subject to tax on its current-year unrelated business taxable income (UBTI)

A. Must make estimated tax payments if its tax can reasonably be expected to be $100 or more.

B. Must comply with the Code provisions regarding installment payments of estimated income tax by corporations.

C. Must pay at least 70% of the tax due as shown on the return when filed, with the balance of tax payable in the following quarter.

D. May defer payment of tax for up to 9 months following the due date of the return.

Answer (B) is correct.

REQUIRED: The timing of payment obligations with respect to UBTI tax.

DISCUSSION: Exempt organizations subject to tax on UBTI are required to comply with the Code provisions regarding installment payments of estimated income tax by corporations [Sec. 6655(g)(3)].

Answer (A) is incorrect. Like a corporation, quarterly payments of estimated tax are required of an exempt organization that expects estimated tax on UBTI to equal or exceed $500 for the tax year. **Answer (C) is incorrect.** Tax on UBTI is due in full when the UBTI return and annual information return are due. **Answer (D) is incorrect.** Tax on UBTI is due in full when the UBTI return and annual information return are due.

15. Which of the following forms is intended for an exempt organization with gross receipts of $100,000 and total assets of $400,000 on December 31, 2022?

A. Form 990.

B. Form 990 Schedule M.

C. Form 990-EZ.

D. Form 990 Schedule O.

Answer (C) is correct.

REQUIRED: The form designed for use by small exempt organizations.

DISCUSSION: Form 990-EZ is a shortened version of Form 990. It is designed for use by small exempt organizations and nonexempt charitable trusts. An organization may file Form 990-EZ instead of Form 990 if it meets both of the following requirements:

1. Its gross receipts during the year were less than $200,000.
2. Its total assets at the end of the year were less than $500,000.

The amounts in this question pass both of these tests.

Answer (A) is incorrect. Form 990 is designed for use by all (large or small) exempt organizations. **Answer (B) is incorrect.** Schedule M is for noncash contributions. **Answer (D) is incorrect.** Schedule O is for supplemental information to Form 990.

Go to Online Course

Access the **Gleim EA Premium Review System** featuring our SmartAdapt technology from your Gleim Personal Classroom to continue your studies.

You will experience a personalized study environment with exam-emulating multiple-choice questions.

APPENDIX A
EXAM CONTENT OUTLINES WITH GLEIM CROSS-REFERENCES

This section contains the Part 2 Exam Content Outlines (ECOs) for 2022/2023.

The ECOs are subdivided into domains, and each domain has one or more topics, which are further divided into specific items. According to the IRS's *Candidate Information Bulletin* (available at www.prometric.com/irs), not every topic in the ECOs will appear on the exam, and the list of topics may not be all-inclusive. However, the ECOs are meant to reflect the knowledge needed for tasks performed by EAs.

Next to each topic, we have provided a cross-reference to the most relevant Gleim study unit(s) or subunit(s).

Domain 1: Business Entities and Considerations (30 Questions)

a. **Business Entities**

1) Sole proprietorships – 1.1
2) Partnerships and qualified joint ventures (QJV) – 1.1, 9.1-9.2, 10.1
3) Corporations – 1.1, 12
4) S corporations – 1.1, 17
5) LLCs – 1.1, 9.1, 12.1
6) Tax-exempt entities and associations – 20
7) Entity type default classifications and elections – 1.1, 17.1
8) Employer identification number – 1.1
9) Accounting periods (tax year) – 1.4
10) Reporting requirements (e.g., Forms W-2, W-4, Form 1099) – 4.1
11) Hobby versus business determination and loss limitations – 8.2

b. **Partnerships**

1) Partnership income, expenses, distributions, and flow-through (e.g., self-employment income) – 2.2, 10
2) Family partnerships – 9.1
3) Partner's dealings with partnership (e.g., exchange of property, guaranteed payments) – 9.3, 10.2-10.3, 11.2
4) Contribution of property and/or services to a partnership (e.g., partnership's basis, property subject to indebtedness) – 9.3
5) Basis of partner's interest – 9.4, 10.1
6) Disposition of partner's interest – 11
7) Partnership formation (e.g., partnership agreement, general vs. limited partners, capital contributions) – 1.1, 9.1, 9.3
8) Dissolution of partnership (e.g., sale, death of partner) – 10.1, 11.1
9) Filing requirements, due dates, penalties, and audit notice requirements – 9.2, 10.1
10) Partnership cancellation of debt – 10.1
11) Partnership level audit and opt-out – 10.1

c. **Corporations in General**

1) Filing requirements, due dates, and penalties – 12.4
2) Earnings and profits – 15.1
3) Shareholder dividends, distributions, and recognition requirements – 15.2-15.3
4) Special deductions and credits (e.g., dividends received deduction, charitable deduction) – 14.1-14.3
5) Liquidations and stock redemptions – 16
6) Accumulated earnings tax – 12.5
7) Estimated tax payments – 12.6
8) Corporate minimum tax credit – 12.5

d. **Forming a Corporation**

1) Services rendered to a corporation in return for stock – 13
2) IRC Section 351 exchange – 13.1
3) Transfer and/or receipt of money or property in addition to corporate stock – 13.1
4) Transfer of property subject to indebtedness – 13.1
5) Controlled groups – 12.2
6) Closely held corporations – 12.1

e. **S Corporations**

1) Requirements to qualify (e.g., qualifying shareholders) – 17.1
2) Election procedure – 17.1
3) Income, expenses, and separately stated items – 17.2
4) Treatment of distributions – 17.3
5) Shareholder's basis (e.g., loan basis, distributions and losses in excess of basis, services for stock) – 17.2-17.3
6) Revocation, termination, and reinstatement – 17.1
7) Debt discharge – 17.2

Domain 2: Business Tax Preparation (37 Questions)

a. **Business Income**

1) Gross receipts and other income – 2.1
2) Cost of goods sold (e.g., inventory practices, expenditures included, uniform capitalization rules) – 1.3, 4.2, 6.1
3) Net income/loss and at-risk limitations – 3.3, 8.2, 10.1, 17.2
4) Cancellation of business debt – 2.1

b. **Business Expenses, Deductions, and Credits**

1) Officers and employees' compensation (e.g., deductibility, fringe benefits, rules of family employment, statutory employee, necessary and reasonable) – 4.1, 5.8, 15.3
2) Business rental deduction, including self-rentals – 4.4, 5.6
3) Depreciation, amortization (start-up and organizational cost), IRC Section 179, depletion, bonus depreciation, and correcting errors – 7.1-7.4
4) Business bad debts – 5.4
5) Business travel, meals, and gift expenses – 5.1-5.2, 5.5, 14.4
6) Vehicle use and expenses – 5.2
7) Interest expense – 4.3

8) Insurance expense – 5.3
9) Taxes (e.g., deductibility of taxes, assessments, and penalties; proper treatment of sales taxes paid, excise) – 2.2-2.3, 4.5, 8.4, 12.5-12.6, 14.1
10) Employment taxes – 2.2, 4.5
11) Casualties, thefts, and condemnations – 6.4, 8.3, 14.4
12) Qualified business income (QBI) (e.g., SSTB, calculations, phase out, UBIA) – 5.9, 10.1
13) Eligibility and deductibility of general business credits (e.g., disabled access credit, R&D credit, small business healthcare tax credit, foreign tax credit) – 8.1
14) Net operating loss deduction – 8.2, 14.5
15) Home office – 5.7

c. **Business Assets**

1) Basis of assets – 6.1-6.2
2) Disposition of property or assets – 2.3, 7.5, 10.2
3) Like kind exchange – 6.3
4) Converted property – 6.1, 6.4
5) Capitalization and repair regulations (e.g., elections) – 2.3, 4.3, 6.1-6.2

d. **Analysis of Financial Records**

1) Proper business type, the use of classification codes, and year to year comparison – 1.1
2) Income statement – 14.1
3) Balance sheet (e.g., proofing beginning and ending balances, relationship to income statement and depreciation) – 14.1
4) Method of accounting and changes (e.g., accrual, cash, hybrid, Form 3115) – 1.2
5) Depreciation recovery (e.g., recapture, IRC Section 280F) – 7.1, 7.5
6) Pass-through activity (e.g., K-1, separately stated items, non-deductible expenses) – 10.1, 17.2, 18.3
7) Reconciliation of tax versus books (e.g., M-1, M-2, M-3) – 14.1
8) Related party activity – 1.2, 10.3, 14.6
9) Loans to and from owners – 10.3

e. **Advising the Business Taxpayer**

1) Reporting and filing obligations (e.g., extended returns and potential penalties, international information returns, Form 1099 series, Form 8300) – 4.1, 9.2, 10.1, 12.4, 17.1-17.2
2) Payments and deposit obligations (e.g., employment tax, excise tax) – 4.1, 4.5
3) Record-keeping requirements (e.g., mileage log, accountable plans) – 5.2
4) Selection of business entity (e.g., benefits and detriments) – 1.1
5) Comingling (e.g., personal usage of business accounts, separation of business and personal accounts) – 5.2
6) Advice on accounting methods and procedures (e.g., explanation of requirements) – 1.2
7) Transfer of property in or out of the business – 9.3, 10.2, 11, 13, 15.2, 16.2-16.3, 17.1-17.3
8) Life cycle of the business (e.g., formation, dissolution) – 9-17
9) Type of industry (e.g., specified service business owners) – 5.9, 10.1
10) Worker classification (e.g., independent contractor versus employee, outside sales, full-time versus part-time) – 4.1, 5.8
11) Deductions and credits for tax planning (e.g., timing of income and expenses, NOL, depreciation versus IRC Section 179 versus bonus depreciation) – 1.2, 7.1-7.2
12) ACA compliance – 8.1, 8.4

Domain 3: Specialized Returns and Taxpayers (18 Questions)

a. **Trust and Estate Income Tax**

1) Trust types (e.g., simple/complex, grantor, irrevocable, tax shelters, foreign) – 18.3
2) Distributable net income and accounting income – 18.3
3) Exclusions, exemptions, and deductions – 18.1, 18.3
4) Fraudulent trusts – 18.4
5) Income (e.g., allocations, corpus versus income) – 18.1, 18.3
6) Separately stated items (e.g., items reported on the K-1) – 18.3
7) Filing requirements, tax years, and penalties – 18.2-18.3

b. **Exempt Organizations**

1) Qualifying for and maintaining tax-exempt status (e.g., IRC 501(c)) – 20
2) Applying for IRS tax-exempt status (e.g., Form 1023, Form 1024) – 20
3) Filing requirements (e.g., Form 990 series) – 20
4) Unrelated business taxable income – 20

c. **Retirement Plans**

1) Employer and employee contributions – 19.1-19.3
2) Reporting requirements – 19.1-19.3
3) Plans for self-employed persons (e.g., SEP and SIMPLE) – 19.1-19.3
4) Prohibited transactions – 19.4
5) Qualified and non-qualified plans – 19
6) Non-discrimination rules – 19.1

d. **Farmers**

1) Farm income (e.g., livestock, crop insurance proceeds, subsidies, patronage dividends, conservation payments) – 2.3
2) Depreciation for farmers – 2.3, 7
3) Disaster-area provisions (e.g., drought, flood, other weather-related conditions) – 2.3, 8.3
4) Farm rental (e.g., Form 4835) – 2.3
5) Farm tax computation (e.g., Schedule J, Schedule SE, estimated tax) – 2.3

e. **Rental Property**

1) Real estate professional qualifications – 3.3
2) Commercial rentals versus residential rentals – 3.1-3.2
3) Mixed use property/vacation home – 3.1-3.2
4) Passive loss limitation (e.g., special $25,000 allowance, MAGI limits) – 3.3
5) Rental income (e.g., deposits, pre-paid rent, not rented for profit) – 3.1
6) Rental expenses (e.g., allocation between personal and rental, repair versus capitalized) – 3.2

INDEX

GLEIM® EA REVIEW

2022 Inflation Adjusted Amounts

$ 0	Personal Exemption	$1,400	Addtl Std Ded, Married
12,950	Std Ded, Single	1,750	Addtl Std Ded, Unmarried
19,400	Std Ded, HH	1,150	Child Std Ded
25,900	Std Ded, MFJ	400	Dependent Child

Income Tax Rate Schedules

Single

$ 0	10%	
10,275	12%	$ 1,027.50
41,775	22%	4,807.50
89,075	24%	15,213.50
170,050	32%	34,647.50
215,950	35%	49,335.50
539,900	37%	162,718.00

Head of Household

$ 0	10%	
14,650	12%	$ 1,465.00
55,900	22%	6,415.00
89,050	24%	13,708.00
170,050	32%	33,148.00
215,950	35%	47,836.00
539,900	37%	161,218.50

Married Filing Jointly

$ 0	10%	
20,550	12%	$ 2,055.00
83,550	22%	9,615.00
178,150	24%	30,427.00
340,100	32%	69,295.00
431,900	35%	98,671.00
647,850	37%	174,253.50

Married Filing Separately

$ 0	10%	
10,275	12%	$ 1,027.50
41,775	22%	4,807.50
89,075	24%	15,213.50
170,050	32%	34,647.50
215,950	35%	49,335.50
323,925	37%	87,126.75

Estates and Trusts

$ 0	10%	
2,750	24%	$ 275
9,850	35%	1,979
13,450	37%	3,239

Credits

Earned Income

1 child	2 children	3 children	0 children	
$10,980	$15,410	$15,410	$ 7,320	Earned Income Limit
$ 3,733	$ 6,164	$ 6,935	$ 560	Max Credit
$20,130	$20,130	$20,130	$ 9,160	Phaseout, Unmarried
$43,492	$49,399	$53,057	$16,480	End Phaseout
34.00%	40.00%	45.00%	15.3%	Credit %
15.98%	21.06%	21.06%	15.3%	Phase %
$10,300	---	---	---	Unearned Income
$26,260	$26,260	$26,260	$15,290	Phaseout, MFJ
$49,622	$55,529	$59,187	$22,610	End Phaseout, MFJ

Child Tax

$ 2,000	Credit Amt
200,000	Phaseout, Single
200,000	Phaseout, HH
400,000	Phaseout, Married

Adoption

$ 14,890		Credit Amt
223,410	$263,410	Phaseout

Elderly

$7,500	$10,000	MFJ with both
5,000	10,000	MFJ with one
5,000	7,500	Single
3,750	5,000	MFS

Savers

$41,000	$44,000	$68,000	MFJ
30,750	33,000	51,000	HH
20,500	22,000	34,000	Single

FICA Limits

$147,000	SS
2,400	Household Emp

Health Savings Accounts

$1,400	Single Minimum	$ 2,800	Family Minimum
7,050	Single Maximum	14,100	Family Maximum
3,650	Single Limited	7,300	Family Limited
		1,000	Over age 55

GLEIM® EA REVIEW

2022 Inflation Adjusted Amounts

$ 0	Personal Exemption	$1,400	Addtl Std Ded, Married
12,950	Std Ded, Single	1,750	Addtl Std Ded, Unmarried
19,400	Std Ded, HH	1,150	Child Std Ded
25,900	Std Ded, MFJ	400	Dependent Child

Income Tax Rate Schedules

Single

$ 0	10%	
10,275	12%	$ 1,027.50
41,775	22%	4,807.50
89,075	24%	15,213.50
170,050	32%	34,647.50
215,950	35%	49,335.50
539,900	37%	162,718.00

Head of Household

$ 0	10%	
14,650	12%	$ 1,465.00
55,900	22%	6,415.00
89,050	24%	13,708.00
170,050	32%	33,148.00
215,950	35%	47,836.00
539,900	37%	161,218.50

Married Filing Jointly

$ 0	10%	
20,550	12%	$ 2,055.00
83,550	22%	9,615.00
178,150	24%	30,427.00
340,100	32%	69,295.00
431,900	35%	98,671.00
647,850	37%	174,253.50

Married Filing Separately

$ 0	10%	
10,275	12%	$ 1,027.50
41,775	22%	4,807.50
89,075	24%	15,213.50
170,050	32%	34,647.50
215,950	35%	49,335.50
323,925	37%	87,126.75

Estates and Trusts

$ 0	10%	
2,750	24%	$ 275
9,850	35%	1,979
13,450	37%	3,239

Credits

Earned Income

1 child	2 children	3 children	0 children	
$10,980	$15,410	$15,410	$ 7,320	Earned Income Limit
$ 3,733	$ 6,164	$ 6,935	$ 560	Max Credit
$20,130	$20,130	$20,130	$ 9,160	Phaseout, Unmarried
$43,492	$49,399	$53,057	$16,480	End Phaseout
34.00%	40.00%	45.00%	15.3%	Credit %
15.98%	21.06%	21.06%	15.3%	Phase %
$10,300	---	---	---	Unearned Income
$26,260	$26,260	$26,260	$15,290	Phaseout, MFJ
$49,622	$55,529	$59,187	$22,610	End Phaseout, MFJ

Child Tax

$ 2,000	Credit Amt
200,000	Phaseout, Single
200,000	Phaseout, HH
400,000	Phaseout, Married

Adoption

$ 14,890		Credit Amt
223,410	$263,410	Phaseout

Elderly

$7,500	$10,000	MFJ with both
5,000	10,000	MFJ with one
5,000	7,500	Single
3,750	5,000	MFS

Savers

$41,000	$44,000	$68,000	MFJ
30,750	33,000	51,000	HH
20,500	22,000	34,000	Single

FICA Limits

$147,000	SS
2,400	Household Emp

Health Savings Accounts

$1,400	Single Minimum	$ 2,800	Family Minimum
7,050	Single Maximum	14,100	Family Maximum
3,650	Single Limited	7,300	Family Limited
		1,000	Over age 55

Education Credits, Exclusion, and Deduction

$2,500 American Opportunity Credit
$2,000 Lifetime Learning Credit Maximum

$ 80,000	$ 90,000	Phaseout, Single
160,000	180,000	Phaseout, MFJ

US Savings Bonds

$ 85,800	$100,800	all other returns
128,650	158,650	joint returns

Student Loan Interest

$ 70,000	$ 85,000	Single
145,000	175,000	MFJ
	2,500	Maximum Interest

Mileage Rates

Jan-Jun	Jul-Dec	
$0.585	$0.625	Business
0.18	0.22	Medical & Moving
0.14	0.14	Charitable
0.26	0.26	Depreciation

Section 179

$1,080,000	Maximum
2,700,000	Phaseout

Medical Savings Accounts

$2,450	Single Minimum	$4,950	Family Minimum
3,700	Single Maximum	7,400	Family Maximum
4,950	Single Out of Pocket	9,050	Family Out of Pocket

Per Diem Rates

$296	High Cost
202	Other Locality
74	M&IE High Cost
64	M&IE Other Locality
69	Meals for Transportation Workers in U.S.
74	Meals for Transportation Workers outside U.S.

Foreign Income Exclusion

$112,000	Foreign Income
16%	Housing
$ 15,680	Housing Limit

Luxury Auto Limits

$11,200 $18,000 $10,800 $6,460 Cars/Trucks
$8,000 Bonus (Special) Depreciation

Eligible Long-Term Care Premiums

Amount	Age
$ 450	40 or less
850	41 to 50
1,690	51 to 60
4,520	61 to 70
5,640	More than 70

Coverdell Savings Account

$ 2,000		Maximum Contribution
95,000	$110,000	Phaseout, Single
190,000	220,000	Phaseout, MFJ

Retirement Amounts

$ 61,000		Maximum Contribution
6,000		IRA
1,000		Over age 50
68,000	$ 78,000	Phaseout, Single
109,000	129,000	Phaseout, MFJ
129,000	144,000	Roth, Single
204,000	214,000	Roth, MFJ
20,500		401(k)/SEP
14,000		SIMPLE
20,500		457 Plan
6,500		Catchup, not SIMPLE
3,000		Catchup, SIMPLE
305,000		Compensation Limit
245,000		Defined Benefit Limit
135,000		Highly Compensated Employee

Education Credits, Exclusion, and Deduction

$2,500 American Opportunity Credit
$2,000 Lifetime Learning Credit Maximum

$ 80,000	$ 90,000	Phaseout, Single
160,000	180,000	Phaseout, MFJ

US Savings Bonds

$ 85,800	$100,800	all other returns
128,650	158,650	joint returns

Student Loan Interest

$ 70,000	$ 85,000	Single
145,000	175,000	MFJ
	2,500	Maximum Interest

Mileage Rates

Jan-Jun	Jul-Dec	
$0.585	$0.625	Business
0.18	0.22	Medical & Moving
0.14	0.14	Charitable
0.26	0.26	Depreciation

Section 179

$1,080,000	Maximum
2,700,000	Phaseout

Medical Savings Accounts

$2,450	Single Minimum	$4,950	Family Minimum
3,700	Single Maximum	7,400	Family Maximum
4,950	Single Out of Pocket	9,050	Family Out of Pocket

Per Diem Rates

$296	High Cost
202	Other Locality
74	M&IE High Cost
64	M&IE Other Locality
69	Meals for Transportation Workers in U.S.
74	Meals for Transportation Workers outside U.S.

Foreign Income Exclusion

$112,000	Foreign Income
16%	Housing
$ 15,680	Housing Limit

Luxury Auto Limits

$11,200 $18,000 $10,800 $6,460 Cars/Trucks
$8,000 Bonus (Special) Depreciation

Eligible Long-Term Care Premiums

Amount	Age
$ 450	40 or less
850	41 to 50
1,690	51 to 60
4,520	61 to 70
5,640	More than 70

Coverdell Savings Account

$ 2,000		Maximum Contribution
95,000	$110,000	Phaseout, Single
190,000	220,000	Phaseout, MFJ

Retirement Amounts

$ 61,000		Maximum Contribution
6,000		IRA
1,000		Over age 50
68,000	$ 78,000	Phaseout, Single
109,000	129,000	Phaseout, MFJ
129,000	144,000	Roth, Single
204,000	214,000	Roth, MFJ
20,500		401(k)/SEP
14,000		SIMPLE
20,500		457 Plan
6,500		Catchup, not SIMPLE
3,000		Catchup, SIMPLE
305,000		Compensation Limit
245,000		Defined Benefit Limit
135,000		Highly Compensated Employee